ANIMALS IN ROMAN
LIFE AND ART

ANIMALS IN ROMAN LIFE AND ART

J. M. C. Toynbee

THE JOHNS HOPKINS UNIVERSITY PRESS

BALTIMORE AND LONDON

Dis Manibus
MITHRAE
felis albae
carissimae amantissimae fidissimae
hunc libellum
dedicavit
magistra

©1973 Thames and Hudson
All rights reserved
Printed in the United States of America on acid-free recycled paper

Originally published in the United States by Cornell University Press, 1973
Published by arrangement with Thames and Hudson, London
Johns Hopkins Paperbacks edition, 1996
05 04 03 02 01 00 99 98 97 96   5 4 3 2 1

The Johns Hopkins University Press
2715 North Charles Street
Baltimore, Maryland 21218-4319
The Johns Hopkins Press Ltd., London

Library of Congress Cataloging-in-Publication Data
Toynbee, J. M. C. (Joceyln M. C.), d. 1985.
Animals in Roman life and art / J. M. C. Toynbee.
p.   cm.
Originally published : London : Thames & Hudson, 1973, in series :
Aspects of Greek and Roman life.
Includes bibliographical references and index.
ISBN 0-8018-5533-0 (pbk. : alk. paper)
1. Animals and civilization—Italy—Rome.   2. Animals in art.
3. Animals in literature.   4. Zoology—Italy—Rome.   5. Rome—
Antiquities.   I. Title.
QL87.T68   1996
636'.00937—dc20   96-26467
                                                        CIP

A catalog record for this book is available from the British Library.

CONTENTS

LIST OF ILLUSTRATIONS

Fig. 1 The 'Great Hunt' mosaic, Piazza Armerina (pp. 40-1)

PREFACE

THE PLACE OCCUPIED BY ANIMALS in Roman life and art has long been recognized; and the present writer is much indebted to the work of predecessors, notably to O. Keller's comprehensive *Die antike Tierwelt* (1909, 1913, reprint 1963) and to G. Jennison's delightful *Animals for Show and Pleasure in Ancient Rome* (1937). Both books draw widely on the ancient literary sources and both are illustrated by some reproductions of ancient monuments. But, since they were written, numerous important articles dealing with individual aspects of the subject have been published and, above all, there has come to light a whole wealth of new and illuminating archaeological evidence bearing upon it. Moreover, since Keller's book includes Oriental and Greek as well as Roman material, the specifically Roman contribution is sometimes difficult to evaluate from its pages; and Jennison confines himself to animals as entertainers and pets. There would, therefore, seem to be room for another, up-to-date study of Roman animals from these and from other standpoints.

It goes without saying that the present book, although arranged according to species, makes no kind of claim to be a complete zoological treatise covering all the fauna of the Roman world. Some categories of creatures – insects, spiders, scorpions and worms, for example – are not included. It is, however, hoped that most of the animals and birds that feature prominently in Roman literature and art have found a place here. Nor has an attempt been made to produce anything approaching a corpus of the literary passages and artistic monuments that are relevant to the theme. Every reader will be sure to note with regret the omission of many a favourite reference and work of art. But perhaps he may feel that what he does find in these pages is reasonably representative. Renderings of fabulous birds and beasts receive only incidental mention.

In this book something is said of zoological collections and displays, of individual creatures, and of renderings of them in art in the Hellenistic world, since these are closely linked with the role played by animals in the life and art of Roman times. But representations of fauna in the paintings and sculpture of Etruria are not discussed or reproduced, inasmuch as their study more properly belongs to that of Greek art in its archaic and early classical phases. In so far as the animal kingdom is concerned, specifically Etruscan influence on Rome would appear to have been small, apart from the role that Etruscan chariot-races may have played in the development of those at Rome.

Since this book is intended for non-classicists as well as for those acquainted with the Greek and Latin languages, all quotations from Greek and Roman authors have been translated. Where such quotations appear in the text they are always translated there, so the sight of them need cause no alarm to the general reader. But the classicist will surely appreciate that some of the original words and phrases used by the ancient writers are much too picturesque and pithy to be wholly relegated to the notes. In the notes some of the delicious Greek and Latin poems on animals, notably on dogs, horses, and donkeys, are quoted in full for the sake of readers who can enjoy them in the original but do not necessarily have at their elbow the anthologies and collections of inscriptions from which they are culled.

In the Appendix on Roman veterinary medicine I have been extremely fortunate in securing the collaboration of Mr R. E. Walker, B.Vet.Med., MRCVS. His specialist, professional knowledge, practical experience and close acquaintance with the works of the Greek and Roman veterinary writers have provided a most valuable contribution such as I myself am quite unqualified to make.

My warm thanks are due to Professor Scullard for constant help and advice. I am also very grateful to Dr Peggy Varley of the Open University for advice on the classification of animals and birds; to the Edward Grey Institute of Ornithology, Oxford, for help with the identification of some birds in works of Roman art; and to Mr Stanley Baron, of Messrs Thames and Hudson, for encouraging me to write on a subject that has always appealed to me. Finally, it is a pleasure to record the great assistance that I have received from members of the staff of Thames and Hudson with the numbering of the numerous notes and with selecting the illustrations from the very large mass of pictorial material available.

Oxford, 1972   J. M. C. Toynbee

CHAPTER I

GENERAL SURVEY

THE VARIETY OF ANIMAL ROLES IN ROMAN LIFE

ONE OF THE MOST OBVIOUS and far-reaching differences between life in the ancient Roman world and that in the mechanized, 'developed' countries of modern times lies in the vastly more extensive part played in the former by animals of all kinds. There were, indeed, few aspects of human activity, either in work or in leisure, in which beasts did not share. Among means of **transport**, horses and mules provided the usual mounts for riders on journeys long or short and of very varied purposes: very rarely Romans rode elephants (pp. 49, 50). Vehicles such as chariots, whether used for travel or in official ceremonies, carriages and carts of many types and waggons for carrying loads were drawn by horses, mules and oxen – sometimes by elephants and other quadrupeds not normally seen in harness. Camels, horses, mules and donkeys carried loads and packs. The **food supply** was, then as now, maintained by the keeping of herds of cattle, goats, pigs and deer, of flocks of sheep and of edible birds, and by fishing in seas, lakes, rivers and streams. Then as now, animal wool, skins, hides and furs produced the basic elements of **dress**; while the feathers of birds were used as **adornment** for human beings and animals such as, for example, racehorses (pp. 180, 185). In **agriculture** ploughing was mainly done by oxen; reaping machines and mills were worked by donkeys (for the *vallus*, see p. 196). **Hunting,** whether for pure sport or for obtaining game for the table, was served by horses and hounds. **War**, needless to say, demanded horses as mounts for cavalry units, and horses and mules as baggage- and draught-animals; very occasionally the Romans used elephants as a fighting arm (p. 37), and the specially trained horses that took part in the elaborate cavalry displays and sports (the ἱππικὰ γυμνάσια of Arrian's *Tactica*) and in parades were equipped with richly embossed chamfrons, complete with perforated eye-guards, and with pectoral ornaments (pp. 170, 171). The ritual of the Roman state **religion** and of private cults required animals for sacrifice in honour of the gods, mostly bulls, heifers, sheep, pigs and goats. **Pets** included not only lap-dogs, watch-dogs and other house-dogs, cats and birds, the commonest domestic pets of modern times, but also monkeys, reptiles, deer, gazelles and even fish. Wild animals, mainly tamed, but occasionally left in their savage state, were kept by individuals in their homes.

Pleasure and scientific interest in animals for their own sake (as well as the needs of the table) were catered for in the case of wealthy private persons and sometimes of emperors by parks and enclosures for quadrupeds (*leporaria, roboraria* – i.e. spaces fenced with oak palisades – θηριοτροφεῖα, *vivaria*), with aviaries (*aviaria*) for birds, and with sea-water ponds (*piscinae*) for sea-fish. The ancient Roman and Italian *leporaria* (enclosures for hares)[1] developed in late republican times into preserves in which not only hares but also such animals as deer, boars, wild goats and wild sheep were kept and fed. Quintus Fulvius Lippinus, Quintus Hortensius and Varro, for example, owned such parks at Tarquinii, Laurentum and Tusculum respectively.[2] Hortensius had a dining-room so constructed as to overlook his park, in order that his guests might see his animals converging on a servant got up as Orpheus when he blew a horn to summon them.[3] The grounds of Nero's Golden House were stocked with all kinds of domesticated and wild animals;[4] and there must have been a very large *vivarium* to house the great collection formed in Rome by Gordian III (238-244) for his Persian triumph, but actually exhibited by Philip the Arabian at the *ludi saeculares* of 248 for the thousandth birthday of Rome. According to the *Augustan History* this menagerie comprised 32 elephants, 10 elks (*alces*), 10 tigers, 60 tame lions, 30 tame maneless lions (*leopardi*), 10 hyenas (*belbi*), 6 hippopotamuses, 1 rhinoceros, 10 white or very large lions (*argoleontes* or *arcoleontes*), 10 giraffes (*cameleopardi*), 20 wild asses and 40 wild horses.[5] The prototype of a menagerie of this size was the famous royal collection made by Ptolemy II (283-246 BC) at Alexandria.[6] Such were the Hellenistic and Roman precursors of the public and private 'zoos' of modern and earlier post-classical times.

Gordian's collection, however, was formed less to gratify his personal pleasure and taste than to enable him to stage a splendid show; and it was as a means of **public entertainment** that animals played their most dramatic role in ancient Roman life. In modern

Europe, at any rate, the interest taken by the general public in wild and unfamiliar birds and beasts is largely satisfied, apart from the occasional visit paid to zoos, circuses and such a place as Longleat, by books, photographs, films and television programmes. The showing of wild animals at travelling fairs is growing rarer; and comparatively few enjoy the sight of horses in the flesh at race meetings and riding competitions. But in Rome and in many other cities of her world a very large proportion of all strata of the population had frequent opportunities of watching and observing at first hand great quantities of creatures of many species both known and strange. In the streets and squares of a town, trained wild beasts owned by one or more individuals could be seen performing singly or in small troupes – beasts that were either 'native' or 'foreign' and 'exotic' according to the location of the town in question. Above all there were the lavish public games and spectacles, organized and paid for by magistrates and successful generals under the late Republic and by emperors in Rome, by local authorities in the provinces, and in the late Empire in Rome by wealthy individuals such as Symmachus, even when a special licence to give them had to be obtained.[7] In Rome, at any rate, as later in Constantinople, the most popular of all displays was chariot-racing in the Circus, with 'star' horses many if not all of which had personal names that were shouted by the onlookers[8] and are often recorded in inscriptions (pp. 177-83).

Next to the races in popularity came the exhibitions of animals held in Rome and elsewhere, first in temporary enclosures and then in permanent amphitheatres as well as in the Circus. Such shows could include the pacific and amusing antics of tamed beasts, of elephants, for instance (pp. 48, 49). But mainly they consisted of the bloody fights of beasts with beasts and of beasts with men, whether unarmed criminals (such as Christian martyrs) or professional fighters (bestiarii), or of staged hunts (venationes), in which professional hunters (venatores) attacked and slew (or were sometimes slain by) the creatures. The earliest recorded beast shows in Rome are the venationes given with lions and leopards (pantherae) in 186 BC by Marcus Fulvius Nobilior[9] and by the curule aediles in 169 BC, when 63 Africanae bestiae (large cats), 40 bears and some elephants appeared in the Circus Maximus.[10] The aediles of 104 BC, Lucius Licinius Crassus and Quintus Mucius Scaevola, showed a large number of lions;[11] and Sulla produced 100 maned lions (iubati), the gift of King Bocchus of Mauretania.[12] From the first, as Rome's annexations and trading connections were extended east and west, most of these shows were characterized by the great variety of creatures exhibited. In his aedileship of 58 B C Marcus Scaurus showed 150 leopards (*variae*), a hippopotamus and 5 crocodiles.[13] In 55 B C Pompey displayed about 20 elephants (pp. 22, 23), 600 lions, 410 female leopards (*variae*), a lynx, a rhinoceros and some apes;[14] and in Julius Caesar's quadruple triumph in 46 B C there featured elephants (p. 47), 400 lions, Thessalian bulls and a giraffe.[15] In 25 B C the praetor Publius Servilius exhibited 300 bears and 300 other African wild beasts.[16]

The beast shows given by Augustus, which included the display of 420 leopards (*variae*),[17] were on an unprecedently generous scale, as the records of the numbers of animals killed on various occasions indicate (p. 21). Gaius' (Caligula's) *venationes* in A D 37, those of Claudius in 41, and those of Nero in 55 likewise ended in death for the exhibits (p. 21). Claudius and Nero both staged bullfights.[18] The shows of Domitian and Trajan were quite gruesome scenes of carnage (p. 22) and even the cultured Hadrian is said to have had many wild beasts, often as many as a hundred lions, killed in the Circus; but presumably the thousand *ferae* which he showed in the stadium at Athens were not publicly slaughtered.[19] Coins of 149 with the reverse-legend MVNIFICENTIA and an elephant (occupying the whole field) and a lion (accompanying the figure of Munificentia) as reverse-types (pp. 53, 63) confirm the *Augustan History*'s account of Antoninus Pius' *munera* at which elephants, hyenas, lions, tigers, rhinoceroses, crocodiles and hippopotamuses made their appearance and are not recorded as having been destroyed.[20] Commodus' role as a slayer of beasts is described below (p. 22). Among the events in the animal displays given by Septimius Severus were the fight, joined at a signal, of 60 boars and the emergence into the arena of 700 beasts (100 on each of seven days) from an ingenious contraption made in the form of a ship that fell apart. The ship's 'passengers' were bears, lions, lionesses, leopards, ostriches, wild asses and bison; all were slaughtered.[21] It was in his aedileship under Septimius (if we can really believe the *Augustan History* that anyone who was not a reigning emperor could give beast shows in Rome at this period) that the future Emperor Gordian I exhibited 100 *ferae Libycae*, 1,000 bears, 200 stags (some from Britain), 30 wild horses, 100 wild sheep, 10 elks, 100 bulls from Cyprus, 300 ostriches with reddened feathers (*miniati*), 30 wild asses, 150 boars, 200 ibexes and 200 gazelles (? *dammae*).[22] Elagabalus had a collection of Egyptian animals (*omnia Aegyptia*) which he showed;[23] and on the occasion of his marriage various wild beasts, including an elephant and 51 tigers, were despatched.[24] The *Augustan History* credits Aurelian with showing animals in the triumph that he celebrated over Queen Zenobia of Palmyra in 274. The participants were 20 elephants, 200 assorted *ferae mansuetae* from Libya and Palestine (afterwards given away to private citizens), 4 tigers, giraffes and elks.[25]

Probus is the last emperor whose beast shows are recorded in a literary source and these were on a truly magnificent scale.[26] On the occasion of his triumph in 281 he exhibited, at a *venatio* in the Circus Maximus (which had been planted with trees to imitate a natural setting), 1,000 ostriches, 1,000 stags, 1,000 boars, gazelles (? *dammae*), ibexes, wild sheep and other grass-eating creatures (*herbatica animalia*). The public was then admitted to the arena and allowed to help itself to the animals. On another day he showed in the amphitheatre 100 maned lions (*iubati leones*), which raised a mighty roar but had to be killed at the doors of their cages, which they seem to have refused to leave: their butchering did not make much of a show for the people (*non magnum praebentes spectaculum quo occidebantur*). After that he put on 100 Libyan and 100 Syrian maneless lions (*leopardi*), 100 lionesses and 300 bears. This time, too, the display appears to have caused some discontent among the populace, for the writer adds that all these wild beasts made a great show, but one that gave little pleasure (*quarum omnium ferarum magnum magis constat spectaculum fuisse quam gratum*). From what we now know of the *Augustan History*'s character, its accounts of the shows just described may well be judged fictitious in some of their details – in the numbers of animals exhibited, for instance. But its lists of species of creatures, at any rate, are confirmed by the archaeological sources.

The exhibitions, fights and *venationes* so far cited were held in Rome and involved great quantities of beasts. Yet shows on a large, but probably less lavish, scale must also have been given by the municipal authorities or by private individuals in the numerous Italian and provincial cities that possessed monumental masonry-built amphitheatres. Puteoli, Verona, Italica, Arles, Nîmes and Carthage are among the most obvious names that spring to mind. But, as inscriptions indicate, at the local shows in lesser towns only a few animals could sometimes be produced. For example, at a four-day show at Minturnae in AD 249 only 10 savage bears (*ursi crudeles*) and on each day 4 grass-eating creatures (*bestiae herbanae*) appeared and were killed: at Beneventum there were 16 bears and only 4 *ferae*, probably felines; and another unnamed Italian town had to be content with 10 grass-eaters and 4 *ferae dentatae*.[27] In the case of other towns of a similar type where the inscriptions do not specify the numbers of beasts exhibited it is likely that they were small.[28]

In fourth-century Syria the beast shows proved so attractive that people waited in the open overnight to make sure of securing places, preferring the hard stones of the street to their comfortable beds.[29]

There can, indeed, have been few cities, whether large or small, throughout the Roman world that did not provide their citizens with the entertainment of watching animals shown and killed; and the preliminary processes of catching the beasts alive in their homelands, of transporting them thence, by land or sea, alive and healthy to their destinations, and of keeping them fit between their arrival in *vivaria* such as the great State-owned one outside the Porta Praenestina in Rome[30] and their removal to cages in the amphitheatres before their appearance in the arenas – all this must have been organized on an enormous scale and have cost enormous sums. Not only had the beasts to be paid for when captured by the local inhabitants, but whole armies of professional trappers and hunters (other than the *venatores* of the shows), keepers, trainers and vets must have been maintained, receiving high wages for what was highly skilled and dangerous work. The sort of problems involved in the supply of beasts is vividly illustrated in Cicero's corresponder.ce, when, on taking up his governorship in Cilicia in 51 BC, he was badgered by his friend Marcus Caelius Rufus, who was standing for the aedileship of 50, to provide him with leopards (*pantherae*) for the *ludi* that he would have to give on his election. This embarrassed Cicero, who did not want to start his term of office with demands from the provincials for leopards on behalf of a personal friend: he did no more than issue a commission (*mandatus*) to professional hunters (*qui venari solent*) to procure the creatures; and he flatly refused to raise subscriptions from the Cilician communities towards defraying the cost of Caelius' shows.[31] Other disappointments were due to natural causes. Maximus, a friend of the Younger Pliny, had ordered a large number of *Africanae* for the show that he was giving at Verona; but the animals were delayed by bad weather and did not arrive in time.[32] Again, Symmachus' letters recount the difficulties that he sometimes encountered in securing the beasts that he needed for his games at the end of the fourth and beginning of the fifth century.[33] On one occasion his animals were shipwrecked; on another, hardly any of the bears that he had ordered actually arrived; and on yet another his crocodiles refused to eat and had to be killed off. But at other times he was successful in obtaining animals from many quarters.

THE ROMAN ATTITUDE TO ANIMALS

The literary and epigraphic evidence for the prominence of animals in so many aspects of Roman life is, as we shall see, abundantly and closely paralleled in Roman art. There beasts and birds of almost every species known to the ancient Romans are lovingly, sensitively, and often very accurately depicted in many media – in sculpture, painting, mosaics, ivory, metalwork, gem- and die-engraving. Not infrequently we find them rendered for their own sakes, out of the context of any human activity, or as accessories to scenes of which the content does not explicitly demand their presence. All this serves to underline what is one of the outstanding paradoxes of the Roman mind – that a people that was so much alive to the interest and beauty of the animal kingdom, that admired the intelligence and skill to be found in so many of its representatives, that never seemed to tire of the sight of rare and unfamiliar specimens, that displayed such devotion to its pets, should yet have taken pleasure in the often hideous sufferings and agonizing deaths of quantities of magnificent and noble creatures. Mass excitement induced by scenes of violent conflict, particularly those in which human dexterity and courage in mastering the beasts (as in Spanish bullfights today) stirred the enthusiasm of the crowds, might perhaps in part explain it. Yet in the written sources the numbers of animals slaughtered on specific occasions are recorded cold-bloodedly and, indeed, as matter for congratulation. In the twenty-six *venationes bestiarum Africanarum* given by Augustus, 3,500 creatures died.[34] In 29 BC wild and tame animals in vast numbers ($\pi\alpha\mu\pi\lambda\eta\theta\hat{\eta}$) perished, including a rhinoceros and a hippopotamus; in 13 BC 600 African beasts were slain; in 2 BC 260 lions were slaughtered in the Circus Maximus and 36 crocodiles in the Circus Flaminius; and in AD 12 there was another slaughter of wild beasts ($\theta\eta\rho\acute{\iota}\omega\nu \ \sigma\phi\alpha\gamma\acute{\eta}$), including 200 lions.[35] In one of Gaius' shows 400 bears and 400 other Libyan beasts were killed; under Claudius, 300 bears and 300 Libyan beasts; and Nero's bodyguard brought down with javelins 400 bears and 300 lions.[36] In Titus' spectacles of A D 80, 9,000 animals, tame and wild, were killed, partly by women.[37]

With Domitian, personal pleasure in animal holocausts is only to be expected: he is said to have slain with arrows 100 wild beasts of different kinds on his Alban estate, deliberately killing some with two successive shots.[38] Trajan, however, beat the record by the butchery of 11,000 beasts to celebrate his Dacian triumph.[39] But for refinement of cruelty to animals Commodus took the palm. He kept animals at home in order to kill them: in public he despatched with his own hands 100 bears, 6 hippopotamuses, 3 elephants, rhinoceroses, a tiger and a giraffe; and according to Herodian, who also mentions lions and leopards as Commodus' victims, he shot ostriches with crescent-shaped arrowheads devised to decapitate the birds, whose headless bodies went on running.[40]

A very few protests raised against such scenes of sadistic barbarity are recorded in the literary sources, the most important being that of the Roman populace itself at the show given by Pompey in 55 B C.[41] On this occasion 20 or 17 elephants, according to Pliny, 18 in Seneca's and Dio Cassius' versions of the incident, were set to fight in the Circus against men armed with javelins, Gaetulians, so Pliny states. In Pliny's account one elephant delighted the spectators by the extraordinary fight that it put up, crawling on its knees, when its feet were wounded, to attack its opponents, whose shields it seized and tossed in the air in such a way that as they fell they described a circle (or formed a circle on the ground round it?) – *decidentia . . . erant in orbem circumiecta*; it was more like watching a clever juggler than an infuriated beast – *velut arte non furore beluae iacerentur*. The crowd was also amazed at seeing another elephant killed by a single blow when a javelin hit it below the eye and penetrated to the head's vital parts. But, when the whole troupe tried to stampede and break down the iron bars enclosing it, the onlookers were thoroughly alarmed; and their compassion and disgust were aroused when the creatures, losing all hope of escape, began to trumpet piteously and beg for mercy, running round the arena and raising their trunks heavenwards in lamentation, according to Dio's description of the scene. Dio further says that they gave the impression of calling for vengeance on their keepers, who had broken the promise made to them before they embarked in Africa that no harm should come to them. At any rate, to quote Pliny's words, the whole crowd wept and rose to its feet, cursing Pompey for his cruelty: *flens universus [populus] consurgeret dirasque Pompeio imprecaretur.* The story thus vividly told by Pliny and Dio is confirmed by Cicero's contemporary reference to Pompey's exhibition. 'The last day of the shows was devoted to the elephants. This stirred the people's wonder, but did not please them at all. In fact, it ended in their pitying the beasts and in their feeling that a certain affinity exists between men and elephants.'[42] 'What pleasure can a cultivated man find in seeing a noble beast run through by a hunting spear?' is Cicero's comment on the general treatment of animals at the shows.[43]

This is unfortunately the first and the last public protest of which we have knowledge. No doubt many cultured and humane individuals were, like Cicero, disgusted by the senseless wounding and slaughtering of beasts, who, as Plutarch sharply remarks, were either forced to make a stand and fight against their will or destroyed without possessing any natural means of self-defence.[44] But the horrifying spectacles of carnage still went on, at any rate in Rome; and if provincial shows involved less bloodshed, the same animals being exhibited on several successive occasions, considerations of expense, rather than feeling for the creatures, may well have been the reason. Our problem still remains.[45]

THE ANCIENT SOURCES

References to animals in Roman life are, of course, scattered throughout the works of Latin and Greek writers of the Roman age. But the most important literary sources that deal in general with the subject are: Varro, *De Re Rustica* (first century BC), Columella, *De Re Rustica* (first century AD), the Elder Pliny, *Naturalis Historia* (first century AD), Martial, *De Spectaculis* (first century AD), Plutarch, *De Sollertia Animalium* (first to second centuries AD), Arrian, *Cynegetica* (second century AD), 'Oppian', *Cynegetica* and *Halieutica* (late second century AD), and Aelian, *De Natura Animalium* (second to third centuries AD).

Of equal if not greater importance are the archaeological monuments. The use of animals for transport and for agriculture is illustrated by equestrian statuary, by numerous funerary reliefs and by some paintings and mosaics. Domestic pets appear both in these media and on *genre* reliefs and minor works of art as well. Apart from the actual remains of horse-armour that survive (pp. 170, 171), the role of beasts in war is portrayed on tombstones and on official State reliefs; and these last are the best and most obvious source for renderings of their place in public religious ritual. Hunting scenes on sarcophagi offer a number of spirited and often naturalistic representations of horses, hounds, lions, boars and so forth. But for the parts played by animals in hunting and in public entertainment, namely by horses in circus-racing and by creatures tame and wild in the spectacles, the mosaic pavements, especially those of Rome, Sicily, North Africa and Syria, are unrivalled as documents. The racehorse mosaics will be treated in detail in the chapter devoted to horses (pp. 177–82); and special mosaic renderings of other individual species, whether shown singly or in groups, will be discussed in the chapters relevant to each kind. At this point, however, something may be said in general of those mosaics which feature varied assortments of animals within the frame of a single picture, whether they be scenes of hunting for sport, where the aim was to kill the quarry, or of the rounding up and capturing alive of beasts for the arena or of the shows in progress. From these again particular figures and groups of individual species will be selected for detailed comment in later chapters.

Hunting for sport in Sicily is illustrated on the 'Little Hunt' mosaic in Room 23 of the great country villa near Piazza Armerina in the centre of the island – a villa whose owner and date within the fourth century, together with the date of its splendid polychrome figured pavements, are still in dispute. Intensive excavation of the site began in 1950 and was completed in 1955. The 'Little Hunt' picture [46] is divided into five superimposed registers, the third and fourth from the top being broken at the centre by a single episode, that of the hunters' picnic alfresco, which occupies both zones. All the quarry could be local and the whole pavement could reflect the pastimes of the villa-owner and his friends. In the left-hand half of the first zone two hounds are being led on leashes to the hunting field; in the right-hand half they have been released to chase a fox. In the second register, to the left of a central group showing a sacrifice to Diana, two huntsmen carry on their shoulders a pole from which a netted boar is suspended, while a hound runs below, its eager head raised towards the prey: on the right a huntsman grasps a dead hare by the hind-legs. In the third and fourth zones, on the left, are two huntsmen, one with a falcon, trapping birds, and a hound in pursuit of a fox; on the right are a hound chasing a hare and a mounted huntsman spearing a hare that has taken refuge in a thicket. Finally, in the fifth register, on the left three stags are being driven into a net by two mounted huntsmen, while on the right four huntsmen on foot and a couple of hounds engage an infuriated boar.

Local fauna, some of them more dangerous and exciting than the fiercest of Sicilian boars, form the quarry on four hunt-mosaics from Antioch-on-the-Orontes. That all these pavements illustrate hunting in the field, not arena *venationes*, would seem to be clear from the landscape elements, trees, shrubs and small plants, that represent the setting of the figures and do not look like artificial scenery (p. 19). Three of the four triangular panels of the Room I mosaic in the Constantinian Villa show, respectively, two huntsmen on foot attacking a lion and a boar with bow and arrow and spear; two mounted huntsmen dealing with a leopard, a bear and a lion; and three mounted huntsmen slaying a bear, a lion and a tiger.[47] On the mosaic of Megalopsychia (*c.* AD 450), the animals in the scenes surrounding her bust-in-medallion, which are encountered by six named huntsmen on foot, are a tigress and her cubs, a lion, a boar, two leopards and a bear, while in the field are four groups of animals hunting other animals – a bear and a bull, a lion and a stag, two dogs and a ram, a lioness and a wild horse.[48] On the fragmentary Dumbarton Oaks mosaic (*c.* AD 500) the quarry consists of a lion, a leopard, a doe, a caracal, a tigress with two cubs, a boar, a small elephant and an ibex.[49] Finally, in the Worcester Hunt (*c.* AD 500), along the sides of the picture, four mounted huntsmen and three huntsmen on foot are engaged with a lion, a leopard, a lioness, a bear, another leopard, a tigress with her cubs, and a hyena. Encircling the central standing figure of the master of the hunt (?) are a boar, already slain, a crouching ibex, a wounded bear, a hyena, another bear, a wounded doe, a stag and a hare.[50] All four of these magnificent pavements are worked in polychrome, and the creatures, despite the late date of the last three pieces, are rendered with superb vigour and great fidelity to nature.

A large mosaic pavement found at Carthage in 1965 depicts partly the hunting and slaughtering for sport of beasts in the African wilds and partly their capture alive for arena displays.[51] Parts of the floor are lost, but the large and reasonably well-preserved portions of it that remain carry a series of self-contained scenes one above the other, separated by ground-lines below the figures but not symmetrically arranged in even registers: the central scene enjoys more space than do the pictures above and to the sides of it. Rocks, trees and shrubs convey the natural setting of the episodes. The smaller scenes are: the enticing of lions into a large cage or travelling-box; the killing of a boar and the conveyance of its corpse from the hunting field in a net; a large-eared African elephant in a python's deadly grip; the pursuit of a jackal by a huntsman and his hound; the capture of two wild asses by lasso; a huntsman on foot attacking a leopard; a huntsman about to slay the lion that has pounced upon the horse from which he has been unseated; and a stag attacked by a leopard – the last scene, like that of the elephant and python, suggesting that strife between the beasts themselves will facilitate their capture or destruction by human hunters. The large central scene presents a mounted hunter who has stolen a baby elephant clattering up the gangway of a ship as though hotly pursued by the desperate mother (cf. pp. 72, 81); she is not actually portrayed but is left to the spectator's imagination, according to the way in which the fragments of the pavement have been assembled. The baby elephant is not very easy to discern. But there does seem to be a greyish feature, ending in a rounded aperture, which sticks out from under the mounted hunter's arm and which could well be the baby's trunk. Moreover, Dr Katherine Dunbabin, who has studied the actual pavement, has suggested that the group of two wild asses on the left should be placed lower down, leaving room above them for the now lost mother elephant.

Two post-reform coins of Maximian (one in almost mint condition), which were found below the mosaic's concrete bed, provide a *terminus post quem* for its creation.

A pavement from the House of Bacchus at Cuicul, in Algeria, shows an animal hunt comprising a boar, a stag, a leopard and four lions.[52]

A mosaic found at Hippo Regius in Algeria provides an extremely detailed and circumstantial picture of a favourite method of taking animals alive.[53] Nets have been stretched out in a circle and fenced on the inner side with a hedge of prickly plants. On one side, between the hedge and the open space enclosed by it and the nets, huntsmen armed with large shields and flaming torches form a close ring, while other huntsmen, two mounted and one on foot, are driving a pair of antelopes and a pair of ostriches into the trap, in which three leopards (one has pinned another huntsman to the ground), a lion and a lioness (or tiger?) are frantically rushing round. Three circular pens behind the ring of shield-bearing huntsmen hold cattle and deer, perhaps to serve as bait and food for the captured beasts; and in the left-hand lower corner of the picture is a mule-cart bringing up a wooden travelling-box for transporting a wild animal: on top of this box is a funnel-shaped object, perhaps a ventilator or a mechanism for closing the open end as soon as the captive was inside.[54] Another such box can be seen on the right-hand side of the mosaic, near one of the cattle-pens. Still further to the right, outside the circle of nets, is a tent and a meal in preparation for the huntsmen. At the top of the picture, on the right, are two antelopes that have escaped the trap and a huntsman chasing a wild ass with a lasso.

For wealth of incident the 'Great Hunt' mosaic in the villa near Piazza Armerina far surpasses all other documentations so far known of the preliminary activities that lay behind the shows. This mosaic completely carpets a corridor (seventy yards long and terminating in an apse at either end), which runs north-south between the eastern side of a great rectangular peristyle (to whose western side the entrance to the villa gives access) and an enormous apsed audience hall, in which the owner of the place presumably received his guests and clients.[55] The 'Great Hunt' thus occupies one of the most important positions, if not the most important one, in the whole house (the audience hall itself has no figured pavement); and its subject, the hunting, capture, embarking and disembarking of wild animals and birds, must have been of paramount interest to the proprietor.[56] And it would seem that this proprietor is himself portrayed in the figure of an elderly, short-bearded man, wearing a round cap and a richly embroidered mantle, leaning on a staff and gazing intently before him, who, with two shield-bearing attendants beside him, stands near the centre of the corridor's southern half.[57] We must think of him as either being present in person at the African or eastern hunting grounds and ports where all the work is going on and keenly watching its progress or, more probably, as following it in his imagination at home. The official view of the Piazza Armerina villa is that it was the place to which the Emperor Maximianus Herculeus retired when his colleague Diocletian forced him, much against his will, to abdicate in May 305. The arguments for and against this theory cannot be rehearsed here. But it may be noted that we have no record that Maximianus had given lavish beast shows in Rome or evinced any lively interest in animal-supply; and the possibility suggests itself that the villa's owner was a private individual who had made a vast fortune for himself by contracting to produce beasts and birds for the arenas of the Roman world. Further proof of this person's special interest in the animal kingdom lies in the fact that wild creatures figure prominently as heads in wreaths on the portico mosaic of the great rectangular peristyle [58] and as protomes and full figures in a floral scroll on the portico mosaic of a large elliptical courtyard.[59] (The athletic and mythological subjects that also feature on the villa's pavements could mean that the owner was in part responsible for other types of display besides beast shows at the spectacles.)

The contents of the corridor mosaic may now be briefly reviewed, starting at its northern end. The scenes form, in the main, two superimposed registers and along the top of the picture small-scale landscape and architectural features indicate locality. First comes a scene, spreading over both zones, of the rounding up of leopards by mounted huntsmen against a wall of shield-bearing huntsmen standing in a row behind a hedge: in the centre of the row is an open travelling-box in which a dead or dying goat is suspended with a view to enticing a leopard to enter, while above the box a hunter grasps with both hands the funnel-shaped object on the roof.[60] The next portion of the pavement is partly destroyed, but it seems to show fleeing animals above and mounted huntsmen below. The following sections present a lion-hunt above and a boar-hunt below; and, after these, a leopard hunting an antelope, a fleeing gazelle or bubal, and another chased by a dog, all above an ox-cart loaded with travelling-boxes of the type already described. In the next upper scene two pairs of huntsmen on foot are carrying, on poles on their shoulders, respectively a beast in a box and a boar in a net, while below two ostriches and what is either a gazelle or a bubal are being taken up the gangway of a large sailing-ship which fills the whole width of the mosaic and has travelling-crates stacked on deck:[61] yet on a second gangway at the ship's other end four men carrying a large box on poles, and an ostrich in the arms of another huntsman, are disembarking. Above this disembarkation are seen first the capture of an elephant, of which only the legs and trunk survive, and then a group of two men with round caps and long staves, apparently officials directing some of the operations. After that comes another sailing-ship, rather smaller than the first, but also filling both zones, from which a bear (?) is disembarking down a gangway on the left, while an African elephant, with concave back and large ears (cf. p. 46), embarks on a gangway on the right and a recalcitrant bull with ropes fastened to its horns is being dragged along with a view to its following the elephant up the gangway.[62] In the register above the embarkation gangway a quartet of more or less quiescent animals, a horse, a camel, a tigress and an antelope, is being led towards the sea. We must be meant to imagine these two sailing-ships as both about to sail across the Mediterranean, say from Africa or Syria, and just arriving at their destination, say at Ostia – an extreme form of the 'continuous' or 'simultaneous' style in Roman narrative art.[63] At the centre of the southern half of the mosaic is the capture of a hippopotamus, above, and of a rhinoceros, below.[64] Then come, in the lower zone, the villa-owner and his attendants, two mounted huntsmen, and a cart drawn by oxen and loaded with slatted crates that are surmounted by the same funnel-shaped objects. Above these groups is the hunting of a lioness (or maneless lion), a leopard, and a maned lion, the last two of the felines having each seized an antelope.[65] The following section shows, above, a leopard stalking either a gazelle or a bubal, and, below, a small boat without sails, up the gangway of which, on the right, a mounted huntsman is fleeing from a tigress in an incident to be discussed in detail later (p. 72).[66] The final portion of the pavement depicts, above, two huntsmen advancing on a lion absorbed in the slaughter of a wild ass [67] and, below, a griffin, popularly believed actually to exist in eastern lands,[68] sprawling on the lid of a slatted crate from one end of which a human face, probably that of a man used as a decoy, peeps out dolefully: the idea was that a griffin could be caught while preoccupied with trying to tear the crate open and get at the man inside.

The mosaic in each of the apses contains a personification of the regions in which the animals of the 'Great Hunt' were taken captive. The northern apse mosaic is very fragmentary, but that at the southern end is very well preserved. Here the female figure, a composite personification, is seated on some rocks, grasping the trunk of a tree in whose foliage exotic birds are sheltering, and holding an elephant's tusk sceptre-wise: a phoenix (Arabia) and an elephant (Africa) flank her on the left, a tigress (Persia or India) and another tusk on the right.[69] This elephant, too, is African, with huge ears and a concave back. All three elephants in the 'Great Hunt' mosaic are completely covered with 'reticulations' – the standard convention in Roman art for representing the creatures' wrinkled hides.[70] (The complete 'Great Hunt' is reproduced on pp. 40-1). (Pl. 1)

We may now turn to the mosaic renderings of fights in the arena
with animals of several species. One of the frieze-like panels from
Torre Nuova, now in the Galleria Borghese in Rome, presents a
combat of men with six different creatures – a wild ass (or boar?), an
ostrich, a bull, an antelope, a lion and a stag.[71] Still more lively and
varied are the scenes on the east and west sides of the mosaic border
surrounding a partly tessellated, partly opus sectile square emblema
from the villa at Zliten in Tripolitania, a piece of controversial date.[72]
That these scenes are arena venationes is certain from the fact that, as in
the Torre Nuova frieze, no landscape elements appear, and that
gladiators occupy the other two sides of the border. Furthermore, at
the extreme left of the eastern frieze, which is relatively complete,
two condemned criminals, each standing in a little two-wheeled cart
and bound to a stake, are about to be devoured by two leopards. One
animal has leapt onto its victim's chest and shoulders and the other,
its hind-legs still on the ground, is on the point of doing likewise.
Then come a venator on foot chasing, with the help of two hounds, an
antelope and a stag, a dwarfish figure facing a boar, and three more
huntsmen, one with a dog assistant, dealing with a stag and a wild ass.
Above the third huntsman from the left a bear and a bull, chained
together, are locked in deadly conflict. The final episode shows a
venator, armed with a whip, pushing a helpless criminal towards a
lion that bounds to the left to seize him, and a second lion which
seems to have hurled another huntsman to the ground before
bounding to the right, perhaps to attack another beast now lost. The
west side of the border is much more fragmentary. The first
surviving figure on the left is that of a hound rushing leftwards in
pursuit of a quarry that has now disappeared. Then come two
ostriches driven by a hound towards the right where two venatores
respectively brandish a stick or sword and a lash. Of the rest of the
menagerie all that remains, in the right-hand half of the frieze, are the
legs and belly of a bull and the hind-legs of a wild ass or horse. Thus
there are at least nine different species in the preserved portions of the
two friezes and it could be that some of the creatures now lost to us
would have lengthened the list.

A mosaic panel discovered at Carthage in 1930 portrays an
assemblage of animals and birds for show set out in five 'columns',
the figures in each column being arranged in superimposed tiers.[73]
The piece has many gaps; but nineteen creatures, wholly or partially
preserved, can be counted, and in the blank left-hand bottom corner

there was room for two more. There are six leopards, two bears, a bull, two boars, two antelopes, two shaggy wild sheep with long, curly horns, two stags and two ostriches. That the picture purports to represent a real exhibition, in which many more beasts actually appeared, is clear from the inscriptions on the bodies of some of the participants – N[umero] followed by a numeral indicating the numbers of each species that were to be seen in the arena. There were 30 bears of one kind and 40 of another, 25 ostriches, 15 antelopes, 10 wild sheep of one kind and 6 of another. The numbers of leopards, boars, bulls and stags are not recorded on such parts of the mosaic as survive; but they may have been given in the missing portions. Similarly, in the reasonably well-preserved surviving section of the pavement showing performing animals from Radez in Tunisia – in which the protagonists are eight bears, seconded by five boars – the solitary bull is marked N XVI on its flank. None of the bears and boars is numbered; nor are the stag and ostrich which complete the menagerie as it has come down to us.[74] It is, however, more than likely, on the analogy of the Carthage pavement, that a bear and a boar in the missing main portion informed the spectator of the numbers of their species that were exhibited on that occasion.

It is, of course, possible that the components of the Carthage and Radez menageries, the numbers of each species said to have been shown, and the names of the Radez bears (p. 96) were the mosaic designer's inventions and bore no relation to fact. On the other hand, there would seem to be no valid reason why these pavements should not reflect historical entertainments that the patrons who commissioned the pictures had themselves witnessed. After all, programmes of the shows in the form of handbills or painted placards giving details of the animal performances might still have been available, after the shows were over, for the artists' information. And bears, like racehorses, may have been 'star' performers who made reputations for themselves in successive appearances and were known to the public by name.

CHAPTER II

ELEPHANTS

ELEPHANTS IN WAR

ELEPHANTS, BY FAR THE LARGEST and most intelligent of animals, renowned for their tenacious memories, patience, gentleness and obedience to man, were not known to the classical world as instruments of war before Alexander's eastern campaigns.[1] At the battle of Gaugamela in 331 BC Darius had fifteen elephants from the Arachosia region, to the west of the Indus, whose satrap fought on the Persian side; but they were not, apparently, put into line against the Greeks. Four years later, in 327, when on his way eastwards from Bactria, Alexander was presented with twenty-five elephants by Taxiles, ruler of Taxila, and other local chiefs, but he used them only for transport. Pressing still further eastwards, he captured at Durta the elephants of a resisting chief; and in the early spring of 326 he acquired fifty-six more beasts as a gift from Taxiles. Alexander's first serious encounter with elephants as armament was on the river Jhelun (Hydaspes), south-east of Taxila, on the far bank of which the local king, Porus, had drawn up a large force of the animals. These at first prevented the Greeks from crossing; eventually, however, the crossing was achieved and, after a desperate battle, the elephants were routed. Porus, meanwhile, had ridden off on an elephant, but he was pursued and submitted, becoming Alexander's ally. A coin struck, probably soon after Alexander's death, to commemorate the battle shows the latter on horseback in pursuit of Porus on his huge elephant.[2] Elephants accompanied the Greeks on their return journey down the Jhelun in the autumn of 326. (Pl. 3)

The grim experience of the fight with Porus' elephants had a lasting effect on the mind of one of Alexander's generals, Seleucus, who after Alexander's death founded the Seleucid dynasty and later made Indian elephants his special arm in war and the emblem of his House. He did, in fact, exchange all the provinces that had been annexed beyond the Indus for large numbers of elephants; and thus succeeded in defeating Antigonus, his rival in Asia Minor, who had only seventy-five elephants, at the battle of Ipsus in Phrygia in 301.

The war arm of Alexander, Porus and the Seleucids, the Indian elephant, is characterized by its convex back and small ears, as contrasted with the African Forest elephant, which has a concave back and very large ears and is smaller than the Indian variety. Coin-types of the Seleucid King Seleucus III, on the one hand, and reverse-types of the Barcid (Carthaginian) silver coinage struck in Spain, on the other, illustrate the difference very clearly [3] – a difference which later artists of the Roman period did not always observe so carefully. While the Seleucids of Syria obtained their elephants from India, their rivals, the Ptolemies of Egypt, got their main supply from Ethiopia, where the animals were hunted and shipped up from the trading posts on the Red Sea to Alexandria. Ptolemy II (Philadelphus: 283-246) and his son Ptolemy III (Euergetes: 246-221) were especially active in this business,[4] valuing the beasts as curiosities and as a source of ivory as well as for use in warfare, for which Indian trainers or mahouts ('Ινδοί) must have been imported. However, at the battle of Raphia in Palestine in 217, Ptolemy IV's 73 African elephants proved, with a few exceptions, greatly inferior to the 102 Indian beasts of Antiochus III. Ptolemy did, indeed, win the battle; but sixteen of his elephants were killed and most of the rest either ran away or were captured, whereas Antiochus lost only five.[5] There is little evidence of the Ptolemies using Ethiopian elephants for warfare after Raphia. (Pls 4, 5)

Meanwhile, early in the third century B C, the Greeks, Romans and Carthaginians west of the Adriatic had had their first experience of elephants in war when Pyrrhus King of Epirus, invited by the Tarentines to assist them in resistance to Rome, landed in Italy in 280 with twenty almost certainly Indian elephants.[6] These he used in his first encounter with the Romans under Valerius Laevinus at Heraclea, stationing them on the wings to terrify the Roman cavalry and securing victory by this means. But later his display of a large and splendid beast to face the Roman embassy that demanded the redemption of prisoners did not produce the request for peace that he hoped for. Next year, in the battle near Venusia with the consuls Publius Sulpicius and Publius Decius Mus, Pyrrhus first placed his elephants on his wings again, but next day he used them to open breaches in the Roman legions; and a second time it was the elephants that gained for him an indecisive victory. In 278 they crossed with him to Sicily;[7] but many of them were lost when the Carthaginian fleet attacked his transports recrossing to Italy in 275. In Pyrrhus' final repulse that year by Manius Curius Dentatus near Beneventum four of his elephants were captured and shown in Rome at the consul's triumph – the Roman people's first sight of such creatures.[8] Since Lucania had been the scene of the elephants' first appearance in Italy they were nicknamed by the Romans 'Lucanian cows'.[9]

There can be little doubt that it was Pyrrhus' elephants that occasioned the earliest representations of the animals in ancient Italian art. Among the types on the heavy brick-like bronze pieces, the so-called *aes signatum*, struck, probably in Rome, during the first half of the third century BC,[10] is the very naturalistically rendered figure in relief of an Indian elephant, with convex back and small ears, walking towards the right.[11] On the other side of the 'brick' is the figure, pacing leftwards, of one of the Italian wild sows whose grunting alarmed Pyrrhus' elephants.[12] Another reflection of Pyrrhus' beasts is on a painted plate from Capena, made in Latium, of third-century BC date, and now in the Villa Giulia in Rome. In the central roundel of this plate is the enchanting portrait of a female Indian war-elephant, with convex back, small ears, and tusks abnormally large for a cow, marching sedately towards the left, either on parade or into battle, and followed closely by her calf – its mother's split-image in physical characteristics. On her back is a lofty tower or howdah (*turris*, πύργος) with battlements, manned by a mahout (*rector*) and two fighting-men.[13] No female elephant would consent to fight if parted from her young and if the latter squealed when wounded or trampled on she immediately rushed to the rescue, abandoning her martial duties. Pyrrhus' elephants would certainly have carried howdahs of the type depicted on the plate – *turrita corpora* and *dorso ferre cohortes ... euntem in proelia turrem*, to quote the phrases used by Lucretius (see p. 347, note 9) and Juvenal (XII, 109, 110) respectively of war-elephants. And although Lucretius wrongly ascribes the invention of the use of elephants in battle to the Carthaginians, whose war beasts do not seem to have been turreted,[14] he rightly associates elephants with India. A fascinating terracotta statuette of an Indian war-elephant of the Roman period, now in the National Museum at Naples, was found at Pompeii. The elephant, which has small ears, wears a heavy saddle-cloth sweeping to the ground, and on it, fastened by chains to the beast's body, is a tall, crenelated tower. In front of the tower sits a mahout, inserting a loaf or cake into the elephant's uplifted trunk.[15] (Pls 2, 6, 10)

But India was not the normal source from which the Carthaginians got their animals. Their elephants were, as we have seen (cf. p. 33), African; and they were obtained in the Atlas region of western North Africa and from the Fezzan further east (see p. 347, note 3). These creatures belonged, as did the Ethiopian elephants of the Ptolemies (cf. p. 33), to the smaller Forest, as contrasted with the larger Bush or equatorial species of African elephant.[16] It was probably the Carthaginians' encounter with the Indian elephants of Pyrrhus in Sicily that first suggested to them the idea of capturing the native animals and training them for war with the aid of Indian mahouts. According to Appian, Carthage had stabling for three hundred elephants.[17]

The earliest recorded instance of the use of elephants by Carthage in war was in 262 BC when Hanno put 50 or 60 in the field against the Romans at Agrigentum. Most of the beasts were captured by the enemy;[18] but that did not deter the Carthaginian generals from using them on subsequent occasions in the First Punic War – for instance in 256-255, against Regulus in Africa, when about 100 were used with success; or in 255 in Sicily, under Hasdrubal, when they mustered about 140, which were, however, lost in 250 in the battle against Lucius Caecilius Metellus at Panormus[19] – here the animals became confused and charged their own side, many being captured by the Romans with their Indian mahouts and despatched to Rome, after being ferried on rafts across the straits to Rhegium.[20] It was in commemoration of this event that the elephant became the emblem of the *gens Caecilia* on the coins issued by its later members.[21] In the 'Truceless War' of Carthage against her rebellious mercenaries from 240-237 Hanno had 100 elephants and Hamilcar 70. In Spain Hamilcar had 100 of the beasts; while Hasdrubal, who succeeded him in Spain, had 200 from 229 to 228.[22]

The most famous of all Carthaginian war-elephants are, of course, those that Hannibal brought with him across the Alps into Italy in 218 BC.[23] In 220 in his campaign against the Spanish tribe of Vaccaei Hannibal had used 40 elephants; but when he set out for Italy he left 21 in Spain and had 37 when he crossed the Rhône. Arrived in Italy the elephants played their part in alarming the local inhabitants; they also fought at Trebia in 218, after which all but one died. The survivor carried Hannibal across the Apennines.[24] Juvenal writes of an 'African beast' in this connection.[25] But a local bronze coin of the third century B C struck in Etruria shows on its reverse an unmistakably Indian elephant with convex back and small ears, which suggests that Hannibal's mount on his journey southwards may have been an Indian beast, obtained by Carthage through Egypt.[26] Two other Italian coin-types struck in the south also depict what are probably Indian elephants, one carrying a tower and both recognizable as Indian from their convex backs, although their ears are distinctly large.[27] It has been suggested that these indicate that Indian elephants may have been among the forty sent as reinforcements to Hannibal in Italy from Carthage in 215.[28] Perhaps the designer of these coin-types had seen both African and Indian beasts and conflated the characteristics of the two species.[29] According to Livy [30] Hannibal used thirty-three of his new elephants in his vain attempt to relieve Capua in 211. Finally, the elephants brought into Italy from Spain by Hasdrubal Barca, Hannibal's brother, made no small contribution to his defeat in 207 at Metaurus. At their first charge the animals threw into confusion the Roman line in front of the standards and even drove the standards from their positions. But later, as the fighting and noise increased, they got out of hand and rampaged up and down between the two armies as though uncertain as to which was their own side, wandering about like ships without anyone to steer them. More elephants were killed by their own drivers (*ipsis rectoribus*) than by the Roman enemy.[31]

Meanwhile in Spain Mago Barca, a second brother, had the twenty elephants sent with him to the peninsula by Carthage in 215; but we do not know what part, if any, the beasts played in the total defeat of Publius and Gnaeus Scipio in 211. In the Spanish campaigns of Publius Cornelius Scipio (Africanus)[32] we hear of elephants fleeing northwards with Hasdrubal Barca after the battle of Baecula in 208. At the battle of Ilipa in 206 Hasdrubal, son of Gisgo, placed his elephants on his wings, but in the course of the conflict they took fright and stampeded, doing as much harm to their own side as to the Romans. Transferred to Africa in 204, Scipio Africanus was faced with elephants again at his crowning victory over Hannibal in 202 at Zama, where some eighty beasts were stationed in front of the first Carthaginian line and opened battle with a charge. But, terrified by the blare of the bugles, some turned against their own side, while the rest were either driven through gaps in the Roman lines or escaped altogether from the field.[33] Once more, as at Ilipa, the Carthaginian beasts proved failures as a war arm. None the less, one of the terms of the peace made by the Romans after Zama was to the effect that the Carthaginians should surrender all their elephants and undertake not to train any more.[34]

An early occasion on which we hear of the Romans using war-elephants themselves was at the battle of Magnesia in 191 against Antiochus III. Lucius Scipio's sixteen elephants did not, however, actually fight, but were kept in reserve, since he knew that his African beasts would not be able to withstand Antiochus' fifty-four Indians, which were both larger and more courageous. These towered above the soldiery and were rendered the more terrifying by their frontlets and plumes and the castles on their backs, each castle being manned by four combatants in addition to the mahout. Antiochus placed two elephants between each of the ten sections of his phalanx. But when it came to the contest the elephants failed to frighten the Romans, who had got used to dealing with the creatures in the Carthaginian wars. Moreover, Antiochus' elephants went wild and fled, so that the Romans were able to cut his phalanx to pieces and captured fifteen of his beasts.[35] Juvenal evidently believed that turreted elephants had been used in war by Roman republican generals, as well as by Pyrrhus and Hannibal;[36] and in 121 BC Gnaeus Domitius Ahenobarbus is said to have employed elephants against the Gallic tribe of the Allobroges at Vindalium.[37] In one of his battles with Jugurtha in 109-108 BC Quintus Caecilius Metellus, faced with forty-four Numidian elephants, captured four and slew the rest.[38] In 80 or 79 BC Pompey in Africa captured from the Numidian King Iarbas many elephants and planned to enter Rome at his triumph in a chariot drawn by four of these beasts; but the gate was too narrow for them and he had to be content with horses.[39]

The last occasion on which elephants played a part on a battlefield in Africa was at Julius Caesar's crushing defeat of the Pompeians at Thapsus in 46 BC. Caesar had already sent to Italy for a few elephants, probably belonging to a State-owned herd (cf. p. 47), not to use in fighting, but in order to train his cavalry to face the animals.[40] In the battle itself the Pompeian elephants were placed on the wings, but they were of no avail. Terrified by the blows inflicted on them by Caesar's slingers and archers, by the whirr of the slings and the impact of the stones and lead, they trampled on the men of their own side and crashed their way back to their own half-finished camp.

Caesar captured sixty-four armed and decorated enemy elephants, complete with their towers and ornaments.[41] It was surely in commemoration of this event that Caesar issued his *denarius*-type of a majestic African(?) elephant with concave back but small ears, walking towards the right and trampling on a dragon – unless the San Caesario and Cadriano hoards which contain it can be proved to have been buried before 49 BC.[42] Were that so, the type could only refer to the belief that 'Caesar' signified 'elephant' in Punic.[43] It has been suggested that in staging elephant fights at his shows (cf. p. 47) Caesar was experimenting with elephants as a war arm in view of his projected Parthian war.[44] Shortly after Caesar's death there was a force of war-elephants in northern Italy which passed from Antony's to Octavian's side.[45] We have no evidence that the elephants which accompanied Claudius to Britain in AD 43 took part in the battle that ended in the Roman capture of Belgic Camulodunum.[46] It was doubtless hoped that the sight of them would be enough to scare the natives. (Pl. 7)

In the fourth century AD Roman armies encountered war-elephants again, this time in the East, in Constantius II's and Julian's Persian campaigns. Ammianus Marcellinus vividly describes the impact made upon the Romans by the creatures' height (*elata in arduum specie*) as they moved slowly along in line with their wrinkled hides and armed men on their backs *(elephantorum agmina rugosis horrenda corporibus leniter incedebant armatis onusta)*.[47] Nothing, he says, could equal the horror caused by their trumpeting and enormous bulk (*adiectis elephantorum agminibus quorum stridore immanitateque corporis nihil humanae mentes terribilius cernunt*).[48] He returns again in other passages to the beasts' great size (*magnitudo corporum*), their stench (*faetor*), and noisy trumpeting (*stridor, fremitus*).[49] In yet another, still more graphic, passage Ammianus dilates upon 'the terrifying aspect of the gleaming elephants with their cruel gaping jaws, pungent smell, and strange appearance'.[50] Julian compares the Parthian (i.e. Persian) phalanx to a wall with the creatures carrying towers.[51] Most of the men on the Roman side must have seen elephants at shows. But it is one thing to watch from a safe distance while tame beasts perform tricks in the arena or meekly draw chariots, and quite another to face them, armed and goaded into fury, on the battlefield. The Persians must have got their beasts from India.

ELEPHANTS FOR DRAUGHT

Our earliest record of elephants used as draught-animals in classical times relates to the reign of Ptolemy I (Soter: 323-283 BC). A gold stater minted by him at Cyrene shows on the reverse Alexander, in Zeus Ammon's guise with thunderbolt and aegis, standing in a chariot drawn by four elephants towards the left[52] – an allusion to his return from India accompanied by elephants (cf. p. 32). The animal here depicted is clearly Indian, with small ears and convex back; and this confirms the belief that Indian elephants were in Ptolemy I's possession (cf. p. 347, note 4). Perhaps the king had staged some show in which a statue of Alexander was carried in an elephant *quadriga*. For we know that in Ptolemy II Philadelphus' famous pageant (πομπή) held at Alexandria in 279 or 278, in which Dionysus' triumphal return from India was represented, a golden statue of Alexander was drawn along in a chariot by elephants, probably four of them; and this chariot was preceded by twenty-four other chariots drawn by elephants, probably four to each chariot. If these conjectures are correct, Ptolemy II would have possessed as many as a hundred Indian elephants before his scheme for capturing and training Ethiopian beasts had got under way (cf. p. 33).[53] Who or what occupied the twenty-four chariots is not recorded. Alexander's return from India was closely linked with Dionysus' legendary triumphal progress from the East.

It was possibly in some measure of conscious imitation of the Hellenistic practice of associating Dionysus and Alexander with elephant-drawn chariots that Pompey planned to enter Rome in triumph driving an elephant team (cf. p. 37). This would have been a gesture for which no Roman precedent existed, inasmuch as it did not merely imply a display of beasts, as in Curius Dentatus' triumph (cf. p. 34), but a claim on Pompey's part to the personal use of creatures well known for their services as draught-beasts to gods and semi-divine rulers. Similarly there was more than a hint at Augustus' possession of quasi-superhuman status in the *denarius* reverse-type of 18 BC which depicts him standing, with laurel branch and sceptre, in a *biga* of elephants that moves slowly towards the left.[54] The animals are Africans, with large ears and concave backs, and they wave their trunks as though to acclaim the emperor – just as elephants are said to have raised their trunks in adoration of the Sun.[55] An *aureus* reverse-type of 17-16 BC, with the legend QVOD VIAE MVN[*itae*] SVNT,

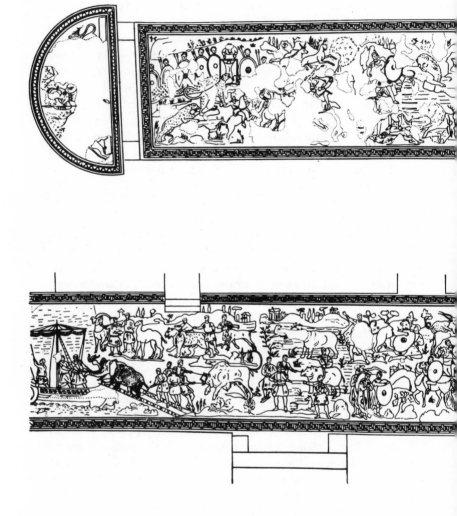

Fig. 1 *The 'Great Hunt' mosaic in the corridor of a Roman villa near Piazza Armerina, Sic*

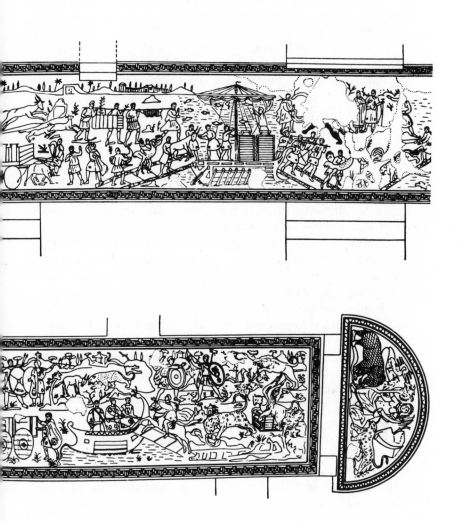

referring to the repair of high roads in Italy, shows a double arch placed on a viaduct and on the summit of the arch Augustus standing to the right in an elephant *biga*, holding a branch and crowned by Victory, who stands behind him in the chariot.[56] This may reflect a statuary group in bronze or marble erected at various points along the Italian highways. That Augustus actually rode in an elephant *quadriga* or *biga* during his lifetime is most unlikely: the elephant teams symbolize the honour paid to him for his achievements; and it was not until after his death, on a *sestertius*-type struck by Tiberius in AD 34-36, that these draught-beasts were used to betoken a scene of full-blown divinization. Here, accompanied by the legend DIVO AVGVSTO S[*enatus*] P[*opulus*] Q[*ue*] R[*omanus*], the radiate statue of Augustus, holding laurel branch and sceptre, is seated on a throne placed on a decorated car, which four elephants, each with a mahout on its neck, draw slowly towards the left.[57]

Tiberius' coin-type doubtless represents the chariot of Divus Augustus which was paraded at the *pompa circensis* in the reign of Claudius (who saw to it that a similar elephant-drawn car was voted to his grandmother Livia [58]), and at that under Nero in AD 59, when the elephants are said to have got as far as the seats of the senators and then flatly refused to proceed any further.[59] *Aurei* and *denarii* issued in 55 in the joint names of Nero and his mother Agrippina show on their reverses an elephant *quadriga* with two male figures side by side, most probably the statues of Divus Augustus and Divus Claudius, each seated on a throne on the decorated car, which moves left-wards.[60] The reverses of *sestertii* struck by Titus in 81-82 feature Divus Vespasianus, holding a sceptre, and Victory, seated on a throne on an ornamented car which four magnificent, probably Indian, elephants, each with a mahout on its neck, are drawing towards the right.[61] A *biga* of elephants for the *pompa circensis* was voted to Julia, daughter of Titus, after her death; and *aurei* reverse-types issued by Domitian present her effigy on its car drawn leftwards with a mahout on the neck of each beast.[62]

According to Martial, Domitian erected in Rome a triumphal arch which was surmounted by two elephant-drawn chariots each carrying a golden statue of himself.[63] A four-way arch with two elephant *quadrigae* back to back on top does, indeed, appear on *sestertii* of 88, 90-91 and 95-96: possibly these three series represent three separate, but similar, monuments.[64] The golden statues suggest the titles of *Dominus et Deus* which the emperor arrogated to himself;[65] and not so many years before his accession there had appeared at Pompeii, shortly before the eruption, a remarkable representation of a goddess riding in an elephant-drawn car. This is the well-known painting on the façade of the house-cum-workshop of the draper (vestiarius) Verecundus in Abundance Street.[66] In a red and gold frontal chariot, to which four elephants are harnessed, stands the statuesque figure of Venus Pompeiana, the city's patron deity, wearing a golden diadem and a sky-blue tunic and mantle, holding a sceptre and the rudder of Fortuna, and accompanied by Cupids. The four grey African elephants are seen from the front, two of them turned inwards three-quarters towards the left and two inwards three-quarters towards the right, while their lowered trunks converge at a central point on the ground. This imposing shop sign can hardly have been the wall-painter's own invention. Was he copying a picture displayed in one of Pompeii's public buildings? Or had he witnessed some pageant in which elephants, hired for the occasion, had drawn a statue of the goddess in the arena? Ironically, the long-lived elephants were meant to signify the town's good fortune and eternity. (Pl. 9)

Alexandrian coins of Domitian, Trajan and Hadrian appear to present the living emperors in elephant quadrigae.[67] Another Alexandrian coin-type, struck under Trajan, shows Isis and Serapis drawn by a similar team.[68] But on the Roman coinage throughout the second century elephant chariots are the exclusive perquisite of imperial Divi, whose images were paraded on them in the pompa circensis, as during the first century. Trajan issued aurei for Divus Nerva[69] and aurei and sestertii for his sister, Diva Marciana.[70] These, and the types struck subsequently for Diva Faustina I,[71] show a biga drawn now to left, now to right, with mahouts on the necks of the beasts. For Divus Antoninus,[72] Divus Verus,[73] and Divus Marcus[74] the cars are quadrigae, with four mahouts apiece. But Diva Faustina II has only a biga of two particularly large, mahout-ridden beasts.[75] The second-century series ends with a bronze medallion (at Bologna) of Divus Pertinax (193), where the image is borne beneath a canopy on a car drawn leftwards by four elephants with mahouts.[76] No third-century coins with such types were struck in Rome. But on the Greek imperial coinage of Asia Minor the pompa circensis elephant-team types were issued, not only for Tiberius, Vespasian, Antoninus Pius and Commodus, but also for third-century emperors – Caracalla, Gordian III and Gallienus.[77]

Meanwhile, on sarcophagi of the second half of the second century AD, carved with Dionysiac processions, two imposing elephants draw the god's chariot rightwards. On those that portray his triumphal return from India he stands erect in his car and is accompanied by camels and Indian prisoners.[78] Other pieces show the usual riotous *thiasos*, with Dionysus leaning forward in his chariot and turning to look backwards.[79] On all these reliefs, even on those that depict the Indian triumph, the elephants appear to be large-eared Africans. On such funerary monuments the long-lived, sun-worshipping animals (cf. pp. 39, 47, 53, 54), symbols of light and of eternity, reinforce the general theme of victory over death and after-life bliss that the Dionysiac processions were intended to convey.

To return to the emperors, Dio Cassius and the *Augustan History* (for what the latter's evidence is worth) record a number of scenes in Rome itself during the first half of the third century in which elephant-drawn chariots played their parts. Caracalla is said to have taken about with him many elephants – presumably harnessed in *quadrigae*, if not marching before him in procession – so that he might seem to be imitating Alexander (or rather Dionysus).[80] Elagabalus drove four elephant *quadrigae* in the Vatican region, destroying such tombs as got in his way.[81] Alexander Severus' triumphal car was drawn by four elephants.[82] The *statuae cum elephantis* decreed to Balbinus and Gordian I doubtless portrayed those personages as carried along by elephant teams;[83] and *quadrigae* of elephants were voted to Gordian III 'so that as victor over the Persians he might enjoy a Persian triumph'.[84]

If these statements are to be believed, there were, in the third century, not only a revival of the Augustan precedent of portraying living emperors in effigy as drawn along by elephants, but also occasions on which they actually rode behind such teams in person. Our next surviving record of imperial draught-elephants dates from the end of the century, when on 1 January 287 Diocletian and Maximian entered on their third and first consulships respectively and marked that event by issuing some remarkable gold medallions of which two examples have come down to us – a ten-*aurei* piece now in Florence and a five-*aurei* piece in Berlin.[85] The obverses of these two pieces bear busts of the two emperors in rich consular dress, while the reverses carry the legend IMPP [*imperatoribus*] DIOCLE-TIANO ET MAXIMIANO CCSS [*consulibus*] and a novel version of the consular procession – a frontal chariot in which the emperors are drawn by four Indian elephants with small ears and convex backs, two turned outwards to the right and two outwards to the left. It is not impossible that these animals did in actual fact draw the consular car. At any rate, the naturalistic way in which they are depicted suggests that these medallions (which have no mint-mark) were designed and struck in Rome where the die-engraver could have seen live elephants. Similarly, an actual consular procession may be reflected on a bronze *follis* issued in Rome in 310 for Maxentius' third consulship, with the reverse-legend FEL[ix] PROCESS[us] CONS[ulatus] III AVG[usti] N[ostri] and the emperor shown in an elephant *quadriga* moving leftwards with mahouts on the animals' necks and a Victory flying above.[86] But since other *folles* with the same consular legend present Maxentius in a frontal four-horse or six-horse chariot,[87] the elephant car could in this case be symbolic rather than factual.

An 'ideal' rather than an actual triumphal or consular procession is almost certainly represented on two fine gold medallions struck for Constantine I's *vicennalia* (celebration of twenty years of rule) in 326, in which year he and his son Constantius II were consuls, the former for the seventh time, the latter for the first. These are a four-and-a-half-*solidi* piece, of which one specimen (in Stockholm) is known, bearing Constantine's portrait, and a two-*solidi* piece of Constantius II, known from three specimens (in Paris, Oxford and Dumbarton Oaks, Washington).[88] Both emperors are shown in elaborate consular costume, holding eagle-topped sceptres. Constantine's medallion has the reverse legend INNVMERI TRIVMFI AVG[usti] N[ostri], that of Constantius, AETERNA GLORIA SEN[atus] P[opuli] Q[ue] R[omani] and both pieces bear the mint-mark PTR (*percussa Treviris*). In this imperial capital north of the Alps the die-cutter would appear never to have seen an elephant, but to have worked from sketches or descriptions of the beasts. For the four elephants that in each case draw the imperial car towards the spectator are comical, man-faced creatures with bulging eyes and enormous ears that seem to sprout from the top of the head. On each type the two pairs of animals are turned outwards three-quarters to right and left respectively; and while the bodies of Constantine's elephants are reticulated and their trunks are waving in the air, the bodies of those of Constantius are almost completely concealed behind their vast heads and thick, rope-like trunks, sweeping almost to the ground. The subsidiary figures in the scenes, four on Constantine's piece and two on Constantius', are not mahouts, but either lictors or palm-bearers. It seems likely that the same die-engraver was responsible for both medallions, despite the differences in detail between the two sets of elephants.

The latest surviving monument dating from classical times of the use of elephants for draught is a panel from an ivory diptych of unknown provenance, now in the British Museum. Its carved relief is a scene of imperial apotheosis.[89] At the top the dead emperor, fully clothed, is carried by two winged *Genii* to heaven, where four persons are waiting to receive him. In the centre his naked soul is rising skywards from the pyre in a four-horse chariot, preceded by two eagles. But the principal group, below and on the right, is that of the emperor's effigy, again completely draped, seated in a gabled shrine which rests on a four-wheeled car drawn leftwards by four powerful, reticulated elephants, whose convex backs suggest that they are Indians. A small figure walks in front to guide them and on their necks are four mahouts, two of whom hold goads and two large, sectioned loaves, presumably for feeding to the beasts. The emperor's hairstyle and beard most closely resemble those of Julian the Apostate, and the piece could date from the late fourth-century pagan revival that he initiated. On stylistic grounds some scholars have assigned the panel to the mid-fifth century. But, while scenes and figures from mythology survived on works of art well into the fifth, and even into the sixth, century as part of the period's cultural inheritance, so uncompromisingly unchristian a scene of pagan religious belief and ritual is, perhaps, unlikely at so late a time. (Pl. 11)

ELEPHANTS FOR SHOW

In using elephants for draught purposes the Romans combined the demands of both utility and display. But the main purpose for which they, in common with other exotic creatures, were maintained in Rome and in other great cities of the Mediterranean world was, as we have seen, public entertainment in the form of pure show. The capture of elephants in Africa and their transport by sea as depicted on the 'Great Hunt' mosaic at Piazza Armerina have already been described (p. 28). Another figured pavement, less spectacular but in its surviving portion, at any rate, devoted wholly to the elephant, comes from a Roman house at Veii. It was found on private property and is still in private hands, but is housed at present in the Louvre; it consists of a portion of the frieze-like polychrome border of a large mosaic floor.[90] The scene presents the embarkation of what is probably, in view of its humped, convex back, an Indian elephant, despite the fact that its rather large ears give it an African touch – an example, perhaps, of the Roman artists' failure always to distinguish carefully between the two breeds. The alert grey beast strides purposefully up the gangway of a ship, so unresistingly that the ropes round its feet – two held by four men on shore and two by four on board – seem to be quite *de trop*, although both groups of men are straining under the effort to hold them. The workmanship of this mosaic, which may date from the early fourth century, is far inferior to that of the Piazza Armerina pavements. The elephant is neatly and realistically portrayed, while the drawing of its human captors is extremely crude. (Pl. 12)

Arrived at their destinations, the captive elephants, whether destined for draught or for show or both, were maintained and trained in enclosures (*vivaria*) as municipally or State-owned herds. As has been suggested, the elephants that Julius Caesar sent for from Italy to join him in Africa probably came from such a herd, kept not far from Rome (cf. p. 37); and Juvenal speaks of 'Caesar's herd' at Laurentum in the late first or early second century A D.[91] An official in charge of the imperial beasts bore the title of *procurator ad elephantos*.[92] Most of the animals were doubtless imported ones, from Africa or India. But Juvenal would seem to be wrong in implying that elephants were never born in Italy – 'that beast does not breed in Latium or anywhere beneath our skies'.[93] For Aelian records that at Germanicus' shows there was a performance by twelve elephants born of a herd near Rome (cf. p. 48).[94]

It is likely that Caesar also drew on the State-owned herd for the forty highly trained elephants which, as symbols of light (cf. pp. 39, 53, 54), escorted him up to the Capitol, walking in two lines, one on each side of him, with lighted torches in their trunks on one of the days of his quadruple triumph in 46 B C.[95] This was an accomplishment that had been learnt by elephants in Hellenistic times: a bronze coin of Antiochus VI of Syria, struck between 145 and 142 B C, shows an Indian elephant holding in its trunk a flaming torch.[96] The practice is probably reflected in a wall-painting from the House of the Vettii at Pompeii, in which three Indian elephants, each flourishing in its trunk a small torch, act as the supports of an elaborate *candelabrum*.[97]

Less agreeable elephant items on the dictator's programme were their fights against other elephants, carrying fighting men in towers, against companies of infantry and cavalry, and alongside infantry and cavalry against other mixed forces of horse, foot and elephants.[98] Fights between elephants had been exhibited in Rome by Gaius Claudius Pulcher as aedile in 99 BC;[99] and they occurred again towards the end of the first century AD.[100] Lucius and Marcus Lucullus as aediles in 79 BC had shown elephants fighting bulls;[101] and gruesome descriptions of similar encounters are given by Martial.[102] The disgusting incident when Pompey brutally slaughtered about a score of helpless elephants has already been described at length (pp. 22-3).

After its despatching of the bull, one of the elephants mentioned by Martial is said to have knelt before the emperor of its own accord – *pius et supplex elephas te, Caesar, adorat*; and it was the harmless, clever and amusing tricks which these animals were taught to perform that provided a light relief to those grimmer forms of elephant entertainment. At the word of command from a minute Ethiopian boy an elephant would kneel and walk the tightrope.[103] A most dramatic exhibition of the last accomplishment was given by an elephant at Nero's festival in his mother's honour in AD 59: it was led up to the highest gallery of the theatre and walked down from that point on ropes, carrying a rider.[104] Somewhat similar is Pliny's spicy anecdote about elephants walking on tightropes in parties of four, each party carrying on a litter another elephant which pretended to be a lady in the throes of childbirth.[105] On one occasion a dinner party was staged in the arena at which elephants took their places among the guests so circumspectly that none of the human diners was trampled on.[106] Another comedy enacted at the shows given by Germanicus (cf. p. 47) drove the spectators almost wild with delight – τὰ δὲ . . . καὶ ἐκμῆναι τὸν θεατὴν ἱκανά.[107] Six male and six female elephants, all appropriately costumed, came in, reclined in their places on couches, and dined with the utmost decorum on the excellent food and drink provided for them.

An elephant could even execute a graceful dance at its dusky master's bidding;[108] and Aelian paints a delicious picture of a dancing display given by the twelve Roman-born elephants at Germanicus' shows (cf. p. 47).[109] Trained by a dancing-master (ὀρχηστοδιδάσκαλος), they entered the theatre in two groups, from right and left, with mincing gait and a saucy swaying of the whole body to and fro. They wore the flowered dresses of dancing-girls, formed into line and wheeled at their teacher's orders, sprinkled the floor with flowers, and beat time with a rhythmical stamping. In the same passage Aelian comments generally on elephants' aptitude for dancing, on their feeling for music and enjoyment of the sound of the pipe, whose notes they could accurately distinguish. Some elephants even tried to read and write. But the most endearing story of all is that of the conscientious elephant who, being somewhat slow at mastering his tricks and frequently scolded and punished in consequence, arose at dead of night to put in some extra practice, all by himself by moonlight.[110]

To turn from history to mythology, there are representations of Dionysus' triumphal return from India in which elephants do not draw the chariot but lend to the occasion a special atmosphere of ostentatious display. A striking instance of this occurs in the relief on a late second-century A D sarcophagus in the Walters Art Gallery, Baltimore.[111] Here the god's chariot is drawn by a couple of leopards, but on the far side of the felines, in the background, can be seen the head and part of the back of an elephant ridden by a Satyr, who urges the animal on with a goad. Marching side by side in front of the leopard *biga* are two more elephants, the one in the foreground covered with reticulations, equipped with a thick, fringed saddle-cloth, and loaded with booty in the form of a huge tusk and a large metal vase. Its companion in the background is larger and very much taller (unless raised in 'vertical perspective' in order to be visible); and whereas the foreground beast is ridden by one Satyr only, grasping a goad, that in the background accommodates both a Satyr with a goad on its neck and a bearded Silenus seated sideways on its rump. Despite the context, all three elephants have the large ears and seemingly concave backs of Africans. Also African is the elephant that walks in Dionysus' Indian triumph on a second-century marble sarcophagus in the Fitzwilliam Museum, Cambridge.[112] (Pl. 8)

PRIVATE ELEPHANTS

As may well be surmised, elephants owned privately and used as mounts were extremely rare in ancient Rome. Only two instances are recorded. Suetonius recounts that Nero's great-grandfather's grandfather, Gnaeus Domitius the tribune (it was actually the father of the tribune), having defeated the Allobroges and the Averni as consul in 122 B C, rode through the province on an elephant in a kind of triumphal procession.[113] Lucius Cornuficius, consul in 35 B C, had in the previous year saved the lives of the soldiers whom he was commanding in the war against Sextus Pompeius. This went to his head; and even when he was in Rome his habit was to ride out to dinner on elephant-back.[114]

ELEPHANTS AS SYMBOLS

We have already seen that in the picture on the floor of the southern apse of the 'Great Hunt' mosaic corridor at Piazza Armerina an elephant accompanies the seated woman who partly represents Africa (p. 29); and it is in personifying Africa in general or parts of Africa that elephants perform their most familiar symbolic role in Roman art.

The commonest form of elephant symbolism in this context is the head-dress consisting of the creature's scalp, with ears, tusks and trunk, which is worn by personifications of Africa in the shape of female heads, busts and full-length figures standing, reclining or seated. The great majority of Roman examples are on coins and medallions, but Roman sculpture, mosaics and metalwork contribute some striking, if less numerous, instances. The symbol was not, however, an invention of the Roman age. Before the end of the fourth century B C Ptolemy I had struck in Egypt coins with a head of Alexander wearing the elephant head-dress on the obverse;[115] and Ptolemy himself appears with the same headgear on a gold coin bearing his own name.[116] Here the references are presumably to Alexander's return from India with elephants in his train; and to Ptolemy's own possession of elephants (cf. p. 347, note 4). Our earliest example of its definite association with the land of Africa is as the head-dress of a female bust on a gold stater struck between 310 and 304 by Ptolemy's son-in-law, Agathocles of Syracuse – a clear allusion to the latter's African campaigns and victory over the Carthaginians in 310.[117] Next we find it used to symbolize parts of Africa on the hellenized royal coinage of Numidia and Mauretania, where female heads and busts wear the head-dress – under Hiarbas (108-81 BC), Juba I (60-46), Bogud (49-38), the Mauretanian inter-regnum (33-25), Juba II (25 BC-A D 23), and Ptolemy (A D 20-40).[118] It may be that it was the earliest of these North African coin-types, those of Hiarbas and Juba I, that inspired the Roman republican series bearing the same device, namely the coins of Pompeius

Magnus (61 BC?), Quintus Metellus Scipio (c. 54-44), Lucius Cestius (44?), and Quintus Cornuficius (43-42).[119] Alternatively, both sets of types could have been inspired, independently of each other, by Hellenistic works. The Roman types all refer to activities in Africa. Under the Empire, renderings of Africa with the elephant head-dress are extremely plentiful on coins and medallions of the second and third centuries. One first-century type, that of Clodius Macer struck in Africa in AD 68, shows the bust.[120] But from Hadrian onwards Africa appears with this headgear as a full-length figure on the 'province' coin series of Hadrian and of Antoninus Pius, on medallions of Antoninus Pius, and on coins and medallions of Commodus, Septimius Severus, Caracalla, Diocletian, Maximianus, Constantius Chlorus, Galerius, Domitius Alexander, Maxentius and Constantine I.[121] M. Jatta, *Le rappresentanze figurate delle provincie romane* (1908), lists a number of non-numismatic representations – sculptures, mosaics, and lamps.[122] To his list may be added such other noteworthy instances as those on the *emblema* of the famous Boscoreale silver *patera*,[123] on a silver cup, also from the Boscoreale treasure,[124] on a Flavian mosaic at Ostia,[125] and on a marriage sarcophagus in the Museo Nazionale Romano, Rome.[126]

But complete figures of elephants, not merely their spoils in the form of a head-dress, also played their part in the art of the Roman world as symbols of Africa and, in particular, of African trade. This, as has been pointed out, was undoubtedly the significance of the massive marble figure of an elephant, slightly over life-size, which was found in 1931, shorn of its trunk and tusks, on the busiest street of Lepcis Magna in Tripolitania, between the Severan Arch and the Forum Vetus.[127] A stout column supports the belly of the beast, which is covered with reticulations and is genuinely African in type, with concave back and large spreading ears. Lepcis was one of the leading emporia for commerce in African ivory and for the export of elephants overseas; and the prominent position of the statue in the city centre is in no way surprising. That elephants were a common sight at Lepcis can be gathered from inscriptions. One, from the Forum Vetus, is a dedication to Liber Pater, one of the city's patron deities, of two tusks of a 'Lucanian cow' (*Lucae bovis*: the Italian nickname had spread to Roman Africa) belonging to the god's 'Indian herd' (*Indorum tuorum*), the last phrase referring either to an actual Indian elephant or, more probably, to the story of Dionysus' return with elephants from India.[128] Another, found in the marketplace, is cut on a statue-base in the form of a small four-way arch and records an honour paid by the local *ordo* to one Porfyrius in return for his gift to the city of four live elephants (*feras dentatas quattuor vivas*).[129] These beasts were most probably for show; and one or more elephants are very likely to have featured in the 'exhibition of 10 Libyan wild animals' (*exhibitionem Libycarum ferarum X*) given by a certain Titus Flavius Vibianus, as recorded in a third inscription, this time from the Severan Forum.[130]

The export of animals from Africa to Rome was largely, no doubt, in the hands of African companies whose headquarters were in one or other of the great provincial cities. One piece of evidence for this comes from the Foro (Piazzale) delle Corporazione at Ostia. This is situated just to the north of the theatre and consists of a great open rectangular space with a temple in its centre and its northern, eastern, and western sides bounded by porticoes which form the frontage of a series of offices set in rows adjacent to one another.[131] Most of these offices are floored with black-and-white mosaic pavements with figure scenes, a number of which are accompanied by inscriptions that indicate the business and provenance of the groups of persons who owned the rooms. Office no. 14 on the east side has a pavement inscribed STAT[io] SABRATENSIVM (office belonging to Sabrata in Tripolitania); and below this inscription is the figure of an African elephant, walking towards the left, executed in black silhouette against a white ground and with white interior lines. It has a drooping trunk and is a somewhat flabby, feeble, badly put together creature, resembling a child's toy that has lost much of its stuffing. But it stands for the city of Sabrata and her trade in animals, mainly elephants, for the Roman arena.[132] Office no. 28 on the northern side of the Foro has a mosaic pavement with no inscription but with the superimposed figures of three animals worked in the same technique. Above is an elephant walking towards the right, more strongly and compactly built than its *confrère* of Sabrata: it has small, cunning eyes and waves its trunk energetically. Below is a stag prancing towards the right; and below that again a boar rushing leftwards.[133] The company that owned this office must have been African, for the elephant is African; and on a mosaic from Utica, now in the British Museum, depicting a swampy African landscape in which hunters in two boats are rounding up animals in a net, a stag and a boar (but no elephant) appear among the quarry, along with ostriches, leopards, and other African species.[134]

Office no. 28 must also have belonged to African traders in beasts for the arena.

Elephants as badges of a family, in allusion to an event in its history associated with the animals, has already been noted apropos of the *gens Caecilia* (p. 35). The earliest examples known to us of this kind of symbolism are on the reverses of the fine silver coins struck by the Barcids in Spain between 237 and 209 B C.[135] Three reverses show an African elephant walking to the right, one with an elegant, long-cloaked rider on its back, perhaps a slim Indian mahout. Here the elephants symbolize both the Barcids' African origin and their use of war-elephants in Spain. It was possibly from these Barcid types that were derived the types of an elephant walking to the right, occasionally to the left, which are frequently found on the royal Numidian and Mauretanian coinage – of Masinissa, Jugurtha, Juba I, the Mauretanian interregnum, Juba II and Ptolemy.[136] Sometimes the elephant is trampling on a serpent; and on one of Juba II's coins it is turreted and flourishes a wreath in its trunk. These beasts are national, dynastic emblems of country and of war arm simultaneously.

As the most spectacular and popular performer at the public shows, the elephant was naturally chosen as the chief symbol of imperial munificence on the Roman coinage of the second and early third centuries (cf. p. 18). The animal is always shown walking towards the right and is generally accompanied by the legend MVNIFICENTIA AVG[usti], on *dupondii* of Antoninus Pius struck in 148-149,[137] on *asses* of Commodus issued in 183 and in 183-184,[138] on *denarii* and *sestertii* of Septimius Severus of the years 196-197.[139] *Sestertii* of Geta struck in 212[140] and *denarii, sestertii* and *asses* of Caracalla struck in 212 and 213[141] carry the elephant type without the legend MVNIFICENTIA, but there can be little doubt that they too commemorate the games. All these elephants are carefully and naturalistically drawn. All have large ears, but the backs of some are convex, indicating some confusion between the African and Indian species on the die-engravers' part. A number have reticulated hides; and on one *as* of Commodus the animal, an African, sports a handsome saddlecloth.

In view of the belief that elephants were worshippers and protégés of Helios/Sol (cf. pp. 39, 47), their role as symbols of light and life and of victory over darkness and death can be readily explained.[142] It was, as we have seen, in this capacity that they carried torches in effigy on Antiochus VI's coinage and in the flesh at Caesar's triumph; and a

Pompeian painting of a *candelabrum* with elephant torch-bearers as its supports has already been cited (p. 47). Another painting from Pompeii (House I, 6, 4) shows a bronze *candelabrum* flanked on either side by a large white elephant;[143] and a third Pompeian picture in the Fourth Style presents a charming group of a female elephant with her young at the foot of an ornamental *candelabrum* shaft.[144]

Closely connected with this association of elephants with light and victory, in addition to their reputation for longevity, is their place in the symbolism of eternity and of the after-life (cf. p. 53). *Dupondii* and *sestertii* of Philip I show on their reverses an elephant walking towards the left and bearing a mahout on its back: the legend reads AETERNITAS AVGG[*Augustorum*].[145] The allusion here is partly, no doubt, to the empire's eternity, which the emperor represents, but also, and probably mainly, to the latter's future apotheosis after death. The function of elephants as draught-beasts for the statues of imperial *Divi* in the *pompa circensis* has been described above (pp. 42, 43). A notable example of their funerary significance as the symbols of conquest of death and of eternal life beyond the grave is the stone figure of an elephant discovered in one of the rock-cut chamber tombs in the necropolis of Carmona (Carmo) near Seville.[146] Is it possible that the *miraculum* (portent) out of regard for which Augustus dedicated four obsidian elephants in the temple of Concord in Rome had some other-worldly intimation?[147]

CHAPTER III

MONKEYS

THE COMMON INDIAN MONKEY does not feature in Ptolemy II's pageant (cf. p. 39 and *passim*); and nowhere in the literature of the Hellenistic period is India mentioned as the source from which apes of any breed were derived, unless the *tityrus* ape, which Theophrastus' 'Complaisant Man' acquired, was an Indian orang-outang.[1] To the Hellenistic and Roman worlds the home of monkeys was normally in Africa, and in particular in Ethiopia and Egypt. Strabo in his account of the Arabian Gulf region says, quoting Artemidorus, that the apes known as κῆβοι (*cebi*) were native there and describes them as lion-faced, with bodies like those of leopards and of the size of deer.[2] Later, in his account of Egypt, he states that the Babylonians near Memphis worship the κῆβος; and he gives a somewhat different picture of it as Satyr-faced and in other respects a cross between a dog and a bear: again he says that Ethiopia is its home.[3] Aelian provides a much more detailed description of the *cebus*' physical characteristics. It lives, he writes, on the shores of the Red Sea, is many-coloured (ἔχειν γὰρ χρόας πολλάς), and is, when fully grown, of the size of an Eretrian hound. Its head, back and spine as far as the tail are red, with a sprinkling of golden hairs. Its face is white as far as the cheeks and from thence three golden stripes descend to the neck. The chest and front legs are white, the teats are of a darkish blue, the belly is white, and its back legs are black. One would not go far wrong, he adds, in comparing its mask with that of a baboon (κυνοκέφαλος).[4] Pliny recalls that in Pompey's *ludi* of 55 BC there were shown *cephi* from Ethiopia with hind-feet resembling human feet and legs and front feet resembling hands. They had never, he declares, been seen in Rome again;[5] and no record has come down to us of their appearance in Roman shows after his time.

The baboon or dog-headed ape is stated by Strabo, in the passages cited above (cf. p. 354, notes 2, 3), to be a native of the Arabian

Gulf area and to be worshipped by the Hermopolitans in Egypt. Pliny speaks of the *cynocephalus* as a native of Ethiopia[6] and remarks on its extreme ferocity.[7] Cicero met at Laodicea a Roman named Publius Vedius whose *cortège* included two carriages, one of which was occupied by a baboon.[8] Baboons may have reached Italy, although we have not any absolutely certain evidence of their presence there (cf. p. 58). The same would appear to be true of two of the other breeds of apes that Pliny mentions – the gentle *satyrus* (cf. Strabo's Satyr-faced κῆβος in Egypt), and the *callitrichis* ('pretty-haired' monkey), which was very different from the others in physique, having a beard and a broad tail flattened out at the base. Pliny adds, in fact, that the latter breed could not live in any other climate than that of its native Ethiopia.[9]

The breed of monkeys best known in Italy was the tailed Barbary ape (*cercopithecus*), of which there is also a tailless variety. Pliny states that it came from Ethiopia and had a black head, hair like that of a donkey, and a voice quite different from that of other monkeys.[10] Juvenal says that it was a sacred beast in Egypt.[11] The Latin word for monkey in general is, of course, *simia*; and it is under that name and under that of *cercopithecus* that apes appear, both as pets and as performers, in Latin literature.

To judge from some passages in Plautus, monkeys were kept as pets in Italy as early as the third century BC. In the *Miles Gloriosus* Periplectomenos, an old gentleman of Ephesus, orders his slaves to remove without more ado anyone seen climbing on the roof of his house and not to accept 'I'm after my monkey' as an excuse for the intrusion.[12] In the *Mercator* Demipho recounts a dream in which he had bought a lovely she-goat and given it to a monkey to look after – presumably a tame ape belonging to his household.[13] The next records of the animal as a household pet date from the second half of the first century AD. Pliny notes the great affection displayed by tame monkeys for the young that they had given birth to *intra domos* and describes how they showed their babies off to everyone and were delighted when people fondled them, taking this as a compliment to themselves; in fact, they were not infrequently known to have killed their offspring by hugging them too tightly.[14] Martial writes of a certain Comius who adored a Barbary ape as ugly as himself.[15]

A couple of domesticated apes may be reckoned as the highlight of a marble relief, perhaps of late second-century AD date, which was found on the Via della Foce at Ostia. It was presumably a shop sign, erected on the façade of the building, and it depicts an intimate interior scene, in which fruit, poultry and small game are on sale. Behind the counter stand two women (or a woman and a young man), the woman to the right handing out figs, from two large bowls or baskets in front of her, to a man on the left, who carries a bulky bag or purse. In the background, behind this man, a dead duck and a dead chicken are dangling from a bar. To the left again two men, one of whom has bought a rabbit, seem to be discussing prices. To the right of the saleswoman, on another section of the counter, is a tall, round wicker basket with a small square one on top of it; and still further to the right there stands a large cage, of the same height as the counter, through the bars of which the heads of two long-eared hares emerge. On the top of this cage two apes are seated side by side, turned three-quarters towards one another and seemingly tailless. The left-hand monkey, who is seated partly on the counter beside the wicker baskets and partly on the hares' cage, is scratching its head. The animals are not tied up and wear gentle, not to say benign, expressions. The conclusion would seem to be that the apes are the saleswoman's pets, put on view to please customers, who would find an added attraction in this engaging little pair.[16] (Pl. 14)

It is, however, as performers, rather than as pets, that monkeys feature most often in the literature and art of Roman times. Aelian declares that in Ptolemaic Egypt baboons had been taught to distinguish letters, to dance, and to play the pipe and harp. They would then demand payment for these accomplishments and pop what they received into a bag that they carried round with them attached to their persons, just like professional beggars.[17] The same author recounts the achievements of the πίθηκοι (probably Barbary apes) of his own day. The ape is, he says, the most imitative of all animals and it will learn to reproduce with the utmost accuracy any bodily action that you teach it. It can dance and play the pipe, if you show it how. Aelian had actually seen a monkey driving a chariot, holding the reins and laying on the whip. Anything else, he adds, that a monkey learns it will perform and it never let its teacher down.[18]

Pliny notes that the various breeds of monkeys are the closest to human beings in appearance and are distinguished from one another by being tailed or tailless (caudis inter se distinguuntur); and also that the tailed kind (quibus in eo genere cauda sit) get depressed when the moon is waning but are thrilled when it is new. To illustrate their surprising intelligence (mira sollertia) he cites their ability to play at draughts (*latrunculis lusisse*) and to spot at a glance imitation nuts made of wax (*fictas cera nuces visu distinguere*).[19] A performing monkey must be meant by the little creature that Juvenal describes as nibbling a rotten apple on the city ramparts of Rome, armed with shield and helmet and learning, under the threat of the lash, to hurl a spear from the back of a shaggy goat.[20] Another performer was the monkey, cited by Martial, which was so clever at dodging the spears that were thrown at it that the speaker in the epigram wished that he could grow a tail and turn into a monkey.[21]

Another short epigram of Martial mentions a person who went about in a Gaulish-style coat or cloak with a hood attached to it, a garment that monkeys used to wear – presumably when performing.[22] This would seem to be precisely illustrated by a Pompeian painting which shows an ape dressed in a sleeved coat with the hood thrown back on the neck and walking on its hind-legs at the end of a lead held by its trainer, who flourishes a whip. The tall jar on the left of the picture may contain the performer's reward after a successful 'turn'.[23] A performing monkey squatting beside its master on a first-century AD lamp in the British Museum is described below (cf. p. 89): so is the relief at Sofia, where the small dog-faced figures, dressed like men, may possibly be performing baboons, rather than human mountebanks wearing dog-masks (cf. pp. 97, 98).

Sometimes performing monkeys were made to play the parts of mythological personages. One of the items observed by Apuleius' Lucius in the Isiac procession (cf. p. 97) was an ape got up as Ganymede (Catamitus): it wore a cap made of woven stuff and a Phrygian-style saffron robe and carried a golden wine cup.[24] A well-known Pompeian painting presents Aeneas fleeing from Troy with Anchises and Ascanius, all in the guise of dog-faced baboons. 'Aeneas' wears the cuirass, boots, and scarlet cloak of a Roman general and 'Ascanius' has his Phrygian cap and *pedum*.[25] In view of the Ganymede episode, this caricature could well reflect a real performance that the artist or his patron had witnessed and in that case attest the presence of a troupe of performing baboons in Italy (cf. p. 56). A similar scene may have lain behind a mosaic from Sousse (Hadrumetum), now in the Louvre, which portrays a monkey got up as Orpheus, playing a guitar in the centre of a group of pacing animals.[26]

Another possible caricature of Orpheus is the colourless glass flask, in the Cologne Museum, in the form of a monkey seated in a basket chair, wearing a *cucullus* (hood), and grasping a *syrinx* in its front paws.[27] It seems likely that the tailless monkey on the peristyle mosaic of the palace of the Byzantine emperors at Istanbul is doing a trick that it has learnt. It stands at the foot of a date-palm tree and reaches up with a long stick to touch a bird perched among the branches. On its back it carries a wicker basket on the lid of which a decoy bird is seated.[18]

It remains to consider three more renderings of apes in Graeco-Roman art. From the Ionian coast comes the bronze figurine of a monkey which was shown at an exhibition held in London in June 1971 and assigned to the first century BC. It is $3^1/_4$ inches high and depicts a monkey, perhaps a performer, wearing a broad collar, sitting up on its haunches, and holding what looks like a tablet.[29] A fragmentary marble relief in the Thorvaldsens Museum, Copenhagen, said to have come from Italy, might date from early imperial times. It bears a very taking and naturalistic portrait of a short-tailed ape seated on its haunches to the left on a ledge, with its face turned three-quarters towards the spectator. The animal wears a rather sad and meditative air, as it gnaws what might be a radish or a long fruit held in its right hand, while its left hand clasps its left leg. What purpose the relief originally served, whether architectural or sepulchral, it is difficult to say. There is a section of leaf-moulding at the top of the fragment and to the left of the ape are the remains of five lines of an inscription – O/MO/RI/O/N.[30] (Pl. 14)

Of controversial breed are the two monkeys on a silver-gilt dish found at Lampsacus in the Troad and now in the Archaeological Museum of Istanbul. The apes, which wear collars and have long hind-legs and long tails, stand to right and left respectively, with their bodies in profile and their faces turned towards us. They flank a central female seated figure, clearly the personification of a country or continent, who is distinguished by her stiff ringlets surmounted by a turban, from which project two horn-like features, probably meant to be feathers. This woman is generally identified as India; [31] and good Indian parallels have been adduced for her garment, head-dress, hairstyle, and throne, with its legs in the form of elephant tusks. The monkeys might, then, be Indian, despite the fact that they do not carry their tails curved along their backs, as Indian monkeys normally do. But the guineafowl above the right-hand ape is definitely African, as could also be the parrakeet above the left-hand ape, as Jennison[32] points out. On the other hand, the woman, for all the resemblance of her ringlets to those of Mauretanians, is unlikely to be Africa, since she lacks Africa's characteristic elephant head-dress (cf. pp. 249, 254). The plate, variously ascribed to the early Empire[33] and, with much greater probability, to the fourth or fifth century A D,[34] must be regarded as the work of a Graeco-Roman artist who confused the fauna of the two continents. The central figure must be India, known to be the home of apes, but these monkeys could be, like the guineafowl and parrakeet, of African species – that is, Barbary apes.[35] (Pl. 15)

CHAPTER IV

FELINES

LIONS

THE SOURCES FROM WHICH LIONS were to be obtained in bulk for display by Hellenistic kings and by Roman magistrates and emperors were Africa, Arabia, Syria and Mesopotamia. The twenty-four lions of great size (λέοντες παμμεγέθεις) that took part in Ptolemy II's pageant (cf. p. 39 and *passim*) could have been secured by him most easily from Cyrenaica or Syria. The hundred maned lions (*iubati*) that Sulla put on show in Rome came from Mauretania, through the offices of King Bocchus (cf. p. 17); and it was probably from Syria, where he had been *quaestor*, that Gaius Cassius ordered for exhibition at his entry into the aedileship the caged lions which were held up at Megara on their way to Italy owing to the civil war. These beasts were the agents of a somewhat piquant incident. When the Caesarian troops that were besieging Megara were about to break in, the Megarians released the lions from their cages, fondly assuming that they would go for the intruders. The animals, however, made straight for the citizens themselves, as the quarry nearest and readiest to jaw.[1]

We have seen that, in the third century, of Probus' 200 maneless lions (*leopardi*) 100 came from Libya and 100 from Syria (cf. p. 19). In the fourth century, Symmachus' phrase *Libyca congressio* used apropos of the lions that he needed for a show seems to indicate, although it does not prove, that it was from Africa that he hoped to get them.[2] It was certainly from Africa that Claudian believed that Stilicho would obtain the 'superb lions' (*eximii leones*) for display at his consular games.[3] This rather scrappy literary evidence, coupled with that of the mosaics (cf. pp. 25-30), suggests, so far as it goes, that North Africa came first and Syria second as the principal sources of supply in Roman times.

The first display of lions in Rome was given by Nobilior in

186 BC. This exhibition and the subsequent shows of lions under the late Republic and Empire have been listed and described in Chapter I (pp. 16-19, 21, 22). At this point mention may be made of a few special incidents relating to lions at the public spectacles which Roman and Greek writers, mainly of the first and second centuries A D, have recorded. Pliny tells us that in the reign of Claudius it was proved to be possible to put a raging lion completely out of action by throwing a cloak over its head.[4] Martial recalls that on one occasion a lion bit the hand of its trainer (magister) and had to be destroyed;[5] on another, a lion was killed in the arena by a woman;[6] on a third, the famous venator Carpophorus slew a lion of unprecedented size;[7] and on a fourth, a tamed tigress ran amok and despatched a savage lion.[8] The poet's sympathy was stirred by the death in a venatio of a particularly splendid lion, the mass of whose golden mane stood erect, crescent-like, above its neck.[9] But the deepest feeling for a noble beast's brave death is that expressed by Statius in a poem addressed to a tamed lion which was killed in the arena by a fera of unspecified breed. He describes the anger of the other lions, shut in their cages, at this outrage; and how the victim itself refused to give in immediately but retained its spirit and its native fierceness (mansere animi virtusque cadenti/a media iam morte redit nec protinus omnes/tergo dedere minae). Senate and people mourned for it and it was the only beast whose loss drew tears from the emperor's eyes.[10]

Several stories are told of lions recognizing and sparing human friends in the arena. Seneca describes a scene in which a lion recognized one of the bestiarii as the man who had once been his keeper and protected him from the attacks of other animals.[11] And there is the famous tale of the condemned slave Androcles, in the reign of Gaius, who was affectionately greeted, with much tail-wagging in the canine manner and licking of hands and feet, by the lion whom he had long ago relieved of a thorn in the pad and who had then shared a cave with him. On the score of this touching episode Androcles was given his freedom and the lion became his constant and tame companion, going the round of the shops with him on a lead, accepting bouquets and collecting money for his friend.[12] One of the sights in the amphitheatre that seems to have impressed Martial most was that of lions trained to seize hares in their jaws and let them go again without doing them the slightest injury: no less than eight of his Epigrams deal with the subject.[13] He also saw a lion and a ram sharing the same cage and dining amicably together off a lamb.[14] A less agreeable sight was that of a tamed lion that suddenly turned wild and killed two boys who were raking over the blood-stained sand in the arena.[15]

The literary accounts of lion shows in the arena have their counterparts in Roman art. On *asses* of Antoninus Pius a lion, standing or reclining, does not, as the elephant does, serve as a complete symbol of imperial munificence (cf. p. 18), but accompanies as an adjunct the female figure that represents it.[16] Some of the most vivid scenes of lion *venationes* are on ivory diptychs of the fifth and sixth centuries. One, carved in Rome *c.* 435, presents in the bottom half of the left-hand leaf one *venator* tackling five maned lions.[17] Another, worked in Constantinople in 517 for Anastasius, has at the bottom of its right-hand leaf a slightly comic scene in which two immense lions, with terrifying, windswept manes, have reduced to panic three *venatores* who have fled for refuge to the wooden boxes from which the beasts have been released.[18] On a third diptych, that of Areobindus, made in 506, are depicted, at the bottom of the right-hand leaf, five men engaging four lions before a semi-circle of spectators.[19] But the most dramatic piece in this series of lion *venationes* is one carved in the Eastern Empire *c.* 450, where both leaves are filled from top to bottom with the grim encounter between eight *venatores* and sixteen beasts – maned lions, some of them spotted, maneless lions and lionesses.[20] The two leaves are almost, but not quite, identical and the groups are tiered one above the other in non-naturalistic vertical perspective, so as to leave no space unoccupied. The rendering of the animals is, however, most realistic. Particularly moving are the beasts, transfixed with spears, which are rolling over on their backs and those which are vainly trying to extract with their teeth the spears that have broken in their bellies and dealt them fatal wounds. There are also two dying maneless lions or lionesses who are lying on their sides howling in their anguish.

Lions as draught-animals have a firm place in mythological iconography, notably in that of Cybele (Magna Mater), where they draw her chariot. Striking instances of this are the bronze group in the Metropolitan Museum of Art, New York, where the goddess is enthroned in a lion *biga*, and the late fourth-century silver-gilt plate from Parabiago, now in Milan, where four bouncing lions are harnessed to the car in which Cybele and Attis are riding side by side.[21] But their function as draught-beasts for deities derives from much earlier times;[22] and it was, perhaps, largely because it hinted at a claim to divinity that Mark Antony's appearance in public, with the actress Cytheris at his side, in a chariot drawn by lions so much shocked the Romans.[23] Coins of Diva Faustina with the legend AETERNITAS show her seated with Cybele's *tympanum* on a throne on a car drawn by two lions towards the left; and Julia Domna during her lifetime was still more closely assimilated to the goddess on a coin that depicts her with the towered crown, as well as with the *tympanum*, drawn leftwards by four lions.[24] The Emperor Elagabalus yoked lions in explicit imitation of the Magna Mater.[25] (Pl. 19)

Elagabalus' draught-animals must have been very thoroughly tamed and trained, as must also have been the lions that were kept as domestic pets. Seneca speaks of lions kept *intra domum*,[26] Epictetus of tame, caged lions, whose owners fed them with their own hands and took them about with them,[27] and from Juvenal we learn that a certain Numitor bought a tamed lion that consumed vast quantities of meat.[28] Caracalla had a large number of lions always about with him: one of them, named 'Scimitar' ('Ἀκινάκης), slept and ate with him and was often caressed by him in public.[29] Elagabalus made pets of maned and maneless lions which would suddenly appear at dinner-parties, greatly alarming the guests, who did not know that they were *exarmati*, with claws and teeth removed; and when, after deep drinking, they had gone to bed, these creatures would suddenly, at dead of night, be let into their rooms, to their even greater consternation.[30]

Some lions may have been bred in Italy, in captivity; but the great majority of those that were maintained for show or as pets must have been imported by sea. A relief on the lid of a mid-third-century sarcophagus in the Villa Medici in Rome shows three mariners operating a ship that is just coming into port, as the lighthouse on the right indicates, the port being probably Ostia. On the deck are ranged three small cages, set frontally, from behind the bars of each of which glares a lion minute in scale but fierce in mien and heavily maned.[31] Very different in dimensions is the gigantic beast which Claudian describes as voyaging from Africa to Italy 'with its tail curled at the poop, while the rest of it reaches to the prow': the ship could hardly get along beneath its weight.[32] This animal, if not wholly mythical, was presumably tame and uncaged. But the caged beasts on reaching Rome seem to have been stacked at the docks until someone came to collect them. For Pliny tells the story of how the sculptor Pasiteles nearly paid with his life for his zeal for modelling from nature. One day when he was at the docks, where the African animals were waiting, he was peering into a lion's cage in order to engrave (or make a relief of?) the creature, when suddenly there burst out of another cage a leopard, from which he only just escaped.[33] The magnificent maned lion, bowing its head in reverence, which eastern barbarians are presenting to the emperor in Constantinople on the so-called 'Barberini ivory',[34] had only the Bosphorus to cross.

Mosaics illustrating the hunting and capture of lions in the field along with animals of different species have been described in Chapter I (pp. 25-30). A painting from the Tomb of the Nasonii in Rome shows a hunt in which only lions, two large maned ones, compose the quarry.[35] In a landscape setting of hills and trees a net has been spread in the middle distance, enclosed by which the beasts are bounding towards a serried row of five huntsmen with interlocking oval shields. In the foreground, to left and right, two more huntsmen, also armed with shields, are fleeing for their lives – not surprisingly, since in the centre yet another huntsman is being crushed beneath his shield by the forepaw of the larger of the two lions.

In the context of a tomb this lion hunt is likely to have had some sepulchral significance; and in Roman funerary art the lion has its place as a symbol of the ravening power of death and of man's victory over it. On the Baltimore sarcophagus carved with Dionysus' Indian triumph (cf. p. 49) this may be the meaning of the little drama near the right-hand end of the procession where a captive lion walks with lowered head before the pair of elephants and a Satyr lays his hand upon its mane and brandishes a knotted club threateningly above it.[36] Strigillated sarcophagi of the late second and early third centuries, mainly of the oval, vat-shaped type with curved ends, carry on the front two lion-masks each with a ring in its jaws as though for lifting the vat.[37] During the third century the lion-mask at the curved ends could be replaced by the complete figure of a lion slaughtering another animal – a boar, an antelope, a goat, a horse, a stag, and so forth. A now fragmentary piece in the Museo Torlonia has on its left-hand curved end an arena lion, attended by its keeper, standing over its prey, an antelope: the lion's face and mane are magnificently carved.[38] A fragment of a sarcophagus (the left-hand curved end) in the Museo Capitolino carries a similar group, the lion's face, with its powerful brow and cheek-bones, its grooved, pointed muzzle, glaring eyes under heavy, beetling eyebrows, and gaping jaws, being very similar to that of the Torlonia beast: but here the lion springs with mighty force upon its prey.[39]

Sometimes the group of a lion attacking its victim appears at each curved end of a sarcophagus of which the front is filled, not with strigillations, but with a figure scene. For instance, there are the Four Seasons flanking a portrait of the deceased on a Vatican piece;[40] and there is the pastoral paradise on Julius Achilleus' sarcophagus in the Museo Nazionale Romano (cf. pp. 165, 283).[41] A large lion-mask (without body or prey) occurs near each end of an oval piece in the Museo Capitolino, brooding over the crowded scene of a lion hunt, which fills every inch of the front.[42] A central male figure on horseback, presumably the deceased occupant of the sarcophagus, gallops towards the right, supported by Virtus (personifying prowess in the hunting-field), other huntsmen, one of them mounted, and dogs; and the company encounters three maned lions and two lionesses. This is the basic scheme – although often only one lion constitutes the quarry and occasionally the Dioscuri on their mounts appear – of the mainly third-century series of lion-hunt sarcophagi of which thirty-six examples are catalogued, illustrated, and discussed by Vaccaro Melucco;[43] a few can be assigned to the first half of the fourth century. Of these only the Capitoline piece just cited combines the lion hunt with lion-masks. All the lion-hunt sarcophagi can be interpreted as allegories of the victory of the soul over death; and this is so even when the prototype of the central mounted huntsman can be traced back to renderings of imperial lion-hunters, those of Hadrian and Commodus, for instance, on medallions, where no funerary association is involved.[44] On nearly all of these sarcophagi the modelling of the lions is extremely naturalistic and vigorous, based ultimately, at any rate, on a study of the beasts from life in the arena.

The view that the lion hunts on the principal faces of sarcophagi are not mere apings by private persons of imperial *virtus* but have an other-worldly significance is supported by another series of sarcophagi on which a lion features prominently, namely those that are carved with the Labours of Hercules, including his wrestling with the Nemean lion.[45] As Hercules earned apotheosis through his toils, so the soul of the deceased triumphs over death and evil. It goes without saying that not every representation of Hercules' struggle with the lion is related to the after-life: a particularly striking instance in a domestic context is a wall-painting from Pompeii.[46] But there can be little doubt of the meaning of a stone group in the round that depicts this subject, found in a cemetery at Cologne.[47]

Lions either by themselves or crouching on their prey are fairly common as the subject of funerary sculpture in the round. A large Augustan tomb now re-erected beside a modern street in Aquileia has lions poised on two of the corners of its enclosure wall;[48] and in the Danubian, German and British Roman provinces lions appear as tomb groups, sometimes with their victim between their forepaws, and are either self-contained monuments or mounted on the coping of the precinct walls of mausolea.[49] The fine marble figure in the Museo Capitolino of a recumbent lion, with forepaws extended, open jaws, and massive head and mane, is of unrecorded provenance: perhaps it, too, once graced a tomb.[50] (Pl. 18)

On two lion-hunt sarcophagi, one at Pisa, the other at Béziers, a lioness is accompanied by three cubs, which shelter beneath her belly and introduce a *genre* touch into the picture;[51] and on one of the two so-called Grimani reliefs of Julio-Claudian date now in Vienna – reliefs on which animals appear to be depicted solely for their own sake – we have the peaceful counterpart of those scenes of stress for mother and offspring. Here a lioness is crouching within a rocky cave, her head turned back concernedly towards her two cubs, which snuggle up against her body. One of them, seen from behind, is busy feeding, while the other rests its right forepaw on its brother's (or sister's) rump. The wavy locks of hair on the mother's neck and shoulders, her fringed hind-legs, and the plump, loose-skinned bodies of the cubs have all been carved with great sensitivity and care.[52] (Pl. 21)

We have seen that the motif of a lion devouring its prey is often to be found in definitely sepulchral contexts as a symbol of the ravening power of death. A painted counterpart of those sculptured reliefs and figures comes from the wall of a tomb at Ostia, where a fine, naturalistically rendered lion stands to the left, its head turned to face the spectator and its right forepaw resting on a bleeding bull's head.[53] Here, the Nilotic landscape beneath the beast and its victim creates an idyllic atmosphere to some extent softening the horror. What the significance of the motif may have been in non-funerary associations is not so clear. A mosaic once in the Palazzo Mignanelli in Rome, and now known only from a drawing at Eton College, shows a frontal lion mangling another feline in a hilly landscape. It is of unrecorded provenance, but could have come from a house rather than from a tomb.[54]

Two *opus sectile* wall-mosaic panels, each showing a yellow-maned lion in profile, to right and left respectively, devouring a dark-grey fawn, come from a building outside the Porta Marina at Ostia. This building, which was neither a house nor a tomb, had religious, in fact Christian, associations, since it contains an *opus sectile* portrait of Christ, also from one of its walls. The lions are arena beasts, with ornamental coloured straps round body and neck.[55] Definitely domestic is the provenance of a mosaic panel found in a private house at Verulamium, near St Albans. This shows a lion striding to the left and holding in its maw the head of an antlered stag which drips abundantly with blood.[56] Lively amphitheatre scenes are, indeed, not uncommon on the floors of private houses (cf. pp. 25-31), whose occupants presumably frequented the shows or had some particular connection with them. On the other hand, to select and isolate this peculiarly grisly motif as the central adornment of the floor of a reception room might seem to be a strange proceeding on a house-holder's part, especially in the case of a citizen of Verulamium, who is most unlikely to have seen lions or any other breed of wild beast in his local arena. He must have been shown the group in an imported copy-book and perhaps have admired for their own sake the vigor-ous drawing and vivid colouring of the animal. (Pl. 16)

In a much lighter vein are those mosaics that depict large and powerful lions submissive to the will and pranks of quite young children in the guise of Cupids. In one of the octagonal panels of the great Dionysiac mosaic found near Cologne Cathedral a Cupid rides sideways on a lion pacing slowly and patiently towards the left.[57] More picturesque is a square mosaic panel from Pompeii, now in Naples, where a Dionysiac Cupid crowned with ivy and gripping a large wine cup rides astride a rightwards-marching lion, which wears a vine wreath round its neck, turns back its head to give a friendly look at its rider, and treads lightly over a beribboned *thyrsus* lying on the ground.[58] Three panels, one circular, from Pompeii, and two square, from Rome and a private Neapolitan collection respectively (the latter now in the British Museum), present a picture which in its general scheme is so much the same in all three cases – although the details differ – that all must have been derived from the same copy-book original. A vast lion sprawls helplessly on its left side towards the right while five, three, or four Cupids fasten chains round its body and legs and tease it with lighted torches, music played on various instruments and so forth.[59] All these mosaics point the contrast between the lion's formidable bulk and the slight proportions of the children whom it serves or by whom it is mastered.

Two remarkable mosaics from Antioch-on-the-Orontes, dating from the first half of the fifth century, were obviously inspired by the proximity of lions in Syria, Mesopotamia and Persia. On one of these a rectangular *emblema*, at the centre of a great expanse of floral carpet, is filled by the powerful form of a lion that advances rapidly towards the left in a setting of bushes and undulating hills. The body, some of the anatomical details of which are inexactly rendered, is in profile, while the face is frontal and has more the look of an angry elderly man than of a lion. Two ends of the Persian royal ribbon flutter from the beast's neck.[60] The second pavement, also rectangular, has an all-over floral trellis design that forms a diagonal network, each of whose compartments holds a small animal or a bird. At the centre the network is interrupted to accommodate the large-scale figure of a lion striding towards the right, with the head in profile and the jaws agape, as though to emit a roar. This beast, in contrast to the heavily built beribboned lion, is springy, lithe and slender and altogether much more naturalistic.[61] Interest in the creatures for their own sake would seem to be the main *raison d'être* for their appearance on these mosaics. (Pl. 20)

In Romano-Christian art one of the most arresting renderings of a lion is in a wall-painting of the fourth century in the recently discovered catacomb by the Via Latina, just to the south of ancient Rome. On the left is Samson, lunging towards the right as he wrestles with the lion, which springs at him and which he grips by the mane and throat. Below, in accordance with the principles of the Roman 'simultaneous' style of composition, the same lion lies dead, as Samson saw it later, with a swarm of bees buzzing round its head. The contrast between the live lion, self-confident, well-knit and sinewy, and the dead beast, lying limp and huddled in a heap, is admirably expressed.[62]

TIGERS

The earliest record of a tiger in the Graeco-Roman world after Alexander is that of the one presented to the people of Athens by

Seleucus I (312-280).[63] He must have got it from India or from Hyrcania, south of the Caspian Sea, or from Armenia, stretching between the south-west shore of the Caspian and the south-east coast of the Euxine. Pliny names the first two of these regions as the homelands of tigers;[64] and Virgil writes of *Armeniae tigres* in a familiar passage of the *Eclogues*.[65] In view of the particularly difficult terrains in which they had to be captured and the very long distances over which they had to be conveyed, tigers were always a relatively infrequent sight in Mediterranean countries. They are not mentioned as featuring in Ptolemy II's great zoological pageant (cf. p. 39 and *passim*) nor, so far as we know, did they appear in any of the shows staged in Rome under the Republic.

Seleucus' gift to Athens was, in fact, a tigress; and in the Roman world, at any rate, it was the female of the species that played the leading role. *Tigris* is always feminine in Latin poetry and in Pliny's account of the breed, although the masculine form is found in other Latin prose. Furthermore, in Roman art, particularly in mosaics, it is nearly always tigresses that are depicted. Virgil, in the passage of the *Eclogues* cited above, implies that tigresses were credited, in one version of the story, with having drawn Dionysus' chariot in his Indian triumph.[66] This is well illustrated by a mosaic pavement from Saragossa in the National Archaeological Museum in Madrid, where two strapping tigresses are harnessed to the god's triumphal car and converse with one another as they stride along towards the right, and by the well-known vine mosaic from El-Djem in Tunisia, where the same service is performed by another pair.[67] Occasionally, however, Dionysus rides a male tiger, as on a mosaic medallion found in London.[68] But on the 'Great Hunt' mosaic at Piazza Armerina the three examples of the species are, as we have seen, all female (cf. pp. 28, 29).

In the winter of 20-19 BC, when he was on the island of Samos, Augustus was presented by an Indian embassy with an unspecified number of tigers.[69] What happened to those beasts we do not know. Perhaps they died before reaching Italy. For Pliny states that the first tiger ever seen in Rome, a tamed tigress in a cage, was exhibited by Augustus in 11 BC, when the Theatre of Marcellus was dedicated.[70] Claudius produced four tigers at a single show;[71] and Seneca reports that in Nero's time an arena tiger was kissed by its keeper.[72] Plutarch has the story, of which the date is not recorded, of how a live kid was put into a tigress' cage; but she refused to touch it, going without food for two days and on the third day breaking out of her prison to search for something else to eat.[73] Very different in temper is the arena tiger in an octagonal mosaic panel from the third-century AD baths at Philippi in Greece, which munches the head of a wild horse or ass, while the decapitated corpse lies prostrate in the background (cf. the Verulamium lion mosaic, p. 68).[74]

Martial, writing under Domitian, mentions harnessed tigresses; [75] and he later records in great detail how, on the occasion of the emperor's return from the Sarmatian war in 93, an unspecified number of tigresses – but certainly more than two – drew chariots in the arena: he compares this scene with that of Dionysus' Indian triumph, in which the god was content with only two tigresses to draw him [76] – as on the Madrid and El-Djem mosaics, although on a mosaic with a vine-scroll border from the Maison du Virgile at Sousse in Tunisia four tigers, two of them, at least, female, pull his chariot.[77] Antoninus Pius showed an unspecified number of tigers (cf. p. 18); Commodus killed one tiger (cf. p. 22); in 205 at Quintillus Plautianus' funeral games ten were killed at once;[78] and Elagabalus exhibited and caused to be killed the unprecedented number of fifty-one tigers (cf. p. 19): he also put tigers in harness.[79] Philip I produced ten tigers from the menagerie that Gordian III had assembled (cf. p. 16). Apart from Elagabalus' tour de force, the number of tigers that could be displayed on a single occasion in Rome was clearly very small, as compared with the enormous numbers of lions, bears and other quadrupeds that could be seen in the arena.[80] It is likely that tigers seldom, if ever, made their appearance in provincial amphitheatres, at any rate in the West.

We have seen that on two of the lion-hunt sarcophagi the artist has shown a lioness accompanied by her cubs in her struggle with her human foes (cf. p. 67). The same motif of mother and offspring appears in a scene of tigress-hunting on two late mosaics from Antioch-on-the-Orontes. In a group on the mosaic of Megalopsychia (c. 450) a huntsman on foot lunges towards the right and aims his spear at the throat of a tigress which springs at him. Under her are two male cubs also springing towards the huntsman, one below the other: the upper one looks up at its mother as though for help or instructions.[81] A very similar group, but with the directions of huntsman and tigress reversed, occurs on the Dumbarton Oaks Hunt (c. 500). Here the lunging huntsman drives his spear into the tigress' chest and the two cubs below her are in line, the hinder one looking back towards its mother.[82] Both sets of beasts are remarkable for the vigour and the naturalism of their drawing. (Pl. 22)

A favourite method in Roman times for obtaining tigers and tigresses for pets or for show in the arena was to steal cubs on the hunting-field. Such a thief was the mounted *raptor* mentioned by Martial (cf. p. 358, note 76); and Pliny has a vivid description of how a huntsman, having seized some cubs, would gallop off with them on the swiftest and freshest of horses. When the outraged tigress discovered her loss she would rush headlong in pursuit and at her furious approach the huntsman would drop one of the stolen cubs in the hope of delaying her onrush. But she would pick it up and as though spurred on by its weight continue the chase, coming ever closer and closer to her enemy until he was safely on shipboard and she was left to vent her fury on the shore.[83] Just such a scene, apart from the ship and shore, appears on a third Antiochene mosaic, the Worcester Hunt (*c.* 500), where a mounted huntsman galloping towards the right turns his head back and extends in his right hand a cub, grasped by its back, that he is about to drop in front of a huge tigress which springs hard on the heels of the horse, with her two other cubs in identical springing attitudes, one above the other, underneath her.[84] A painting from the Tomb of the Nasonii in Rome shows two tigers pursuing leftwards three mounted huntsmen who are fleeing for their lives to the gangway of a ship. Two more huntsmen are on foot and one of them holds in his left hand a cub that he is just going to drop, while he parries with his shield a tigress' attack.[85] In this context the tiger hunt could have the same significance as the lion hunt on sarcophagi (cf. p. 66). (Pl. 23)

If the ship and the shore of which Pliny writes and which the Nasonian tomb-painting depicts are to be thought of as really part of the story of tiger-hunting, they could have been located only on the southern Armenian coast of the Euxine, since no tigress could have pursued a huntsman to one of the Syrian ports. Similarly, we must imagine ourselves transported from an African or Syrian to a Black Sea port in the scene on the 'Great Hunt' mosaic at Piazza Armerina in which a mounted huntsman on the left, pursued by an enormous tigress on the right, hurtles up the gangway of a ship.[86] He reaches safety with a captured cub grasped in his left hand, while the tigress pauses to pick up a round, convex mirror, thrown to the ground by the huntsman, in which she sees a reduced reflection of herself and imagines it to be her offspring. This is the famous 'mirror trap'; and

1, 2 *Above*, Africa (?) personified, the apsidal end of the 'Great Hunt' mosaic, Piazza Armerina. (*see also* Fig. 1), and, *below*, an Indian war-elephant and calf on a Campanian plate (pp. 29, 34).

3–7 Elephants on coins. *Top, left to right*, deka-
drachm of Alexander the Great, Alexander attacking King Porus; an African elephant with mahout
on a double shekel of the Barcids in Spain, and an
Indian elephant on a tetradrachm of Seleucus III,
(pp. 32, 33). *Above*, an elephant on a piece of *aes
signatum* (see Plate 58 for the reverse); *left*, an
African (?) elephant on a *denarius* of Julius Caesar
(pp. 34, 38).

8, 9 *Above*, The Triumph of Dionysus with African (?) elephants on a sarcophagus relief, and, *below*, a wall-painting of Venus in an elephant *quadriga*, in the Via dell'Abbondanza, Pompeii (pp. 43, 49).

10, 11 A terracotta war elephant with a mahout and turret on his back; he is attacking a Celtic warrior with his tusks (p. 348, n. 13). *Right*, The apotheosis of Antoninus Pius, or Julian, in an elephant *quadriga* on a leaf from an ivory diptych (p. 46).

12 Embarking an elephant up a gangway, the 'Great Hunt' mosaic, Piazza Armerina (*see also* Fig. 1 and p. 28)

13, 14 Reliefs of monkeys; *above*, sitting on a shop counter above hares in a cage, and, *left*, quietly contemplating (pp. 57, 59).

15 Silver dish with a personification of India with monkeys and birds beside her and leopards on leads beneath her feet (p. 59).

16, 17 Detail of a mosaic with a lion killing a stag, *left*, and the two leaves of an ivory diptych, *right*, showing a lion *venatio* (pp. 68, 63).

18 The Corbridge Lion, a powerful Roman-British sculpture of a lion attacking a goat, probably originally from a tomb (p. 67).

19–21 *Above*, a silver *patera* with Cybele and Attis in a lion *quadriga*; *below*, *left*, a beribboned lion mosaic, and, *right*, a marble relief of a lioness with her cubs (pp. 63, 69, 67).

22, 23 Details of mosaics from Antioch-on-the-Orontes showing a tiger hunt in progress and a mounted huntsman stealing a tiger cub (pp. 71, 72).

24 The 'mirror trap': a tigress deceived by her own reflection on the 'Great Hunt' mosaic, Piazza Armerina (see also Fig. 1, p. 72).

the mosaic illustrates very clearly a passage of Claudian where the poet describes how a Hyrcanian tigress, whose cubs have been stolen to be the pet of a Persian king, pursues the mounted robber, her stripes blazing with anger, and would have eaten him were she not checked by the mirrored image of herself.[87] Claudian does not mention the thief's escape on shipboard, as shown on the Piazza Armerina mosaic and in the painting from the Nasonian Tomb. But a relief on a sarcophagus lid in the Villa Medici in Rome may present the same scene as that on the mosaic. A mounted huntsman rushes towards the right up the gangway of a ship and was once holding something, possibly a tiger cub, in his now vanished extended right hand. Two felines, perhaps tigers, although there are now no indications of their stripes (these could have been added in paint), are hot in pursuit. One pauses to pick up a round, cake-like object which might be meant to be a convex mirror. If she is a tigress, the artist has forgotten to carve her udders.[88] (Pl. 24)

Apart from these hunting scenes and the Dionysiac processional mosaics (pp. 70, 71), renderings of tigers and tigresses in the art of the Roman age are relatively rare, as compared with those of other felines – lions and leopards, for instance. The following examples may be briefly described. On the well-known mosaic, now in Berlin, from Hadrian's Villa, which depicts a battle between Centaurs and a lion, tiger and leopard, the tiger (this time apparently male) occupies a central position on the stage. It crouches towards the left, with the claws of its forepaws plunged in the prostate body of a Centauress whom it has mortally wounded, and looks back, snarling, at a rearing Centaur who is about to bring a large piece of rock crashing down upon it.[89] The handsomest pictures wholly devoted to a tigress and her prey are panels of fourth-century date worked in *opus sectile*. One comes from the building outside the Porta Marina at Ostia which produced the lion panels (cf. p. 68): a tigress shown in profile to the left, with red, black and white body-stripes and a yellow and white head, slays a yellow fawn.[90] Two panels very similar in style to that at Ostia, from the basilica of Junius Bassus in Rome and now in the Palazzo dei Conservatori, would appear to have been made as pendants, although in detail they are not completely identical. One presents the tigress in profile to the right, the other to the left; and both beasts are yellow all over with black markings and white udders. Each has sprung on to the back of a helpless white calf whose hind-quarters are crushed to the ground. Both of the panels are very well preserved; and the bold drawing, to which the *opus sectile* technique lends itself so well, brings out admirably the tigresses' relentless strength and massive bulk.[91]

LEOPARDS AND CHEETAHS

These two breeds of large spotted cats, very similar to one another in physique, were procured for the Roman world from Asia and Africa. Thirty of these creatures had taken part in Ptolemy II's pageant, differentiated by the names παρδάλεις (fourteen) and πάνθηροι (sixteen), the former leopards, the latter probably cheetahs.[92] The king could have obtained his beasts from either continent. The *pantherae* which, according to Livy, Marcus Fulvius Nobilior showed in 186 BC (cf. p. 17) probably came from the East, since Livy does not mention Africa; whereas Pliny in his section on leopards refers to the animals as *Africanae* when recalling the senatorial decree that forbade their importation into Italy.[93] The date of this decree is not recorded. But it must soon have been shelved, for the aediles of 169 showed sixty-three *Africanae bestiae*, all most probably of the leopard class (cf. p. 17). The animals displayed by Marcus Scaurus, Pompey and Augustus (cf. p. 18) are described by Pliny in the section just cited as *variae*, 'spotted animals'. Although the context suggests that these *variae* came from Africa, it is possible that those of Scaurus were obtained from Syria, where he had been governor. The leopards that Marcus Caelius Rufus pressed Cicero to get for him from Cilicia (cf. p. 20) are called *pantherae*.

The earliest extant use of the Latin word *pardus* for leopard dates from the time of Nero;[94] and Pliny distinguishes *pardi* and *variae* (spotted females), found, he says, in Africa and Syria, from *pantherae*, the latter probably being cheetahs, since they have a light coat as a background to their spots.[95] The tame animals that Elagabalus introduced into his guests' bedrooms, along with lions and bears (cf. p. 64 and p. 356, note 30), are called *pardi*.[96] Since Roman art makes no very clear distinction between the two breeds, the general term 'leopard' will be used here in describing representations of the creatures in sculpture, painting, mosaic work and so forth.

The capture of leopards in the wild by enticing them into a travelling-box in which a bait has been placed is, as we have seen, illustrated on the 'Great Hunt' pavement at Piazza Armerina (p. 28). Another illustration of a similar device for taking these animals alive is a painting from the Nasonian Tomb.[97] On the right are six huntsmen in a row with interlocking shields, one of whom has either killed or badly wounded with his spear a leopard rolling over on its back with all four paws in air – obviously too dangerous a beast to be caught intact. But on the left is a row of five shielded huntsmen, one of whom, sheltering his head and body with his shield, kneels on the roof of a travelling-box, one end of which is open with its door, hinged to the base, lying on the ground. Inside the box there is a mirror in which the leopard, stepping across the door, sees the reflection of itself. Imagining it to be an enemy, it will, in another moment, push the mirror aside and enter the box. As soon as it is in the man on the roof will hook up the door with his spear and secure it behind the imprisoned and apparently unwounded animal. On the 'Great Hunt' mosaic two more leopards illustrate the stage before their rounding up and capture has begun, when they are still at liberty to stalk and seize their prey in the wilds (cf. pp. 28, 29).

The purpose of capturing and transporting leopards was, of course, as in the case of other wild animals, to display them and then to fight and ultimately slaughter them in arena *venationes*. In the Borghese Gallery in Rome is a much repaired and patched up mosaic panel found at Torre Nuova, of which the main figures seem to belong to the original picture, with two extraneous pieces added at the sides.[98] It depicts in two tiers an arena episode of the cruellest and grimmest kind. Above are three dying leopards, each transfixed by a murderously barbed spear, writhing in agony, one rolled over on its back, the other two sprawling on their bellies. Below, two *venatores*, one of them labelled MELITTO, are each driving a spear into a leopard's chest, from which gush streams of blood. A dying leopard, also speared, lies on its belly in the background. The build of the leopards on this pavement is clumsy and over-heavy. But the realism with which their anguish is portrayed is excruciating; and this picture raises in a most acute form the problem of how householders could wish to perpetuate such scenes of carnage on the floors of their homes.

Equally vivid and only a little less gruesome is the painted frieze of a leopard *venatio* high up on one of the long walls of the *frigidarium* of the extra-mural 'Hunting Baths' at Lepcis Magna in Tripolitania.[99] On the opposite long wall are the very scanty remnants of a painted lion hunt; and the possibility suggests itself that these *thermae*, which are not associated with a private house and are too large to have served for purely domestic use, belonged to a guild (*collegium*) either of professional hunters (*venatores*) or of merchants who traded in beasts for the local arena and for export to arenas abroad. In the leopard hunt the huntsmen, four of whom have their names inscribed beside them – NUBER, [V?]ICENTIVS, [L?]IBENTIVS and BICTOR [= Victor] – are engaging six leopards, the names of three of which – RAPIDVS, FVLGENTIVS and GABATIVS [?] – are likewise extant. The meaning of the first two leopards' names is self-evident, while that of the third remains obscure. Each of the three beasts in the foreground faces to the left as a hunter, lunging to the right, drives his spear into the creature's chest or head. Blood flows freely from the wounds. The leopards' coats, skilfully shaded and showing orange, brown, mauve and grey spots on a buff ground, are most realistically done, as are also the animals' expressions of rage, grim determination, or pain. The mosaic of Magerius, from Smirat, now in the Sousse Museum, shows a *venatio* with four leopards named, respectively, VICTOR, CRISPINVS, LVXVRIVS and ROMANVS.[100] (Pl. 27)

Another series of renderings of the leopard in the art of the Roman age is mythological, where the animal appears as the mount, draught-beast and companion of Dionysus and of personages connected with him. Among the most striking Hellenistic forerunners of Roman representations of the god on leopard-back are the pebble mosaic of the late fourth century B C, found at Pella in Macedonia in 1957, on which Dionysus, naked, vine-crowned, and brandishing a beribboned *thyrsus*, sits lightly on a lithe and slender beast that prances to the left, his right arm clasping its neck;[101] and the well-known *opus vermiculatum* piece of *c.* 100 B C in the House of the Masks on Delos, where the god, fully draped, ivy-crowned, and flourishing a *thyrsus* and a tambourine, is poised on the back of a leopard running to the right, looking back at its rider, and wearing round its shapely neck a garland of ivy bound with a scarlet scarf.[102] Similar in composition to the latter piece is a Roman mosaic from Zliten in Tripolitania, which shows Dionysus seated half-draped, holding a *thyrsus* and a wine cup, on a leopard that gallops to the right, while glancing back towards the god.[103] (Pl. 26)

The species of the Zliten beast, being spotted, is not in doubt. But when we turn to Roman sculpture, to the renderings of this motif on sarcophagi, there is much less certainty about the nature of the animal that Dionysus rides, since the markings of the coat, which must once have been added in paint, have now disappeared. Here the beast often has a short ruff of hair round the throat, starting from below the ears, fringed legs, and sometimes a tuft at the end of the tail.[104] The beast on the most spectacular sarcophagus of this series, the early third-century Badminton/New York piece depicting Dionysus flanked by figures of the Seasons, displays these traits very clearly.[105] It is possible that these creatures were meant, not for leopards, but for tigers; and F. Matz opts for tigers in his publication of the great sarcophagus just cited.[106] On the other hand, the leopard is the god's traditional mount; and on a mosaic panel, now in the British Museum, from a Roman villa at Halicarnassus, the definitely spotted animal that runs beside the dancing figure of the god, labelled ΔΙΟΝΥΣΟΣ, must be intended for a leopard, despite its ruff, fringed legs and thickened tail-end.[107] We may then, tentatively at least, include the beasts on these Dionysiac sarcophagi among renderings of leopards. A Maenad, seen from behind, rides what is most likely to be a leopard in circular stucco relief on the vault of the vestibule of the Underground Basilica near the Porta Maggiore in Rome.[108] There again we note the animal's slight ruff and tufted tail.

More distinctively leopard-like are the two carved felines that so frequently draw Dionysus' triumphal chariot on sarcophagi, whether the car contains Dionysus alone or Dionysus accompanied by Ariadne or, as very occasionally, Ariadne alone.[109] An outstanding example is the Baltimore Indian triumph piece, already quoted in other contexts (pp. 49, 65), where each animal is ridden by a small, curly-haired boy,[110] as it is on a Capitoline sarcophagus:[111] on one in Copenhagen the riders are Cupids.[112] A member of the god's train leads the harnessed creatures, which pace along sedately, looking straight before them and not, as in the scenes in which he rides upon the beast's back, turning back to view their master.

A late and somewhat crudely worked version of this processional theme occurs on a polychrome mosaic from the House of Liber Pater at Sabratha in Tripolitania.[113] The central portion of this pavement is filled by three medallions, of which the middle one contains a lion's head.[114] The upper one shows Dionysus, accompanied by Ariadne and a Victory, in a car drawn by two greenish-grey leopards which converse with one another and are led by Pan. The lower roundel holds a fine and most expressive leopard's head. The beast's coat is worked in brown, grey and white *tesserae*: round its neck is a thick shaded collar; and in the field surrounding it are sprays of flowers.[115]

Although less delicately drawn than the lion's head, it is much superior, both in execution and in feeling, to the leopards' heads in the triumph scene. (Pl. 25)

Two particularly pleasing Campanian paintings present the leopard as Dionysus' playmate. In one the god stands beneath a vine, while the animal, one forepaw raised, looks up expectantly at the wine cup held in its master's hand.[116] In the other, Dionysus is seated and extends his wine cup towards the leopard, which stands on its hind-legs and rests its forepaws affectionately on the god's knees.[117] On sarcophagi carved with the finding of Ariadne an alert leopard is seated on the ground beside Dionysus' legs and peeps round curiously at the sleeping maiden.[118] In renderings of Dionysus drunk and supported by members of his entourage a crouching leopard sometimes joins the party, as in the marble group from the Walbrook Mithraeum.[119] In the outer, Dionysiac frieze on the great Oceanus silver dish from Mildenhall in Suffolk, Dionysus, who has beaten Hercules in the drinking contest, rests his left foot nonchalantly on the back of his crouching leopard, which looks up angrily, jaws agape, as though protesting at this indignity.[120]

Among other representations of leopards in Dionysiac contexts are an amusing painting from Pompeii in which two of these animals slink up cautiously to sniff at a pair of cymbals, presumably dropped on the ground by a Maenad;[121] and the square panel immediately below the central picture of the drunken Dionysus on the pavement at Cologne Cathedral (cf. p. 68).[122] On this mosaic a female leopard strides along in solitary state towards the left with lowered head. She wears a bright blue collar and her spots form dark-red circles on a grey-green coat, largely worked in iridescent *tesserae* of glass paste. She recalls, in fact, the *virides pardi* of Claudian's line.[123]

Most unusual is the theme of a pair of leopards drawing a racing chariot, as on three late mosaic panels from Andania in the Peloponnese, where the charioteers are respectively named Enenion, Eunouda and Hieronas.[124]

LYNXES AND CARACALS

Four specimens of these animals, described as λυγκία, walked in Ptolemy II's pageant (cf. p. 39 and *passim*).[125] But we are not told whether these were spotted lynxes proper or unspotted ones, that is, caracals. Ptolemy could have procured them from Asia or from

Ethiopia, of which latter region Pliny states the lynx to be a native.[126] The spotted lynx was also found in Europe; for Pliny notes that the creature called *chama*, characterized as wolf-like in shape but leopard-like in spots, was known as *rufius* in in Gaul: Pompey showed one for the first time in Rome in his *ludi* of 55 BC.[127] After that the lynx is not recorded as appearing in the Roman shows. Aelian writes that the Moors say that lynxes are more snub-nosed than leopards, have hairy tips to their ears, are possessed of a wonderful spring, and hold their prey in an extremely powerful grip.[128] No certain rendering of a spotted lynx is extant in Roman art, so far as the present writer is aware. But on the Dumbarton Oaks Hunt mosaic an unspotted caracal is fleeing for its life towards the right, just to the left of the group of the tigress and her cubs (cf. p. 25).[129] The literary sources mention lynxes as one of the species of beasts reputed to have drawn the chariot of Dionysus.[130]

THE DOMESTIC CAT

Small cats, kept as household pets and imported no doubt in the first instance from Egypt, first appear in Italy on works of Greek art of the fifth and fourth centuries BC from the south of the peninsula. Silver coins of Tarentum and Rhegium, of the second half of the fifth century, carry the type of a naked youth, who probably represents the city-founder, seated on a chair towards the left and playing with, or accompanied by, a little feline. Sometimes this creature squats on its haunches with head and forepaws lifted towards an object that the youth holds up above it – now a bird, now what has been described as a distaff, but is possibly a cake or piece of meat (Tarentum).[131] Another version shows the cat leaping behind the youth's chair (Tarentum);[132] on yet another it sports with a ball beneath it (Rhegium).[133] On all of these variants the cat is so lifelike in its attitudes that the die-engravers must be held to have studied the movements of the animal in their homes. (Pl. 31)

The same must be true of the painters of those Apulian and Campanian vases on which a house-cat is portrayed, as on three examples in the British Museum collection. On one, a *kotyle* (Apulian: 400–380 BC), a naked youth stands three-quarters towards the right and holds in his raised right hand a tiny bird, which a small mottled cat, clinging to the youth's back, eyes greedily, one forepaw lifted to strike the fatal blow.[134] The second vase, a *lekane* (Campanian: *c.* 330 BC), presents a group of two women facing one another, that on the right naked and seated towards the left, that on the left draped and standing towards the right. Between them is a partly striped and partly mottled tabby, reared on its hind-legs and with its forepaws and eager gaze raised towards a bird that the seated woman holds above its head. On her lap is a ball, probably of wool, and two more such balls are held by her companion – all for the cat to play with. Even if the women are, as has been suggested, Aphrodite and Peitho, the episode is clearly drawn from daily life.[135] Such, too, is the nature of the group of a white goose confronted by a cat in the lower tier of a toilet scene on a *pelike* (Apulian: *c.* 350 BC).[136] (Pl. 30)

Undoubtedly the most familiar rendering of a cat dating from Roman times is a mosaic panel, now in the Naples Museum, from Pompeii, which contains two superimposed scenes divided from one another by a horizontal line.[137] In the upper portion a well-fed striped and spotted cat stands towards the right, with its left forepaw planted firmly on the back of a large bird, perhaps a partridge, and its round eyes expanded in anticipation of the pleasure of plucking and mealing off its victim. In the lower zone are two fat ducks accompanied by four much smaller birds, several fishes, water-lily buds, and shells – a sight to make the mouth of the beast above water still more. It can hardly be denied that this picture was either derived from a copy-book or was itself the original that copy-book compilers used, in view of the fact that, as in the case of the teased lion mosaic motif (cf. pp. 68, 69), two more versions of it have come down to us, both from the neighbourhood of Rome. The one that is nearest to the Pompeian piece, now in the Museo Nazionale Romano, was found on the Via Ardeatina and is also a panel in two tiers. The group in the upper tier repeats that on the Pompeian panel almost line for line, although the cat has no spots but is wholly striped and the bird's head and neck are less naturalistic, while in the lower zone the two ducks appear alone.[138] The third mosaic, in the Vatican, from Tor Marancio, is a somewhat freer version and is the least well-drawn of the three. The cat's attitude is the same, but the bird is a cock and there is no line dividing the upper from the lower zone, the latter containing two ducks and some fruit.[139] Another cat mosaic from Pompeii, in the Naples Museum, depicts a different theme. In the centre of the picture there stands on a high pedestal an ornamental, two-handled bowl, on the rim of which are perched two parrots and a dove. On the ground, to the right of the pedestal, a long-eared mottled cat crouches to the left, with large round eyes and glinting teeth. It seems to realize that the birds are out of reach; but its raised right forepaw indicates the longing that they stir in it.[140] (Pl. 29)

The two mosaics in Naples are, so far as the present writer knows, the only extant renderings of cats in Pompeian art. No mural paintings portray them; furthermore, no skeletons of cats or larva-formed moulds of their decayed corpses have as yet been reported from the excavations of the site. Is this due to chance? Or did the cats have some uncanny premonition and escape in time from the doomed towns? Or did the citizens of these Campanian towns not keep cats? However that may be, house-cats and their habits were certainly familiar to contemporary Roman writers. Seneca asks why chickens are afraid of cats, but not of dogs;[141] and Pliny had obviously observed, closely and at first hand, the tactics of the household fowler and mouser. 'How silently', he writes, 'and with how light a tread do cats creep up to birds, how stealthily they watch their chance to pounce on tiny mice. When they need to do their business they dig a hole in the earth and bury every trace, realizing that the smell would give them away.'[142] In Petronius' *Satyricon*[143] one of the characters relates how his little boy (*cicaro*) is mad on birds (*in aves morbosus est*) and how, annoyed by this, he has killed the child's pet goldfinches (*cardeles*), pretending that the *mustela* had eaten them (*dixi quod mustela comedit*) (cf. p. 278). This convenient scapegoat, which was obviously about the house, was probably a weasel or a polecat, rather than an ordinary cat, although the latter possibility cannot be wholly excluded.

Three monuments of early imperial times attest the presence of the house-cat in Italy. A terracotta lamp, now in the British Museum, presents on its *discus* a juggler or mountebank squatting on the ground as he conducts a performance of his private animals.[144] On the spectator's left is an ape (cf. p. 58), while on the right, scaling a ladder, is what would seem to be undoubtedly a cat. Above the ladder are two rings, which may be meant for the cat to jump through – unless we are to think of them as an item in the ape's 'turn'. Ascribable to the second century on the score of its lettering is a tombstone now in the Palermo Museum, but found in Rome. It was erected by a certain Calpurnia Felicla for her husband, Ger-mullus, and for herself.[145] Below the inscription there stands towards the right, on a ledge, a stocky, thick-coated little cat, with ears pricked and its tail waving across its back. The animal is clearly an allusion to the dedicator's name – 'Felicla' ('Kitty'). Thirdly, a small and daintily carved marble relief in the Museo Capitolino, perhaps of Hadrianic date, depicts a pet cat learning to dance to music.[146] On the left a girl, seated towards the right on a high-backed chair, plays the lyre. In the centre a cat is standing on its hind-legs, its head and forepaws raised towards a brace of ducks that dangles above it from the branch of a tree (the lesson must be taking place in the courtyard or garden of the house), hung there, no doubt, as an incentive. (Pl. 32)

Cats in the Roman provinces are represented by a now lost mosaic panel from Orange, on which a somewhat evil-looking animal crouches on the ground towards the right, with arched back and a dead mouse between its forepaws.[147] On a mosaic from Volubilis in Morocco a cat named 'Vincentius' and wearing a red collar and bell is slaying a mouse or rat named 'Luxurius'.[148]

Pet cats also feature in Gallo-Roman stone sculpture – in a fragmentary figure in the round from Auxerre, where a heavy collar encircles the animal's neck; on the funerary stelai of young boys and girls, where the dead child either sits or stands with its favourite on its lap or in its arms, a piece from Bordeaux (Musée d'Aquitaine), showing a particularly realistic rendering of the cat, which is held up to face the spectator by its little mistress, who grasps it by the forepaws, while its hind-legs and tail, playfully nipped by a cock, hang down in front of her; and on a table-leg from Mont Auxois, now in the Alesia Museum, where a young boy, worked in high relief, holds a sprightly little cat, wearing a collar and bell and comfortably couched towards the left on a fold of the child's tunic, while its mask and tall, pricked ears are turned towards the viewer.[149] Further north, the skeleton of a cat (?) came to light in the Deep Room in the villa at Lullingstone in Kent: it died in the final fire that destroyed the house.[150] (Pl. 28)

On the whole, domestic cats, although sometimes trained to do tricks and undoubtedly treated by some of their owners as pets, seem to have been chiefly valued as destroyers of vermin. Such portraits of them by the hands of Roman artists as we possess are, if often lively and realistic, relatively few. No other personal name of a pet cat has been recorded, so far as the present writer is aware.

CHAPTER V

CAT-LIKE GROUPS

ICHNEUMONS

THE ICHNEUMON, akin in physique to the Indian mongoose, was in ancient times a specifically Nilotic creature. Pliny recounts its hatred, and destruction, of snakes and describes how it plasters itself with several coatings of mud before attacking another of its enemies, the crocodile.[1] According to Strabo the inhabitants of Herakleopolis worshipped ichneumons as being most destructive of crocodiles and asps; they eat the eggs of their foes and put on 'breastplates of mud' (πωλῷ θωρακισθέντες) before attacking them.[2] The same process is compared by Plutarch in one passage to the donning of a cuirass by a hoplite before going into battle,[3] in another to the action of an athlete.[4] Aelian also compares the precautions thus taken by the ichneumon to those of a soldier who arms himself for the fight with his full panoply.[5] The same writer speaks of the animal's destruction of asps' eggs; of its enmity to the asp and crocodile; and its worship by the Herakleopolitans in Egypt as sacred to Leto and the Eileithyiae.[6] Cicero writes of the ichneumon's *utilitas*, presumably as a slayer of obnoxious creatures.[7] According to Martial these animals, so dangerous in their wild state, were sometimes tamed and kept as pets in Rome.[8]

Occasionally ichneumons are portrayed in art. A fine bronze statuette, now in the Ashmolean Museum, Oxford, shows the animal standing quietly, its fur unplastered and no enemy in sight: it is possibly of Ptolemaic date, but could be earlier.[9] On a Nilotic mosaic from Pompeii it advances against a rearing snake;[10] on one side of the base of the famous Vatican Nile it appears in relief with tail raised for onslaught on a crocodile;[11] and in the Nile group itself it and its crocodile foe are carved in the round, by the knee and feet of the god respectively confronting one another and sported with by some of the *putti*.[12] (Pl. 33)

HYENAS

The hyenas most familiar to the Graeco-Roman world would appear to have been of the smaller, striped variety, common in Asia and Africa. Pliny, after relating a number of fantastic tales about the animal, states that Africa is its native home.[13] He also recounts the belief that when a lioness is crossed with a hyena it gives birth to a *corocotta*,[14] a term used for the hyena itself, so it would seem, by other writers, as, for instance, by Diodorus Siculus, who describes it as a mixture of dog and wolf of Ethiopian origin.[15] Pliny furthermore devotes a long passage to the supposed remedies to be derived from a hyena's corpse.[16]

If the *Augustan History* is to be believed, Antoninus Pius *corocottas exhibuit* at a show in Rome,[17] a statement that contradicts Dio Cassius' declaration that the κοροκόταs killed in AD 202 at the shows held in honour of Caracalla's marriage with Plautilla was the first specimen of the breed, mistakenly described as 'Indian' (unless 'Indian' is used here generally for 'Asiatic'), to appear in Rome, so far, at least, as the historian knew. Dio says that it combines the colouring of a lioness and of a tigress, both of which it resembles in its general appearance, while being at the same time a curious mixture of dog and fox.[18] Again the *Augustan History* records that there were ten hyenas in Gordian III's collection, exhibited by Philip I (cf. p. 16).[19]

Renderings of hyenas in the art of Roman times are very rare. On the 'Worcester Hunt' mosaic pavement from Antioch-on-the-Orontes a striped hyena is running for its life towards the right, just to the right of the group of a mounted huntsman with a stolen tiger cub (cf. p. 25).[20]

CHAPTER VI

BEARS

OF THE WILD AND DANGEROUS ANIMALS of the Roman world that were hunted and killed in the field, captured alive for display in public and private spectacles, and occasionally tamed, bears were among the most ubiquitous. In the first place, Italy itself supplied them. Martial speaks of the 'Lucanian bear';[1] and when Horace wrote of the bear that prowls around the sheepfold of an evening he must certainly have had in mind the Italian countryside.[2] Bears were also natives of several areas in Greece. Pausanias mentions them in Attica, in the region of Mount Taygetus, and in Arcadia.[3] He also states that Thrace produced white bears;[4] and the single great white she-bear that walked in Ptolemy II's pageant (cf. p. 39 and *passim*)[5] may well have been of Thracian origin – if it was not a straw-coloured Syrian beast (cf. p. 95). In the temple of Eros at Thespiae in Boeotia Hadrian dedicated, with verses of his own composition, the spoils of a she-bear slain by him on the hunting-field.[6] It seems that some at least of the bears with which Demochares of Plataea in Apuleius' *Metamorphoses* was intending to entertain the populace were local animals (cf. pp. 98-9).

Across the Aegean, bears were to be found in Asia Minor: Hadrian also hunted and destroyed a she-bear in Mysia, on the spot on which he founded the town of Hadrianotherae.[7] 'Oppian', in his account of the method used for catching bears alive (cf. p. 95), locates them in Armenia.[8] The Emperor Julian, invading Babylon in AD 363, found among other beasts in the royal animal reserve that provided the king with quarry for his sport some Persian bears noted for their excessive savagery.[9] To turn to the West and North, Claudian knew of Spanish bears[10] and Martial of bears imported for the slaughter of criminals in Rome from Scotland, recently opened up to the Roman world by the conquests of Agricola.[11] Martial also tells of how the famous *venator* Carpophorus plunged his hunting spears into a bear that rushed headlong at him – a bear that had once been king of all the beasts beneath the Arctic sky.[12] 'Arctic' could mean Caledonia or northern Germany or even the polar regions; for according to Calpurnius Siculus bears, which must certainly have been polar bears, could be seen in Rome chasing seals.[13] Calpurnius' *Eclogues* are generally assigned, for linguistic reasons, to the time of Nero; but another view would place them in the third century A D, on the ground that Pliny never mentions polar bears.[14]

But Pliny, for all the knowledge of the habits of bears that he displays, was not infallible in this regard and could have overlooked the polar species just as he failed to take account of the existing literary evidence for bears in Africa. After describing how in 61 B C Domitius Ahenobarbus as aedile produced in the Circus a hundred Numidian bears and as many Ethiopian *venatores* to fight with them, he adds 'I am surprised that the bears are said to have been Numidian, since it is a well-known fact that no bears are to be found in Africa.'[15] But the evidence of literature for bears in Africa, both accessible to Pliny and of later times, and the later evidence of archaeology, is overwhelming. Strabo informs us that the Mauretanians dressed and slept in bear skins;[16] Virgil speaks of a shaggy Libyan she-bear;[17] Martial tells us of Libyan bears in harness,[18] Juvenal of Numidian bears slaughtered in Domitian's private arena at Albano;[19] and Dio Cassius writes of the slaying of 'bears and other Libyan beasts' in the shows given by Publius Servilius as praetor in 25 B C and by the Emperor Gaius in A D 37.[20] To these passages must be added the witness of the African mosaic pavements featuring bears, some of which will be discussed below (pp. 96, 97). There can be little doubt that Pliny's confident assertions about the absence of bears in Africa were simply wrong. Throughout the Roman world – east, west, north, south, and centre – bears were to be obtained.

Reference has already been made to Hadrian's bear-hunting exploits in Greece and Mysia. The Hadrianic *tondo* on the Arch of Constantine, which shows an imperial bear hunt, may have been meant to illustrate one of these achievements; but the relief itself provides no clues through which the scene's precise locality can be determined. Most of the bear's head is lost; but its movement and shaggy coat are admirably carved.[21] A bear hunt, seemingly in the field, appears on a rock-cut relief at Byblos in the Lebanon, where a hunter drives his spear into the chest of a huge shaggy beast that rears on its hind-legs towards him.[22] One of the reliefs (that on the east side) on the mausoleum at Hermel, also in the Lebanon, depicts a bear running towards the right, confronted by one hound and pursued by another, while around it all manner of implements symbolic of the chase are hurtling through the air – hunting spears, quivers, arrows, and a curious object with a cord or rope wound round it, perhaps for ensnaring the creature's paws.[23] The relief on the west side presents a she-bear standing to the left with two cubs, one behind and one in front of her. The former cub licks a wounded forepaw, the latter dances on its hind-legs, unaware apparently of the danger it is in. The same array of weapons as on the east face menaces the family.[24] These Lebanese bears could have been of the local straw-coloured species (cf. p. 93).

The object of the bear hunts described above was either pure sport or restriction of the numbers of these potential devourers of human beings and of their flocks and herds. Equally important was the still more difficult task of taking bears alive and transporting them, in extra-strong and heavy boxes, to the arenas and other public places in which they were to be displayed. One of the methods followed for their capture is described in great detail by 'Oppian'.[25] When the animal's lair had been located a run was dug from it and a net spread at the opposite end. On one side this run was lined by armed men in ambush, while along the other side was stretched a rope hung with coloured ribbons and feathers. This latter contraption was the scare (*formido*), quoted by Seneca as a cause of terror to wild beasts.[26] The bear was then roused from its lair by the blast of a trumpet and driven by beaters down the run into the net. The mouth of the net was then closed by cords drawn by men hidden on either side and the enmeshed beast finally hauled into a travelling-box.

The great public shows in which bears featured in substantial numbers, beginning with the show of 169 BC, have been listed in Chapter I. There was also, no doubt, as in Horace's day, bear-baiting on a smaller scale.[27] Sometimes in the public spectacles the bears are not described or represented as being hunted and killed, but as being just displayed before the audience or as being put through the performances, not all of them bloodless, for which they had been trained. The bears that Martial saw in harness have already been cited. On another occasion he witnessed a she-bear sent up to the arena from its cage below to devour a criminal who had been cast in the role of Orpheus.[28] Two fragments, now in the Bardo Museum in

Tunis, of a mosaic pavement from Kourba (Curubis) show seven bears in all, playing and sparring with one another without any trace of *bestiarii* or *venatores*. On the one fragment are two superimposed registers, each containing two bears, of which one in the upper register has the name [PL?]OTINA inscribed beside her. Of the three bears on the second fragment one is named LEANDER, another INVICTVS. The surviving beasts' lively attitudes and expressions make it all the more regrettable that so much of these scenes has been destroyed. [29]

A troupe of performing bears occupies the surviving portion of another pavement in the Bardo Museum, found at Radez (cf. p. 31). Here again, no hunters are in evidence and the eight extant bears appear to be mainly sporting, more or less amicably, with other creatures – five boars, a bull, a stag and an ostrich. The names of six of the bears are preserved – 'Nilus', 'Fedra' (who is swarming up a pole), 'Alecsandria', 'Simplicius' ('Frank'), 'Gloriosus' and 'Braciatus' ('Brawny').[30] Another performing she-bear, labelled *EIPHNH*, appears on a gem, a heliotrope, now known only from a drawing. She stands on her hind-legs, with her forepaws resting on the flank of her trainer, *MAPKEΛΛOΣ*, who carries a whip and what is either a succulent joint of meat or a cloth (*mappa*).[31] An incised marble tablet from Narbonne depicts another bear performance. In the background a bear, directed by its trainer, is balanced on a horizontal bar. In the foreground a much larger, spotted bear is reared on its hind-legs and rests its forepaws on the hands of a man who is squatting in a tub, while its gaping jaws almost touch his head. Is the beast playing with its trainer, pretending that it will devour him? Or has the creature run amok and does it really mean to eat the man, who has vainly jumped into the tub for refuge? Or is this no performing bear, but a killer of criminals? It is not easy to decide.[32] Bear performers are featured in two small bronzes in the Museum of Fine Arts in Boston, Massachusetts. One is dated *c.* 50 BC and depicts the animal reared on its now vanished hind-legs and holding a stick in its mouth and right forepaw; the other, in the form of a late Roman *ampulla*, presents the creature squatting on its rump and wearing harness.[33] (Pls. 34, 38, 39)

It is recorded that the shows of Carus, Carinus and Numerianus in the late third century AD included bears acting a mime and an acrobat running up a wall to escape from a bear's pursuit.[34] The latter item is illustrated vividly on a much later monument, an ivory diptych, now at Zürich, which was carved for Areobindus in 506 in Constantinople. In the lower scene on the left-hand leaf, above a group of three *venatores* fighting a couple of bears, a man is running up a wall built of ashlar blocks, while a bear is seizing one of his ankles (cf. p. 63).[35] In the Isiac procession that Apuleius' hero Lucius witnessed there was a tame she-bear dressed up as a matron and carried on a *sella* (sedan chair).[36]

Archaeological and literary evidence, additional to that already cited in Chapter I, for bear *venationes* is fairly plentiful. A fragmentary pavement from Khanguet-el-Hadjaj in Tunisia, bearing the figure of the *venator* Lampadius with his name inscribed beside him, shows, above him, two superimposed registers, in each of which there stands a frightened bear.[37] Protomes of bears, along with those of many other beasts and birds that featured in *venationes*, occur in the 'peopled' floral scroll mosaic of the curvilinear peristyle in the villa at Piazza Armerina[38] and on a pavement of the baths of Thuburbo Majus in Tunisia.[39] On a mixed animal *venatio* mosaic at Cos (cf. p. 359, note 100), on which 16 *venatores* are contending with 18 beasts, there are 7 bears, 6 of them named in Greek – 'Norike' (two bears – perhaps denoting their place of origin), 'Drakontis', 'Dionysos', 'Xanthias', and 'Tachine' ('Swift').[40] Yet another fragmentary Tunisian pavement, from the House of the Peacock at Carthage, portrays a *venator* named BONIFA[TIVS] and two bears called CRVDELIS and OMICIDA.[41] With these names that describe straightforwardly the creatures' natures may be contrasted those of 'Mica Aurea' ('Grain-of-Gold') and 'Innocentia' ironically bestowed on two particularly savage man-eating bears that Valentinian I kept in first-rate condition for the arena in cages placed near his bedroom, with guards posted to ensure that nothing was done to 'sabotage' their bloodthirsty ferocity. 'Innocentia', having done her stint of providing human corpses for burial, was honourably retired and set free to roam the woods, where she could do no harm.[42]

A fourth-century limestone relief in the Sofia Museum, of which the upper part is broken off, is carved with an animated bear *venatio*. Seven bears survive and four *venatores*, together with the figure of a man armed with conical helmet, round shield and heavy spear, in the centre of the picture, who seems to be in charge of the proceedings. Some of the bears are attacking humans, the rest pitted against other animals – three bulls, a stag (?) and a ferocious crocodile (cf. p. 219) seen behind the central personage. Below him is a stage, on which a bear-cub (?) is seated on a high-backed chair and accompanied by four standing, small-scale figures, either mountebanks wearing dog-masks or, possibly, baboons dressed like men (cf. p. 58). On the left a similar, but slightly larger, mounted masked man or ape gallops into the lists.[43]

In Symmachus' shows (cf. pp. 20, 21) bears were obviously a most important item, several times referred to in his correspondence. On one occasion he complains that the bears which he had ordered never arrived (*ursorum defectus*).[44] On another, he requests the swift and safe transport of Italian bears, as many as possible (*ursi quam plurimi . . . ex Italia*) for his *munus* and begs his correspondent to see to it that inferior bears are not fraudulently substituted for them during the journey (*ne qua eos fraus avara commutet*).[45] In another letter he thanks a friend for undertaking to secure a good quantity of bears for a spectacle to be given by his son.[46] Later letters mention bears from overseas (*de transmarinis locis ursi*)[47] and a consignment of Dalmatian bears which he expects to appear shortly (*plures de Dalmatia ursos*).[48] Symmachus also writes of 'bear-dealers' (*ursorum negotiatores*).[49]

Bear *venationes* were still a popular form of entertainment in the Eastern Empire during the late fifth and early sixth centuries, to judge from their appearance on ivory diptychs carved in Constantinople. In addition to the Zürich piece cited above (cf. pp. 96-7), there is another made for Areobindus in 506, now in Leningrad, where, in the lower scene on the right-hand leaf, are an acrobat turning a somersault and attacked by a bear, and two men, each slung up in a basket, similarly threatened.[50] The same motifs occur again on the right-hand leaf of a diptych, now in Berlin, which was worked for Anastasius in 515;[51] and in the lower scenes on both leaves of a piece, now in the Louvre, made in the Eastern Empire in *c.* 400, are *venatores* attacking bears and scaring or provoking them with cloths (*mappae*).[52]

A private bear show on a large scale, or rather an attempted show, is luridly described by Apuleius.[53] For the splendid *munus* that he proposed to stage, Demochares of Plataea had expended large sums on procuring a vast number of immense bears (*immanis ursae comparabat numerum copiosum*), which he had either caught locally or bought or received as gifts from friends (*domesticis venationibus captas, praeter largis emptionibus partas, amicorum etiam donationibus . . . oblatas*). But he had no luck. All of them died as the result either of their long captivity (*diutina captivitate fatigatae*), or of the wasting effect of the broiling heat (*aestiva flagrantia maceratae*), or of lack of exercise (*pigra etiam sessione languidae*), or of a sudden infection (*repentina correptae pestilentia*). Whereupon the populace fell on the carcases and feasted off the flesh. Then two of the characters in Apuleius' tale who witnessed this scene seized the largest of the dead bears, skinned it, dressed up one of their companions, a certain Thrasyleon, in the skin, hired a cage, and put him into it. Demochares, being shown Thrasyleon in the cage and tricked into believing it to be a real bear presented to him by a friend in Thrace, was overjoyed and caused the cage to be placed in his house. But at dead of night the two friends came and released Thrasyleon, so that he could run about the place, where he was unfortunately hunted and eventually torn by the master's hounds and run through by a man with a hunting spear. The comedy had, in fact, turned into a very gruesome human *venatio*.

Occasionally we hear of bears kept as domestic pets, such as those which Seneca describes as living in the house and being fondled by humans with impunity.[54] In theory, at any rate, the Gaulish goddess Artio had a tame bear, delightfully portrayed in a bronze group now in the Bern Historical Museum. The bear slinks up to its mistress from the forest, symbolized by a tree, and seems to cause her some embarrassment by its affectionate forwardness.[55] (Pl. 37)

There are some works of Roman art in which a bear appears to have been depicted simply for its own sake. A square mosaic panel in the Landesmuseum at Trier shows a bear that has found its way into an orchard designated by three trees. The largest of the trees, that on the left, is an apple tree and against its trunk the intruder, reared on its hind-legs, rests its forepaws, ready to snatch the fruit in its open jaws.[56] A life-like study of a rough-coated bear is the subject of a cameo found at South Shields in County Durham. The beast, which is worked in the·white upper layer of the stone against the background of the lower brown layer, stands towards the right, its head slightly raised, its ears flattened back, and its forepaws clutching its prostrate prey, probably a goat. Since it seems unlikely that the stone, an Indian sardonyx, would have been imported into this province in an unworked state, the model must have been a bear seen in some Mediterranean arena, rather than in northern Britain.[57] (Pls. 35, 36)

On the other hand, we can assign to Romano-British workmanship the miniature figures in the round of bears carved in Yorkshire jet that are found on British sites – York, Malton and Colchester – and also exported to the Rhineland, to Cologne and Trier, where there is no evidence for the manufacture of objects of this material or of deposits of it. Some of these tiny creatures stand on platforms, others have holes pierced through them so that they could be worn round the neck as amulets. One was found at Malton in a child's grave and may have been the infant's plaything. [58]

CHAPTER VII

CANINE ANIMALS

WOLVES

THE WOLF, IN ROMAN TIMES INDIGENOUS to Italy and Sicily and particularly common in the northern and western provinces, but also an inhabitant of eastern lands,[1] is familiar in Latin literature as the slaughterer of sheep and goats – the shepherd's and herdsman's inveterate foe. Sacred to Mars,[2] it features most frequently in Roman art in the form of the famous *Lupa Romana*, the She-wolf suckling the Twins, standing to right or left with her head turned back towards the infants. On the Roman coinage this time-honoured scene made its first appearance on the reverses of silver didrachms struck between 269 and *c.* 242 BC, mainly in southern Italy, with the legend ROMANO in the exergue.[3] One of its latest numismatic occurrences is on the VRBS ROMA bronze medallions issued *c.* AD 330 by Constantine the Great. Here the group is either free-standing and accompanied by a couple of stars in the sky above[4] or contained within a rocky cave, above which two stars are twinkling and on either side of which stands the figure of a shepherd, a *pedum* in his left hand, while his right hand is raised in a gesture of astonishment.[5] On these medallions the group is a symbol of Eternal Rome, as it also is on the numerous reliefs of the Roman age that depict it. Among provincial reliefs with this motif one of the most striking is that at Avenches (Aventicum) in Switzerland, where the group is ensconced in a cave that is flanked by a tree on either side; and the *Lupa*, who stands towards the left, turns back her head and extends her tongue to lick the back of one of the Twins.[6] In Britain the motif appears on a badly battered, but still clearly recognizable, relief from a temple pediment at Corbridge (Corstopitum) in Northumberland, where the She-wolf stands towards the right against the background of a spreading vine;[7] and in an excessively provincial form on the well-known mosaic pavement, now in the Leeds City Museum, from Aldborough (Isurium Brigantum) in Yorkshire: here the *Lupa* stands beneath the *Ficus Ruminalis* with her right forepaw raised and kicked out behind her as though to indicate the Twins who, instead of sucking her, are dancing a jig beneath her belly.[8] This last *Lupa* is far from being true to nature, since her teats are absent and her upstanding ears are more like those of a cat or lynx. (Pls 40, 41)

According to Paulus/Festus Roman hunting dogs (*canes venatici*) sometimes wore a collar with iron spikes (*mellum* or *millus*) against the attacks of wolves.

FOXES

Foxes, native to Italy, were the victims of a barbarous ritual enacted in Rome on 19 April each year during the festival of Ceres, when a number of the creatures were let loose in the Circus Maximus with lighted torches tied to their tails and allowed to burn to death. Ovid explains this custom by the tale of how a vixen, having been caught by a child and wrapped in straw and hay, which was then set alight, had escaped into the cornfields and burnt the crops: atonement for this was supposed to be the purpose of the rite that was still carried out in Augustan times.[9] This passage immediately recalls the episode of Samson catching three hundred foxes, turning them tail to tail, putting a lighted torch between each pair of tails, and then releasing the animals in the cornfields of the Philistines.[10] And the liveliest rendering of foxes in Roman art known to the present writer is the wall-painting that presents a free version of this story in the new fourth-century Christian catacomb on the Via Latina.[11] Here a trio of sprinting foxes represents the three hundred; but the animals, which are painted in various shades of yellow and red, are not tied tail to tail and no torches are visible. Fox hunts are occasionally depicted on mosaic pavements (cf. pp. 24, 105).

The *aurita lagalopex* that one of Martial's friends kept as a pet was probably a long-eared fox.[12]

DOGS

Hunting Dogs
The various breeds of dogs known to have been used for hunting in the Graeco-Roman world are described at length by Aymard in Chapter XII of his *Essai sur les chasses romaines* (1951), where full

references to ancient writers on the subject will be found. No more, therefore, need be attempted here than to list the main characteristics of the principal types of dogs that the Romans employed in the chase and to mention some probable representations of them in works of art.

The war dogs of Asia Minor that feature on the great frieze of the Altar of Zeus at Pergamon as the comrades of Hekate, Artemis and Asteria[13] were used for hunting such big game as boars and antelopes. They were extremely strong and muscular, with heavy muzzles, large, solid heads, powerful necks encircled by a great ruff of hair, straight, upstanding ears, and long, tufted tails. Marble statues in the Uffizi in Florence, a bronze in the Museum of Art and History in Geneva, and two mosaics in the Roman Antiquarium, depicting an antelope and a boar hunt respectively, portray examples of the breed.[14] Indian dogs, tall, strong, short-eared, and short-coated, were acclimatized in Mesopotamia in antiquity. In the Roman period they were used for hunting in eastern lands, at least, as a papyrus dated after 29 BC indicates.[15] The Greek Philostratus mentions Indian dogs in his description of a picture of a boar hunt; [16] and Indian dogs were among the 2,400 hounds that walked in Ptolemy II's procession (cf. p. 39 and *passim*).[17]

Of the Greek hounds the Cretan, also listed by Philostratus in the passage just cited, were tall and strong, with an elegant, long, sinewy body, lean flanks, a long head, short, straight ears, and a long, thick tail. According to Claudian they had a shaggy coat.[18] They specialized as harriers, but were reputed to have the strength of bears or of any other fierce animal.[19] This breed is generally mentioned by Latin writers in the context of mythological episodes. Of the two types of Molossians from Epirus, one was employed for hunting. This was a massive, heavily built dog, with a smooth coat, a large, blunt-nosed head, half-pricked ears and a tufted tail. Martial describes a *venatio* in Rome at which a hind, chased by swift Molossians, stayed her flight as though in suppliant prayer before the emperor's feet and was left untouched by the hounds (cf. p. 144); [20] and Claudian has a simile of Molossian dogs guiding the huntsman to his prey by their subtle scent.[21] The enormous dogs depicted in the boar-hunt scene on the Villelaure mosaic may be Molossians.[22] More famous still were the Laconians, frequently mentioned in the literary sources, lightly built and characterized by Claudian as being svelte (*tenues Lacaenae*).[23] And when at Trimalchio's famous feast draperies embroidered with hunters and *totus venationis apparatus* were spread in front of the diners' couches, it was Laconian hounds that raised a great din outside the dining-room and then burst in, running this way and that round the table – preceding the huge boar on a dish, which a servant, dressed as a hunter, cut open with a hunting knife.[24]

Of the physique of the Italian breeds, the Umbrian and the Tuscan, no descriptions survive in literary sources. Virgil characterizes the former as lively and keen;[25] and the dog that lies curled up asleep on an *aes grave* coin struck at Hatria in Picenum might be a portrait of it.[26] As to the Tuscan, Aymard suggests that it may be represented by the hound that is dealing with the boar in the right-hand part of the scene on a Meleager sarcophagus in the Palazzo dei Conservatori: this hound has a long muzzle, partly drooping ears, a rough coat and a long, curving tail.[27] But the identification is purely conjectural.

To turn to the Western provinces – Gaulish dogs enjoyed a high reputation in Graeco-Roman times, in particular the breed known as *vertragi*, famed as the swiftest of harriers. Arrian says that their name was derived from the Celtic word for speed;[28] and he later gives a minute account of their physical characteristics.[29] They had large, supple ears, long necks, long muzzles, broad chests, long paws, muscular hind-quarters, lean flanks and long, thin tails ending in a tuft. Their portrait may perhaps be recognized in the dog attacking a hare in the left-hand part of the Conservatori Meleager sarcophagus cited above; and in the superb bronze running dog from Moudon in Switzerland, now in the Bern Museum.[30]

A British breed of rough-haired dogs, Agassaeans, small and lean in build, but strong, keen-scented, and very swift, was so highly esteemed that it was exported to the Continent for hunting.[31] The bronze figurine of a dog found in Coventina's well at Carrawburgh (Procolitia), Northumberland, shows a stocky little beast, with a heavy, blunt muzzle, short, upstanding ears, shaggy coat and legs and a short, curly tail: it may depict, to some degree at least, this British type.[32] Claudian declares that British dogs were strong enough to break the necks of mighty bulls.[33] Possibly the poet had in mind dogs of yet another breed that crossed the Channel and even made their way to Rome, namely, the Irish hounds (*Scottici canes*) which, according to Symmachus, aroused great interest in the capital.[34] A portrait of one of these may be detected in the beautifully modelled bronze figurine from the temple of Nodens at Lydney in Gloucestershire. It presents a lithe and sinewy animal, slightly rough-coated, with long ears, a long, pointed muzzle and powerful legs and haunches: there is a heavy collar round the slender neck.[35] Its counterpart in relief may be seen in the long-eared hound with pointed snout that lies tightly curled as though for sleep, but with one round, watchful eye wide open, on the lid of a small bronze box found in the Roman villa at Witcombe, also in Gloucestershire.[36] In the case of the latter bronze the tail is concealed. But the long-tailed, long-eared creatures, with long heads and slender legs, that, worked in *en barbotine* technique, hurtle round the bodies of Castor-ware beakers in pursuit of stags and hares, might well be akin to the Irish species, although their coats are smooth.[37] Very similar, also, is the bronze smooth-coated dog, long-eared and long-snouted, in the Cologne Museum, which sits on its haunches with its head pointing skywards, as though about to howl piercingly.[38] Possibly related to the same breed are the two seated hounds, one of which playfully gnaws the other's ear, in the two well-known and heavily restored marble groups in the Vatican and British Museum.[39] (Pls 44, 45, 46, 47)

It may be that the dogs that feature on some North African mosaic pavements in scenes of hare, antelope and boar hunts depict local species. A very well preserved panel from Oudna in Tunisia, now in the Bardo Museum, Tunis, presents a scene of rapid movement in which two mounted huntsmen and a hunter on foot are urging on two sinewy, long-eared and long-tailed hounds that fly like the wind, one above the other, the upper one, named EDERATVS ('Ivy-crowned'), in pursuit of a hare and the lower, named MVS-TELA ('Weasel'), hard on the heels of what appears to be a bushy-tailed fox.[40] Similar in build are the hounds named FIDELIS and CASTVS that are chasing an antelope and other creatures into nets on a pavement from Constantine (Cirta) in Algeria.[41] Very different are the solidly built, blunt-nosed and short-eared animals, with short, cheekily upturned tails, that are taking part in a boar hunt on an apse-shaped mosaic from Carthage, now in the Bardo Museum.[42] On the 'Little Hunt' mosaic in the Piazza Armerina villa in Sicily (cf. pp. 24, 25), the pavements of which were probably the work of African artists and craftsmen, both of these types of hound are represented – the slenderer, long-eared, long-tailed kind for hare and fox hunts, the heavier, blunt-nosed variety with the short, upturned tail, for work with boars.[43] The hound that is 'assisting' with the capture of a rhinoceros on the 'Great Hunt' pavement in the villa (cf. pp. 29, 127) is of the more elegant, long-tailed species.

The hunting dogs that feature on a Thessalian grave relief are on too small a scale and are too crudely carved for their breed to be determined.[44] Their interest lies in their personal names. The deceased, a certain Rufus, is portrayed twice on horseback. Above he is accompanied by a dog chasing a hare with the inscription Ἰούλιος ὁ συνκαμώ[ν] μοι ('Julius, my colleague') beneath it. Below he has two canine comrades, also hot on the heels of a hare, named ΝΕΙΚΗ ('Victory') and ΛΑΔΑΣ, Ladas being the name of a celebrated Spartan runner[45] who came to be regarded as a kind of personification of swiftness of foot, so allusions to him in Latin literature suggest.

The training of hunting dogs must have started when they were still puppies; and it must have been a highly skilled affair. Apuleius speaks of hounds that were 'mindful of their careful training' (sollertis disciplinae memores) on the occasion of what was supposed to be a goat hunt, in a passage that implies that the instructions imparted to dogs varied in accordance with the different types of quarry with which they had to deal.[46] In this instance the dogs, a pack of highly-bred hunters taught to encircle their prey (canes venationis indagini generosae), fanned out when released, blocked every entrance to the thicket in which the goats were thought to be lurking, and, at a given signal, raised a tremendous cry. This caused to leap from the thicket no goat, but a wild boar of unprecedented size and ferocity, which ripped up and killed the first hounds that had the rashness to set upon it and then charged right through the net that was meant to hold it. The unhappy hounds, expecting goats, had obviously flown straight at the boar's tusks.

Sheep Dogs

An equally important and familiar role played by dogs in the life of the Roman world was that of guarding and rounding-up flocks of sheep. Both Molossians and Laconians were imported for this purpose from Greece into Italy. Horace writes of these beasts as 'the shepherd's friendly force' (Molossus aut fulvus Lacon/amica vis pastoribus);[47] and Virgil impresses on the owners of flocks the importance of taking proper care of their dogs and of feeding them on rich whey.[48] In return for this, he continues, they will keep off from the sheepfolds night robbers, wolves, and (by poetic licence) Spanish marauders. They can also be used for hunting wild asses (another poetic licence), hares and deer, while their barking will rouse boars from their woodland lairs and drive great stags into nets on the hills.

In pastoral scenes in Roman art, for example on sarcophagi, shepherds are frequently accompanied by dogs – for instance, on a piece from the Isola Sacra necropolis just to the north of Ostia.[49] Columella advises farmers to give short, two-syllabled names to their dogs, so as to ensure a quick response when they are called; and he gives as examples 'Scylax' ('Pup'), 'Lacon' ('Spartan'), 'Spoude' ('Speed'), 'Alce' ('Force'), and 'Rome' ('Might') in Greek, 'Ferox', 'Celer', 'Lupa', 'Cerva' ('Doe'), and 'Tigris' in Latin.[50]

Dogs as House-guards

Another invaluable type of business dog was the house-guard or watch-dog. Imported Molossians also served in this capacity in Italy. Lucretius paints a vivid picture of Molossian hounds (*canes Molossûm*) now snarling and barking, now sporting with their pups, licking them, tossing them and pretending to swallow them, now baying when left alone to guard the house (*deserti baubantur in aedibus*).[51] At his *cena* Trimalchio gives orders to have his enormous watch-dog Scylax brought in on its chain, introducing it to his guests as the guardian of his house and slaves (*praesidium domus familiaeque*).[52] Whereupon the host's boyfriend, Croesus, eggs on his indecently fat (*indecenter pinguis*) black puppy Margarita ('Pearl') to attack Scylax, who fills the room with hideous barking (*taeterrimo latratu triclinium implevit*) and nearly tears 'Pearl' to pieces. Scylax appears again later on his chain (*catenarius*) at the front door of the house by which Trimalchio's dinner-guests are trying to escape, and he raises such a din that one of the party falls headlong into the fishpond. The narrator of the tale promptly follows suit, declaring that he is terrified even of a painted dog.[53]

Petronius' *pictus canis* immediately recalls the well-known Pompeian black-and-white mosaics at the entrances to private houses, which depict a watch-dog on a chain. The most famous of these is the one now in the Naples Museum inscribed CAVE CANEM ('Beware of the Dog') and presenting an alert beast at bay, with hindquarters raised, forepaws extended, ears pricked and teeth bared to bark furiously at a visitor or intruder – *Hylax in limine latrat* ('"Barker" is giving tongue at the door'), as Virgil puts it.[54] It has a feathery tail, fringed legs, and white markings on its mainly black coat.[55] Another piece, still *in situ* in the house of Paquius Proculus, shows a similar, but completely black, dog lying across the threshold of the half-open door, also rendered in mosaic, to a knob on which it is chained.[56] Among casts of dead bodies in the Pompeian Antiquarium, made by pouring liquid clay into the holes left by them in the ash, is that of a probably chained house-dog wearing a heavy collar and curled in the agonized attitude in which death overtook it in its struggle to break free.[57] It would have been of much the same type as the mosaic dogs just cited.[58] (Pls 43, 50)

Draught-Dogs and Performing Dogs
Dogs were occasionally put in harness in Roman times and taught to draw carts and even chariots. Dio Cassius relates how in Nero's reign the horse-breeders and charioteers, encouraged by the emperor's enthusiasm for the races, got above themselves and treated the magistrates most insolently. Whereupon Aulus Fabricius, the praetor, finding them unwilling to enter their horses for the contests on reasonable terms, dispensed with their services, trained dogs to draw chariots, and produced them in the Circus. The dogs would seem to have acquitted themselves well; for the Whites and Reds, at any rate, climbed down at once and entered their chariots.[59] Elagabalus is also said to have harnessed to his chariot a team of four large dogs.[60]

In the Archaeological Museum at Verona is a fragmentary tombstone with part of the relief in the panel below the inscription surviving. It shows a child, with whip and reins in its hands, seated in a high, light cart drawn by a dog. The animal, which is somewhat pig-like, trots towards the right between shafts or side-straps attaching the cart to a collar round its neck.[61]

Of performing dogs none can have outshone the brilliance of the one whose consummate acting in a mime in the Theatre of Marcellus, when the Emperor Vespasian was present, is described by Plutarch.[62] It was given food on which was poured what was believed by the audience to be poison, ate it, began to shiver, stagger and nod, and finally dropped down seemingly dead. When dragged and hauled about by other actors in the mime it showed no signs of life. Then, at a given cue, it began to stir slightly, as if roused from a deep sleep, raised its head and looked round, and running to one of the actors fawned on him. So the audience was led to suppose that what the dog had swallowed was not poison, but a sleeping-draught.

Pet Dogs
Of all the pet animals whose names, descriptions, and portraits have

come down to us in literature, epigraphy and art of the Roman age, the dog is by far the most fully and charmingly documented. In the numerous scenes and contexts that relate to daily life in which pet dogs appear there are many named characters that had an actual, historical existence; others are fictitious, but generally true to life as described; while others again, those that are represented unnamed in sculpture, painting or mosaic-work, are clearly based on living animals that the artists had personally observed. As man's most faithful friend, whose affection for his master or mistress was held to outlive death, the dog occurs very frequently in funerary art as a symbol of the fidelity that links together dead and living human beings. But it is not always easy to distinguish between mere emblems of this kind and the real, individual pets of the deceased in the little creatures that sometimes nestle beside the *gisants* figures on funerary couches and on the lids of sarcophagi or in the larger ones that occupy the lids of ash-chests. At any rate, there can be no doubt that love for canine pets in particular was one of the most attractive features of the ancient Roman character.

To begin with fiction, Trimalchio had, besides his disagreeable watch-dog, a little pet dog, whose effigy, he directed, was to be placed at the feet of his own sepulchral statue, while on his right hand there was to be a statue of his wife Fortunata leading her little dog with its body-belt on.[63] 'Pearl', the revoltingly fat black puppy of Trimalchio's boyfriend, Croesus, has been mentioned already. Another fictitious pet was the greedy Melitaean lap-dog Πλαγγών ('Dolly'), its mistress' gentle plaything, as Alciphron describes it, who three days after jumping up to steal the joint lay prostrate as a clammy corpse.[64] To return to 'Pearl', we may perhaps gain some idea of her obesity from the marble figure of a very fleshy and self-satisfied looking animal carved in the round and now in the National Museum in Athens.[65] This dog, whose head, with its mean little rounded ears, is too small for its bulky body, lies towards the right on a very thick mattress which fills the whole area of a funerary couch that has a dolphin (symbol of the journey of the dead overseas) carved on each of its two terminals. Its body is shown in profile, but it turns its head (the end of the muzzle is broken off) to stare boldly at the spectator with its large, round, bulbous eyes and crosses its fore-paws complacently. Round its corpulent neck is a heavy, studded collar with a bell depending from it. The couch and its occupant form the lid of a rectangular marble ash-chest – uninscribed, so we do not know whether the remains inside were those of the dog or of its master. But there can be little doubt that we have here the portrait of a once living animal, whom somebody had doted on and grossly overfed.

The same doubt as to the owner of the ashes housed within it applies to the circular stone *cinerarium* made in the form of a wicker basket, again uninscribed, in the Aquileia Museum: on the lid sprawls a hound more prepossessing than its Athenian counterpart and slenderer in build, with short ears, a ruff of hair round its neck, and a short, expressive tail.[66] If the chest were for a human, rather than for a canine, burial the dog could well have been the devoted pet of the deceased, realistically portrayed and at the same time an emblem of faithfulness. The last is almost certainly the role of the engaging little cur carved in relief in a sunk panel on a marble slab in the *columbarium* of the Vigna Codini by the Via Appia, just to the south of Rome. It stands in profile towards the right, with ears pricked, right forepaw raised and upward-curling tail. The epitaph, in a mixture of Latin and Greek and cut on either side of the picture, reads SYNORIS GLVCON DELICIV[*m*] ('Synoris, sweet pet'), and most probably refers to a baby slave-girl, whose favourite the dog could have been.[67] The shaggy-coated seated bitch, with left forepaw raised, on a fragmentary tombstone from Narbonne, inscribed CYTHERIS L[*iberta*], could also be interpreted either as an actual pet or as merely an emblem of fidelity.[68] (Pl. 48)

Certainly a real pet was 'Parthenope' of Mytilene, who is carved in relief on her own tombstone. She reclines on a funerary bed and her epitaph below her portrait explains that she earned her fine monument by devotion to her master and urges the passer-by to make as good a friend who will cherish him in life and death.[69] Two more tombstones, both of humans and both in the form of *stelai*, may be cited as showing the portraits of canine characters that actually once existed. The first is the *stele* from Pergamon of the gladiator Chresteinos, beneath whose lengthy epitaph, which his wife Antonia caused to be composed for him, is a touching little picture in relief. His pet dog named Μούρδων (a name perhaps to be connected with *mordere*, 'to bite', and translatable as 'Holdfast') stands towards the left between two crowns with lifted head and forepaw raised towards what appears to be a hand with the thumb up.[70] The second piece, now in the British Museum, carries an even more affecting scene, also worked in relief, in a sunk rectangular panel. It shows a little girl, with her hair stiffly waved after the fashion set by the Empress Julia Domna, seated towards the right on a stool and reading an open scroll held in both hands. Before her is a book-stand, on which another open scroll awaits her perusal; while behind her, seated patiently upon its haunches, is a long-tailed, collared dog with lifted head and its right forepaw raised to touch the cushion on the stool in the vain hope of distracting its beloved mistress from her studies or, perhaps, of recalling her from that other world beyond the grave in which she must now pursue them. The Greek inscription below the picture tells us that this studious child was called ABEITA ('Avita' in Latin) and that she died at the age of 10 years, 2 months.[71]

To turn to the dogs that accompany the reclining figures of the dead on the lids of sarcophagi or on funerary couches – while they could be nothing more than emblems of faithfulness, there would seem to be no reason for rejecting the belief that some at least of them recall the actual pet that the deceased had loved in life. The same could, of course, be said in the case of the dogs carved beside, or at the feet of, medieval and Renaissance *gisants* effigies. A funerary relief in the former Lateran collection, found in the burial ground of the Volusii in Rome, shows the half-draped recumbent figure, tipped up on its left side, of a Flavian lady, Ulpia Epigone, beneath whose left armpit is ensconced a tiny lap-dog, the end of its muzzle unfortunately broken off.[72] On a funerary couch in the Vatican a boy, perhaps of early third-century date, lies on his back, holding poppies in his right hand, while a little dog with a very curly tail strikes a playful attitude beside him.[73] On the lid of a third-century oval sarcophagus, again in the Vatican, a young boy reclines and strokes with his right hand the head of a little dog which opens its mouth in response and scratches its ear with its right hindpaw.[74] Yet again, on another third-century sarcophagus lid from the Monteverde catacomb, a boy lies on his back with his hand outstretched to caress a minute dog that nestles beside his legs.[75] On the lids of Asiatic sarcophagi of the late second and early third centuries found in Anatolia or imported into Italy similar pet dogs have their place beside the effigies of the dead. Examples are the now headless little animal crouched at the foot of the lid of Claudia Antonia Sabina's sarcophagus at Sardis;[76] and the diminutive seated beast beside the pillow of the dead girl on the great sarcophagus found at Melfi.[77]

Two bronze figurines of smooth-coated dogs in the Carlisle Museum, Tullie House, and Stuttgart Museum respectively, both looking up and with the right forepaw raised in greeting, could well portray pet dogs in intimate conversation with a master or mistress whose presence is left to the spectator's imagination.[78] The Stuttgart dog, which wears a rounded collar, seems to have parted with its tail. But the wiry and crooked tail of the British beast, found at Kirkby Thore (Bravoniacum) in Westmorland, is remarkably expressive. Undoubtedly household pets are two of the dogs that appear in the figure-groups on the probably sixth-century peristyle mosaic in the palace of the Byzantine emperors at Istanbul. One group shows a small boy seated on a rock and clutching with both hands a fat and floppy-eared puppy which is objecting strongly to being squeezed.[79] The second scene is that of a seated woman who is suckling her child, while the long-tailed house-dog squats beside her, nose in air and jaws agape, as it howls with jealousy.[80] (Pls 42, 49)

In addition to the epitaphs of favourite dogs, named and unnamed, that were inscribed, and often accompanied by their portraits, on their own or on their owners' tombstones (cf. pp. 109-11), there are a number of other Greek and Latin verse epitaphs and epigrams, in inscriptions and in literature, on named pets with descriptions of their physique, achievements and characters so detailed that they compensate for the absence of their pictures. The majority of the subjects are bitches and some of them were used for hunting as well as being greatly cosseted by their masters or mistresses. Some were still alive at the time when the poems were composed. But most of these verses were written to commemorate the loss by death of beloved companions and their owners' anguish, which is timeless in its poignancy and forges a direct link between those Roman men and women and ourselves today.

Tiny 'Kalathine' ('Midget'), so named because she was small enough to travel in a lady's handbag (*kalathos*), was in labour with pups, but Leto's daughter Artemis (as birth-goddess) granted her an easy delivery in answer to her prayer, as she does to women when they pray to her. For the goddess, says the poet, knows how to save her canine fellow-huntresses.[81] The Cretan 'Gorgo', being pregnant when she was hotly pursuing a stag, prayed to Artemis in her double role (as birth-goddess and as huntress) and gave birth to her offspring in the very act of slaying her quarry. Swift Eleutho (Artemis) granted her the double gift of good sport and good delivery. Now she's suckling nine pups. So the young deer of Crete had better learn to take advice and give the pups of whelping bitches a very wide

25, 26 Two mosaics showing leopards drawing Dionysus and Ariadne in a chariot, and being ridden by Dionysus (pp. 85, 84).

27 A wall-painting of a leopard *venatio* in which the leopards are individually named (p. 84).

28–31 The domestic cat seen as a pet held by a child on a grave stele, watching birds on a mosaic, being teased by two women on an Apulian vase, and playing with the city-founder on a coin of Rhegium (pp. 98, 88, 87).

32 The *discus* of a
Roman lamp showing
a performing cat
climbing a ladder
while his trainer
squats nearby with a
monkey (p. 90).

33 The confrontation
of an ichneumon
(mongoose) with a
snake on a mosaic
from Pompeii (p. 91).

SIMPI ICIVS

XVI

GIORIOSVS

BRACIATVS

34–36 *Above*, named bears on a mosaic; *left*, a relief of a bear guzzling apples, and, *below*, a bear cameo (pp. 96; 363, n. 56; 99).

37 The goddess Artio with her bear (p. 99).

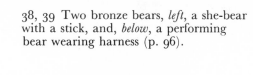

DEAE·ARTIONI
LICINIA·SABINILLA

38, 39 Two bronze bears, *left*, a she-bear with a stick, and, *below*, a performing bear wearing harness (p. 96).

40, 41 The *Lupa Romana* on an *aureus* of Hadrian and a mosaic from Aldborough (pp. 101, 102).

42 Bronze dog from Germany (p. 365, n. 32).

43, 44 The '*Cave Canem*' mosaic from Pompeii, and a marble group of hounds playing (pp. 107, 105).

45–47 Three breeds of dog:
above, a terrier from North
Britain; *right*, a howling hound
from Germany, and, *below*, an
Irish wolf-hound from
Gloucestershire (pp. 104, 105).

48–50 *Above*, grave relief of Synoris with a dog, from the *columbarium* of Vigna Codini, Rome; *left*, mosaic of a boy squeezing a puppy, and, *below*, a cast of a dead dog, killed in the eruption of Vesuvius in AD 79 at Pompeii (pp. 110, 112, 108).

berth.[82] Much less happy was the fate of Midas' hunting dog 'Lampon' ('Flash'), who died of thirst in spite of fighting desperately for his life. He dug with his paws on a damp piece of ground, but the sluggish water was slow in coming from the hidden spring and the poor beast fell dead from exhaustion before it gushed forth. Perhaps the Nymphs had a spite against Lampon for having killed so many of their stags.[83]

Among the Latin epitaphs we have that of 'Myia' ('Fly'), who was sweet and gentle and while she was alive slept on her master's breast, her heart ever set on bed and sleep. How tragic was her death, poor 'Fly'! She would only bark, and then unstintedly, if a rival lay beside her mistress. But now a tall tombstone covers her, poor 'Fly'! Insensible, she cannot ever be angry again, nor can she ever again leap on her master in rapture and smile at him with coaxing jaws.[84] Another epitaph, put into the dog's own mouth, is that of the Gallic hunting bitch, 'Margarita', who was called after the pearls of ocean and was as brave as her name was beautiful. She was trained to face boldly the dangers of the woods and to chase shaggy beasts on the hills. She was never chained up nor did her snow-white body ever feel the lash. She lay on her master's or mistress' lap and always knew where to find a cosy bed on which to sleep off her weariness. She could almost talk, dumb animal as she was, and no one ever feared her barking. But things went wrong with her whelping and she died. Now a little marble slab marks the spot where the earth enfolds her.[85] A third poem, in the words of the bereaved master, tells how he carried his little darling 'Patrice' to the grave in floods of tears, after fondling her joyfully in his arms for fifteen years. No longer will she give him countless kisses or snuggle happily against his neck. Full of sorrow he has laid her in the marble tomb that she deserves, so that he shall ever have her company when his own time comes. Clever as a human in her ways she was: what a darling he has lost! Patrice used to share her master's meals. Seated on his knee she begged coaxingly for bits and her cunning tongue knew how to lick round the cup that his hands held out to her. When he came home tired out she would greet him with the joyous wagging of her tail that told him of all her love for him.[86]

Martial has two familiar epigrams on favourite bitches. Lydia, another huntress, was reared among the amphitheatre managers, fierce in the woods, gentle at home, and most devoted to her master Dexter. She did not die useless, of length of days, but was slain by the lightning blow of a foaming boar's tusk. She did not complain of her sudden and untimely death, since she could not have perished in a nobler cause.[87] But the most delightful of all dog poems of the ancient Roman world is Martial's hendecasyllabic tribute to Issa, whose name might be translated as 'Missy', *issus* being used in Roman baby language for *ipse*. Well known as these verses are, they deserve full quotation in the poet's own words:

> Issa's more of a rogue than Lesbia's sparrow,
> Issa's purer by far than kiss of ring-dove,
> Issa's more of a coax than all the maidens,
> Issa's worth all the costly pearls of India,
> Issa's Publius' darling lady puppy.
> If she whimpers you'll think that she is speaking,
> Sorrow and joy she feels as much as he does,
> Snuggling close to his neck she sleeps so softly
> That you'd scarcely believe the pet was breathing.
> If in the night she finds that Nature's calling,
> Never a spot she'd leave on master's bedspread,
> But with her paw a gentle tap she gives him,
> 'Please put me down' – and then, 'Please pick me up now'.
> Modest and chaste a little lap-dog is she,
> One who knows naught of love, nor could we ever
> Find for this tender maid a spouse to match her.
> So, lest death should bear off the whole of Issa,
> Master has had a portrait of her painted,
> Where you will see so true a likeness of her
> That Issa's self is not more truly like her;
> Place side by side the real and painted Issas:
> Either you'll think that both are living Issas
> Or you'll believe that both are in a picture.[88]

Dogs of Death and Healing

The link between death and healing, at first glance by no means obvious, lies in the ancient concept of Mother Earth in whose depths the deceased were believed to dwell, according to the most widespread Graeco-Roman notion of the after-life, but who also brings forth from her kindly bosom new life, new strength and new prosperity for the living. Hence the same animal, the dog, has in this context a two-fold significance. In the guise of the triple Cerberus it functions as the watch-dog that guards the entrance to the kingdom of the dead or, as a triple or single beast, it attends on underworld divinities – Pluto, Serapis and Hekate. At the same time, as supposedly possessed of healing qualities,[89] the dog appears as the companion of Asklepios/Aesculapius, who was also, most probably, by origin a chthonian god, and of other health-bringing deities, male and female. At Asklepios' great shrine at Epidaurus inscriptions record the cures of children by the licking of a dog.[90] A stone block from the healing centre at Bath is carved in relief with a dog, a snake and a scene from the legend of Aesculapius.[91]

As a symbol of death, the dog is found in provincial graves of the Roman period in the form of clay or bronze figurines:[92] the dead were also 'healed' by rebirth into the after-life. And it could be that the dogs which feature on sepulchral monuments, whether as emblems of fidelity or as portraits of the pets of the deceased (cf. pp. 109-11), had, secondarily, something of this significance.[93] As attributes of Mother-goddesses who belonged both to the underworld and to this world as the source of its fertility, dogs function in their double death-and-healing role. A now headless clay figurine from Canterbury shows a seated Mother-goddess wrapped in a thick cloak and holding on her lap a sprightly little hound with pricked ears and tail held erect.[94] Nehalennia, the Mother-goddess of the Lower Rhine, shown seated on her monuments, also has a dog as attribute, seated or crouched beside her.[95] Another Gaulish Mother-goddess, Epona, patroness of horses and their grooms (cf. pp. 197-9), is sometimes seen riding with a small dog perched on her lap.[96] Yet another Gaulish goddess, Sirona, associated with a healing spring and with the healing god Apollo, is depicted seated with a little lap-dog; [97] and stone sculptures from the shrine, at the sources of the Seine, of the healing goddess Sequana show devotees grasping a puppy with both hands and pressing it against their bodies – perhaps illustrations of the superstitious notion that a human ailment could be made to pass from him or her into a *catulus*.[98] It was probably because Coventina's well on Hadrian's Wall had healing properties that the bronze figurine of a shaggy British dog was thrown into it (cf. p. 104).

Perhaps the most convincing evidence for the link between dogs and healing deities is that supplied by what we might describe as the 'British Epidaurus', the cult-centre of the Romano-Celtic god Nodens at Lydney in Gloucestershire.[99] It dates from the late 360s;

and it comprises, besides a substantial temple, a large guest-house for accommodating pilgrims, a bath-building, and a long, narrow building or *abaton*, divided into small rooms for the 'incubation' of patients, comparable to the one at Epidaurus. Among the most notable finds from the site are renderings of dogs in bronze – not only the fine statuette in the round of a hound lying on the ground with extended forepaws, which has already been connected with the *Scottici canes* that made such a 'hit' in Rome in Symmachus' time (cf. p. 104),[100] but also three very crudely worked figurines in the round[101] and three no less crudely fashioned thin bronze plates, the last obviously intended to be fixed to the walls of the temple or some other building nearby.[102] Furthermore, there is a gable-topped bronze plate with the figure of a shaggy little dog in the begging attitude above and below it an inscription recording the payment of a vow to Nodens by one Pectillus.[103] There can be little doubt that all these canine portraits were the votive offerings of pilgrims.

CHAPTER VIII

RHINOCEROSES

OF THE TWO TYPES OF RHINOCEROS known to the Greeks and Romans, the one-horned Indian and the two-horned African, the former was first encountered by the Macedonians on Alexander's Indian campaigns.[1] The Ethiopian rhinoceros that took part in Pompey's pageant (cf. p. 39 and *passim*) was presumably of the two-horned African kind;[2] as is also the animal labelled *PINOKEPΩΣ* in one of the painted friezes of the second-century BC Tomb I at Marissa in Palestine (cf. p. 347, note 3), which has a large horn on the tip of its nose and a very small one just above it.[3] Diodorus Siculus in his account of Ethiopia, however, attributes to that country the one-horned rhinoceros, which he describes as snub-nosed ($\sigma\iota\mu\acute{o}s$), an allusion to the way in which the horn on the tip of the nostrils curves back along the nose – a horn as hard, he says, as iron.[4] The mistake could have originated from the fact that of the two types of African rhinoceros, the *bicornis* (two-horned) and the *simus* (snub-nosed), the latter has a rear horn so small as sometimes to pass unobserved.[5] Strabo repeats the error. In his section on the Arabian Gulf, which he does not seem ever to have visited in person, he says that the area produces the rhinoceros and twice claims to have seen one (precisely where he does not state) with a single, curved-back (snub-nosed) horn harder than any bone.[6] But Strabo may be describing an Indian rhinoceros seen by him in Rome. Pliny confirms the Ethiopian origin of the rhinoceros when listing as products of that country *rhinocerotum cornua* and mentioning the tracks (*vestigia*) of these beasts near Meroe.[7]

The rhinoceros with which Lucilius in the second century BC compares a personage described as *troncus*, that is, with jutting mouth and somewhat prominent teeth, could have been of either the one-horned or the two-horned variety.[8] The poet must undoubtedly have had some description or possibly some representation in mind, since the actual animal is most unlikely to have reached Italy at so early a date. On the other hand, if G. Gullini is right in identifying the famous Nile mosaic, now displayed in the museum at Praeneste, with one of the *lithostrota* which Sulla caused to be laid in the temple of Fortuna there, we have on it the earliest evidence for a certainly two-horned rhinoceros in Italy.[9] Here the animal, labelled *PINO-KEPΩΣ*, which survives in one of the original, unrestored portions of the pavement, stands three-quarters towards the right, looking back towards the left, with the two horns on its nose clearly visible. This rendering is likely to have come from an Alexandrian copy-book imported into Italy by visiting mosaicists from Egypt. According to Pliny it was a one-horned beast that figured in Pompey's games of 55 BC and which was, so he says, a common sight by his time.[10] But here again an Ethiopian *simus* may have been mistaken for an Indian animal. Pliny goes on to say that another rhinoceros bred in Italy (*hic genitus*) prepared to fight its enemy, an elephant, by filing its horn on a stone and then proceeded to direct its main attack on the soft belly of its adversary. The rhinoceros, he continues, is as long as an elephant, but has much shorter legs, and is of the colour of box wood (*buxus*). (Pl. 51)

Conflicting with Pliny's account of Pompey's games and hence almost certainly wrong is Dio Cassius' statement that the rhinoceros slain along with a hippopotamus in the shows of 29 BC was the first ever seen in Rome: it was, he claims, a one-horned specimen, in other respects resembling an elephant.[11] The date of Augustus' exhibition of a rhinoceros at the Saepta is not recorded, nor are we told whether it was one- or two-horned.[12] Peculiar is the rendering of a fine rhinoceros, standing towards the left, on a marble relief now in the Naples Museum, from Pompeii.[13] On the tip of the nose is one very large horn, which at first sight suggests the Indian beast, until one observes what appears to be a second, very small, horn, sprouting from the back, well to the rear of the ears. If the sculptor intended to portray the two-horned African, he must have worked from a description only. In Domitian's reign we have certain evidence for the two-horned rhinoceros' appearance in the Roman shows. Martial describes a rhinoceros which, after being goaded into fury by its trainer, tossed in the air on its two horns a heavy bear, just as a bull tosses dummies heavenwards; another time it tossed a vast bull as though it were a dummy.[14] What must surely be a portrait of this 'star' rhinoceros features on bronze *quadrantes* issued by Domitian at an unspecified date. The creature stands sometimes to the left, sometimes to the right, and has two horns upon its nose.[15] (Pl. 52)

Two-horned rhinoceroses were seen in Rome by Pausanias in the second century. He describes them as 'Ethiopian bulls', with one horn on the tip of the nose and another higher up.[16] We are not informed whether the rhinoceroses shown by Antoninus Pius[17] and slain by Commodus[18] and Caracalla[19] had one or two horns. The rhinoceros that Elagabalus kept was almost certainly from Egypt.[20] Nothing is said of the horns of the *rhinoceros unus* that Gordian III obtained and Philip I showed.[21] But the rhinoceros that is being captured in the 'Great Hunt' mosaic at Piazza Armerina is definitely of the one-horned Indian breed. The animals stands stolid and immovable, with a cunning twinkle in his eye as though he were rather enjoying the situation, in a swamp or river: a thick rope has been flung around his body and attached to it are two slighter ropes held by two of the five huntsmen whose combined efforts, supported somewhat ineffectively by a dog, have as yet failed to dislodge him from his native waters.[22] If, as is very probably the case (cf. p. 105), this Sicilian pavement was the work of immigrant African mosaicists, they must have copied their rhinoceros, not from nature, but from a pattern-book in which an Indian animal was portrayed.

CHAPTER IX

HIPPOPOTAMUSES

TO THE GRAECO-ROMAN WORLD the hippopotamus was essentially a
Nilotic beast. Pliny twice associates it with the Nile and remarks on
its amphibious nature (*victus gemini*);[1] and it is, as will be seen below,
in Nilotic contexts that most of its representations in the art of
Roman times occur. Pliny also gives an accurate account of the
animal's physical features – its cloven hooves, resembling those of a
bull, its horse-like back, mane, and neigh, its snub snout (*rostro
resimo*), tail, and tusks like those of boars, and its impenetrable hide –
first-rate material for shields and helmets.[2] Diodorus Siculus
describes how the hippopotamus can be caught, wounded and killed
with barbed iron harpoons – a task requiring a large band of hunters
(πολυχειρίᾳ τῶν τυπτόντων).[3] But since hippopotamuses were taken
alive to appear at Roman shows, the wounds thus inflicted were by
no means always fatal, but would merely leave the creatures scarred.[4]

Probably the earliest rendering of a hippopotamus that has survived is that in the painted animal frieze in Tomb I, of second-
century date, at Marissa (cf. p. 347, note 3),[5] where the lumbering,
ungainly body and long, heavy snout are characterized in a lively
manner, while the red colouring is, of course, wholly fanciful. If the
Sullan date for the Nilotic pavement at Palestrina (Praeneste) be
accepted (cf. p. 126), this, based on an Egyptian copy-book, would
probably be the context of the animal's first appearance in the art of
the Roman West. At the bottom of the scene, on the left-hand side, are
two hippopotamuses, both original parts of the mosaic and both
naturalistically drawn. The head of one is seen emerging from the
Nile, while the complete figure of the other stands among reeds on
the bank. Both are open-mouthed and roaring.[6] A number of
Nilotic pavements from Pompeii and Herculaneum feature the beast
no less faithfully. Now it rears its head and shoulders, with jaws
agape, from the water;[7] now it is harpooned by a Pygmy standing

on its back in a scene of contest between Pygmies and Nilotic creatures;[8] now a pair of hippopotamuses appears in a landscape setting of palm-trees, shrubs and water.[9] Alexandrian copy-books must also lie behind these Campanian mosaics. On the famous Nile mosaic from the Villa del Nilo at Lepcis Magna the Nile-god rides on a hippopotamus.[10] (Pl. 53)

Meanwhile, the actual animals were appearing at the Roman games. Pliny states that the first hippopotamus ever seen in Rome was displayed, along with five crocodiles, in a temporary tank or channel in Marcus Scaurus' spectacles of 59 BC.[11] In the shows of 29 BC one hippopotamus was killed;[12] and in displays most probably of Neronian date (cf. p. 94) there featured a hippopotamus from the Nile.[13] Live models may, then, have served the sculptor or sculptors of the famous Vatican Nile, on whose base is a scene in relief of seven hippopotamuses which threaten crocodiles and boating Pygmies.[14] And while the die-engravers of late first- and early second-century imperial coin-types of Alexandria, where a hippopotamus accompanies the figure of the Nile-god, would have copied local beasts,[15] those who designed the Nile types with a hippopotamus as adjunct on Hadrian's Roman coinage could have seen the animals in the capital.[16] The same could also be true of the designers of Nilotic pavements in Rome – for instance an elaborate one from the Aventine, where two hippopotamuses appear in a context of boating Pygmies, crocodiles, and buildings;[17] and another which presents a Pygmy harpooning a hippopotamus partially screened by a thicket of reeds.[18] On the other hand, it is no less possible that these Roman mosaicists based their compositions on Egyptian copy-books (see above). Some doubt exists as to the nature of the beast portrayed on a circular mosaic from Rome now known only from a drawing in the Eton College collection. Here the creature standing beside a palm-tree has the build of a hippopotamus, while the curved projection near the nostril suggests, if it is not a piece of foliage, the horn of a rhinoceros.[19] Tunisian mosaicists could have used either copy-books or living models at the shows for their renderings of hippopotamuses fighting Pygmies in Nilotic landscapes.[20]

To return to the shows in Rome: Commodus slew with his own hand six hippopotamuses, five of them on a single occasion.[21] Elagabalus kept an unrecorded number of the animals for display;[22] and in Gordian III's collection, put on show by Philip I (cf. p. 16), there were six hippopotamuses.[23]

If the *Augustan History* may be credited, Firmus, who held Egypt temporarily during Aurelian's reign [24] had a tame hippopotamus on which he sat or rode. [25]

Our latest extant evidence for arena hippopotamuses is on the 'Great Hunt' mosaic at Piazza Armerina and is somewhat disappointingly uninformative. In the register above the rhinoceros episode (cf. p. 127) there stands in water, quite passively and facing towards the left, a large hippopotamus whose head is unfortunately lost, while its body and legs are naturalistically represented. [26] No hunters accompany it, so the method that would have been employed for taking the animal alive remains unknown.

Most unusual in its context is the small bronze figurine of a hippopotamus found in a cremation grave at Bingen on the Rhine. It carries on its back an *uraeus*-snake, which is suitable enough. But the other objects in the burial were numerous doctor's implements; and the medical significance of this Nilotic animal is by no means obvious (cf. p. 235). [27]

CHAPTER X

BOARS AND PIGS

ALMOST EVERY COUNTRY of the ancient Roman world from Britain in the north to North Africa in the south was plentifully supplied with the large tusked wild pig or boar and its female counterpart the wild sow. In Italy these animals abounded; and according to tradition their earliest appearance in 'Roman history' was in the person of the famous white sow with her thirty piglets that Aeneas saw on landing on the Italian coast, exactly as Apollo's priest and the Tiber-god had foretold.[1] In Roman art the sow and young are either shown alone, as in marble groups in the Vatican and in Copenhagen;[2] on coin-types of Vespasian, Titus and Antoninus Pius;[3] and on a bronze medallion of Antoninus Pius;[4] or they are combined with the scene of Aeneas' landing, as on another bronze medallion of Antoninus Pius[5] and on a marble relief in the British Museum.[6] Aeneas promptly sacrificed the entire family to Juno,[7] an episode also represented in art, as on the Ara Pacis Augustae, on an Augustan altar in the Vatican and on a bronze medallion struck for Marcus Aurelius as Caesar, where the artist was obviously much indebted to the Ara Pacis relief.[8]

The earliest truly historical occasion on which wild pigs intervened in Roman affairs was during the Pyrrhic war, when the king's Indian elephants were much discomforted by the grunting of the south Italian sows – an occurrence commemorated on the *aes signatum* 'bricks' on which the figure of an elephant and that of a sow, whose dorsal bristles run from head to rump, are 'muled' (cf. p. 34).[9] Under the late Republic we hear of boars kept in the private parks (*vivaria*) of the wealthy Roman gentry (cf. p. 16). These were doubtless locally obtained and some at least must have been partially tamed, since they had been trained to come running when a keeper dressed as Orpheus announced their meal time. Such wild pigs would have been maintained partly for the pleasure that the sight of them gave to their owners and partly for commissariat, to be killed and served to guests on special occasions. Of Trimalchio's dinner-party in Nero's time the *pièce de resistance* was an enormous wild pig, carried in on a dish with a cap of liberty on its head and two little baskets made of palm-leaves hanging from its tusks, containing two different kinds of date: around it lay piglets made of pastry, as though sucking at its udders, indicating that the creature was a sow; and its inside had been stuffed with live birds which flew out when the sow's side was cut open with a knife.[10] But this was obviously an exceptionally ostentatious way of serving the animal. As for the smaller kinds of pigs reared and maintained on farms – some of those animals would have been kept for domestic consumption and for breeding purposes; but most of them would have been despatched, whether as full-grown animals or as sucking-pigs, to the pork-butchers in the nearest town, and have ended their days as table meat in the form of pork, ham and sausages (cf. pp. 151, 152). (Pl. 58)

Another reason for keeping boars in the late republican *vivaria* would have been the joys of hunting, primarily for its own sake as a form of field-sport, secondarily as a means of provisioning the table more exciting than direct slaughtering. An extract from such a hunting scene appears on the reverse of a *denarius* stuck *c.* 60 BC by Gaius Hosidius Geta, where we see a huge boar, very naturalistically drawn and facing towards the right, attacked by a dog and pierced by a spear: on the obverse is a bust of Diana with a bow and a quiver on her back.[11] Less expertly worked is the figure of a wild sow pierced by a spear on an Augustan *denarius* struck by the moneyer Marcus Durmius in 18 BC: but the beast's attitude, with hind-quarters hunched and the forelegs stiffly extended, is realistic.[12] Another excerpt from a boar-hunt scene, this time in sculpture in the round, is the well-known marble group from Pompeii, now in the Naples Museum, of a boar being savaged by two hounds.[13] (Pl. 54)

Numerous sarcophagus reliefs depicting the boar hunts of Adonis, Meleager and Hippolytus present in mythological guise hunting in the field as it was practised in the Roman Empire during the second and early third centuries AD.[14] Hadrian's boar-hunting is shown in one of the *tondi* (cf. pp. 94 and 357, note 44) on the Arch of Constantine: the emperor is on horseback and accompanied by two other riders, one of whom has been identified as Antinous. The great shaggy beast is emerging towards the right from its cover of trees and reeds.[15] This *tondo*'s pair contains a scene of sacrifice to Diana. Marcus Aurelius in his *Meditations* expresses admiration for the sight of foam flowing from a boar's mouth;[16] Dio Cassius records that when the emperor was still young and vigorous boar-hunting was one of his favourite pastimes [17] – a statement borne out by bronze medallions struck for him as Caesar with the reverse-type of the prince on horseback hurling his spear at a boar.[18] (Pl. 56)

Boar-hunting in a northern Roman province is illustrated vividly by the text cut on an altar found in Britain, at Stanhope in County Durham. It is dedicated to Unconquered Silvanus by one Gaius Tetius Veturius Micianus, prefect of the Sebosian squadron, in fulfilment of a vow and in thanksgiving for his capture of an outstandingly splendid boar that no one before him had succeeded in bagging.[19] The inscription is probably not earlier than the third century. That the animal was killed is very probable, although the text does not explicitly say so. A number of small bronze renderings of boars found in Britain, for instance, at Aldborough (Isurium Brigantum) in Yorkshire, Colchester (Camulodunum), Wattisfield in Suffolk, and Findon in Sussex, may well be the votive offerings of hunters.[20]

In the case of boar hunts on a small scale involving one (as above) or a handful of huntsmen, the dead or wounded beast was brought home upside down in a net slung on a pole and carried on the shoulders of two assistants. This process is portrayed in the second register from the top on the 'Little Hunt' mosaic at Piazza Armerina (cf. p. 24), where the animal, whose eyes are open, seems to be still alive. This stage is far from being reached in the scene in the bottom register, where it looks as if the maddened boar would have to be killed on the spot, unless it succeeds in slaying all its human and canine adversaries first (cf. p. 25). Almost identical with the first of the 'Little Hunt' groups just described is that at the top of the apsidal pavement from Carthage (cf. p. 105); while the lowest scene on the mosaic shows a single boar, relatively mild compared with the second 'Little Hunt' beast, engaged by three huntsmen and a pair of dogs. In the centre of the Carthage piece a hunter and two dogs are driving another single boar into a net that has been erected in a semi-circle to contain it.

If the Piazza Armerina 'Little Hunt' represents sports on a Sicilian gentleman's estate, the Carthage mosaic may well depict the taking of boars alive for amphitheatre display. The pavement from Radez, on whose surviving portion is presented an arena sparring match

between boars and performing bears, has already been described
(p. 96): on the *venatio* mosaic at Cos (cf. p. 359, note 100 and pp. 97,
144, 150) there are three boars named 'Gorgonis', 'Polyneices' and
'Solon'; and the appearance of boars at the spectacles in Rome is
attested by literary passages ranging in date from the first to the
fourth century A D. Calpurnius Siculus under Nero saw in Rome
what seems to have been African wart-hogs – *non sine cornibus apros*.[21]
Martial saw a boar in purple harness;[22] and the group of two boars
harnessed to a cart, containing a mask, on the Bacchic mosaic from
Walraumsneustrasse at Trier may have been inspired by some arena
episode.[23] Martial also witnessed the slaughter of a bear by Carpophorus, the famous *venator*, and saw a pregnant wild sow giving birth
to her young as she died, in a scene in which Diana was portrayed as
hunting woodland beasts; the new-born piglets immediately got up
and scuttled away.[24] In A D 202, when Septimius Severus returned
from the East and celebrated his *decennalia* (ten years of rule), sixty
wild boars, the property of the emperor's son-in-law, Plautianus,
proceeded to fight one another at a given signal.[25] Gordian I's
exhibition (cf. p. 18) included 150 boars;[26] and when Probus landscaped the Circus and filled it with animals, 1,000 boars, presumably
tamed, were among the creatures that members of the populace were
permitted to appropriate (cf. p. 19). Finally, for Stilicho's spectacles
in the second half of the fourth century there was brought from Germany an immense boar, so old that its tusks had grown curved.[27]

Another profitable market for the pig-breeder's stock was provided by the state religion's need of animals for sacrifice. If wild boars
were captured for this purpose they would have had to be tamed and
reduced to a suitable state of decorous quiescence before appearing
for slaughter at the ceremonies. But most sacrificial pigs probably
came from farms. Sows were regularly offered to Ceres. Among the
many sculptured reliefs that present the most solemn of all Roman
offerings, the *suovetaurilia* (sacrifice of pig, sheep and bull), are two in
the Louvre, one in the Palazzo dei Conservatori in Rome, one on the
Augustan arch at Susa in northern Italy (here the pig is of mammoth
proportions), three on Trajan's Column in Rome, one, of Antonine
date, on the Arch of Constantine in Rome, and one on the Diocle-
tianic basis in the Roman Forum.[28] On the back of each of the two
so-called 'Anaglypha' or 'Plutei Traiani', sculptured panels of
Hadrianic date now housed in the one-time Roman Curia, the three
stately victims of this ceremony (the sacrifice itself is not represented)

march slowly in procession towards the left, headed by the pig, a fine medium-sized boar, which has fillets depending from its head and an elaborate body-belt, embroidered with meander pattern.[29] A bronze relief in the British Museum shows a wreathed youth urging forward a pig due for sacrifice.[30] The animal wears a plain body-belt; and the fact that on the reverses of some bronze *quadrantes* of Trajan and Hadrian (which have on the obverse a bust of Hercules combined with the emperor's name and titles) the boar walking towards the right sometimes wears a double body-belt suggests that we should interpret it as a sacrificial victim.[31] On the other hand, arena animals are sometimes shown belted (cf. p. 68).[32] (Pl. 57)

Among the Gauls the boar enjoyed special prominence and sanctity. A standing figure of the animal frequently topped their native standards, as can be seen from the reliefs depicting Gaulish arms on the Roman arch at Orange; [33] and from a similar relief from an arch at Narbonne, where the beast's dorsal bristles and corkscrew tail are most expertly characterized.[34] A neat little boar, again with corkscrew tail, stands demurely in relief on an altar of Roman date at Avignon, surmounted by the punning Gaulish emblem of a cock.[35]

A sprinting boar was also one of the emblems of the Twentieth Legion.[36] (Pl. 55)

It remains to look at a few works of art in which boars and pigs seem to have been rendered purely for their own sakes – unconnected with any of the contexts discussed above. A marble relief in Madrid shows a boar trotting purposefully leftwards. It has been heavily restored, ear, snout, all four legs and portions of the belly being modern work.[37] A magnificently naturalistic bronze figurine of late Hellenistic or early imperial date, now in the Museum of Fine Arts in Boston, Mass., is the portrait of a wild sow at bay, with shaggy coat and ruff and a short, curly tail. She is balanced on her hind-legs with her fore-legs raised in the air, as though about to hurl herself against a foe.[38] From Pompeii comes the bronze statuette, now in the Naples Museum, of a sprinting pig, no less faithful to nature, if in a calmer vein.[39] A nicolo gem in the Lewis Collection at Corpus Christi College, Cambridge, presents another racing pig, with its name CER/TVS ('Sure-and-Steady') inscribed partly above and partly below it.[40] Finally, three glass perfume vessels in the Cologne Museum, one of a boar and two of pigs, provide delightful examples of the Rhineland glass-workers' fantasy (cf. p. 58). The boar is made of cobalt blue glass. Its ears are pricked, its short tail curls upwards, and its powerful dorsal bristles are rendered by a thick, zigzag thread. The stopper was at the rump.[41] The two pigs are mainly of colourless glass. Of one, the eyes and the two rings round its snout and chest respectively are worked in dark, reddish brown glass: here the stopper was at the end of the tail.[42] The second pig has lost its tail and its eyes and neck-ring are of opaque blue.[43] (Pls 59, 60, 61)

CHAPTER XI

CAMELS

BOTH OF THE TWO MAIN BREEDS of camel, the two-humped Bactrian camel from central Asia and the one-humped dromedary native to northern Africa, Arabia and western Asia, were familiar to the Graeco-Roman world. Pliny describes the physical differences between them and remarks on the services that all camels perform both as beasts of burden and as cavalry in war.[1] Cicero notes the usefulness of the camel's length of neck.[2] The black Bactrian camel was first introduced into Egypt by Ptolemy I.[3] But it is the dromedary that is generally represented in Roman works of art. Two sets of camels, of unspecified breed, walked in Ptolemy II's zoological procession (cf. p. 39 and *passim*). First were seen six teams of camels, three on each side of a chariot.[4] Later on came camels carrying spices, 300 pounds of incense, 300 of myrrh, 200 of saffron, casia, cinnamon and orris, and of all the other spices that there are;[5] and it was Ptolemy II who first provided camel transport for the spice trade on the desert route between Coptos on the Nile and northern Berenice on the Red Sea.[6] Strabo speaks of merchants with camel caravans who travelled all night with their eyes on the stars and made their way like sailors, carrying their water with them.[7] *Denarii* issued in 58 BC by the aediles Marcus Aemilius Scaurus and Publius Plautius Hypsaeus show the Nabataean King Aretas III kneeling as a suppliant, with an olive-branch, beside a loaded camel, symbol of the important role played by Petra, his capital, in the caravan trade. The type commemorates, somewhat disingenuously, Scaurus' expedition against the Nabataean Arabs in 62 BC, when Aretas bought him off with a substantial bribe.[8] A camel accompanies the figure that personifies Arabia on the *Arabia adquisita* coin reverse-type of Trajan and on the *restitutori Arabiae* reverse-type in Hadrian's 'province' coin series.[9] Bronze and terracotta statuettes and lamps of the late Hellenistic and Roman periods, in the form of saddled, harnessed and loaded camels have come to light in Syria and elsewhere.[10] (Pl. 63)

It is, not surprisingly, in the art of Palmyra, the greatest caravan city of the Roman world and controller in chief of trade between the Mediterranean countries and the East that camels are most frequently and most realistically represented. One of the best portrayals of the beast is on a stone relief found in the Polish excavations at Palmyra in 1960.[11] A cameleer stands facing the spectator, a long staff in one hand and with the other leading by the bridle towards the right a camel seen in profile. The creature has an elaborately embroidered saddle-cloth on which rests a tall, hood-like receptacle with a curved top, covered with a sheepskin. On the right side of its rump is a large circular object, perhaps a water container. On another stone relief is depicted a priest sacrificing to two rider-gods who advance towards the left and are named, in the inscription below the scene, as Arzu and Azizu.[12] The god on the right rides a horse, but the one in front of him, holding a spear, is mounted on a camel, on whose back is spread a fringed and embroidered saddle-cloth, while the same round object dangles against its rump. Yet a third stone relief, from the temple of Bel and hence carved c. AD 32, presents a camel led by a driver towards the left and carrying, again on an ornamental saddle-cloth, the hood-like receptacle with rounded top: a group of heavily veiled women follows behind and the cortège may have some cultic significance.[13] Palmyrene clay tesserae carry renderings of loaded camels.[14] A limestone frieze, found in Syria and thought to be Palmyrene, has been recently acquired by the Cleveland Museum. It is broken off at both ends, but the portion that remains presents an impressive procession of noblemen mounted on horses and camels and advancing towards the right. On the left are three camel-riders, each of whom holds in his camel by a short rein, so that the animals' heads are pulled right back: their expressions suggest displeasure.[15]

In southern countries camels were occasionally used in agriculture. Ploughing with camels, as well as the loading of camels with packs, is illustrated on reliefs from some of the native mausolea of the Roman period at Ghirza and elsewhere in Tripolitania.[16]

As an instrument of war dromedaries ridden by Arab archers were among the forces of Antiochus III at the battle of Magnesia in 189 BC.[17] At the defeat of Marcus Licinius Crassus at Carrhae in 53 BC the Parthian army under Surenas included teams of camels carrying large reserve supplies of arrows which completely non-plussed their Roman opponents.[18] The lesson of the usefulness of camels on campaign was, however, learnt by Rome; for when

Corbulo entered Armenia in AD 62 a great force of camels loaded with corn accompanied his army.[19] Ten *dromedarii* (camel-riders) were enrolled in AD 156 in the *Cohors I Augusta Praetoria Lusitanorum* in Egypt;[20] and in the early third century the *Cohors XX Palmyrenorum* at Dura-Europos on the Euphrates included at least 34 *dromedarii*.[21] These camels, whose own requirements were low and whose carrying capacity was very high, were probably used for the transport of water and rations of food for men and horses. Camels again appear in the train of Roman troops in the time of Constantine. On his Roman arch, in the *profectio* frieze carved by a contemporary sculptor, a camel laden with a pack marches with the soldiery.[22] The importance of camels in the Roman army of the late Empire is well attested by a passage in Procopius' *Anecdota* or *Secret History*, where are listed the follies committed by the Emperor Justinian in the sixth century.[23] For a long time (ἐκ παλαιοῦ), says Procopius, it had been the custom for the State to maintain a large number of camels to carry all the supplies (ἅπαντα τὰ ἐπιτήδεια) that the Roman army needed on campaign. This meant that the soldiers did not have to requisition food from the local farmers and were always well provisioned. But Justinian abolished practically the whole of this invaluable camel service (ἀλλὰ καὶ ταύτας περιεῖλεν Ἰυστινιανὸς σχεδόν τι ἁπάσας), with disastrous effects on the army's commissariat.

Camels are occasionally mentioned as items in the public shows. Claudius put on a camel fight in the Circus, whether of camels with men or of camels with camels is not made clear.[24] Nero pitted against one another camel *quadrigae*;[25] and Elagabalus is said to have given in his private circus a display of camels in harness, four to each chariot.[26] A mosaic found on the Aventine shows a man riding a camel and leading a lion by a rope – obviously an arena episode.[27] In a rare Dionysiac context is the camel ridden by a Silenus on a mosaic in the House of Dionysus at El-Djem (Thysdrus): a leopard walks beside it.[28]

Camels also find a place in Romano-Christian art. On the lid of a mid-fourth-century sarcophagus under St Peter's in Rome, one scene, that on the left of the inscription tablet, depicts Joseph being pulled by his brothers out of the well to be sold to the merchants, one of whom leads a camel with one hand and grasps a heavy goad in the other. This is just possibly a two-humped Bactrian beast, since there is room for a second hump behind the wing of the Victory who supports the tablet. In the right-hand scene, that of the Adoration of the Magi, all three camels are in the background with their backs concealed, so that we cannot tell whether they were one- or two-humped.[29] In the catacomb of Domitilla near Rome a fourth-century painting of Christus/Orpheus and the beasts includes a camel and a dromedary on the spectator's left, with their gaze fixed on the musician (cf. p. 290).[30] Camels are not very frequent in pagan Orpheus scenes (cf. pp. 289, 291, 293). But dromedaries are very well represented in a later work of Romano-Christian art, the sixth-century illuminated Vienna Genesis, particularly in the three scenes that illustrate the story of Rebecca at the well.[31] (Pl. 64)

Another late surviving portrait of a camel in the art of the Roman age, dating probably from the sixth century, is a scene on the peri-style mosaic of the imperial palace at Istanbul. A camel-driver with a long staff leads towards the right a somewhat meagre and depressed-looking beast, on the back of which two boys are riding jauntily, one of them holding a bird.[32] It is one of those enchanting episodes from daily life which are so prominent a feature of this wholly secular production of the Christian Empire. (Pl. 62)

CHAPTER XII

GIRAFFES

THE GIRAFFE, FOUND ONLY IN AFRICA, was known to the Graeco-Roman world as καμηλοπάρδαλις, *camelopardalis, camelopardalus,* or *camelopardus*. One specimen of the breed walked in Ptolemy II's pageant (cf. p. 39 and *passim*).[1] A late Hellenistic rendering of the animal occurs in one of the painted friezes in Tomb I, of second-century B C date, at Marissa in Palestine.[2] Here the artist seems to have worked, not from life, but from some none too accurate description. For although the long neck and buff coat picked out with red and brown spots indicate (quite apart from the fragmentary inscription beside the beast) that a giraffe is what he meant to paint, the spots should be white, the head should be smaller, and the hind-legs should be shorter, instead of equalling the fore-legs in length (with the result that the hind-quarters do not slope steeply down towards the tail, as they ought to do). The rear effect is, in fact, more like that of a deer.

Truer to nature are the descriptions given by Pliny and Dio Cassius apropos of the first giraffe ever seen in Rome in Julius Caesar's *ludi* of 46 B C. Pliny states that the Ethiopians call it a *nabun*, that it has a neck like that of a horse, legs and feet like those of a bull, a head like that of a camel, and a tawny skin spangled with white spots – hence its name *camelopardalis*. He adds that it was mainly admired for its unusual looks, since it made no display of ferocity, earning for itself the nickname of 'wild sheep'.[3] But Pliny's comparison of the giraffe's neck with that of a horse fails to do justice to the former's phenomenal length; and he does not mention the giraffe's short hind-legs and sloping back. These features are, however, noted in Dio's more exact account, also apropos of Caesar's games. The beast is, he says, very like a camel, apart from the fact that its legs are not equal in length, the hind-legs being much shorter, and that the back, starting from the rump, slopes up gradually and rises to a great height. The weight of the body, he continues, rests on the fore-legs; the neck is unusually long; and the skin is spotted like a leopard's – hence its name, a

mixture of camel and leopard.[4] Varro writes of a giraffe recently
introduced from Alexandria, shaped like a camel and spotted like a
leopard;[5] Horace speaks of a beast of mongrel breed, half camel, half
leopard, as attracting, along with a white elephant, the attention of
the crowd at the shows;[6] and Strabo in his section on the Arabian
Gulf region gives an accurate description of the animal's spotted skin,
low hind-quarters and hind-legs, and tall, erect neck.[7]

One of the very few renderings of a giraffe in Roman art is in a
painting discovered in the *columbarium* of the Villa Pamfili on the
outskirts of Rome: a giraffe, very accurately drawn, with a bell
round its neck and obviously being shown, is led along on a leash by
its trainer.[8] Pausanias saw at a show in Rome what he calls 'Indian
camels with leopards' colouring';[9] and the same erroneous notion
that giraffes came from India appears again on the Baltimore
sarcophagus depicting Dionysus' Indian triumph (cf. pp. 49, 65, 85).
Here, near the head of the procession on the front, in the background
behind the lion threatened by a Satyr, tower the long neck and small
head of a spotted giraffe, excellently carved.[10] (Pl. 65)

From the end of the second century AD onwards all our information on the subject of giraffes in Roman times is in the context of
public spectacles. On one day Commodus killed a giraffe with his
own hand, entirely unaided.[11] Gordian III's zoological collection in
Rome, subsequently displayed by Philip I (cf. p. 16), included ten
giraffes;[12] and an unspecified number of giraffes walked in the
triumphal procession staged by Aurelian in 274 to mark his victory
over Queen Zenobia of Palmyra.[13] In the *Aethiopica* of the third-
century 'novelist' Heliodorus there is the story of how a king named
Hydaspes was presented with a giraffe by the embassy of a people
called Auxomitae.[14] A number of the creature's characteristics are
vividly retailed – its camel-like size and head, its leopard-like
colouring and spotted skin, its long, swan-like neck, its rolling eyes,
its curious gait, and its extreme docility, such that only a slender rope
was needed for leading it. The populace, assembled for the function,
were amazed at the sight and spontaneously dubbed it *camelopardalis*.
Furthermore, its strange appearance so scared the four white horses
and two bulls that were standing at an altar to be sacrificed to Helios
and Selene respectively that they broke loose, bolted, and dashed
frenziedly round the arena. The scene as it stands is, of course,
fictitious; but it could well be based on some spectacle involving a
giraffe that the writer had personally witnessed.

CHAPTER XIII

DEER AND ANTELOPES

DEER

DEER, OF WHICH ITALY FURNISHED a plentiful supply, were not only hunted for sport and food, but were also maintained for the pleasure that their beauty afforded on the country estates of wealthy late republican Romans. Varro lists *cervi* among the animals that obeyed the summons of Quintus Hortensius' 'Orpheus' (cf. p. 16).[1] That stags were sometimes kept as pets is suggested by the popularity of scenes of Cyparissus, with the favourite stag that he accidentally shot, in Pompeian wall-paintings[2] and on some mosaics.[3] This practice is also likely to be reflected in Virgil's intimate picture of the pet stag beloved by Silvia, daughter of Latinus' shepherd-in-chief, Tyrrhus[4] – a stag remarkable for its beauty and for the size of its antlers which let its mistress deck its head with garlands, groom it, and bathe it:

> *omni Silvia cura*
> *mollibus intexens ornabat cornua sertis*
> *pectebatque ferum puroque in fonte lavabat.*

It fed at the family table and roamed by day, but never failed to return home at nightfall. Martial compares a tamed and harnessed stag at the shows both with Cyparissus' and with Silvia's darling;[5] and the Virgilian passage may well have inspired the designer of a bronze medallion reverse-type of Antoninus Pius, struck between 140 and 144, where a long-robed Diana stands beside a stag that turns back its head affectionately towards her as she strokes it.[6] Other stags and fawns attending on Diana in works of Roman art are too numerous to list, although the fourth-century silver plate in the Berlin Museum, with Diana mounted on a fine running stag, perhaps deserves special mention.[7] (Pls 67, 70)

The hunting and capture of deer, whether for sport, for the table, for taming as pets or for training for the shows, is vividly illustrated by the scene in the bottom left-hand corner of the 'Little Hunt' mosaic at Piazza Armerina (cf. p. 25).[8] A net has been spread in an arc and secured between two tree-stumps; and into this trap two huntsmen are driving three handsome red stags, the foremost of which has already got its antlers entangled in the meshes of the net. Since no dogs are taking part the aim of the hunt would seem to be, not to kill the animals, but to capture them unwounded and alive.[9] Roughly contemporary with this Sicilian pavement are the fourth-century deer-hunt scenes on the Christian mosaic pavement found at Hinton St Mary in Dorset in 1963.[10] Here the pursuers are hounds; but again neither wounding nor killing is depicted and the quarry appear to be rather enjoying the chase. The episodes would seem, in fact, to symbolize, at least in part, the teeming life of the animal kingdom (cf. pp. 284, 285). In two of the lunettes that surround the Christ bust two dogs pursue respectively a stag and a hind, in a third a dog barks furiously at a stag which turns back its head nonchalantly to nibble at a tree. On one of the two rectangular panels that flank the Bellerophon roundel a dog is chasing a stag, on the other a dog is hard on the heels of a stag and a hind, while the latter turns back her head to cast a somewhat saucy look at her pursuer. (Pl. 72)

To judge from the literary accounts, deer, whether doing 'turns' or merely displayed, were a frequent item in the spectacles. Martial has the story of a deer (*damma*) which, chased by Molossian hunting dogs in the arena, successfully eluded its pursuers, then came to a standstill, suppliant-wise, at the emperor's feet – whereupon the hounds refused to touch it.[11] He also witnessed arena *dammae* fighting one another.[12] Pausanias saw and admired white deer in Rome, but, annoyingly, he forgot to ask the source of this rarity, whether it was one of the continents or the islands.[13] Gordian I's collection contained *dammae ducenti* and two hundred stags with antlers shaped like the palm of the hand, including some British stags (*cervi palmati ducenti mixtis Britannis*).[14] *Mille cervi* and an unspecified number of *dammae* were among the animals introduced into Probus' landscaped Circus.[15] On the *venatio* mosaic of Cos (cf. p. 359, note 100, and pp. 97, 150, 205) there is a stag named 'Cupid' (Ἔρως).[16]

A particularly arresting spectacle was that of stags in harness, since stags are held to be extremely hard to train.[17] Martial writes of stags champing jagged golden bits.[18] Pausanias witnessed a procession at Patrae in Greece in which the virgin priestess of Artemis took up the rear in a chariot drawn by stags.[19] The scene on the Bacchic mosaic from Walraumsneustrasse in Trier (cf. p. 134) of two stags drawing a cart loaded with branches may reflect an arena episode.[20] Elagabalus is said to have driven a four-in-hand of huge stags in public;[21] and of Aurelian it is recorded that in his triumph over Zenobia he drove a similar equipage to the Capitol.[22]

Among other renderings of deer in Roman art one of the most naturalistic is that of the dainty dappled hind which suckles the infant Telephus in the famous 'Finding of Telephus' painting from Herculaneum.[23] Fine late antique (Christian-period) representations of the stag chastizing a snake, a symbol of the fight between good and evil, are to be found on the peristyle mosaic of the palace of the Byzantine emperors at Istanbul[24] and on the sixth-century mosaic pavement in the church at Qasr El-Lebia in Cyrenaica.[25] (Pls 66, 71)

Elks were a species of deer from northern lands known to the Romans. Calpurnius Siculus mentions them as woodland beasts.[26] Pliny remarks on their northern origin, but rather oddly calls them bullock-like;[27] and Pausanias describes them as wild animals from Celtic countries, the males having horns on their eyebrows, while the females have no horns at all.[28] The Gordians' collections each contained *alces decem*;[29] and an unspecified number of *alces* walked in Aurelian's triumphal pageant.[30] One leaf of an ivory diptych, carved in the Eastern Empire some time after 400 and now in the Liverpool Museum, shows a *venatio* in which a single *venator* has taken on five magnificent antlered beasts, while three keepers peep nervously from behind the doors of three of the cages from which the animals have been released.[31] The scene is rendered in the vertical perspective usually employed for diptych *venationes* (cf. p. 63). One animal is dead, two appear to be mortally wounded, another seems to be escaping back into its cage, and in the centre the *venator* drives his spear into the neck of the creature that confronts him. These animals are generally described as elks,[32] although one authority, in a postscript to Delbrueck's discussion of the piece, classes them as Mesopotamian fallow deer.

ANTELOPES

Three types of antelopes are recorded as walking in Ptolemy II's pageant.[33] First came twelve teams of *koloi* (κόλων δεκαδύο) drawing chariots. *Koloi* are described by Strabo as being intermediate in size between a stag and a ram, white in colour, swifter than either of those animals, and coming from the countries north and east of the Black Sea.[34] They have been identified as 'Saiga' antelopes.[35] Next came seven pairs of *oryges* (ὀρύγων ἑπτά), also drawing chariots. These were 'Beisa' or 'Sabre' antelopes with very long and sharp horns. Thirdly there were fifteen teams of *boubaloi* (βουβάλων δεκαπέντε), to be identified with the Tora hartebeests, which are characterized by fairly short, ringed horns that diverge in a U-shaped form and by their long, somewhat cow-like faces. The last two types are those that feature most frequently in Roman literature and art and both were of African provenance. Pliny lists *oryges*, *pygargi* and *strepsicerotes* (twisted horned ones) as species of antelopes imported into Italy from overseas.[36] He names Africa as the native land of *oryges*: [37] states that the *strepsiceros* is called *addax* in the African language; [38] and describes the *oryx*'s main features.[39] Columella lists *oryges* along with roebucks, deer, stags and boars as being kept in the parks of wealthy Romans for 'style', pleasure and financial gain.[40] Antelopes are occasionally mentioned as appearing in the shows. According to Martial the *oryx* was extremely fierce and destructive of hounds in the arena *venationes*.[41] Symmachus asked a friend abroad to procure for him *pygargi* and *addaces* as being new and foreign animals essential to the splendour of his praetorian games in Rome.[42] They seem to have been something of a novelty again in late antique spectacles.

'Sabre' antelopes are often depicted in Roman works of art as the prey of large felines. They are seen in the grip of ravening lions on the curved ends of some third-century sarcophagi (cf. p. 65); [43] and their slaughter by two leopards and a lion is graphically presented in the upper zone of the 'Great Hunt' mosaic at Piazza Armerina.[44] To the right of the leopard-and-antelope group towards the left-hand end of this pavement are two creatures fleeing rightwards that could be either *boubaloi* antelopes or gazelles, with a dog in hot pursuit of one of them (cf. p. 28). The same doubt as to the precise species represented is raised by the beast that a leopard is stalking in the group above the boat near the right-hand end of the same pavement and by the animal that is being carried up the gangway of the left-hand transport ship at the centre of the corridor.[45] But it is certainly a captured 'Sabre' antelope that is being led along by a rope, in the wake of a captured tigress, above the group of four men who are hauling a very recalcitrant wild bull towards the gangway of the right-hand transport ship at the centre.[46] How this antelope had been taken the Piazza Armerina pavement does not tell us; but there can be little doubt that a net had been spread to trap it. On the hunt mosaic from Hippo Regius (cf. pp. 26, 27) two 'Sabre' antelopes are being rounded up into a net and two more that have managed to dodge the trap are escaping at the top of the picture. Again, on the hunt mosaic from Constantine (Cirta), in the zone in which the dog 'Castus' is operating (cf. p. 105), a 'Sabre' antelope is running head-long into the net. (Pl. 68)

The gazelle (*dorcas*), a small and particularly attractive species of antelope renowned for its speed, was, according to Aelian, a native of Egypt,[47] Ethiopia,[48] Libya,[49] Icarus, an island in the Red Sea,[50] and Armenia.[51] When Pliny includes *dammae* along with *oryges*, *pygargi* and *strepsicerotes* in his list of animals sent to Italy from overseas (cf. p. 146) – *haec transmarini situs mittunt* – he probably means by the word gazelles.[52] Creatures that might be gazelles on the 'Great Hunt' mosaic have already been noted above; and a gazelle would seem to be the hapless victim of an onslaught by a pair of leopards in a group on the peristyle mosaic of the palace at Istanbul.[53] Arrived in Italy alive the gazelle could be tamed and shown. Martial recommends it as a pet for a child and describes how members of the crowd in the amphitheatre would flutter their togas as a sign that they wanted it dismissed unharmed.[54] An arena episode may lie behind the well-known painting from the House of the Vettii at Pompeii, where pairs of slender, high-stepping gazelles are driven by Cupids standing in light carts.[55] As domestic pets gazelles made, so 'Oppian' declares, ideal foster-mothers for puppies destined to be trained as hunting dogs, since it was believed that their quality of fleetness of foot could be imbibed along with their milk.[56] (Pl. 69)

Closely related to antelopes and gazelles is the ibex, a native of the Alps. Its very curly horns are marked by bold, transverse rings, it has a smooth coat and a short tail, and the male has a very small, short beard. Pliny notes its remarkable speed – *ibices pernicitatis mirandae*.[57] There were two hundred *ibices* in Gordian I's collection[58] and an unspecified number in Probus' show.[59] The ibex appears to feature twice on the Istanbul palace pavement.[60] Four of these animals are very vividly portrayed in relief on a fifth-century round silver dish with niello inlay now in the Metropolitan Museum of Art, New York: they are being shot by King Peroz I of Persia, who hunts them in his park on horseback.[61]

CHAPTER XIV

CATTLE

BISON, AUROCHSES AND ZEBUS

A SPECIMEN OF THE MANED BISON (*bison*, *vison*), known in northern Europe in Roman times, is mentioned by Martial as having been confronted in the amphitheatre by the famous *venator* Carpophorus.[1] Pliny remarks on its mane and German origin;[2] and the arena bulls described by Calpurnius Siculus as having some an ugly hump on the shoulders, others a shaggy mane on the lofty neck, a rough beard below the chin, and dewlaps stiff with quivering bristles sound like humped oxen (zebus) and bison.[3] But the Paeonian (Macedonian) βίσων ταῦρος of which Pausanias writes as having to be caught in an enclosed hollow in the ground because no net would hold it[4] may have been not a bison, but the maned *bonasus* (perhaps the musk ox) to which Pliny alludes as a Paeonian *fera quae bonasus vocatur equina iuba*:[5] bison are said by Pliny in another passage not to have been used by the Greeks for medical experiments.[6] Seneca knew of, and may well have seen at a show, shaggy-backed bison;[7] and Martial saw ugly bison, presumably a pair of them, drawing a Gallic two-wheeler.[8] Bison were among the animal 'passengers' in the arena 'shipwreck' staged by Septimius Severus (cf. p. 18): Dio Cassius notes them as a kind of cattle, but foreign in both species and appearance.[9]

The aurochs (*urus*), the wild ox now extinct in Europe, was known to Julius Caesar in Germany.[10] He describes it as slightly smaller than an elephant, resembling a bull in general look, colour and shape, very strong and swift (*magna vis et magna velocitas*), and showing mercy to neither man nor beast that came in its way. It had to be caught in a pit (*fovea*) and it was impossible to tame. Pliny, writing of its German origin, also comments on its strength and speed (*excellentique et vi et velocitate uri*). Furthermore, he declares that ignorant folk (*imperitum vulgus*) call this creature a *bubalus*, which is an African antelope (cf. p. 146) somewhat resembling a steer and a stag.[11] This very mistake was in fact made by Martial, who couples with the *vison* the *atrox bubalus*, by which he must mean the *urus*, as yielding to Carpophorus.[12] Pliny couples *uri* with *bisones* as not being used by the Greeks for their remedial qualities.[13] *Uri* were known to Virgil.[14]

The twenty-six all-white Indian oxen that took part in Ptolemy II's procession may well have been humped oxen or zebus.[15] According to Calpurnius Siculus these animals were probably seen in the amphitheatre in Nero's time;[16] and sixteen zebus appear on a *venatio* mosaic from El-Djem (Thysdrus) in North Africa.[17] We shall meet the zebu again on biblical mosaics of the later Empire (cf. pp. 285-6).

BULLS, OXEN AND COWS

Bulls, presumably wild ones captured for the purpose, were frequent sights in the arenas of Rome and of other cities of the Roman world. The commonest bull shows appear to have consisted of fights between bulls and men and between bulls and other animals. Julius Caesar was the first to exhibit in Rome the Thessalian method of men fighting bulls on horseback: the horseman galloped alongside the bull, seized it by the horn and killed it by twisting its neck.[18] A mosaic pavement found on the Aventine in Rome, on which a horseman is dashing after a bull, may be an illustration of this exploit.[19] Claudius and Nero followed the Dictator's example by putting on similar displays: in the former's the horsemen first tired out the bulls by chasing them round the Circus and then, leaping on their backs, seized them by the horns and brought them to the ground.[20] At Pompeii bulls and bullfighters were announced for a show in the forum.[21] The *Augustan History* has a tall story of how the Emperor Gallienus crowned a *venator* who had failed ten times to strike the death-blow at an enormous bull, with the comment 'It's a feat to fail so many times to strike a bull.'[22]

As early as 79 BC the aediles Lucius and Marcus Lucullus had exhibited a fight between elephants and bulls (cf. p. 48).[23] Conflicts of this kind were seen by Martial: on one occasion the bull was pursued with flares through the arena to stir it to fury, tossed dummies high into the air, and perished on the fiery tusk of the elephant that it vainly thought to toss with equal ease.[24] Another Aventine mosaic pavement shows a bull and an elephant locked in deadly combat.[25] Fights between bulls and bears tied together were witnessed by Seneca;[26] and this again is paralleled in art, in a Pompeian painting[27] and on a Zliten mosaic (cf. p. 30). A fight between a rhinoceros and a bull has been already noted (cf. p. 126). Three passages in Martial's *Epigrams* allude to shows in which lions were let loose on bulls.[28] A similar episode occurs on the left-hand leaf, now in the Cluny Museum in Paris, of an ivory diptych carved for Areobindus in Constantinople in 501.[29]

Occasionally we hear of wild bulls being tamed and trained as performers. Pliny saw some bulls in a show which, at the word of command, fought and let themselves be whirled round and caught by the horns as they fell, got up again, then lay down and were lifted off the ground: they even stood like charioteers in racing *bigae*.[30] Martial saw a bull in the arena leap high into the air and then carry heavenwards, probably on some mechanical contraption, a man got up as Hercules.[31] One of his *Epigrams* gives a vivid picture of some very well-trained bulls that quietly submitted to the antics of a troupe of acrobats, who stood on the animals' backs, hung on the tips of their horns and ran along their shoulders waving weapons all over them.[32] The one hundred Cypriot bulls in Gordian I's collection seem to have been merely displayed.[33]

The capture of a vast, red and very recalcitrant wild bull in some overseas land, for transport to the arenas of the capital or of some other large and important city, is dramatically presented on the 'Great Hunt' mosaic at Piazza Armerina.[34] The beast, which has a slight mane on its head and a small hump above its shoulders, is leaping into the air, with all four feet off the ground and with lowered head in a menacingly butting attitude. A red bar is fixed between the tips of its horns and round their base has been thrown a rope held by four men who are straining with might and main to haul the animal to the gangway of a transport ship, which an elephant, prodded from behind by another hunter, is mounting more or less obediently (cf. p. 29). North African mosaics with scenes of animal *venationes*, such as those from Carthage (cf. pp. 30, 31) and Radez (cf. pp. 31, 96), show wild bulls; and on the Cos mosaic (pp. 97, 144) there are three named fighting bulls, 'stars' of the arena – 'Aeris' ('Airy-Fairy'), 'Arkodamos' ('Bear-Slayer'), and 'Stadiarches' ('King of the Stadium'). In one of the lunettes containing hunted animals that surround the scene of Venus at her toilet on the mosaic pavement from Rudston in Yorkshire there is a bull rushing towards the left with the words TAVRVS OMICIDA inscribed beside him. These could mean either 'the man-slaying bull' or 'the bull named Homicide'.[35] (Pl. 74)

Another branch of Roman-age art in which wild, or at any rate non-domestic, bulls are represented is that of wall-paintings and mosaics featuring Graeco-Roman myths in which these animals play a leading role. Such myths are those of Dirce, punished for being trampled to death by an infuriated bull;[36] of the routing of the Cretan (Marathonian) bull by Hercules;[37] of Europa, whether playing with or mounted on the bull/Jupiter;[38] and of Pasiphae, who fell in love with a splendid bull and for whom Daedalus made a false cow in wood.[39] This last story Martial saw enacted in an arena tableau – the mating of Pasiphae with a bull in dummy form: thus the myth, old as it is, can, he says, be credited, since seeing is believing.[40] A pair of bulls driving Selene's chariot is, of course, a very familiar art motif.[41] So, too, is the bull of the famous Mithras Tauroctonos episode.[42] (Pl. 73)

As contrasted with the free-ranging cattle on the ranches of southern Italy, whose chief function was the reproduction of their kind, the domestic cattle bred and maintained on the farms of Italy and the Roman provinces were used for three main purposes. They worked, as draught-animals on the farms or for the army or for hunters in the field; they served the State religion as sacrificial animals; and they formed a more important item than has generally been supposed in human diet, both in military and in civilian contexts.

The breeds of cattle kept in Italy and the areas of their production, both Italian and foreign, have been listed and described elsewhere.[43] Here mention need only be made of the most important, the large white animals from Umbria, the small Alpine breed, and the Epirote breed held to be the best in the whole Roman world. We may turn at once to their uses.

First, diet. It has long been popularly believed that the Romans ate comparatively little beef and veal. Recent investigations[44] have, however, shown that the army ate meat at all periods, the supplies coming, in the case of cattle, from local provincial herds, by requisition or purchase, or from the pasture lands reserved for the military units, or from sacrificial beasts, whose carcases must have been disposed of as food for the troops. An analysis of the animal bones found on thirty-three military sites in the provinces of Britain and Germany has revealed that the largest percentage comes from the domesticated ox. As the soldiers in the army and civilians in the towns came from much the same social background, it seems unlikely that the populations of Rome and other cities were averse to eating meat when the carcases of sacrificial animals were on the market.

Good-looking bulls and oxen, trained to docility, were needed for the great State sacrifices, for the *suovetaurilia* in particular (cf. pp. 134, 164); and on reliefs on which such ceremonies are portrayed we can observe these dignified and patient animals walking in procession or standing at the altar awaiting death. A much less orderly sacrifice of bulls, probably to the *Divi* (deified emperors), is rendered in mosaic in the barracks of the *vigiles* (fire brigade) at Ostia.[45] Cows were sacrificed to Hercules and Juno.[46]

On the farms, while the bulls' main duty was to breed, both cows and oxen were first and foremost working animals. Fresh cow's milk seems to have been seldom drunk in Italy; and there was a general practice of allowing cows to calve only every second year so as to conserve their capacity for work.[47] But the working animal *par excellence* was the ox, which had to be carefully broken in for its most important jobs, those of drawing waggons, carts, ploughs and so forth. There were, it appears, professional trainers who acquired young oxen from the owners of herds, broke them in, and sold them to farmers.[48] One of the most attractive renderings in art of oxen ploughing is the small bronze group, two inches high, found at Piercebridge in County Durham and now in the British Museum: the ploughman wears the peasant hood (*cucullus*) familiar on provincial monuments of Gaul and Britain.[49] Here the oxen move obediently and placidly along. But on the well-known mosaic pavement from Cherchel (Caesarea) in Algeria, in the two superimposed friezes which each show a scene of ploughing in an olive-yard, the beasts strain forwards restively and have in each case to be menaced with a goad.[50] Pliny writes of a two-wheeled plough in *Raetia Galliae* drawn by two or three teams (i.e. pairs) of oxen (*protelis binis ternisque sic arant*); and Palladius gives a detailed description of a heavy Gallic reaping-machine (*carpentum*) which was pushed by a yoked ox walking between short yoke-beams (cf. p. 196).[51] Cato records the transport by oxen (*vectura boum*) of an olive-mill (*trapetus*).[52] Oxen were also used, with horses, for threshing (cf. p. 184).[53] (Pls 75, 76)

A group depicting a pair of oxen drawing a farm cart, which rumbles along on two solid wooden wheels, is seen on the front of a

51–53 Two details from the Praeneste mosaic show, *above*, a rhinoceros, and, *below*, hippopotamuses being hunted in a Nilotic landscape. *Right*, a rhinoceros on a *quadrans* of the Emperor Domitian (pp. 126, 128).

54, 55 *Below*, a wild boar attacked by
a hound on a *denarius* of *c.* 60 BC,
and, *right*, a boar as the emblem
of the 20th Legion on a terracotta
antefix (pp. 132, 135).

56, 57 *Above*, a boar hunt with mounted horsemen and nets on a
sarcophagus relief, and, *below*, a pig, sheep and bull being led
forward for sacrifice at the *suovetaurilia* (pp. 132, 134).

58 Wild sow on a piece of *aes signatum* (p. 131, and see Plate 6 for the obverse).

59–61 Two glass pigs from German graves and a bronze wild sow at bay (pp. 135, 136).

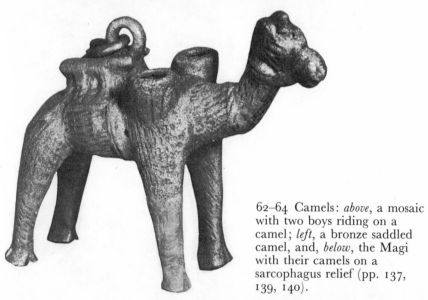

62–64 Camels: *above*, a mosaic with two boys riding on a camel; *left*, a bronze saddled camel, and, *below*, the Magi with their camels on a sarcophagus relief (pp. 137, 139, 140).

65 A rare representation of a giraffe on a sarcophagus relief (p. 142).

66 Wall-painting of a hind suckling Telephus (p. 145).

67, 68 *Left*, a silver plate with Diana riding on a stag and holding her bow, and, *below*, an antelope being carried aboard a ship on the 'Great Hunt' mosaic, Piazza Armerina (*see also* Fig. 1, and pp. 143, 146).

69 Wall-painting of Cupids in gazelle-drawn carts (p. 147).

70–72 Stags on mosaics: *left*, Cyparissus mosaic at Leicester; *centre*, a stag and snake at Istanbul, and, *below*, a stag and hind hunt from Hinton St Mary (pp. 143–5).

73 A relief of Mithras ritually slaying the sacred bull attended by other animals associated with the cult: a dog, a snake, a scorpion and a raven (p. 151).

74 The capture of a wild bull on the 'Great Hunt' mosaic, Piazza Armerina (see also Fig. 1, and p. 150).

third-century Christian sarcophagus carved in relief with a picture of the pastoral paradise (cf. Chapter XXIII) and the large-scale figures of a sheep-bearning shepherd at one end and an *orans* at the other.[54] Another Cherchel mosaic, this time with a vintage scene, presents a pair of oxen drawing a two-wheeled cart loaded with a round bin or basket full of grapes;[55] and in each of the vintage-scene panels on the vault of the ambulatory of Santa Costanza in Rome are two groups of a pair of oxen drawing a cart with solid wooden wheels and a heavy cargo of grapes.[56] A peaceful trio of oxen, one red, one white, and one black, off duty and resting while their herdsman entertains them with his pipe, appears in a probably second-century AD mosaic panel from the Roman villa at Corinth.[57] Vespasian's *denarius* reverse-type of two oxen standing quietly beneath their yoke may symbolize the Flavian programme for the restoration of Italy's agricultural prosperity.[58]

Apart from their farm work draught-oxen had another function in civilian life, that of drawing carts or waggons on the hunting field. On the border of a fragmentary mosaic at Boscéaz, near Orbe, in Switzerland two oxen advance briskly towards the right as they pull a four-wheeled waggon laden with a huge pile of hunting nets.[59] On the 'Great Hunt' pavement at Piazza Armerina there are two groups each of a pair of oxen drawing on a cart, with four solid wheels, a travelling-box for captured wild animals.[60] These groups vividly illustrate a passage of Claudian which describes the transport of amphitheatre beasts by land on waggons (*per terram pars ducta rotis*), although the mosaic oxen do not turn to look with terror at their savage burden or attempt to pull away from the pole of their cart as do the oxen in the poem (*quotiensque reflexi/conspexere boves, pavidi temone recedunt*) (cf. pp. 28, 29).[61] (Pl. 77)

A fourth-century wall-painting in the Christian catacomb found on the Via Latina, on the outskirts of Rome, in 1956 (cf. pp. 69, 102), illustrates the use of ox-drawn vehicles for transporting a whole family and its effects to a new home. It depicts Jacob and his sons arriving in Egypt in three typically Roman two-wheeled carts, each pulled by a pair of oxen. The animals are stepping out bravely, straining at their loads, towards the strongly walled city that represents their goal.[62] According to Procopius, writing in the sixth century AD, oxen were in his time still used to haul barges, laden with goods, up the Tiber to Rome.[63]

Oxen also served as draught-animals in the train of the Roman armies. On Trajan's Column a pair of them appears twice in the story of the first Dacian war, pulling now a covered two-wheeled cart, now three wine-barrels on an open type of two-wheeled cart.[64] On the Marcus Column they are more in evidence. For example, three unharnessed military oxen and a two-wheeled cart drawn by a pair feature in the 'rain miracle'; [65] and above a group of prisoners being led before the emperor a pair seems to be drawing a vehicle of some kind.[66] Four more groups towards the termination of the frieze show the animals at work. Two pairs draw each a cart, loaded with arms, which has two solid wooden wheels; [67] and two pairs pull each a waggon that has four such wheels, on which has been placed a small boat stuffed with arms.[68] Local oxen appear on both Columns in scenes that present the capture of the enemy's livestock by the Romans; and we may reckon as native animals the oxen that draw four-wheeled carts for the transport of barbarian women on the Marcus Column[69] and of a whole Dacian family on a relief from the *Tropaeum Traiani* at Adamklissi in Rumania.[70] But the beasts that operate on the Columns alongside the Roman troops must have been brought to the front, already trained to face the noise and bustle of warfare, from within the empire – in many cases, doubtless, requisitioned from the civilian population of the provinces.

Occasionally oxen draw chariots in processions of a mythological character. In a Pompeian painting a pair draws Bacchus and Ariadne in their triumphal car.[71] In another Pompeian painting two beasts pull the chariot in which a mountainous Silenus is seated with the infant Bacchus on his lap.[72] Possibly some dramatic pageantry in which oxen had taken part lay behind these scenes.

Among other naturalistic renderings of cattle in the art of Roman times special mention may be made of the imposing figure of an ox on an *aes signatum* (cf. pp. 34, 131); [73] of the butting bull *aureus* and *denarius* reverse-types struck for Augustus in Gaul[74] and revived by Vespasian at the Roman mint; [75] of Vespasian's *aureus* and *denarius* reverse-types, also from the Roman mint, of a cow,[76] which may, like his yoked oxen type (cf. p. 161), have had a propagandist significance; and of the study of cows on a relief in the Munich Museum.[77]

CHAPTER XV

SHEEP AND GOATS

SHEEP

WILD SHEEP (MOUFFLONS), with their shaggy coats and picturesquely curly horns, have already been noted on the Carthage *venatio* mosaic with the creatures ranged in 'columns' (cf. p. 31). Also from Africa came the fierce wild rams, with wool of a marvellous colour (*silvestres et feri arietes miri coloris*), that were shipped to Cadiz (Gaditanum), along with other animals, for persons giving shows (*munerarii*). Marcus Columella, the writer's uncle, bought some of them, took them to his estate, tamed them and mated them with 'coated' sheep (*mansuefactos tectis ovibus admisit*), the offspring being mated in their turn with Tarentine sheep.[1] Wild sheep (*oves ferae*) were among the animals maintained by Quintus Fulvius Lippinus on his estate at Tarquinii;[2] and we hear of them again as appearing in the late imperial spectacles of Gordian I[3] and Probus.[4]

Of the eastern domesticated breeds of sheep three sorts are recorded as having walked in Ptolemy II's pageant: 130 Ethiopians, 300 Arabians and 20 Euboeans.[5] Strabo also mentions the white-fleeced sheep (πρόβατα λευκύτριχα) of the Nabataeans in northern Arabia and the 'goat-haired' (τῶν προβάτων αἰγυτριχούντων) Ethiopian kind.[6] Of the Italian breeds by far the most famous were the fat-tailed Tarentines, which pastured by the banks of the river Galaesus, whose wool was prized as the very best for making garments, and whose praises were constantly sung by Roman poets.[7] Another greatly valued breed came from Spain and was renowned for its wool's natural golden hue.[8]

Sheep husbandry in Italy is chiefly known to us from the pages of Columella, who migrated thither from his native Spain. Some flocks were allowed to range freely; others were folded and stalled on farms. Of the sheep's products, both in Italy and in other countries where flocks of sheep were kept and sheep farming practised, by far the most important was the wool from which clothes, blankets, rugs and carpets were manufactured. In Italy the shearing season ran from the end of May to the end of June. Next came milk; and Columella recommends that, in order that the maximum supply be achieved, some at any rate of the lambs that are still too young to graze should be taken by the shepherds from their dams and despatched to the butchers in the nearest town.[9] Lamb was a not unimportant item in the Roman diet (cf. pp. 151, 152). The third valuable commodity was the cheese made from ewes' milk.[10] Lambing was a very tricky business; ewes in labour needed to be treated with as much care as midwives bestow on women.[11]

Sheep were, like pigs and cattle (cf. pp. 134-5, 152), also bred as sacrificial animals.[12] A sheep was, of course, part of the great *suovetaurilia* offering (cf. pp. 134, 152); and both sheep and lambs were sacrificed to many deities, major and minor, such as Jupiter, Juno, Janus, Mars, Terminus, Faunus, Silvanus and so forth.[13] In the imperial cult male lambs were offered to *Divi*, female ones to *Divae*. In the mysteries of Attis the worshipper was drenched with the blood of a ram (*kriobolion*).

It goes without saying that sheep appear extremely frequently in Roman and Romano-Christian art, particularly in pastoral scenes. Only a few examples need be cited here. One of the most attractive is the so-called Grimani relief in the Vienna Museum, pendant to that of the lioness and cubs (p. 67), which shows a fleecy ewe suckling her lamb within a rocky cave surmounted by a shrine and a gnarled tree; the lamb seems to have upset a milk bowl as it tugs strenuously at its mother's teats.[14] One unusual Christian sarcophagus of the third century, with the 'Good Shepherd', bearing a sheep and accompanied by others, at the centre of the front, has, at each of its rounded ends, the head and forequarters of a vast ram, taking the place of the lions and their prey on the pagan pieces (cf. pp. 65, 66).[15] Among mythological representations in which a ram plays a leading role is the scene of Phrixus and Helle carried by this animal across the sea.[16] (Pl. 80)

GOATS

In the *Fasti* Ovid asks the goddess Flora why at her festival unwarlike wild goats or roes (*umbelles capreae*), and not lionesses from Libya, are displayed within a net in the Circus.[17] These creatures, native to

Italy,[18] were probably not picturesque, spirited or rare enough to make an exciting show; and we do not hear of them again in the context of the Roman public spectacles – unless the roe that Martial saw poised on a rock and ignoring the hunting dogs was in a staged *venatio*.[19] But on the farms domesticated goats were a valuable economic asset. Their hair and skins were used for making rough country clothes. They were eaten, particularly as kids. Above all, they supplied abundant milk, which was both drunk fresh and converted into cheese. Virgil states that many goat-owners kept the new-born kids away from their mothers (presumably not all the time), so as to increase the milk-supply for human use.[20]

It is, therefore, not surprising that milking scenes are a favourite context for the goat's appearance in works of Roman art. The *denarius* reverse-type of a herdsman milking a she-goat issued by Vespasian at the Roman mint probably proclaimed, as did the yoke of oxen and possibly the cow (cf. pp. 161, 162), his agricultural programme for Italy.[21] Sarcophagi with pictures of the pastoral paradise (cf. Chapter XXIII), whether pagan or early Christian, often present a goatherd seated just outside the door of a reed-built hut and milking goats. There is, for instance, just such a group in the left-hand portion of the front of the mid-third-century pagan sarcophagus of Julius Achilleus;[22] and the same theme occurs by itself, on a larger scale, on one of the short sides of another piece.[23] Both of these are now housed in the Museo Nazionale Romano. More elaborate is the group on the peristyle mosaic of the imperial palace at Istanbul. Here the goatherd, seated on the right outside his reed-built hut, is milking a pair of stalwart nanny-goats into a bowl, while on the left is a boy in charge of a large pitcher full of milk.[24] (Pls 79, 81)

Goats peacefully grazing or resting are a common idyllic art motif. On one of the mosaic panels, now in the Vatican, from Hadrian's Villa at Tibur a herd is depicted beside a stream in a rocky landscape, well supplied with shrubs which some of the beasts are cropping: a standing statue of Dionysus watches over them.[25] A fragmentary pavement from the Roman villa at Corinth (cf. p. 161) shows a pair of goats lying on the ground beneath a tree.[26] The goat's destructive habit of nibbling every leaf or branch within its reach, fatal to vineyards and orchards, is often represented, as on a terracotta lamp in the British Museum, where a goat is standing on its fore-legs against a tree-trunk to attack the greenery, unrestrained by its herdsman and his dog, which slumbers in a tight ball under the marauder's very nose.[27] Several carved sarcophagi feature a goat similarly reared up and browsing on leafage.[28] As a naturalistic rendering of the animal the impressionistic painted portrait of a goat in Nero's Golden House is unsurpassed.[29] (Pl. 82)

Goats were also trained for draught. In Ptolemy II's pageant there were sixty pairs of he-goats, each pair drawing a chariot.[30] In a painting from the House of the Vettii at Pompeii Dionysus, reclining on a four-wheeled cart with a Cupid as coachman, is drawn along by a pair of goats.[31] Goat carriages seem to have been used by Roman children in actual life; for on a young boy's sarcophagus, now in the Louvre, which depicts a succession of events in his life from early infancy to school days, the child stands, grasping reins and whip, in a light two-wheeled cart to which a goat is harnessed between shafts.[32] In fancy, if not in reality, goats functioned as beasts of burden, as on another painting from the House of the Vettii, where two Cupids are conducting to market a goat whose back is loaded with a flower basket.[33] (Pl. 83)

Goats served as relatively cheap and easily obtainable sacrificial victims. A Pompeian landscape painting shows a goat being led up for sacrifice at a shrine in wild and rocky country.[34] Kids are constantly mentioned in Latin literature as offerings made to such rustic gods as Faunus, Silvanus and the deities of springs.[35]

Among mythological renderings of goats are the painting from the Golden House of the she-goat Amalthea carrying on her back the infants Jupiter and Juno; [36] and two paintings, one from Herculaneum, the other from Pompeii, of Pan and a he-goat sporting together.[37] Sheep and goats represent, of course, the saved and the damned in early Christian art, as on the Last Judgment mosaic in S. Apollinare Nuovo, in Ravenna.[38] (Pl. 84)

CHAPTER XVI

EQUINE ANIMALS

ZEBRAS

THE ZEBRA, APTLY DESCRIBED in Greek as the 'tiger-like horse' (ἵππος τιγροειδής) or 'tiger-horse' (ἱππότιγρις), appears to have played only a very minor role in Graeco-Roman life and was seldom, so far as the present writer is aware, portrayed in the art of Roman times (cf. pp. 286, 287). Plautianus, Septimius Severus' praetorian prefect, is recorded as having sent centurions to collect some zebras from the islands in the Red Sea, where they were sacred to Helios, for the shows of *c.* A D 200.[1] In *c.* A D 212 Caracalla had a zebra killed in the ring.[2] That is all that we know about these picturesque creatures in the Roman world. They were, presumably, rare and hard to come by.

HORSES

Wild Horses

Wild horses were probably considered to be too much like their domesticated counterparts in appearance to be worth exhibiting often; and we hear only of the 30 and 40 that formed part of the Gordians' collections.[3] That they were sometimes hunted is proved by the presence of one among the huntsmen's quarry on the fifth-century mosaic of Megalopsychia from Antioch-on-the-Orontes (cf. p. 25). A pavement at Cherchel in Algeria shows a wild horse being torn to pieces by a lion.[4]

The Uses of Domesticated Horses

The main uses to which domesticated horses were put in Roman times are, of course, very well known. Varro classifies these uses as for war, transport, the breeding of their own kind and of mules, and racing in the Circus.[5] Here transport (*vectura*) includes both riding, whether for short-distance locomotion, long-distance travelling or hunting, and the drawing of vehicles by horses, mainly at special ceremonies. Vegetius, writing in the late fourth century, lists the horse's most important uses as war, racing in the Circus and riding; while its more menial functions (*viliora ministeria*), to which he refers in passing, cover, besides breeding, such occasional farm and factory work as threshing corn and turning mills.[6] All these aspects of equine activity will be described and discussed individually below.

Sources of Supply

As regards the most important regions of the Roman world from which horses were obtained, Varro singles out the Peloponnese, Thessaly and Apulia as productive of the best studs (*greges*).[7] Vegetius names a number of areas in northern and central Europe, together with Epirus and Dalmatia, as the main sources of supply of horses for the army; Cappadocia, Spain, Sicily and Africa for Circus horses; Persia, Armenia, Epirus and Sicily for mounts.[8] Under the late Empire the chief emperor-owned stud farms of racers were in Cappadocia and Spain; and it was laid down by law that retired racehorses from these particular studs were to be maintained for their remaining days on fodder from the State granaries (*ex horreis fiscalibus alimoniam praebere decrevimus*).[9] That the owners of studs, whether emperors or private individuals, had branded on their horses either their own names in the genitive case or stud-marks is proved by representations in art of racers (cf. pp. 180, 183), by an African hunt mosaic, where a horse is adorned with a Maltese cross,[10] and by a passage in Apuleius which describes how an errant horse was recovered by the recognition of the mark on its back (*notae dorsualis agnitione*).[11] The horses mentioned by Tacitus as being requisitioned unremittingly by Rome from the provinces of Gaul were for military use;[12] so were the Mauretanian horses, whose portraits are seen on Trajan's Column carrying Moorish riders with their characteristic corkscrew curls and accompanying the personification of Mauretania in Hadrian's 'province' coin series.[13]

Horses in War

To judge from the archaeological monuments, above all from the sculptured friezes on the two great Roman Columns, the draught-beasts employed in the Roman army were oxen (cf. pp. 161, 162) and mules (cf. pp. 190, 191), the latter being also used for carrying military packs (cf. p. 191); and unlike a number of their foreign foes the Romans did not fight from horse-drawn chariots. In Roman warfare the essential function of horses, on whose intelligence in battle Pliny comments,[14] was to serve as mounts for the emperor and his entourage when they took the field, for generals, and especially, of course, for allied and auxiliary units of cavalrymen. The conditions under which these cavalry horses served – their rations of food, the tactics for which they were trained and the arms that were carried by their riders, their stabling in fortresses and forts, and the items of their equipment – are discussed in Chapter III of the Appendix to this book. Part III of Book II of Paul Vigneron's *Le cheval dans l'antiquité gréco-romaine* (1968) – 'Les techniques d'utilisation dans les combats' – really contains a history of the development of Roman cavalry from late republican to early imperial times and provides full accounts of the problems confronting it, of its methods and tactics, of the effect on it of lack of stirrups, and of the arms and armour of the riders, together with detailed descriptions of the part that it played in individual battles, whether for success or failure. Scene after scene on the Columns, the reliefs on battle sarcophagi, of which the great Ludovisi piece in the Museo Nazionale Romano is an outstanding example,[15] and other reliefs depicting military activities, the carved tombstones of cavalrymen in particular,[16] show the Roman warhorse on duty, whether waiting with its rider behind the lines, moving up towards the front or deeply involved in an attack. One scene on Trajan's Column presents the transport by river, in a flat-bottomed boat, of three decidedly restive cavalry horses.[17] There is no need to go over all that evidence in detail again here. The present section on the Roman war-horse will be confined to an aspect of its service which neither the Appendix nor Vigneron's book covers and which is not depicted in works of art, namely its share in the quasi-dramatic sports or exercises (ἱππικὰ γυμνάσια) which were held in the army in times of peace and in quiet intervals between campaigns and for which the horses were trained and provided with special equipment.

These military sports were doubtless influenced to some extent by the *lusus Troiae*, which Vigneron does mention,[18] that is, the highly intricate riding exercises carried out by youths and boys of noble birth who rode in labyrinthine formation in two or three separate bands, each of which in turn broke up into two or three companies, wheeling, attacking, separating and joining up again in a mock fight.

The institution was held to be of very ancient origin and its performance is described in great detail by Virgil apropos of Anchises' funerary games.[19] There are many references in Seneca, Dionysius of Halicarnassus, Tacitus, Suetonius, Plutarch and Dio Cassius to its celebration in late republican and early imperial times;[20] and a very intensive training of the horses must have been involved. But Arrian in his *Tactica*, published in AD 136, although he gives a very long and circumstantial account of the military ἱππικὰ γυμνάσια,[21] says nothing of the Roman *lusus Troiae*, but maintains that these army sports were taken over by the Romans from the Celts and Iberians, nationalities that formed a very large proportion of the cavalry *auxilia*. Their circling and wheeling evolutions and division into opposing companies, now advancing, now retreating, were as complex as those of the *lusus* and must have entailed for the horses a no less exacting training.

Arrian paints a vivid picture of the riders' equipment: crested face-mask visor-helmets, coloured jerkins in place of breastplates, tightly fitting trousers, light painted shields, and streaming pennons made of coloured cloth. Of these items the helmets and shields, with the addition of richly ornamented greaves and knee-guards (which Arrian does not mention), have been confirmed by archaeological finds, notably at Dura-Europos, so far as the shields are concerned, and by the treasure unearthed at Straubing in Bavaria in 1950, in which face-mask visor-helmets of two very different types indicate two opposing companies.[22] But in our present context it is the horse equipment that is of special interest – the saddles or saddle-cloths (ἐφίππια) that protected the creatures' flanks and the chamfrons (προμετωπίδια) that fitted closely round their heads. Both are cited in Arrian's account. But it was not until the Straubing discovery of seven complete, and one fragmentary, bronze chamfrons, all splendidly embossed, that the nature of the latter class of items could be properly appreciated.[23]

All of these chamfrons consist of three separately made pieces hinged together, a central piece covering the horse's nose and two lateral pieces, each with an eye-guard, covering the horse's cheeks. In five cases the coverage is virtually complete, the straight, rectangular central portion protecting most of the animal's nose, the lateral portions, with straight inner and curving outer sides protecting the cheeks. The remaining two chamfrons leave much more of the horse's head exposed. The central piece is octagonal and the lateral pieces pear-shaped, with an outward curving point, forming a stylized bird's head, at the top. In two cases the eye-guards consist of heads, in high relief, of Medusa and of Ganymede, pierced with holes to permit a limited amount of vision. The rest have eye-guards that are hemispheres of openwork geometric design. The embossed relief-work on these chamfrons is extremely complicated and ornate and includes figures and busts of Mars, busts of Minerva and of Ganymede, Medusa heads, figures of the Dioscuri, of Victories, of lions, sea-dragons, snakes, eagles, snaky-legged monsters, and so forth – mostly themes of a military or apotropaic character. Two chamfrons carry curious curved objects and a casket with a pyrami- dal lid – possibly of ritual significance, since so much of this Roman sports equipment, whether human or equine, is of a religious character. A leather chamfron, with round lateral holes for the now- vanished eye-guards and adornment in the form of leaves, circles and other patterns, partly tooled and partly picked out with minute bronze studs, came to light in the frontier post of Newstead, Melrose.[24]

A type of ornamental bronze object not listed by Arrian, but very probably worn by horses in the ἱππικὰ γυμνάσια, is a broad, curving pectoral band (balteus) on to the outer surface of which bronze figures in the round of Roman and barbarian horsemen locked in battle have been welded. The best and most complete example was found at Aosta and is now in the local museum.[25] Here the workmanship is very fine, while a piece from Brescia is more provincial in style.[26] There is also a detached figure of a horseman from such a balteus in the Bologna and in the Stara Zagora (Thrace) Museums.[27] (Pl. 86)

Horses for Riding in Civilian Life
The head-harness of the civilian mount comprised much the same items as that of the cavalry mount, namely bridle-bits (frena), reins (habenae, lora), halters (capestra), stallion-muzzles (fiscellae), blinkers, and metal discs attached to straps (phalerae). These are described in detail by Vigneron;[28] and some of them are also mentioned on Chapter III of the Appendix to this book. In civilian life the equi phalerati used for riding[29] could be quite spectacularly adorned with golden discs, silver bridle-bits, figured pectorals (see above), and tinkling bells, like the unhappy ass in Apuleius' *Metamorphoses* whose master insisted on riding it as though it were a Thessalian or Gallic horse, beasts from those countries being among the best types

of mounts.[30] In the same passage Apuleius distinguishes between *purpurea tapeta* (purple saddle-cloths) and *fucata ephippia* (coloured saddles). In both military and civilian contexts it is often only the *tapetum* that is visible in works of art; and in literature the word *ephippium* may have been applied to it loosely. But a group on the Marcus Column shows a cavalryman leading his horse, on the back of which the saddle-cloth (*tapetum*) is surmounted by a leather saddle (*ephippium*) with a wooden bow at back and front, the two objects being quite distinct.[31] It is likely that civilian saddles were of much the same type, with wooden bows and a leather seat between them. For spurs (*calcaria*) there is abundant evidence in Latin literature.[32] But of stirrups there is no trace in either literature or art. No equine of any kind was shod in Roman times. But quantities of iron 'hipposandals' of various shapes, tied to the horses' hooves by leather thongs, have come to light on Roman sites and must have given some protection from the worst effects of being ridden or driven over hard roads or rough terrain (but cf. p. 322).[33]

Horse-grooms were known as *equisones*, *agasones* and *calones*.[34] Columella lays it down that the body of a horse should be cleaned every day with as much care as that of a human and that its back should be rubbed by hand.[35] As regards civilian stabling, Cato distinguishes between the horse stable proper (*equile*) and a mere stall (*stabulum*).[36] Vegetius recommends that the manger (*alveus, patena, praesepe*) should be kept very clean and be divided into compartments (*loculi*) so that the horses do not poach on one another's food, and that the hay-rack (*iacea* or *occa*, *cratis*) should not be placed too high up or too low down; and Varro directs that mares in foal should be separated in the stable by boards (*longurii*) to prevent them from fighting.[37] A rock-cut stable with manger can be seen at Tiddis (Castellum Tidditanorum) in Numidia.[38] There is also the stable discovered at Pompeii in the house of Popidius Secundus. Its plan shows an internal courtyard, on one side of which is the large compartment enclosing the horses' stalls, with rooms for the grooms on the other side.[39]

The most imposing representations in Roman art of horses as mounts are, of course, the large-scale equestrian statues of bronze and marble. Of these the most famous and most constantly reproduced is the bronze Marcus Aurelius on the Capitol.[40] The splendid beast lifts its right fore-leg and wears elaborate head-harness with *phalerae*. The bridle is lost, but the emperor must have held it in his left hand, while his right hand is raised in greeting; and he has a double saddle-cloth, each fold of which is scalloped along its lower edge. The marble groups from Herculaneum, now in the Naples Museum, of Marcus Nonius Balbus and Marcus Nonius Balbus Junior are of the same general type as the imperial group in Rome, the horses wearing ornamental head-harness, but lifting the left fore-leg.[41] In all these three cases the riders are in military dress, but their contexts are civilian. Two fine bronze horses' heads with decorative harness, from Wertach near Augsburg and Herculaneum respectively, most probably once formed part of equestrian groups.[42] A fascinating and comparatively recent discovery of equestrian bronzes was made at Cartoceto di Pergola in central Italy. The pieces, now in the Ancona Museum, are gilded and include two heads of horses with *phalerae* embossed with busts on their harness, parts of their bodies with pectorals and saddle-cloths, and parts of two riders, of one of whom the head and most of the body were capable of restoration.[43] These, like the Balbi statues, must have formed part of a series of family portraits.

In view of the absence of stirrups (which must, however, have been somewhat compensated for by the fact that Roman horses were smaller than they are now), long-distance riding, whether for private purposes or in the service of the State post, must have been very tiring to the rider, who was always liable to be thrown if the horse, whether his own or hired, finding itself in strange surroundings or frightened by some unaccustomed sound or sight, reared and suddenly bolted. Attempts by persons on State service to cover long distances at great speed involved constant changes of horses, which could be worn out or even killed by being made to go too fast.[44] A more considerate traveller, seeing that his horse was tired, would dismount, wipe the sweat carefully from its head, stroke its ears and unbridle it; and when he reached a lodging he would make it his first care to produce money for the purchase of its hay and oats.[45]

Hunting on horseback in the Roman world was of two main types. When the aim of the expedition was the capture or slaughter of powerful, spirited and savage animals that fought back at their human foes – large felines, bears, boars and wild bulls, for example – the hunt could sometimes take the form of a veritable battle between men and beasts, the former consisting of one or more horsemen accompanied by an army of huntsmen on foot, beaters, hounds and so forth, as the lion-hunt and boar-hunt sarcophagi (cf. pp. 66, 132) clearly demonstrate. On the Piazza Armerina 'Great Hunt' pavement the mounted huntsmen carry oval shields resembling those of cavalrymen.[46] The horses, when faced with menacing and roaring creatures in the wild were probably much more terrified and far less confident than they appear to be as portrayed in art. There is, however, a hunt mosaic on which a mounted huntsman accompanied only by his dog has taken on a boar single-handed; and there the horse wears an air of distinct alarm.[47]

In the second type of hunting on horseback the quarry were timid animals such as deer, antelopes, wild asses, foxes and hares that offered no resistance but fled headlong from their pursuers. To judge by the monuments, men, dogs and horses all partook lightheartedly in this form of sport, the horses galloping at top speed on a loose rein. Hare-hunting was particularly popular in Gaul,[48] Africa and Italy. Martial describes a friend as running down the cunning hare with his strong mount; [49] and later he counsels another friend, Priscus, to be more sparing of his tearing hunter and not to dash so violently after hares, since such riding often ends in breaking up the rider rather than the hare.[50] On the 'Little Hunt' pavement at Piazza Armerina, where the quarry are boars, foxes, hares and stags, two horses, in the second register from the top, are held in readiness by grooms while the master of the hunt sacrifices to Diana; below, in the centre, the same two mounts are tethered to trees, while the hunting party enjoys its picnic; to the right of this group a mounted huntsman spears a hare in its form; and in the left-hand half of the lowest zone a couple of mounted huntsmen are rounding up three deer in a net.[51] On a pavement from Constantine (Cirta) in Algeria five men, each on a spirited mount and accompanied by hunters on foot and the dogs 'Fidelis' and 'Castus' (cf. p. 105), are after a stag, a wild ass (?), and a couple of antelopes.[52] On a mosaic panel from Oudna in Tunisia two men each ride a hunter that is almost flying through the air, in the wake of the hounds 'Ederatus' and 'Mustela' (cf. p. 105) which are gaining on a hare and a fox respectively.[53] A mosaic from Lillebonne in Gaul shows mounted huntmen in a stag hunt; another African pavement four riders in a hare hunt; and yet another African piece, a fragment of a pavement from Utica, a single rider who has caught a deer with a lasso.[54] On a hunt mosaic from Djemila (Cuicul) in Numidia a horse has no bridle-bit, merely a rein held in its rider's left hand that passes loosely round its chest, although in this case the quarry is a large and angry boar.[55] The same would appear to have been the case with the horse in a relief on one of the tomb-monuments from Neumagen, now in the Trier Museum.[56] Here a huntsman, returning home on horseback from the chase and attended by a groom and a hound, triumphantly holds up a large hare by the hind-legs. The mount's muzzle has been broken off, but it does not seem to have ever had head-harness or a bridle-bit, only a rein round its chest. It has a saddle-cloth fringed along the lower edge.

Of the mythological mounts and riders portrayed in Roman art the Dioscuri are so familiar and ubiquitous that no examples need be cited here. Less well known are the Rider-gods, shown either singly or as a pair in association with a Mother-goddess, that are the Oriental, Thraco-Phrygian or Danubian counterparts of the Dioscuri, their cult being widespread in the Near East, Anatolia, and the Danubian countries.[57] Thrace was the centre of the cult of a single Rider-god, who is not a member of a pair or connected with a goddess, but always appears alone or with a human attendant.[58] The story of Hercules' capture of the horses of Diomedes, king of the Thracian Bistones, and of their riders' discomforture is dramatically depicted in mosaic in the central portion of the floor of the great three-apsed hall of the Piazza Armerina villa. Five of these magnificent creatures have survived, with their decorative head-harness and bridle-bits.[59] The iconography of Bellerophon and Pegasus in Roman art is the subject of a recent study.[60] Particularly attractive from the equine standpoint are the scenes of the grooming of Pegasus by the Nymphs. The best example is a mosaic from Lepcis Magna, where six Nymphs are carrying out the operation – placing a wreath round the animal's neck, washing its tail, attending to its feet and fore-legs, and holding in readiness various objects for the toilet, while a Cupid hovers in the background.[61] On the mosaic fragment of a similar scene from Sabratha in Tripolitania one Nymph, apparently engaged in binding a shaded ribbon round the top of Pegasus' tail, alone survives.[62] But on the rectangular field of a late Roman red pottery dish from Egypt almost the entire picture is preserved. One Nymph offers the steed a bowl of oats, another is dressing its right fore-leg, while a third pours water on its tail. A small palm-bearing boy is in attendance.[63] (Pl. 94)

Horses for Draught

According to Varro practically all the traffic on the roads in Roman

times consisted of carts and carriages drawn by pairs of mules
(cf. p. 185);[64] and horses, apart from those employed in chariot-
racing (cf. pp. 177-83), were comparatively rarely used for pulling
vehicles. When they were, their equipment was much the same as
that of mules and could comprise shafts attached to a yoke (*iugum*)
on, or fastened to a collar round, the neck; a pole (*temo*), attached to
the yoke at one end, at the other to the front of the car and separating
two horses or two pairs of horses in a row; or, if the horses were
harnessed in two pairs one behind the other, a long pole passing
through the centre of both pairs; or a pole parting the two horses of
the second pair only, while those of the leading pair had reins
fastened at one end to their collars, at the other to the termination of
the pole. As with racing chariots, so with other vehicles drawn by
three or four horses in a row, the two inner horses could be yoked
and separated by a pole, while the one or two outer animals were
merely attached by a rein to the front of the car. Less clear is the
method used when it was a case of more than two pairs of horses in
action, one pair behind the other. Octavius' dream that he saw his
son, afterwards Augustus, mounted on a chariot drawn by twelve
glitteringly white horses may have been based on something actually
witnessed;[65] and Nero is said to have driven a ten-in-hand at
Olympia.[66]

It was, in fact, mainly on such ceremonial occasions as the
triumphal and consular procession of the emperors that horses served
as draught-animals outside the Circus, generally in teams of four
(*quadrigae*).[67] Such processional scenes appear repeatedly on State
reliefs, as for instance on those on the Arch of Titus, on the Arch of
Constantine (Marcus Aurelius), on the Severan Arch at Lepcis
Magna,[68] and on coins and medallions.[69] The fine bronze horse
wearing a collar from the basilica at Herculaneum was probably part
of a *quadriga* group; as were also the famous four bronze horses,
likewise equipped with collars, of controversial, but probably
Roman, date that now adorn the façade of St Mark's, Venice.[70]
Occasionally private persons drove in horse-drawn vehicles. On a
fourth-century sarcophagus relief, now in the Stockholm National
Museum, two women in a carriage fitted with a high-backed seat are
being pulled by a pair of horses, with a coachman holding the reins
and an outrider accompanying them.[71] On a tombstone in the
Museo Lapidario Maffeiano at Verona two men are seated in a light
carriage drawn by a mare with her foal trotting along below her

belly.[72] Martial has an epigram addressed to a chaise (*covinnus*) drawn by ponies (*mannuli*);[73] Horace twice alludes to *manni* in contexts that imply their use for driving;[74] and Ovid speaks of a two-wheeled carriage (*esseda*) whirled along by *manni*.[75] Horses were also sometimes put to draw carts as a mark of disgrace.[76]

The possibility of a certain amount of stylization in the rendering of horse equipment in Roman art must always be borne in mind; and, in particular, it is probable that too much may have been made, on the score of the monuments, of the supposed strangling effect of the neck-, as opposed to the shoulder-, collar on horses and mules, an effect that is often held to have greatly restricted their capacity for drawing heavy loads.[77] All the same, we have no reason to suppose that the representations on reliefs, mosaics, and so forth were wildly inaccurate; and with these reservations in mind we can accept their evidence. A marble relief in the Ashmolean Museum, Oxford, of a racing *biga* that has come to grief gives a very clear picture of the yoke and pole.[78]

Racehorses

The sport of chariot-racing in ancient Rome has already been thoroughly surveyed elsewhere.[79] There is no need to repeat and illustrate here what is said and shown there on the architectural and technical arrangements of the Circus, the organization of the races, the performances of acrobats (*desultores*) in connection with them, the factions, the spectators' reactions, and the breeding, length of service, retirement and funerary inscriptions of the horses. It is proposed in this section to concentrate chiefly on some of the other personal aspects of the animals, particularly on their names and on the representations of them in various artistic media. There can be little doubt that the horses knew their own names and that the winners understood that they were being praised when their names were yelled by the enthusiastic crowd (cf. p. 17). Ovid's account of the pleasure that they registered after victory – tossing the head in response to the people's acclamation – need not be wholly fanciful.[80] Nor is it impossible that racehorses sometimes rehearsed in their sleep the excitements of the Circus – sweating and panting and straining every nerve as though for victory while their limbs were at rest, as Lucretius pictures them.[81]

Of the names of beasts of Roman times that have been recorded [82] those of racehorses, which run into hundreds, greatly outnumber those of other species. The most fruitful source of knowledge is the inscriptions, mostly found in Rome, giving the names of victorious steeds [83] and the inscribed spells (defixionum tabellae) comprising a number of texts in which adherents of one or other of the great Circus factions invoke some demon or malignant deity to bring disaster in the coming races on the charioteers and horses, all of whom are named, of the rival factions.[84] Much further information is furnished by archaeological monuments. Only a small selection of the names in different categories can be cited here. It will be noted that nearly all the names are masculine.

Some names denote colour or markings – for example, 'Aureus', 'Candidus', 'Purpureus' ('Roan'), 'Polyeides' ('Dapple'), 'Glaucus' ('Grey'), 'Roseus' ('Bay'), 'Maculosus' ('Piebald'). Others allude to speed – 'Celer' ('Swift'), 'Cursor' ('Runner'), 'Dromos' ('Racer'), and 'Volucer' ('Flyer'). The last was the name of a famous racehorse of the Greens, much beloved by the Emperor Lucius Verus, who carried a golden statuette of it about with him, fed it on grapes and nuts instead of barley, and presented it with brightly coloured horse-cloths (saga fuco tincta) and a tomb on the Vatican.[85] General good looks are referred to by such names as 'Calimorfus' ('Beauty'); lightness and agility by 'Agilis', 'Penna' ('Feather'), 'Passerinus' ('Sparrow'), the last a 'star' mentioned twice by Martial,[86] and 'Incitatus' ('Bounce'),[87] which was also the name of the Emperor Gaius' favourite. According to Suetonius [88] Gaius posted soldiers on the day before the races to preserve silence in its neighbourhood, lest its rest should be disturbed, gave it a marble stable (equile), an ivory manger (praesepe), purple blankets (tegamenta), jewelled collars (monilia), and a ménage of its own with slaves and furniture for the better entertainment of the guests invited in its name. He even considered it for the consulship. 'Valens' and 'Adamas' ('Cast-Iron') denote strength, 'Farus' ('Lighthouse'), 'Phosphorus' ('Morning-Star'), and 'Lampas' fiery breath or fiery eyes. 'Crinitus' ('Long-Locks') and 'Cirratus' ('Curly-Locks') refer to manes. Names derived from weapons – 'Sagitta' ('Arrow'), 'Sica' ('Dirk'), 'Ballista' ('Cannon-Ball') are suggestive of physical prowess.

Psychological characteristics are described by such names as 'Ferox' ('Hotspur'), 'Eustolus' ('Ready'), 'Volens' ('Willing'), 'Astutus' ('Cunning'), 'Animator' ('Life-and-Soul-of-the-Team'). Among the most popular names are naturally those that allude to victory and triumph over rivals – 'Victor', 'Polyneices' ('Ever-Victorious'), 'Palmatus', 'Laureatus', 'Praeclarus' ('Renown'), 'Felicissimus' ('Lucky'), 'Dominator', 'Pertinax' ('Will-to-Victory'), the last a horse of the Greens favoured by the Emperor Commodus.[89] Closely allied are the titles of honour – 'Caesareus', 'Basilius', 'Regalis', 'Patricius'.

Especially attractive are the playful and endearing names, such as 'Amor', 'Cupido', 'Amicus' ('Pal'), 'Gemmula' ('Jewelette'), 'Amandus' ('Darling'), 'Mirandus', 'Blandus' ('Coax'), 'Puerina' ('Girly'), 'Iuvenis' ('Laddy'), 'Fastidiosus' ('Choosy'), 'Garrulus' and 'Verbosus' ('Chatterbox'). More solemn are the names denoting virtues – 'Dicaeosyne' and 'Elpis' ('Justice' and 'Hope'). There are also terms of abuse playfully used as names – 'Lues' ('Pest'), 'Parasitus' ('Toady'), 'Latro' ('Thief').

A large number of names are those of gods and heroes – 'Sol', 'Phoebus', 'Castor', 'Achilles', 'Ajax', 'Diomedes', 'Alcides' (Hercules), 'Admetus', and so forth. There are also many names taken from places, countries, cities and such natural features and forces as mountains, rivers and winds. Examples are 'Romanus', 'Italus', 'Pompeianus', 'Hirpinus', 'Macedo', 'Gallus', 'Aegyptus', 'Indus', 'Roma', 'Corinthus', 'Olympus', 'Caucasus', 'Euphrates', 'Tigris'.[90] The Emperor Hadrian's favourite hunter was called 'Borysthenes' ('Dnieper'); and the epitaph placed on its tomb was found at Apt in southern France.[91] There are the horses named after other creatures – 'Leo', 'Pardus', 'Lupus', 'Bubalus', 'Catta' ('Puss'), 'Aquila', 'Palumbus' ('Dove'); those whose names are playfully derived from professions and occupations – 'Advocatus', 'Patronus' ('Barrister'), 'Scholasticus' ('Student'), 'Agricola', 'Nauta' ('Sailor-Boy'); and those called by such familiar or famous proper names as 'Marcus', 'Domitius', 'Roscius' (the celebrated actor), 'Darius', 'Socrates', 'Antiochus'.[92]

Of the works of art depicting racehorses with their names inscribed beside them mosaic pavements are both the most attractive and the most informative. One at Barcelona, which presents a race of four *quadrigae* in progress, yields no less than twelve names, including 'Regnator' ('Emperor'), 'Eridanus' ('Po'), 'Spumosus' ('Foam'), and 'Luxuriosus' ('Sybarite').[93] A *bigae* race pavement showing two chariots, found on the Via Flaminia a few miles north of Rome, gives two names – 'Olympus' and 'Romanus'.[94] Another mosaic rendering of a Circus race, found on the Via Imperiale in Rome and now in the Museo Nazionale Romano, is somewhat disappointing in that it produces the names of only four racehorses out of the eight *quadrigae* teams in action.[95] Among the North African mosaics showing racing scenes is a fragmentary one from Dougga (Thugga) in Tunisia, where a frontal chariot driven by the charioteer 'Eros' is pulled by four horses, two of which are named 'Amandus' and 'Frunitus' ('Jolly').[96] It is a pity that we do not know the names of the four racers in a particularly fine *quadriga* team worked in mosaic in a villa at Munzach, near Liestal, in Switzerland.[97]

In another series of mosaics on which named racehorses are portrayed the animals are shown off duty. A pavement from Roman Spain, found in a villa in Portugal at Torre di Palma in 1947, presents five named horses, each in one of five separate squares set quincuncially against a geometric ground. In the centre is the favourite, 'Lenobatis' ('Wine-Treader'), who faces the spectator and wears a handsome pectoral ornament. The other four, 'Hiberus' ('Spaniard'), 'Leneus' ('Bacchus' Own'), 'Pelops' and 'Inachus' (a river in the Argolid), are arranged in two pairs above and below Lenobatis, each horse facing towards the centre and drawn in profile. All wear plumes on their heads.[98] Spain was, as we have seen, one of the most important sources of supply for Circus horses; and Spanish horses are mentioned several times by Symmachus as those which he particularly wished to procure for the races that he planned to provide.[99] Possibly the owner of the villa at Torre di Palma kept a stud and supplied racers for the shows. Or he may have been merely a Circus 'fan' who had backed these particular animals. A square mosaic panel from the Roman villa at Duenas, near Valladolid in northern Spain, contains the figure of a racehorse of which the head and neck, the hind-legs and the tail are preserved. It is held by a groom, wears scarlet head-harness, and has inscribed on its neck 'Amoris', perhaps the owner's name.[100]

To return to North African pavements, a panel from Cherchel shows the figure of a horse labelled 'Muccosus' and with 'Pr[*asinus*] Cl[*audii*] Sabini' branded on its flank: it is 'Snuffler' (?) or 'Slobberer' (?) of the Greens, owned by Claudius Sabinus.[101] On a pavement from Ferryville in Tunisia 'Diomedes' and 'Alcides' are tethered on either side of a post.[102] Other, more ambitious, pavements present whole stud-farms, two of this type having come to light in the same villa at Sousse (Hadrumetum), also in Tunisia. On one are two pairs of horses, with a Cupid holding a garland above the back of each steed, the members of each pair facing one another from either side of a palm-tree: rocks, shrubs and grazing goats occupy the centre of the picture. The names are 'Campus' ('Field'), 'Dilectus' ('Pet'), 'Hipparchus' ('Chief'), and 'Patricius' ('Noble'), the first and the last having the owner's name, 'Sorothi', inscribed on their flanks.[103] The second pavement, clearly by the same hand, features an African landscape with buildings, rocks, shrubs and a variety of grazing beasts. Inset are four medallions, each of which originally contained two horses, again confronting one another from either side of a palm-tree, but the right-hand horse in each of the two medallions on the right side of the picture has disappeared. The names are 'Amor', 'Dominator' ('Boss'), 'Adorandus' ('Angel'), 'Crinitus' ('Long-Locks'), 'Ferox' ('Hotspur'), and 'Pegasus'. Four of the horses have 'Sorothi' on their flanks.[104] Yet another stud pavement, this time divided into three tiers, was found at Constantine but has been destroyed, surviving only in a drawing. Here are six horses in their stable, three in the central and three in the lowest tier, while in the upper tier are the buildings of the owner's villa, inscribed 'Pompeianus'. The inscriptions in the central tier, reading from left to right, are 'Altus' ('Lofty'), with the caption *unus es, ut mons exultas* ('You're only one, but you're proud as a mountain'), 'Pullentianus' ('Dusky'), and 'Delicatus' ('Dandy'); below we read *vincas, non vincas, te amamus, Polidoxe* ('Whether you win or lose, we love you, Polidoxus ["Renown"]'), 'Titas' ('Titan'), and 'Scholasticus'. The mangers, to which the horses are tethered, were not in the original mosaic, but are a product of the draughtsman's fancy.[105]

The most remarkable mosaic presentation of a racehorse stud so far known was found in 1960 in the main room (*oecus*) of a huge Roman building on the site of ancient Carthage.[106] It consists of a grid of *opus sectile* (marble inlay) panels alternating originally with 98 mosaic panels, of which 61 have survived in whole or in part. Each of these panels contains a racehorse, some of the animals having names or symbols, presumably denoting their owner, branded on them. All have plumes and ribbons tied round their tails. What is so unusual about this equine portrait gallery is the fact that each horse is accompanied, not by its inscribed name, but by a large single figure or by a scene of figures on a much smaller scale or sometimes by both. These secondary motifs fall into several categories such as deities, personifications, mythological episodes and *genre* figures and activities; and Salomonson has made the most acceptable suggestion that they are symbols standing for the horses' names. With the aid of the lists of horse names already compiled from literary, epigraphical and monumental sources he is able to deduce from the motifs one or more possible names for almost every horse. For example, the horse accompanied by the She-wolf and Twins could have been called 'Roma', 'Romanus', or 'Lupercus' (after the Lupercal where the episode took place);[107] that accompanied by a Cupid with a flaming torch could have had the name of 'Cupido', 'Amor', or 'Phosphorus'.[108]

The occupier of the house who commissioned this mosaic could perhaps have been the owner of a very large stud that supplied racers for all four factions;[109] or the pictures may commemorate some very special races that he himself had staged. To the question as to why he chose this cryptic and roundabout way of naming the steeds Salomonson provides no answer, beyond suggesting that it was a means of showing off his erudition and of setting the tongues of his guests wagging with curiosity. Could it be that, if the owner of an exceptionally large stud, he hoped in this way to avert the effect of curses laid by charioteers upon their rivals and the rival teams in *defixionum tabellae*, where individual horses are specified by name? An ill-disposed person seeing the mosaic might either fail to grasp the meaning of the accessory figures and scenes or hit upon the wrong interpretations of them where there were several possible ones to choose from. Meanwhile the horses could have conferred upon them with impunity the honour of having their names recorded, even if the public, in this case, did not know those names and so could not shout them during the races.

One more African mosaic relating to the Circus horses may be mentioned as depicting an uncommon theme. It comes from Medeina (Althiburus) in Tunisia, is now in the Bardo Museum, and shows the transport of three racers across the Mediterranean, perhaps to Italy. The animals are labelled 'Ferox', 'Icarus', and 'Cupido' and the flat-bottomed boat in which they are travelling is identified, both in Latin and in Greek, as 'Hippago' and ΙΠΠΑΓΩΓΟΣ.[110]

Of the six known monuments with reliefs portraying named horses[111] the most impressive is the marble basis set up *c.* 490 in Constantinople in honour of the celebrated charioteer Porphyrius, whose figure is depicted on the front.[112] On each of the sides and on the back there is a racing *quadriga* and each of the twelve horses has its name inscribed in Greek.[113] Three of these names – 'Halieus' ('Fisher'), 'Anthupatos' ('Proconsul'), and 'Kynagos' ('Hunter') – denote professions: a curious name, unparalleled elsewhere, is 'Palaistiniarchos' ('Lord of Palestine'). Also of special interest is the marble funerary *cippus* of Titus Flavius Abascantus, an imperial judicial functionary (*a cognitionibus*), which is now in the Palazzo Ducale at Urbino. Above the main inscription the dead man reclines at the celestial banquet, and in a panel below it is a charioteer holding a wreath of victory and driving a *quadriga* towards the right. This scene, which in the context can only designate victory over death, is surmounted by another text in much smaller lettering – *Scorpus Ingenuo Admeto Passerino Atmeto* ('Scorpus wins with the horses *Ingenuus* ["Free-Born"], *Admetus*, *Passerinus* ["Sparrow"], and *Atmetus* [Greek for "Unconquered"]'). Scorpus was a famous charioteer of Domitian's day, mentioned several times by Martial.[114]

Named racehorses also appear in a variety of 'minor' works of art – glass vessels, bone, ivory, and stone counters, terracotta lamps, lead *tesserae*, bronze contorniates, bone knife-handles, and intaglios.[115] Only a few of these items can be described here. Of the six ivory counters found in a sarcophagus near the church of San Sebastiano, just to the south of Rome, each incised with a named charioteer on one side and a named racehorse on the other, one portrays the horse 'Amicus' ('Pal'), which has its owner's name, 'Antoni', inscribed on its flank, another shows 'Pyrobolus' ('Flame-Thrower'), with a stud-mark, or good-luck emblem, in the form of a solar disc above its fore-legs.[116] Of the eight contorniates with horses, two may be singled out for mention. One has on its reverse a charioteer holding by the bridle 'Turificator' ('Incense-Offerer', that is, 'Snorter', with steaming breath) and 'Astutus' ('Cunning'); the other piece presents a frontal *quadriga* with the charioteer Eugenius driving 'Achilles', 'Sidereus' ('Star'), 'Speciosus' ('Beauty'), and 'Dignus' – all names known elsewhere.[117] A lamp in the British Museum displays on its *discus* the triumphal procession of the horse 'Roma'.[118] Finally, a bone knife-handle shows on one side a charioteer's cap and the name 'Euprepes', on the other a horse's head labelled 'Nereo' and a palm-branch – 'Euprepes has won with the horse Nereus'.[119] (Pl. 87)

Horses in Gladiatorial Shows
Occasionally horses were employed in the Circus or arena to pull the

light chariots (*essedae*) from which gladiators sometimes fought. Cicero writes of the horses of gladiators being no less terrified than the gladiators themselves by a sudden hissing.[120] Suetonius mentions *essedarii* in connection with gladiatorial combats;[121] and gladiatorial inscriptions from the Greek provinces refer to ἱπποδιώκται (drivers) and ἐσσεδάριοι (charioteers).[122]

Performing Horses

Horses but rarely appeared as performers in Roman times. A lamp in the Louvre shows a horse being taught to dance on its hind-legs.[123] According to Dio Cassius Titus gave a water-show, flooding the theatre and causing horses, bulls and other tamed animals to perform in the water all the various tricks that they had learnt to do on dry land.[124]

The Horse on the Farm and in the Factory

On the farm one of the horse's most obvious duties was that of breeding other horses and mules. Two fine farm-horses, one peace-fully grazing, the other a mare suckling her foal, appear on the peristyle mosaic of the imperial palace at Istanbul.[125] The horse was also used, along with oxen, for threshing, as a mosaic from Zliten in Tripolitania demonstrates.[126] But one of the least agreeable aspects of the Roman treatment of horses was the use of animals that either were intractable, or had failed to make the grade as racers or whose days as racers or hunters were past, to turn mills, whether in town or country, for grinding corn and pressing olives. A sarcophagus in the Vatican shows such a mill in the form of two superimposed cone-shaped stone features on a circular base and fitted with a wooden frame, to which a horse is chained. It wears blinkers and is made to work the mill by walking in a circle round and round it, under the eye of an attendant.[127] Apuleius paints a grim picture of the wretched beasts at a baker's mill – the old mules (*muli senes*) and sickly horses (*cantherii debiles*). Their necks were covered with sores, their nostrils rattled with incessant coughing, their sides were worn bare by their harness, their ribs were broken with perpetual beatings, and their hooves were flattened with the endless pacing round and round (*multivia circumcursione*).[128] Juvenal describes how the offspring of famous racers who were never victorious were put to draw carts like mules, till their necks were sore, and made to turn mills;[129] while

Columella directs that unmanageable stallions should be put to the mill as a punishment.[130] But to end one's days at the mill was an even bitterer fate for horses that had once been Circus favourites; and three epigrams in the *Greek Anthology* witness to the fact that at least some human beings had an understanding of what their degradation meant to 'Eagle', 'Pegasus', and another aged racehorse, whose toil in rotating the mill seemed to mock their one-time laurels (στεφέων ὕβρις).[131] These did not share the good fortune of the emperor-owned racers that were put out to grass at the State's expense (cf. p. 168).

The Dead Horse

The skins of dead horses obviously served all manner of purposes. Their tails and manes could be made into helmet decorations or into ropes for working war-machines.[132] The eating of horses was revolting to the Romans, who only resorted to it when sheer starvation was the alternative.[133]

MULES

Varro defines the offspring of a mare and a jackass as *mulus*, that of a stallion and a jenny as *hinnus*, noting that the latter is of smaller build.[134] The term *mula* can be used to denote a she-mule, as in the famous proverb 'when a mule foals', that is, never, since mules are sterile.[135] But Pliny uses *mula* for a mule in general, when describing the animal as of unrivalled strength for work of all kinds; although he also says that 'the ancients' called the offspring of stallions and jennies *hinnuli*, that of mares and jackasses *muli*. He further remarks that the *mulae* born of the union of mares and tamed wild asses (*onagri*) are swift, very strong in the feet, lean in body, and of stubborn temper.[136] The whole purpose of breeding mules in the Roman period, as in earlier and later times, was to exact from them services of the most laborious kind – mainly as draught-animals and as beasts of burden.

Draught-Mules

Pairs of mules, rather than horses, were, as we have seen, regularly used for drawing vehicles on the highways of the Roman world. The numismatic evidence suggests that they also served on some ceremonial State occasions to draw the *carpentum* or two-wheeled covered carriage in which Roman matrons in early times and later State priestesses had the privilege of driving through the city on a feast-day and on the day preceding.[137] Under the early Empire the *carpentum* could be granted as an honour to ladies of the imperial House, first under Tiberius to Livia by a motion of the Senate, which also decreed a *supplicatio* (solemn public prayer) on the occasion of the empress' illness in AD 22.[138] A *sestertius* reverse-type issued at that date, with the legend S[*enatus*] P[*opulus*] Q[*ue*] R[*omanus*) IVLIAE AVGVSTAE, shows a *carpentum* adorned with figures in relief and drawn towards the right by a pair of long-eared mules.[139] Gaius, when he instituted games in the Circus in honour of the memory of his mother, Agrippina I, provided a *carpentum* to convey her image in procession;[140] and he issued a *sestertius* with her portrait on the obverse and a reverse with the legend S[*enatus*] P[*opulus*] Q[*ue*] R[*omanus*] MEMORIAE AGRIPPINAE accompanying the scene of two mules drawing a *carpentum*, similar to Livia's, towards the left. On both of these *sestertii* the animals wear collars set quite low on the neck, bits, and bridles.[141] We know from literary sources that in Claudius' British triumph in 44 his wife Messalina followed his chariot in a *carpentum*;[142] and that in 51 Nero's mother, Agrippina II, drove in a *carpentum* to the Capitol.[143] No coin-types commemorate these events, but there can be little doubt that in these cases too the vehicles were drawn by mules. (Pl. 89)

Mule-drawn also were the carriages used by the officials of the State post (*cursus publicus*). When in 97 Nerva remitted to Italy the expenses of this post he issued a *sestertius* type with the legend VEHICVLATIONE ITALIAE REMISSA and a picture of two mules quietly grazing, with the pole of their carriage and their reins and collars shown tipped up behind them.[144] A tombstone in the Belgrade Museum carries the inscription of Lucius Blassius Nigello, a *speculator* (that is, a member of the military police) attached to the Seventh Claudian Legion, and a relief that depicts him travelling by the *cursus publicus* on his official duty. He is seated on a bench in a light four-wheeled carriage, with a driver on the box, and he holds a short staff or a scroll, while behind and back to back with him there rides on the baggage his servant, who holds his master's badge of office – a long staff or spear, which appears to have a wreath or a metal circlet attached near its upper end.[145] The vehicle is drawn by three high-stepping mules, wearing collars to which their reins are fastened, and advancing rapidly towards the right. This would be the quick post (*cursus velox*). In contrast to this is the slow post (*cursus clabularius*) depicted on a tomb relief now in the Avignon Museum. The vehicle in this case in a heavy four-wheeled coach (*raeda*), inside which the heads and shoulders of two travellers are visible through windows. On the box is a driver and next to him, on the roof of the coach, there is seated in a kind of chair a man who may well be an agent of the State, since the servant seated behind and back to back with him holds a long staff round which a scarf is tied, again apparently an emblem of office. The two mules that draw the coach towards the left have each round its neck a choking collar from which project vertically two curious scimitar-shaped features, and to these the driver's reins are fastened. The animals also have traces running horizontally from their collars to the front of the coach and a horse-cloth secured by straps. They appear to be standing stock still, making little if any progress despite the fact that the driver, urged by the official traveller on the roof, is brandishing his whip.[146] No inscription has survived ; but it seems very likely that the person whom the stone commemorates was someone who had to travel on imperial business. (Pls 88, 90)

But it is to the social and economic life of the provinces, particularly of Gaul, that most of the funerary reliefs presenting mule-drawn vehicles are related. In the Langres Museum is a piece put together from a number of fragments which shows a four-wheeled chaise carrying a driver and two passengers and drawn rightwards by two pairs of mules, one behind the other. All four animals wear collars and are stepping out briskly. The two next to the carriage are clearly yoked together, the driver's reins being fastened to the yoke. The pole that must have passed between these mules is not visible in the carving; but the reins of the leading pair, attached at one end to the creatures' collars, must have been fastened at the other end to the pole's termination, just below the heads of the beasts behind. This pair, immediately controlled by the driver, would, when checked or urged on, automatically have caused the two in front to stop or press forward.[147] This quartet seems to accept its task quite lightheartedly. But on another relief from Langres two mules plod laboriously along towards the right with lowered heads, straining under the weight of a vast wine-barrel on the four-wheeled cart that they are forced to draw. These two must have been equipped with yoke and pole, although the details are far from clear. In the background is a third mule, attached to the cart by long reins and serving as a kind of trace-horse. It tosses its head and appears to be taking only a minor share of the burden. There is a driver on the box.[148]

Somewhat similar to the second Langres relief is a fragmentary one found at Neumagen in the Mosel valley and now in the Trier Museum. It comes from the monument of one Lucius Securius. Here again are three mules pulling rightwards a now-vanished vehicle, two smaller beasts in the foreground and a larger one in the background. The former two, carrying a common yoke to which their reins are fastened, are straining forwards with lowered heads, while the background mule, its head erect, is controlled by reins and a rope attached to its collar and wears a head-plume.[149] Draught-mules appear on two reliefs on the tower tomb erected at Igel near Trier for the Secundinii, a local Treviran business family. On one of these two men, seated in a high, two-wheeled gig, are driving two high-stepping mules between shafts that are attached at one end to their collars, at the other to the front of the car. The cortège is emerging from a city gate and passes a milestone inscribed LIIII.[150] The second scene shows a four-wheeled covered cart also emerging from a city gateway and pulled by three mules past a tree.[151] The cart could have contained merchandise and perhaps some human passengers as well. For a very similar covered cart, on a tomb relief now let into one of the outer walls of the church at Maria Saal near Klagenfurt, in Austria, has a door in one of its sides through which a small figure seated inside can be discerned. A driver with a long whip is on the box of the cart, which is drawn by two stout mules wearing collars and an ornamented yoke with the reins attached to it.[152] (Pl. 85)

A number of other Treviran grave monuments, now in the Arlon Museum in southern Belgium, show pairs of draught-mules in action. On one side of the 'Pilier du Drapier' are two superimposed scenes, the upper one featuring a man driving two spanking beasts in a two-wheeled cart towards the right, while the lower one shows a man leading slowly through a city gate a loaded cart, also two-wheeled and pulled by a pair of mules. Perhaps we may see in each of these scenes the same man, the same cart, and the same mules, in the morning hurrying gaily to town, in the evening returning somewhat wearily to the farm with heavy purchases.[153] A fragmentary relief carries the greater part of the figures of two splendidly conditioned mules, the one in the background tossing its head, which are speeding past an uninscribed milestone. There is now no trace of the vehicle to which they were harnessed between shafts fixed at one end to their collars; and the yoke to which their reins may have been fastened is not clearly shown.[154] A complete relief in the Buzenol-Montauban Museum in the same Treviran region gives a good idea of what the Arlon piece was like before it was broken. Two men are seated in a high two-wheeled gig and drive a pair of mules almost identical with those at Arlon: they run between shafts and have collars and reins, possibly also a yoke.[155]

Occasionally in this Treviran series of draught-scenes only one mule is used. A relief found at Trier in 1931 and now in the local museum shows a very small two-wheeled cart, consisting only of the driver's box, on which is seated an elderly peasant driving a weary mule towards the left past a milestone. The animal, whose tongue is hanging out, stumbles along between shafts that are attached to a particularly thick and heavy collar round its neck.[156] On yet another Arlon piece a peasant leads by the bridle a solitary mule again walking between shafts that are fixed to the front of a small cart equipped with two immense wheels and loaded with an enormous circular basket or bin. The contents of this receptacle look like either manure for the fields or a mass of clay that is being conveyed to a factory for the purpose of manufacturing building bricks and tiles.[157] (Pl. 96)

In an altogether lighter vein are the portraits of draught-mules on a black-and-white mosaic pavement in the Baths of the *Cisarii* (drivers of gigs) near the Porta Romana at Ostia. These consist of four self-contained groups. One shows a single mule drawing a four-wheeled cart with a single driver. Another features a similar cart with two mules, in which three men appear to be going for a joy-ride, while a fourth man, striding along on foot, leads the way. In both of these groups the animals have light collars, head-harness, and, of course, reins, but no shafts. In the third group a couple of mules is being pulled, clearly most unwillingly, by a groom or driver towards the vehicle (not shown) to which they are to be harnessed. An inscription names them as 'Pudes' ('Bashful') and 'Podagrosus' ('Gouty'). Fourthly, two mules labelled 'Potiscus' ('Thirsty Fish') and 'Baro-sus' ('Mollycoddle') are drinking, unharnessed, side by side, while their driver holds their pole and yoke.[158] In all these scenes the stubborn mulish character comes across with lively realism and not a little humour.

A number of vivid literary passages describe draught-mules in civilian life. Martial complains of the pedestrian's inability, when he wants to cross a road, to find a gap in the endless droves of mules that file along roped to waggons loaded with blocks of marble.[159] According to Suetonius, Nero never travelled with less than a thousand carriages drawn by mules with silvered hipposandals.[160] A mule on the towpath hauled the boat or barge in which Horace travelled along a canal in the Pomptine Marshes on his famous journey to Brundisium.[161] In his account of Alexander's funeral in 322 B C Diodorus Siculus relates that the funerary chariot was drawn by means of four poles to each of which was fastened four teams with four mules (ἡμίονοι) harnessed in each team, making in all sixty-four mules selected for their strength and size;[162] and it may have been the case that mules were sometimes used, on a far less lavish scale, to draw the biers at Roman funerals. The most attractive picture of all is in Claudian's poem on the draught-mules of Roman Gaul. They obey their master's every word and understand the meaning of his different cries, needing neither rein nor yoke and never tiring. He has only to shout and they go fast or slow, turn left or right. Covered with tawny pelts they haul along the rumbling carts, each of them loyally doing his share of the toil (consensuque pares et fulvis pellibus hirtae/esseda concordes multisonora trahunt) (cf. pp. 26, 27).[163]

The use of draught-mules in the Roman army is well attested in works of art, particularly on the friezes of the two Columns. On Trajan's Column they appear seven times. A pair stands within a Roman strongpoint, attended by a soldier and waiting to be harnessed; two light two-wheeled carts are each driven by a soldier and drawn by a pair of mules; two two-wheeled carts, one covered, the other loaded with vessels and other items, are pulled along in file each by a pair of mules; a pair draws two wine-barrels on an open two-wheeled cart; two pairs pull each a similar cart containing a ballista (war-engine); two more mules draw a two-wheeled cart piled with shields; and finally a pair pulls a two-wheeled cart loaded with baggage, again inside a Roman strongpoint.[164] On the Marcus Column draught-mules appear in six scenes. One pair draws a war-engine in a two-wheeled cart in the episode of the 'rain miracle'; another a wine-barrel on a two-wheeled cart; while in each of the other four scenes two mules pull a four-wheeled cart piled with arms and other baggage.[165] A fragmentary tombstone found at Strasbourg (Argentorate) and now in the local museum features a soldier, with his sword under his arm and a whip in his hand, driving past a tree a four-wheeled cart loaded with military supplies and drawn by a pair of spanking, and unusually long-eared, mules.[166] (Pls 78, 91)

Pack-Mules

In both civilian and military life the mule, even more than the donkey, was the pack-animal *par excellence*. Roman pack-saddles were of two types. One type resembled a riding-saddle, with a rigid framework of wood, the load being fastened on with straps: a horse-cloth *stratum*[167] was spread on the animal's back beneath it. There is a very clear rendering of it on Trajan's Column, where a mule, attended by a soldier, stands waiting to receive its burden.[168] The second and more common type of saddle was soft, most probably of wickerwork, like a panier, or of some other pliant material, and better adapted to the creature's back. Such saddles were known as *clitellae*, explained by Festus as 'the objects carried by mules by which their packs [*sarcinae*] were fastened on'.[169] Trajan's Column again provides an excellent illustration in a scene in which two mules carry paniers filled with vessels from the captured Dacian treasure: under each of these receptacles is spread a fringed *stratum*.[170] On a long journey the mules' *clitellae* would be removed for a time to rest them, as Horace indicates.[171] Horace also pictures the sharp contractor hurrying along with his mules and bearers laden with building materials.[172] In a narrow frieze on the Igel Monument two pack-mules, probably carrying bales of cloth, are depicted traversing hilly country.[173] Pack-mules were accompanied by muleteers (*muliones* – a word also used to signify dealers in mules),[174] as in a painting from the House of Julia Felix at Pompeii, where a very long-legged mule bears a large panier beneath which a *stratum* is spread.[175] (Pl. 92)

Pack-mules were also pressed into the service of the hunt. The rounded end of a third-century sarcophagus is carved with a fervid scene of huntsmen returning from the chase with a mule that carries the game, legs in air, on its back;[176] and the topmost frieze of an elaborate African hunt mosaic shows again the homecoming from the field with huntsmen conducting a prancing mule on whose back an animal, perhaps a netted boar, has been bound.[177] Horace writes of beasts of burden loaded with hunting-nets; and of a sham hunter, Gargilius, who rides through the city in the morning with every kind of gadget for the hunt and returns with a mule bringing home on its back a purchased boar.[178]

Sometimes a muleteer would expect his beast to carry himself as well as its load, as in the episode humorously portrayed in mosaic in the peristyle of the palace of the emperors at Istanbul. Here a crafty-eyed, rebellious mule has with one vicious and successful upward kick of its hind-legs rid itself of pack-saddle, bundles of faggots and rider all at one swoop.[179] (Pl. 98)

From republican times onwards pack-mules formed an indispensable adjunct to the Roman army, as passages in Livy and Caesar testify.[180] According to Suetonius, Gaius on one occasion forced his praetorians to carry their standards on mule-back.[181] On Trajan's Column two mules bearing heavy burdens on saddles of the stiff type are conducted by a soldier; another mule is almost hidden by its load of arms – two large shields and a helmet; and in a third scene two soldiers are piling pack after pack upon a mule's back, while a third soldier holds its head.[182]

Other Uses of Mules

Very occasionally mules seem to have been employed as mounts in place of horses. On a relief on the 'Pilier du Cavalier' at Arlon there is a rider apparently on mule-back;[183] and the animal from whose back on Trajan's Column a Dacian messenger has slithered in the emperor's presence is certainly a mule.[184] Apuleius' reference to the use of aged mules for turning mills has been already cited (p. 184); and when Gaius, then in Gaul, sent to Rome for all the paraphernalia of the old palace in order to sell it to the provincials, he requisitioned animals from the bakeries (*pistrinensia iumenta*) to transport the stuff in the public vehicles (*meritoria vehicula*) that he also commandeered. Since the result of this action was a shortage of bread in Rome, the animals in question must have been the mules or donkeys that had turned the corn-mills.[185]

DONKEYS

The Wild Ass

The wild ass, native to Africa, Syria and Asia Minor,[186] seems to have occupied a higher place in the estimation of the Roman world than did the wild horse. It is represented rather more frequently in art, particularly in hunting scenes, and, according to our records, it appeared somewhat more often in the shows. It was valued when tamed for breeding purposes; and its flesh was served as food at table.

In the wild the ass was killed and eaten by the larger felines, as is portrayed in an Algerian mosaic pavement from Cherchel, where it forms a lion's prey (cf. p. 29).[187] Sometimes the object of its human hunters was to kill it, probably for eating purposes, if not simply for sport; this is illustrated by a second-century AD fresco painting, now in the Louvre, from Dura-Europos, where a mounted huntsman wearing Parthian dress is shooting at a pair of onagers that flee before him.[188] Ammianus Marcellinus describes how the animal would defend itself by kicking up stones behind it at its pursuers, so as to wound or even kill them.[189] More often the aim was to take the ass alive by means of a lasso thrown round its neck, as Arrian and Aelian state[190] and as hunt mosaics, such as those from Hippo Regius and Carthage (cf. pp. 26, 27), show. The main reason for their capture was doubtless to tame them as breeders. Pliny and Varro both name Phrygia and Lycaonia in Asia Minor as the best sources of the creatures; and Pliny notes that as a sire the foal of a wild ass and a domestic she-ass is the best of all,[191] the males being mated with mares to produce mules.[192] Another purpose of taking them was display. In Ptolemy II's procession there were four pairs of the animals in harness, along with seven teams of what may have been a species of them, known as 'ass-deer' (ὀνέλαφοι);[193] and it seems very likely that the onagri that accompanied the Roman Vedius, whom Cicero met at Laodicea (cf. p. 56), were tamed and perhaps put to draw carriages.[194] They also featured in venationes (cf. p. 30).

The wild ass was shown, and apparently admired, at the spectacles in Martial's time.[195] Ὄναγροι were among the 'shipwrecked' animals in Septimius Severus' show (cf. p. 18); [196] and 20 and 30 of them respectively graced the Gordians' collections.[197] According to Pliny, the foals of African asses, called lalisiones, were the most tasty.[198]

The Domesticated Donkey

The Roman attitude to domestic donkeys was, in general, unsympathetic and harsh. They were looked upon as stupid, if extremely strong, capable of bearing the severest beatings, and fit for the roughest types of work. Pliny writes of the vilis asellus used for ploughing in Africa;[199] and Varro describes how the valuable donkeys of a certain owner have only one little slave to tend them and are given very little barley to eat and only water used for household purposes to drink.[200] Columella paints a detailed picture of the *vilis vulgarisque asellus* and of the services expected of it.[201] It requires, he says, very little fodder, since it feeds on leaves, thorns of briar bushes, or bundles of twigs, and actually thrives on chaff. Furthermore, it endures the neglect of a careless master and will bear most patiently blows and hunger (*plagarum et penuriae tolerantissimus*). It takes longer to break down than any other animal, needs little care, and will undertake essential tasks beyond its share (*supra portionem*), such as breaking up easily worked soil with a light plough, for instance, in Baetica in Spain and all over Libya.[202] It can also draw heavy loads on carts. Columella then quotes Virgil's description of the donkey-driver loading his slow beast's sides with olive oil or cheap fruit and later returning home from town with a millstone or a lump of black pitch as its burden.[203] He concludes with the remark that the animal's almost invariable task (*paene solemnis est huius pecoris labor*) is turning a mill and grinding corn (cf. pp. 195, 196). Ovid notes the wretched lot of the long-eared ass, its perpetual beatings and tardy progress.[204] Plautus twice refers to floggings as its special mark.[205] Apuleius calls it the most ill-starred of quadrupeds, pitful and miserable;[206] and dilates in many other passages on the cruel treatment it receives.[207]

Columella, Varro and Pliny all name Arcadia as the prime source from which working donkeys are obtained, Varro adding the Peloponnese and Varro and Pliny adding Reate in central Italy as supplying some of the best and largest specimens.[208] Columella insists three times on the value of the ass's dung as manure.[209] Pliny cites ploughing and mule-breeding as among the donkey's chief services.[210] Cato lays down among the items of equipment needed for an oliveyard of an area of 240 *iugera* three pack-asses to carry manure and one ass for the mill (*asini ornati clitellarii qui stercus vectent tres, asinus molarius*), together with manure hampers, manure baskets, three pack-saddles and three pads (*instrata*) for the asses, and a donkey-mill. A vineyard of 100 *iugera* needs two draught-donkeys (*asini plostrarii*) and one donkey for the mill, together with one donkey-yoke, three sets of donkey-harness, three pack-saddles, three baskets for wine-lees, and three donkey-mills.[211] Varro also mentions asses working mills and carrying loads for agricultural purposes; and he draws a vivid picture of trains of pack-asses, owned by merchants from Brundisium and Apulia, that carry oil or wine or corn or any other type of merchandise to the south Italian seaports for shipment abroad.[212]

The pack was, indeed, one of the donkey's special grievances. Horace describes the stubborn ass that lowers its head when a heavy load is piled on it.[213] In Apuleius' *Metamorphoses* the ass Lucius complains that his driver heaped on his back bundles of wood heavy enough for an elephant rather than an ass to carry (*ut fascium molem elephanto non asino parem putares*); and if the bundles slipped to one side he added stones to balance them on the other.[214] In another passage we are told how one of this ass's owners, a gardener, drove him laden with vegetables to the nearest town and then, having sold his produce, mounted the beast and rode it home. Later the donkey had to carry to a town several miles off, not only a sack and empty wineskins, but also the person of the gardener himself.[215] Later still the ass passed into the hands of a soldier who decked it and loaded it up for the journey as though it were an 'ass at arms' (*onustum et prorsum exornatum armatumque militariter perducit ad viam*). The animal had to carry on its back a glittering helmet, a burnished shield, and a spear with a very long shaft (cf. p. 191).[216] On the peristyle mosaic of the imperial palace at Istanbul a boy offers a nosebag to a pack-ass. But the animal turns its head away and looks back ruefully at its load.[217] (Pl. 97)

But the donkey's greatest misery of all was toiling at the mill. Apuleius' horrifying description of the scene at a baker's mill in which the ass Lucius was forced to work in blinkers (*luminibus obtectis*), alongside horses and mules, has already been quoted (p. 184). And when to mill-work was added threshing in the company of horses (cf. p. 184), and the prospect of being put to draw the plough (cf. pp. 194, 196), the patient ass was at the end of its endurance, a state to which a poem in the *Greek Anthology* gives moving expression. 'Why do you drive me, the slow-footed, braying ass, round and round with the threshing horses? Is it not enough that, driven in a circle and blindfolded, I am forced to turn the heavy millstone? But I must compete with horses too. Is the next task in store for me to plough with my neck's strength the earth that the share sends curving?'[218] Donkeys at the mill appear in a number of works of art. On the stone frieze of the tomb in Rome of Eurysaces the master-baker each of two corn-mills is worked by an ass.[219] On a somewhat crudely moulded terracotta relief on the façade of Tomb 78 in the Isola Sacra necropolis near Ostia we see an animal that could be a horse or a mule, but whose length of ears rather suggests an ass, turning a mill;[220] and they are certainly donkeys that work the mill on the *discus* of each of two clay lamps in the British Museum collection.[221]

An agricultural task for donkeys apparently rather less arduous than working mills, threshing, ploughing and carrying loads of manure was that of pushing the lighter type of reaping machine (*vallus*), described by Pliny as a very large frame fitted with teeth, driven through the corn by a pack-animal (*iumentum*), and used on the large estates of Gaul (cf. p. 152).[222] That donkeys worked this machine is known from a tomb-relief found in two fragments at Buzenol-Montauban, which shows a man walking backwards as he clears the teeth of chaff, the two wheels (one in very low relief), and the head and neck with halter and the forepart of the body of a donkey between shafts, leisurely propelling the contraption forward. A fragment found at Arlon long before the Buzenol discovery, but not until then fully recognized for what it is, completes the picture with the rump and tail of the animal and a man between the shafts pushing behind it.[223] (Pl. 95)

Again according to Apuleius donkeys could be made to do tricks, for all their alleged stupidity. On one occasion the ass Lucius was brought to table and encouraged, not only to eat the delicate fare set before it, but also to gulp down a cup of wine at a single draught. After this it was taught to perform a number of turns – to recline at table on its elbow, to wrestle, and to dance on its hind-legs; also to answer when spoken to by lifting its head if it did not want anything and by bowing if it did, winking with first one eye and then with the other at the cup-bearer if it felt like a drink.[224] At the festival of Isis Lucius saw an ass got up as Pegasus with wings glued to its back (*pinnis agglutinatis*).[225]

Ass's milk was held to have a purgative value;[226] and was noted for its thickness.[227] It was also used by ladies of fashion for a beauty-bath.[228] The dead ass was valued for its skin and its carcase was given to the poor for food.[229]

Of the donkeys of mythology that feature in art none is more famous than the ass that serves Silenus as a mount. One of its most attractive portraits in this capacity is that on a mosaic pavement, now in the Sfax Museum, from La Chebba in Tunisia. Here Silenus lolls jovially on the creature's back, holding a tambourine and a long staff.

But the donkey's expression indicates that it does not find the tweaking of its right ear by the Pan in front of it, or the twisting of its tail by the Satyr behind it, at all amusing. A bell is suspended round its neck and there is harness on its head, but its bridle is hanging loose.[230]

The donkey's roles in biblical episodes are depicted in works of early Christian art. Balaam and his talking ass, waylaid by the angel, appears twice among the fourth-century paintings in the recently discovered catacomb on the Via Latina.[231] On one of the panels on the sixth-century ivory throne of Archbishop Maximianus at Ravenna is represented the arrival of Mary and Joseph at Bethlehem. Mary is seated on an ass, with her right arm flung round Joseph's shoulders, while an angel leads the weary animal by the bridle.[232] In one of the late fourth-century paintings under the church of Santa Maria in Stelle, near Verona, Christ is shown entering Jerusalem on the back of a long-eared, high-stepping donkey.[233]

EPONA, PATRONESS OF EQUINES

The goddess Epona, patroness of equine animals and of their owners and grooms, has already been mentioned in connection with dogs of healing and the underworld, a dog being one of her attributes in a number of representations of her (cf. p. 123). The dog, together with such other of her emblems as the cornucopia, the *patera* and the basket or bowl of fruits or cakes, expressed her role as a Mother-goddess, sometimes associated with the *Matres*,[234] and bestower of well-being and fertility both in this world and in the world beyond the grave. But it was to horses, mules and donkeys that Epona's motherly care in this world was mainly directed; and it is in their company that she features in most of the works of art connected with her.[235]

Epona was known and worshipped in Italy and in other Mediterranean lands. Juvenal says that a certain Lateranus, mad on horses, swears only by Epona and her images painted in the reeking stables.[236] Apuleius describes a small shrine of the goddess, with her image carefully decked with garlands of fresh roses, on the central pillar of a stable in Thessaly.[237] It is possible that we have such an image of her in the figure of a veiled woman riding a donkey towards the left that was painted in a niche in a Pompeian house. It is true that this figure seems to hold a human baby, which Epona does not do in any of her well authenticated portraits: but that might be just a symbol of her generally maternal character.[238] The African Tertullian accuses the pagans of worshipping every kind of pack-animal and whole horses, together with their goddess Epona;[239] and Minucius Felix complains that they treat as sacred whole asses in their stables, along with Epona as their own and the animals' patron-ess.[240]

But Epona's name is said to be of Celtic derivation; and the vast majority of her monuments come from the northern and western provinces, with a few from Italy, Africa and Spain. Some of these monuments are merely dedicatory inscriptions; but many more show her portrait in bronze, terracotta and, above all, stone; once she appears in wood.[241] One figured and inscribed monument, a bronze plaque from Alise-Sainte-Reine (Côte-d'Or), now in the Saint-Germain Museum, depicts, not the goddess herself, but two of her protégés – a man in a two-wheeled gig driving a yoked mule between shafts.[242] But mostly she is either riding on an animal, nearly always on a horse, or she sits or stands between two or more beasts. When she rides she is usually in the side-saddle attitude, as in three fine bronze groups, now in the Cabinet des Médailles, Paris, from Bâgé-le-Châtel (Ain), Reims and Loisia (Jura) respectively; in the last case her mare's foal trots beside it.[243] Numerous stone and most of the terracotta representations show her in the same pose. But in other groups she rides astride, as in one terracotta piece[244] and on two particularly fine stone reliefs from Luxemburg.[245] On a stone relief from Bregenz in Austria she is seated side-saddle on a large horse while four other equines press around her.[246] (Pl. 93)

To turn to the non-mounted renderings of Epona, a bronze group in the British Museum, said to have been found in Wiltshire, shows her enthroned between two foals.[247] On two stone reliefs from Köngen (Württemberg) and Kapersburg (Hesse) respectively she is seated in the centre with a basket or bowl on her lap and is flanked by outwards facing horses.[248] On two stone reliefs from Bulgaria she stands, in one case, and is seated, in the other, between two horses that face towards her and on whose heads she lovingly lays her hands.[249] Most unusual is a stone relief from Beihungen (Württemberg), now in the Stuttgart Museum, with two superimposed sculptured registers. In the upper one the goddess is centrally enthroned, with two horses advancing towards her from the left and four from the right. In the lower register three mules draw a four-wheeled cart or carriage rightwards towards the scene of the sacrifice of a pig, presumably in Epona's honour.[250]

This wealth of votive monuments offered to the patroness of equines is an index of the care and affection that individual owners of these animals frequently bestowed upon them, especially on their horses.

CHAPTER XVII

HARES, RABBITS AND MICE

HARES

THE 'LEPORIA', OR GAME RESERVES, on the country estates of late republican times, which then contained animals of several kinds, including deer, cattle and boars, were, so Varro tells us, called by that name because 'our remote ancestors' (*tritavi*) had kept only hares in them.[1] A little later,[2] when writing of the estate at Tarquinii of Quintus Fulvius Lippinus (cf. p. 16), he explains how these reserves were carefully fenced in and planted with spreading trees, bushes and thick grass in which the hares could hide themselves during the daytime, safe from preying animals and the attacks of eagles, whose habit of swooping down and carrying off the succulent little creatures in their claws is often illustrated, as for instance on a mosaic from Palestrina in the Vatican.[3] Everyone knows, Varro says, that if a few male and female hares are put in a *leporium* it will be full in no time, so prolific are these quadrupeds (*tanta fecunditas huius quadripidis*).[4]

Varro then describes the two main types of hare proper. The common Italian kind has short fore-legs, long hind-legs, long ears, and a coat that is dark (*pullus*) on the head, back and sides, but white on the belly. To this class also belong the very large (*praemagni*) hares found in Transalpine Gaul and Macedonia and the more moderately sized animals found in Spain and Italy. Hares of the second type, natives of the Alpine regions of Gaul, are completely white. The last, he remarks, seldom found their way to Rome, although Calpurnius Siculus mentions snow-white hares (*nivei lepores*) among the marvels at the spectacles in Nero's time (cf. p. 94).[5] Martial's favourite 'turn' at the shows, that of lions taught to play with hares without doing them the slightest harm, has already been recorded (p. 62); and, along with 'unwarlike wild goats' (*imbelles capreae*), the timid hare (*sollicitus lepus*) was netted in the Circus at the feast of Flora (cf. p. 164).[6]

But the main Roman sport where hares were concerned was the
hunting of them in the open field. Virgil writes of chasing the long-
eared hares;[7] and we have already noted Martial's allusions to
hunting hares on horseback (p. 174), the relief at Trier from one of
the Neumagen tombs, on which a mounted huntsman, reaching
home, holds up by the hind-legs the large hare that he has killed
(p. 175), and the huntsman on foot doing the same on the Piazza
Armerina 'Little Hunt' mosaic (p. 24). Again, mention has been
made apropos of harriers and horses of the Oudna hunt mosaic
(p. 105), of the 'Little Hunt' pavement at Piazza Armerina (pp. 105,
174), and of the Castor-ware hare and hound hunt cups (p. 105). A
mosaic group from Carthage in the British Museum shows another
fleeing hare with a hound in hot pursuit.[8] Other mosaic renderings of
hare hunts show the little creature cowering in its form in the vain
hope that it will not be seen. Such a situation is clearly portrayed in
the Piazza Armerina 'Little Hunt', where a very plump hare
crouches in a thicket at the foot of a tree, while a mounted huntsman
is about to strike it with a cruel double-barbed hunting-spear
(cf. p. 24). In the central zone of a pavement from El-Djem, now in
the Bardo Museum in Tunis, the form consists of a thick wreath of
grass and leaves in the centre of which the hare is sheltering. The two
harriers that have been unleashed for the attack are hesitating near the
form, uncertain, so it seems, as to where the hare can be, and one of
them is looking back at the huntsman behind as though for instructions.[9] On another Piazza Armerina pavement the hunters are
children on foot, one of whom lunges towards the right and drives
his hunting-spear into the breast of a very fine red hare, while blood
flows freely from the wound.[10] (Pls 102-4, 106-7)

It is, of course, as a trophy of the hunting-field that a hare appears
in art as an attribute, grasped by either the hind-legs or the fore-legs,
of figures that personify the months and seasons. Such is the case with
'October' in the illustrated calendar of A D 354;[11] and with the child,
that may also be 'October', on one of the short sides of the Christian
sarcophagus of Junius Bassus in the Vatican, dated A D 359.[12] On
season-sarcophagi the dead hare is the attribute now of 'Autumn',
now of 'Winter'.[13] On a mosaic pavement from Eleutheropolis in
Palestine the hooded bust of 'Winter' grasps a hare.[14] The chief
purpose of killing hares in the field was to eat them, since their flesh
was regarded as a first-class delicacy.[15]

A happier fate awaited the hare that was taken alive, tamed, and kept as a pet. A wall-painting from the Roman villa in Trastevere in Rome shows a woman musician seated, while the girl who stands before her presents her with a tiny hare.[16] Two other Roman paintings depict in a each case a girl seated beside a herm and fondling a hare that is perched on its haunches on her knee.[17] A stone tomb-relief found in Roman Lincoln and now in the cathedral cloisters, of which only the upper part survives, represents a boy who is cuddling his pet, a hare, against his breast.[18] It is possibly the portrait of a favourite hare that is carved in low relief at the top of the tombstone, found at Housesteads and now in the Museum of Antiquities of Newcastle upon Tyne, of an army doctor attached to the First Tungrian Cohort.[19] Alternatively, the animal, renowned for its productivity as we have seen, may appear here as a symbol of after-life fertility.

On the peristyle mosaic of the great palace of the Byzantine emperors at Istanbul a boy is capturing a sleeping hare by popping a basket over it – perhaps to keep it as a pet.[20]

Hares, like bears (cf. p. 99 and p. 363, note 56), seem to have impressed the Romans by their partiality for fruit; and when they are depicted in art purely for their own sake they regale themselves on figs and grapes. A pilaster from the Lateran collection is carved with a 'peopled' vine-scroll, on one of the stems of which is balanced a wicker basket heaped with figs: a hare has climbed onto the pile and is feeding busily.[21] On a mosaic panel found at Gurgi in the Tripoli oasis a hare is crouching, eager with anticipation, before three enormous figs.[22] A hare is guzzling grapes in a painting from a tomb south of Rome[23] and in a painted panel now in the Naples Museum.[24] Finally, in the vine-scroll border on the ivory episcopal throne at Ravenna, dating from the sixth century, there are hares either eating grapes or reaching up to get at them.[25]

RABBITS

The Romans rightly regarded rabbits as generically inseparable from hares; and Varro describes a third type of hare, found in Spain, as similar to the Italian hare, but lower in build and known as the *cuniculus*.[26] He derives their name from the fact that they dig tunnels, that is, burrows, for themselves under ground (*cuniculi dicti ab eo quod sub terra cuniculos ipsi facere solent*); while Martial playfully suggests that it was from rabbits' burrows that humans borrowed the idea of siege-mines in warfare.[27] Catullus' famous phrase *cuniculosa Celtiberia*[28] could, indeed, mean 'Spain full of mines', since the peninsula was rich in its mineral resources of gold, silver, copper, lead, and iron. On the other hand, it could equally well be translated as 'rabbity Spain'; for the rabbit was held to be so characteristic of the country that it appears as the adjunct of a number of the figures of 'Hispania' in Hadrian's well-known 'province' coin series.[29] Furthermore, Strabo declares that Spain bred few baneful wild beasts (ὀλέθρια θήρια) apart from the burrowing rabbit (λαγιδεύς or λεβηρίς), which ruins plants and crops by gnawing away at the roots. This happens all over Spain, as far north as Marseilles, and the creatures even infest the islands. He has a tale of how the inhabitants of the Balearic Isles sent an embassy to Rome asking that another land might be given them, since they were being driven out of their own by the rabbits, whose increase they were unable to control. In less extreme cases, Strabo says, rabbits were regularly hunted in Spain with the aid of wild cats brought in from Libya.[30] Pliny dilates on the Spanish rabbits' extraordinary fertility (*fecunditas innumera*) and their ravaging of crops; and he maintains that the Balearic islanders petitioned Augustus for military aid (*auxilium militare*) wherewith to destroy them.[31] He also declares on the authority of Marcus Varro that a city in Spain was undermined by rabbits.[32] Such yarns are doubtless apocryphal. But they are at least evidence of the close association in the Roman mind of rabbits with Spain.

A large-scale rendering in Roman art of an animal that is more like a rabbit than a hare is a painting in the Naples Museum, found at Herculaneum. The little beast has a dark back and dark ears, but light cheeks, paws and belly. It is sniffing greedily at four huge figs that lie on the ground in front of it.[33] (Pl. 105)

MICE

A dead mouse slain by a domestic cat appeared, as we have seen, on a mosaic pavement, now lost, from Orange (cf. p. 90). A charming bronze figurine of a living mouse, with its nose resting on its forepaws and its long tail curled above its back, was found in a grave in Roman York[34] and has its counterpart in a little bronze in the Bibliothèque Nationale in Paris.[35] The British Museum collection of bronzes includes a number of such tiny mice, one standing on its hind-legs and blowing on a trumpet, others intent on eating fruit or cakes.[36] A small brown fieldmouse is poised on an acanthus tendril on a mosaic from Zliten in Tripolitania.[37] A house-mouse approaches an open walnut on a mosaic in the Lateran collection. Above the figures in the well-known relief at Reims of the Gaulish god Cernunnos, seated cross-legged with Apollo and Mercury standing on either side of him, is a low pediment in the centre of which a large mouse, or possibly a rat, is sculpted.[38] It is very naturalistically worked; but its meaning in this context remains a mystery. (Pls 99–101)

The dormouse (*glis*, *nitella*) was another special treat at the Roman table. *Glires*, sprinkled with honey and poppy-seeds, were served at Trimalchio's feast;[39] and some very big ones appeared at a meal described by Ammianus Marcellinus.[40] Martial, in his account of the villa at Baiae of his friend Faustinus, writes of a country visitor (*rusticus salutator*) bringing sleepy dormice as an offering;[41] and in another poem he calls the creature *aurea nitella*.[42] He also makes a dormouse say that its whole winter is passed in sleep and that it is all the fatter at that season for feeding on sleep alone.[43] Varro writes of special pens (*gliaria*) and tubs (*dolia*) in which dormice were kept for the purpose of fattening them on acorns, chestnuts and walnuts [44] – an end that was also achieved, Pliny says, by a diet of beech-nuts.[45]

A delightful couple of dormice of the squirrel-tailed variety, common in Europe, can be seen lurking in the vine-scroll on the Lateran pilaster already mentioned (p. 202). They seem to be busy with a bowl of nuts.[46]

CHAPTER XVIII

SEA-MAMMALS

THE ROMANS RECOGNIZED THE CETACEANS, namely the seal (φώκη, *phoca, vitulus marinus*), the dolphin (δέλφις, *delphinus*) and the whale (κῆτος, φάλαινα, *balaena*), as being true mammals that breast-feed their young with milk, in spite of their similarity to fish in outward appearance and their purely aquatic mode of life. Pliny states that seals, dolphins and whales all suckle their offspring.[1] Aelian couples the porpoise (φώκαινα) with the dolphin as having milk[2] and compares dolphins to human women in that they have breasts and abundance of milk for feeding their young.[3] 'Oppian', who calls the dolphin more godlike than any other creature, makes the same comparison[4] and he comments on the plentiful milk-supply of seals.[5]

SEALS

Apart from the passages cited above there are but few literary allusions to seals and, so far as the present writer knows, but one representation of them in Roman art. Roman writers were, it seems, mainly impressed by their capacity for sleep. Virgil pictures a scatter of them lying asleep on the shore.[6] Pliny notes that the 'sea-calves' known as *phocae* can breathe and sleep on land;[7] and that their nickname of 'calves' was derived from their habit of lowing in their sleep.[8] Juvenal complains that night traffic in Rome makes enough din to keep even seals awake.[9] As we have already seen (p. 94 and p. 362, note 13), Calpurnius Siculus saw seals sparring with polar bears at a Roman show in Nero's time; and further evidence for performing seals is found in Pliny's account of how seals respond to training, greet the people with noises and bows (reading *nutu*), and when called by name answer with a hoarse roar.[10] We cannot but regret that only one personal name and only one portrait of this engaging animal has come down to us – 'Euploia' ('Fair-Sailing') on the Cos mosaic (cf. pp. 359, note 100, 97 etc.).

Seal-skins were held to give protection against thunderstorms. Augustus, who was terrified of thunder, always carried a seal-skin round with him *pro remedio*;[11] and Pliny declares that some people take refuge from a thunderstorm in seal-skin tents, believing that the seal was the only animal that lightning never struck.[12]

DOLPHINS

More is heard of dolphins in the literary sources. The Romans were particularly taken with the creature's snub-nosed beak (*rostrum simum*) and Pliny maintains that the dolphins themselves knew and actually liked the name 'Snub-Nose' that was given them in consequence.[13] But the Roman world was captivated most of all by the dolphin's extraordinary friendliness to man, of whom it felt no fear, by its alleged passion for music, especially for part-singing and the strains of the water-organ, and its delight in sporting round ships and racing them.[14] Pliny recounts the story of how dolphins helped fishermen in a marsh near Nîmes to catch a huge shoal of mullets (*innumera vis mugilum*) when summoned by the local population on the shore calling 'Snub-Nose' as loudly as it could (*totusque populus e litore quanto potest clamore conciet Simonem*) and how they duly received their portion of the spoils from their friends' hands (*partesque e manibus accipiant*).[15] Aelian tells a similar tale.[16]

Particularly charming is Pliny's story of the dolphin inhabiting the Lucrine Lake in Augustus' time that was so enamoured of a poor boy of Baiae that it came when he called 'Snub-Nose', took bits of bread from him, and carried him on its back all the way across the water to Puteoli, where he went to school, and home again. When the boy fell ill and died, the dolphin died too of a broken heart (*desiderio expiravit*).[17] Both the Elder and the Younger Pliny tell the tale of the tame dolphin of Hippo Diarrhytus on the north coast of Africa.[18] It fed out of people's hands and let itself be stroked (*ex hominum manu vescens praebensque se tractandum*), played with boys when they went swimming, and carried one special boy to and fro on its back. Crowds of people from the town came to see the sight. The governor, Octavius Avitus, is said to have had ointment poured on it out of superstition, a proceeding which the dolphin greatly resented and which caused it to keep away for some time. But when it returned to its gambols it came to an unhappy end. For the little township, being unable to afford the expense of entertaining all the local magistrates who flocked to see the spectacle, and regretting the loss of its one-time seclusion and peace, had the poor beast privately killed.

There can be little doubt that these dolphin stories of the Roman period are, to some extent at least, fictitious. All the same, the docility and friendliness of the creatures, so far as human beings are concerned, have been confirmed by observation and photography in modern times, when strong attachments between dolphins and children in particular have been recorded.[19] It was probably some experience of this kind with the animals that first inspired the Greek myth of Arion carried to safety, out of the reach of the pirates who had captured him, on the back of a music-loving dolphin in return for a lyre recital. The episode is often portrayed in Roman art, for example, on a pavement at Piazza Armerina,[20] on a mosaic from Thina in Tunisia,[21] and in a Pompeian painting.[22] Hence, too, the constantly repeated theme in the art of Roman times of Cupids riding dolphins. For instance, Galataea's message to Polyphemus is delivered by a Cupid on dolphin-back in a painting from Herculaneum;[23] there are two Cupids on dolphins on a pavement from the Villa del Nilo at Lepcis Magna;[24] and a Cupid on dolphin-back forms the central picture of one of the best-preserved mosaics in the palace at Fishbourne near Chichester.[25] An especially delightful version of the theme is on one of the short sides of the 'Marriage of Peleus and Thetis' sarcophagus in the Villa Albani collection in Rome: here a Cupid mounted on a dolphin holds in one hand a bridle, in the other an open sunshade.[26] Variants of the Cupids and dolphins motif in paintings from Pompeii and Herculaneum show a Cupid standing on the backs of a pair of dolphins and driving them with whip and bridle,[27] or standing in a racing *biga*.[28] (Pl. 109)

Besides their ubiquitous appearance in marine scenes, whether alone or mounted, and as allusions to, or symbols of, the sea in other contexts, dolphins, again either mounted or alone, frequently feature in funerary art as symbols of the journey of the soul across the ocean to the Blessed Isles. An outstanding instance of this is on the lid of a fourth-century Christian sarcophagus found beneath the floor of Old St Peter's in Rome.[29] At the centre of the lid is a framed panel designed to hold the name, age, etc. of the deceased, but never actually inscribed; and converging on it from left and right are eight portly dolphins rolling across the waves, two by two, with Neptune's trident emerging from the water between the two pairs on either side. They have come to escort the dead; and the carver has adopted a purely pagan theme and given it a Christian interpretation. On the south-eastern fringe of the Roman world the Nabataean Arabs worshipped Atargatis, the dolphin-goddess.[30]

The dolphin, says Pliny, is the swiftest of all animals, not only of sea-beasts;[31] and it was surely as symbols of speed that figures of dolphins adorned the *spina* (central wall) of circuses. A vigorous bronze dolphin of early imperial date, now in the British Museum, is a natural form for a water-spout to take. (Pl. 110)

WHALES

The whale, for which *balaena* is the usual Latin term, is located by Juvenal in the seas around Britain[32] and by Pliny in the Indian Ocean, where he couples with the *balaena* the smaller *pistris*, which may have been a lesser whale or a shark: the former, he says, extends over four *iugera*, the latter over twenty cubits.[33] Almost certainly a type of whale is the *physter*, which Pliny locates in the Gallic ocean and describes as rising up like a huge column and spouting streams of water over ships.[34] Ausonius locates the *balaena* in the Atlantic.[35] According to Pliny, whales reached the Mediterranean;[36] and Dio Cassius recounts how in the reign of Septimius Severus a huge whale (κῆτος ὑπερμέγεθες) was washed up on shore in the Portus Augusti near the Tiber mouth. A model was made of it for display at a wild beast show and fifty bears were driven into it.[37] There can be little doubt that the *orca*, which appeared in the harbour of Ostia in Claudius' time, was a kind of whale. The emperor ordered it to be caught in nets and he himself and members of his praetorian cohorts made a spectacle for the Roman people by attacking it. It sunk a boat with its spouting (*refletu beluae oppletum unda*).[38]

No renderings of whales, so far as the present writer is aware, are known in Roman art. But we do know the personal name, 'Porphyrios' ('Purple'), of one late Roman whale, which according to Procopius[39] annoyed the city of Constantinople and neighbouring towns for fifty years, eluding all the means devised by the Emperor Justinian for its capture. But at last, when pursuing dolphins one day, it came too close to land, got struck in the mud, was dragged to shore with ropes by the local people, and finally killed. It was 30 cubits (about 45 feet) long and 10 cubits (15 feet) broad.

CHAPTER XIX

FISH, CRUSTACEANS AND MOLLUSCS

IT GOES WITHOUT SAYING that fishing for food in seas, lakes, rivers and streams, whether privately for immediate home consumption or on a large scale for the market, was the activity concerned with these creatures that occupied by far the most important place in the life of the Roman world at large – as, of course, it has done and does in other areas and in periods before and since Roman times. Innumerable fishing scenes, *genre*, with human figures, and mythological, frequently with Cupids thus employed, in works of art of all kinds – mosaics, paintings, reliefs, metalwork and so forth – illustrate the universal interest both in angling from the shore and in catching fish in bulk in nets or wicker baskets (*nassae*) from boats. More specifically Roman was the practice in Italy, particularly under the late Republic and early Empire, of keeping fish in artificially constructed ponds (*piscinae, vivaria*), comparable to some extent to modern aquaria, largely for show and for the pleasure that they gave their owners.

Varro, who had two small oblong *piscinae* in the aviary built on his estate at Casinum,[1] distinguishes two types of fish-ponds.[2] First there were the fresh-water ponds (*dulces*) kept by ordinary people for profit (*apud plebem et non sine fructu*), the content of them being sold on the market for the table; and secondly the sea-water ponds (*salsae, maritimae*) owned by the high-born rich (*nobiles*); and it is of the latter type, described by Varro as designed more for a spectacle than to line the purse (*magis ad oculos pertinent quam ad vesicam*), that he and other writers have naturally most to say.

According to Pliny the fashion for owning *vivaria* for fish, including the somewhat lamprey-like sea-eels or *murenae*, was started before the end of the second century BC by Licinius Murena, who earned thereby this nickname for himself and his descendants.[3] About the same time, that is, before the Marsic War (91–89 BC), the first oyster ponds (*ostrearum vivaria*) were made by Sergius Orata, his motive being ostentation, not gluttony (*nec gulae causa sed avaritiae*).[4] No expense was spared. Lucius Lucullus is reported to have had a channel dug through a hill in order to bring sea-water to his fish-ponds near Naples.[5] The lengthy instructions for the making of fish-ponds that Columella gives[6] indicate how widespread the practice was; and Cicero scathingly dubs some of the people whom he dislikes 'fish-ponders' (*piscinarii*).[7] It is true that sometimes these *vivaria* did serve the interests of greed. Seneca says that some people fattened sea-fish in them for the purpose of keeping their tables well supplied however stormy the weather at sea might be;[8] and Martial describes how in the villa of his friend Apollinaris at Formiae, the *mensa* could always be furnished, however fiercely a storm was raging, by the master letting down his line from his bed or couch to catch turbots (*rhombi*) or bass (*lupi*).[9]

But more often, it would seem, the denizens of the ponds were not eaten, but cherished as pets and lived to a ripe old age. In the same poem[10] Martial pictures the dainty sea-eel (*delicata murena*) swimming up in answer to its master's voice (*natat ad magistrum*), a favourite mullet (*mugil notus*) being called by an usher, and old mullets of another type (*mulli*) coming forward when summoned to appear. Cicero writes scornfully of prominent persons who imagine themselves in heaven if the bearded mullets in their ponds come to be fondled (*ad manum accedunt*).[11] Varro recounts[12] how his friend Quintus Hortensius, with whom he often stayed at Bauli, never ate the contents of his ponds, but always sent to Puteoli to buy fish for his table from the market there.[13] He adds that Hortensius would part more willingly with carriage-mules (*raedariae mulae*) from his stables than with a bearded mullet (*barbatus mullus*) from his ponds; and that when his fish were off colour he was no less attentive to them than he was to sick slaves. Gaius Hirrius was so devoted to his *murenae*, for which he was the first to make a separate pond (*murenarum vivarium privatim excogitavit ante alios*), that he would only lend them (refusing to part with them at any price) to Julius Caesar for show at the banquets that he gave in honour of his triumph – 2,000 *murenae* in Varro's version of the incident, 6,000 in Pliny's.[14] *Murenae* would, indeed, appear to have been special favourites. Aelian has a story of the female *murena* belonging to 'the Roman Crassus' which her master adorned with ear-rings and a jewelled necklace, as though she were a pretty girl. She came swimming up when he called her, recognizing his voice, and ate promptly and eagerly what he offered her. When she died he wept and buried her.[15] According to Macrobius the Crassus in question was the censor and orator; and when the *murena* died he went into mourning (*atratus*) and grieved for her as though she were his daughter.[16] Pliny recalls the similar tale of Varro's friend, the orator Hortensius (cf. p. 210), who wept for the death of the *murena* that he kept in his pond at Bauli; and the story of Antonia, the wife of Drusus, who came into possession of the same villa and decked with ear-rings the *murena* that she loved.[17]

These engaging stories may well be, in part at least, fictitious; and it may be hoped that the less pleasing tales of Vedius Pollio fattening his *murenae* on the flesh of delinquent slaves were also exaggerations.[18] Perhaps apocryphal are the fish that died at the age of sixty, having been put by this same Pollio into the emperor's fish-ponds at Pausylipon near Naples, and the two fish of the same age and kind that Seneca stated to be still living on.[19] The species to which these ancient ones belonged is not recorded; and the same is the case with the tame fish in several imperial villas that fed from the hand (*e manu vescuntur pisces*)[20] and came up sometimes one by one when called by name (*ad nomina venire, quosdam singulos*).[21] Nor are we told the species of the pet fish (*pisces delicati*) that lived in Domitian's fish-pond (*lacus*) at Baiae: they knew their master and licked his hand (*norunt dominum manumque lambunt*), had personal names, and came swimming up when called at the sound of their master's voice (*nomen habent et ad magistri/vocem quisque sui venit citatus*).[22]

To return to the eating of fish, there are Juvenal's well-known tale of the monstrous turbot (*spatium admirabile rhombi*) of Domitian's reign[23] and Martial's remark that one can never find a dish big enough to hold a turbot.[24] From Martial too we learn that the sturgeon (*acipensis*) was considered to be fare fit for the emperor's table;[25] that the gudgeon (*gobius*) was regularly served at dinner-parties as an *entrée*;[26] and that the entrails of the wrasse (*scarus*), but not the rest, make a tasty dish.[27] The famous fish-sauce (*garum*) is mentioned by several writers, notably by Martial, who calls the kind that was made from mackerel (*scomber*) an expensive gift, and by Pliny, who says that the best and most costly came from the fish-ponds (*cetaria*) at New Carthage in Spain and went by the name of 'sauce of the allies' (*garum sociorum*).[28] Ausonius' well-known catalogue of river-fish to be found in the Moselle[29] was inspired largely by interest in the creatures for their own sake, but also, to some extent at least, by their value as food. The fourteen species that he lists are the chub (*capito*), trout (*salar*), roach (*rhedo*), grayling (*umbra*), barbel (*barbus*), salmon (*salmo*), eel-pout (*mustela*), perch (*perca*), pike (*lucius*), tench (*tinca*), bleak (*alburnus*), shad (*alausa*), gudgeon (*gobius*), and sheet-fish (*silurus*).

That fish were regarded as symbols of the living dead in pagan religious thought seems to be proved by their frequent presence in funerary art. One of the clearest instances of this is a relief from one of the mausolea at Ghirza in Tripolitania, where eight large fish are swimming round, and nibbling at, a central rosette, emblem of life beyond the grave.[30] It is just possible that this traditional association of the fish with immortality may have helped to popularize in early Christian thought, art and epigraphy the significance of ἰχθῦς as an acrostic for Ἰησοῦς Χριστός, Θεοῦ υἱὸς σωτήρ ('Jesus Christ, Son of God, Saviour') and as a Eucharistic symbol.

We turn now to what might be described as the equivalent in representational art of the sea-water *piscinae* or *vivaria* described above, namely the floor-mosaics, often in baths, ornamental fountains and pools, that portray assemblages of fish, generally of marine varieties, a theme that was widespread throughout the Roman world. The earliest of these pavements are the late Hellenistic pieces from Pompeii and other sites in Italy; and on these the creatures depicted are those that were seen and captured off the Italian coasts. As Doro Levi has pointed out,[31] these works seem to have formed the models that passed into the pattern-books and were thus repeated far and wide, since there is no trace of the incorporation into these designs of fauna peculiar to the shores of the countries in which the mosaics were laid. On pavements of this early date, down to the first half of the second century AD, the fish are very carefully and naturalistically drawn and modelled and their species can often be identified. But the third, fourth and later centuries witnessed a gradual schematization of forms, a hardening of outlines, and an increasingly conventionalized treatment of such features as eyes, tail and fins. Hence the difficulty frequently encountered in the later period of distinguishing individual fish, in Italian as well as in provincial works.

Sea-fish and other creatures obviously often play a leading role in fishing scenes, as at Piazza Armerina,[32] or in harbour scenes, as in the Terme del Faro (Lighthouse Baths) at Ostia,[33] where they are accompanied by fantastic beasts; or they associate as accessories with marine deities, as on the famous Triumph of Neptune mosaic from Cirta in Algeria[34] and on pavements at Antioch-on-the-Orontes.[35] But from the zoological point of view the most interesting pieces are those which display fish, lobsters, polypi, etc. for their own sake, unaccompanied by figures of men or gods (as in the case of two square polychrome mosaic panels in the Museo Nazionale Romano), or with these in a quite subordinate capacity.

Of such marine studies the most familiar and the earliest are two polychrome mosaics from Pompeii, both of them *emblemata* (central panel-pictures), one from the House of the Faun, with an exquisitely naturalistic floral scroll surrounding it,[36] the other from House VIII, 2, 16.[37] The close similarity between them, both in style and in content, strongly suggests that they are from the same workshop or at least from the same copy-book. In each of them the central feature is a group depicting a fight to the death between a lobster, a *polypus* and a *murena*, whose hostility to one another (they were, presumably, never actually put into the same *piscina*) was observed and described by Aristotle, Pliny, Aelian and 'Oppian', the account of their deadly conflicts by the last-named being particularly vivid and detailed.[38] On both pieces the *polypus* and lobster are inextricably entangled, while the *murena* is rushing to the fray, its jaws agape to bite. Among the surrounding fish on the House of the Faun *emblema* can be distinguished a torpedo (top centre), two wrasses (top right-hand and bottom left-hand corners), a large bass or *labrax* (bottom centre), with a mullet (*mullus*) just to the left of it, another *mullus* to the left of the central group and a dog-fish to the right of it, with what may be a *scorpaena* just above it, and a smaller bass (top left-hand corner). On the other piece a torpedo and a prawn (*palaemon*) occupy the space immediately above the fight. Below it is a large bass, with a dog-fish and a wrasse between it and the left-hand margin of the picture. Between the central group and the right-hand margin of the picture are another dog-fish and a squid (*loligo*); and above these are a *scorpaena* (?) and another wrasse. To the left of the torpedo (reckoning from the top downwards) are a brown mullet (*mullus*), a grey mullet (*mugil*), and perhaps a small striped bass; and the small fish below the head of the big bass may be another, smaller *mullus*. (Pl. 108)

The probably first-century BC fragmentary fish-mosaic in the three-lobed chamber of the Temple of Fortuna at Palestrina (Praeneste)[39] shows marine creatures very similar to those on the two

Pompeian pieces, including lobsters and prawns, but also dolphins; and there is a *polypus* and *murena* conflict. The triple conflict of *polypus*, lobster and *murena*, which grasps one of the legs of the *polypus* firmly in its jaws, occupies most of the field (the rest being filled with fish) of a polychrome mosaic panel of unrecorded provenance, now in the Victoria and Albert Museum in London.[40] Style and technique suggest that it is later than the Pompeian and Praeneste pieces, perhaps of the late first, or even of the early second, century A D. Definitely later, perhaps of the late second or early third century, is the version of the fight on a polychrome mosaic *emblema* from the villa at Gurgi in the Tripoli oasis.[41] The picture is in a roundel, of which a small segment at the top is occupied by a couple of men in a small sailing boat, while in the centre are a *polypus* and a *murena* interlocked, the latter of unrealistically large size and fiercely biting its opponent: a dolphin and some fish fill the remainder of the field. The somewhat crude drawing and diminished fidelity to nature indicate the devolution of the original model.

From the northern provinces two examples of the sea-fauna theme on mosaics may be cited. A square swimming pool in the villa at Münsingen in Switzerland had an all-over assemblage of dolphins, *murenae* and other sea creatures, now in the Bern Museum, on its floor: these would have been seen through water.[42] The pavement would appear to date from the late second or early third century. The second example comes from Britain, from a villa at Lufton, near Yeovil in Somerset; and it is a first-class illustration of how the rendering of fish had degenerated into stylization and convention by the fourth century.[43] On the floor of the ambulatory that surrounds an octagonal plunge in the bath-block are seven polychrome panels carrying a procession of twenty-nine fish, many of which are blowing bubbles from their noses. But despite the fact that some attempt has been made by the mosaicist to vary them in minor details, it is virtually impossible to identify their species or even to designate them as marine or fresh-water creatures. Only the two eels, wound tightly round, as though intent on strangling, two of the fish, are certain; and of these we cannot tell whether they are river-eels or sea-eels. The procession affords a pleasing pattern, but is frustrating for the naturalist.[44]

Among the small molluscs that live on land the snail (*coclea*) was highly esteemed as an eatable by rich and poor Romans alike. Pliny says that Fulvius Lippinus was the first to introduce snail-preserves (*coclearum vivaria*), on his Tarquinian estate, shortly before the outbreak of the Civil War in 49 BC.[45] Lippinus kept the different species apart, namely the white snails from Reate, the very big ones from Illyricum, the prolific ones from Africa, and the 'Solitan' ones (also African) renowned for their particularly high quality (*nobilitas*). He fattened his snails for the cook-shop (*ganea*) on must (*sapa*) and spelt (*far*), amongst other things. Varro[46] gives careful instructions for choosing the right spot for a snail-enclosure (*coclearium*) and for watering, feeding, and fattening the creatures, again on must and spelt. He lists the whitish (*albulae*) snails from Reate, the big ones from Illyricum, and those of moderate size from Africa. Martial mentions snails as the kind of gift that a poor client might make to his patron at the Saturnalia.[47] A naturalistic picture of a snail, not in a *vivarium*, is grouped with the renderings of a goat, a mouse, and a bird's nest on the 'peopled' acanthus-scroll mosaic from Zliten in Tripolitania (cf. pp. 379, note 26, 280).[48]

CHAPTER XX

FROGS AND TOADS

ONE SPECIAL FEATURE OF FROGS (*ranae*, βάτραχοι) as noted by Roman writers is their greenness.[1] Another, not unexpectedly, is their incessant croaking. Cicero declares that fresh-water frogs (*aquae dulcis alumnae*) announce a coming change of weather by particularly strident croaks;[2] and the croaking of the frogs of the Pomptine Marshes kept Horace awake when journeying to Brundisium.[3] Various portions of a frog's interior were used for remedies and charms.[4]

To turn to frogs in Roman art, a minute frog, now unfortunately headless, appears at the base of the acanthus-scroll dado on the north exterior side of the precinct wall of the Ara Pacis Augustae in Rome.[5] The fact that a tiny lizard (σαύρα) is also found in the same stretch of dado, and again on the south side (cf. p. 220), and that a frog and a lizard appear together, again on a very small scale, on an ancient column-capital reused in the church of San Lorenzo fuori le Mura in Rome, recalls Pliny's story of the two Spartans, Sauras and Batrachos, who were supposed to have signed their names by means of the figures of lizards and frogs carved on the bases of the columns of the temples (which they did not, in fact, build) in the Portico of Octavia in Rome.[6]

This tale sounds most unlikely to be true and may well have been invented to explain the presence of the creatures on the temple columns. They could have been carved there, as on the Ara Pacis and San Lorenzo capital, for the artists' pleasure in depicting them. Alternatively, and perhaps more probably, they were put there for their apotropaic value. That they had such a value is clear from the well-known bronze votive hands of the Anatolian mystery-god Sabazius, which give the 'Latin blessing' with the thumb and first two fingers upright and the third and fourth fingers bent down across the palm. Of these there are examples in the British Museum, at Avenches (Aventicum) in Switzerland, and in the library of the Great St Bernard hospice;[7] and on all of these the figures of frogs, lizards, snakes and tortoises are worked in high relief. Frogs, tortoises and snakes also appear in high relief on certain terracotta cult-pots at Augst and Windisch in Switzerland.[8] The frog-seal that Maecenas used had, no doubt, an apotropaic significance;[9] and bronze seal-boxes with a stud in the form of a frog on the lid have come to light in Roman Britain.[10] Frogs were also associated with the Nymphs and with fountains.[11] (Pl. 114)

In ancient Egyptian religion the frog was the animal companion of the Birth-goddess Heket; and it is in line with this tradition that a frog is rendered in relief on the *disci* of terracotta lamps from Roman Egypt, dated by their shape and on stylistic and archaeo-logical grounds to the third and fourth centuries A D.[12] These lamps were mostly found in houses, not in graves, and would therefore seem to have had more to do with birth into this world than with rebirth after death. Other lamps of the same series do, in fact, show a pair of foetuses. They may well have been lighted when births were taking place to enlist the help of Heket and drive away the demons of darkness.

The toad (*bufo, rubeta,* φρύνη) was distinguished from the frog by the Romans by the pale colour of its skin. Varro writes of the *rana lurida*,[13] Pliny of the *rana rubeta* ('bramble toad');[14] and the latter emphasizes its poisonous character.[15] So far as the present writer knows, no clear representation of a toad, as distinct from a frog, survives in Roman art.

CHAPTER XXI

REPTILES

CROCODILES

OF THE NILOTIC ANIMALS none would appear to have fascinated the Romans more than the crocodile. The tame, sacred crocodiles of Arsinoe (Crocodilopolis) were, in fact, one of Egypt's chief tourist attractions in Roman times. A papyrus of 112 BC preserves the letter of an important Egyptian official, Hermias, to a local one, Horus, enclosing a copy of a letter to a certain Asklepiades that announces the impending visit of a Roman senator, Lucius Mummius, on a sight-seeing trip (πρὸς θεωρίαν) up the Nile from Alexandria to Arsinoe.[1] The distinguished visitor is to receive on landing the regulation gifts and suitable accommodation; and Asklepiades is to see to it that titbits (ψωμίον) are ready for the crocodile named Petesuchos and the other crocodiles, so that Mummius may have the pleasure of seeing the creatures fed. About a century later Strabo describes his own visit to Arsinoe in the course of his tour of Egypt, when his host took him to the lake in which the tame, sacred crocodile Suchos lived in solitary state and was fed with bread, meat and wine by the tourists who came to see the sight (πρὸς θέαν).[2] Strabo's host brought with him a cake, some roast meat and a jug of honey-wine. The beast was already lying on the shore; and the priests came, opened its jaws, popped in the cake and meat, and poured the wine down its throat. Suchos then sprang back into the lake and swam to the opposite shore, where the process of feeding it was repeated for the benefit of another party of tourists. The names Petesuchos and Suchos alike denote the god believed to be incarnate in a crocodile. According to Plutarch[3] and Aelian[4] these tame, sacred crocodiles would come when their attendants called them, recognizing their voices, and allowed themselves to be touched and handled, even opening their jaws so that their keepers could put their hands inside, clean their teeth, and remove any bits of food that had got stuck there.

We first hear of crocodiles in Rome in 58 BC, when Marcus Scaurus as aedile showed five in a temporary channel or tank (*euripus*) along with a hippopotamus (cf. p. 18 and p. 345, note 13). Strabo, writing under Augustus, states that some crocodiles brought to Rome for a spectacle were accompanied by men from Tentyra, near Coptos, who prepared a pool for them with a platform on one side of it. They entered the pool, dragged the crocodiles in nets onto the platform so that the spectators could see them, and then dragged them back again into the water.[5] Perhaps these crocodiles were the same as the thirty-six that were later slaughtered in the Circus Flaminius, flooded for the purpose, in 2 BC, in the games held to celebrate the dedication of the temple of Mars Ultor in that year.[6] The next recorded show of crocodiles, unspecified as to number, was that given by Antoninus Pius;[7] and we are told that Elagabalus maintained one crocodile in Rome.[8] The procuring of crocodiles for display was one of Symmachus' major preoccupations, so far as concerned his public shows (cf. p. 21). Of all the exhibits to be seen in Rome crocodiles, he maintains, were by far the most in demand for a theatrical display;[9] and in another letter he writes that, with heaven's help, he hopes to get for his praetorian spectacles a new pleasure for his fellow citizens, namely crocodiles.[10] Get them and exhibit them he did; but he did not succeed in preserving them for long. For in yet another letter he explains that he had tried to keep them for his correspondents to see when they came to Rome; but since they had refused to eat for fifty days and were wasting away, he had had most of them killed off, as was indeed the custom at public entertainments, at a second show. Two were still lingering and being kept for his friends, although their 'hunger-strike' left little hope of their surviving much longer.[11]

The earliest surviving representation of a crocodile in Hellenistic art would appear to be that in the painted animal frieze of the second-century BC Tomb I at Marissa (cf. p. 347, note 3).[12] The Palestinian artist has given us quite an accurate portrait of it. In Italy the best rendering of the beast is on the Nilotic landscape pavement at Palestrina (Praeneste), where the whole animal forms part of one of the unrestored, original portions.[13] Other Nilotic scenes in paintings and mosaics from Pompeii, Rome, other Italian sites, and Africa often present the creatures in conflict with Pygmies or men.[14] The confrontations of crocodiles and ichneumons carved in relief and in the round on the Vatican Nile have already been described (p. 91). An

enigmatic scene on three sixth-century mosaic pavements in Cyrenaica, two in the cathedral at Cyrene and one in the church at Qasr
El-Lebia, shows a crocodile trying to drag a cow into the Nile. In two
cases a man on the bank is pulling back the cow by its tail.[15] (Pl. 113)

As a symbol of Egypt the crocodile appears alone on *aurei* and
denarii struck by Augustus in the East in 28 BC with the legend
AEGYPT or AEGYPTO CAPTA to commemorate the conquest of
Egypt; beside a palm-tree on coins struck under Augustus, also
referring to the conquest of Egypt, at Nîmes (Nemausus) with the
legend COL[*onia*] NEM[*ausus*]; and beside a female bust personifying Egypt on a mosaic in the baths that underlie the barracks of the
vigiles (cf. p. 51) at Ostia.[16]

LIZARDS

The lizard (*lacerta, lacertus*, σαύρα, σαῦρος), a harmless little reptile, was
noted among the Romans for its scaly back and brilliant colouring
– 'the painted lizard with its rough back', as Virgil describes it.[17]
According to the lines on 'September' in the *Carmina Tria De
Mensibus*, probably of fourth-century AD date, it was sometimes
treated as a plaything, being caught, tied to a string, and made to
dance up and down when dangled in the hand.[18] The famous bronze
statue by Praxiteles known to us from Pliny as *Apollo Sauroctonos* and
preserved in marble copies of the Roman period, is described by
Pliny as portraying the youthful god ambushing with an arrow the
lizard that is creeping up towards him;[19] and the marble copies show
the little creature running up the tree-trunk that serves as Apollo's
support. It is, however, possible that the youth did not really mean to
kill the lizard, but was merely playing with it. Such, at any rate,
might appear to be Martial's interpretation of the copy or copies that
he had seen – 'spare the lizard, artful boy, as it creeps towards you: it
wants to perish at your hands' (by which phrase the poet may be
alluding to the lizard's unsuspecting approach).[20]

We have already noted the lizards in the company of frogs in
Augustan sculpture either as a *genre* or as an apotropaic motif and as
certainly the latter in the company of frogs, tortoises, and snakes on
the bronze Sabazius hands (cf. pp. 217, 235). The belief that the lizard
sleeps all through the winter to wake up with the return of spring
may explain its presence, along with a butterfly, beside the figures of
sleeping Cupids, where it could symbolize death and resurrection.[21]

Figures of lizards are sometimes carved in relief on marble ash-chests or funerary *cippi* (memorial bases) below or beside the inscribed text and may perhaps occasionally have the same significance there, as, for instance, when it is represented as gaily catching a fly.[22] But in other cases, as when it is attacked by two small birds[23] or captured by a heron,[24] it can hardly be a resurrection symbol, but would seem to form part of one of those natural history idylls that in sepulchral contexts are allegories of life in general (cf. Chapter XXIII).

TORTOISES

Pliny, in his section on antidotes against poisoning to be derived from animals, lists five types of tortoise (*testudo*, χελώνη) – land tortoises (*terrestres*), sea tortoises (*maritimae*), river tortoises (*fluviales*), those that dwell in muddy water (*lutariae*), and those that live in fresh water (*quae in dulci aqua vivunt*).[25] In the last he presumably distinguishes those inhabiting clear lakes, pools and streams. To the Romans one of the most important aspects of tortoises was the suitability of their shells for making lyres, a discovery ascribed in mythology to Hermes/Mercury. Pausanias in the second century AD saw at Argos a statue of Hermes constructing a lyre from a tortoise shell;[26] and in the temple of Hermes Akakesios at Megalopolis in Arcadia he noticed a statuary group of the god of which only a marble tortoise (χελώνη λίθου) had survived.[27] Here, by virtue of his invention of the lyre, the whole animal has become one of the god's recurrent attributes, as in numerouus Roman-age renderings of Mercury; for example, in the marble group of him seated on a rock, which was found in the Walbrook Mithraeum in London, where the tortoise sprawls just below Mercury's left foot.[28] Another seated Mercury, the marble figure from the Mithraeum at Merida (Augusta Emerita) in Spain, shows the tortoiseshell lyre below the god's left hand.[29] In yet another passage Pausanias states that Mount Parthenion in Arcadia produces tortoises whose shells are particularly good for making lyres (ἐς λύρας ποίησιν χελώνας ἐπιτηδειοτάτας); but the local inhabitants, believing the creatures to be sacred to Pan, were afraid to catch them themselves and would not allow strangers to take them captive.[30]

The use of objects made of tortoiseshell is cited by several Latin writers as a mark of ostentation and luxury. Varro mentions tortoise-shell inlay on a couch.[31] Velleius Paterculus speaks of the tortoiseshell adornments (*apparatus e testudine*) of Julius Caesar's Alexandrian triumph.[32] A couple of lines in Ovid's *Metamorphoses* suggests that in the homes of the wealthy it was used, along with ivory, as wall-inlay in private rooms.[33] Virgil pictures the clients of the great in Rome gaping at the doors inlaid with handsome tortoiseshell as they make their morning calls;[34] and Lucan describes how on the doors of Cleopatra's palace skilled hands had fixed the shells, studded with emeralds, of Indian tortoises.[35] Seneca had seen vastly expensive tortoiseshells embellished with elaborate markings (*video elaboratam scrupulosa distinctione testudinem*) and the variety of their colours enhanced by dyes resembling their natural tints.[36] Juvenal scoffs at a baby's cradle made of tortoiseshell – *testudineum conopeum* (literally, a mosquito-net).[37] According to the *Augustan History* Clodius Albinus' father, learning that the babies of the imperial family were bathed in tortoiseshell tubs (*alvei testudinei*), caused the shell of a giant tortoise, that had been given to him as a present, to be used for his own infant's warm-water ablutions (*excaldationes*).[38]

Other gifts of tortoises are recorded. Some Indians presented Alexander with an unspecified number of shells – *dorsa testudinum*.[39] An Indian delegation gave Augustus a giant river-tortoise three cubits long.[40] But we have no evidence that the monster was ever publicly exhibited. Everyone is familiar with the word *testudo* as applied to the formation of legionaries approaching the walls of an enemy city or fortress with their interlocked shields held above their heads [41] – an allusion to the impenetrability of the creature's shell. The use of the tortoise as an apotropaic symbol has already been described (pp. 217, 220).

The Romans valued the tortoise's shell for its practical and ornamental potentialities; but for the animal itself they appear to have had little liking. No pet tortoises or tortoises with personal names have been recorded. In the famous tortoise riddle quoted by Cicero its extreme slowness of locomotion (*tardigrada*) and its grim cast of countenance (*aspectus trux*) are emphasized.[42] Seneca classes it among the most loathsome and sluggish beasts (*foedissima pigerrimaque animalia*);[43] and in early Christian thought and art it appears as an embodiment of evil in combat with the cock that symbolizes vigilance. In late Greek the word for tortoise is ταρταροῦχος, dweller in Tartarus or Hell; and an early Christian inscription, a curse incised on a tablet of lead, addresses 'the most unclean spirit of a tortoise' – *immondissime spirite tartaruce*.[44] St Jerome writes of 'the sluggish tortoise, burdened and heavy with its own weight . . . signifying the grievous sins of the heretics;'[45] and where the motif of the fight occurs twice on the floor-mosaics of the fourth-century cathedral at Aquileia in northern Italy the tortoise is most likely to represent heresy about to be defeated by Catholicism.[46] The group in the north hall of this church complex is the better drawn of the two. If looks could kill, the tortoise would get the best of it. But of course the cock is going to win and receive the handsome, two-handled prize-vase that surmounts a tall stand in the background. (Pl. 115)

SNAKES

Snakes, at any rate the non-poisonous varieties, were in the main of good repute in the pagan Graeco-Roman world, in contrast to the evil character ascribed to them in general in Jewish and Christian literature and thought (cf. p. 145). They were prized as zoological exhibits, kept as pets, regarded as representing the beneficent spirits of the dead, associated with deities of healing and fertility and with the 'saving' gods and goddesses of the mystery cults; they had apotropaic and prophetic qualities; and their decorative potential was fully recognized by craftsmen.

Diodorus Siculus vividly describes the difficult and dangerous capture, in the marshes of the upper Nile, of a vast snake, 30 cubits (45 feet) long, for Ptolemy II's collection in Alexandria.[47] The hunters first attempted, unsuccessfully and with the loss of some of their number, to take it with nooses and ropes. They then waited till they saw it leave its lair, when they blocked up the lair and made a hole close by, in which they placed a plaited basket with cords attached to its mouth. When the creature returned and found the obstruction in its lair, the hunters raised a great din and the snake fled in terror into the hole and into the basket inside it. The cords closing the mouth of the basket were then drawn and the snake was conveyed alive to Alexandria. There it was preserved on show in the royal palace and became very tame through being kept on a low diet, providing a most unusual and astonishing spectacle (μέγιστον καὶ παραδοξότατον θέαμα) for visitors from abroad. According to Aelian[48] this same Ptolemy also received at Alexandria two great snakes from Ethiopia, 14 and 13 cubits long respectively; while one of his successors, Ptolemy Euergetes (145-116 BC), was presented with three snakes 9, 7 and 6 cubits long respectively. All these presumably also found a place in the royal collection. Among the Indians' gifts to Augustus were some large vipers (ἐχίδναι) and a snake 10 cubits long;[49] and Suetonius claims that the emperor showed in front of the Comitium a snake 50 cubits (75 feet) long.[50]

Again from Suetonius we learn that Tiberius had among his pets (in oblectamentis) a snake (serpens draco) which came to an unpleasant end. For one day, when the emperor went to feed it with his own hands as usual, he found that the ants had eaten it.[51] Seneca saw tame snakes at dinner-parties gliding harmlessly among the cups and over the diners' laps;[52] and Martial knew a lady called Glaucilla who twined a clammy snake round her neck.[53] According to Pliny the yellow anguis Aesculapius, introduced into Rome from Epidaurus, was often kept as a household pet (volgo pascitur et in domibus);[54] and both he and Aelian give accounts of the tameness of Egyptian asps. Pliny tells the tale of a family in Egypt with an asp that came regularly to be fed at table (ad mensam) and one day gave birth to young while in the house. When the asp was out, one of these lusty infants killed the householder's son. The mother, returning for her usual meal and realizing what her offspring had done, punished it with death and was never seen in the house again.[55] Aelian asserts that asps are perfectly harmless, gentle and tame if treated with respect and fed along with the children. After dinner place barley soaked in wine and honey on the table, snap your fingers, and the asps will all assemble from their lairs round the table, rear their heads, and lick off the food prepared for them 'gently and by degrees' (ἡσυχῇ καὶ κατ' ὀλίγον) – their table manners were perfect.[56]

The Egyptian snakes (dracunculi), known as 'good spirits' (agathodaemones), that Elagabalus kept in Rome were probably harmless.[57] But the serpentes in the collection made for him by the Marsic snake-charming priests of central Italy seem to have been venomous; for when he let them loose before dawn, as the crowds started queuing for the games, many people were bitten and fled in terror.[58] Virgil paints a vivid picture of how poisonous snakes were charmed with massage and incantations by one of these Marsic priests.[59] In a lengthy passage Lucan lists the deadly snakes of Libya and describes the deaths from snake-bites of Cato's soldiers.[60]

From archaic Greek times snakes had been believed to embody, or at least to be the close attendants on, the spirits of the dead, as is proved, for instance, by the well-known tombstone, now in Berlin, from Chrysapha in Laconia, where a vast but kindly snake rears itself

75, 75 Oxen ploughing: Trajan as a colonist on a *sestertius*, and a bronze Romano-British group from Piercebridge (pp. 152, 377, n. 50).

77, 78 Draught-animals: *above*, mosaic of oxen with hunting nets in a cart, and, *below*, draught-oxen and mules drawing wine-barrels on a relief on Trajan's Column (pp. 161, 162, 191).

79–81 Goats being milked,
above, on a sarcophagus relief,
and, *below*, on a mosaic at
Istanbul. *Right*, a marble relief
of a ewe and her lamb (pp.
165, 164).

82, 83 *Right*, a wall-painting of a goat in Nero's Golden House, Rome, and, *below*, a sarcophagus relief of a child driving a goat-cart (p. 166).

84 Mosaic in S. Apollinare Nuovo, Ravenna, showing Christ with the sheep and the goats (p. 166).

85 A relief of a cart drawn by two mules passing milestone LIIII (p. 188).

86 A bronze horse's *balteus* decorated in high relief (p. 171).

87–89 *Left*, a racehorse on a bone counter; centre, mules grazing on a *sestertius* of the Emperor Nerva, and, *right*, a memorial *sestertius* showing the *carpentum* of Agrippina I drawn by mules (pp. 183, 186).

90 A relief of the mule-coach of the *cursus publicus* (pp. 186–7).

91, 92 Mules on Trajan's Column; *above*, drawing *ballistae*, and, *below*, *left*, carrying Dacian treasure (p. 191).

93, 94 *Above*, *right*, a relief of the goddess Epona riding her pony with a dog on her lap; *right*, a Late Antique terracotta dish depicting the grooming of Pegasus (pp. 123, 175, 197).

95, 96 A relief of a donkey pushing a *vallus*, and another of a mule drawing a cart with clay or manure (pp. 196, 189).

97, 98 Two mosaics at Istanbul, one of a donkey refusing its fodder and the second of a rider thrown by a mule (pp. 195, 192).

99–101 The two small bronzes *above* show a mouse peeping out from behind a Satyr mask held in its paws before its face, and another mouse strenuously blowing a trumpet. A more typical mouse appears in the mosaic *below* about to start nibbling a halved walnut (pp. 203–4, 387, n. 36).

over the back of the chair on which the deceased, a man and wife, are seated side by side.[61] This traditional belief was, of course, carried on into late republican and early imperial times. Very familiar is Virgil's description of the huge, harmless, slippery snake with its seven coils and resplendent rainbow hues that glided peacefully round Anchises' tomb and adjacent altars and consumed the food and drink there set out – a snake that Aeneas thought might well be his father's 'familiar' (*famulus*).[62] Valerius Flaccus also writes of 'snakes, the shades' familiars' (*angues/umbrarum famuli*).[63]

Familiar, too, are the Pompeian paintings of snakes that accompany the figures of the *Genius Paterfamilias* and domestic *Lares* (household gods) in many *lararia* (shrines) in private houses. Quotation of a few examples must suffice. A niche (*aedicula*) in the House of the Vettii has painted on its back wall the *Genius Paterfamilias* between two dancing *Lares*, while beneath this group a large crested and bearded snake approaches with eager, open jaws an altar on which rests a large egg, symbol of life.[64] Here the snake represents the dead founder of the family. Another painting, now in the Naples Museum, shows the *Genius*, flanked by the *Lares*, sacrificing at an altar and, below, two snakes, one with, one without, a crest and beard, gliding from either side towards a central altar on which two eggs are placed, the snakes in this case representing the founding ancestor and ancestress.[65] In yet another picture, painted at the base of the wall below the projecting bracket-like *lararium*, two similar, but rearing, snakes, male and female, open their jaws to devour the two eggs that again surmount the central altar.[66] One unusual painting, now at Naples, contains a view of the vine-clad Vesuvius, at the foot of which stands Bacchus in the form of a great bunch of grapes with human head, hands and feet and, below him, a single male snake rearing towards an altar.[67] In all of these paintings the vegetation through which the snakes are moving may symbolize the fertile landscape of the world beyond the grave; while the upper portion of the last-mentioned picture suggests the Bacchic paradise in which the dead have gone to dwell. (Pl. 112)

Representation of the dead is probably the true explanation of the snake in a painting in a lunette of the new fourth-century Via Latina catacomb – a painting interpreted as the 'Death of Cleopatra', almost certainly erroneously, since the eruption of a scene from Roman history into a catacomb repertory is highly unlikely. The picture in question shows a half-draped woman with a blue nimbus reclining in a garden planted with crimson roses and leaning against a basket up which a snake is gliding close to her arm. She raises her eyes and right hand heavenwards as though in ecstasy and the nimbus and garden suggest that the deceased has gone to dwell in paradise with her *famula*.[68]

Closely connected in the Roman mind with death and the afterlife were the concepts of healing and fertility (cf. p. 122). The snake-entwined staff of Asklepios/Aesculapius is too well known to require further comment. The god's female collaborator, Hygieia/Salus, is generally depicted as nourishing the healing snake. For example, coins and medallions of Hadrian, Antoninus Pius, Faustina II, Lucius Verus and Commodus present on their reverses Salus either standing and feeding a snake that is coiled round a tree or seated and extending a bowl towards the snake that rears in front of her.[69] As the givers of fertility and teachers of the cultivation of the earth to man, Demeter/Ceres and Triptolemus use snake-drawn cars, as on the silver *patera*, now in Vienna, from Aquileia[70] and on the reverses of medallions of Antoninus Pius and Faustina I.[71] The snake that inhabits the earth in which the seed is sown ensures its rebirth as corn.

It was, indeed, as a symbol of eternal rebirth that the snake, which renews its skin every year, played an important role in the iconography of those mystery-cults that promised immortality and victory over death to their adherents. In the temple of the Syrian mystery-deities on the Janiculum in Rome there came to light the bronze statuette of a mummy-like male personage, perhaps a god, tightly draped as in a shroud and wound round seven times from feet to shoulders by a snake, whose head appears above the figure's brow. The seven coils of the snake and the seven eggs between the convolutions may allude to the seven planetary births and rebirths through which the soul must pass before attaining to its final immortality.[72] This little bronze immediately recalls the snake-entwined Mithraic figure generally depicted with a lion's head[73] or, as on a unique relief at Modena, with a human head and in the act of being hatched from an egg.[74] There can be little doubt that in Mithraism the snake was held to be beneficent. In numerous versions of the scene of Mithras slaying the primeval bull (Mithras Tauroctonos), an allegory of life through death, the snake along with the dog is lapping up the life-giving blood, while the scorpion, perhaps the incarnation of evil, attacks the bull's genitals.[75] Again, in the painting of Mithras as hunter in the Mithraeum of Dura-Europos, a snake is speeding along beside the god's horse to help and protect him as he pursues the wild animals that signify the powers of ill.[76]

In the cult of Isis the sacred snake, the *uraeus*, is worn as a head-dress by the goddess and by her ministers, male and female, or as wound round the arm.[77] It is seen, too, on one side of an altar in the Museo Capitolino, curled on the lid of a round wicker *cista mystica* (holy basket), with the inscription ISIDI SACR[*um*].[78] A silver bowl in Leningrad shows a girl kneeling before a large *cista mystica*: with one hand she raises its conical lid and with the other holds a goblet from which a snake, rearing out of the *cista*, is about to drink.[79] There is no indication here as to the deity with which the snake and *cista* are associated. But on the two large silver coins (*cistophori*) struck in Asia Minor in 39 BC by Mark Antony as the 'New Dionysos', with the reverse-legend III VIR R P C (*triumvir reipublicae constituendae*), the two snakes that flank the *cista mystica* in the centre of the field clearly allude to the Bacchic mysteries. In the case of one piece a bust of Octavia appears above the basket, but on the other piece a figure of Bacchus himself surmounts it.[80]

The apotropaic use of snakes on the bronze Sabazius hands and on cult vessels of clay has been already noted (pp. 217, 220). Apotropaic, too, is likely to have been the purpose of the two entwined snakes that top the staff (*caduceus*, κηρύκειον) that was the distinguishing mark of heralds and of Hermes/Mercury as the gods' messenger. The alleged prophetic powers of snakes are recorded in Propertius' and Aelian's accounts of the annual ritual enacted at the shrine of Juno Sospita at Lanuvium in central Italy, where a girl was detailed to offer the goddess' sacred snake its yearly tribute of food.[81] If the girl were truly a virgin the snake would emerge from its hole and snatch its barley-cake (μάζα) eagerly and a fertile year (*fertilis annus*) was predicted for the farmers. Otherwise the creature would reject the offering. Aelian also describes a grove in Epirus sacred to Apollo, which was fenced in and inhabited by snakes that were believed to be the god's pets (τοῦ θεοῦ ἄθυρμα).[82] When the snakes took their food well, fertility and plentiful crops were predicted for the coming year. A snake given out to be the incarnation of the god Glykon played the leading role in the false oracle established at Abonuteichos (later renamed Ionopolis) in Paphlagonia by the charlatan Alexander.[83] The cult was founded *c.* AD 150, attracted numerous believers, and enjoyed a widespread reputation until the middle of the third century at least. The striking marble figure (2 feet 2½ inches high) of a coiled snake that holds erect its partly human, partly camelian, long-haired head, which was found at Constanta (Tomi) in Rumania, may perhaps be a portrait of the pseudo-Glykon.[84] (Pl. 111)

Finally, the coiled snake was an obvious theme for goldsmiths making bracelets and armlets, the long body often delicately incised with scales and, in the case of bracelets, twin snake heads flanking the clasp.[85]

CHAPTER XXII

BIRDS

OSTRICHES

THE OSTRICH, KNOWN TO THE GRAECO-ROMAN WORLD in North
Africa, Syria and Mesopotamia, bore the names of *struthio* (derived
from στρουθός, the Greek for 'sparrow'), *struthiocamelus* (an allusion
to its long, curving, camel-like neck), and μεγάλη στρουθός ('big
sparrow', to distinguish it from the small and ordinary bird,
although it is sometimes called just στρουθός); Pliny gives a detailed
and accurate description of it.[1] It is, he says, the largest of birds, as tall
as an African or Ethiopian when on horseback, but swifter. Its wings
are not used for flying, but as a help in running. It has cloven hoofs,
like those of a deer, and with these it will, when hunted, throw up
stones at its pursuers. It can digest anything that it swallows indiscri-
minately (*sine dilectu*). It is remarkable for its stupidity (*stoliditas*), for if
it sticks its head into a bush it imagines itself to be completely hidden.
The chief value of the ostrich is its eggs, which are large enough to be
used as vessels, and its feathers, which can serve as plumes on
helmets.[2] In a later passage Pliny states that the ostrich is the only bird
which has, like human beings, lashes on both its eyelids.[3] Diodorus
Siculus provides a very similar account, adding that it is its weight
that makes the ostrich unable to fly and that it sometimes throws up
stones behind it violently enough to wound its hunters: he, too,
comments on its folly and sluggishness of mind (ἀφροσύνη καὶ νωθρότης
ψυχῆς), and Xenophon had already noted the creature's extraordinary speed and the way in which it uses its wings like sails when
running.[4]

Most picturesque of all are the lines in which Claudian compares
Eutropius to an ostrich: 'Even so the great Libyan bird, hard pressed
by the cries of the hunters, speeds across the burning sand and rushes
through the dust with wings curved like sails before the breeze; but
when it hears the clear sound of feet behind it, it forgets to flee and

stands with eyes closed, hiding its head and imagining, poor fool, that it cannot be seen by those whom it itself cannot see.'[5] Lucian lists ostriches among the quarry of the Garamantian tribes of the Sahara and states that they prized the birds' eggs both as food and for their use as cups, and even caps, when split in two.[6]

Eight pairs of ostriches walked in harness in Ptolemy II's procession;[7] and in Rome, as early as the time of Plautus (251-184 B C), an ostrich could be seen scuttling across the Circus, under the name of *passer marinus* ('sparrow from overseas').[8] The next public appearance, so far as our extant records go, of the birds in the capital was on the macabre occasion of Commodus' slaughter of an unspecified number with crescent-shaped arrow-heads that neatly beheaded the creatures, while their bodies went running on (cf. p. 22 and p. 346, note 40). Herodian, in his description of the incident, calls the birds Mauretanian and comments on the speed with which they move and the way in which they fold their wings ($\kappa\delta\lambda\pi\omega\sigma\iota\varsigma$ $\pi\tau\epsilon\rho\hat{\omega}\nu$) to catch the wind. Ostriches were among the 'passengers' in Septimius Severus' arena 'shipwreck' (cf. p. 18); Gordian's exhibition included 300 Mauretanian ostriches with reddened wings (*miniati*) (cf. p. 18); and, if we can credit the *Augustan History*, Probus put 1,000 of these birds into his 'landscaped' Circus (cf. p. 19) – a number that might indicate the presence of an imperial ostrich-farm in Italy.

But it is the mosaic pavements, particularly those in North Africa and Sicily, that provide our best evidence for the capture and transport of ostriches and for their display and slaughter in *venationes*. An apse-shaped mosaic, now in the British Museum, from Utica shows a net stretched in a semi-circle in terrain so marshy that the hunters have had to take to a couple of boats in order to secure their prey.[9] Conspicuous among the creatures netted is a prancing ostrich worked in red, buff, pink and dark-grey *tesserae*. The pavement with a netting scene from Hippo Regius includes, as we have observed (p. 26), a pair of ostriches. Their transport is dramatically illustrated on the 'Great Hunt' pavement at Piazza Armerina (cf. p. 28), where two men are each carrying an ostrich in his arms up the gangway on the left of one of the transport-ships, while another man carries a bird down the gangway on the right of the same ship, which is conceived of as simultaneously leaving a port in the country in which the capture took place and arriving at a port in the land for which the birds were destined.[10] According to Synesius of Cyrene ostriches were still being shipped abroad from there in the early fifth

century, presumably for amphitheatre shows. He explains to Pylae-
menes, one of his correspondents, that he has got some ostriches,
taken in the hunt under peaceful conditions, but cannot send them at
once by sea owing to enemy activity: he promises, however, to send
them later by another boat.[11] (Pl. 116)

The protomes (busts) of ostriches appear, along with those of other
arena animals, in the octagons and medallions that compose a
number of North African mosaic pavements, for instance one from
Djemila (Cuicul)[12] and two from Kasbat (Thuburbo Majus).[13]
Ostrich protomes also occur at Piazza Armerina on the floors both of
the great rectangular, and of the curvilinear, peristyle: on the former,
the bird peeps coyly from the centre of a wreathed medallion, on the
latter it inhabits an acanthus-scroll.[14] A complete ostrich features on a
mosaic, apparently used for some kind of game, from Tebessa
(Theveste).[15] The ostrich in the mosaic of performing bears from
Radez, that on a piece from Carthage with N XXV inscribed upon
it, and the two in the arena-shows mosaic from Zliten have been
already mentioned (pp. 30, 31).

On all the pavements just cited the ostrich is only one among
many other creatures that met their end in *venationes*. But on a
polychrome mosaic from Kef (Sicca Veneria), now in the Bardo
Museum at Tunis, it virtually dominates the scene, its only competi-
tors for the onlookers' attention being deer.[16] This pavement is
apsidal in shape, the apse being fenced all round by stretches of
hunting-nets to enclose the herd of deer and flock of ostriches. The
nets themselves recall those on the piece from Hippo Regius
(cf. p. 26). Here, however, the scatter (*sparsio*) of roses and rose-petals
over the entire area within the nets indicates that the scene is that of
an arena *venatio* about to start, not that of the rounding up of animals
on the hunting-field for transport alive. Furthermore, at each of the
three gaps in the nets, forming entrances to the arena, are two men
each restraining with the greatest difficulty an enormous hound from
dashing at the captives. The deer occupy the apex of the apse; and in
the foreground, along its chord, are the ostriches. The pavement has,
unfortunately, numerous lacunae. But the total number of the birds,
which are nearly life-size and very realistically drawn, can be seen
from the surviving heads, bodies and legs to be no less than twenty.
Unlike the deer, which are rushing round excitedly, the ostriches
stand motionless, as though paralysed with fear. And well they may
be; for in a moment, at a given signal, the frantic dogs will be

released to tear the splendid birds to pieces, before doing likewise to the deer – a ghastly sight, presumably enjoyed by the amphitheatre crowds, which the mosaicist has mercifully spared us, not from any feeling for the victims, but in order to display to full advantage the munificence of the wealthy man who gave the show.

Ostrich-hunting in the field in northern Africa is illustrated by the sculptures in relief from the Ghirza mausolea (cf. pp. 138, 212). One frieze-block shows a couple of these birds and an antelope moving towards the left. No humans are visible on the surviving fragment, but these creatures were obviously represented as being the Berber huntsmen's usual quarry.[17] A second block presents a mounted huntsman, preceded by two large dogs, galloping towards the right in pursuit of an immense ostrich. Despite the crudeness of the carving and the fact that the rider is far too small in proportion to the dogs and bird, this is a spirited enough episode from local daily life.[18]

Difficult to believe are the stories about Elagabalus recorded in the *Augustan History*. On one occasion he gave ten ostriches as prizes for his guests in a lottery. The writer does not tell us what use the winners were supposed to make of these birds; were they to keep them as pets or to eat their flesh and eggs? In another passage the emperor is said to have produced ostriches at dinner-parties for consumption; and in yet another, to have served up the heads of six hundred at a single banquet so that the guests might eat the brains.[19] No less incredible is the report that Firmus, prefect of Egypt in Aurelian's time (cf. pp. 351, note 84, 130), ate an ostrich daily.[20] According to Aelian, the stones that were found in the stomachs of dead ostriches were regarded as a remedy for indigestion.[21]

Finally, there is the use of ostriches as mounts. Catullus writes of the 'winged horse' (*ales equus*) of Ptolemy II's Queen Arsinoe; and Pausanias mentions having seen a bronze statue of her riding on an ostrich.[22] 'Oppian' states that this 'mixture of sparrow and camel' can carry a boy on its back;[23] and Firmus again is described as riding on the backs of huge ostriches and so producing the effect of flying.[24] That the birds could at least have supported the burden of a light-weight woman or boy may possibly be true.

EAGLES

The eagle as the constant companion and attribute of Jupiter in Roman literature and art is too familiar to require detailed documentation. Cicero quotes a Latin version of Aeschylus' *Prometheus Bound* in which the bird is called the god's satellite (*Iovis satelles*);[25] and Virgil writes of it as the god's weapon-bearer (*Iovis armiger*), an allusion to the fact that it is often shown in art as clutching in its claws a thunderbolt.[26] In representations of Jupiter the eagle either stands on the ground beside him or perches on his hand. The adoption of the eagle by Roman emperors when rendered in the guise of Jupiter is illustrated by the well-known Vienna cameo ('Gemma Augustea'), where an eagle stands beneath Augustus' throne;[27] and by two marble statues of Claudius, a standing one in the Sala Rotonda in the Vatican, where the eagle beside the emperor's feet is partially restored,[28] and a seated one from Lepcis Magna, where the bird perches on a globe held in Claudius' extended right hand: most of the right arm and hand is a restoration, but parts of the original globe and eagle were found with the statue.[29] The famous bronze statuette of an eagle, 6 inches high, discovered at Silchester (Calleva Atrebatum) in Hampshire may once have rested on the hand, or on a globe held in the hand, of a bronze statue of an emperor as Jupiter, if not of Jupiter himself.[30] The wings are missing (it seems that the original pair had been replaced in antiquity by a secondary pair), but from the careful finish of the feathers beneath where they once were it is almost certain that they were raised and spread for flight.(Pl. 121)

As a symbol of Roman imperial victory and might a magnificent, naturalistic eagle is carved in relief on a portion of a marble frieze found in Trajan's Forum and now in the portico of the church of the Holy Apostles in Rome.[31] The bird is perched within a heavy oak-wreath, just above the bow of ribbon that secures the bottom of the wreath and flutters out on either side of it. The eagle's head is seen in profile against the front of the wreath, peering towards the spectator's left, while its powerful wings are spread behind it. Another such symbolic eagle is that on the famous onyx cameo in Vienna. The bird, which is worked in brown against a white background, is shown in a frontal pose, but with its beak turned towards the spectator's right. It balances on one claw on the stem of a palm-branch and the other grips a laurel-wreath.[32] (Pl. 120)

The eagle-standard (*aquila*) was introduced into the Roman army by Marius as the collective emblem of a whole legion, in contrast to the standards of individual maniples (*signa*). The bird, which was first of silver, later of gold, stood with spread wings on a thunderbolt and surmounted a long pole. In war-time camps and in permanently occupied fortresses it was lodged in a special chapel in the headquarters building and received religious veneration as the legion's own divine protector (*proprium legionis numen*).[33] To lose its eagle was, of course, the greatest disaster that could befall a legion. A tombstone at Mainz bears the figure of Gnaeus Musius, eagle-bearer (*aquilifer*) of Legio XIV Gemina, grasping his eagle-topped pole in his right hand.[34] Good illustrations of the legionary *aquila* and of the eagle that sometimes tops a manipular *signum* are to be found on some of the panels of Marcus Aurelius' time that adorn the attic of the Arch of Constantine in Rome.[35]

The eagle as the symbol and agent of apotheosis after death is a frequent theme in Roman art both in imperial and in private contexts. A cameo in the Cabinet des Médailles in Paris shows Germanicus mounting to the sky on the back of an eagle, while Victory crowns him.[36] On the vault of the passageway of the Arch of Titus the emperor is being carried heavenwards on eagle-back.[37] At the funeral of an emperor an eagle was released from the top of the pyre to represent the soul of the departed making for its dwelling in the sky; and on the base of the Roman Column of Antoninus Pius, in the relief in which a winged male *Genius* conveys aloft on his back the imperial pair, Antoninus and Faustina I, two eagles are seen flying upwards, to right and left of the emperor and empress.[38] On the funerary altars of private persons dating from the first century AD eagles often feature, sometimes two at the corners or one perched below the inscription panel on the bottom of the swag of leaves and fruit that is suspended round the text: a fine example of the latter is the exquisitely carved altar of Amemptus, freedman of the Empress Livia, in the Louvre.[39] On one of the reliefs from the late first-century AD Tomb of the Haterii near Rome an eagle surmounts the capital of each of the four columns on the façade of the temple-like mausoleum which forms the central motif of the picture; and just above the roof of this building is a horizontal frieze showing four swags of fruit supported in the beaks of five eagles.[40]

Among the numerous representations of the Rape of Ganymede by the eagle in Roman art – in painting, mosaic and sculpture – are works of a funerary character. The myth is here an allegory of the soul's 'rape' from the body at death and of its journey heavenwards.[41]

Another art-motif is that of the fight between an eagle and a snake – splendidly illustrated in polychrome on the peristyle mosaic of the imperial palace at Istanbul.[42] A mosaic panel in the Vatican depicts an eagle tearing a hare,[43] recalling the famous classical Greek coin-type of Akragas (cf. p. 200).

Of relations between eagles and human beings in the Graeco-Roman world little is recorded. The tale of a tame eagle related by Aelian is taken, so he tells us, from the Hellenistic historian Phylarchus.[44] This bird had been owned and reared since it was an eaglet by a boy who had treated it, not as a mere plaything, but as a favourite and even as a younger brother. When the boy fell ill, the eagle stayed by his side, refusing to eat when the boy refused his food. And when the boy died it threw itself into the flames of the funeral pyre.

STILT-WALKERS AND WADERS

Cranes

Pliny, Plutarch, and Aelian all describe in much the same terms the habits of the crane (*grus*, γέρανος) as observed in their day. They fly very high, choose a leader to follow, and have some of their number stationed at the ends of their lines, whose business it is to keep the flock together by their cries. At night they post sentries which are said to hold in their claws stones that by their fall wake the birds up, should they have dozed off. The rest sleep standing first on one foot and then on the other, with their heads tucked under their wings, except for the leader, who keeps a good look-out with head erect, ready to give warning.[45] Cicero, Martial, Plutarch and Aelian write of the V-shaped or triangular formation in which they fly when migrating.[46] Claudian paints a vivid picture of a noisy flight of cranes tracing this letter in the sky against the clouds, when they exchange their summer abode in Thrace, by the river Strymon, for the winter warmth of the Nile.[47] The birds' raucous cries are noted by Lucretius;[48] and Horace speaks of catching with a noose the stranger crane that comes to winter in Italy.[49]

According to Pliny an unusual type of crane with a tufted crest (*cirrus*) and a crane of smaller size (*vipio*) were found in the Balearic Islands.[50] Pliny also says that tamed cranes will execute a kind of dance moving gracefully in circles, one bird performing at a time on some occasions.[51] In AD 80 Titus staged a public crane-fight.[52] The eating of cranes at feasts is mentioned by Horace, Statius and Aulus Gellius;[53] and Pliny states that in his day cranes were much in demand for food, although Cornelius Nepos gives evidence that storks were preferred to cranes in Augustus' time.[54] The great flock of cranes which Varro's friend Seius kept on his estate was probably for eating purposes.[55]

Cranes are represented in Roman art in scenes depicting their fight with Pygmies.[56] A bird that is probably a crane appears near the top of the mosaic pavement in the south transept of the church of the Multiplication of Loaves and Fishes at Tabgha in Israel.[57] This mosaic and its pendant in the north transept of the church, which are unlikely to be earlier than the fifth century although no sure dating criteria for them exist, show all-over polychrome designs of birds and plants, some Nilotic, and a definitely Nilotic feature in the shape of a Nilometer just to the right of the crane. Six silver two-handled goblets, dating from the first century AD, four found in a rich burial at Vize (Bizye) in Thrace and two at Boscoreale near Pompeii, carry in relief on each side a pair of lively cranes, sometimes with a snake or a butterfly in the beak.[58] An as yet unexplained rendering of a trio of these birds occurs in two provincial carvings from Roman Gaul. In one of the reliefs on the boatman's monument in Paris, now in the Cluny Museum, there is depicted a bull with two cranes on its back and one on its head and the legend TARVOS TRIGARANVS above it;[59] and on one side of an altar at Trier dedicated to Mercury and Rosmerta a man is shown felling a tree in the foliage of which are three cranes and the head of a bull.[60]

Storks

The stork (*ciconia*, πελαργός) was especially renowned in the Graeco-Roman world for its alleged piety towards its aged parents. Aelian describes how willingly the younger birds care for the old ones, being prompted by their nature to do this (αἰτία τούτων φύσις). Similarly, when they have nothing to feed their young with they will disgorge the food that they themselves have eaten previously and give it to their offspring.[61] Aelian states that pelicans and herons do the same. In the doggerel verses recited by Trimalchio, the stork, with its slender legs and noisy rattle, is called a model of piety, as well as a beloved foreign guest, exiled by winter and a token of warm weather to come (i.e. when it leaves for the North).[62]

It is as an adjunct of Pietas that the stork is featured in Roman numismatic art. On *denarii* of Quintus Caecilius Metellus, issued *c.* 77 BC, the bird appears in the field beside the head of Pietas on the obverses; while on the reverses of *aurei* and *denarii* struck by Mark

Antony *c.* 41 BC one or two storks attend Pietas' standing figure.[63] Again, the stork accompanies the standing figure of Pietas, with hands uplifted in the praying attitude, on coins issued by Hadrian.[64] On a third-century Christian sarcophagus in the church of Santa Maria Antiqua in the Roman Forum the figure of an *orans* (Christian at prayer), itself modelled on the pagan Pietas, has a stork beside it.[65]

According to Juvenal and Seneca the stork catches snakes and lizards as food for its young;[66] and from Pliny we learn that it was a criminal offence in Thessaly to kill a stork on account of its usefulness in keeping down snakes.[67] In Italy, on the other hand, the stork was eaten and was, as we have already seen, preferred to the crane in Augustus' time. Horace declares that the stork was safe in its nest until a glutton of praetorian rank set the fashion for serving it at table.[68]

Herons

The heron (*ardea, ardeola,* ῥωδιός, ἐρωδιός) is distinguished from most types of crane by its crest (cf. p. 243). Pliny lists three kinds – the white (*leucon*), the speckled (*asterias*), and the dark (*pellos*).[69] An exquisitely naturalistic painting from Pompeii, now in the Naples Museum, seems to show the white variety confronting a rearing and infuriated snake: the bird is mainly cream-coloured with a few brown and black feathers, and has red legs and a red bill.[70] Two graceful birds, one with a very clear crest, are rendered on a Roman relief from Siebenbürgen (Déva) in Hungary.[71] On the Tabgha church mosaics, in the north transept, there are three crested herons, all, it seems, of the speckled kind, one near the top right-hand corner, one near the centre, and one in the bottom right-hand corner; and in the south transept, at the top of the pavement, there is a crested heron of the dark type.[72] (Pl. 118)

Ibises

Pliny twice mentions the *ibis* as being the Egyptian bird *par excellence*;[73] and Juvenal writes of Egypt reverencing the ibis gorged on snakes.[74] As is very well known, the bird was sacred to the goddess Isis; and as such it appears in Hadrian's 'province' coin series as an adjunct of Aegyptos, who reclines, holding the *sistrum* (rattle) of Isis, while the bird is seen at her feet, either standing on the ground or perched on a low column.[75] Two fine ibises, facing one another and crossing bills, feature on a Nilotic mosaic from the House of the Faun at Pompeii.[76] At the bottom of the mosaic in the north transept at Tabgha, near the centre, is an ibis-like bird about to devour a snake. Schneider identifies it, without mentioning its colour, as a flamingo,[77] although it has not got the flamingo's downward-curving hook at the end of its bill. If it is red, a flamingo it must be. But since I have not seen the original and have not had access to a coloured reproduction of it, I cannot decide. (Pl. 117)

Flamingos

The flamingo (*phoenicopterus*), a native of southern Mediterranean lands, is most often referred to in the literary sources as a dish served at luxurious banquets. Juvenal decribes a feast at which the diners partook of a huge flamingo.[78] But the special delicacy seems to have been its tongue.[79] The birds that 'owe their name to their red feathers' (*rubentibus pinnis*) kept by Martial's friend Faustinus on his estate at Baiae were probably also for eating.[80]

Flamingos were among the victims sacrificed to the godhead of the Emperor Gaius; and on the day before his death he was sprinkled with a flamingo's blood as he sacrificed.[81]

Among representations of flamingos in Roman art (cf. pp. 286-7) is a mosaic panel from the floor of the *triclinium* of a house discovered at El-Djem. The bird shown here, which has its characteristic downward-curving hook at the end of its beak, is crouching on the ground, a captive, with a cloth tied round its legs and wings.[82] Flamingos also appear on the great bird-inhabited vine-scroll mosaic from Justinian's sixth-century church at Sabratha in Tripolitania, where the birds are symbols of the blessed souls in Paradise.[83] (Pl. 119)

Porphyrions

The finest specimens of this galinule (*porphyrio*, πορφυρίων) are said by Pliny to come from Commagene and to hold a morsel in one foot to the beak while feeding.[84] Athenaeus states that it comes from Libya and can be domesticated, quoting Aristotle for its long red legs and completely red bill.[85] According to Aelian it was never eaten but was kept for its beauty either as a pet in a wealthy house or to adorn a temple.[86] Pliny also mentions a more familiar (or more splendid? – *nobilior*) kind found on the Balearic Islands and brought thence to Italy; and again a type called *himantopus*, smaller than the other porphyrions, but with legs as long as theirs. It came from Egypt and very soon died when taken to Italy.[87]

PELICANS

According to Pliny, the pelican (*onocrotalus*: 'shrill as an ass') came to Italy from the northernmost coast of Gaul.[88] It is, he says, very much like a swan to look at (he does not note its enormous, shears-like beak), but differs from it in possessing in its jaws a pouch resembling a second stomach (*alterius uteri genus*). In this the insatiable bird first stores the food that it has caught and then gradually returns it to its mouth, passing it into its true stomach (*vera alvus*) when it has chewed it. Since Pliny also refers to its extraordinary appetite (*mira capacitas*), the 'foul throat of the Ravenna pelican', of which Martial writes, may allude, not to Ravenna as a place in which the bird was found, but to the gluttony of its inhabitants.[89]

I can recall only one portrait of a pelican in Roman art, on the fifth-century AD 'animal paradise' mosaic in the church at Dag Pazari in Southern Anatolia (cf. p. 287).

PARROTS

The parrot (*psittacus*, ψιττακός, ψιττακή, σιττακός) is almost unanimously pronounced by Greek and Roman writers to be of Indian origin. This was, of course, the green bird: of the grey bird from West Africa there is no trace in any of the ancient sources, literary or archaeological. Aristotle, in a probably interpolated passage, calls it 'the Indian bird', notes its power of human speech, and observes that it grows more saucy than ever when given wine to drink.[90] Aelian, besides remarking on its Indian origin and habit of chattering like a human,[91] also describes how the parrots crowd round the Indian princelings in their royal parks and how they are never killed in India because the Brahmins regard their convincing imitation of human speech as a sign of sacredness.[92] The Greek world does not seem actually to have seen the parrot before Alexander's Indian campaign, when Nearchus, one of his generals, made this portent (θαῦμα) of a talking bird known in the West;[93] and cages of parrots were carried in Ptolemy II's pageant.[94] Pausanias and Solinus both insist on India as the sole source from which parrots reached the Roman world.[95] Pliny also names India as their source;[96] but in another passage, apropos of Nero's Ethiopian expedition, he says that parrots, presumably the green East African birds, were first sighted after the island of Gaugades, between Syene and Meroe, had been reached.[97]

Pliny,[98] Solinus,[99] and Apuleius[100] all give, in much the same terms, minute descriptions of the parrot's appearance and habits. It is completely green apart from a red-gold (*miniatus, puniceus, mineus*) band of feathers forming a kind of collar (*torques*) round its neck. Its head is so hard that the only way to correct it when it makes mistakes in its talking lessons is to hit it with an iron bar (*radius, clavicula*). Owing to the weakness of its legs it lands on its beak, which is equally hard. Pliny adds that it can be taught to greet emperors (*imperatores salutat*) and notes, like pseudo-Aristotle, how impudent it gets when tipsy (*in vino praecipue lasciva*). In yet another passage he remarks on the friendship of parrots and turtle-doves.[101]

Varro states that parrots sometimes appeared in public shows.[102] But the best-known parrot passages in Latin literature are concerned with the birds as the personal pets of individuals, who taught them to repeat words and phrases and to take their place in human company. A parrot would say 'How d'you do?' (*chaere, ave*) to its master and even to the emperor.[103] Very familiar is the elegy composed by Ovid on the death of the favourite of his mistress Corinna,[104] the bird 'sent from eastern India'. The poet calls upon the other birds to mourn for it, in particular the dove, whose friendship with the parrot (cf. above) is compared with that of Orestes with Pylades. He calls it the 'glory of the birds' (*avium gloria*) and describes its green feathers, brighter than emeralds, and its red and yellow beak. No bird was a better talker or could chatter more coaxingly. It took but little food, since it was too keen on talking to have time for heavy feeding.[105] It was content with nuts and plain water; and its dying words were 'Good-bye, Corinna' (*Corinna vale*).

No less familiar is Statius' poem on the death of the beloved parrot (*voluptas*) of his friend Melior.[106] Only the day before it had joined the company at dinner, enjoying the dainty morsels that it collected and walking from couch to couch until well past midnight, answering when spoken to. Melior had given it a spacious cage that gleamed with shining tortoiseshell and had rows of silver bars joined with ivory. Statius describes the bird as the 'emerald emperor of the East' (*plagae viridis regnator Eoae*), who greeted kings (*salutator regum*) and spoke the name of Caesar (*nomenque locutus Caesareum*). It could share in all its master's moods, whether grave or gay; and when it was released from its cage Melior was never lonely.

To turn to a much less agreeable aspect of the Roman scene so far as parrots were concerned – Elagabalus is said to have produced at feasts dishes filled with parrots' heads and to have fed parrots to his lions.[107]

Among the earliest renderings of parrots in Graeco-Roman art is the green bird now in the Berlin Antiquarium, from one of the mosaics in the royal palace, built by Eumenes II (197-159), at Pergamon.[108] A wall-painting in the 'House of Livia' on the Palatine in Rome depicts a rustic shrine, in which the central feature is a huge votive hunting-club: a long-tailed bird that may well be a parrot is perched in profile to the right of the club on a tall, apparently circular, pedestal.[109] The mosaic from Pompeii, on which a cat watches three birds balanced on the lip of a large bowl, has already been mentioned (pp. 88-9). Two of these birds are parrots – one completely green with a red neck-band, the other partly blue, with red feathers on body and tail: the third bird is a dove, whose friendship with the parrot is noted by Pliny and Ovid (cf. p. 248).[110] From Pompeii again comes a fragment of painting, now in the British Museum, which presents a green bird with a parrot's long tail and hooked beak, walking among cherries towards the left. The band round the neck is now pale mauve, a colour which also occurs round the eye, along the top of the head and body, and in the wings. Possibly this mauve represents an original red.[111] In a painting in the second-century Tomb of Marcus Clodius Hermes under the church of San Sebastiano by the Via Appia, just south of Rome, a parrot is seen in profile approaching from the left a large bowl piled with fruit.[112] Most spirited and naturalistic is the painted parrot perched among flowers on a low pillar in the Domitilla catacomb, also just to the south of Rome.[113] A parrot appears on two mosaic pavements from El-Djem in Tunisia. On one, which consists of a series of square panels each containing the figure of a bird or beast, the parrot has two curious horns sprouting from its head.[114] A more naturalistic parrot, with green body and red neck-band, occupies one curvilinear compartment of an elaborately designed pavement.[115] (Pl. 122)

On the silver dish from Lampsacus (cf. p. 59) a parrot stands towards the right on the left of the central seated figure personifying India.[116] A parrot forms the subject of some bronze figurines;[117] and was a favourite device on gems.[118] A beribboned parrot appears as a repeating, all-over floor-mosaic motif at Antioch-on-the-Orontes (cf. p. 288).[119]

PEACOCKS

That the peacock (*pavo*, ταώς) originally came from India is recognized by Aelian, who states that the largest specimens were to be found there;[120] and India was probably the source of the peacocks displayed in cages in Ptolemy II's procession.[121] In late republican and early imperial Italy peacocks were kept and bred in large flocks,[122] both for pleasure (*ad delectationem*) and for profit (*ad fructum*), as Varro tells us.[123] When sold they fetched remarkably high prices, at any rate in his day; and were to be carefully selected for their beauty, nature having given them the palm for beauty before all other birds. He recommends feeding them on barley and providing peacock-houses (*tecta*) with separate pens and walls carefully plastered to prevent the entry of snakes and harmful beasts. In front of each peacock-house there was to be a run, kept scrupulously clean, in which the birds could go to feed on sunny days.

Columella[124] regards the keeping of peacocks more as a hobby for cultivated householders than as an occupation for countrymen; and he too remarks on the pleasure that their beauty gives. He suggests keeping them on small wooded islands off the coast of Italy, where they would be perfectly safe, since they cannot fly high or far and no thieves or dangerous animals could get at them. In such circumstances they could wander freely and find most of their own food, needing only to be summoned at a fixed time by their keeper for a small extra feed of barley. But if kept on the mainland they would need a peacock-house (*stabulum pavonum*), for the making of which Columella gives instructions, as also for encouraging the birds to mate and for supervising the laying of eggs and the hatching of chicks. It is, he points out, a sign of the male bird's urge to mate when it covers itself with the jewelled feathers of its wings, as though in self-admiration, and is said to 'make a wheel' (*rotare dicitur*).

Pliny notes the friendship between peacocks and pigeons (*columbae*).[125] Alexander Severus is recorded as possessing aviaries in which he kept, besides peacocks, pheasants, poultry, ducks, partridges and no less than 20,000 ring-doves (*palumbae*), his special favourites.[126]

Varro relates that Quintus Hortensius was the first to serve peacocks at a banquet.[127] Other gourmands (*luxuriosi*) soon followed his example, with the result that the prices of their eggs and of the birds themselves rose to fantastic heights. Cicero writes of having demolished peacocks (*pavones confeci*) at wealthy persons' tables.[128]

Vitellius served to his guests the brains (*cerebella*) of pheasants and peacocks.[129] Juvenal speaks of a person going to his bath stuffed with peacock;[130] and Martial castigates the habit of handing over to a cruel cook the bird admired for the jewelled feathers that it spreads.[131] He also disapproves of the practice of making fans, to keep dirty flies off food, from the feathers of a peacock's tail, once the pride of that glorious bird.[132] Peacocks were among the victims sacrificed to the Emperor Gaius' godhead (cf. p. 246).[133]

In the sphere of Graeco-Roman myth and cult, the peacock was sacred to Hera/Juno. Ovid tells the story of Juno taking Argus' hundred eyes and placing them like glittering jewels in the tail of her bird; and he writes of 'Juno's bird, who carries the stars on its tail'.[134] Varro speaks of peacocks in the grove of Juno on the island of Samos (*Sami in luco Iunonis*).[135] Early imperial Greek coins of Samos carry a head of Hera on the obverse and a peacock in profile on the reverse; while Hera's frontal cult-statue, flanked by two peacocks, appears on the reverse of a coin struck at Samos for Julia Mamaea, mother of Alexander Severus.[136] In the Heraion at Argos Pausanias saw the image of a peacock made of gold and precious stones that had been dedicated by Hadrian.[137] On the Roman imperial coinage the peacock is a constant adjunct of figures of Juno; and on coins and medallions of Hadrian and Antoninus Pius, with reverse-types symbolizing the Capitoline Triad, a frontal peacock with tail spread represents Juno, along with an eagle and an owl that stand respectively for Jupiter and Minerva.[138]

Just as emperors appropriated Jupiter's eagle when assimilated to him (cf. p. 241), so Juno's peacock was the badge of empresses and other ladies of the imperial House. Coins of Domitilla (either the wife or the daughter of Vespasian), of Domitia (the wife of Domitian), and of Julia (the daughter of Titus) bear on their reverses a profile peacock, in the last case a frontal one with spread tail, often with the legend CONCORDIA AVGVST., a reference to harmonious relations within the imperial family comparable to those that supposedly existed between Jupiter and Juno.[139] Domitia was, in fact, entitled 'the Roman Juno' by Statius.[140] The reverse of a gold coin of Sabina, the wife of Hadrian, shows a peacock, but is legendless.[141]

As Lucina, Juno was goddess of childbirth; and this may be the reason why a fine frontal peacock, with its tail spread, appears on medallions of Faustina II, whose main preoccupation was with her duty to produce heirs for Marcus Aurelius.[142] This may also explain another of her medallion types which shows a child, probably the infant Juno, riding on peacock-back between two armed dancers (*Curetes*).[143] The impressive frontal peacock, displaying its tail and accompanied by the legend IVNONI REGINAE, on a bronze medallion of Salonina, the wife of Gallienus, betokens her sovereignty as an emperor's spouse.[144]

The peacock's tail, circular like the vault of heaven when spread and jewelled as with stars, made the bird a natural symbol of the sky to which the dead ascend and hence of apotheosis and immortality. Coins struck for the consecration of the Empresses Faustina I, Faustina II, Julia Domna (the wife of Septimius Severus), and Paulina (the wife of Maximinus: 235-238) bear the legend CONSECRATIO and a peacock standing either in profile or facing with spread tail. Some of the coins of Faustina II, Julia Domna and Paulina show a peacock soaring heavenwards with the deified empress on its back; and one consecration type of Faustina II consists of an empty, draped throne in front of which a peacock stands.[145] This last device denotes the deified empress' assimilation to Juno, as is indicated by the numerous Antonine coin-types that portray an empty, draped throne with the legend IVNONI REGINAE accompanying it.

As a symbol of immortality the peacock features in pagan tomb-art, as, for instance, in a painting in the second-century Tomb of the Aelii under St Peter's in Rome;[146] and in the shape of the great bronze peacock from Hadrian's Mausoleum, now in the Giardino della Pigna in the Vatican.[147] And it was, of course, from pagan art that the early Christian Church borrowed the bird as an emblem of everlasting life both in funerary and in ecclesiastical contexts. Of the peacock's very numerous appearances in both of these spheres only a few examples can be cited here. They occur in catacomb-painting, as, for instance, on the ceiling of the chamber of the *velatio* (veiling of a virgin) in the Priscilla catacomb[148] and on the back wall of cubiculum E in the new Via Latina catacomb.[149] On one rounded end of a third-century Jonah sarcophagus, now in the British Museum, a peacock stands on one leg beneath a gourd-tree, clutching an enormous fruit, perhaps a pomegranate, in its other claw.[150] On the symbolic Ravenna sarcophagi dating from the fifth and sixth centuries pairs of confronted peacocks are a favourite motif.[151] Turning to non-sepulchral works of Christian art, we may note the blue-green and golden peacock that steps daintily towards the right through a vine-scroll on a fifth-century mosaic fragment, now in the Aquileia Museum, from the Beligna church.[152] On the sixth-century ivory throne of Bishop Maximianus at Ravenna, on the broad horizontal vine-scroll border just below the seat, two profile peacocks flank the central monogram.[153] The most striking renderings of all are on the great Justinianic vine-scroll pavement at Sabratha (cf. pp. 246 and 394, note 83). To the left of the huge leaf-calyx from which the vine-scroll springs a large peacock stands towards the right and must once have been balanced on the right by a similar, leftward-facing, bird, now lost, its place being filled with ancient patching.[154] In the topmost of the four 'mandorlas' formed by the interlacing of the vine-stems a magnificent peacock faces the spectator, its gorgeous tail spread halo-like in a circle.[155] (Pl. 123)

In view of its highly decorative qualities it is not surprising to find the frontal 'wheel-making' peacock sometimes rendered for its own sake, without any apparent mythological or symbolic allusion attached to it. Instances of this are to be found on polychrome mosaic pavements in various quarters of the Roman world. Such are the apsidal mosaic from Bir-Chana in Tunisia;[156] an octagonal panel in a geometric surround in a private house at Aquileia;[157] and a 'medallion' within an octagon, unfortunately partly damaged, also in a geometric setting, in a private house of Roman Leicester (Ratae).[158] (Pl. 124)

GUINEAFOWL

Guineafowl (μελεαγρίδες, gallinae Africanae, Numidicae) were known to the Greeks of the classical period, but were still sufficiently rare in the Hellenistic age to be carried in cages in Ptolemy II's pageant.[159] Athenaeus gives a detailed description of their physical characteristics.[160] They are, he says, of the same size as a high-bred cock, with a head small in proportion to the body and a comb projecting from the top of the head like a peg. Their cheeks are red, their necks black and thicker and shorter than the cock's. Their entire body is black, thickly speckled with white feathers set at regular intervals in lozenge shapes; and their wings, too, are speckled with white markings forming serrated patterns lying parallel to one another.

Varro characterizes the guineafowl as big, speckled (variae), and hump-backed (gubberae), giving meleagrides as their Greek name; and says that in his time they had recently begun to be served at table as a

delicacy and fetched high prices on account of their rarity.[161]
Columella seems to distinguish between the African and Numidian
bird and the *meleagris*, stating that the former has a red head
(*galea* = 'helmet') and crest; whereas in the latter both are dark
blue.[162] Pliny, while mentioning the fighting of *meleagrides* in
Boeotia, gives Africa as the source of this 'hump-backed fowl'
(*gallinarum genus gibberum*) and declares that all types are now well-
known in Italy.[163] Martial lists *Numidicae guttatae* ('speckled') among
the livestock on the farm of his friend Faustinus at Baiae.[164] According to Statius guineafowl were among the presents thrown to the
people at the Saturnalia; and they played the part of mourners for
Melior's parrot.[165] Suetonius distinguishes *Numidicae* and *meleagrides*
in his list of the victims sacrificed to Gaius' godhead.[166]

Among the portraits of guineafowl in art is that on the Lampsacus
silver dish (cf. pp. 59, 249), where an unmistakable specimen, but
with the head incorrectly rendered, stands to the right of India,
opposite the parrot, the artist having erroneously imagined it to be an
Indian product. The most attractive picture of guineafowl is on the
great vine-scroll pavement from Justinian's church at Sabratha
(cf. pp. 246, 394, note 83), where in the 'mandorla' just below the
frontal peacock, two of these birds, symbolizing, as do all the other
birds, Christian souls in bliss, stand tail to tail amid the grapes, leaves
and tendrils. Their necks are too long and skinny – certainly not
thicker and shorter than a cock's – and are speckled instead of black
(cf. p. 253). But their cheeks are brilliant red and their bodies and
wings dark brown to black flecked with regular rows of tiny white
squares. The effect is that of a couple of dazzling check sports-
suits.[167] (Pl. 125)

PHEASANTS

Pheasants (*phasianae*, φασιανοί) were, like the guineafowl, known to
Greece in the fifth and fourth centuries B C; but they do not seem to
have been common there. They owe their name, of course, to the
fact that they were imported in the first instance from Colchis, land
of the river Phasis. A cage or cages containing some featured in
Ptolemy II's pageant;[168] and there appears to have been a flock of
them in a kind of zoo in the royal palace at Alexandria under
Ptolemy VIII (145-116), from whose *Commentaries* Athenaeus quotes
a passage relating to these birds.[169] The king refers to a type of

pheasant called *tetaroi* which had been procured from Media and bred by placing the eggs under guineafowl. As a result large numbers were raised for food and their flesh was held to be a rich delicacy (βρῶμα πολυτελές). Ptolemy himseelf had never tasted pheasant, but kept the birds as a treasure (κειμήλιον); and he would have been truly shocked by the practice, obtaining in Athenaeus' day, of serving up a whole pheasant to each guest at a feast on top of all their other food. Alexander Severus, like Ptolemy VIII, had pheasants in his aviary.[170] Pheasants are on the list of Gaius' sacrificial victims.[171]

Columella,[172] Pliny,[173] Statius,[174] and Martial[175] all refer to Colchis or Phasis as the pheasant's original home. Columella and Statius imply that the birds were eaten; and those kept at Baiae by Martial's friend Faustinus almost certainly appeared at table eventually. The story is told of Elagabalus that on certain days pheasant was his only fare, all his dishes being piled with nothing else.[176] His lions also dined on pheasant.[177] Other emperors were more frugal. Pertinax never gave pheasant at his private parties and never sent it to his friends as a present.[178] Alexander Severus only ate it on certain feastdays;[179] Tacitus only on his own or his relatives' birthdays.[180] The austere Julian forbade the ordering and serving of pheasants altogether, so far as his own table was concerned.[181]

On the *triclinium* mosaic from El-Djem now in Tunis, with its series of panels of animals and birds (cf. pp. 246, 249), a pheasant stands towards the left between two shrubs;[182] and on the Sabratha Justinianic pavement a large, brightly coloured pheasant stalks the vine-scroll just above the profile peacock (cf. p. 253).[183] (Pl. 126)

PARTRIDGES

The partridge (*perdrix*, πέρδιξ) was probably not native to Italy originally; and Strabo mentions a partridge larger than a vulture among the rare gifts presented to Augustus by the Indian envoys (cf. p. 224).[184] In Italy the bird was kept for fighting.[185] It was also erroneously believed to talk.[186] A mosaic fragment from Carthage, now in the British Museum, depicts a red-legged partridge standing towards the right. It has a pinkish-brown head, a dark-blue beak, a grey tail, and blue, green, grey, buff, grey-pink and orange tints in its plumage.[187] The month for hunting partridges seems to have been July; for a decoy partridge in a cage stands at the feet of the figure that personifies that month on the lost calendar mosaic from Carthage.[188]

The francolin (*attagen Ionius* or *Ionicus*), a type of partridge said by Pliny to have once been rare but to be found in his day in Gaul, Spain and the Alps,[189] must also, from its epithet, have been known in Asia Minor. According to Horace and Martial it was eaten as a delicacy.[190] A panel on the El-Djem *triclinium* mosaic features two of these birds marching one behind the other between two plants.[191]

CAPERCAILZIES

The capercailzie (*tetrao*) a member of the grouse tribe, reached Italy, says Pliny, from the Alps and northern Europe and is larger than a vulture. Pliny also states that when kept in captivity in reserves (*vivaria*), it loses its flavour, 'obstinately holds its breath' (*contumacia spiritu revocato*), and speedily dies.[192] Birds of this breed were among the Emperor Gaius' sacrificial victims.[193]

QUAILS

The quail (*coturnix*, ὄρτυξ), known to classical Greece, was kept for fighting in Italy, so Pliny implies;[194] and W. Helbig records a wall-painting from Pompeii in which a pair of quails are preparing themselves for battle.[195] In another passage Pliny calls the quail a small bird and describes its migratory habits.[196] According to Varro these birds were, in his day, fattened for eating and fetched high prices.[197] But by Pliny's time they had come to be rejected as a table dish on account of the belief that their favourite food was poisonous seed.[198] In Plautus' day they were playthings for children; and 'quail' was used as a term of endearment.[199] On the Justinianic church mosaic at Sabratha, in the 'mandorla' just below that in which the guineafowl are shown, is a fat, short-necked, humped bird standing in a cage which might be a quail, although its tail does not dip at the end as it should.[200] Here it would be a symbol of the soul still imprisoned in the body and longing to escape into the heavenly vineyard where, among the other fowls of the air that are feeding freely, are three very similar birds, one with dipping tail, that might be quails too.[201] (Pl. 127)

POULTRY

The keeping of domestic cocks and hens (*galli, gallinae, galinacei*) was another practice in which the Graeco-Roman world was anticipated by the city-states of classical Greece. In Italy fighting cocks were kept for sport as early as the second century B C, as is indicated by Lucilius' lines on 'the victor cock that struts proudly along, rising on tiptoe as it goes.'[202] In Columella's time there were professional cock-trainers (*lanistae*), who might lose all their outlay on their birds in gambling, should another victor cock win the bet.[203] A relief, said to be preserved in the Evangelical School at Smyrna and probably of Graeco-Roman date, shows a victorious cock strutting towards the left and holding a large palm-branch.[204] A cock-fight in which four birds are engaged—one is already dead—is vividly portrayed in a painting from the House of the Vettii at Pompeii.[205]

Common farmyard or barnyard poultry kept in the country were known as *gallinae villaticae* or *cohortales*.[206] Breeds imported into Italy came from Tanagra (in Boeotia), Chalcis (in Euboea), and Media (Persia) and were noted for their beauty and suitability as fighters.[207] Both Varro and Columella remark on the big profits made by the specially skilful poultry-farmers on the island of Delos;[208] and both writers give lengthy and minute instructions about the keeping, breeding, feeding and fattening of poultry in Italy, about the construction of hen-houses (*gallinaria*), and about the duties of the poultry-keeper (*gallinarius, pastor*).[209] Cato mentions the fattening of hens.[210] Pliny praises the Adriatic birds and says that even bantams (*pumiliones*) are not sterile;[211] whereas Columella disapproves of bantams (*pumiles aves*) on account of their lack of fertility and general unprofitability, while admitting that their diminutiveness could be a source of pleasure.[212]

There was also a wild type of poultry (*gallinae rusticae*),[213] rarely found in towns and only seen in cages in Rome, where such birds sometimes appeared in public shows along with parrots (cf. pp. 248 and 394, note 102).[214]

Cocks were sacrificed to the *Lares*;[215] and a cock, one of the adjuncts of Mercury, frequently accompanies him in works of Roman art.[216] A polychrome mosaic panel, perhaps from Jerash (Gerasa) in Transjordania and now in the Birmingham Museum and Art Gallery, shows a group of poultry, two cocks and a hen, along with an owl and a duck.[217] On a pavement at Piazza Armerina, depicting boys hunting animals and birds, a large and powerful cock attacks a fleeing child.[218] Among the birds on the Justinianic mosaic at Sabratha are two handsome cocks and the group of a hen with her chicks (cf. pp. 287 and 394, note 83).[219] (Pl. 131)

PIGEONS AND DOVES

Pigeons (*columbae*), ring-doves (*palumbae*), and turtle-doves (*turtures*) were again all known to the Greeks of the pre-Graeco-Roman period. Pliny describes their habits;[220] and Varro and Columella both give elaborate instructions for keeping, rearing, and fattening them and for the construction of pigeon-houses and dovecotes (*peristera* or *peristerotrophia* from περιστερά = pigeon, *columbaria*, *avaria*).[221] Often, says Varro, one of these houses could hold as many as five thousand birds; and one of the duties of the pigeon-keeper (*pastor columbarum*) was to keep the houses clean. According to Varro and Columella a pair of particularly good pigeons could be sold for 1,000 *sestertii*. Columella further states that people can be found to pay as much as 4,000 *nummi* (*sestertii*) for a pair to keep as pets for pleasure (*oblectamenta deliciarum possidendi habendique causa*). Varro mentions birds on farms so tame that they will feed on household fare inside the house-door (*intra limina ianuae*). Pliny writes of many people carrying their love of pigeons to insane lengths (*harum amore insaniunt multi*), building towers for them on their roofs and boasting of the high breeding (*nobilitas*) and pedigrees (*origines*) of individual birds: as early as before the civil war of 49 BC a Roman knight, Lucius Anxius, had advertised pigeons for sale at 400 *denarii* per brace.[222]

In towns the pigeons lived on roofs, as Plautus and Juvenal indicate.[223] They were also kept as pets. Martial speaks of the 'darling pigeon' (*delicium columba*) of his friend Stella.[224] Trimalchio ordered the erection at his tomb of a statue of his wife Fortunata holding her dove;[225] and a dove is most probably the bird caressed by the figure of the dead on tombstones.[226] Alexander Severus' partiality for pigeons had been already noted (p. 250). A third-century AD Greek metrical inscription found at Dama in the Hauran (Syria) records a pigeon-lover above whose tomb was erected a fine and conspicuous tower for these birds (πέλειαι) to live in.[227] Turtle-doves were a special delicacy.[228]

Carrier pigeons (*columbae tabellariae*) functioned in both public and private contexts in the Roman world. Frontinus tells the story of how the consul Hirtius communicated by 'pigeon post' with Decimus Brutus when the latter was besieged by Mark Antony at Modena (Mutina) in 43 BC. He shut up pigeons in the dark, starved them, fastened letters to their necks by a hair, and then released them as near to the city walls as he could. The birds, hungry for light and food, made for the highest buildings and were caught by Brutus, who was thus informed of everything, especially after he had put food in certain spots and taught the pigeons to alight there.[229] On the other hand, Pliny states that it was Decimus Brutus who sent the pigeons as messengers (*internuntiae*) to the consul's camp, fastening letters to their legs and thus defeating all Antony's efforts to cut him off from the outside world.[230]

Martial relates that a man sent a missive to his sister Aratulla by a pigeon, a winsome bird that glided through the silent air and fluttered down into her lap as she sat.[231]

Doves are familiar as the sacred birds of Venus. A stele in the British Museum of Trajanic date depicts a girl in the guise of Venus Victrix with a dove at her feet.[232] The dove as a symbol of the soul at peace in early Christian art is too well known for individual examples to need citing here.

The earliest recorded instance of the rendering of doves for their own sake in Graeco-Roman art is that of Sosus of Pergamon's mosaic panel (*emblema*). On this there was a 'wonderful dove' (*mirabilis columba*) drinking and casting the shadow of its head on the water. Other doves were sunning themselves and pluming their feathers on the lip of a bowl.[233] Of this picture several copies or adaptations have come down to us from Roman times, notably the mosaic panel, now in the Museo Capitolino, from Hadrian's villa at Tivoli (Tibur).[234] Pictured, too, for its own sake is the pair of pigeons nestling on an open acanthus-flower on one of the Zliten mosaics.[235]

SWANS

Neither Varro nor Columella nor any other Roman writer mentions the keeping of the swan (*cygnus*, *cycnus*, κύκνος, *olor*) on ponds or lakes on country estates for the pleasure that its beauty affords. Pliny describes the birds' wedge-shaped formation in the air when migrating, declares that they will sometimes eat one another, and expresses disbelief in the story of their dying song.[236] Cicero, on the other hand, does not discount the tradition of their death-song, of their power of divining when their end is at hand or of their sense that death is something good and even pleasurable: hence their dedication to Apollo[237] – by the Romans as by the Greeks before them. Besides music and divination the swans' origin in northern lands was held to connect them with Apollo as coming himself from the Hyperborean regions.

This association of the swan with Apollo is reflected in works of Roman art. For example, in a painting from Herculaneum the god's tripod, flanked by two griffins, is surmounted by a swan.[238] On the Ara Pacis Augustae, the fact that Augustus placed himself under Apollo's patronage is indicated in the great acanthus-scroll dado on the exterior of the precinct walls, where graceful swans, either frontal or turned three-quarters to right or left, are poised at regular intervals, with wings spread and necks bent, on the flower buds that top acanthus-stems, just below the upper edge of the dado.[239] It may also have been the Apolline connection that determined the choice, on the same monument, of a swan to carry the Nymph with flying veil who personifies the *aura* (breeze) that blows over inland streams and lakes. The powerful bird with neck outstretched bears the girl through the air, above reeds and other water-plants and water gushing from an overturned urn, in the left-hand section of the famous *Terra Mater* or *Italia* relief.[240]

A marble altar of Augustan date in the Arles Museum shows on its principal face a heavy laurel-wreath suspended between the beaks of two splendid swans, whose heads and bodies, worked in high relief, occupy the picture's lateral edges, while their legs, also in high relief, are carved on the altar's sides. One wing of each bird, in low relief, fills the space above the wreath on the front, the other wing being spread across each side-face of the block. On the back are two palm-trees linked by a swag of fruit. The altar, being uninscribed and containing no space or panel for an inscription, is unlikely to be sepulchral. The swans suggest that it was dedicated to Apollo, the laurel-wreath and palm-trees perhaps alluding to the victories of Augustus as the god's protégé. The spot where the altar was found, the theatre, further suggests an Apolline association.[241]

The swan as a symbol of a happy death does, however, also have a place on funerary altars, as on one in the Louvre, where two swans flank an olive-tree;[242] and on another in the Louvre, where two swans flank the central Medusa-head just below the inscription-panel that was never actually inscribed.[243]

In the Roman world, as among the Greeks, the swan was also sacred to Aphrodite/Venus; and in Latin poetry she is described as carried through the air drawn by a team of swans.[244] Horace in one passage calls the birds 'dazzling' (*purpurei*). Representations of Leda and Jupiter in swan disguise are, of course, very numerous in works of Graeco-Roman art.[245]

The fact that on the lost calendar mosaic from Carthage (cf. pp. 255, 396, note 188) the figure of 'November' is accompanied by a swan suggests that it was in that month that the bird arrived to winter in North Africa. According to Athenaeus swans were eaten;[246] and in the same passage he mentions their love for their young, their belligerency, which sometimes extends to the killing of their own kind, and their death-song.

On the pavement in the north transept of the church of the Loaves and Fishes at Tabgha (cf. pp. 244-6) a bird that is very probably a swan can be seen about halfway down the mosaic on the left-hand side.[247] On the Justinianic mosaic at Sabratha a swan figures twice in the vine-scroll.[248]

GEESE

The goose (*anser*, χήν) had been domesticated in the Greek world as early as Homeric times, when Penelope was cheered in Odysseus' absence by the sight of her flock of twenty geese which she had in the house (κατὰ οἶκον).[249] Among Roman writers Varro and Columella give the most detailed information about the keeping of geese on the farms of Italy.[250] Varro uses the Greek term *chenoboscion* for the place in which the geese are fed and mentions the large flocks of these birds maintained by Scipio Metellus and Marcus Seius. For breeding he counsels large (*ampli*) and white (*albi*) birds as against those of the grey or mottled variety (*varium genus*), which is wild and not easy to tame. He also gives advice on the supervision of mating and egg-laying. Geese, he says, need plenty of water in which to swim and coops floored with soft straw for the female birds. Great care must be taken to keep weasels or polecats (*mustelae*) and other harmful creatures out of the goose enclosure. The birds prefer damp places; and their naturally voracious appetites can be satisfied with endive (*seris*), barley, corn and mash (*farrago*). Varro then gives instructions for the fattening of the birds on barley-meal and flour.[251] After they have fed, their place must be well cleaned out, since they like it clean but never leave it clean themselves.

Columella declares that of all amphibious animals the goose gives the countryman the most satisfaction, because it needs very little tending and keeps better watch than a dog – after which he recalls the story of how the cackling of geese had given warning of the night attack of the Gauls on the Capitol in 390 BC, 'when the dogs didn't make a sound' (canibus silentibus). Geese need water and plenty of grass, but must be kept away from crops or they will devour them. Their goslings are of value and they shed their feathers twice a year. Coops (harae) must be provided in bushes in quiet corners of the yard where the females can make their nests and lay their eggs. Columella also uses the Greek term chenoboscia for the birds' feeding-places. The enclosure (cohors) must have walls fifteen feet high with a verandah (porticus) inside and a room (cella) for the keeper (custos). The coops must be so constructed that no snakes, vipers, cats (feles) or mustelae can find a way in. Columella then lists the various types of green food and cereals to be fed to geese. For breeding the white (albi) birds are to be preferred to the grey or mottled (varii), which are less profitable and valuable. There follow details on the subjects of mating, the rearing of goslings, and fattening.

A picturesque commentary on the keeping of domestic geese in Italy in early Hellenistic times is provided by an Apulian pelike (two-handled pitcher) now in the British Museum. The painting shows, above, a toilet scene in the house and below it a large spotted cat is advancing rapidly on a white goose that stands its ground, facing its enemy, with flapping wings and beak poised for the counter-attack.[252] Whether this bird was a pet, living partly indoors, or one of the farmyard flock, we cannot tell. But similar incidents must sometimes have occurred in some of the Italian country houses of the Roman period (cf. p. 88).

Pliny, in his main passage on the goose,[253] remarks on the excel-lence of a stuffed goose's liver as food[254] – a discovery made either by Scipio Metellus or by his contemporary, the knight Marcus Seius. He relates the remarkable feat of driving a flock of geese on foot all the way to Rome from the land of the Morini in central Gaul: such birds as got tired were sent to the head of the column and automati-cally pushed forward by the rest. The white geese can be plucked twice a year for profit and their feathers grow again, those nearest to the body being the softest. The best goose feathers come from Germany, where are to be found small, white birds called gantae, providing plumage that can be sold for 5 denarii per pound. Pliny declares that some of the commanders of auxiliary units on the German frontier have got into trouble for taking whole cohorts of their men off sentry duty and sending them off to capture these birds.

Luxury, he says, has reached such a pitch that even men must have goose-feather pillows under their heads. In another passage Pliny describes the wedge-shaped migratory formation of the wild geese.[255]

According to Caesar the Britons before the Roman conquest abstained from eating geese (as also from eating hares and poultry), keeping them for pleasure and amusement, presumably as pets.[256] On the other hand, the cackling geese that wandered about, with the crowd of other birds, in the dirty farmyard of Faustinus at Baiae probably ended their days on their owner's table;[257] and such may well have been the fate of the two stout geese that a boy drives before him on the palace peristyle mosaic at Istanbul.[258] (Pl. 132)

In the Roman world geese, like swans, were regarded as sacred to certain deities. It was, of course, because they were Juno's sacred birds that the geese on the Capitol were spared by the starving Roman garrison when the Gauls were besieging it and so saved the situation, while men and dogs were sound asleep, by giving the alarm with their cackling and the noisy flapping of their wings (*clangor alarumque crepitus*).[259] In the art of the northern provinces the goose is the adjunct of Mars Thincsus, originally a Germanic god. Examples of this are a small altar in the museum at Housesteads (Vercovicium) on Hadrian's Wall and an arch, again from Housesteads but now in the museum at Chesters (Cilurnum), also on the Wall, where the warrior god stands in the central arched panel at the top of the arch.[260] On both of these reliefs the bird stands on the ground beside the god's feet. The goose was also sacred to the fertility god Priapus. Petronius tells the story of a visitor to a certain house, who, on reaching the door, was attacked by three sacred geese which rushed at him and stood around him, cackling like mad things (*rabioso stridore*). One of them, the ringleader and chief of the savage trio (*dux et magister saevitiae*), gave him a vicious jab in the leg with its bill, whereupon he wrenched a leg off a table and slew the ferocious creature. On discovering this, the old woman who fed the geese exclaimed in horror that the visitor had committed a dreadful sin in killing 'the darling of Priapus, beloved of all matrons' (*Priapi delicias, anserem omnibus matronis acceptissimum*).[261] Finally, in Roman Egypt the goose was sacred to Isis and Osiris. A Pompeian painting shows Osiris with the head of a bull and holding a *sistrum* (rattle), while to the left of him his goose is nibbling a plant.[262]

Since the wild goose seems to have been hunted in winter, one

bird, or a brace of birds, appears as the attribute on sarcophagi of the
personification of that season, held in the figure's hand.[263] Among
renderings of geese for their own sake in Graeco-Roman art
are the bronze statue of a goose, 23 inches high, now in the
British Museum, which was found in the hippodrome in Istanbul
and probably once served as part of a fountain, since its beak forms a
spout;[264] and the two geese, accompanied by snails, ducks, and a
basket for catching fish, on a 'still-life' mosaic panel now walled up
in the vestibule of the sacristy of Santa Maria in Trastevere in
Rome.[265] There is an expressive goose in the top right-hand coner of
the mosaic in the north transept of the Tabgha church.[266] On the
Sabratha Justinianic vine-scroll pavement are three grey birds, probably geese, although one is somewhat too long in the leg, and a white
goose.[267]

DUCKS

Ducks (*anates*, *νῆτται*) are among the birds most prominent in the
accounts of Italian aviaries of the first centuries B C and A D, of which
the earliest were those of the knight Marcus Laenius Strabo at
Brundisium and of Lucullus at Tusculum,[268] and the most famous
and minutely described, that of Varro at Casinum.[269] In his aviary
Varro made a pond with a platform (*falere*) above it and along this
platform were hollowed out 'docks' (*navalia*) as shelters for ducks.
From one side of the platform Varro's guests, when dining alfresco,
could watch the ducks coming out into the pond and swimming
around. Later on Varro[270] gives general instructions for the keeping
of flocks of ducks and for the building of a duck 'nursery' (*nessotrophion*). The place chosen must be either swampy, which the ducks
like best, or where there is a pond, natural or artificial, into which
they can go down gradually (*gradatim*). The birds should have an
enclosure fifteen feet high with a wide ledge (*crepido lata*), to hold
covered resting-places (*cubilia tecta*), along the entire wall on the inside.
In the run (*vestibulum*) in front of the ledge there must be a trough for
their food and water. The walls of the enclosure must be smoothed
with plaster to keep out cats (*feles*) and other animals; and the whole
must be covered with a wide-meshed net to keep eagles out and the
ducks in. For food ducks need wheat, barley, grape-skins, and
sometimes aquatic creatures such as water-crabs. Varro also mentions a species of duck called *phaleris*, of which the best specimens,

102–104 Hares on mosaics at Piazza Armerina. *Above, left*, a mounted huntsman with a two-pronged spear stabs at a hare in its form and, *right*, a hunter holding up his kill by its hind-legs. *Below*, a child impales a hare on his spear, encouraged by his companion (p. 201).

105–107 *Above*, a wall-painting of a rabbit with some figs; *left*, a hare pursued by hounds on a Castor-ware beaker, and, *below*, a relief of a successful mounted hare-hunter holding up his catch (pp. 201, 203).

108–109 Two marine mosaics: *above*, various fish, from Pompeii, and, *below*, Cupids riding on dolphins, at Lepcis Magna (pp. 207, 213).

110 A fountain spout in the form of a bronze dolphin (p. 208).

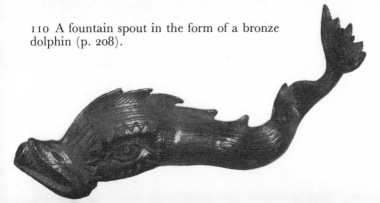

111, 112 *Above*, a statue of a coiled snake at Constanta, and, *below*, a Pompeian wall-painting of snakes from a *lararium* (pp. 233, 235, 236).

113 Wall-painting of Pygmies with crocodiles and a hippopotamus in a Nilotic landscape from Pompeii (p. 219).

114, 115 Reptiles on a bronze votive hand at Avenches, and a mosaic of a tortoise fighting a cock at Aquileia (pp. 217, 220, 223, 235).

118 Wall-painting of a heron attacking a snake (cf. Plate 33, and p. 245).

◁ 116, 117 Long-legged birds on mosaics: *left*, an ostrich being carried aboard a transport ship, on the 'Great Hunt' mosaic, Piazza Armerina (*see also* Fig. 1); *below*, ibises wading, a detail of a Nilotic landscape from Pompeii (pp. 238, 245).

119 A flamingo represented in a vine-scroll on a mosaic from Justinian's church, Sabratha (p. 246).

120, 121 The Roman eagle seen as the imperial
emblem, *above*, on a cameo holding a wreath and
palm, and, *below*, a rare representation in the
round of a bronze eagle from Silchester (p. 241).

according to Pliny, came from Seleucia in Parthia and the Roman province of Asia.[271]

Columella also describes the ideal *nessotrophion*, which, like Varro's, is to have a wall fifteen feet high, to be covered with lattice-work or a wide-meshed net to keep the ducks in and eagles and hawks out, and to be plastered over inside and out to prevent the entry of cats (*feles*) and ferrets (*viverrae*). There should be a pond in the middle, but its edges are not to be reared on steps (*gradus*), but should slope down gradually (*paulatim clivo subsidere*). The floor of the pond should be plastered over, except in the centre, where water-plants should be allowed to grow. Columella then gives instructions about the mating of ducks and the rearing of ducklings.[272]

Ducks, like quails, were sometimes given to children as pets (cf. p. 256); and duckling ('duckie') could sometimes be used as a term of endearment.[273] Ducks were eaten, but Martial says that, although a duck should be served whole, only the breast and neck are tasty: the rest can go back to the cook. Trimalchio calls the duck low-class food.[274] Both Pliny and Aelian mistakenly believed ducks to be prophets of wind.[275]

The wild duck, apparently hunted in winter, is an attribute of 'Winter' in works of Roman art, as, for instance, on the Parabiago *patera* in Milan, where the little hooded figure that personifies the season carries a brace of ducks in the fold of his cloak.[276] Rendered for their own sake they form the subject of a mosaic panel in the Metropolitan Museum of Art, New York, where is depicted a complete family: a duck and a drake, with a band of white round its neck, standing on the edge of a pond in which three ducklings are paddling.[277] Two ducks occupy the lower register of all three cat-and-bird mosaic pictures (cf. p. 88). On the piece in the Naples Museum the ducks are shown among lotus-buds; and ducks are a constant motif in Nilotic landscapes.[278] On the Tabgha pavements, with their Nilotic features (cf. p. 244), ducks appear singly or in a pair balanced on the top of lotus-flowers: in one case a single bird peeps down inquisitively over the flower's edge.[279] (Pl. 134)

CROWS AND RAVENS

Crows (*cornices*, κορῶναι) and ravens (*corvi*, κόρακες) were among the most remarkable of all the talking birds whose accomplishments Roman writers have recorded. Macrobius[280] has the story of how, on Octavian's return to Rome after his defeat of Antony at Actium, a workman came up to him holding a crow which he had taught to say *ave Caesar victor imperator* ('Hail Caesar, victorious general'). Octavian, full of admiration for the courteous (*officiosus*) bird, bought it for 20,000 sesterces. But one of the workman's mates, annoyed that none of this bounty had come his way, told Caesar that the man had also another crow and asked him to order it to be produced. When it arrived it repeated the lesson it had learnt: *ave victor imperator Antoni* ('Hail Antony, victorious general'). Octavian, far from being angry, merely told the owner of the crows to share the money with his mate; and he bought both a parrot and a pie that gave him the same greeting. All this encouraged a cobbler to try to teach a crow to give a similar salutation; and exasperated when the bird often made no response he used to say 'All my labour and expense wasted'. At last the crow began to repeat its lesson. But when Octavian heard it as he was passing by, he said 'I've enough people greeting me like that at home'. Whereupon the bird, remembering the words that it had heard its master utter in complaint, came out with 'All my labour and expense wasted'. At this Octavian burst out laughing and had the crow bought for a higher price than he had ever paid for a bird before.

Suetonius declares that a few months before Domitian's assassination a crow alighted on the Capitol and announced in Greek ' All will be well' (ἔσται πάντα καλῶς) ; [281] and Pliny says that in his own day in Rome there was a crow from Baetica in southern Spain which belonged to a knight and was remarkable for its very black colour and for its ability to repeat sentences and words, constantly adding to its repertory.[282]

Pliny also relates the tale of a talking raven in Tiberius' time.[283] This bird, hatched in a nest on the Temple of Castor and Pollux, flew down to a cobbler's shop nearby, took up its abode there, and soon picked up the habit of talking. Every morning it flew to the speakers' platform (*rostra*) in the Forum and greeted first Tiberius, Germanicus and Drusus Caesar by name and then the Roman public passing by: then it returned to the shop. This performance it kept up continuously for several years. But the owner of the next-door shop, perhaps jealous of the bird or annoyed at the mess that it made, killed it. Public indignation at this outrage reached such a pitch that the murderer was driven from the neighbourhood and ultimately done away with. Meanwhile, crowds of people attended the raven's funeral: the corpse was carried on a draped bier, borne by two negroes and preceded by a piper, to its pyre by the Appian Way.

In Asia a certain Monoceros is said to have used ravens in hunting, for tracking down and driving out the game. He carried them down to the forest on his head and shoulders.[284]

Allegedly gifted with prophetic powers, the raven is described in Latin literature as sacred to Apollo/Helios; and it often appears on Mithras Tauroctonos reliefs (cf. p. 151) just below the sun-god's figure or bust in the upper left-hand corner of the picture.[285] There is also some evidence in Roman Gaul of the association of ravens with Celtic gods, with Lugus, who seems to have been linked with Mercury, and other unnamed deities.[286] The British Museum possesses the bronze figure of a raven, about 16 inches high and holding what looks like a large nut in its left claw.[287]

PIES

As a talker the pie (*pica*, κίττη) of Roman times rivalled the crows and ravens. Pliny declares that its speech is more articulate (*expressior*) than a parrot's, that pies like (*adamant*) uttering words, which they not only learn but enjoy, practising their lessons in their heads carefully and thoughtfully (*meditantes intra semet cura atque cogitatione*) and making no secret of their concentration on them (*intentionem non occultant*). Pies will die, he says, if a difficult word beats them and their memory fails them unless they hear the same word repeatedly, but they cheer up wonderfully (*mirum in modum hilarari*) when they do hear it spoken. Their gift of speech compensates for their lack of beauty.[288]

Trimalchio kept a spotted pie (*pica varia*) in a golden cage hung over his front door so that it might greet visitors.[289] Martial writes of the 'greeting pie' (*pica salutatrix*) belonging to a certain Lausus; and later he makes a pie say that it greets its master in such intelligible words that no one would believe that it was a bird unless they saw it.[290]

Plutarch, in a charming passage on talking birds in general – starlings, crows, and parrots, which can be taught to utter words and imitate the flow of human speech (τὸ τῆς φωνῆς πνεῦμα), retails the following story of a pie.[291] This wonderful talker belonged to a barber in Rome and was famed for its ability to reproduce, not only human words, but also the noises made by animals and the sounds of musical instruments. But one day, after hearing trumpets played at a funeral, it became completely silent, greatly to everyone's astonishment and alarm. The bird must be ill, people said; when suddenly from its throat came blazing forth (ἀνέλαμψεν), none of its former mimicries, but only trumpet music, with all its sequences and every change of rhythm, pitch and tone precisely rendered. The pie had spent its interval of silence in rehearsing all this in its head.

STARLINGS

The starling (sturnus, ψάρ) was also a talker. Statius, listing it among the mourners for Melior's parrot (cf. p. 248), describes it as 'storing in its memory the words that it has heard'.[292] Pliny says that in his day the young Caesars, Britannicus and Nero, kept a starling and nightingales that had learnt to speak in Greek and Latin (Graeco ac Latino sermone) and were for ever practising (meditantes assidue), adding new words and longer sentences to their repertory every day.[293]

NIGHTINGALES

The nightingale (luscinia, luscinius, lusciniola, ἀηδών) was again a talking bird. But it was as a songster that the Roman world knew it best. Plutarch, in the passage already quoted (cf. p. 275 and p. 399, note 291), says that nightingales are taught the art of singing as nestlings by the mother-bird and learn it, not for pay or glory, but for the joy of rivalling one another in the beauty of song. Pliny grows quite ecstatic about the nightingale's music, with its great range and variety of tones and notes pouring from the tiny throat, for the brief fortnight in early spring during which its sings its sweetest.[294] He declares that the prices paid for these lovely songsters can sometimes be as great as those paid for slaves and that a white nightingale once fetched 6,000 sesterces, the purchaser wishing to present it to Agrippina II, the mother of Nero. There are cases, he adds, of these birds being taught to start singing at the word of command and to sing antiphonally with a choir in a concert (cum symphonia alternasse).

Martial maintains that a lady of his acquaintance, one Telesilla, had a burial mound erected over the body of her dead pet nightingale.[295] But there were also some gourmands barbarous enough to eat these little creatures. Horace speaks of people who make a habit of dining expensively on nightingales.[296] Elagabalus was credited with often consuming their tongues.[297]

BLACKBIRDS

Philostratus, in a passage on the training of talking birds and singing birds,[298] couples nightingales with blackbirds (*merulae*, κόψιχοι, κόσσυφοι) as capable of being taught to speak like human beings and to trill like pipes. Blackbirds were also, along with nightingales, kept as pets, as in the case of the young son of Pliny the Younger's acquaintance, Regulus, who had these birds, in company with parrots and animals of various kinds, killed at the boy's funeral pyre, so that he might have them with him in the after-life.[299] On the other hand, blackbirds could be snared for eating and appear with pigeons as a dish.[300]

White blackbirds were a great rarity and were exhibited as such, with parrots (cf. p. 248), in public shows in Rome.[301] Pliny and Pausanias both state that they were found on Mount Cyllene in Arcadia, Pliny adding, incorrectly, that they existed nowhere else.[302]

THRUSHES OR FIELDFARES

The thrush (*turdus*, κίκλη), if it were not rather the fieldfare that the ancient writers had in mind, was not renowned for talking: the talking thrush owned by Agrippina II was, in fact, said to be unprecedented.[303] These birds' chief function in the Roman world was to serve as food. Varro states that from the aviary on his maternal aunt's farm in the Sabine country five thousand *turdi* were sold for three *denarii* apiece and that in that region large flocks of them were found.[304] He also describes the type of enclosure in which the fattened birds (*pingues turdi*) should be kept – either a large domed building (*testudo*) or a peristyle covered with tiles and netting in which several thousand thrushes and blackbirds could be maintained; and he gives all the details of its essential internal equipment – poles and rods for the birds to perch on, recesses (*caveae*) furnished with shelves (*tabulatae*), water and cakes (*offae*) for their drink and food, and so forth. The walls must be well plastered to keep out vermin and other small pests; and the windows must be few, so that the imprisoned birds do not see trees and birds outside and so grow thin with longing to be free.[305] Pliny quotes Cornelius Nepos, who died during Augustus' principate, as saying that the practice of fattening thrushes (*turdos saginari*) had been introduced a little before his time.[306] Plutarch tells us that Pompey's doctor prescribed a thrush for him as invalid diet. But when Pompey heard that thrushes were only to be found in the aviary where his enemy Lucullus was fattening them, he refused to have one.[307]

Thrushes were, indeed, held to be special delicacies, as Horace and Martial indicate.[308] At Trimalchio's banquet the *turdi* that escaped from the interior of the great boar's body when it was cut open were caught by fowlers as they flew round the room and were doubtless killed, plucked, cooked and eventually consumed.[309] The custom was to string the dead birds on hoops before they passed into the hands of the cook. Martial twice mentions such a hoop (*corona*) with fat thrushes hanging from it;[310] and on one of the panels on the *triclinium* mosaic from El-Djem is depicted just such a hoop on which five birds are suspended.[311]

FINCHES

The most acceptable suggestion has been made that Lesbia's famous 'sparrow' (*passer*) was, in fact, a bullfinch,[312] with whose habits and characteristics Catullus' account of the favourite corresponds.[313] It sported with the girl, nestled and hopped about on her lap, playfully nipped her finger-tips, now frolicking with her, now consoling her when sad. It was 'honey-sweet' (*mellitus*), knew its mistress as well as a child knows its mother, and was for ever chirruping for her alone (*ad solam dominam usque pipilabat*). *Passer* was certainly used as a term of endearment, as by Plautus[314] and by Marcus Aurelius apropos of the little daughter, Gratia, of his tutor Fronto.[315]

The goldfinch (*carduelis*, ἀκανθυλλίς) could, according to Pliny, be taught to do tricks (*imperata faciunt*), not only singing to order, but doing things with its feet and beak as though they were hands.[316] They were also children's pets. At Trimalchio's banquet one of the guests relates how, growing weary of his boy's craze for birds (*morbosus in aves*), he has killed the child's three pet goldfinches and said, as a reason for their disappearance, that the *mustela* (weasel or polecat) has taken them (cf. p. 89).[317] From Herculaneum comes a painting of two small birds facing one another in a floral setting. The

smaller and more colourful bird on the right, with green head, back
and wings and red throat and breast, could well be a finch of some
kind. The larger, all-yellow bird on the left might be a water-pipit.[318]

A particularly pleasing instance of the Roman artists' interest in
nature for its own sake is the rendering of parent birds at their nests,
generally in the act of feeding their demanding nestlings. In funerary
art, on sepulchral altars, for example, the motif might perhaps
symbolize the piety of the deceased towards their children or other
relatives. But in other contexts it is difficult to find any reason for its
presence other than sheer delight in its intrinsic charm.

Of the funerary altars of the first century AD whose carved
decoration comprises the bird's-nest motif, the most notable is one in
the former Lateran collection.[319] The back is unworked and in the
inscription-panel on the front, accompanied by decorative features
of a common kind, only the stock D M has been engraved. But on
each of the sides the spectator's attention is focused on a large nest
lodged within the curve of a heavy fruit-swag that is suspended
between two *candelabra*. On one side this nest-scene is perfectly
preserved. The two parent birds appear to be eagles just returned
from a foraging sortie. The mother is inserting succulent morsels into
the gaping mouths of her eaglets, while the father is ripping up a snake
that he has caught for them. On the other side all that remains is the
nest, one nestling, now headless, the entire form of one of the parents
and the legs and tail of the other. This, too, appears to be an eagle
family.[320] (Pl. 128)

Another sepulchral monument carved with a bird's nest, on which
the motif would seem to be just a part of the natural setting of the
episode depicted, is the Triumph of Dionysus sarcophagus at Baltimore (cf. pp. 49, 65, 85, 142). Here, on the extreme right of the front,
just above the head of the Satyress who leads the cortège, is an eagle's
nest built in an oak-tree.[321] In the nest are three eaglets, not clamour-
ing for a meal, but sheltering contentedly beneath their mother's
wing. The father bird is perched some distance to the left and surveys
his brood with an air of detachment.

Yet another sculptural example, of a purely decorative character,
is on a flat pilaster, in the former Lateran collection, carved all over
with a two-dimensional vine-scroll, the technique of which suggests

an early third-century date. The nest, whose owners are of an indeterminate species, is ensconced among the grapes and vine-leaves and contains three nestlings looking up with heads erect and beaks agape towards their parent, which bends down to feed them from its perch on a stem above them.[322]

A polychrome mosaic rendering of the bird's-nest theme is on the acanthus-scroll pavement from Zliten (cf. pp. 379, note 26, 215), where an open flower forms the nest.[323] Five nestlings with wide-open beaks strain up ravenously towards the mother-bird, who perches on one of the petals of the flower, holds a large worm or insect tantalizingly in her beak, and contemplates her offspring somewhat severely, as though rebuking them for greediness. All the birds have green bodies and red heads and backs and could be red-backed shrikes.[324] (Pl. 129)

Most striking for their realism and vivacity are the scenes from the family life of storks embossed on two silver cups, dating from early imperial times, in the Boscoreale treasure found near Pompeii and now in the Louvre.[325] Tiny nestlings are extending their little heads and beaks and the parent birds are busily employed in feeding them or in rushing off to fetch new supplies. One father is disputing with another in the air over the possession of a large insect. Two adult birds appear to be employed by the parents as assistants; and one of them is passing to the mother's beak an insect for her young, while the father darts away for more. But in the other case the 'baby-sitter' has shockingly neglected its charges and allowed a crab, in the parents' absence, to drive the nestlings out and occupy the nest, from which the mother, all too late, is vigorously ejecting it: the father, returning with a snake, turns its head to glare furiously at the hunched and shame-faced culprit. There can be little doubt that the designer of the decoration on this pair of cups has worked from his own observation of the ways of storks. (Pl. 130)

BIRDS IN HARNESS

The harnessed ostriches in Ptolemy II's procession (cf. p. 238) could really have drawn reasonably large carts or chariots. But the birds depicted in Roman art as harnessed to miniature vehicles – swans, parrots, ducks, pigeons, and so forth – are obviously *jeux d'esprit*, designed for sheer amusement. Among the earliest of these are two Campanian paintings. One, from the House of the Vettii at Pompeii, shows a Cupid, whip in hand, driving towards the left a tiny chariot pulled by a pair of swans.[326] From Herculaneum comes the portrait of a green parrot drawing towards the left a little carriage with a locust as coachman.[327]

Possibly of third-century AD date is the great polychrome Dionysiac mosaic found in 1941 close to Cologne Cathedral.[328] In two of the small hexagonal panels along the right-hand margin of the pavement are pairs of birds in harness; and these were doubtless balanced by similar groups in the two, now destroyed, corresponding panels along the opposite margin. Of the two well-preserved panels one contains two green parrots, with red neck-bands, red beaks, red legs and some red feathers in their wings, drawing towards the left a cart that is loaded with harvest implements – a rake and a sickle, suggesting that summer is the meaning of the scene. The birds are very well drawn, apart from the fact that they are made to extend three toes to the front and one to the back, instead of two to the front and two to the back, as they should do.[329] In the second bird panel a cart piled with grapes is being pulled towards the right by two porphyrions, with bluish-purple bodies, red beaks and long red legs.[330] This group must stand for autumn; and the two vanished bird-teams on the other side are likely to have represented spring and winter, while their species remains unknown. (Pl. 135)

The most entertaining and complete example of the use of this motif in Roman art is the very well-preserved mosaic pavement known as the 'Little Circus' in the Piazza Armerina villa. Across the centre of the picture runs the *spina*, above and below which two racing chariot-groups are moving towards the left and right respectively. The charioteers appear to be children, as are also the three *sparsores* ('sprinklers'), each of whom carries an amphora (from which to sprinkle perfume on the course) and encourages one of three of the charioteers; and a child, too, is the backer of the fourth and winning chariot, below the *spina* on the right, who offers his charioteer a palm. All four chariots are *bigae*, each drawn by a pair of birds. Of the birds above the *spina*, those on the right are red flamingos, those on the left white ducks; while below, on the left are two greenish-blue porphyrions with red crests and red legs, on the right, the two greyish-green wood-pigeons that have won the race. From the colour of the birds it is clear that the four famous Circus factions are represented – the Reds (*russati*) by the flamingos, the Whites (*albati*) by the ducks, the Blues (*veneti*) by the porphyrions, and the Greens (*prasini*), in this case victorious, by the pigeons. There is also no doubt that; as at Cologne, each team also symbolizes a season. The ducks have reeds round their necks and stand for winter, the porphyrions, each with a large bunch of grapes suspended round its neck, must stand for autumn. Both the pigeons and the flamingos seem to have neck-wreaths of flowers; and if the designer of the pavement meant to show the seasons in their proper sequence, working backwards and starting with winter, the pigeons should be summer and the flamingos spring. The seasonal order would then be winter (ducks), spring (flamingos), summer (pigeons), and autumn (porphyrions), as contrasted with the racing order which is spring (last), winter, autumn, summer (first). On the other hand, the red flamingos would seem to be more congruous with the flaming heat of summer and the green doves with the freshness of spring.[331] (Pl. 133)

CHAPTER XXIII

THE ANIMAL PARADISE

FUNERARY PASTORAL SCENES

IN TOMB ART, SCENES FROM THE FARMYARD and from pastoral life depicting animals are not allusions to the one-time occupations of the dead, but symbolize the existence of idyllic peace and plenty awaiting them beyond the grave.[1] Such must be the meaning of the ox and ram painted in a rural setting in the large lunette that spans the west wall of Mausoleum F (First Tomb of the Caetennii) in the Vatican necropolis.[2] A notable example of this pastoral paradise is carved on the front of a marble sarcophagus found in Rome inside the Aurelian Walls and therefore earlier than *c.* 275, when those walls were built to define and defend the city boundary, inside which no new burials could be made. The inscription on the lid gives the name of the occupant of the sarcophagus, one Julius Achilleus (cf. p. 165), described as a *vir perfectissimus* (V C), who had been, no farmer, but head of one of the imperial bureaux, the *e* or *a memoria*, in which official State documents were drafted, and before that director, receiving a salary of 200,000 sesterces (*procurator ducenarius*), of the *Ludus Magnus*, the chief gladiatorial training school in Rome. Yet his tomb is decorated with a lively rural scene, with the gate of a farmyard in the background and within it three horses running free, two oxen, a large herd of goats, some nibbling at trees (cf. p. 166), others being milked by a goatherd seated at the entrance to a straw hut, and a flock of sheep, which includes two butting rams and is tended by a seated shepherd.[3] A sarcophagus with carving so similar to that on the Julius Achilleus piece that it must have come from the same, or a closely related, workshop used to be in the Lateran collection and is almost certainly Christian, since the two large-scale figures at the ends of the front are a sheep-bearing 'Good Shepherd' and a female *orans* (praying figure) with her box of Scriptures beside her.[4] Between these figures is a rustic scene with the same farmyard gate, sheep, including butting rams, goats, some brought along for milking, and a waggon with two solid wheels pulled by a pair of oxen (cf. pp. 152, 161). There is quite a large number of other sarcophagi with pastoral scenes dating from the third century, some with sheep-bearing 'Good Shepherds' and *orantes* that are likely to be Christian, others with shepherds or herdsmen standing or seated as they watch their sheep or goats, which are probably pagan, or at least 'neutral'.[5] (Pls 140, 141)

In the catacombs there are pastoral paintings in which a shepherd, accompanied by animals and birds, does not bear an animal upon his shoulders and is not necessarily meant to represent Christ. Such is a third-century scene in the Domitilla catacomb, where a shepherd holding a *syrinx* (pipe) is seated in the centre with a horned sheep and two ewes to the left of him and two ewes and a ram to the right, all in a setting of flowering shrubs and other plants.[6] In a lunette painting of the fourth century in the Priscilla catacomb the shepherd stands in the centre, flanked by trees, and extends one hand to caress the muzzle of a sheep, while another sheep grazes peacefully beside it. On either side of this group and facing towards it are birds, a cock on the left and a hen on the right, drawn on a disproportionately large scale, but clearly integral parts of the picture.[7]

ANIMALS AS SYMBOLS OF TEEMING LIFE

Closely related to these scenes of farm animals quietly resting, grazing or at work are those, occurring in funerary or other religious contexts, which include wild fauna, as well as domestic birds and beasts, and which would seem to lay stress on the teeming life of paradise. 'Paradise' is, of course, derived from *paradeisos*, an Oriental word first used by Xenophon to denote the extensive parks of the Persian kings, well stocked with trees and other plants and with fauna of all kinds. In such scenes the creatures either run, sometimes chasing one another in lively movement, or they stand or walk sedately as though on show. A pagan instance of this is in the border of the probably second-century floor-mosaic, of which the Rape of Persephone forms the central picture, in Mausoleum I (Tomb of the Quadriga) beneath St Peter's. Of this border only fragments remain – two tigers confronting one another from either side of a chalice, two antelopes, and some partially destroyed animals that might be boars.[8] On the mid-fourth-century Christian pavement from Hinton St Mary in Dorset, now in the British Museum, three of the lunette-shaped panels that surround the bust of Christ in the larger part of the room, and the two rectangular panels that flank the roundel with Bellerophon and the Chimaera in the smaller part, all contain groups of hounds pursuing deer.[9] It is noteworthy that in none of these groups is there any trace of wounding or killing taking place, although the dogs are mostly shown as hard on the heels of the stags and does, which seem almost to enjoy the chase. In one of the lunettes a stag turns its head round nonchalantly to nibble at a tree, quite unmoved by the springing hound that confronts it and barks at it furiously. In one of the rectangular panels, in which a stag and a doe flee side by side, the doe looks saucily back at the pursuer. The vigorous life here depicted could either point to the next world or to the natural world here and now as part of God's creation (cf. p. 144).

Teeming life must also be the meaning behind the groups of animals, peaceful and wild, that are embossed on the flanges and on the lids of such late antique silver bowls as those from Mildenhall in Suffolk, where the context is not specifically either funerary or religious.[10]

Both in pagan and in Jewish/Christian thought friendship and peace between wild and tame animals normally inimical to one another is a token of the Golden Age to come in this world. Hints of this appear in pagan Roman literature as early as Augustan times, in Virgil's *Eclogues* – 'the herds will not fear the mighty lions', 'the timid deer will, in the age to come, drink beside the hounds';[11] and in one of Horace's *Epodes* – 'the trusting herds do not fear the ravening lions'.[12] It has been suggested that coin-types of Philip the Arabian, who celebrated the Secular Games in 248, showing the figure of Dacia standing between an ox and a lion and an eagle and a lion, were partly meant to indicate the same idea.[13] But the first definite allusions to this aspect of the Golden Age in art are on Christian mosaics, mainly of the fifth and sixth centuries, in the eastern provinces.

In the north chapel of the church at Ma'in near Madaba in Transjordania is a mosaic pavement inscribed with the words of Isaiah XI ('and the lion eats straw like the ox'), below which is a mutilated and clumsily restored (in ancient times) picture preserving the outline of a humped ox (zebu) standing to the right with a tree behind it and obviously once balanced by a lion standing towards the left.[14] Undoubtedly also intended to illustrate the Isaiah passage, although no Scriptural text accompanies it, is the long mosaic panel in the 'Hall of Philia', dating from the fifth century, which came to light between Antioch-on-the-Orontes and Daphne.[15] The contents of this panel are groups of two animals confronting one another from either side of a tree. First come a lion and a zebu (cf. p. 148); secondly, a tigress and a boar; thirdly, a leopard and a goat; fourthly, a lioness and a stag; while of a fifth group only the figure of a bear survives. On the trunk of the tree in the first group is inscribed the word 'Friendship' ($\Phi I/\Lambda I A$) – hence the name assigned to the building. It is true that the expressions of the felines are not altogether friendly, but the other beasts show no fear of them. A similar group on a church mosaic at Madaba consists of a lion and a zebu cropping the same bush.[16] These groups, if not literally illustrative of the Isaiah text, must have been influenced by the prophet's picture of fraternization between such animals as wolf and lamb, leopard and kid, calf and lion, cow and bear, as well as between lion and ox. (Pl. 143)

Much more thickly populated, if not directly alluding to the Golden Age, is the teeming bird and beast paradise on the ambulatory mosaic of the late fifth- or early sixth-century quatrefoil *martyrium* (martyr shrine) at Seleucia, the port of Antioch.[17] This mosaic consists of two series of animals and birds set back to back, but in almost all cases moving in the same direction – eastwards. Most of the larger animals are in the outer row, most of the smaller animals and birds in the inner one. Trees and bushes indicate the park-like setting. The best preserved of the quadrupeds are a zebra, a large deer, a horse turning back its head and obviously neighing, and a dark grey elephant with the tip of its trunk turned upwards and the concave back of an African, but with an Indian's small ears (cf. p. 33). There is also, this time advancing westwards, a lioness which prowls along with lowered head, open jaws and swishing tail, followed by her two cubs, whose gait and expressions exactly reproduce their mother's. Among the fragmentary animals may be noted a giraffe. The birds include a heron, peacocks, a pheasant, an eagle, a flamingo, ducks and a swan.

More recently discovered are the animal *paradeisoi* on church mosaics found in southern Anatolia and dating from the fifth or sixth century. One of these, excavated in 1952 at Ayas (Elaeusa) on the Cilician coast, is on the floor of the apse and of the *bema* (area in front of the apse) of the church.[18] In the apse are two eagles, some small birds and a fish. Across the *bema* is a broad horizontal panel with fauna in two tiers. Those below include a leopard, a bustard, a partridge (?), a bull and a bear; above are a dog chasing (but not killing) a hare and a duck. These pictures are of late fifth- or early sixth-century date. Another animal mosaic was brought to light inland in the mountains of Isauria, at Dag Pazari, in 1957. It lies in the narthex of the church and consists of two sections, an earlier and a later, both of the fifth century.[19] The earlier pavement, at the northern end of the narthex, consists of a series of circles, some of which enclose a bird, for instance, a peacock and a goose. The later, southern, section is filled by a vine, issuing from a two-handled vase, the spreading branches of which are 'peopled', as in Justinian's pavement at Sabratha (cf. Chapter XXII *passim*), with living creatures. The beasts include fat-tailed sheep and a hare perched above a bunch of grapes. Among the birds are a pelican (cf. p. 247), a flamingo, a hen and her chicks (cf. p. 257), a heron, an ibis, a guineafowl and a duck. These birds and beasts are better drawn and more naturalistic than those at Ayas.

In Syria a favourite form of paradise mosaic was the all-over vine-scroll forming regular rows of circular medallions in which human figures mingle with the animals and birds. On the pavement of a room in the monastery at Beisan the pictures include a huntsman attacking a lioness and her cubs, two men leading each a donkey, a seated shepherd piping to his dog, which turns its head away as though it could not care less for the music, and a Negro leading a long-necked spotted beast, a kind of cross between a camel and a giraffe.[20] The floor of the funerary chapel at Beisan originally contained fifty-six vine-medallions containing men, animals and birds. Among the fauna are peacocks, a loaded donkey and a cock-fight.[21] A very similar vine-scroll-medallions pavement, now in the Louvre, from Kabr-Heram near Tyre shows *inter alia* a leopard, a lion, a bear, an ostrich, a hound and a lioness.[22] Inset in a geometric background on the nave mosaic of the church of SS Cosmas and Damianus at Jerash are square panels, the majority of which contain a bird or an animal. This paradise includes peacocks, pheasants, a camel, a wild ass, a jackal, a hare, a gazelle, lions, an elephant, a bear, a flamingo, ducks, an ibex and a guineafowl.[23] Yet another mosaic paradise of vine-scroll medallions is in the synagogue at Gaza: among its creatures are a lioness suckling her cub, a zebra, two giraffes, and two flamingos.[24]

The collections of animals and birds described in this section, and those yet to be described in the sections below, must have been compiled, not from observation of the actual creatures, but from copy-books in which pictures of fauna circulated through the mosaicists' workshops and through those of craftsmen using other media. The same applies to the all-bird vine-scroll paradise on Justinian's mosaic at Sabratha, frequently alluded to in Chapter XXII. Such copy-books could either have been derived from illustrated zoological and ornithological manuals ('bestiaries') or they could themselves have been the sources on which the book-illustrators drew. The connection, however it came about, between mosaics and manuals is particularly clearly shown in the case of birds. A large mosaic *in situ* in the Roman town of Italica near Seville consists of a grid of squares in each of which is a single bird. In the Vienna National Library is preserved the sixth-century *Anicia Codex*, which contains a treatise on birds by Dionysius of Philadelphia, who probably lived in the second century A D. The treatise is illustrated by pictures in the form of a grid of squares each containing a different bird, as on the mosaic – pictures that may, perhaps, have been based on illustrations executed prior to the sixth century.[25] A very similar mosaic grid occurs on the floor of Room II in the sixth-century 'House of Ktisis' at Antioch. Each alternate square is occupied by a single bird, two of the birds being beribboned parrots (cf. p. 249 and p. 395, note 119): each of the alternating squares hold a flower.[26]

ORPHEUS

Of assemblages of animals and birds that are linked with individual personalities in Roman times, by far the most numerous and varied in their media are those that illustrate the familiar theme of Orpheus and the beasts. The great majority of these are pagan in character. But two are Jewish; and there is a small series of renderings of the story which are either definitely Christian or were at any rate created under an officially Christian Empire. The sculptural versions, worked in stone, marble or ivory, range in date from the second or first century B C to the fourth or fifth century A D. There are a few painted representations. But most of the Orpheus scenes are on mosaics, at least sixty in all being known; and these are spread geographically from Lincolnshire in the West to Edessa in the East. As regards the fauna repertory, many of the same animals and birds constantly recur. But there is also a number of more unusual creatures that only put in an occasional appearance.

The basic significance of the motif is idyllic, denoting heavenly peace and a Golden Age to come, here or hereafter, in which nature, wild and domestic, is to be completely tamed in mutual friendliness and to be enthralled by the harmony and order that music implies. This explains the occurrence of the theme in funerary and other religious contexts and in connection with fountains as places of refreshment and rest. Hence, too, its popularity on the floors of people's homes and as a decoration for small, portable objects of secular use. But another, secondary reason for its remarkable vogue in so many areas of the Roman world cannot be excluded. It obviously provided an opportunity almost as ample as that which the *venatio* pictures offered for the representation of animals and birds of all kinds as items of interest and entertainment in their own right.

The earliest known rendering of Orpheus and the beasts in Roman art is a statuette carved in peperino stone, found in a cemetery region outside the Porta Tiburtina in Rome and clearly from a tomb. It dates from the early first, or late second, century B C. The musician wears a pine-wreath, parts his lips in song, and is naked. His arms and lyre have disappeared. An owl perches on his left knee; and at his feet are a feline of some sort, on whose back rests another owl, also a lion, a dog, and another, indeterminate, quadruped.[27] The theme appears again in pagan funerary contexts on some *stelai* from the Danubian provinces, notably on the well-known tall monument at Petau (Petovio) in Austria, where it occupies the central and largest sculptured panel. The fauna include a very rare crocodile (cf. p. 290), a relatively infrequent camel (cf. pp. 140, 291, 293), an elephant, a monkey, and a snake, as well as other beasts.[28] Another Orpheus *stele* was found at Intercissa.[29] The mausoleum of Quintus Apuleius Maximus Ridens at El-Amrouni, now in Tunisia, has carved on its west façade a relief of Orpheus with animals that include one fabulous creature, a griffin (cf. pp. 29, 290, 291), along with a monkey, a lion, a lioness and so forth.[30] (Pl. 139)

In Romano-Christian sepulchral art Orpheus represents Christ, the Logos, the Divine Musician and Tamer, as in the comparison made between them by Eusebius.[31] In unequivocally Christian contexts he is shown fully draped, in tunic as well as in cloak; and his audience is generally small and wholly tame – one or two sheep and sometimes birds in a tree beside him. Such are the scenes in a third-century vault-painting in the Callixtus catacomb[32] and in the central panel of a late third-century strigillated sarcophagus found at

Ostia.[33] But in the central panel of a very similar sarcophagus in the crypt of the church of San Gavino at Porto Torres in Sardinia there appears a griffin (cf. pp. 289, 291) balancing a ram at Orpheus' side, suggesting that Christ is the new Apollo, lord of music and the sun.[34] A fourth-century painting on the lunette of a tomb-recess (*arcosolium*) in the Domitilla catacomb portrays Christus/Orpheus playing to a larger assembly, which consists of a camel, a dromedary (cf. pp. 140, 289, 291), two other fragmentary animals and some birds.[35] Still more complex is the company that is grouped round Orpheus on a sixth-century mosaic pavement, now in the Istanbul Archaeological Museum, from a Christian funerary chapel in Jerusalem. Here, in addition to a rare crocodile (cf. p. 289), a white cow (?), a brown bear, a lioness, a rat and some birds, are two fictitious creatures, a Centaur and a Pan, symbolizing the natural passions of mankind that Orpheus tames.[36]

A religious, but non-funerary, Orpheus is to be found in the under-layer of painting on the Torah Shrine of the third-century synagogue at Dura-Europos on the Euphrates, a symbol of the Messianic Age that is to come. The musician, who wears his usual dress and Phrygian cap, is seated with his lyre and an eagle is perched behind his shoulders, while approaching him from the right are a lion, a duck or dove, and possibly a monkey.[37] Another, much later, Jewish religious rendering is on the sixth-century mosaic pavement of the synagogue at Gaza (cf. p. 296). Here we have a David/Orpheus, the Messianic king, nimbed (cf. p. 402, note 52) and arrayed as a Byzantine emperor with crown, golden tunic and purple mantle. All that remains of his animal audience is the forepart of a lioness, bowing to the music, and what may be the uplifted trunk and head of an elephant. David's name is inscribed in Hebrew beside his head.[38]

The association of Orpheus and the beasts with fountains is attested in the late first century A D by Martial, who states that one can see on the Esquiline, after crossing the Subura, Orpheus wet with spray at the crown of his drenched theatre (*theatrum* means here either 'audience' or, more probably, 'theatre-shaped pool') and the wild beasts and royal bird (the eagle) marvelling at his music.[39] This fountain was known as the *Lacus Orphei*.[40]

No less definitely linked with a piece of ornamental water is a two-dimensional marble sculptural rendering of the Orpheus motif that came to light in a *nymphaeum* (public fountain) at Byblos in the Lebanon. Intended to be viewed only from the front, it is worked in very high relief, the figures of man and animals being deeply undercut so as to stand out almost in the round against a dark background of shadow. The scene rests on a low pedestal and would seem to have crowned some portion of the fountain's structure. Orpheus, seated at the centre, is ringed all round by birds and beasts, which include an elephant, an ox (?), a monkey, a cock, a swan, possibly a pelican (cf. pp. 247, 287), and an unreal creature in the shape of a Sphinx (cf. pp. 29, 289, 290). The technique of the carving, in particular that of the hard, deeply drilled grooves that mark the folds of the musician's drapery, is strongly suggestive of a late, fourth-century date. In the same *nymphaeum* there were found other marble sculptures, purely pagan or 'neutral' in content – Hygieia, Naiads, a headless youth (*ephebus*), portions of a group of Achilles and Penthesilea, the portrait-statue of an elderly, clean-shaven man, and two bodiless heads.[41] These are not easy to date stylistically from the published photographs. They could well be earlier than the Orpheus, since work of different periods might have been assembled to adorn a fountain. On the other hand, the sculpting of such non-Christian subjects in the fourth century would by no means be surprising.

We know from Eusebius' (?) *Vita Constantini* that in this period public fountains could be seen in Syria and Palestine decked with Christian groups – the Good Shepherd and Daniel and the Lions.[42] These are said to be made of bronze plated with shining gold. But in the Istanbul Museum there is a Good Shepherd marble figure on a low pedestal so similar in style and form to the Byblos Orpheus that it must have served the same purpose of a fountain ornament.[43] Above the Shepherd's head is a curious funnel-shaped feature, which, together with the pedestal, is paralleled on an Orpheus group in marble in the same museum that closely resembles the Byblos group (although the latter lacks the 'funnel'), is clearly contemporary with it, and must come from the same workshop or at least from the same artistic *milieu*.[44] Here only Orpheus, one headless animal, and some beasts in low relief on the base have survived. But in two more precisely similar Orpheus groups, one in the Sabratha Museum, the other in the Byzantine Museum in Athens,[45] the animal audience is very well preserved. On the former, this includes an eagle and other birds at the top, a Sphinx and a griffin (cf. pp. 29, 289, 290), a camel (cf. pp. 140, 289, 293), an elephant, an ox, a lion, a bear, and a monkey close to Orpheus' head. In the Athens group there are an eagle and other birds, again a Sphinx and a griffin, a camel, an elephant, a stag, a lion, other felines, a bear and a monkey in the same position. There is also in the Aquileia Museum a fragment consisting only of the funnel-shaped feature and Orpheus' head.[46] The question arises, could all these Orpheus fountain groups, forming as they do a homogeneous series, possibly be Christian? An argument against this possibility is the fact that in every case Orpheus is semi-nude, instead of being fully draped (cf. p. 289). This argument is, however, not completely conclusive, since the Good Shepherd figure in catacomb painting and on Christian sarcophagi sometimes has part of his chest exposed. (Pl. 137)

Forty-seven Orpheus floor-mosaics, mostly found in domestic contexts, but including the funerary Christian piece from Jerusalem (cf. p. 290), have been catalogued by Henri Stern.[47] Eight more were listed by R. M. Harrison;[48] and to these at least four must now be added – from Vienne, Mytilene, Adana in Cilicia, and Panik in Yugoslavia.[49] As compositions these Orpheus pavements show considerable diversity, which suggests that the arrangement of the birds and beasts around the normally central figure of Orpheus and the shape of the picture, whether circular, polygonal or rectangular, were the free choice of individual designers or of local workshops. For example, the unbroken concentric circles of animals and birds seem to have been peculiar to a school of mosaicists in what is now Gloucestershire, as exemplified at Cirencester and Woodchester.[50] On the other hand, the scheme in which a circular field is divided into eight wedge-shaped segments, in which the creatures stand or move around the central Orpheus, is found both in Britain, at Horkstow in Lincolnshire and at Withington in Gloucestershire, and in Morocco, at Volubilis – a fact that is suggestive of a pattern-book origin for all three.[51] And there can be little doubt that it was from copy-books that the individual items of fauna were culled. Not only are the same beasts often very similarly drawn on different pavements, but some scenes contain animals, such as the elephant at Horkstow, that the local designer can never have seen in life. Again, there is often little attempt to draw the various creatures to scale. There are, indeed, some cases in which a unified picture is achieved by making the larger quadrupeds and some of the smaller animals focus a concentrated and ecstatic gaze on Orpheus and sometimes open their mouths or raise one paw as though accompanying him with song or beating time to the music.[52] But on other pavements the beasts are scattered somewhat haphazardly over the field and even turn their backs on Orpheus, only their heads being twisted round towards him.[53] In these cases the fauna would appear to have been lifted straight from copy-books and just dumped, as it were, on the mosaic. (Pl. 136)

Here only a few of these domestic pavements can be commented upon apropos of further points. In the centre of the room from which the Blanzy-les-Fismes mosaic (now in the Laon Museum) came was a circular fountain;[54] and at Woodchester, in the lost central portion, there may well have been once an octagonal water-basin, causing the displacement of Orpheus from his normal central place to the circle of the birds.[55] These further illustrate the fountain associations of Orpheus (cf. pp. 290, 291). At Trinquetaille (Arles), at Sant'Anselmo in Rome, and at Piazza Armerina the not so frequent camel appears (cf. pp. 140, 289, 291).[56] Snakes and a tortoise figure prominently at Sparta;[57] and a snake wound round a tree is an unusual motif found at Ptolemais and at Tobruk.[58] At Piazza Armerina we meet an armadillo, at the bottom left-hand corner of the picture (also interrupted by a fountain), and some particularly gorgeous birds – a crimson-headed, green-bodied woodpecker, a green parrot with crimson neck-band (cf. pp. 248, 249), a splendid peacock, and a shining white goose.[59] There are occasional touches of humour, as at Perugia, where a monkey pulls a bird's tail;[60] and when a bird pauses to clean its claw – a pheasant at Woodchester and a long-legged wader at Ptolemais.[61] On a pavement from Yvonand (Vaud) in Switzerland there appears a peculiarly endearing little animal not as yet mentioned in this book – a squirrel (*sciurus*, σκίουρος, 'shadow-tail'), which is seated on the ground with tail erect, facing Orpheus on the left.[62] A squirrel is probably also represented on the one-time Lateran vine-scroll pilaster, above the bird's nest (cf. p. 279).[63] That it was sometimes kept as a pet seems to be implied by Martial, who lists it among the precious things which the little dead slave girl, Erotion, outshone; compared with her, he says, the squirrel is no darling (*inamabilis sciurus*), suggesting that it was in itself most lovable.[64] Pliny mentions the squirrel's exceptionally bushy tail (*villosior cauda*), which serves it for a covering, and describes its habit of storing food for the winter and its way of sitting up and using its forepaws like hands to bring food to its mouth.[65]

Finally, there are two ivory *pyxes* (caskets) so similar that they must be the products of the same workshop and of the same late fourth- or early fifth-century date – one in San Colombano at

Bobbio, the other in the Bargello in Florence.[66] Both show on one side Orpheus and the beasts, with a Centaur and a Pan included in the audience (cf. p. 290). In each case Orpheus is fully draped. On the other side are horsemen fighting large felines – a subject which suggests that the caskets were made for non-liturgical, secular use, although the Orpheus scenes could have conveyed a Christian meaning.

ADAM

Obviously much indebted to the Orpheus scenes is the only rendering of the Roman period known to me of Adam with the animals in Paradise. This is on the left-hand leaf of the ivory diptych in the Bargello in Florence, of which the right-hand leaf shows scenes from the life of St Paul: it probably dates from the closing years of the fourth century.[67] Adam is seated among trees in the upper right-hand corner of the picture, with the birds and beasts, which he is presumably naming, filling the remainder of the field in superimposed tiers. Passing from the top downwards, we can identify an eagle, a dove (?), a leopard (?), a bear (erroneously furnished with a tail), a lion, a wolf, a boar, a minute hound, an African elephant with enormous ears, a horse, a goat, a snake, an ox, a sheep, an antlered stag and a tiny fawn. Apart from his gaffe about the bear's tail, the artist has carved the individual creatures naturalistically, although his lion is larger than his elephant, his boar also disproportionately large, and his goat almost as big as his horse and his ox. Lion, wolf, boar and horse are open-mouthed, as though they were answering to the names assigned to them. A Romano-Christian Eden such as this must lie behind the scene of Adam and Eve in Paradise with the animals reworked in Carolingian times on half an ancient diptych.[68] (Pl. 138)

One medieval representation of the Christian Paradise may be noted here for the sake of its quite remarkable resemblance to the Orpheus pavements. It is the early fourteenth-century painting in the Holkham Bible Picture Book of the Creator seated in the centre with his right hand raised to call into being the birds and animals that surround him on every side.[69] Above him, in the tree-tops, are numerous birds and below his feet ducks and a swan, all clearly drawn from life. Ranged in tiers on either side of him are the animals, among them a lion, a very strange elephant, a dromedary and an antelope, all presumably culled from bestiaries, as well as the more familiar quadrupeds, on ox and a doe, for instance, which could be seen in England. Such a Roman work as the Palermo Orpheus pavement is immediately recalled.[70]

NOAH

Of the renderings in Romano-Christian art of Noah's Ark in which the birds and animals saved from the Flood are depicted, the earliest, probably dating from the Constantinian period, is the scene carved in the centre of the front of a stone sarcophagus at Trier.[71] Noah and his family, eight persons in all, are standing in the Ark and in front of them, along the vessel's edge, are the figures of nine creatures, birds and quadrupeds. The dove is just returning with the olive-branch; and just outside the Ark, on the left, there stands the raven, already on dry land, and looking up as though to announce the recession of the waters.[72]

Next in date is the square mosaic picture, worked in polychrome and laid, in the late fourth or early fifth century, in the nave of the basilica at Misis (Mopsuhestia) in Cilicia.[73] In the centre is the Ark, a square box on four legs open at the top and equipped on one side with a small arched door. Inside it is inscribed *KIBΩTOΣ NΩE P[ύσιος]* ('Noah's saving Ark'). One bird can be seen already within and the tail of another is vanishing through the door. Round the Ark on all four sides there pace or stand in two tiers the birds and beasts, waiting their turn to enter, birds in the inner or upper zone, quadrupeds and an ostrich in the outer or lower register. Fifteen quadrupeds and sixteen birds, including the ostrich, are wholly or partly preserved; and there is room for two or three more animals in one of the damaged corners of the square. It remains a mystery how so great a company will squeeze into the box and as to how the larger creatures will contrive to effect an entry through the door. The quadrupeds include a gazelle, a lion, a goat, a donkey, a bear, a tiger, a lioness, a stag and a dromedary. Among the birds, besides the ostrich, are a guineafowl, a goose, a cock, a pheasant, a lark, a peacock, a swan, a porphyrion and a stork. No fighting is taking place. The use of copy-books for the individual creatures is betrayed by the fact that they do not overlap one another, no attempt being made to pair them, a male and female of every kind, that they are not drawn to scale – the goose is almost as large as the lion, for example – and that they do not all face in the same direction as they should if proceeding to the same goal. As is so often the case with these menageries, the birds are truer to nature than are the quadrupeds. No human beings feature in this picture. (Pl. 142)

A third version of the Noah's Ark theme is Jewish, on the late fifth- or early sixth-century mosaic pavement of the synagogue that was found six inches below the floor of the 'Synagogue Church' at Jerash in Transjordania.[74] The scene is worked in a long horizontal panel, in the left-hand upper corner of which the names of Shem and Japhet, two of Noah's sons, are inscribed in Greek: but no human figures are preserved. The creatures are arranged in three super-imposed friezes and are all moving rightwards. Above are birds, including a cock, a peacock and an eagle. In the centre are the large animals – a deer, a gazelle, a hind, a sheep, a goat, two horses and an ass. Below are two snakes, a spotted hare and other small quadrupeds.

Roughly contemporary with the Jewish pavement is the minia-ture illustrating the Noah's Ark story in the Vienna codex of the Book of Genesis (cf. p. 140 and p. 373, note 31).[75] In this case the artist has followed the biblical text much more closely and has shown the animals in pairs emerging from the Ark with Noah and his family. We see two dromedaries, two elephants, a lion and a lioness, two donkeys, two horses, a bull and a cow, and some other paired quadrupeds. For his arrangement of the beasts, at any rate, this painter would not seem to have depended on a copy-book.

THE GOOD SHEPHERD

The Good Shepherd figure in Romano-Christian art is normally shown with a sheep, either ewe, ram or lamb, laid across his shoulders. This was, of course, the usual way of carrying a small, portable animal in ancient times; and the Christian motif was obviously derived from pagan models – archaic and classical Greek, Hellenistic, and imperial Roman. In pagan Roman art the animal-bearing figure appears either as a *genre* motif in pastoral scenes or as the personification of a season, winter or spring; and when such a figure occurs alone or unaccompanied in sarcophagus reliefs by personages or themes that are unequivocally Christian, even when of third- or fourth-century date, it cannot be interpreted with any certainty as representing Christ.[76] This applies to the famous ex-Lateran marble statuette[77] and to a number of other statuettes and to ivory figurines forming the handles of knives in various collections,[78] including a somewhat crude, but engagingly childlike, marble statuette in the Byzantine Museum in Athens.[79] It could also apply to the fountain figures in Istanbul and Alexandria,[80] although, as we have seen (p. 291), shepherd groups definitely held to be Christian were adorning public fountains in the fourth century. If pagan, these figures are purely *genre* in character. There is no literary, epigraphical or clinching archaeological evidence for T. Klauser's theory that the sheep-bearing figure symbolized the pagan virtue of *philanthropia*.[81] It is only in the Gospels that we find the motif definitely equated with the virtue of love of mankind [82] – a love that is visually expressed in early Christian art by figures of Christ or of his followers with a sheep on their shoulders.

In definitely Christian works of art the Good Shepherd figure is, indeed, not always meant for Christ himself, but could stand for any 'philanthropic' Christian; and it must do so when two or even three sheep-bearers feature in the same picture. Normally the Good Shepherd's Paradise is as thinly populated with creatures as is that of the Christus/Orpheus – one or two sheep at his feet and sometimes a dog, in addition to the sheep on his shoulders and some birds in a tree. The painted versions in the catacombs are very well-known,[83] as are those carved on the often-published third-century sarcophagi.[84] Less familiar is a very finely carved group on the fragment of a third-century strigillated sarcophagus from the San Sebastiano catacomb, just to the south of Rome.[85] Here the shepherd wears a short, long-sleeved tunic, a cape, leggings and boots – the regular peasant costume – holds a *syrinx* in his left hand and grasps with his right the hind-leg of the enormous ram that he is carrying: from his right arm is slung his scrip and by his left leg is his dog, which looks up lovingly at its master. Very similar is the early fourth-century floor-mosaic group in the one-time cathedral at Aquileia, where the sheep-bearing shepherd wears the same type of dress, holds a *syrinx* and is accompanied by another sheep that stands behind his legs and gazes up at him.[86]

A particularly striking sculptured Good Shepherd is in the central *aedicula* (niche) on the front of a large sarcophagus found in a Christian cemetery at Salona in Dalmatia and now in the Split Archaeological Museum.[87] Here the sheep-bearer, both of whose hands are employed in grasping the fore-legs and hind-legs of his burden, wears a short tunic, a cloak and boots, and he is accompanied by two more sheep, one on either side of him, while two trees indicate the pastoral setting. In the two lateral *aediculae* are the portrait-statues of a man and wife, each surrounded by a crowd of small figures, male and female, clearly the beneficiaries of charitable foundations that they had made. Its Christian location does not prove this sarcophagus to be Christian, for in the same cemetery there was a pagan mythological sarcophagus reused for Christian burial; and if the Good Shepherd piece could be proved to be pagan it would offer strong support to Klauser's theory of the sheep-bearer as a symbol of pagan *philanthropia*. On one short side there is a mourning Cupid, obviously of pagan derivation. But the other short side shows beneficiaries in the *orans* attitude praying for their dead benefactors at the tomb-door – surely an exclusively Christian scene.

Two undoubtedly Christian painted versions of the sheep-bearer theme show the shepherd with a whole flock of sheep. One is the third-century painting accompanied by other Christian scenes on the attic of the Tomb of Marcus Clodius Hermes under the church of San Sebastiano (cf. p. 249).[88] The other is in the third-century baptistry of the house-church at Dura-Europos.[89] In a painting in the Hypogeum of the Aurelii on the Viale Manzoni in Rome the reader seated with an open scroll on a flowery hill, on the slopes of which a flock of sheep is grazing, probably represents, not the Good Shepherd, but a heterodox (Gnostic) teacher.[90]

The Good Shepherd is not always animal-bearing. On a fourth-century circular Christian mosaic in a private house at Aquileia he stands with a *pedum* (shepherd's crook) in his left hand and originally a *syrinx* in his upraised right hand, which was subsequently altered so as to show him making the gesture of greeting or benediction. He has a blue nimbus and wears exceptionally rich clothes – embroidered and pearl-sewn tunic and cloak, the latter purple, and long blue trousers. On the ground beside him are a milk-pail, a sheep with a bell round its neck, and a bearded goat. Approaching his head from the right is a dove, the normal Christian symbol of the soul.[91] This version of the shepherd at once recalls the famous wall-mosaic in one of the lunettes of the 'Mausoleum of Galla Placidia' at Ravenna, dating from *c.* 450.[92] Here the shepherd, again nimbed and clad in a purple mantle and golden tunic, is seated among rocks and shrubs with a flock of six sheep, three on either side of him and all of them turning their heads towards him. He playfully tickles the chin of the animal next to him on the right. (Pl. 144)

By far the most populous animal paradise over which the Good Shepherd rules is that on a late fifth-century polychrome mosaic pavement from a villa at Jenah in the Lebanon, just to the south of Beirut.[93] That the villa was at some time Christian is attested by the cross and A and Ω inserted in the pavement of another floor;[94] and there would seem to be little reason for doubting that the figured picture, if earlier than these, is of Christian inspiration. The picture consists of a tall, rectangular panel, intended to be viewed along its long axis, of which about a third has been destroyed, while the rest is very well preserved. In the centre stands a youthful, non-sheep-bearing shepherd with a staff in one hand and his dog beside him. But his 'flock' is as varied as the largest of Orpheus' audiences on mosaics. Not only do we find here domestic animals, such as a sheep and a goat, but also wild fauna, including two zebus with prominent humps (cf. pp. 148, 285, 286), a bear, a leopard, a lioness, an antelope, two gazelles or hinds, a stag and possibly a lion, of which the head is lost. Among the birds are a guineafowl, an ibis, a porphyrion, a pheasant, a stork, a duck, a goose, a beribboned parrot (cf. pp. 249, 288) and an ostrich. The creatures are, on the whole, very naturalistic; and all are feeding or strolling peacefully in an Eden rich in trees, shrubs and water-plants.

ROMAN VETERINARY MEDICINE

R. E. Walker, B.Vet.Med., MRCVS

CHAPTER I

THE PRACTITIONER

LATE IN THE FOURTH CENTURY A D Publius Vegetius Renatus compiled a work on the diseases of horses and mules which is known to us as the *Mulomedicina*.[1] Vegetius tells us that he felt obliged to write the book for several reasons. Prominent among his motives were his own love of horses; his concern that contempt for veterinary medicine had led to its practice by poor-quality individuals; and an opinion that the books available were badly written. In defence of his opinions Vegetius gives us an eloquent and perceptive insight into Roman attitudes toward animals and veterinary medicine. A better foundation for the study of these matters can scarcely be found. In the Prologue to the *Mulomedicina* Vegetius surveys the veterinary literature of his day critically and as the works that he cites have survived we are able to assess his views. As a Roman educated to admire eloquence of speech and literary style he is repelled by the works of Chiron[2] and Apsyrtus[3] which are crudely written or at least badly translated from Greek originals. He admits however that they have presented material which is detailed and comprehensive. Pelagonius[4] and Columella[5] are praised for their style but they are criticized for inadequate treatment of the subject-matter. Pelagonius omits causes and signs of disease and Columella does not write enough because he is preoccupied with agriculture.

Vegetius gives a very clear statement of his intent. He has brought together all that he could find written in Latin, consulted with veterinarians and doctors, and finally reduced and abridged the material as well as his 'ordinary abilities' would allow. The result is a fine work written by a man who does not claim to be a veterinarian. The only criticism that can be made is that in polishing the rough but highly technical texts of Chiron and Apsyrtus, Vegetius has sometimes lost the sense of vital procedures. Restoration is possible in most cases by reference to the sources. The defence of the veterinary art is conducted on two fronts, the persuasion of the Roman upper classes that the medical attendance of animals was not a base occupation and insistence that the veterinarian himself should not be regarded as inferior to the physician. The argument embraces the economic value of horses, their noble virtues, the value of knowledge for its own sake and even includes that invincible gambit, 'the animal cannot speak for itself whereas a man can describe his symptoms'. Apart from providing a fine exercise in rhetoric and revealing much about Vegetius, this introduction can hardly be surpassed as an apologia for the veterinary art in any period of history.

The Sources

The *Mulomedicina* is dominated by the Hellenistic [6] tradition of horse medicine as embodied in the works of Chiron.[7] In addition Vegetius includes a section on cattle diseases by request of his friends and in view of the current heavy mortality among oxen. Vegetius includes Columella's chapters on cattle with the addition of descriptions of forms of plague relevant to his own times.[8] It is not possible to trace Greek horse medicine back in time beyond Chiron, but Columella gives a list of over fifty Greek and Latin writers whose books contributed to his volumes. Prominent among the Greeks are Democritus, Aristotle and Theophrastus. A strong Punic tradition is represented by Mago the Carthaginian whose works are held in high esteem.[9] Among Latin authors cited by Columella we find Celsus, who is credited with five books on agriculture. Assessment of the actual content of Columella's veterinary chapters is extremely complicated, but it is obvious that Punic, Greek and Roman influences are interwoven. Celsus[10] and Varro[11] are important for the information they give regarding the veterinary practitioner.

The Practitioner in Literary Sources

Varro makes an important distinction between two types of veterinary treatment. Some treatments may be administered by an intelligent herdsman, others require the attention of the *medicus*. Varro tells us that his herdsmen were required to copy out treatments for cattle, oxen, sheep and goats from Mago's books. He remarks that horses have a great many diseases and methods of treatment and indicates that this complexity led to those who treated animals in Greece being known as ἱππιατροί or horse doctors. The picture which Varro gives is of a strong Punic influence being established on the farms and among the herdsmen to be perpetuated by tradition and in the form of copybooks. The practice of horse medicine would seem to have achieved some importance in Greece; and possibly a basis for the evaluation of the status of the veterinarian is to be found at this point. Support for this would seem to be given by the anecdote related by Valerius Maximus concerning the veterinarian Herophilus.[12] The events are contemporary with Varro and the title of Herophilus is *equarius medicus*, which would appear to be the literal translation of the Greek. This man's adventures lead us to the belief that he must have enjoyed some education which would have assisted him in his deceptions. Further support for the higher status of the ἱππιατροί can be derived from the Greek grave monuments. It is perhaps no coincidence that in the later Roman Empire we find Apsyrtus enjoying prominence as Constantine's chief army veterinarian and the Greek literature on horse diseases far outweighing the Latin works.

Columella refers to practitioners as *veterinarii*, as does the Latin translation of Chiron. Vegetius uses the title *mulomedicus* consistently throughout his books.

The Practitioner in Official Documents

The *Edict* of Diocletian refers to the veterinarian as *mulomedicus*.[13] In the *Theodosian Code* the expression used is again *mulomedicus*.[14] The *Digest* mentions the occupation *veterinarius*.[15] These official references, although only three in number, are most interesting. The *Edict* of Diocletian, intended to control inflation by fixing

122 A wall-painting of a parrot with cherries (p. 249).

123, 124 A sarcophagus relief of a peacock with its tail closed and, *right*, a mosaic at Aquileia showing a peacock with its tail fanned (pp. 252–3).

125 Guineafowl in a vine-scroll on a mosaic from Justinian's church, Sabratha (p. 254).

126, 127 Two mosaic details from Justinian's church, Sabratha, showing, *above*, a pheasant and a parrot in a vine-scroll, and, *left*, a quail (?) in a cage (pp. 255–6).

128, 129 *Left*, relief on an altar of two eagles feeding their young in a nest, and, *below*, a mosaic from Zliten showing a bird's nest in an acanthus-scroll with a field-mouse on a branch above the nest (pp. 279, 280).

130 Storks' nests on two silver cups from Boscoreale (p. 280).

131 A humorous mosaic at Piazza Armerina with a cock chasing a boy (p. 257).

132 A mosaic at Istanbul showing a young child herding geese (p. 263)

133 Birds harnessed in chariots, part of a comic circus scene mosaic at Piazza Armerina (p. 281–2).

134 A mosaic of a duck and drake with their ducklings (p. 273).

135 A mosaic representation of a pair of parrots harnessed to a small cart, at Cologne (p. 281).

136–138 Orpheus with the wild beasts is seen, *above*, on a mosaic at Lepcis Magna and, *below, left*, in a marble group at Sabratha. His Christian counterpart, Adam with animals in Paradise, appears on an ivory diptych leaf (pp. 291, 292, 294).

139 Mosaic of an owl perched on the evil eye (pierced by a spear) and mobbed by animals, birds and reptiles (p. 402, n. 27).

140, 141 Two views of the pastoral paradise: *above*, on a pagan sarcophagus and, *below*, on a Christian one (pp. 283, 284).

142–144 Mosaics of, *above*, Noah's Ark at Misis; *centre* an animal paradise, Antioch-on-the-Orontes, and, *below*, the Good Shepherd, 'Mausoleum of Galla Placidia', Ravenna (pp. 295, 286, 298).

prices, must be aimed at veterinarians engaged in private practice. When Vegetius reproves *mulomedici* for avarice in their fees and for compounding medicines whose cost exceed the value of the patient he is again obviously addressing private practitioners. The *Theodosian Code* refers to *mulomedici*; but these are hereditary public slaves paid by issues of food and clothing and cannot be the object of legislation such as Diocletian's or criticism such as that of Vegetius. The directive of the Emperors Valentinian and Valens certainly suggests that slaves in the service of the *cursus publicus* were being paid illegally, but the passage is difficult to interpret. It is not clear whether the services that they were charging for were those that they would normally have performed for the livestock and transport of the *cursus* or services outside the scope of this organization. If the first case, it is puzzling that anyone using the *cursus* should have been prepared to pay charges when the whole advantage of the travelling arrangements was the fact that the expense was born by the imperial exchequer. In the second case, the directive does not seem expressly to forbid such private enterprise although it must be admitted that Roman legal definitions often seem to lack precision. In any event there would seem to be evidence that the term *mulomedicus* was generally in use in the later Roman Empire in respect of veterinarians in private practice. It is interesting to note that the Greek text of the *Edict* of Diocletian translates *mulomedicus* as ἱππιατρός; clearly no other term existed in the Greek world.

The *Digest* gives us a military title, *veterinarius*, among the *immunes* or soldiers exempted from general duties and fatigues by virtue of special skills. It is dangerous, however, to attempt to draw conclusions from the list of *immunes*. It seems only too likely that Paternus was writing down the names as they came to mind rather than in relation to some headquarters hierarchy. Similarly it is not possible to say that the term *veterinarius* was formal and therefore exclusively military. It might be argued that Paternus was closer in time to the translator of Chiron, who prefers the term *veterinarius*, and that this term may have enjoyed an earlier vogue before the *mulomedicus* of the *cursus* became officially established.

At this point a reference to the military handbook *liber de munitionibus castrorum* is necessary.[16] This book discusses the layout of a Roman army camp in general terms and as an exercise for the uninitiated. At the centre of the camp with the headquarters and hospital is the site of the *veterinarium*. Apparently without exception veterinary historians have interpreted this to mean that 'veterinary hospitals' were part of the regular establishment of a Roman camp. Attractive as it is, this view cannot stand unchallenged. The *veterinarium* can only be the park or picket lines of the vast concourse of baggage-animals or *veterinae*. These animals were herded together under restraint, at the part of the camp least likely to be reached by enemy missiles, for safety and for fear of pandemonium should they be alarmed and stampede. That this point would be the station of the *veterinarii* and similar *immunes* is indisputable, but the meaning cannot be 'hospital'.

The Practitioner in Inscriptions
Only a few relevant inscriptions are recorded, but their variety is striking. The eight inscriptions surviving yield the terms *mulomedicus* (3), *medicus veterinarius* (2), *medicus iumentarius* (1), *medicus pecuarius* (1) and *medicus equarius et venator* (1).

The proper response to such a wide variety of terms should perhaps be to suspect informality rather than complex specialization. In addition, when dealing with tombstones we should perhaps never forget the effect that pride and fond memory may have had on the choice of titles by the heirs and sorrowing relatives. Faced with a similar plethora of titles the student of the term *medicus ordinarius* and its variants must tread warily. From the veterinary point of view the inscriptions appear to reflect the predominant interest of the deceased commemorated or dedicator of the tombstone. The *mulomedicus* is, as indicated, civilian. The *medicus pecuarius* is appropriate to the herds and flocks maintained by garrisons. *Medicus jumentarius* and *veterinarius* are concerned with draught-animals; and it is to be noted that the three mentioned in the inscriptions were freedmen. A most interesting inscription is that of the *medicus equarius et venator*. Apollodorus is equally proud of both of his qualifications and although he cannot be identified as a soldier both of these occupations are listed by Paternus among the *immunes*. The two occupations enjoy the same status because in the case of the military personnel it is the rank of *immunis* that matters not the speciality. It is singularly difficult for the modern reader to understand social status in ancient times and particularly hard for the modern professional man to comprehend his ancient counterpart's position in society. In Roman times social status was governed by two factors, possession of Roman citizenship or military rank. It was possible to enjoy military rank and no mean status in relation to civilian pursuits without citizenship. But a slave would not aspire to military rank. The gulf between the *immunis* with the duties of *medicus equarius* and the later hereditary slave *mulomedicus* was enormous. Similarly the Roman citizen practising as *medicus equarius*, *mulomedicus* or ἱππιατρός might enjoy significant social advantages over the auxiliary soldier with the rank of *immunis*, whatever his veterinary title.

Completion of our picture of the practitioner requires a study of his scientific equipment.

Greek and Roman Veterinary Theory

Celsus makes only one reference to veterinary medicine, but it is a most interesting observation.[18] In a detailed discussion of the relative merits of rational and empirical medicine he tells us by way of illustration that those who treat cattle and horses depend only upon ordinary knowledge. That is to say that the empirics treat a sympton with a remedy which experience has shown will be effective in alleviating that symptom, regardless of causes. Included in this condemnation of 'symptomatic treatment' are those in charge of large hospitals who presumably have not time to trouble with deliberations on causes. The reason that the veterinarian is an empiric is given as being the result of the inability of the animal to describe its complaint. By implication those who treated horses and cattle did not reason or inquire into the workings of the body and attempt to implement rational therapy. This description of veterinary medicine certainly applies to the greater part of Columella's chapters on disease, where there is no inquiry into causes or theory. Varro tells us that his herdsmen had manuals copied from Mago's books and makes it clear that these would only cover simple matters, while the veterinarian is to be called in for complexities; he still gives a brief discourse on disease in general. He divides the topic into three parts, causes, symptoms and therapy. The first division perhaps sets Varro slightly apart from the empirics.

Causes of disease – Varro

In broad terms animals become sick as a result of the effects of heat, cold, overwork, insufficient work or being given food or drink immediately after work. The symptoms shown by an animal that has been overworked and has a consequent fever are an open mouth, fast panting and a hot body. The treatment prescribed is rational; the animal is bathed with cold water, rubbed down with oil and warm wine, nourished with food, covered against chilling and given tepid water if thirsty. If treatment is not effective the animal is bled from the head.[19]

No further discussion takes place on the subject. We are told that other diseases have other symptoms and causes and referred to the writings which the flock-master is obliged to maintain in his possession. The observations are only those derived from common experience, and the treatment (cold applications for fever) shows simple reasoning and is quite rational. It is, however, at this point that the reasoning scientist parts company with the empiric. The Hippocratic treatise *Ancient Medicine* notes the paradox that cool applications to the body evoke a hot response within the body and the scientific study of medicine begins. The fruits of Greek scientific writing and study were available to the Latin writer on veterinary matters and the bibliography of Varro and Columella indicates that use was made of them all.

Democritus of Abdera

A great deal of information on animal disease was elicited from the study of dissections. Ammianus Marcellinus gives an oblique indication of the importance of Democritus in the study of pathology.[20] The author delivers an attack on gourmets and cooks, comparing their concentration on the process of preparation and cooking to the examination of dissected animals by Democritus and others intent on discovering the means of curing future generations of internal disorders.

Our knowledge of this pathological study is confined to glimpses in Aristotle's work or scraps preserved by curiosity collectors such as Aelian.[21] Direct references abound in Aristotle and the picture hinted at by the fragments is impressive. It is in Aristotle that we find a description of pulpy kidney, a sheep disease, complete with observations on its occurrence and the conditions favourable to its onset, with a detailed scientific argument as to its causes and the way in which death is brought about. This particular passage is not ascribed to any author, but it must be representative of the standard of investigation carried out by Democritus and 'other dissectors'.[22] By studying Aelian we can see how the technical works were discarded by the sophists where incomprehensible and preserved only where some entertaining paradox made a conversation piece. Study of Roman veterinary medicine should concentrate on elucidating the interweaving of Greek scientific theory and empirical practice. In general terms it appears that much of the Greek knowledge remained in Greek hands to reach its highest practical application in the late Roman Empire and the earlier Byzantine period. The greater part of Roman practice was most probably the empirical practice of countryfolk with a strong admixture of the North African tradition. Collections of prescriptions in handbook form provided the flock-master with his guide and possibly the *mulo-medicus* of the imperial post and the *immunis* in the army with the basis of their practice.[23] Higher scientific considerations would, for obvious reasons, most likely have been neglected. It is clear from a study of Chiron that if the veterinary practitioner was to be placed in relation to any school of medical theory, he was certainly a 'methodist' with a basic understanding of disease processes that can be traced to Democritean atomic theory. But it is to be doubted that this aspect of veterinary medicine enjoyed much discussion in abstract terms. Such niceties would have been misplaced on the farm and in the military camp against a background of stark practicality. In the field of private practice, however lucrative, scientific discourse would have been deemed ludicrous by a society in which dissection of animals and such topics had become uncouth along with their practitioners. Similarly the silence of the patient would have removed from the veterinarian the most direct stimulus for discussion and explanation.

CHAPTER II

THE PRACTICE IN CIVILIAN LIFE

THE HORSE

Breeding

VARRO, COLUMELLA AND PLINY give some account of the details of horse-breeding. Vegetius is informative about types of horse and their respective uses. Columella emphasizes the importance of a high standard of pasture and nutrition to both mare and stallion. Mating is timed so that birth after eleven months should take place at a time when the spring pasture is ready for mother and foal – that is to say, the spring equinox, but not later than the solstice. Varro points to the need for a competent stallion groom, the *origa*, whose duty is to bring the stallion into the mare twice daily until she is ready to mate. The mare is tied and the *origa* ensures that mating is accomplished successfully and that the stallion's seed 'is not wasted' as a result of his overeagerness. Since *origa* is derived from *auriga* ('steersman' or 'charioteer') we may be sure that the groom would direct the stallion's penis by grasping it to ensure penetration and that his name would combine both elements of rustic ribaldry and some reflection of the courage of the charioteer. Varro says that the mare defends herself when she has conceived, which suggests that repeated matings were supervised. As the mare would also defend herself in the earlier stages of heat, we would expect some precaution to be taken to protect the valuable stallion from damage. Some of the danger is removed in modern times by the use of the 'teaser' stallion which is brought up to the mare to test her reaction. The stud horse is not risked until the reaction is favourable. Columella describes the use of a badly bred ordinary horse in this manner.

Columella urges special care for the pregnant mares. The advice is sound in general. The mare and foal, and especially the foal, are afforded sufficient room and comfort, being neither exposed to cold nor physically disturbed. Both mother and foal are put out to pasture as soon as possible. Of special interest are the instructions in the event of abortion or harm incurred during labour. The remedy recommended is to crush polypodion fern (*felicula* or *filicula*) and administer it in tepid water through a horn. What Columella fails to make clear is exactly by which route the medication is given. Polypodion is found twice in Vegetius (*filicis radix*: II 48, 3.4; III 28, 17) used as an application to disperse or drive away inflammations and swellings. Pliny (XXVI, 37) tells us that it can be used as an aperient to bring away bile and phlegm, but is harmful to the stomach. The dried powder will consume polyps in the nostrils if administered as a snuff. In view of the generally harsh properties of this medicament and its use as an application, rather than internally, it is tempting to suggest that it was administered directly into the genital tract as a cleansing agent rather than by mouth. Its action would be to disperse or 'consume' detritus and portions of retained foetal membranes, most likely after-effects of abortion or difficult delivery. Precedent is to be found for such a treatment in Columella's discussion of the goat (VII, 7, 4).

Management

Vegetius discusses the general management of the stable (I, 56). He emphasizes the importance of diligence and attention to health as a means of avoiding sickness. The *dominus* must visit the stable frequently for an inspection. The standing for the horses must be raised and constructed of hard wood. The gully for the urine should connect to a drain so that the horses' feet are kept dry. The manger should be kept clean and efficient partitions provided to prevent feed-stealing among the horses to the detriment of weaker individuals. The hay rack should be suitably positioned in accordance with the horses' height so that it may be reached comfortably. The stable must be well lighted, not dark and gloomy. In summer the horses should be out in the open air by day and night. In winter the stable should be warm, but not hot, lest the horses are chilled on emerging. Twice daily the bodies of the horses must be groomed and handled thoroughly to promote docility and tone up the skin. The water should be clean and cool and preferably running water, which is less likely to be tainted, should be used. The quality of the feed is of great importance. Fodder such as hay and chaff must be good, clean, and not musty. Similarly the barley must be neither too old nor too new. It must not contain dust and stones or be mouldy. The feed should be given in several small amounts rather than as one large feed, to facilitate digestion.

A place should be provided and softly littered for the horses to roll on if they wish. Such exercise is beneficial and provides an opportunity for detecting signs of ill-health; that is to say, the ailing horse will be disinclined to frolic and its illness will therefore be detected in the early stages. The importance of careful exercise and strict supervision of it by the grooms is stressed. Vegetius includes a discussion of various routine treatments which are representative of general practice.

Nutrition

The foals were turned out to grass with their dams within ten days of birth. According to Varro they were then brought in at five months of age and introduced to bran and barley meal. Suckling was expected to have ceased by the time the offspring were yearlings and they were separated from their dams at two years of age. At three years of age the horse was put on a purgative diet of green forage for ten days. Small amounts of barley were introduced into the feed for four days in gradually increasing quantities. The amount given on the fourth day was maintained for ten days. This slow introduction to a ration of barley is necessary and must be approved. The amounts are not quoted and presumably would have varied with the type of horse and the extent of its activity. Vegetius does give details of a ration for fattening a horse. Four *modii* of barley are mixed with eight *sextarii* of beans, eight *sextarii* of chickpeas, four *sextarii* of wheat, four *sextarii* of fenugreek and one *sextarius* of vetch. One *modius* of the mixture is soaked in water overnight and fed in two portions on the following day. The season is winter and the horse is kept indoors on this diet for twenty-one days. It is intended that he should fatten, but not unduly. The daily intake of barley in this ration was just over 9 lb, which was high by Roman standards, the cavalry ration being 3 ½ lb daily. (The whole question of rations is discussed below, in Chapter III.)

Medical Treatment of Horses

The treatments of horses require considerable space for full discussion. The *Edict* of Diocletian provides a most convenient indication of those facets of veterinary medicine that came most readily to the Roman mind as being representative of the whole subject.

Blood-letting. The bleeding operation referred to in the *Edict* under the name of *depletura* was of great importance. Bleeding was an essential part of routine management of the horse, quite apart from its use in specific therapy. The intention was to purify the system by drawing off corrupted blood. Nemesianus gives a poetic description in his *Cynegetica*: 'In the early spring feed the colt with soft grain and then open a vein to let its chronic ailments escape with the tainted blood. Soon strength will return to his strong heart and the well built limbs will quickly be penetrated with a new strength. Soon a better and more wholesome blood will warm every vein in the horse's body.'[2]

The rationale behind bleeding is the beginning of the *Mulomedicina Chironi*.[3] Vegetius follows it exactly. The belief was that the blood becomes corrupted by indigestion and fatigue (Chiron), and Vegetius adds humours. The corrupt blood runs throughout the whole body causing pain and lassitude. In this way constriction and tension are caused by the inflation of the veins which can only be relaxed by drawing off blood. Vegetius recognizes the custom of spring bleeding (described by Nemesianus) but recommends that young animals should only be bled from the palate to relieve the head, eyes and brain.

On the day prior to bleeding the horse was kept on a light diet in order that the body should not be disturbed by the circulation of undigested food-residues in the blood. The horse was placed on level ground and a cord or thong passed around the base of the neck. The cord was tightened and held by someone standing at the horse's shoulder. The effect of this was to 'raise' or obstruct the flow of blood within the jugular vein so that it would stand out prominently. The hair was flattened by sponging with water to make the vein even more distinctly visible. The left hand of the operator was used to steady the vein by pressure of the thumb (which would also further raise the vein by added constriction of the blood flow) and the sharp *sagitta* stabbed through the skin with the right hand. The exact manner of holding the *sagitta* and the dangers of its misuse are carefully described by Chiron and Vegetius. It was appreciated that deep penetration by the *sagitta* could result in complete transfixion of the vein and danger to the oesophagus, carotid artery and trachea. That it was possible to kill the horse by careless technique is made clear. The site of the puncture is carefully chosen as at least one hand's-breadth below the bifurcation of the jugular vein at the angle of the jaw.

Striking the bifurcation was likely to be fatal. To prevent overpenetration of the vein, the *sagitta* was held between finger and thumb so that only the point protruded. The middle finger of the hand rested on the neck as an additional safeguard. Only the point was allowed to penetrate the vein. Green forage was offered to the horse so that its chewing movements would promote blood flow from the puncture. The blood flow was watched, and when the dark or 'corrupted' blood was replaced by bright red 'healthy' blood the vein was closed by a *fibula* pierced through the skin and application of a plaster. The horse was then placed in a dark, warm stable and fed green fodder and water for seven days and nights. The operation was obviously a lengthy one and this is no doubt the explanation of the very high fee allowed for it by the *Edict* of Diocletian. Some medicinal virtue was ascribed to the extracted blood. This was carefully caught in a bowl and mixed with vinegar and oil. The mixture was applied to the body, especially the part in particular need of cure. The value of this method of treatment by antipathy is explained by Chiron.

After the seven days the horse was brought out into the sun and a second bleeding effected from the palate. Feeding was carefully supervised for several days during which time the transition from green fodder and bran to barley was made. After about fifteen days the horse was taken to the sea or a river and bathed, provided the day was warm. The body was rubbed with wine and oil in the sun to repel chills. Work was not resumed for a further ten days. Racehorses were rested for forty days.

The severity of this bleeding is apparent in the descriptions. Serious depletion of the blood volume will without doubt result in colour changes as the proportion of arterial blood with its brighter colour due to higher oxygenation becomes greater. That the horses bled in this manner often suffered a severe shock is revealed by Chiron, who orders that the horse should not be moved, after bleeding, for at least two hours! The prolonged aftercare is a measure of the weakness of the horse, as are the numerous warnings against bleeding old, very young, weak, castrated or valuable breeding stock.[4]

Purging of the Head (purgationes capitis). The great importance attached to the head is reflected in a lengthy passage in Chiron (*De Capitis Valitudinibus*), in which the various afflictions of the head (*de capitis dolore*) are included in their entirety. Vegetius compresses the matter into the beginning of his second volume and paraphrases the authors cited above as 'other authors'.[5]

Vegetius explains the ancient view of the importance of the head. As the repository of sight, hearing, taste and smell-appreciation, it is pre-eminent and rules the other members of the body. Thus the danger from diseases of the head is all the greater. Corruption of the blood by undigested food-residues leads to inflation of the cerebral veins and distension of the membranes enclosing the brain. Simple distension leads to insomnia, headache, depression and weakness. Rupture of the membranes (meninges) causes great pain and staggering. As one side of the brain is affected the animal may circle round as the result of the weighing down of the head on that one side. Should the corrupted blood penetrate to the substance of the brain from the membranes, the horse will become frenzied and completely uncontrollable. All the symptoms that can be attributed to disorders of the brain, circling, ataxia, head-pressing, stupor and sight impediments, are discussed in detail with careful speculation as to the exact causes.

Other Purgings (purgationes). The treatments for this wide range of diseases are directed at cleansing the brain and its blood-vessels of corrupted matter and harmful distensions. Not only bleeding but cauteries are employed. General purging of the intestines is undertaken and local purging of the head with medicaments introduced into the nostrils. The choice of veins is made with due consideration for the seat of the disease. Eye symptoms merit bleeding from the veins under the eyes. Drooping, heavy heads are bled from the palate. Staggering and mental disturbance are countered with bleeding from the temples. Due care is taken to nourish the horse and its comfort is attended to with provision of a cool, dark stable and a soft bed of chaff. Nothing is neglected and a great number of potions and drenches are described, as is carefully supervised heat treatment in the *caldarium* of the bath house. That these procedures should have been chosen as representative by the financial advisers of Diocletian is an indication of the prominence that they were accorded.

Clipping (tonsurae). As representing a minor veterinary activity the *tonsura* at first appears an odd choice. Vegetius, however, devotes some space to its discussion.[6] In his view attention to the appearance of the horse is of some importance. A badly trimmed mane is a disgrace to the honourable rider. He disapproves of the close clipping of the mane as practised on racehorses and some saddlehorses in order to increase their strength (by preventing a waste of nourishment in maintaining the hair). Of the fashions available Vegetius favours the Persian, according to which the mane is exactly polled on the left side, while the right side of the neck is adorned with the uncut mane. Vegetius quotes Virgil (*Georgics* III, 86): *densa iuba et dextro iactata recumbit in armo.*

Care of the Feet (aptaturae pedis). The care of the hooves would have been a very common and important duty of the *mulomedicus*, especially in the service of the imperial *cursus publicus*. Vegetius includes care of the feet in his section on routine management. After a journey the feet of the draught-animals must be carefully searched after washing. To nourish the hoof and repair what the journey has worn away the use of a special ointment is urged. Tar, wormwood, garlic, pig's fat, old oil and vinegar are mixed and boiled. With this the hooves and coronets are anointed. The soles and frogs are to be purged with the *ferramentum* (that is pared with the tool or paring iron), which cools and refreshes and strengthens the hoof.

A number of these paring irons have survived. They consisted of a sharp gouge or shovel blade which could be used literally to plane the horn of the hoof. The edges of the blade were sharply upturned to facilitate the cutting out of the indentations of the frog and the angle of the hoof wall and sole. The handle had a curious offset feature which protected the knuckles of the operator from being barked on the hoof after each powerful planing motion. A remarkable continuity of design and use, which persisted until the nineteenth century, was established in farrier's practice. The use of the 'desperate buttress' was only terminated when the positively harmful effects of overtrimming the hoof were demonstrated by enlightened students of shoeing and general hoof surgery. The Roman examples of *ferramenta* exhibit lavish decoration with griffin handles and elaborate statuettes of goddesses and horses mounted on the shanks against the guard.[7]

A certain amount of confusion attaches to the interesting objects known as 'hipposandals' or *soleae ferreae*. An explanation of their function is simple, if two facts are appreciated. First, the purpose of the *solea spartea* and *solea ferrea* is to protect the actual dressing (that has been applied to the foot) from being dislodged or soiled by the normal stamping and scuffing of the patient. In short these devices are analogous to the modern poultice boot or the elaborate arrangements of plaited straw and calico which the nineteenth-century practitioner used to protect medicaments applied to the foot.

The second point is that variations in type must be related to their use for all species of draught-animal, not merely for the horse. The ox hoof may require dressing as a whole or only one or other claw. The suitable *solea* will be either the 'half-sandal' or of the rather elongated plate variety. The horse's hoof is essentially rounded and the bearing surface is a thin area of the outer wall. The sole is markedly concave and therefore wear on a dressing will take place mainly at the outer edge and under the heel. The *solea* for a horse may dispense with the centre of the sole plate. This is a great convenience when the iron stock to hand is in the form of bars, since it is not necessary to beat out the metal laboriously to fill the lacuna enclosed by turning the iron into the basic shape.

A special use for the *solea ferrea* is embodied in the treatment for hip injuries (*de vitiis coxarum*).[8]

Columella describes lameness in cattle and mentions the *solea spartea*. Lameness is described as being due to down-flow of blood into the animal's feet. The inflammation is demonstrated by pressure on the hoof which elicits a pained response when the affected part is touched. An incision is made with a knife (*cultellus*) between the claws and bandages dipped in salt and vinegar are applied. The foot is then covered with a *solea spartea* and the greatest care is taken to prevent the ox from wetting its foot by keeping it in a dry stall. The *solea spartea* is mentioned three times as used in this manner to protect dressings applied to a foot. Vegetius describes various treatments for the foot; he also mentions the *solea spartea* and instructs the reader to shoe the foot (*calceabis*). When a foot is affected by a suppuration it is searched and pared. Blackening of the horn and local tenderness betray the presence of pus below the surface. The spot is cut through and the pus allowed to escape. Linen cloths soaked in oil, vinegar and salt are placed on the hoof, which should then be shod.

Whether the *solea spartea* was constructed in the manner of the nineteenth-century apparatus of plaited straw or as a complete basket work of spanish broom is not certain. It is obvious that it must have been rather tedious to make and unlikely to be used more than once. A far more rapidly applied, and readily reusable, device would be the *solea* made of iron.

The only occasion that the *solea ferrea* is actually specified in the veterinary literature is in Chiron's discussion of hip lameness in the horse (*coxa misera*). The *solea spartea* or the vague *calcea* are not indicated. Blood is let from the thigh veins of a horse with hip pain and mixed with sulphur, nitre and bay-berries. The mixture is applied to the surface of the hip and rubbed well against the fur. For three days the hip is fomented with warm water in which vervain has been boiled. Each treatment is repeated three times daily. The foot which is sound is shod with the *solea ferrea*, the idea being that the horse is raised up and the lame leg rested on the ground more comfortably. Vegetius, polishing and rearranging Chiron's material as is his custom, says that the *solea spartea* may be used if the *solea ferrea* is not available. His intrusion is inappropriate and raises the suspicion that he has not grasped the sense of the passage. (Cf. de Blundeville, *The True Art of Paring and Shoeing all manner of Hooves* [1565], Chapter xxxi, *Of the paten shoe*: 'Because every smith knoweth the use of the Shoe and how to make it I shall not need to use many words, but onlie show you that it is a necessarie shoe for a horse that is hurt in the hip, or stifle, to be put upon the contrary foote to the intent that the sore leg may hang, and not touch the ground.' It may be that de Blundeville reading the *Hippitriaka* could see that which eluded Vegetius, but his condensed style at this point suggests the possibility that the art of making the 'raising *solea*' may have been lost by the sixteenth century.)

Clearly those *soleae* which are occasionally found fitted with little legs or feet were intended for this type of treatment.[9]

THE OX

Breeding
For a general discussion of the role of animal husbandry in the agricultural economy of Roman times, see K. D. White, *Roman Farming* (1970).[10] The selection of breeding stock tended to emphasize those characteristics which would yield animals built for the plough and heavy draught duties. There was no pre-occupation with milk production, although cows obviously were milked. Columella recommends that heifers should not be allowed to rear their calves if they have conceived before reaching two years of age. The heifer should be separated from the calf at birth. The udder should be eased for three days to relieve pain and then the heifer should not be milked (*postea mulctra prohiberi*).[11] The heifer was in short 'dried up'. Pliny gives a clear indication of Roman attitudes toward milk consumption. He tells us that the Alpine breed, although noted for giving most milk, also does most work, and these combined functions must have been more important than milk production alone. That no special concern was given by the Romans to the maintenance of a supply of cow's milk is made plain by the observation that mating is allowed only in the month following 4 January (Columella gives July), while those nations that live on milk (*gentibus quidem quae lacte vivunt*) arrange mating throughout the year so as to have cows in milk at all times.

Calf-rearing
Columella gives a good account of calf-rearing.[13] Where there is abundant fodder cows are bred every year. If fodder is scarce, then preference is given to maintaining

the cow's strength for working. If the cow is not a working animal it is still considered unwise to breed annually, as the calf requires milk for the space of a year. The difficulty of rearing a calf and working the cow as a draught-animal is solved if cows from Altina can be procured as sucklers, since they are high yielders. Early weaning is achieved by a diet of crushed beans and wine. The new-born calf may be given toasted millet ground up and mixed with milk. Varro suggests that the dams can be relieved of some of the burden of suckling if the calves are encouraged to accept some green fodder. At six months, he suggests, wheat bran, barley-meal and choice grass should be offered to them.

Castration, according to Varro, should not take place in animals under two years of age. Columella mentions the Punic custom of castrating much younger calves.[14] By that method the testicles were compressed with a cleft stick of fennel and gradually destroyed. *Sed fissa ferula comprimere testiculos, et paulatim confringere* presents a slight difficulty of interpretation. The notion of 'breaking up' that *confringere* gives is perhaps too violent and sudden to agree with *paulatim* or 'little by little'. There is no doubt that clamping the scrotum and spermatic cords between pieces of wood and cutting off the blood-supply would result in the slow atrophy of the testicles. Thus *confringere* should probably be read as 'destroy' or 'bring to naught' rather than 'break up'. The operation would then exactly resemble that of castration by means of a rubber ring or Burdizzo emasculators, as practised in modern times. The advantages claimed by Mago – that no wound is caused, and that it is best to castrate a beast when young – would be in accordance with modern opinion as to the degree of 'setback' that is suffered as a result of the shock of surgical castration. On the other hand, late castration would enable greater growth and a better conformation for draught-work to be gained.

Adult castration is of some interest, as the bulls were 'cut proud' which in modern times has been recognized as a means by which certain characteristics of male behaviour and physical conformation may be retained. The belief has been that failure to remove the whole of the epididymis or duct system of the testicle will result in a horse (for example) exhibiting the behaviour of a stallion (aggression and interest in mares), although sterile. The same observation seems to have been made in the Punic practice. After clamping the cords (cremasters) between two lathes of wood the scrotum is incised and the testicles exposed. The epididymal tissues are removed from the testicles and left attached to the spermatic cords and cremaster muscles (collectively known as *nervi*). Haemorrhage was considered less likely to occur and the steer kept the form of an entire male. That such a castrated animal could impregnate a cow immediately after operation puzzled the ancients who naturally were unaware of the presence of spermatozoa in the epididymis. The castrated bull was carefully rested and fed as a sick animal. Pitch was applied to the wound as a fly repellent.

Nutrition

K. D. White gives a most excellent account of ration scales for working oxen and fodder crops are analysed carefully with regard to season.[15] Space does not permit any account to compare with this survey. But the questions raised when considering herd economics must be discussed. Oxen were very much in demand for draught and ploughing duties. Mature beef seems to have been little used as an item of diet. The fate of steers not trained to the yoke would appear to have been most commonly sale as sacrificial victims. These two demands seem to have provided the Roman cattle-breeder with outlets for his stock not represented in modern times. The idea of a dairy industry simply cannot be countenanced, but cows were in demand for calf-rearing and their milk-producing capacities were valued in this respect. Although beef finds little mention, there are frequent references to the consumption of veal.[16] We may confidently assume that surplus calves would provide meat. The lack of fodder for winter feeding would preclude rearing animals for beef and in any event there seems to have been a certain prejudice against slaughtering oxen. This may have been exaggerated by the ancient authors, but there is no evidence that beef was held in such culinary esteem as to induce the Roman populace to pay the higher price for it that overwintering stock would merit.

The importance of veal in the soldiers' diet is illustrated by A. H. M. Jones. He tells us that the ration scales for the late Roman period included bread, meat, wine and oil. The meat was either veal or pork. A diet for AD 360 was two days of veal and one of pork. Two days of biscuit alternated with one of bread and wine alternated with *acetum* daily.[17] For a garrison peacefully deployed with its granaries and storehouses amid the pasturage for their own flocks this seems reasonable. On active service bread gave way to biscuit and salt pork took precedence over fresh meats. Again this would seem to be reasonable under conditions of warfare with problems of transport and the perishable qualities of foodstuffs. The problems of foul water-supply must have been avoided by the use of the dilute *acetum*. The rather seasonal production of calves must have presented difficulties in maintaining an even supply of veal, but sufficient evidence seems to exist for veal being considered the third most important of the cattle-breeder's sources of income.

Management

Columella tells us that he favours stables for oxen which combine covered quarters for winter and open quarters for summer.[18] The stalls should be nine or ten feet wide so that the ox is comfortable and the herdsmen can work round the animals easily. Palladius prescribes a stall eight feet wide and fifteen feet long for a pair of oxen. Vitruvius gives an allowance of seven feet by fifteen as a maximum and a length of ten feet as a minimum. Drainage is important and the feed racks should be comfortably positioned. Straw for the bedding is to be stacked in August. Cattle kept for breeding purposes can winter in the open but it is deemed wise to call them in to well-constructed yards with stalls in which the cows will not be crowded.

Medical Treatment of Oxen

Our main source is Columella. His passages cannot be interpreted until the treatments for the African diseases, such as rinderpest and bovine malignant catarrh, have been sorted out from those of mild diseases such as coughs and diarrhoeas and the many injuries suffered by the working ox. Our earliest record of the major cattle plagues is the Papyrus of Kahun.[19] It is not surprising to find descriptions of such plagues in Columella in view of his avowed debt to Mago and the Punic traditions of veterinary medicine. If the diseases crossed to Spain with the Punic colonizers, Mago's prescriptions may have found their way into local traditions before a Latin translation of his works was formally approved by the Roman Senate. Perhaps the most interesting aspect of Columella's treatments of cattle plagues is their great antiquity. A comparison of passages in his work and the Egyptian papyrus shows a most remarkable number of parallels:

Columella VI, 6.3: 'If indigestion is neglected, inflation of the stomach and a greater pain in the intestines follows, which prevents the animal from feeding, makes it bellow, prevents it from resting and forces it to lie down frequently, tossing its head and lashing its tail.'

Pap. Kah., lines 20–2: 20 '... if afterwards/21 he is stretched out *itn* and he falls to the ground/22 It is called the hidden bendings.'[20]

Columella VI, 6.4: '... draw off the faeces by inserting the greased hand [*uncta manu*].'

Pap. Kah., lines 23–8: 23 '... I must thrust/24 my hand into the interior of his rudder/28 ... the hand is *kmya*.'[21]

Columella VI, 6.1: 'Sometimes, however, medicine is of no avail and blood and mucus flows from the belly.

Pap. Kah., line 29: 29 'You must remove the blood clots and the matter or mucus. ...

Columella VI, 9.2: 'The symptoms of fever are tears from the eyes, a heavy head, contracted eyes, a flow of saliva from the mouth, an unusually slow and impeded respiration.'

Pap. Kah., lines 35–8: 35 'If I see a bull with *nft* [dyspnoea or panting – literally wind]/36 then his eyes are discharging,/37 his temples are heavy, the roots/38 of his teeth are red (the gums are inflamed).'

Columella VI, 8.4: 'If the violent flux and the pain in the intestines has not ceased and the animal refuses food, and its head is very heavy and it frequently blinks and tears flow from its eyes. ...'

Pap. Kah., lines 53–4: 53 '... if he is not well and he is heavy/54 under your fingers and blinks his eyes. ...'[22]

The classic pictures of the fevered ox with its head hanging and tears streaming is a recurrent theme in descriptions of cattle diseases which span a score of centuries. The Egyptians bathed the feverish beasts and bled them from the nose and the tail. These are the procedures found in the accounts of Varro and Columella. It seems reasonable to suggest that as the diseases spread through Africa in the last two millenia B C so the experience of treating them passed from the Egyptian to the Canaanite and into the Punic sphere of influence. Further evidence of the African influence in Columella's pages comes from analysis of VI, 7.4: '... and slime from his nostrils, the middle of his forehead should be burned down to the bone. ...' At first sight the treatment is meaningless, but Celsus provides information which makes interpretation of the procedure possible. In VII, 7, he tells us that troublesome eye discharges were attributed to the drainage of matter via the superficial blood vessels of the scalp. Various methods are discussed for the division of these vessels. The method favoured in Africa is that by which the crown of the scalp is burned down to the bone so as to cause flaking and sealing of the vessels. There can be little doubt that this method of treating humans was readily adapted by the Punic practitioners to the imagined needs of the ox with bovine malignant catarrh.

By the time Vegetius came to consider cattle diseases (under the stimulus of the outbreak of severe plagues) the ancient treatments contained in Columella's chapters were apparently no longer associated with the new manifestations of the very same conditions.[23] Rinderpest and the other epizootic virus diseases are described as varieties of the *malleus* and in the same terms as the horse plagues. This confusion may to some extent be blamed on Columella's muddled presentation. There may well have been a long period of relative freedom from visitations of cattle plague and, as I have already indicated, Vegetius may have felt competent to provide the knowledge required by reference to the horse literature.

The Medical Handbooks

It may be that Columella was the only Latin author to provide any extensive account of cattle diseases. The subject may not have been considered worthy of attention in the form of a special treatise. Small handbooks must have provided such information as was necessary for the herdsman or flock-owner. A convenient Latin distillation from Punic sources of the type that Columella gives may have provided the source for abbreviated notes such as appear in Gargilius Martialis in the form of eighteen simple prescriptions. The account of cattle diseases in the *Mulomedicina Chironis* (IX) is actually prefaced by a complete page of Columella's preamble to his Book VI. The thirteen prescriptions for cattle that follow are only brief notes, but distinct parallels can be seen between them and passages in Columella and Martialis. Pelagonius is only a little more comprehensive, with thirty-five prescriptions for the same range of simple conditions.

THE SHEEP AND GOAT

Breeding

Lambing time appears to have been later in Roman practice than in modern times.[24] The rams were turned into the ewes in May, so that the lambs would be born in autumn, after the grape harvest. It was considered that the great heat of summer would be fatal to the lambs born in spring. The early rains of autumn would have caused some grass growth in time for the lambs. The idea that cold water could cause abortion might have influenced the avoidance of a winter pregnancy such as spring lambing would entail. Certainly the ewe herself was regarded as delicate, although the ability of lambs to survive birth in the depths of winter was recognized. The same water-supply was used throughout the five months' gestation period, as change of water was considered injurious to the womb, apart from being likely to 'spot' the wool.[25] Damp was deemed harmful to the ewe and the folds were to be kept dry and softly littered. The delivery of the lambs was closely supervised. Columella attaches great importance to the *magister* having veterinary knowledge and being equipped to perform the operation of embryotomy or surgical division of the retained foetus if necessary. No details of the operation are given other than that if the foetus is trapped transversely it is divided with a knife (*ferrum*) without causing the death of the mother.[26] Celsus describes the operation on the human being, stipulating the use of the *uncus* with its inner curvature specially sharpened.[27] This instrument would have resembled the embryotomy knife of modern veterinary practice. No doubt the plain, blunt *uncus* (hook) would have been used for traction on the retained foetus. The newborn lamb was kept penned with its mother in a warm pen. Experience of lamb dysentery may have inspired Columella's instruction that some of the rich colostrum should be drawn off before the lamb suckled lest it cause harm to the lamb.[28]

Management

For the first few days of life the lambs were kept in pens to restrain over-exertion while playing. The ewes were allowed out to grass and suckling took place in the morning and evening. Fold feeding with lucerne and shrub-trefoil and bran is recommended by Columella. If it could be afforded barley flour was fed (*si permittat annona*).[29] Weaning took place when the lamb was four months old. Castration of the lambs took place when they were five months old. The location of the sheep farm decided the fate of the lambs. Close to a town lambs were sent to the butcher. Transport costs would be very small and no expenditure on fodder would be incurred. This procedure had its essential complement in the simultaneous release of the mother's milk for consumption in the same town in the form of cheese.[30] The profit from the actual meat must have been too small for transport of fat lambs from distant pastures to have been contemplated. Wool and milk were the prime considerations in sheep-breeding, with the possibility of occasional lamb sacrifices providing a demand for victims.

Medical Treatment of Sheep

The general health of the flock was considered to be affected by the weather. In particular the sun could be harmful and steps were taken to drive the sheep when grazing so that they faced away from the dangerous rays.[31] In cold weather the flock was allowed to drink only once a day. Columella makes the most interesting observation that the sheep would suffer catarrh (*gravedo*) and intestinal upsets if allowed to graze on pastures before the sun had removed the hoar-frost.[32] The ancient experience of pulpy kidney in sheep allowed to feed on rich pasture has been noted above (p. 315). The condition known as 'braxy' is another disease in the group caused by clostridial organisms. The factor of prime importance in the pathogenesis has been recognized as the ingestion of frozen grass or fodder. Death is rapid, but preceded by obvious abdominal pain. On occasions the stomach (modern abomasum) is obviously inflamed when examined post-mortem. The best method of control is still to keep sheep in the fold overnight and feed hay in the morning before allowing the sheep out to frozen pasture. There can be no doubt that the ancient shepherds had made several correct observations in relation to the clostridial diseases.[33] The type of management recommended by Columella for keeping the fleece of valuable wool-bearers clean must have helped to reduce the extent of exposure to the ground contaminated with clostridial organisms. Shelters are to be kept free from mud and faeces, urine is to be swept away, and for preference boards with holes in them should be used for flooring the pens.[34] The standard of hygiene incidentally brought about by concern for the fleece must to some extent have countered the effects of concentrating large numbers of sheep on permanent fold sites year after year. Columella also recommends scattering flocks as widely as possible in the event of plague.

The most important conditions from the point of view of the sheep-owner must have been those which threatened the fleece. Thus we find Columella preoccupied with treatments for the various types of parasitic mange to which sheep are susceptible. To prevent scabies the sheep are to be anointed for three days after shearing with the juice of boiled lupins, dregs of old wine and olive lees. Then they are bathed in the sea or a salt solution. Vigilance for the early signs of irritation on the sheep is urged. Prompt treatment of lesions involved scraping them and applying remedies such as hemlock juice which had been salted and stored in pots in a dungheap for a whole year. Ground sulphur and liquid pitch boiled over a low fire were considered efficacious. The information given by Columella adds up to a complete picture of sheep scab or psoroptic mange. A high degree of resistance would prevail in flocks in a healthy condition and well-nourished sheep would suffer only a low incidence of infestation. In these cases an apparent good response would have been observed. Where a flock was in poor condition generally the mange might have spread with astonishing virulence causing a heavy mortality. Several common sheep ailments such as foot-rot and orf are described.

Columella's section on goats is brief, as the same general rules apply to their diseases as apply to those of the sheep and oxen.[35] Three observations, however, are of particular interest. Roman flocks were plagued by parasitic diseases such as liver fluke and stomach worm, in which fluid would be observed under the skin of affected individuals (*hydrops* or anasarca). Retained foetal membranes (*secundae*) are treated with an application administered directly into the genital tract of liquid wax (*ceratum liquidum*).[36] Third, and perhaps most important, is Columella's recommendation to slaughter sick goats and salt the flesh. This habit must have been an important factor in exposing the populace to serious disease from infected meat.

THE PIG

Breeding
Pig-rearing seems to have been organized in two ways; the production of sucking-pigs close to towns and the raising of stock for breeding porkers in more remote districts.[37] This seems to have been economic, even though the long journeys entailed could reduce the weight of the porker – a fact which was recognized, so that when under Aurelian the guild of pork butchers was obliged to administer a pork issue to the populace of Rome they were able to claim a fixed rebate for the

loss incurred by driving the pigs.[38] Milling of white bread left a surplus of wheat bran which enabled the bakers to feed and fatten porkers. Castration of pigs took place when they were six months old and Columella gives a careful description.

Diseases of Pigs

It is impossible to isolate specific pig diseases from Columella's general remarks in respect of fevers and malaise. In any event the presence of enzootic foot and mouth would account for a great many symptoms and degrees of illness relative to the native immunity of the herd and its standard of nutrition. One matter must be discussed in some detail. Columella mentions that pain from a diseased spleen often attacked pigs (solet etiam vitiosi splenis dolor eas infestare).[39] He also mentions vomiting pigs and scrofulous tumours (strumae) on the neck. The treatment for the strumae is to bleed the pig from under the tongue and to rub the mouth with salt and flour. The one condition in the pig which will invariably present the appearance of an obviously diseased spleen to the dissector (or butcher) is anthrax. Prior to death the pig may show oedematous swellings in the throat due to infection of the lymph glands. The swellings are hot and blood-stained froth may be seen in the mouth. Fever and lethargy are characteristic signs. Death may not ensue for several days. The enormous demand for hams, pork and sausage in Roman times and efforts to provide quotas for free distribution, plus a lack of concern about butchering diseased animals, must have exposed the people to serious risk of anthrax.[40]

THE DOG

Breeding

Accounts of dog-breeding and management are embodied in the Cynegetica of Xenophon, the Cynegetica of Nemesianus, Columella (VII, 12), and Varro (II, 9). General agreement exists on breeding from bitches at least two years of age and arranging for litters in the spring or early summer. The first litter is to be ruthlessly discarded, according to Columella and Nemesianus. Varro is the most solicitous for the bitch's welfare, although even the hunting fanatic Xenophon allows his bitches to rest during gestation. Varro recommends barley bread as being more nourishing for the bitches and likely to encourage a greater milk supply. Varro alone mentions provision of a soft bed of chaff for the puppies. Again agreement exists on the need to kill weak puppies, although Nemesianus is alone in advocating the cruel expedient of setting fires around the bitch and her litter in order to see which puppies she elects to save first!

Weaning is recommended by Varro after two months and then by degrees only. Columella recommends goat's milk as a replacement for any deficiency in the mother's supply, to be given to puppies up to four months of age.

Nutrition

Varro has the best account, recognizing that the dog is omnivorous, feeding on scraps of meat and bones as well as on barley bread soaked in milk. Bone soup and broken bones are given for the savour of the marrow and to strengthen the jaws. The dogs, however, are not allowed the flesh of the flock that they are to guard.

Similarly Varro warns against purchasing sheep dogs from hunters and butchers. His reasons are that the former will chase off after game and the latter are lazy ; and so both would be unsuitable for the care of a flock. One would chase the sheep and the other would have an appetite for fresh meat! Columella adds boiled bean liquor to the diet of bread but warns against madness if the beans are too hot. Xenophon warns against overfeeding. Varro is careful to recommend kennels with beds of leaves or fodder for rainy days to protect the dogs from mud and chills.

Medical Treatment of Dogs
The information on dog diseases is very limited and is confined to the phenomena which would impress the casual observer rather than the serious student. From time to time dogs would have been observed to eat grass and vomit or suffer diarrhoea. Distempered dogs would suffer coughs and various degrees of nervous disease ranging from violent fits to paralysis of the hind-limbs. The infestation with fleas and ticks and the sores and inter-digital cysts that trouble dogs would have been observed by the herdsmen and treated as a matter of routine. Rabies was recognized and its transmissible nature known. All of these symptoms could be conveniently grouped under the headings of *lytta*, *podagra* and *cynanche* (madness, lameness and cough). Thus cures for rabies would appear successful where the 'madness' was merely a fit or a manifestation of distemper such as encephalitis. A great number of diseases could be grouped under *podagra*: conjecture about individual diseases is therefore fruitless. Columella widens the field with his remark that the other diseases of dogs should be treated according to the instructions for treating those of the other animals.

GENERAL ASPECTS OF VETERINARY PRACTICE

Injuries Attributable to Accidents or Bad Management
Both Vegetius and Columella give examples of common mishaps and the appropriate treatments. The ox was obviously at great risk of injury when struggling to move heavy loads or draw ploughs through obstacles in the ground. Injuries to the shoulders sustained in this way were treated by letting blood from the forelegs (Columella, VI, 16). If the neck was severely bruised blood was drawn from the ear and applications of salt and groundsel made to the swelling (VI, 14.3). If the swelling prevented work the beast was rested and treatment applied in the form of bathing with water and massaging with pitch, beef marrow, goat's fat and stale oil. Columella describes treatments for injuries to the ox's feet caused by the ploughshare (VI, xv). The wounds were dressed with pitch and axle-grease, bound up with sulphur and wool and cauterized through the dressing with a red-hot iron. Penetrating wounds of the hoof caused by pieces of wood or stone were cauterized as above and protected for three days with the *solea spartea* (VI, 15). The dangers of sores being infested with the larvae of the blow-fly were recognized. The maggots were dislodged with cold water or pounded leek and salt. The unpleasant wounds resulting from 'fly-strike' were dressed with bandages and pitch, oil and axle-grease (VI, 16.3).
Vegetius (II, 45-7) and Chiron (VII, 1-8) discuss a range of injuries and serious

fractures in horses. Vegetius illustrates a remarkable degree of perseverance in his accounts of the fixation of fractured legs and the supporting of the horses (II, 47).

Vegetius also mentions briefly the harm caused by bad hay and barley (II, 136–137). Part of his treatment is to stand the horse in a cold stream, from which we may deduce that laminitis is the condition involved. Further discussion of laminitis due to lack of care when feeding barley is to be found in *De Pletura* (II, 108).

In an important passage Vegetius discusses the way in which injuries to the horse's back due to harness may be avoided (II , 59). The saddle-cloths should be sufficient in quantity and soft. They should be washed and brushed to remove adherent material or anything of a rough nature that might cause damage to the skin. The saddle-cloths should be large enough and the saddles should fit properly. Apart from suffering abscesses, bruises and galls from badly fitting pack-saddles, the animals will be harmed by enormous loads and these should be moderate. Once caused, the injuries are treated with hot onion poultices (II, 60; I, 63), which will disperse watery swelling overnight. Hard callouses are treated with fomentations of barley meal and colewort. Open sores are dressed with honey and linen cloths.

The crisis when a horse accidentally inhales a medicinal drench is described accurately and the dangers well understood by Vegetius (II, 140) and Chiron (V, 44). The dangers of careless use of the *sagitta* when bleeding the horse have already been mentioned. Another danger was that the opened vein would not close when required to do so, which could be fatal in a horse already bled to the point of suffering shock. At first the animal's own dung was plastered over the wound. Light cautery was attempted if this failed. Alternatives included wool soaked in oil and binding a piece of wood across the vein.

Evaluation of Roman veterinary medicine in the light of modern knowledge and practice has been undertaken by a small number of medical historians.[41] It is a procedure of doubtful value and tells us nothing about the part played by veterinary medicine and its practitioners in Roman life. To criticize ancient medicine for its employment of blood-letting and cauterization is easy from a modern standpoint, but not likely to advance understanding of the subject. The ancient theories of the workings of the body were mistaken.[42] As more intricate and involved theories were evolved so practitioners were led farther from the truth until the most inquiring intellects lost contact with the realities of the subject. Inevitably a reaction against an excess of theory was prompted by the hard-pressed practitioner confronted with the evidence of his eyes and the urgent need for helpful treatments. In his *Proemium* Celsus is preoccupied with an attempt to defend the theorists of the Coan school against the disciples of Themison, the 'methodists'.[43] At some time in the first century BC Themison of Laodicea formalized the teachings of his master Asclepiades of Bithynia who had first propounded the simplified doctrine which came to be known as 'methodism' (*methodos*). The various states of disease were explained by the theory of *strictum* and *laxum*. In the simplest terms the body was composed of solid matter and fluid matter. The fluid was dispersed around the atoms of solid material. The gaps between the atoms permitted the fluids to flow around them. Disease was explained as being the result of constriction or relaxation of these gaps or pores causing disturbance of the flow of the body fluids. Food was held to leave the stomach unchanged and to be diffused throughout the body. These 'methodist' concepts are clearly illustrated in Chiron (I) in the explanations for the procedure of blood-letting. It would appear that 'methodism' found ready acceptance in the veterinary sphere and probably remained strongly entrenched long after its fall from favour in the field of human medicine. The clear relation between food and disease in animals, as exemplified by the horse with acute laminitis after overfeeding on barley or the ox with bloat after eating rich greenstuffs, would have supported 'methodist' beliefs. The susceptibility of the horse to tetanus (*De Roborosis*, Vegetius II, 88) would have supplied frequent examples of a disease epitomizing the concept of *strictum*.

Surgery

Surgical procedures appear to have been limited to minor operations such as castration and draining guttural pouch abscesses. Chiron (II) defines surgery (*chirurgia*) as those procedures in which the knife or cautery effects the cure, and Vegetius follows his text exactly (II, 13 *et seq.*). Chiron's account of castration in the horse (VII, 68, 101) is almost identical with Celsus' description of ablation of the testicle in medical practice (VII, 22.5). An attempt to echo the medical texts may perhaps be seen in the discussion of fracture of the skull as an introduction to the subject.

Some rather startling statements are to be found in Pliny and Columella. Pliny (VIII, 78.209) tells us that sows are sterilized in the same way that camels are, by being fasted for two days and then hung up by the forelegs. The *vulva* (? womb) is then excised. Columella tells us that an operation is performed on sows by which the *vulva* is made to suppurate and scar over (VII, 60.5: *feminis quoque vulvae exulcerantur*) in order to prevent breeding. Columella states that he cannot see the advantage of such a procedure. Pliny says that the operation 'makes the pigs fatten', and it must therefore involve removal of the ovaries. The operation Columella describes is a curious procedure. Similar problems are raised by the astonishing statement of Pliny (XI, 80.205) to the effect that runners troubled by enlargement of the spleen undergo surgical removal of the organ. He also tells us that animals survive after removal of the spleen through an incision. Further, he says that removal of the spleen was considered by some people to deprive the patient of the ability to laugh. These passages suggest that there existed a certain amount of surgical expertise which has not found expression in the literature or has been lost. It is interesting to speculate that experimental surgery was conducted for private interest rather than for publication. Galen's public demonstrations on the pig certainly lend support to such an hypothesis.

The difficulties of transmitting the more technical procedures by means of the written treatise are obvious. Those individuals most concerned (students of medicine) would attend the operations for practical tuition. The difficulties of technical expression and illustration would possibly have made written accounts purposeless, since the lay reader would have been unable to understand. In this way a curious gap between the lay public and the initiated may have developed. It may also have been fostered by a profession jealous of its secrets and anxious to retain some expertise that was not common knowledge. The relative absence of surgical accounts in the veterinary literature may perhaps be explained along these lines.

The great problem of lucid explanation of technical procedures is demonstrated in *De Dysenteria* (Vegetius II, 75; Chiron V, 29), which is concerned with prolapse or eversion of the rectum. The surgical reduction of this condition is almost impossible to understand without the aid of diagrams and an understanding of the anatomy of the various layers of the bowel. Vegetius writes: 'If a horse suffers from dysentery, its rectum may be reversed [everted], and if it is to be cured it must be cut round with the utmost caution, lest the intestine which precedes the rectum be touched. The intestine, if it is damaged, does not return but remains and the rectum is laid open. The intestine comes out easily and the danger to life is immediate.' The operation which is here so inadequately described is that of 'submucosal resection of the rectum'. The essence of this operation is that the thick mucosal lining of the rectum is carefully cut away so as to denude the muscular coat and outer covering of the rectum. This is then tucked back within the pelvic cavity and the cut edges of the mucosal lining reunited. If the rectum is cut through, egress of the intestine is quite unimpeded and the outcome is disastrous.

This example shows the way in which the best of the technical achievements of the ancient surgeons were probably lost in the process of copying, even when an initial attempt to transmit them was made.

Similar effects of copying and translation can be seen in Vegetius (I, 49-51: Chiron III, 4), in whose work the differential diagnosis of various types of colic in the horse can be recognized. Much restoration and correction is required before definite diagnosis can be made from the information given in the ancient text. It is here, apropos of the practical consideration of the ailments of the digestive system, that Vegetius expresses his scorn for ignorance among *veterinarii* (*imperitia veterinariorum*) and for old wives' spells (*praecantationes anicularum*). He has borrowed his knowledge of this important topic from the practical treatise of Chiron. The Greek veterinarian is the source of Vegetius' critique and is far more blunt; those who seek to cure the complicated digestive disturbances of the horse with spells and spurious medicines are *minus intelligentes* and *idiotae et minus scientes* (Chiron III, 4).

CHAPTER III

SOME NOTES ON CAVALRY HORSES IN THE ROMAN ARMY

The Function of Cavalry
FROM THE TIME OF XENOPHON ONWARDS the strengths and weaknesses of cavalry were understood completely and its employment was as effective and successful as at any time in its more recent history.[1] A convenient picture of Roman cavalry in action is to be found in Caesar's campaign at Ilerda in 49 B C.[2] At the outset he was in extreme difficulties, but the arrival of his Gallic cavalry transformed the situation dramatically. Within a short space of time this body of horsemen had gained mastery of the countryside, annihilated isolated bodies of infantry, extricated hard-pressed legionaries and so demoralized the Pompeian cavalry as to render it quite ineffective. The enemy, unable to send out foragers or watering parties, were reduced to extreme privation and obliged to surrender.

From this account we can draw up a list of the duties of cavalry. It was expected to act as the eyes of the commander by carrying out observation and reconnaissance; to forage for supplies and prevent the enemy from sending out foragers; to overpower the enemy cavalry and drive them from the field; to isolate and overpower bodies of enemy infantry as opportunity arose; and to support the infantry in pitched battles. The cavalry was not expected to operate as an independent arm. Indeed it was recognized by Xenophon that cavalry had great need of attached infantry and should never be used without such support. In order to perform these varied duties it had to be equipped to fight in different ways, and to be capable of both speed and endurance.

Roman Cavalry in the First and Second Centuries A D
Josephus describes the Roman cavalryman as being equipped with helmet, cuirass, lance and three or four javelins in a quiver.[3] The sculptured gravestones and bas-reliefs confirm the use of this equipment, and show a general absence of horse-armour. In practice, it would seem that the Romans had adopted a method of cavalry fighting that embodied the best of the Greek styles[4] and still enabled the various duties of their own cavalry to be efficiently performed. Thus in the cavalry *mêlée* or against disordered infantry the cavalry could use the spear or lance with effect and against steady infantry they could dash up and discharge javelins. By not attempting to close with the enemy infantry cavalrymen could avoid wounds being inflicted on their mounts. Missiles could be deflected with the large shield and the use of horse-armour could be dispensed with. This would have conferred the

special advantage of sparing the horses much overheating in sustained actions. Mounted archers, who had been used experimentally during the civil wars of the late Republic, were established in regular units during the Flavian period.

The Gyrus

In the *Germania* Tacitus mentions the *gyrus* (or training ring).[5] He tells us that the German horses were neither beautiful nor noted for speed. Their riders used only the shield and spear and could perform only the most simple of mass manoeuvres in battle. They were restricted to advancing in formation and making carefully dressed wheels to the right. The Roman cavalry, on the other hand, were trained in the *gyri* (training rings) in which individual horses could be exercised on the lunging rein and taught to wheel and turn in any direction. The movements required by the javelin attack would have been practised in this way. When Pliny tells us that the horse can aid its rider in the throwing of the javelin by swaying its body it is obviously a reference to this type of training.[6]

An important insight is to be derived from Tacitus' remark on the German cavalry. The limited training and the exclusive use of the lance as a weapon are perhaps to be linked. A restriction on freedom of movement must have been the almost inevitable result of the employment of the lance. Having charged into the enemy ranks a lancer *must* break through. Should he fail he must either ride backwards or break away and expose his back. His fellows massed behind him would cause crowding and compound the disastrous effects of failure.[7] In any event, should a breakthrough be effected at any one point, those lancers committed to the remainder of the enemy's line would have to disengage and ride to the point where a gap had been made, in order to exploit their comrades' success. In practice this would have been most difficult and a better alternative would have been the adoption of the wedge formation. This tactic would enable the cavalry to follow their leader, who could see enemy weaknesses and exploit them; and at the same time maintain a compact formation.

Cataphractarii and Clibanarii

There must, then, have been a tendency for the *contarius* (lancer) to adopt mailed body armour to some extent. This change appears at least from the time of Hadrian, although a like protection was seemingly not extended to the horse. These mailed *contarii* were called *cataphractarii*. An early use of cataphracts by Vespasian may be implied in a passage of Josephus.[8] Having breached the walls of Jotapata Vespasian ordered some of his cavalry to dismount and form the spearhead of the assault party about to attack the breach. The cavalrymen 'covered in armour on every side and with lances (*conti*) couched' were to be first to enter the town. It seems reasonable to assume that full armour was an important qualification for this duty.

With the increasing use of *cataphractarii* the Romans later took the final step of imitating their enemies and extending armour to the horses themselves, apparently from early in the fourth century, thus, incidentally at least, going some way to meet a dominant consideration in cavalry tactics, namely the inability of the horse to tolerate wounds. In general the character of the armies of the late Empire changed dramatically. The legions had been modified by reduction in numbers and reform of armament; only a proportion of the infantry were now javelin-men in the old legionary style. An emphasis on missile-throwing and projection is reflected in the literature and in the military architecture of city walls. Some legions were armed entirely with *ballistae* (*legio ballistaria*).[9] One of the effects of such innovations must have been to expose the horses of the fourth- and fifth-century cavalry to unendurable torment. To operate on the battlefields of the late Empire the cavalry must have been obliged to adopt more, and heavier, armour.[10] The javelin attack would have become impractical and highly dangerous to man and horse. The effect would have been to oblige the *cataphractarius* to transform into the *clibanarius*, with mail armour for man and horse. The tactic would have been the wedge formation used to exploit opportunities made for the cavalry by their own artillery.

Such a body of horse would be unsuitable for the varied general duties that we have discussed; and the use of a separate light cavalry would have been necessary.

Training
Provision seems to have been made for training in inclement weather, in the form of large riding halls.[11] These are recognizable in the excavated remains of many Roman forts and are in most cases arranged across the front of the headquarters building. There is no doubt that the training of men and horses took place in these structures. Here and on parade grounds and outdoor training areas the men learned to vault onto wooden horses and, no doubt, onto their own mounts. Here, we may imagine, the javelin-men practised in the *gyrus* with dummy targets, and the *contarii* could train their horses not to flinch and shy. At intervals, at least every month, the *ala* would ride out and practise the *ambulatura* or route march, and evolutions of the type that Xenophon recommended. The results of such training would have been assessed at the reviews and parades. Some interesting information about cavalry training is preserved in Hadrian's address to his troops at Lambaesis.[12] The base of a monumental column has survived and bears the remains of a number of addresses which Hadrian made to the various units attached to the legion which he had reviewed. In his remarks to the cavalry he comments on their exercises, saying 'You chose to demonstrate to me the hardest [exercise] of all, javelin-throwing at full gallop and in full armour'. His personal views on cavalry tactics are revealed – 'I do not care much for open order tactics. . . . When you charge, let it be knee to knee . . .'. Hadrian claims that he 'follows the best authority' on the subject and perhaps the fact that he feels that he needs to justify his views is itself suggestive of some controversy. The coincidental formation of the first recorded unit of regular *cataphractarii*, the *ala I Gallorum et Pannoniorum catafractata*, during Hadrian's reign suggests that Roman ideas on cavalry tactics were undergoing change at this period. Lessons may have been learned from the fact that Trajan's army had had to contend with the Sarmatian *cataphractarii* and to face sophisticated artillery.[13]

Equipment
A detailed survey of Roman horse trappings and equipment is contained in Vigneron's book, which has many illustrations.[14] The Roman cavalryman was obviously proud of his horse's harness and decorations. Many ornate remains have

been discovered. Harness was decorated with a type of *phalera* similar to those awarded to the soldier for gallantry. Polybius states that voluntary acts of valour, not expressly required, by which an enemy was killed were rewarded by presentation with a *phiale* (cup?) to the infantryman and horse-trappings to the cavalryman.[15] Various types of bronze and enamelled medallions and pendants have been found. Saddles appear to have been made of leather and bronze with cloths either side, presumably to protect the calves of the rider from becoming slippery with the horse's sweat and so imperilling his grip. The saddle of Genealis, a Thracian *eques* whose tombstone is in Cirencester Museum, has a substantial knee-roll on either skirt to afford greater security of seat to the rider. Several scenes on Trajan's Column depict shields and helmets hung from projections on the cantle and pommel of troopers' saddles.

A great variety of bits has survived, ranging from the simple snaffle bit to elaborate and quite savage ones of Thracian and Asiatic type. Xenophon discusses bits and points out that the discs, commonly found in the Greek type, are designed to prevent the horse from gripping the bit between his teeth.[16] Stallion muzzles have survived and a very fine example is in the British Museum. The difficulties of controlling stallions and preventing fighting and aggressive behaviour may appear greater to the modern observer than was in fact the case. Xenophon is adamant that vicious horses should be rejected for military service as being likely to do more harm than the enemy.[17] With training, and riders accustomed to uncastrated mounts, the Roman charger was probably spirited but docile and well-disposed to its fellows. It must be remembered that stallions of small stature do not present the same handling difficulties that are posed by the modern throughbred of 16 hands and more in height, whose sole purpose is breeding. It may be that the cavalrymen could manage stallions and mares in the same unit, which is almost unthinkable in these days. Evidence for this is provided by a list of remounts for the *cohors XX Palmyrenorum* which quite clearly includes mares.[18] British regimental experience of stallions is related by H. C. B. Rogers, *The Mounted Troops of the British Army*, 1959. The 10th Hussars were ordered to India in 1846 and on arrival were given entire mounts – 'but in spite of the trouble they gave in biting and kicking and occasionally fighting with one another, the troopers became devoted to them.'

Horse-armour

Actual representations of horse-armour in Roman times are rare and depict Rome's enemies, such as the Sarmatians on Trajan's Column and the *graffito* of a charging *clibanarius* at Dura-Europus.[19] The Sarmatians are depicted in scale armour. The horses wear eye-protectors and are enveloped in fanciful skin-tight scale-armour which includes the heads and legs. This is quite impossible. If in fact the Romans did use horse-armour as early as the second century, the silence of the artists is puzzling; but if they did not, a passage of Arrian is equally puzzling.[20] Writing in the time of Hadrian he mentions that armoured cavalry exist and the horses have frontlets and side coverings. Arrian has possibly failed to distinguish sharply enough between the practice of the parade ground and that of the battlefield, but more probably, in regard to the horses, he is referring to some protective material which was lighter than metal armour, a possibility which is strengthened by the fact that he emphasizes that the cavalryman's body-armour is of mail, canvas and horn. However that may be, no Roman horse-armour is represented in surviving grave sculpture or any of the narrative reliefs. In a similar way, although horse-armour is described by Xenophon, none of the Athenian sculptures depict it.[21] This is difficult to explain. Perhaps bulky armour was considered unaesthetic by the sculptors as it would hide the lines of the horse's head and body and detract from the artistic result. This may explain the curious depiction of Sarmatian armour on Trajan's Column where the armour follows the horses' contours exactly. Frontlets may have been depicted by means of paint or perhaps it just happens that no gravestone of a fully armed *clibanarius* has survived, a fact which would support the view of his late appearance on the scene.[22]

Practical considerations may have militated against the constant use of horse-armour. The Roman light horse would not, in any event, have adopted armour, since sweating would have presented severe problems in protracted action. The armoured blankets would have become soaked after a time and any rations or equipment attached to the saddle would be likely to become similarly sweat-soaked. In general it seems likely that the *clibanarii* would be severely limited in their range of activity.

Stabling

A detailed discussion of military stabling is to be found in I. A. Richmond's report on his excavations at Hod Hill.[23] This first-century Roman fort accommodated a legionary cohort and a half-*ala* of cavalry. The stable blocks were thoroughly investigated and are of considerable interest. Two types of stable division were noted. In one type of compartment, measuring 11 feet by 12, three horses might have been tethered to the cross-wall with a 6-foot alley behind them for access by the grooms. A larger type of compartment measured 11 feet by 18 and would have held two such rows of three horses each, providing a 6-foot alley between the rows. Complete excavation of one compartment revealed that the floor was formed by natural chalk rock. It was possible to see the effects of the horses' hooves on the floor. The fore-hooves had made a narrow strip of wear about 18 inches from the cross-wall. The hind-hooves had made a larger area of wear about three feet from the narrow patch. The hind-hoof trampling appeared to be associated with the dark staining appropriate to the effects of dung. Richmond pointed out that this evidence reinforces the conclusion that the Roman cavalry horses were small by modern standards.[24] A complex of buildings in the southern corner of the fort was tentatively identified by Richmond as a *veterinarium* for baggage-animals and the quarters of an officer. These quarters appeared to comprise a small suite of rooms with a closet and a wash-place. The size would indicate an officer below the rank of decurion but still of some importance. In view of the context Richmond made the cautious guess that this may have been the station of the *mulomedicus*.

No evidence was found to support this, but the possibility of the existence of such accommodation merits discussion. From what we have seen of Roman veterinary activities it is possible to make certain suggestions in respect of veterinary accommodation. A definite point within the fort for the treatment of horses must have been necessary, since such treatment could not take place among horses tethered abreast in their stables. The operation of bleeding, for example, required close confinement of the horse in comfortable, quiet surroundings. The operations which involved use of the cautery would require a hearth for heating the irons. Sufficient space would be required for casting down horses and provision for operations to take place under cover in inclement weather must have been made. Restraint of horses during operations and treatments may well have been achieved by means of the stocks described by Columella and Vegetius. Future excavations on other sites may reveal sluices, hearths, stalls and even the post-holes of stocks,[25] in a context that will allow identification of veterinary activity to be made. It seems reasonable to relate the paired stable blocks of Hod Hill with paired *turmae*, but Richmond's calculations indicate that the accommodation is sufficient for more than an establishment of 30 troop horses and 4 officers' remounts per *turma*. Richmond, however, located the baggage-animals at his hypothetical *veterinarium*. This may be questioned, since the grooms of the cavalry were clearly accommodated in the ends of one block in each pair of stables, and it seems unlikely that the pack-animals would be so far removed from their charge. Indeed the allowance of only one pack-animal to each officer and 4 to each *turma* brings the total of horses and baggage-animals to 82 which is very close to Richmond's figure of 84.

Rations

Our source for the ration-scales of Roman cavalry mounts in Republican times is Polybius.[26] The monthly ration for a Roman cavalryman was 2 *medimni* of wheat and 7 *medimni* of barley. The auxiliary or allied cavalryman was allotted 1⅓ *medimni* of wheat and 5 *medimni* of barley. The ration for a foot-soldier was ⅔ *medimnus* of wheat. It would appear that the Roman cavalryman was allotted sufficient wheat for three men and that his auxiliary counterpart was allotted enough for two men. A comparable proportion is evident in the barley ration. The result of Polybius' translation of Latin terms into Greek must be examined before deductions can be drawn. At the rate of 4½ *modii* to the *medimnus* the ration for a man is 3 *modii* of wheat per month. The ration of barley, if we take the Greek measure as exact, would be 31½ *modii* for the Roman cavalryman and 22½ *modii* for the auxiliary troops. If, however, we accept that Polybius converted the Roman measure to its nearest equivalent in *medimni*, the rations are respectively 30 *modii* and 20 *modii* giving a ration of 10 *modii* per month per horse or ⅓ *modius* per day. If we accept Pliny's weight for Roman barley (15 *librae* to a *modius*) the cavalry horse was allowed 5 *librae* of barley per day or 3½ modern pounds weight.[27]

Evidence from a papyrus suggests that in the later Empire the barley ration for a horse was the same. A sixth-century papyrus gives a daily scale of ⅒ *artaba* of barley per horse. At the rate of 3⅓ *modii* to the *artaba* the ration is again ⅓ *modius* or 3½ lb.[28] Further evidence is to be found in the annual requisitions of barley for the *ala Heraclia* at Coptos in A D 187. This unit was allowed twenty thousand *artabai* of barley from the previous year's harvest. This quantity used at the rate of ⅒ *artaba* daily would be sufficient to feed 548 horses for 365 days. It is necessary to give brief consideration to the strength of cavalry units during the Principate in order to understand the significance of this figure.[29]

It is generally accepted that the *ala quingenaria* comprised 16 *turmae* each containing 30 men. The manual *De Munitionibus Castrorum* tells us that the officers' remounts totalled 64 at the rate of two for each decurion and one for each *duplicarius* and *sesquiplicarius*. This gives a total for the *ala quingenaria* of 544 horses which is remarkably close to the computed figure above. Again it is obvious that the ration is calculated as a round number of *artabai*, which can hardly be a coincidence and is therefore very strong evidence for the authenticity of the figures given in *De Munitionibus Castrorum*.[30]

Remounts and Servants

The question of remounts is in itself most interesting. The Polybian ration-scales suggest that the Roman *eques* was expected to maintain three horses and two attendants to ride and care for them. The cavalryman of the Italian allies was expected to maintain two horses and one attendant. The *eques* was selected on the basis of wealth and his pay was subject to deductions for his rations. It is clear, then, that he was expected to maintain the number of horses and servants as a requirement of his position. The establishment of 300 cavalry per legion at this time is generally considered to be a low figure and indicative of a certain lack of interest in cavalry on the part of the Romans. This view is perhaps a little unjust, as the allied complement of cavalry was three times the Roman number, whereas only an equal number of allied infantry was employed, according to Polybius. In addition, access to fresh mounts would have trebled the staying power of the Roman contingent. The allies with one remount per man would have a doubled staying power.

The Augustan reforms, which put the Roman army on a regular footing, must have resulted in the adoption of a system of single mounts. The increasing demand for manpower and garrisons would have rendered the Republican remount establishment grossly expensive. The greater part of the duties of the reformed army was that of policing frontiers and a larger cavalry force in general was required. Some echoes of the lavish remount scale appear to have lingered in the allotment of three horses for the decurion and two each for the *duplicarius* and *sesquiplicarius*. Recognition of the advantages given by close support of cavalry by infantry seems to be indicated by the creation of units of auxiliary troops containing both cavalry and infantry. A quingenarian cohort of six centuries had 120 cavalry attached and a milliarian cohort of ten centuries had 240 horsemen. Obviously these units would have been ideal garrison troops with a capacity for patrol and police work that infantry could not undertake alone, and for small-scale conflicts that cavalry could not deal with unaided.[31]

It is impossible to be definite about the establishment of servants or attendants in Imperial times. No doubt the decurion still required two attendants for his remounts. Some cavalry tombstones depict an attendant either holding spare javelins or leading his master's mount. Traditionally the allied cavalryman had one attendant and in the time of Xenophon the Greek trooper had a single attendant. Men would be required to lead the mules or pack-horses needed to carry the tents and personal effects. Servants seem to have been employed in foraging on behalf of their masters. The actual numbers may well have depended on the inclination of the troopers to own slaves or share them with comrades, and have been an informal or unofficial matter.

The Standard of Nutrition of Cavalry Horses

The 3 ½ lb of barley was supplemented by hay and fodder crops. The quantities actually given to the horses must have varied according to the amount available and the individual appetite of the horse. The sixth-century A D scale was one sixth of a load of hay per day.[32] It is not clear what this represents in modern terms, but some official figure was clearly necessary to control direct requisitions by troops billeted on the local population.

In general the rations might seem small by modern standards, especially when compared with the 9 ½ lb of grain issued to the British cavalry in 1917 as a daily ration.[33] The horses of the Roman cavalry were small, as their stabling has indicated. The rations are suitable for horses of between 12 and 14 hands and would be adequately completed by up to 10 lb of hay or green forage. Direct evidence of the small stature of the cavalry mounts is afforded by the equine skeletal remains excavated at Newstead and evaluated by Professor Ewart. The material discovered related to ponies of under 14 hands in most instances. One or two bones could be associated with horses of 15 hands.[34] That the Romans constantly tried to improve the stature and appearance of their horses may be assumed and is illustrated by Columella's remarks on the use of inferior stallions as 'teasers' prior to the matings with better breeding stock. We may, perhaps, infer from Vegetius' fattening ration for a horse, which contains 9 lb of barley in addition to wheat and green fodder, that his horses were of somewhat greater size than those of earlier times.[35] The quest for size and spectacular appearance has often been detrimental to performance. The Roman horses may have been small but there is no reason to suppose that their hardiness or endurance was impaired by this fact. In general the opposite situation has been recorded by authorities on the history of cavalry. The small pony type of horse has made an excellent mount for light cavalry duties.[36] Comparison could be made with the light cavalry of the Bashi Bazouks or Armenians in the Crimean War. These horses were between 14 and 14.3 hands in height and while fed only chopped straw and a little barley (when available) could endure conditions which the best British horses could not support. The astonishing performance (to British eyes) of the 'native' stallion is well illustrated by the experience of the 19th Hussars in Egypt in 1885. This regiment took over some Syrian Arab stallions, since their English horses were unsuitable for use in the desert. These Arabs were about 14 hands and existed on 6 lb of barley or dhoora (millet) and 10 lb of dhoora stalk per day. They made a forced march of 336 miles across the desert at a rate of 26 miles per day and on a ration of 5 to 6 lb of grain daily. For a period of 55 hours in the final advance the horses had no water and only 1 lb of grain.[37]

Pliny mentions that the Sarmatian horsemen could travel 150 *milia* (138 miles) without drawing rein.[38] This startling statement can be matched by modern experience. Rogers relates that an officer in India rode 400 miles in five days for a wager and won it without the least harm to his mount, which was an Arab of 14.3 hands height. He also quotes a French authority who relates that horses of the Sahara could travel from 75 to 90 miles per day and even, if required to do so, between 150 and 180 miles over stony desert in one day.[39] The nineteenth-century literature on cavalry abounds with references to the endurance of the small and powerful horses of the Arab, Persian and Turcoman type. There is little reason to doubt that the Roman cavalry functioned perfectly well on the fodder and grain provided for its use.[40]

Transport of Rations

The question of carrying rations on the march has been discussed exhaustively in respect of the infantryman in Roman times. Troops seem to have been expected to carry three days' rations in ordinary circumstances and up to seventeen days' rations in emergencies. From the point of view of the cavalry this merits serious consideration. Three days' barley would have weighed 10 lb and would not have been a problem. Barley for seventeen days, however, would weigh 68 lb. The trooper armed with helmet, cuirass, lance, three javelins in a quiver and a large shield in addition to his cloak and personal rations (30 to 40 lb for 17 days) would scarcely be able to carry 68 lb of grain. It is possible that for forced marches or even long patrols the cavalry would require a pack-animal for each cavalryman. If the servant's rations and utensils for cooking and the tools for cutting forage are included the pack-animal seems to be essential. The carrying power of the small horse should not be underestimated, however, as Rogers cites a case of a Persian horse 14.3 hands in height which carried a large British artilleryman, who weighed with his equipment 22½ stone, on a march of 800 miles.

NOTES

ABBREVIATIONS

AJA	American Journal of Archaeology
Aymard	J. Aymard, Essai sur les chasses romaines, 1951
BCH	Bulletin de Correspondance Hellénique
BMQ	British Museum Quarterly
CGCBM	Catalogue of Greek Coins in the British Museum
CIG	Corpus Inscriptionum Graecarum
CIL	Corpus Inscriptionum Latinarum
CRAI	Académie des Inscriptions et Belles Lettres: Comptes Rendus
CREBM	Coins of the Roman Empire in the British Museum
DC	Dio Cassius
DNA	Aelian, De Natura Animalium
DS	Diodorus Siculus
DSA	Plutarch, De Sollertia Animalium
Hinks	R. P. Hinks, Catalogue of Greek, Etruscan, and Roman Paintings and Mosaics in the British Museum, 1933
IG	Inscriptiones Graecae
ILS	H. Dessau, Inscriptiones Latinae Selectae, 1892–1916
JDAI	Jahrbuch des Deutschen archäologischen Instituts
Jennison	G. Jennison, Animals for Show and Pleasure in Ancient Rome, 1937
JRS	Journal of Roman Studies
Keller	O. Keller, Die antike Tierwelt I, 1909; II, 1913; Register 1920 (reprinted 1963)
MAAR	Memoirs of the American Academy in Rome
MAH	Melanges d'Archéologie et d'Histoire
NC	Numismatic Chronicle
NNM	Numismatic Notes and Monographs
PBSR	Papers of the British School at Rome
Pernice	E. Pernice, Die hellenistische Kunst in Pompeji VI: Pavimente und figürliche Mosaiken, 1938
Pliny, NH	Elder Pliny, Naturalis Historia
RE	Pauly-Wissowa, Real-Encyclopädie der classischen Altertumswissenschaft
RIC	Roman Imperial Coinage
RPGR	S. Reinach, Répertoire de peintures grecques et romaines, 1922
SHA	Scriptores Historiae Augustae
Vigneron	P. Vigneron, Le cheval dans l'antiquité gréco-romaine, 1968

CHAPTER I

1 Varro, *De Re Rustica* III, 3, 2.
2 ibid. III, 12, 13; Pliny, *NH* VIII, 78 (211).
3 Varro, *De Re Rustica* III, 13.
4 Suetonius, *Nero* 31, 1: *cum multitudine omnis generis pecudum et ferarum.*
5 SHA, *Gordiani Tres* 33, 1, 2.
6 Athenaeus V, 201B, C.
7 Symmachus, *Epistolae* II, 46, 76, 77; IV, 7, 8, 12, 58–60, 63; V, 56, 62, 82; VI, 33, 35, 43; VII, 48, 59, 82, 98, 105, 106, 121, 122; IX, 15, 16, 20, 27, 117, 135, 141, 144, 151.
8 Younger Pliny, *Epistolae* IX, 6, 2: *equos illos, quos procul noscitant, quorum clamitant nomina.*
9 Livy XXXIX, 22, 1, 2.
10 Livy XLIV, 18, 8. This show may have served as a precedent for the games which were held by Lucius Aemilius Paullus in Macedonia after his victory over Perseus, and which the Seleucid King Antiochus IV sought to outdo by getting up, in *c.* 165 BC, a great parade at Daphne, near Antioch: this included an elephant *quadriga*, an elephant *biga* and a single file of 36 caparisoned elephants (καθ'ἕνα δὲ εἵποντο ἐλέφαντες διεσκευασμένοι τριάκοντα καὶ ἕξ: Athenaeus V, 194C, 195A; Polybius XXXI, 3, 11).
11 Pliny, *NH* VIII, 20 (53).
12 Pliny, loc. cit.; Seneca, *De Brevitate Vitae*, 13, 6.
13 Pliny, *NH* VIII, 24 (64) (leopards); 40 (96) (hippopotamus and crocodiles).
14 ibid. VIII, 2 (4); 7 (20, 21) (elephants); 20 (53) (lions); 24 (64) (leopards); 28 (70) (lynx and apes); 29 (71) (rhinoceros); DC XXXIX, 38, 2–4; Cicero, *Ad Familiares* VII, 1, 3.
15 Pliny *NH* VIII, 20 (53); 70 (182);

Suetonius, *Iulius* 37, 2; DC XLIII, 22, 23.
16 DC LIII, 27, 6. All were slaughtered.
17 Pliny, *NH* VIII, 24 (64).
18 Suetonius, *Claudius* 21, 3; DC LXI, 9, 1.
19 SHA, *Hadrianus* 19, 7; 19, 3.
20 SHA, *Antoninus Pius* 10, 9; *CREBM* IV, 1940, 300, 301, nos 1838–42, pl. 45, nos 1, 2.
21 DC LXXVI, 1. For representations of this ship on the reverses of Severan coins, see *CREBM* V, 1950, pls 34, 4 (Caracalla); 35, 19 (Septimius); 39, 6 (Geta); 40, 17 (Caracalla).
22 SHA, *Gordiani Tres*, 3, 6, 7.
23 SHA, *Elagabalus* 28, 3.
24 DC LXXX, 9, 2.
25 SHA, *Aurelianus* 33, 4.
26 SHA, *Probus* 19.
27 *ILS*, 5062, 5063a, 5054.
28 E.g. ibid., 5055 (Panormus), 5059 (Allifae), 5060 (Telesia), 5061 (Salernum).
29 Libanius, *Epistolae* 1399: οὐδὲν δὲ οἷον οἱ θηρίων πρὸς ἀνθρώπους ἀγῶνες ... τούτων [*sc.* θηρίων] δὲ εἵνεκα ὑπαίθροι ταλαιπώρουσι μαλακωτέρους τῶν εὐνῶν ἡγούμενοι τοὺς λίθους.
30 Procopius, *Bellum Gothicum* I, 22, 10; 23, 13–19. The βιβάριον mentioned here was probably the great imperial one. *ILS*, 2091 is a votive tablet of AD 241 recording a *custos vivari cohortium praetoriarum et urbanarum* found between the Castra Praetoria and the Servian Wall. These cohorts would have had their own shows in the nearby Amphiteatrum Castrense. For a provincial military *vivarium*, fenced by a centurion of the Sixth Legion at Cologne, see *ILS*, 3265. But this may have con-

tained animals, not for show, but for commissariat use.

31 Cicero, *Ad Familiares* II, 11, 2; VIII, 6, 5; VIII, 8, 10; VIII, 9, 3; *Ad Atticum* VI, 1, 21; Plutarch, *Cicero* 36, 5.

32 Younger Pliny, *Epistolae* VI, 34.

33 See note 7.

34 *Res Gestae* XXII.

35 DC LI, 22, 5; LIV, 26, 1; LV, 10, 7, 8; LVI, 27, 4, 5.

36 DC LIX 7, 3; LX, 7, 3; LXI, 9, 1.

37 DC LXVI, 25, 1.

38 Suetonius, *Domitianus* 19.

39 DC LXVIII, 15.

40 SHA, *Commodus* 8, 5; DC LXXII, 10, 18, 19; Herodian I, 15, 5, 6; Ammianus Marcellinus XXXI, 10, 18, 19; cf. C. Robert, *Die antiken Sarkophagreliefs* III, 2, 1904, pl. 81, no. 236, where a *putto* in a hunting scene is performing the same operation on an ostrich. Commodus' beast shows are recorded on coins with the reverse-legend MVNIFI-CENTIA and an African elephant as reverse-type: *CREBM* IV, 1940, 788, 794, no. 543, pl. 105, no. 13.

41 Pliny, *NH* VIII, 7 (20, 21); DC XXXIX, 38, 2–4; Seneca, *De Brevitate Vitae* 13, 6.

42 Cicero, *Ad Familiares* VII, 1, 3: *extremus elephantorum dies, in quo admiratio magis vulgi atque turbae, delectatio nulla exstitit: quin etiam misericordia quaedam consecuta est. atque opinio eius modi esse quamdam illi beluae cum genere humano societatem.*

43 ibid.: *quae potest homini esse polito delectatio, cum . . . praeclara bestia venabulo transverberatur?*

44 DSA 7: τὰ μὲν ἀναγκάζωσι τολμᾶν ἄκοντα καὶ μάχεσθαι, τὰ δὲ μηδ' ἀμύνεσθαι πεφυκότα διαφθείρωσιν.

45 R. Auguet, *Cruauté et civilisation: les jeux romains*, 1970, 97–150, 235, 236, hardly touches on the problem of cruelty to animals.

46 B. Pace, *I mosaici di Piazza Armerina*, 1955, fig. 30.

47 D. Levi, *Antioch Mosaic Pavements*, 1947, II, pls 56b, 57a, b.

48 ibid. I, 324, fig. 136; II, pls 77, 78.

49 ibid. I, 359, fig. 148; II, pl. 86a.

50 ibid. I, 364, fig. 151; II, pls 170–3.

51 *CRAI*, 1967, 263–78, with fig. Cf. also the general animal hunt mosaic from Apamea-on-the Orontes: J. Balty, etc., *Belgian Archaeological Research in Apamea*, 1970, pl. opposite p. 40.

52 P. A. Février, *L'art de l'Algérie antique*, 1971, pl. 85.

53 Jennison, pl. opposite p. 145; Aymard, pl. 3a.

54 Such boxes were the *domus ilignae* and *caveae* described by Claudian, *De Consulatu Stilichonis* III, 323, 325.

55 G. V. Gentili, *La villa erculia di Piazza Armerina: i mosaici figurati*, 1959, fig. 1.

56 ibid., fig 5: this provides an excellently clear, continuous outline drawing of the whole mosaic. Cf. W. Dorigo, *Late Roman Painting*, 1971, plan C, 140–2.

57 Gentili, op. cit., pl. 31.

58 ibid., pl. 15.

59 ibid., pl. 14b.

60 ibid., pl. 24.

61 ibid., pls 25, 26.

62 ibid., pls 28, 29.

63 For the transport of wild animals by sea, cf. Claudian, *De Consulatu Stilichonis* III, 325–7.

64 Gentili, op. cit., pl. 27.

65 ibid., pls 30, 34.

66 ibid., pls 32, 33.

67 ibid., pl. 35.

68 Philostratus, *Vita Apollonii* 3, 48.

60 Gentili, op. cit., pl. 36.

70 Pliny, *NH* VIII, 10 (30), writes of the elephant's *cancellata* ('lattice-like') *cutis*, which could expand and

contract for the purpose of catching and killing flies.

71 Dorigo, op. cit., pl. 116.

72 S. Aurigemma, *I mosaici di Zliten*, 1926, 131–201, figs 75–8, 111–

25, pl. D; *La mosaique gréco-romaine*, 1965, 147–55, fig. 1.

73 *Karthago*, 1951/1952, 129–53, figs 1–6: Bardo Museum, Tunis.

74 *PBSR*, 1948, pl. 10, fig. 30.

CHAPTER II

1 For the narrative of these campaigns, see W .W. Tarn, *Alexander the Great*, 1948. For a general survey of some aspects of the elephant in ancient times see W. Krebs, 'Zur Rolle der Elephanten in der Antike', *Forschungen und Fortschritte*, 1967, 85–7; H. H. Scullard, *The Elephant in the Greek and Roman World* (forthcoming in this series).

2 *BMQ*, 1926, 36, 37, pl. 18b.

3 Seleucus III: *CGCBM: the Seleucid Kings of Syria*, 1878, pl. 7, no. 7; Barcids: H. H. Scullard, *Scipio Africanus: Soldier and Politician*, 1970, pls 6, 8, 12: cf. *NC*, 1948, 160, figs 3, 4. The elephant in one of the painted friezes of Tomb I (second century BC) at Marissa in Palestine is African: it has very large ears and its back, covered with a large white cloth, is concave (J. P. Peters and H. Thiersch, *Painted Tombs in the Necropolis of Marissa*, 1905, pl. 10). For some remarkably naturalistic prehistoric rock-incised drawings, found in the Fezzan area of northern Africa, of African elephants with concave backs and enormous ears, see *Africa Italiana*, 1940, 72, 75, figs 7, 10. For a good rendering of an Indian elephant, with small ears and convex back, see G. Brett and others, *The Great Palace of the Byzantine Emperors, Report 1*, 1947, pl. 41 (sixth century AD).

4 DS III, 26, 27, 36 (3); Strabo XVI, 4, 5; *RE* XXIII, 2, 1959, cols 1648–50, 1674; *NC*, 1950, 275, 276 and note 15. For the virtual certainty that

Ptolemy I (Soter: 323–283) captured some of Perdiccas' Indian elephants in 321 and for Diodorus Siculus' statement (XIX, 83, 84) that in 312 he captured all Demetrius' Indian elephants, see *NC*, 1950, 272, 273 and notes 6, 7. For the evidence that Ptolemy III also secured some Indian elephants, see ibid., 276.

5 Polybius V, 84, 86. For Sir William Gowers' vindication of Polybius' statement that the African Forest elephants at Raphia were inferior in size to the Indian, see *African Affairs*, July 1948, 173 ff. For the likelihood that the exceptional elephants which fought well for Ptolemy IV were Indian, and for the record that *he* captured all Antiochus' Indian elephants, see *NC*, 1950, 276, 277.

6 Plutarch, *Pyrrhus* 15; for references to the later activities of Pyrrhus' elephants in Italy and Sicily, see ibid., 20, 21, 24, 25.

7 DS XXII, 8, 2.

8 Seneca, *De Brevitate Vitae* 13, 3: *primus Curius Dentatus in triumpho duxit elephantos*; Eutropius II, 14: *[Curius] primus Romam elephantos quattuor duxit.*

9 Lucretius, V, 1302–4: *inde boves lucas turrito corpore taetras,/anguimanus* ['snake-handed', a reference to the elephants' trunks: cf. II, 537, 538: *anguimanus elephantos, India quorum/ milibus e multis vallo munitur eburno*] *belli docuerunt vulnera Poeni/sufferrte et magnas Martis turbare cateruas*; Varro, *De Lingua Latina* VII, 39, 40; Pliny,

NH VIII, 6 (16): *elephantos Italia primum vidit Pyrrhi regis bello et boves lucas apellavit in Lucania visos anno urbis CCCCLXXII*; J. M. Reynolds and J. B. Ward-Perkins, *The Inscriptions of Roman Tripolitania*, 1952, 92, no. 295: *dentes duos lucae bovis*.

10 E. A. Sydenham, *The Coins of the Roman Republic*, 1952, xv, xxiii; H. Mattingly, *Roman Coins²*, 1960, 4, 5, 49.

11 G. Macdonald, *Coin Types*, 1905, 29, fig. 3; *NC*, 1948, 158, fig. 1.

12 Macdonald, op. cit., 31, fig. 4; cf. Pliny, *NH* VIII, 9 (27).

13 P. Ducati, *L'Italia antica* I, 1936, 400 (colour reproduction); J. D. Beazley, *Etruscan Vase-Painting*, 1947, 211-15, pl. 39, fig. 1. There may be some connection between the picture on this plate and the story in Florus (I, 13, 12) of Pyrrhus' female elephant with a calf in the king's last battle in Italy: *NC*, 1950, 273, note 9. For early Hellenistic renderings of turreted Indian war-elephants, see M. Rostovtzeff, *The Social and Economic History of the Hellenistic World* 1941, I, pl. 52, fig. 2 (terracotta statuette from Myrina: Paris, Louvre); pl. 53, fig. 1 (silver *phalera*: Leningrad, Hermitage); P. Bieńkowski, *Les Celtes dans les arts mineurs gréco-romains*, 1928, fig. 213 (terracotta statuette from Myrina: Athens, National Museum). The elephant of the Louvre statuette is overpowering a Galatian foe and may represent one of the animals that fought in Antiochus I's battles against the Galatians. For a discussion of Indian elephants under Alexander and his successors, and the view that the fighting-tower (also called θωράκιον) was a Hellenistic, not an Indian, invention see *BCH* XCVI, 1972, 473-505. For two Seleucid war-elephants named 'Ajax' and 'Patroclus', see Pliny *NH* VIII, 5 (12).

14 *NC*, 1948, 161, 162 and note 6.

15 Bieńkowski, op. cit., fig. 215; *Notizie degli Scavi*, 1897, 25, fig. 3. For other Roman terracotta and bronze statuettes, etc., representing war-elephants with towers, see Bieńkowski, op. cit., figs 214, 216, 217, 225. Other reminiscences of Pyrrhus' elephants in south Italian art are the tiny Indian beast below Taras on a dolphin on a coin of Tarentum and the large Indian beast that occupies the reverse of a coin of Capua: G. de Beer, *Hannibal*, 1969, figs on pp. 235 and 246.

16 *NC*, 1948, 160, 161. According to Pliny, *NH* VII, 11 (32), elephants were still to be obtained from the same North African sources in the first century A D: *elephantos fert Africa ultra Syrticas solitudines et in Mauretania: ferunt Aethiopes ac Troglodytae.* Cf. *NH* V, 1 (15).

17 *Libyke* 95.

18 Polybius I, 19, 2.

19 Polybius I, 32, 9; 38, 2; 40, 15.

20 The numbers of elephants captured range from 60 to 140 or 142 in the ancient sources: e.g. Pliny, *NH* VIII, 6 (16): 140 or 142; Seneca, *De Brevitate Vitae* 13, 8: *idem narrabat Metellum victis in Sicilia Poenis triumphantem unum omnium Romanorum ante currum centum et viginti captivos elephantos duxisse*; DS XXIII, 21: 60. Polybius I, 40, 15, does not give the number. On their transport from Sicily to Italy see Frontinus, *Strategemata* I, 7, 1: *Lucius Caecilius Metellus, quia usu navium, quibus elephantos transportaret, deficiebatur, iunxit dolia construavitque tabulatis ac super ea positos per Siculum fretum transmisit.* ('Lucius Caecilius Metellus, lacking ships for the transport of his elephants, fastened together jars, covered them with planking, and then loading them with

elephants ferried the beasts across the Sicilian strait.')

21 Elephant's head on centre of round shield: 158-120 BC (Sydenham, op. cit., 57, no. 480); Jupiter in *biga* drawn by elephants with large ears and concave backs: 158-120 (ibid., 58, no. 485, pl. 18); elephant's head above prow: 158-120 (ibid., 58, 61, nos 486, 497); elephant's head on centre of round shield: 90-78 (ibid., 113, no. 719); elephant walking left, with large ears and concave back: 90-79 (ibid., 122, no. 750, pl. 21); elephant walking right, with largish ears and straight back: 54-44 (ibid., 175, no. 1046, pl. 27).

22 Polybius I, 74, 75; DS XXV, 10, 3; 12.

23 For full discussions of Hannibal's elephants in Italy, see *NC*, 1948, 162-8 (H. H. Scullard) and 1950, 278-83 (Sir William Gowers and H. H. Scullard).

24 Polybius III, 14; 33; 42; 46; 47; 53; 74; 79.

25 X, 158: *cum Gaetula ducem portaret belua luscum.*

26 *NC*, 1948, 163, fig. 5; 1950, pl. 16a. A coin issued in Etruria is most unlikely to portray one of Pyrrhus' Indian elephants; the obverse shows a negro's head. Cato recorded the name 'Surus' of a Carthaginian elephant – surely an Indian: Pliny, *NH* VIII, 5 (11).

27 *NC*, 1948, 162, fig. 6; 1950, pl. 16b, c. Cf. *NC*, 1964, pl. 5, figs 5-7, portraying Indian elephants, whereas the beast in fig. 9 is African, with concave back and a bell round its neck.

28 *NC*, 1950, 280, 281; Livy XXIII, 13, 7. On the other hand the foreparts of two long-eared, unmistakably African elephants, rudely carved on two stone blocks found at Alba Fucens, may represent African members of this reinforcement seen

on the occasion of Hannibal's march northwards from Capua through central Italy in 211: *L'Antiquité Classique*, 1960, 51-60, pls 4a, b.

29 The Sark hoard, of first-century BC date and probably of Thracian origin, contains a silver-gilt *phalera* embossed with the figure of a reticulated and turreted elephant, which has the convex back of the Indian, but the large ears of the African species: *Archaeologia*, 1971, pl. 12b.

30 XXVI, 5, 4.

31 Livy, XXVII, 48, 10; 49, 1. For similar panic and confusion among the Carthaginian war-elephants in a battle between Marcus Claudius Marcellus and Hannibal in 209 BC, see Livy XXVII, 14.

32 For the narrative of these campaigns, see H. H. Scullard, *Scipio Africanus: Soldier and Politician*, 1970, chapters II–IV.

33 Livy XXX, 33. These elephants may well have been some of those that Hasdrubal, son of Gisgo, was set to capture in 205: Appian, *Roman History* VIII, 9: Καρχηδόνιοι δὲ ταῦτα πυνθανόμενοι Ἀσδρούβαν μὲν τὸν Γίσκωνος ἐπὶ θήραν ἐλεφάντων ἐξέπεμπον.

34 Livy XXX, 37, 3: *traderent elephantos quos haberent domitos neque domitarent alios.*

35 Livy, XXXVII, 39-44: *sedecim elephantos post triarios in subsidio locaverunt, nam praeterquam quod multitudinem regiorum elephantorum – erant autem quattuor et quinquaginta – sustinere non videbantur posse, ne pari quidem numero Indicis Africi resistunt, sive quia magnitudine – longe enim illi praestant – sive robore animorum vincuntur . . . eminentibus tantum inter armatos elephantis magnam terrorem praestabat. ingentes ipsi erant. addebant speciem frontalia et cristae et tergo impositae turres turribusque superstantes praeter rectorem quaterni armati . . . ne* interpositi quidem elephanti militem Romanum deterrebant, adsuetum iam ab Africis bellis et vitare impetum beluae... quindecim cum rectoribus elephanti [capti].

36 XII, 107–10: si quidem Tyrio parere solebant/Hannibali et nostris ducibus regique Molosso/horum [i.e. the elephants of the imperial herd in Juvenal's own day] maiores ac dorso ferre cohortis/partem aliquam belli et euntem in proelia turrem.

37 Florus I, 38 (III, 2, 5): maximus barbaris terror elephanti fuere; Orosius, Adversus Paganos V, 13, 2: Gnaeus quoque Domitius proconsule Allobriges Gallos iuxta oppidum Vindalium gravissimo bello vicit, maxime cum elephantorum nova forma equi hostium hostesque conterriti diffugissent.

38 Sallust, Jugurtha 53: elephanti quattuor capti, reliqui omnes, numero quadraginta, interfecti.

39 Plutarch, Pompey 14, 4; Pliny, NH VIII, 2 (4).

40 DC XLIII, 4, 1.

41 Bellum Africanum 83–6; DC XLIII, 8, 1 and 2.

42 Sydenham, op. cit., 167, no. 1006 and note, pl. 27.

43 SHA, Aelius Verus 2, 3.

44 Jennison, 57.

45 Cicero, Oratio Philippica V, 17, 46: quod C. Caesar pro praetore Galliae provinciae cum exercitu subsidio profectus sit, equites sagittarios elephantos in suam populique Romani potestatem redegerit; DC XLV, 13, 4: καὶ τούς τε ἐλέφαντας τοὺς τοῦ Ἀντωνίου πάντας ἔλαβεν ἐξαπίνης παρακομιζομένοις σφίσιν ἐντυχών.

46 DC LX, 21, 2.

47 XIX, 2, 3.

48 XIX, 7, 6.

49 XXV, 3, 4 and 11; 6, 2 and 3.

50 XXV, 1, 14: post hos elephantorum fulgentium formidatam speciem et truculentos hiatus vix mentes pavidae perferebant ad quorum stridorem odor-

emque et insuetum aspectum magis equi terrebantur.

51 Oratio II, 65 C: καὶ ἐῴκει τείχει τῶν Παρθυαίων ἡ φάλαγξ· τὰ μὲν θηρία τοὺς πύργους φέροντα.

52 CGCBM: Cyrenaica, 1927, cxl, 73, pl. 28, nos 6–11; NC, 1950, pl. 17, no. 4. Cf. the seated statue of Zeus beneath a canopy which is drawn along on a car by two elephants on a Hellenistic gem from Iraq, now in the British Museum: BMQ, 1938 (1939), 17, pl. 9d; S. Weinstock, Divus Julius, 1971, pl. 25, no. 5.

53 Athenaeus V, 200F, 202A; NC, 1950, 274, 275. Dionysus himself appeared in the pageant on elephant-back.

54 CREBM I, 1923, 3, 10, nos 7–9, 52–4, pl. 1, nos 5, 6, 19; 2, no. 9.

55 DNA VII, 44; DSA 17, 972 BC. Cf. the famous ivory diptych leaf of c. 500 in the Louvre, where in the bottom panel an elephant brought by barbarians as a gift to the emperor raises its trunk to greet its new master, shown on horseback in the central picture: R. Dellbrueck, Die Consulardiptychen, 1926–29, 188–96, no. 48.

56 CREBM I, 1923, 75, no. 432, pl. 10, no. 6.

57 ibid., 134, 135, 138, nos 102, 108, 125, pls 24, no. 9; 25, no. 2. Cf. the elephant car that drew the statue of Drusilla, Gaius' sister, to the Circus: DC LIX, 13, 8.

58 Suetonius, Claudius 11, 2: aviae Liviae divinos honores et circensi pompa currum elephantorum Augustino similem decernenda curavit.

59 DC LXII, 16, 4: καὶ οἱ ἐλέφαντες οἱ τὴν τοῦ Αὐγούστου ἀρμάμαξαν ἄγοντες ἐς μὲν τὸν ἱππόδρομον ἐσῆλθον καὶ μέχρι τῆς τῶν βουλευτῶν ἕδρας ἀφίκοντο, γενόμενοι δὲ ἐνταῦθα ἔστησαν καὶ περαιτέρω οὐ προεχώρησαν.

60 *CREBM* I, 1923, 201, nos 7, 8, pl. 38, nos 4, 5. The elephants may be Indian.

61 ibid. II, 1930, 269, nos 221-3, pl. 51, no. 5.

62 ibid., 350, 351.

63 *Epigrams* VIII, 65: *stat sacer et domitis gentibus arcus ovat./hic gemini currus numerant elephanta frequentem,/ sufficit immensis aureus ipse iugis* ('A consecrated arch stands in triumph over the conquered tribes. Here are two chariots with many an elephant; and he [Domitian] himself in gold guides the mighty teams.') Domitian may be the clean-shaven emperor who stands in an elephant *quadriga* surmounting a triumphal arch on the well-known Torlonia harbour relief of Severan date: R. Meiggs, *Roman Ostia*, 1960, 158, 159 and pl. 20, where reference is also made to a Vatican sarcophagus depicting two arches with elephant-drawn chariots on them.

64 *CREBM* II, 1930, 364, 399, 407, pls 71, no. 6; 81, no. 1.

65 Suetonius, *Domitian* 13, 2.

66 A. Maiuri, *La peinture romaine*, 1953, colour plate on p. 147.

67 *CGCBM: Alexandria*, 1892, nos 339, 508-14, 859-63, pl. 27.

68 J. Vogt, *Die alexandrinische Münzen* II, 1924, 29.

69 *CREBM* III, 1936, 144, no. 706, pl. 24, no. 12.

70 ibid., 126, 230, 231, nos 655, 1086, 1087, pls 21, no. 9; 44, no. 8.

71 ibid. IV, 1940, 46, 50, 56, 232, 235, 241, 255, 256, pls 7, no. 15; 8, no. 11; 9, no. 50; 34, no. 11; 35, no. 11; 38, no. 9. Some types show the image seated beneath a canopy.

72 ibid., 528, pl. 72, no. 5. The image is under a canopy or shrine as in the types cited in notes 73-5.

73 ibid., 612, pl. 81, nos 8, 9.

74 ibid., 763, pl. 101, no. 9.

75 ibid., 652, pl. 86, no. 8.

76 F. Gnecchi, *I medaglioni romani* II, 1912, pl. 91, no. 10. Cf. DC LXXXV, 4, 1: the statue was of gold and drawn into the Circus.

77 For references, see F. Matz, *Der Gott auf dem Elefantenwagen*, 1952, 33, note 1.

78 E.g. Matz, op. cit., pls 1a (formerly Palazzo Albani-Del Drago, Rome), 1b (Villa Medici, Rome).

79 ibid., pls 2 (Museo Nazionale Romano, Rome); 3 (former Lateran Collection, Rome).

80 DC LXXVIII, 7, 4: ἐλέφαντας πολλοὺς συμπεριήγετο, ὅπως καὶ ἐν τούτῳ τὸν Ἀλέξανδρον, μᾶλλον δὲ τὸν Διόνυσον, μιμεῖσθαι δόξῃ.

81 SHA, *Elagabalus* 23, 1: *fertur . . . elephantorum quattuor quadrigas in Vaticano agitasse dirutis sepulcris quae obsistebant.*

82 SHA, *Alexander Severus* 57, 4.

83 SHA, *Maximini Duo* 26, 5.

84 SHA, *Gordianus Tertius* 27, 9; *utpote qui Persas vicisset, ut triumpho Persico triumpharet.* Firmus, who controlled Egypt temporarily under Aurelian, is said to have driven an elephant: SHA, *Firmus* 6, 1: *elephantum rexisse.*

85 Gnecchi, op. cit. I, pl. 5, nos 1, 2; J. M. C. Toynbee, *Roman Medallions*, 1944, 88.

86 *RIC* VI, 1967, 378, nos 215, 217, pl. 6.

87 ibid., 378, no. 216 and note 8; 383, no. 264.

88 ibid. VII, 1966, 207, 208, nos 467-9, pl. 5, nos 468, 469; Toynbee, op. cit., 52, 88, 89, pl. 4, no. 3.

89 Delbrueck, op. cit., 227-30, no. 59; J. M. C. Toynbee, *The Art of the Romans*, 1965, pl. 96 and p. 263, where the resemblance of the emperor to Antoninus Pius is noted.

90 *MAAR*, 1936, 183, 184, pl. 46, fig. 3; *MAH*, 1970, 787-807, figs 3, 6-11 and colour plate. The scene is now mounted as two separate panels.

91 XII, 102–6: *elephanti,/nec Latio aut usquam sub nostro sidere talis/belua concipitur, sed furva gente petita/ arboribus Rutulis et Turni pascitur agro/Caesaris armentum.*

92 ILS, 1578 (a tomb inscription found in Rome): *D[is] M[anibus] Ti[berio] Claudio Spectatori. . . . procuratori Laurento ad elephantos. Cornelia Bellica coniugi b[ene] m[erenti].*

93 See above, note 91.

94 *DNA* II, 11.

95 Suetonius, *Julius* 37, 2,: *ascendit Capitolium ad lumina, quadraginta elephantis dextra sinistraque lychnuchos gestantibus;* DC XLIII, 22, 1: πολλῶν δὲ ἐλεφάντων λαμπάδας φερόντων ἐκομίσθη. For displays of elephants by Philip the Arabian and Aurelian, cf. pp. 16, 19.

96 *CGCBM: the Seleucid Kings of Syria* 1878, 66, 67, nos 42–8, pl. 19, no. 12.

97 *Monumenti Antichi,* 1898, 339, fig. 46.

98 Appian, *Bellum Civile* II, 102: ἐλεφάντων τε μάχην εἴκοσι πρὸς εἴκοσι; DC XLIII, 23, 3: καί τινες καὶ ἀπ' ἐλεφάντων τεσσαράκοντα ἐμαχήσαντο; Suetonius, *Iulius* 39, 3: *pugna divisa in duas acies, quingentis peditibus, elephantis vicenis, tricentis equitibus hinc et inde commissis;* Pliny, *NH* VIII, 7 (22).

99 Pliny, loc. cit. (19).

100 DC LXVI, 25.

101 Pliny, loc. cit. (19).

102 *De Spectaculis* 17 and 19.

103 Seneca, *Epistolae* 85, 41: *elephantum minimus Aethiops iubet subsidere in genua et ambulare per funem.*

104 DC LXI, 17: ὅτε δὴ καὶ ἐλέφας ἀνήχθη ἐς τὴν ἀνωτάτω τοῦ θεάτρου ἀψῖδα καὶ ἐκεῖθεν ἐπὶ σχοινίων κατέδραμεν ἀναβάτην φέρων; Suetonius, *Nero* 11, 2: *notissimus eques Romanus elephanto supersidens per catadromon decucurrit.* Cf. Pliny, *NH* VIII, 3 (6), where elephants

are said to be able to climb down, as well as up, ropes. Nero seems to have been first in the field with this form of entertainment, *pace* Suetonius, *Galba* 6, 1: *novum spectaculi genus elephantos funambulos edidit.*

105 Pliny, *NH* VIII, 2 (5).

106 Pliny, loc. cit.

107 *DNA* II, 11.

108 Martial, *Epigrams* I, 104, 9, 10: *et molles dare iussa quod choreas/nigro belua non negat magistro.*

109 DNA, loc. cit.

110 Pliny, *NH* VIII, 3 (6): *certum est unum tardioris ingenii in accipiendis quae tradebantur saepius castigatum verberibus eadem illa meditantem noctu repertum;* Plutarch, *DSA* 12 (968 C): εἷς ὁ δυσμαθέστατος ἀκούων κακῶς ἑκάστοτε καὶ κολαζόμενος πολλάκις ὤφθη νυκτὸς αὐτὸς ἀφ' ἑαυτοῦ πρὸς τὴν σελήνην ἀνατατπόμενος τὰ μαθήματα καὶ μελετῶν.

111 K. Lehmann-Hartleben and E. C. Olsen, *Dionysiac Sarcophagi in Baltimore,* 1942, 12–16, 26–33, 70–2, figs 5–8. Cf. fig. 39.

112 L. Budde and R. Nicholls, *Catalogue of Greek and Roman Sculpture in the Fitzwilliam Museum,* Cambridge, 1964, pl. 54, no. 161.

113 Suetonius, *Nero* 2, 1; *in consulatu Allobrogibus Avernisque superatis elephanto per provinciam vectus est turba militum quasi inter solemnia triumphi prosequente.*

114 DC XLIX, 7: τοσοῦτον γάρ που καὶ ὁ Κορνουφίκιος ἐπὶ τῇ τῶν στρατιωτῶν σωτηρίᾳ ἐφρόνει ὥστε καὶ ἐν τῇ 'Ρώμῃ ἐπὶ ἐλέφαντος, ὁσάκις ἔξω τῆς οἰκίας ἐδείπνει, ἀνακομίζεσθαι. According to SHA, *Aurelianus* 5, 6, Aurelian before he came to the throne was presented with a splendid elephant for his personal use; but he immediately gave it to the reigning emperor: *donatus eidem etiam elephantus praeci-*

puus quem ille imperatori obtulit, solusque omnium privatus Aurelianus elephanti dominus fuit. But cf. ibid. 33, 4, for the twenty elephants that walked in Aurelian's triumphal procession after his victory over Zenobia, queen of Palmyra, as emperor. See Nicephorus, ed. C. de Boor, 1880, 22 for the four elephants displayed by Heraclius in 629 in the hippodrome in Constantinople 'to the city's delight' (ἐπὶ τῇ τῆς πόλεως τέρψει).

115 CGCBM: The Ptolemies, Kings of Egypt, 1883, pl. 1, nos 1, 2, 3, 5, 6, 8.

116 Revue Numismatique, 1883, pl. 4, no. 1.

117 J. M. C. Toynbee, The Hadrianic School, 1934, pl. 10, no. 5.

118 J. Mazard, Corpus Nummorum Numidiae Mauretaniaeque, 1955, nos 93, 94, 95, 97, 103, 118, 122, 125, 130, 133, 134, 296, 400-2, 497. All of these types are drawn and photographed in the Corpus.

119 Sydenham, op. cit., nos 1028, 1051, 1153, 1355, pls 27, 28, 29.

120 CREBM I, 1923, 286, note, pl. 49, no. 8; Africa Italiana, 1940, 76, fig. 13.

121 E.g. Toynbee, op. cit., pls 1, nos 23, 24; 2, nos 1-14; 7, nos 1-6; 10, nos 10-25.

122 30-4, nos 8 (fig. 1); 9 (fig. 7); 10; 11; 12 (fig. 8); 13; 14; 20-7.

123 Monuments Piot, 1899, pl. 1: Louvre.

124 ibid., pl. 32, fig. 2: Louvre.

125 G. Becatti, Scavi di Ostia IV, 1961, pl. 122, no. 68 (above).

126 Toynbee, op. cit., pl. 23, no. 2.

127 Africa Italiana, 1940, 67-86, fig. 1.

128 ibid., 79, fig. 15; Reynolds and Ward-Perkins, op. cit. (note 9), 92, no. 295, pl. 8. Cf. Martial, Epigrams V, 37, 5: modo politum pecudis Indicae dentem ('the newly polished tusk of India's beast').

129 Africa Italiana, 1940, 82, 83, figs 17, 18; Reynolds and Ward-Perkins, op. cit., 159, no. 603.

130 Africa Italiana, 1940, 84, 85, fig. 19; Reynolds and Ward-Perkins, op. cit., 150, 151, no. 567.

131 Becatti, op. cit., 66, fig. 19.

132 ibid., 69, 70, no. 95, pl. 93: the mosaic is attributed to AD 190-200.

133 ibid., 76, 77, no. 109, pl. 93: the mosaic is attributed to c. 150.

134 Hinks, 119, 120, no. 45, fig. 137.

135 Cf. p. 33, and note 3, above.

136 Mazard, op. cit., nos 17, 73-5, 90, 119, 123, 135-9, 276, 403-5.

137 CREBM IV, 1940, 301, nos 1840-2, pl. 45, no. 2.

138 ibid., 788, 794, no. 543, pl. 105, no. 13.

139 ibid. V, 1950, 47, 56, 148, 153, 168, nos 169. 168, 602, pls 9, no. 15; 10, no. 18; 25, no. 6.

140 ibid., 429.

141 ibid., 438, 439, 474, 475, nos 47, 236, 239-41, pls 68, no. 14; 74, nos 15, 18.

142 A tetradrachm of King Antialkidas of Bactria (c. 130-110 BC) has on its reverse the standing figure of a bearded god with radiate crown and behind him an elephant with a bell hung round its neck and a victory above its head: Bulletin of the Fine Arts Museum, Boston, 1948, 41, fig. 5.

143 Matz, op. cit., pl. 4.

144 V. Spinazzola, Le arti decorative in Pompei, 1928, pl. 107.

145 M. Bernhart, Handbuch zur Münzkunde der römischen Kaiserzeit, 1926, pl. 58, nos 7, 9.

146 Ars Hispaniae, 1947, 53, 54, fig. 32.

147 Pliny, NH XXXVI, 67 (196): dicavit ipse [sc. Augustus] in templo Concordiae obsidianos IIII elephantos. The Loeb Library translation (vol. X, 155) of pro miraculo by 'as a curiosity' can hardly be right. As a symbol of a

political move, defection from Rome
to Hannibal during the second Punic
war, an African elephant appears on

the reverse of a bronze coin of
Atella: de Beer, op. cit., fig. on
220.

CHAPTER III

1 Characters IV, 9: ἀμέλει δὲ καὶ
πίθηκον θρέψαι δεινὸς καὶ τίτυρον
κτήσασθαι ('He's a one for keeping
a monkey and acquiring a tityrus
ape').

2 XVI, 4, 16: γίγνονται . . . καὶ
κήβοι λέοντος μὲν πρόσωπον
ἔχοντες, τὸ δὲ λοιπὸν σῶμα
πάνθηρος, μεγέθος δὲ δορκάδος.

3 XVII, 40, 1: τιμῶσι καθ'
ἑαυτοὺς ἕκαστοι . . . κῆβον δὲ
Βαβυλώνιοι οἱ κατὰ Μέμφιν. ἔστι
δὲ ὁ κῆβος τὸ μὲν πρόσωπον
ἐοικὼς σατύρῳ, τἆλλα δὲ κυνὸς
καὶ ἄρκτου μεταξύ, γεννᾶται δ'ἐν
Αἰθιοπίᾳ.

4 DNA XVII, 8.

5 NH VIII, 28 (70): iidem [sc.
ostenderunt] ex Aethiopia quas vocant
cephos, quarum pedes posteriores pedibus
humanis et cruribus, priores manibus
fuere similes. hoc animal postea Roma
non vidit.

6 NH VI, 35 (184): VII, 2 (31):
nomadum Aethiopum . . . gens . . .
animalium quae cynocephalos vocamus
lacte vivit.

7 NH VIII, 80 (216): efferatior
cynocephali natura.

8 Ad Atticum VI, 1, 25: erat praeterea
cynocephalus in essedo.

9 NH VIII, 80 (216): sicut mitissima
[sc. natura] satyri. callitriches toto paene
aspectu differunt. barba est in facie, cauda
late fusa primori parte. hoc animal
negatur vivere in alio quam Aethiopiae
qua gignitur caelo.

10 NH VIII, 30 (72): Aethiopia
generat . . . cercopithecos nigris capitibus,
pilo asini et dissimiles ceteris voce.

11 XV, 4: effigies sacri nitet aurea
cercopitheci.

12 160–3: quod ille . . . se sectari
simian dicat.   i

13 229–33: visus sum/in custodelam
simiae concredere. In Poenulus 1073,
1074 Plautus describes how a Carthaginian boy was bitten on the hand
by his pet ape in play.

14 NH VIII, 80 (216): simiarum
generi praecipua erga fetum adfectio.
gestant catulos quae mansuefactae intra
domos peperere, omnibus demonstrant
tractarique gaudent, gratulationem intel-
legentibus similes: itaque magna ex parte
complectando necant.

15 Epigrams VII, 87, 4: si Comius
similem cercopithecon amat.

16 R. Calza and M. F. Squarciapino, Museo Ostiense, 1962, 20, no. 8
(134); 128, fig. 4.

17 DNA VI, 10: ἐπὶ τῶν
Πτολεμαίων οἱ Αἰγύπτιοι τοὺς
κυνοκεφάλους καὶ γράμματα
ἐδίδασκον καὶ ὀρχεῖσθαι καὶ
αὐλεῖν και ψαλτικήν. καὶ μισθὸν
κυνοκέφαλος ἐπράττετο ὑπὲρ
τούτων καὶ τὸ διδόμενον ἀργύριον
φασκώλιον ἐμβαλὼν ἐξηρτημένον
ἔφερεν, ὡς οἱ των ἀρειρόντων
δεινοί.

18 ibid. V, 26: μιμηλότατόν ἐστιν
ὁ πίθηκος ζῶον, καὶ πᾶν ὅ τι ἂν
ἐπιδιδάξῃς τῶν διὰ τοῦ σώματος
πραττομένων ὁ δὲ εἴσεται ἀκριβῶς
ἵνα ἐπιδείξηται αὐτό. ὀρχεῖται
γοῦν ἐὰν μάθῃ καὶ αὐλεῖ, ἐὰν
ἐκδιδάξῃς. ἐγὼ δὲ καὶ ἡνίας
κατέχοντα εἶδον καὶ ἐπιβάλλοντα
τὴν μάστιγα καὶ ἐλαύνοντα. καὶ
ἄλλο δ' ἄν τι μαθὼν καὶ ἄλλο οὐ
διαψεύσατο τὸν διδάξαντα. For
dancing apes, which, however, aban-
doned their performances at the sight

of food, see Lucian, *Piscator 36* (Egyptian king); *Apologia 5* (Cleopatra). For ape musicians, see J. Déchelette, *Les vases céramiques ornés de la Gaule romaine* II, 1904, 307, 308, pl. 4. For an ape driving a *biga* of camels, see Helbig, *Führer*³ II, 1913, 181, no. 1424 (relief in the Museo Nazionale Romano).

19 *NH* VIII, 80 (215).

20 V, 153-5: *tu scabie frueris mali, quod in aggere rodit/qui tegitur parma et galea, metuensque flagelli/discit ab hirsuta iaculum torquere capella.*

21 *Epigrams* XIV, 202: *callidus emissas eludere simius hastas./si mihi cauda foret, cercopithecus eram.*

22 ibid. XIV, 128: *Gallia Santonico vestit te bardocucullo,/cercopithecorum paenula nuper erat.*

23 P. Gusman, *Pompéi*, 1890, fig. on 285; *RPGR*, 255, no. 7. Cf. Claudian's description, *In Eutropium* I, 303-7, of an ape dressed up in rich clothes, but with his back and behind left bare, brought by a boy to a banquet to amuse the guests.

24 *Metamorphoses* XI, 8: *vidi . . . simiam pileo textili crocotisque Phrygiis Catamiti pastoris specie aureum gestantem poculum.* Cf. the relief on a Roman clay lamp in the Louvre, where an ape, wearing a Phrygian cap, enacts the part of Ganymede

carried up to heaven by an eagle: W. C. McDermott, *The Ape in Antiquity*, 1938, pl. 10.

25 A. Ruesch, *Guida illustrata del Museo Nazionale di Napoli* I, 1911, 291, no. 1265; *RPGR*, 176, no. 2.

26 ibid., 427, fig.; McDermott, op. cit., pls 6, 7.

27 F. Fremersdorf, *Römisches Geformtesglas in Köln*, 1961, 78, 79, no. 292, pls 177-9.

28 G. Brett and others, *The Great Palace of the Byzantine Emperors, Report 1*, 1947, pl. 33.

29 R. Symes, *Ancient Art*, 1971, no. 2, with illustration.

30 Keller I, p. 4, fig. 1.

31 *JDAI*, 1900, 202-15, fig. 6 on p. 203; E. H. Warmington, *Commerce between the Roman Empire and India*, 1928, 143 and pl. opp.; D. E. Strong, *Greek and Roman Gold and Silver Plate*, 1966, 198, 199.

32 P. 120, note 1.

33 Warmington, loc. cit.

34 Strong, loc. cit.

35 McDermott, op. cit., includes a very valuable collection of literary references to monkeys in the life of the Roman world and a most useful catalogue of Roman monuments (figurines, pots, paintings, mosaics and reliefs) on which monkeys are portrayed in manifold capacities.

CHAPTER IV

1 Plutarch, *Brutus* 8, 4.

2 *Epistolae* II, 76: *et de leonibus fama conticuit, quorum adventus posset efficere ut ursorum defectum congressio Libyca repensaret.*

3 *De Consulatu Stilichonis* III, 333-8.

4 *NH* VIII, 16 (54).

5 *De Spectaculis* 10.

6 ibid., 6b.

7 ibid., 15: *stravit et ignota spectandum mole leonem.*

8 ibid., 18.

9 *Epigrams* VIII, 55, 9, 10: *o quantum per colle decus quem sparsit honorem/ aurea lunatae, cum stetit, umbra iubae.* Seneca, *Epistolae* 41, 6 writes of lions being put before the public with gilded manes (*aurata iuba*) and covered with gold-leaf (*bracteatus*); and he contrasts these degraded, submissive, 'made-up' creatures with the noble savagery of their free kinsmen in the wilds.

10 *Silvae* II, 5.

11 *De Beneficiis* II, 19, 1: *leonem in amphitheatro spectavimus, qui unum e bestiariis agnitum, cum quondam eius fuisset magister, protexit ab impetu bestiarum.*

12 Aulus Gellius V, 14: *tum caudam more atque ritu adulantium canum clementer et blande movet hominisque se corpori adiungit cruraque eius et manus . . . lingua leniter demulcet . . . leonem, loro tenui revinctum, urbe tota circum tabernas ire, donari aere Androclem, floribus spargi leonem*; *DNA* VII, 48.

13 I, 6; 14; 22; 44; 48; 51; 60; 104 (ll. 12–22).

14 IX, 71.

15 II, 75.

16 *CREBM* IV, 1940, 300, nos 1838, 1839, pl. 45, no. 1.

17 R. Delbrueck, *Die Consulardiptychen*, 1926–29, no. 37.

18 ibid., no. 21.

19 ibid., no. 9.

20 ibid., no. 60: Hermitage, Leningrad.

21 E. Strong, *La scultura romana* II, 1926, pl. 48; W. F. Volbach, *Early Christian Art*, 1961, pl. 107.

22 E.g. Lucretius II, 600, 601: *hanc* [*sc.* Cybelem] *veteres Graium docti cecinere poetae/sedibus in curru biiugos agitare leones.*]

23 Pliny, *NH* VIII, 21 (55): *iugo subdidit eos* [*sc. leones*] *primusque Romae ad currum iunxit Marcus Antonius. . . . ita vectus est cum mima Cytheride*; Plutarch, *Antonius* 9, 5: λέοντες ἅμασιν ὑπεζευγμένοι.

24 *CREBM* IV, 1940, 241, 249, no. 1505, pl. 36, no. 1; V, 1950, 308.

25 SHA, *Elagabalus* 28: *iunxit sibi et leones, Matrem Magnam se appellans.*

26 *De Ira* II, 31, 6.

27 IV, 1, 25: λέοντας τρέφουσιν ἡμέρους ἐγκλείσαντες καὶ σιτίζουσι καὶ κομίζουσιν ἔνιοι μεθ' αὐτῶν.

28 VII, 75–7: *nec defuit illi/unde emeret multa pascendum carne leonem/ iam domitum.*

29 DC LXXVIII, 7, 2.

30 SHA, *Elagabalus* 21, 25: *habuit leones et leopardos exarmatos in deliciis.*

31 M. Cagiano de Azevedo, *Le antichità di Villa Medici*, 1951, no. 61, pl. 31, fig. 50.

32 *De Consulatu Stilichonis* III, 357, 358: *caudamque in puppe retorquens/ad proram iacet usque leo: vix sublevat unum/tarda ratis.*

33 Pliny, *NH* XXXVI, 4 (40): *accidit ei, cum in navalibus, ubi ferae Africanae erant, per caveam intuens leonem caelaret, ut ex alia cavea panthera erumperet, non levi periculo diligentissimi artificis.*

34 Cf. p. 350, note 55.

35 *RPGR* 300, no. 2.

36 K. Lehmann-Hartleben and E. C. Olsen, *Dionysiac Sarcophagi in Baltimore*, 1942, figs 7, 8. For a first-rate portrait of a lion on a late Dionysiac mosaic at Sabratha in Tripolitania, see S. Aurigemma, *Tripolitania: I mosaici*, 1960, pl. 13.

37 *La Critica d'Arte* I, 1936 (G. Rodenwaldt, *Römische Löwen*), pl. 157, fig. 7: Villa Doria Pamfili, Rome. Cf. a similar sarcophagus in the Vatican (Belvedere), but with straight ends: W. Amelung, *Die Sculpturen des vaticanischen Museums*, vol. II of plates, 1908, pl. 29.

38 *La Critica d'Arte* I, 1936, pls 152, fig. 1; 153, fig. 3; 154, fig. 4. Cf. a mosaic panel from Nennig: K. Parlasca, *Die römischen Mosaiken in Deutschland*, 1959, pl. 39, fig. 1.

39 *La Critica d'Arte* I, 1936, pl. 156, fig. 6; H. Stuart Jones, ed., *The Sculptures of the Museo Capitolino*, 1912, pl. 17, no. 5. Cf. A. Frova,

L'arte di Roma e del mondo romano, 1961, pl. 5. See A. Vaccaro Melucco, 'Sarcofagi romani di caccia a leone', Studi Miscellanei XI, 1963–64, Appendix B, for a list of other sarcophagi and fragments of sarcophagi with groups of this type. Cf. also Archeologia Classica, 1952, pls 60–7.

40 Amelung, op. cit., pl. 16.

41 Frova, op. cit., fig. 289.

42 Stuart Jones, op. cit., pl. 17, no. 2; La Critica d'Arte I, 1936, pl. 152, fig. 2; Vaccaro Melucco, op. cit., pl. 12, no. 27.

43 See note 39.

44 F. Gnecchi, I medaglioni romani, 1912, III, pls 146, nos 3, 4, 7; 151, no. 14. On the Hadrianic lion-hunt tondo on the Arch of Constantine a magnificently maned lion is stretched dead in the 'exergue' of the circular relief: Strong, op. cit., fig. 137.

45 E.g. ibid., pl. 59.

46 RPGR, 191, no. 4.

47 F. Fremersdorf, Die Denkmäler des römischen Köln II, 1950, pl. 68.

48 G. Brusin and V. de Grassi, Il mausoleo di Aquileia, 1956.

49 J. M. C. Toynbee, Death and Burial in the Roman World, 1971, 278, 279, where references will be found.

50 Stuart Jones, op. cit., pl. 8, no. 25a. For lions sprawling on the lids of stone ash-chests see V. S. M. Scrinari, Sculture romane di Aquileia, 1972, pls 315, 320, 321.

51 Vaccaro Melucco, op. cit., pls 17, fig. 39 (Pisa); 18, fig. 41 (Béziers).

52 Strong, op. cit. I, 1923, fig. 50.

53 R. Calza and M. F. Squarciapino, Museo Ostiense, 1962, 109 and fig. 57. A mosaic from Hadrian's Villa, now in the Vatican, shows a still more dramatic scene of a lion attacking a bull in a mountainous landscape, but without any funerary association; G. E. Rizzo, La pittura ellenistico-romana, 1929, pl. 184 (above): cf. the mosaic group in the

schole of Trajan at Ostia (Scavi di Ostia IV, 1961, pl. 96).

54 RPGR, 356, no. 1; PBSR, 1914, 38, pl. 16, IV, 3. Cf. the mosaic from Bad Kreuznach showing a lion slaying a bull: Parlasca, op. cit., pl. 91, fig. 3.

55 G. Becatti, Scavi di Ostia VI: edificio con opus sectile fuori Porta Marina, 1969, pls 59, figs 1, 2; 60, gs 1, 2. In the Ostia Museum there is an incomplete opus sectile panel, found earlier near the Porta Marina, which must belong to the same series. It shows the body, encircled by an ornamental strap, and the hindquarters (the head and fore-legs are missing) of a lion pacing to the left and devouring its prey: Calza and Squarciapino, op. cit., 107 and fig. 56.

56 J. M. C. Toynbee, Art in Roman Britain, 1963, 197, no. 179, pl. 208.

57 O. Doppelfeld, The Dionysiac Mosaic at Cologne Cathedral, 1964, figs 10, 17.

58 RPGR, 79, no. 1; Pernice, pl. 59.

59 RPGR, 82, nos 1–3; Hinks, 65, no. 1, pl. 25; Pernice, pls 60, 61.

60 D. Levi, Antioch Mosaic Pavements, 1947, I, 313–15; II, pl. 70b, c. For a very similar, but not beribboned, lion on a Western mosaic, see R. Massigli, Musée de Sfax, 1912, 6, no. 12, pl. 6, fig. 1 (from the baths at Thina).

61 Levi, op. cit. I, 321–3; II, pl. 74a.

62 A. Ferrua, Le pitture della nuova catacomba di Via Latina, 1960, pl. 109.

63 Athenaeus XIII, 590A. In the Ny Carlsberg Glyptotek, Copenhagen, there is a bronze statuette 6 cms high of a handsome tigress of mid-Hellenistic date: she advances towards the right, the long stripes on her fur are rendered by inlaid strips of copper, and her eyes are filled with metal of a lighter colour: F. Poulsen, Catalogue of Ancient Sculpture in the Ny Carls-

berg *Glyptotek*, 1951, 604, Br. i;
2. *Tillaeg til Billedtavler*, pl. 17.
64 *NH* VIII, 25 (66): *tigrim Hyrcani
et Indi ferunt*. Cf. Pomponius Mela
III, 43: *tigres ferunt ubique Hyrcaniae*;
Martial, *Epigrams* VIII, 26: *Gangeticus
raptor, in Hyrcano . . . equo.*
65 V, 29, 30.
66 *Daphnis et Armenias curru subiun-
gere tigres/instituit, Daphnis thiasos
inducere Bacchi.*
67 The tigresses are in both cases
led by Pan: *Ars Hispaniae*, 1947,
153, fig. 147; *Mosaiques de Tunisie*,
1914, pl. 67. On the Dionysiac
mosaic panel, now in the National
Archaeological Museum at Lisbon,
from the Torre di Palma villa, two
male tigers, led by Pan, draw the
god's triumphal car: *O Arqueólogo
Português*, 1962, pls 15 and E; cf.
Parlasca, op. cit., pl. 41, fig. 4
(Trier). The sex of the two frontal
tigers that draw Dionysus' frontal
chariot on the mosaic from the House
of the Triumph of Dionysus at
Antioch-on-the-Orontes cannot be
determined: Levi, op. cit. II, pl. 16c.
68 Hinks, 98, fig. 108. For a Hellenistic precursor of this motif, see the
late second-century B C mosaic in the
House of Dionysus at Delos, where
the god, ivy-crowned, winged, and
brandishing a *thyrsus*, rides on a
magnificent tiger, whose neck is
wreathed with vine-leaves and
grapes: *Délos*, 1922, pl. 52; C. M.
Havelock, *Hellenistic Art*, 1971,
colour pl. 8.
69 DC LIV, 9, 8: καὶ οἱ Ἰνδοὶ . . .
φιλίαν τότε ἐσπείσαντο, δῶρα
πέμψαντες ἄλλα τε καὶ τίγρεις.
70 *NH* VIII, 24 (65): *idem* [*sc.
Augustus*] *Quinto Tuberone Paullo
Fabio Maxumo coss.* IIII *nonas Maias
theatri Marcelli dedicatione tigrim primus
omnium Romae ostendit in cavea man-
suefactam*. Cf. Suetonius, *Augustus* 43,
4: *tigrim in scaena*.

71 Pliny, loc. cit.: *divus vero
Claudius simul quattuor* [*sc. tigres
ostendit*].
72 *Epistolae* 85, 41: *osculatur tigrim
suus custos.*
73 *DSA* 20 (974, C).
74 *BCH*, 1935, pl. 16 (fig. on left).
75 *Epigrams* I, 104, 2, 3: *improbaeque
tigres/indulgent patientiam flagello.*
76 *Epigrams* VIII, 26: *non tot in
Eois timuit Gangeticus arvis/raptor, in
Hyrcano qui fugit albus equo,/quot tua
Roma novas vidit, Germanice, tigres,/
delicias potuit nec numerare suas./ vincit
Erythraeos tua, Caesar, arena trium-
phos/et victoris opes divitiasque dei;/
nam cum captivos ageret sub curribus
Indos,/contentus gemina tigride Bacchus
erat* ('The robber in the East by the
banks of the Ganges, pale with fear
on his Hyrcanian mount, did not
dread as many tigresses as your
Rome, Germanicus, has but lately
seen, nor could she count all the
scenes that delighted her. Your arena
shows, Caesar, have outdone the
eastern triumphs of the victor god
and all his wealth; for when Bacchus
drove captive Indians beneath his
yoke, he was content with only two
tigresses to draw him.')
77 *Mosaiques de Tunisie*, 1914, pl.
142.
78 DC LXXVI, 7, 5: τίγριδες
δέκα ἅμα ἐσφάγησαν.
79 SHA, *Elababalus* 28, 12: *iunxit et
tigres.*
80 For a single arena tiger, wearing
a bell round its neck and accompanied by two *bestiarii*, see a black-
and-white mosaic in the Museo
Nazionale Romano: *MAH*, 1938, fig.
on p. 45.
81 Levi, op. cit., pl. 77a.
82 ibid., pl. 86a.
83 *NH* VIII, 25 (66): *totus eius
foetus, qui semper numerosus est, ab
insidiante rapitur equo quam maxime
pernici atque in recentes subinde trans-*

fertur. at ubi vacuum cubile reperit foeta . . . fertur praeceps, odore vestigans. raptor appropinquante fremitu abicit unum e catulis. tollit illa morsu et pondere etiam ocior acta remeat iterumque consequitur ac subinde, donec in navem regresso irrita feritas saevit in litore. Cf. Pomponius Mela III, 43.

84 Levi, op. cit., pl. 172b. Cf. the unpublished (?) mosaic pavement from the Central Church at Cyrene, now in the museum, on which a fleeing mounted huntsman dangles a tiger-cub in front of a pursuing tigress, unaccompanied, in this case, by other cubs.

85 P. S. Bartoli and G. P. Bellori, *Picturae antiquae cryptarum Romanarum et sepulchri Nasonum*, 1791, 55, pl. 15, fig. 1.

86 G. V. Gentili, *La villa erculia di Piazza Armerina*, 1959, pl. 33.

87 *De Raptu Proserpinae* III, 263–8: *arduus Hyrcana quatitur sic matre Niphates,/cuius Achaemenio regi ludibria natos/advexit tremebundus eques: fremit illa marito/mobilior Zephyro totamque virentibus iram/dispergit maculis timidumque hausura profundo/ore virum vitreae tardatur imagine formae.* The ancients accepted the theory of impregnation by wind.

88 Cagiano de Azevedo, op. cit., no. 61, pl. 31, fig. 49.

89 Rizzo, op. cit., pl. 185; R. Bianchi Bandinelli, *Roman Art to A.D. 200*, 1970, pl. 306 (detail of tiger in colour).

90 Becatti, op. cit., pls 61, figs 1, 2; 62, fig. 3.

91 E. Nash, *Pictorial Dictionary of Ancient Rome* I, 1961, 194, figs 217, 218. For mosaics from Roman Germany showing a tigress killing a wild ass and a wild horse respectively, see Parlasca, op. cit., pl. 35, fig. 2 (Nennig); pl. 91, fig. 4 (Bad Kreuznach). For a late antique tiger hunt in mosaic, see *The Great Palace of the*

Byzantine Emperors Report 1, 1947, pls 37, 55.

92 Athenaeus V, 201C. The English word 'panther', often used loosely for 'leopard', is best avoided: see Jennison, 183.

93 *NH* VIII, 24 (64): *senatusconsultum fuit vetus, ne liceret Africanas in Italiam advehere. contra hoc tulit ad populum Gnaeus Aufidius tribunus plebis, permisitque circensium gratia importare.*

94 Lucan VI, 183.

95 *NH* VIII, 23 (62, 63): *pantheris in candido breves macularum oculi . . . quidam ab eis* [*sc. pardis*] *pantheras candore solo discernunt.*

96 SHA, *Elagabalus* 25, 1.

97 Aymard, pl. 33a.

98 ibid., pl. 16; W. Dorigo, *Late Roman Painting*, 1971, pl. 115.

99 *PBSR*, 1948, pl. 11, fig. 32; *Archaeologia*, 1949, 181, pls 42, 43.

100 *CRAI*, 1966, 137, fig. 1. For a leopard named *ANΔPOMAXH* on a mixed animal *venatio* mosaic at Cos, see *PBSR*, 1948, 36. For other leopard *venationes* on mosaics, see Parlasca, op. cit., pl. 39, fig. 2 (Nennig); pl. 90, fig. 4 (Bad Kreuznach).

101 *La mosaique gréco-romaine*, 1965, fig. 2 after p. 56. For a list of classical Greek and Hellenistic versions of the theme, see F. Matz, *Ein römisches Meisterwerk: der Jahreszeitensarkophag Badminton–New York*, 1958, 15–18.

102 *Délos*, 1933, pl. 3; Havelock, op. cit., colour pl. 18.

103 *RPGR*, 106, no. 7: for further references, see Matz, op. cit., 17, F.3.

104 E.g. R. Turcan, *Les sarcophages romains à répresentations dionysiaques*, 1966, pls 40a (Los Angeles): 47a (Ostia); 48a (Salerno, Duomo); 50a (Frascati, Villa Aldobrandini); 51a (Beneventum); 51d (Besançon); Stuart Jones, op. cit., pl. 53, no. 86 (Museo Capitolino); Amelung, op.

cit., vol. I of plates, 1903, pl. 86 (Vatican); G. Pesce, *Sarcofagi romani di Sardegna*, 1957, fig. 8.

105 Matz, op. cit., pls A, D, E.

106 ibid., p. 8.

107 Hinks, 137, no. 540, fig. 155.

108 *Monumenti Antichi*, 1926, pl. 5.

109 E.g. Turcan, op. cit., pls 10c (Copenhagen); 11a (Munich); 35 (Lyon); 37a (Museo Torlonia, Rome); 57a (Palazzo Doria-Pamfili, Rome); 58a (Louvre). For a late classical Greek rendering of this theme, see the pebble mosaic from Olynthus, on which two slender, rearing leopards, conducted by Hermes, draw the god's chariot: *AJA*, 1934, pl. 29.

110 Lehmann-Hartleben and Olsen, op. cit., fig. 7.

111 ibid., fig. 39.

112 ibid., fig. 40.

113 Aurigemma, op. cit., pls 10, 11, 12.

114 Cf. note 36, above.

115 Aurigemma, op. cit., pl. 14.

116 *RPGR*, 106, no. 6.

117 ibid., 107, no. 9.

118 E.g. Lehmann-Hartleben and Olsen, op. cit., figs 9, 42.

119 Toynbee, op. cit., pp. 128–30, no. 12, pl. 34.

120 ibid., 169–71, no. 106, pl. 117.

121 *RPGR*, 356, no. 4.

122 Doppelfeld, op. cit., figs 11, 17.

123 *De Consulatu Stilichonis* III, 345.

124 *Archaiologikon Deltion*, 1967, pl. 145b. But see Martial, *Epigrams* I, 104, 1, 2 on leopards in harness at the shows: *picto quod iuga delicata collo/ pardus sustinet*. ('The leopard carries on its spotted neck a dainty yoke.')

125 Athenaeus V, 201C.

126 *NH* VIII, 30 (72): *lyncas . . . Aethiopia generat.*

127 ibid., 28 (70): *Pompei Magni primum ludi ostenderunt chama quem Galli rufium vocabant, effigie lupi, pardorum maculis.*

128 *DNA* XIV, 6: ἐπεί τοι καὶ ἐκεῖνα οἱ αὐτοὶ [*sc.* the Moors] ὑμνοῦσι λύγκας εἶναι, φασὶ δε αὐτὰς παρδάλεως μὲν ἔτι καὶ πλέον σιμάς, ἄκρα γε μὴν τὰ ὦτα λασίους. θηρίον δὲ τοῦτο ἀλτικὸν δεινῶς καὶ κατασχεῖν βιαιότατά τε καὶ ἐγκρατέστατα καρτερόν. For an animal labelled ΛΥΝΞ with very long, tufted ears, see J. P. Peters and H. Thiersch, *Painted Tombs in the Necropolis of Marissa*, 1905, pl. 15: second century B C.

129 Levi, op. cit. II, pl. 86a.

130 E.g. Virgil, *Georgics* III, 264: *lynces Bacchi variae*; Propertius, *Elegies* III, 17, 8: *lyncibus ad caelum vecta Ariadne tuis.*

131 *CGCBM: Italy*, 1873, 171, nos 81, 84; Keller I, pl. 2, fig. 4; M. P. Vlasto, 'Taras Oikistes' (*NNM*, 1922), pls 9, nos 38d, e, A; 10, nos 41a, b, 42a, 47, A; 11, nos 47, B, a, b; 48a, b.

132 ibid., pls 9, nos 40a, b; 10, no. 40c; *Sylloge Nummorum Graecorum II: the Lloyd Collection* (British Museum), 1933, pl. 4, no. 138.

133 ibid., pl. 22, no. 683; H. Herzfelder, *Les monnaies d'argent de Rhegion*, 1957, pl. 5, nos 48, 49.

134 H. B. Walters, *Catalogue of Greek and Etruscan Vases in the British Museum* IV, 1896, 65, F. 126; Keller I, 77, fig. 24.

135 Walters, op. cit., 104, F. 207; Keller I, 78, fig. 25.

136 Walters, op. cit., 153, 154, F. 308.

137 Anderson, photo 25772, Napoli; Pernice, pls 62, 63, fig. 1.

138 Gabinetto Fotografico Nazionale neg. no. E. 23092.

139 Anderson, photo 23824, Roma; Pernice, pl. 63, fig. 2. A stylized version of this cat-and-bird motif is embossed on one of the silver-gilt *phalerae* in the Sark Hoard (cf. p. 349, note 29): a powerful and thick-tailed

domestic cat with spotted coat
demolishes a cock: *Archaeologia*,
1971, pl. 13a.

140 Alinari, photo 39164, Napoli;
Pernice, pl. 66.

141 *Epistolae* 121, 19: *quare pulli
felem timeant, canem non timeant.*

142 *NH* X, 94 (202): *feles quidem
quo silentio, quam levibus vestigiis
obrepunt avibus, quam occulte speculatàe
in musculos exiliunt. excrementa sua
effossa obruunt terra intelligentes odorem
illum indicem sui esse.*

143 46.

144 Levi, op. cit. I, 275, fig. 107.

145 Keller I, 76, fig. 23; *CIL* VI,
14223: *Diis Manibus/Calpurnia Feli-
cla/Germullo coniugi/suo benemerenti et/
sibi. vixit ann[os] XXXXV/Calpurnia*

Felicla v[ixit] an[nos] L; L. Bovina,
*Iscrizioni latine lapidarie del Museo di
Palermo*, 1970, 154, 155, no. 180, pl. 89.

146 Stuart Jones, op. cit., 271, 272,
no. 120, pl. 63.

147 *Mosaiques de la Gaule* I, 1911,
pl. 108.

148 *Latomus*, 1961, 52–71, pl. 1,
fig. 1. This could be a parody of a
gladiator's victory over a rival, since
enicesas ('you've won') is written
below the cat.

149 *Revue archéologique de l'Est et du
Centre Est*, 1958, 128–36, figs 34–8;
Gallia, 1953, 85–9, figs 1–4.

150 G. W. Meates, *Lullingstone
Roman Villa*, 1955, 123, 124. For the
careful cremation-burial of a cat at
Wroxeter, see *Britannia*, 1972, 316.

CHAPTER V

1 *NH* VIII, 35, 36 (87, 88): *inter-
necivum bellum [sc.* of the snake] *cum
ichneumone. notum est animal hac
gloria maxima in eadem natum Aegypto,*
etc.

2 XVII, 1, 39.

3 *DSA* 10 (966, D): οὐθὲν
ἀπολείπει θωρακιζομένου πρὸς
μάχην ὁπλίτου.

4 ibid., 31 (980, E): ὥσπερ
ἀθλητήν.

5 *DNA* III, 22: ὡς ἀνὴρ πανοπλίᾳ
φραξάμενος.

6 ibid. VI, 38; VIII, 25; X, 47.

7 *De Natura Deorum* I, 101: *possum
de ichneumonum utilitate dicere.*

8 *Epigrams* VII, 87, 5: *delectat
Marium si perniciosus ichneumon.*

9 *Ashmolean Museum: Report of the
Visitors*, 1970–71, pl. 4b.

10 Keller I, fig. 57. The long-
headed animal confronting a rearing
snake on the wall of the Walbrook
silver casket may be an ichneumon:
J. M. C. Toynbee, *A Silver Casket and*

Strainer from the Walbrook Mithraeum,
1963, pl. 6.

11 W. Amelung, *Die Sculpturen des
vaticanischen Museums* I, 1903, 129.

12 ibid., pl. 18, no. 109.

13 *NH* VIII, 44 (105, 106); 46 (108):
hyenae plurimae gignuntur in Africa.

14 ibid. VIII, 45 (107).

15 III, 35, 10: μεμιγμένην μὲν ἔχει
φύσιν κυνὸς καὶ λύκου.

16 *NH* XXVIII, 27 (92–106).

17 SHA, *Antoninus Pius* 10, 9.

18 LXXVI, 1, 4: τὸ δὲ ζῷον τοῦτο
Ἰνδικόν τε ἐστι καὶ τότε πρῶτον
ἐς τὴν Ῥώμην, ὅσα καὶ ἐγὼ
ἐπίσταμαι, ἐσήχθη. ἔχει δὲ χροιὰν
μὲν λεαίνης τίγριδι μεμιγμένης,
εἶδος δὲ ἐκείνων τε καὶ κυνὸς καὶ
ἀλώπεκος ἰδίως πως συγκεκρα-
μένον.

19 SHA, *Gordiani Tres* 33, 1: *belbi, id
est hyenae, decem.*

20 D. Levi, *Antioch Mosaic Pavements*, 1947, I, 364, fig. 151.

CHAPTER VI

1 *De Spectaculis* 8: *ursus Lucanus.*

2 *Epodes* 16, 51.

3 I, 32, 1: Πάρνης παρεχομένη θήραν . . . ἄρκτων; III, 20, 5: δι᾽ ὅλον τὸ Ταύγετον ἄγραν . . . ἄρκτων; VIII, 23, 9: ὅσοι δρυμοὶ τοῖς Ἀρκάσιν εἰσὶν ἄλλοι παρέχονται τοσάδε, . . . ἄρκτους.

4 VIII, 17, 3: ἄρκτους τῶν Θρᾳκίων λευκάς.

5 Athenaeus V, 201C: ἄρκτος λευκὴ μεγάλη μία. It is most unlikely to have been a polar bear.

6 G. Kaibel, *Epigrammata Graeca*, 1878, no. 811.

7 SHA, *Hadrianus* 20, 13: *oppidum Hadrianotheras, in quodam loco illic et feliciter esset venatus et ursam occidisset, aliquando constituit.*

8 'Oppian', *Cynegetica* IV, 354, 355: ἄρκτοισιν δὲ πόνευσι κλυτὴν περιώσιον ἄγρην,/ Τίγριν ὅσοι ναίουσι καί Ἀρμενίην κλυτότοξον.

9 Ammianus Marcellinus XXIV, 5, 2: *erat etiam in hac eadem regione extentum spatium et rotundum . . . continens . . . et ursos, ut sunt Persici, ultra omnem rabiem saevientes.*

10 *De Consulatu Stilichonis* III, 309–13: *speluncas canibus Thero rimatur Hiberas/informesque cavis ursos detrudit ab antris,/quorum saepe Tagus manantes sanguine rictus/non satiavit aquis et quos iam frigore segnes/Pyrenaea tegit latebrosis frondibus ilex.* ('Thero scours with her hounds the caves of Spain and drives from their rocky lairs the uncouth bears, whose thirsty jaws, dripping with the blood of victims, Tagus' waters have often failed to satisfy – beasts that lurk, when sluggish with the winter's cold, beneath the shelter of the oak trees of the Pyrenees.')

11 *De Spectaculis* 7, 3: *Caledonicus ursus.*

12 ibid., 15, 3, 4: *ille* [*sc. Carpophorus*] *et praecipiti venabula condidit urso,/primus in Arctoi qui fuit arce poli.*

13 *Eclogues* VII, 65, 66: *aequoreos ego cum certantibus ursis/spectavi vitulos.*

14 Jennison, 70, 71, 188, 189.

15 *NH* VIII, 54 (131): *annalibus notatum est Marco Pisone Marco Messala consulibus a.d. xiv kal. oct. Domitium Ahenobarbum aedilem ursos Numidicos centum et totidem venatores Aethiopes in circo dedisse. miror adiectum Numidicos fuisse, cum in Africa non gigni constet.* Cf. VIII, 83 (228): *non esse . . . in Africa ursos:*

16 XVII, 3, 7: τὰς [*sc.* δορὰς] δὲ . . . ἄρκτων ἀμπέχονται καὶ ἐγκοιμῶνται.

17 *Aeneid* V, 37: *Acestis/horridus in . . . pelle Libystidis ursae.*

18 *Epigrams* I, 104, 5: *quod frenis Libyci domantur ursi.*

19 IV, 99, 100: *comminus ursos/figebat Numidas Albano nudus arena/venator.*

20 LIII, 27, 6: Πούπλιός τε Σερουίλιος . . . στρατηγῶν ἄρκτους τε τριακοσίας καὶ Λιβυκὰ ἕτερα θηρία ἴσα ἐν πανηγύρει [festival] τινὶ ἀπέκτεινεν. LIX, 7, 3: τότε δὲ καὶ ἄρκτους τετρακοσίας μεθ᾽ ἑτέρων Λιβυκῶν θηρίων ἴσων ἀπέκτεινε [*sc.* Gaius].

21 Aymard, pl. 39.

22 *Syria*, 1940, pls 15, fig. 1; 17.

23 Aymard, pl. 21c; *Syria*, 1938, pl. 12, fig. 1.

24 ibid., pl. 13, fig. 2.

25 *Cynegetica* IV, 354–424.

26 *De Ira* II, 11, 5, 6: *cum maximos ferarum greges linea pinnis distincta contineat et in insidias agat, ab ipso affectu dicta formido . . . metuitur . . . a feris rubens pinna.*

27 *Epistles* II, 1, 185, 186: *poscunt/ . . . ursum . . . his nam plebecula gaudet.*

28 De Spectaculis 21a: Orphea quod subito tellus emisit hiatu/ursam invasuram, venit ab Eurydice [because she wanted Orpheus back in Hades].

29 Karthago, 1951/1952, 154, 155, figs 10, 11.

30 Mosaiques de Tunisie, 1914, pl. 511a; PBSR, 1948, pl. 10, fig. 30. A mosaic from El-Djem depicts a somewhat similar assemblage of bears (unnamed) with boars and bulls, in two groups flanking a standing figure of Dionysus: Monuments Piot, 1934, pl. 9, fig. 1.

31 PBSR, 1948, pl. 10, fig. 29. For other references to bear-keepers or trainers (ursarii), see ILS, 3267; F. Bücheler, Carmina Epigraphica, 1930, no. 465; G. Brambach, Corpus Inscriptionum Rhenanarum, 1867, no. 211 (ursarius attached to a legion on the Rhine).

32 E. Espérandieu, Recueil général des bas-reliefs de la Gaule romaine, I, 1907, 386, no. 609, with fig.

33 M. Comstock and C. Vermeule, Catalogue of Greek, Etruscan and Roman Bronzes in the Museum of Fine Arts, Boston, Mass., 1971, 147, no. 172 with fig.; 346, no. 486 with fig.

34 SHA, Carinus 19, 2: tichobaten, qui per parietem urso eluso cucurrit, et ursos mimum agentes.

35 R. Delbrueck, Die Consulardiptychen, 1926-29, pl. 9.

36 Metamorphoses XI, 9: vidi et ursam mansuem cultu matronali, quae sella vehebatur.

37 Mosaiques de Tunisie, 1914, pl. 465, fig. 1; Aymard, pl. 34.

38 B. Pace, I mosaici di Piazza Armerina, 1955, fig. 34.

39 Karthago, 1953, 157, 159, figs 4, 5.

40 L. Robert, Les gladiateurs dans l'orient grec², 1971, 191, no. 191a, C; PBSR, 1948, 36. For further scenes of bear venationes, see K. Parlasca, Die römischen Mosaiken in

Deutschland, 1959, pl. 37, fig. 3 (Nennig); pls 90, fig. 3; 91, fig. 1 (Bad Kreuznach).

41 Karthago, 1951/1952, 144-6, figs 7-9.

42 Ammianus Marcellinus XXIX, 3, 9: quod cum duas haberet ursas saevas hominum ambestrices, Micam Auream et Innocentiam, cultu ita curabat enixo, ut earum caveas prope cubiculum suum locaret, custodesque adderet fidos visuros sollicite nequo casu ferarum deleretur luctificus calor. Innocentiam denique post multas quas eius laniatu cadaverum videret sepulturas ut bene meritam in silvas abire dimisit innoxiam.

43 H. Peirce and R. Tyler, L'art byzantin I, 1932, pl. 13; D. Levi, Antioch Mosaic Pavements, 1947, I, 276, 277, fig. 108; Jennison, pl. opp. p. 70.

44 Epistolae II, 76.

45 ibid. VII, 121.

46 ibid. IX, 132: abundantissime gaudeo, tibi esse curae ut filii mei editio ursis pluribus instruatur.

47 ibid. IX, 135.

48 ibid. IX, 142.

49 ibid. V, 62.

50 Delbrueck, op. cit., pl. 12.

51 ibid., pl. 20.

52 ibid., pl. 57. Cf. Seneca, De Ira III, 30, 1: ursos . . . mappa proritat.

53 Metamorphoses IV, 13-21.

54 De Ira II, 31, 6: intra domum ursorum . . . ora placida tractantibus. Cf. SHA, Elagabalus 25, 1.

55 J. M. C. Toynbee, The Art of the Romans, 1965, 48, 248, 249, pl. 32.

56 B. Schindler, Landesmuseum Trier, 1971, fig. 154. The greed of bears was a favourite topic: e.g. the relief from one of the Neumagen tombs, in the Trier Museum, of a bear guzzling a pile of apples on the ground and the same motif on a mosaic at Ostia: W. von Massov, Die Grabmäler von Neumagen, 1932, 188, 189, no. 238, fig. 120; G. Becatti, Scavi

di Ostia IV, 1961, pl. 96; the bear that is climbing a tree and shaking down apples on the sixth-century peristyle mosaic in the palace of the Byzantine emperors at Istanbul: G. Brett, etc., *The Great Palace of the Byzantine Emperors Report 1*, 1947, pl. 44; the bears gorging themselves on grapes in the 'peopled' vinescroll on the sixth-century ivory throne of Archbishop Maximianus at

Ravenna; F. W. Volbach, *Early Christian Art*, 1961, pls 232, 233. **57** J. M. C. Toynbee, *Art in Roman Britain*, 1963, 185, no. 139, pl. 158. For a very naturalistic rendering of a bear devouring a lamb, see D. Talbot Rice, etc., *The Great Palace of the Byzantine Emperors, Report 2*, 1958, pl. A. **58** Toynbee, op. cit., 183, 184, no. 135, pl. 156.

CHAPTER VII

1 E.g. Christ's parable of the Good Shepherd.

2 E.g. Horace, *Odes* I, 17, 9: *Martialis . . . lupus*; Virgil, *Aeneid* IX, 565, 566: *agnum Martius a stabulis rapuit lupus*.

3 E. A. Sydenham, *The Coinage of the Roman Republic*, 1952, 2, no. 6, pl. 13. The type appears on the Roman imperial coinage of Domitian, Titus, Trajan, Hadrian, Antoninus Pius, and Marcus Aurelius.

4 F. Gnecchi, *I medaglioni romani* II, 1912, pl. 132, nos 7, 8.

5 ibid., pl. 132, no. 9.

6 F. Stähelin, *Die Schweiz in römischer Zeit*[3], 1948, 453–6, fig. 113. Cf. Virgil, *Aeneid* VIII, 633, 634: [*fecerat*] *illam* [*sc. lupam*] *tereti cervice reflexa/mulcere alternos et corpora fingere lingua*.

7 *Archaeologia Aeliana*, 1943, 173, 174, pl. 10E.

8 J. M. C. Toynbee, *Art in Roman Britain*, 1963, 198, no. 184, pl. 220.

9 *Fasti* IV, 681–712: *cur igitur missae vinctis ardentia taedis/terga ferant volpes, causa docenda mihi est/ . . . qua fugit, incendit vestitos messibus agros/ . . . utque luat poenas gens haec Cerialibus ardet,/quoque modo segetes perdidit, ipsa perit*.

10 Judges XV, 4, 5.

11 A. Ferrua, *Le pitture della nuova catacomba di Via Latina*, 1960, pl. 31,

fig. 1. Cf. the same scene in the mosaic Samson cycle in the north aisle of the late fourth-century basilica at Misis-Mopsuhestia in Cilicia, where two foxes survive: L. Budde, *Antike Mosaiken in Kilikien* I, 1969, 69 and figs 145, 147.

12 *Epigrams* VII, 87, 1: *si meus aurita gaudet lagalopece Flaccus*. For fox-hunting on mosaics cf. pp. 24, 105.

13 H. Kähler, *Der grosse Fries von Pergamon*, 1948, pls 6, 7, 10, 37, 41.

14 Aymard, pls 9 (Uffizi); 8b (Geneva); 6, 14 (Rome).

15 ibid., 245, note 4.

16 *Imagines* I, 28, 5.

17 Athenaeus V, 201B: ἤγοντο καὶ κύνες δισχίλιοι τετρακόσιοι, οἱ μεν Ἰνδοί, οἱ λοιποὶ δὲ Ὑρκανοὶ καὶ Μολοσσοὶ καὶ ἑτέρων γενῶν.

18 *De Consulatu Stilichonis* III, 300: *hirsutae . . . Cressae*.

19 Philostratus, *Vita Apollonii* VIII, 30, 2: ἀξιοῦσιν αὐτοὺς οἱ Κρῆται μήτε οὖν ἄρκτων μήτε τῶν ὧδ᾽ ἀγρίων λείπεσθαι.

20 *De Spectaculis* 30.

21 *De Consulatu Stilichonis* II, 215: *ducunt ceu tenera venantem nare Molossi*.

22 Aymard, pl. 22. Cf. ibid., pl. 19.

23 See note 18. For other literary references, see Aymard, 254, note 3.

24 Petronius, *Satyricon* 40: *extra triclinium clamor sublatus est ingens, et ecce canes Laconici etiam circa mensam discurrere coeperunt.*

25 *Aeneid* XII, 753: *vividus Umber.* Cf. Silius Italicus, *Punica* III, 295, 296: *exigit Umber/nare sagax e calle feras.*

26 Keller I, 124, fig. 49; Aymard, pl. 10b.

27 ibid., pl. 11.

28 *Cynegetica* III, 6: αἱ δὲ ποδώκεις κύνες αἱ Κελτικαὶ καλοῦνται μὲν Οὐέτραγοι φωνῇ τῇ Κελτῶν . . . ἀπὸ τῆς ὠκύτητος.

29 V, 7-9.

30 M. Pobé and J. Roubier, *The Art of Roman Gaul*, 1961, pl. 195. Cf. the vigorously carved head of a Gaulish hunting dog, wearing a collar with ring, on a fragmentary relief from Neumagen: W. von Massow, *Die Grabmäler von Neumagen*, 1932, no. 37, p. 88, fig. 58.

31 Strabo IV, 5, 2: ταῦτα δὴ κομίζεται ἐξ αὐτῆς [*sc. Britannia*] . . . καὶ κύνες εὐφυεῖς πρὸς τὰς κυνηγεσίας. 'Oppian', *Cynegetica* I, 468-80; Nemesianus, *Cynegetica* 225, 226: *divisa Britannia mittit/veloces nostrique orbis venatibus aptos.* 'Oppian' remarks on their cruel claws and teeth.

32 Chesters Museum: Toynbee, op. cit., 150, no. 59, pl. 62. Cf. the bronze figurine of a blunt-nosed, curly-tailed, shaggy-coated dog in the Stuttgart Museum: Stuttgart Museum picture postcard.

33 *De Consulatu Stilichonis* III, 301: *magnaque taurorum fracturae colla Britannae.*

34 Symmachus, *Epistolae* II, 77: *ut nunc septem Scotticorum canum probavit oblatio, quos praelusionis die ita Roma mirata est, ut ferreis caveis putaret advectos.*

35 J. M. C. Toynbee, *Art in Britain under the Romans*, 1964, 126, 127, pl. 34b, c.

36 ibid., 334, pl. 79b.

37 E.g. ibid., 410, pl. 93.

38 F. Fremersdorf, *Die Denkmäler des römischen Köln* I, 1928, pl. 116.

39 Vatican negative VI, 32, 7; British Museum no. 1250.

40 *PBSR*, 1948, pl. 8, fig. 23. Cf. Aymard, pl. 25b.

41 *PBSR*, 1948, pl. 8, fig. 22.

42 M. Yacoub, *Musée de Bardo*, 1970, 99, fig. 111, inv. no. 1515; Aymard, pl. 5b.

43 G. V. Gentili, *La villa erculia di Piazza Armerina*, 1959, pls 16, 22.

44 V. Béquignon, *Recherches archéologiques à Phères de Thessalie*, 1937, 92-4, no. 69, pl. 23, fig. 4; *PBSR*, 1948, 33, 34, pl. 9, fig. 24.

45 Pausanias II, 19, 7; III, 23, 1.

46 *Metamorphoses* VIII, 4, 5.

47 *Epodes* VI, 5.

48 *Georgics* III, 404-6: *nec tibi cura canum fuerit postrema, sed una/velocis Spartae catulos acremque Molossum/ pasce sero pingui.*

49 G. Calza, *La necropoli del porto di Roma nell' Isola Sacra*, 1940, fig. 117: the dog is on the ground in the right-hand group.

50 *De Re Rustica* VII, 12, 13.

51 V, 1063-72.

52 Petronius, *Satyricon* 64.

53 ibid. 72.

54 *Eclogues* VIII, 107.

55 Alinari, photo 12051, Napoli. Cf. the epitaph of a watch-dog, set to guard carriages, who never gave a false alarm by its barking (*raedarum custos, nunquam latravit inepte*) until death claimed him and silenced him (*nunc silet et cineres vindicat umbra suos*): *Anthologia Latina*, 1174.

56 A. Maiuri, *Pompeii*[8], 1956, pl. 49, fig. 86; Pernice, pl. 40, fig. 2.

57 Maiuri, op. cit., 103, pl. 64, fig. 111.

58 For a third mosaic watch-dog from Pompeii, now in the Naples Museum, of a similar type, completely black, wearing a crimson collar and tied up by a crimson leash, see A. Maiuri, *La peinture romaine*, 1953, 112. Cf. also Pernice, pl. 44, fig. 1.

59 DC LXI, 6: Αὖλος Φαβρίκιος στρατηγῶν ἐκείνοις μὲν μὴ βουληθεῖσιν ἐπὶ μετρίοις τισὶν ἀγωνίσασθαι οὐκ ἐχρήσατο, κύνας δὲ διδάξας ἕλκειν ἅρματα ἀντὶ ἵππων ἐσήγαγε.

60 SHA, *Elagabalus* 28, 1: *canes quaternos ingentes iunxit ad currum*.

61 Unpublished (?): photo Roger Wilson.

62 *DSA* 19 (973E, F, 974A).

63 *Satyricon* 71: *valde te rogo ut secundum pedes statuae meae catellam ponas . . . ad dexteram meam ponas statuam Fortunatae meae . . . catellam cingulo alligatam ducat*.

64 *Epistolae* II, 19, 3: Πλαγγὼν δὲ τὸ Μελιταῖον κυνίδιον ὅ ἐτρέφομεν, ἄθυρα τῇ δεσποίνῃ προσηνές, ὑπὸ τῆς ἄγαν λιχνείας ἐπὶ τὸ κρέας ὁρμῆσαν κεῖταί σοι τρίτην ταύτην ἡμέραν ἐκτάδην νεκρὸν ἤδη μυδῆσαν. 'Oppian' would have classed her among the 'little good-for-nothing, gluttonous, table-fed house-pets' with which he compares the British hunting dogs for size (loc. cit., note 31, ll. 462, 473). A terracotta cut-out relief 4 cm. long in the British Museum (1914.5–16.4), said to have come from near Smyrna and probably to be dated to the first century B C, may portray Dolly's breed (R. H. A. Merlen, *De Canibus*, 1971, pl. 13 opp. p. 96). A white Melitaean male dog, described as a most faithful guard, was playfully named 'Taurus' (*Anthologia Graeca* VII, 211). The Melita from which these dogs (*catuli Melitaei*) came is not Malta but the island of Meleda off the coast of Illyricum: Pliny, *NH* III, 26 (152).

65 Unpublished (?): photo Bernard Ashmole.

66 G. Brusin, *Il R. Museo Archeo-*

logico di Aquileia, 1936, 53, fig. 42; V. S. M. Scrinari, *Sculture romane di Aquileia*, 1972, pl. 316; cf. also pl. 319.

67 *PBSR*, 1948, pl. 10, fig. 27.

68 E. Espérandieu, *Recueil général des bas-reliefs de la Gaule romaine* I, 1907, 456, no. 770.

69 *BCH*, 1880, 494; *IG* XII, 2, no. 459. For other Greek epitaphs of dogs, see G. Kaibel, *Epigrammata Graeca*, 1878, nos 329 (unnamed: Mytilene); 332 ('Philokynegos' ['Hunter']: Pergamon); 626 ('Theia': Rome); 627 (unnamed: near Florence). Cf. the Greek inscription on a square funerary chest found near Frascati reading ᾿Ακρίδι κυναρίῳ ('To "Grasshopper", tiny doggie'): *IG* XIV, no. 1360; and SHA, *Hadrianus* 20, 12: *canes sic amavit* [*sc. Hadrianus*] *ut eis sepulchra constitueret*.

70 M. Fraenkel, *Inschriften von Pergamon* II, 1895, 895, no. 577; *PBSR*, 1948, pl. 9, fig. 25.

71 A. H. Smith, *A Catalogue of Sculpture in the Department of Greek and Roman Antiquities in the British Museum* I, 1892, no. 649; *CIG*, 6866: *ΑΒΕΙΤΑ ΖΗΣΑΣΑ ΕΤΗ Ι/ ΜΗΝΑΣ ΔΥΩ/ΧΑΙΡΕΤΕ*.

72 F. Cumont, *Recherches sur le symbolisme funéraire des Romains*, 1942, pl. 43, fig. 2; *PBSR*, 1948, pl. 9, fig. 26.

73 Cumont, op. cit., pl. 41, fig. 4.

74 ibid., pl. 40, fig. 1.

75 ibid., 497, fig. 105.

76 C. R. Morey, *The Sarcophagus of Claudia Antonia Sabina and the Asiatic Sarcophagi: Sardis V* I, 1924, 7, fig. 3.

77 ibid., fig. 39 between pp. 34 and 35.

78 Carlisle: J. M. C. Toynbee, *Art in Roman Britain*, 1963, 150, no. 58, pl. 64; Stuttgart: Stuttgart Museum picture postcard.

79 *The Great Palace of the Byzantine Emperors, Report 1*, 1947, pl. 34.

80 ibid., pl. 32.

81 *Anthologia Graeca* IX, 303: τῇ
βαιῇ Καλαθίνῃ ὑπὸ σκυλάκων
μογεούσῃ/Λητωὶς κούφην εὐτο-
κίην ἔπορεν,/μούναις οὔ τι γυναιξὶν
ἐπήκοος, ἀλλὰ καὶ αὐτὰς/συνθή-
ρους σῴζειν Ἄρτεμις οἶδε κύνας./
(Adaios).

82 ibid. IX, 268: Κρῆσσα κύων
ἐλάφοιο κατ᾽ ἴχνιον ἔδραμε Γοργὼ/
ἔγκυος ἀμφοτέρην Ἄρτεμιν
εὐξαμένη,/τίκτε δ᾽ ἀποκτείνουσα.
θοὴ δ᾽ ἐπένευσεν Ἐλευθὼ/ἄμφω
εὐαγρίης δῶρα καὶ εὐτοκίης./καὶ
νῦν ἐννέα παισὶ διδοῖ γάλα.
φεύγετε, Κρήσσαι/κεμμάδες ἐκ
τοκάδων τέκνα διδασκόμεναι.
(Antipatros of Thessalonika).

83 ibid. IX, 417: θηρωτὴν Λάμπ-
ωνα, Μίδου κύνα, δίψα κάτεκτα/
καίπερ ὑπὲρ ψυχῆς πολλὰ πονησά-
μενον./ποσσὶ γὰρ ὤρυσσεν νοτε-
ρὸν πέδον, ἀλλὰ τὸ νωθὲς/πίδακος
ἐκ τυφλῆς οὐκ ἐτάχυνεν ὕδωρ./
πῖπτε δ᾽ ἀπαυδήσας, ἡ δ᾽ ἔβλυσεν·
ἦ ἄρα Νύμφαι/Λάμπωνι κταμένων
μῆνιν ἔθεσθ᾽ ἐλάφων. (Antipatros
of Thessalonika).

84 F. Bücheler, *Carmina Epigraphica*, no. 1512: *quam dulcis fuit ista,
quam benigna,/quae cum viveret, in sinu
iacebat/somni conscia semper et cubilis./
o factum male, Myia, quod peristi./
latrares modo, si quis adcubaret/rivalis
dominae, licentiosa./o factum male,
Myia, quod peristi./altum iam tenet
insciam sepulchrum,/nec saevire potes nec
insilire/nec blandis mihi morsibus renides.*

85 ibid., no. 1175: *Gallia me genuit,
nomen mihi divitis undae/concha dedit,
formae nominis aptus honor./docta per
incertas audax discurrere silvas/ collibus
hirsutas atque agitare feras./non gravibus
vinclis unquam consueta teneri/verbera
nec niveo corpore saeva pati./molli
namque sinu domini dominaeque iace-
bam/et noram in strato lassa cubare
toro./ et plus quam licuit muto canis ore
loquebar,/ nulli latratus pertimuere meos./*

*sed iam fata subii partu iactata sinistro/
quam nunc sub parvo marmore terra
tegit.*

86 ibid., no. 1176: *portavi lacrimis
madidus te, nostra catella,/quod feci
lustris laetior ante tribus./ergo mihi,
Patrice, iam non dabis oscula mille/
nec poteris collo grata cubare meo./
tristis marmorea posui te sede merentem/
et iunxi semper manibus ipse meis./
moribus argutis hominem simulare para-
tam,/ perdidimus quale, hei mihi,
delicias./tu, dulcis Patrice, nostras attin-
gere mensas/consueras, gremio poscere
blanda cibos,/lambere tu calicem lingua
sapiente solebas,/quem tibi saepe meae
sustinuere manus,/accipere et lassum
cauda gaudente frequenter/et mi omnes
gestu dicere blanditias.*

87 *Epigrams* XI, 69: *amphitheatrales
inter nutrita magistros/venatrix, silvis
aspera, blanda domi,/Lydia dicebar,
domino fidissima Dextro./ .... /non me
longa dies nec inutilis abstulit aetas,/
.... /fulmineo spumantis apri sum
dente perempta./ .... /nec queror
infernas quamvis cito rapta sub umbras/
non potui fato nobiliore mori.*

88 ibid. I, 109: *Issa est passere
nequior Catulli,/ Issa est purior osculo
columbae,/Issa est blandior omnibus
puellis,/Issa est carior Indicis lapillis,/
Issa est deliciae catella Publi./hanc tu, si
queritur, loqui putabis;/sentit tristi-
tiamque gaudiumque./collo nixa cubat
capitque somnos,/ ut suspiria nulla sen-
tiantur;/et desiderio coacta ventris/gutta
pallia non fefellit ulla,/sed blando pede
suscitat toroque/deponi monet et rogat
levari./castae tantus inest pudor catellae,/
ignorat Venerem; nec invenimus/dignum
tam tenera virum puella./hanc ne lux
rapiat suprema totam,/picta Publius
exprimit tabella,/in qua tam similem
videbis Issam,/ut sit tam similis sibi nec
ipsa./Issam denique pone cum tabella:/
aut utramque putabis esse veram/aut
utramque putabis esse pictam.* For still
further names of dogs, whether kept

as pets or for business purposes, see *PBSR*, 1948, 26–9. There is also the dog 'Monnus' on a mosaic at Ostia: *Scavi di Ostia* IV, 1961, pl. 159, no. 61.

89 See *MAH*, 1968, 247-53, for a list of the remedies given by Pliny (*NH* XXIX and XXX) that could be obtained from dogs for the cure of all manner of diseases and ailments. The relief from Mavilly (ibid., 274, fig. 14) would appear to represent, not a healing divinity, but a human doctor, with his pet dog and eagle, treating an ophthalmic patient.

90 *IG* IV, nos 951, 952. Cf. Aelian, *DNA* VIII, 9: τρωθέντες δὲ ἔχουσι [*sc.* dogs] τὴν γλῶτταν φαρμάκον, ἥπερ οὖν περιλιχμώμενοι τὸ τρωθὲν μέρος εἰς ὑγίειαν ἐπανάγουσιν.

91 B. Cunliffe, *Roman Bath*, 1969, 198, pl. 64.

92 *Latomus*, 1957, 62. E.g. the clay seated dog at Cologne wearing collar and bell (or amulet?): F. Fremersdorf, *Neuerwerbungen des Römisch-Germanischen Museums, 1923–1927²*, 1964, pl. 56.

93 The dog that lies beside the dead man's legs on the funerary couch of Gaius Julius Maternus, in the funerary banquet scene on his tombstone at Cologne, could be either a symbol or a pet: F. Fremersdorf, *Die Denkmäler des römischen Köln* II, 1950, pl. 50.

94 *Latomus*, 1957, pl. 7, fig. 4.

95 Fremersdorf, op. cit. (note 93), pl. 30; A. Hondius Crone, *The Temple of Nehalennia at Domburg*, 1955, pls on pp. 23, 25, 27, 29(?), 33, 35, 39, 41, 43, 45, 49.

96 R. Magnen and E. Thevenot, *Épona*, 1953, pls 13, 25, 31.

97 *Germania*, 1941, pl. 16, no. 10.

98 Pliny, *NH* XXX, 14 (42, 43); Espérandieu, op. cit. III, 1910, nos 2407, 2408 (Dijon Museum).

99 R. E. M. and T. V. Wheeler, *Report on the Excavation of the Prehistoric, Roman, and Post-Roman Site in Lydney Park, Gloucestershire*, 1932.

100 ibid., pl. 25.

101 ibid., pl. 26, nos 117, 118, 120.

102 ibid., pl. 26, nos 115, 116, 119.

103 ibid., pl. 34, no. 2.

CHAPTER VIII

1 Curtius, *History of Alexander* VIII, 19, 16: *eadem terra* [*sc.* India] *rhinocerotas alit, non generat*. Curtius seems to imagine that rhinoceroses are not indigenous in India, although they can be reared there.

2 Athenaeus V, 201C.

3 J. P. Peters and H. Thiersch, *Painted Tombs in the Necropolis of Marissa*, 1905, pl. 10.

4 III, 35, 2, 3: ῥινόκερως . . . ἐπὶ δ' ἄκρων τῶν μυκτήρων φέρει κέρας, τῷ τύπῳ σιμόν, τῇ δὲ στερεότητι σιδήρῳ παρεφερές.

5 See *Antiquity*, 1950, 61–71.

6 XVI, 4, 15: ἡ χώρα . . . φέρει

. . . ῥινοκέρωτας . . . κέρας σιμὸν στερεώτερον ὀστέου παντός . . . ἀπό γε τοῦ ὑφ'ἡμῶν ὁραθέντος . . . ἐκ μὲν δὴ τοῦ ὑφ'ἡμῶν ὁραθέντος ταῦτά φαμεν ἡμεῖς.

7 *NH* VI, 34 (173); 35 (185).

8 *Satires* III, 5, ed. Muller, 1872: *broncu Bovillanus dente adverso eminculo hic est/rhinoceros*.

9 G. Gullini, *I mosaici di Palestrina*, 1956, 11, 12, pl. 21. There is no clinching evidence for the identification, often made, of *lithostrota* with pavements composed of a patchwork of irregular pieces of coloured marbles.

10 NH VIII, 29 (71): *iisdem ludis et rhinoceros unius in nare cornus, qualis saepe visus.*

11 LI, 22, 5: ῥινόκερως ἵππος τε ποτάμιος πρῶτον τότε ἐν τῇ Ῥώμῃ ὀφθέντα ἐσφάγη ... ὁ δὲ δὴ ῥινόκερως τὰ μὲν ἄλλα ἐλάφαντί πῃ προσέοικε, κέρας δέ τι κατ᾽ αὐτὴν τὴν ῥῖνα προσέχει.

12 Suetonius, *Augustus* 43, 4: *rhinocerotem apud Saepta.* Was this in 29 BC?

13 Keller I, 388, fig. 135.

14 *De Spectaculis* 22, 1–6: *sollicitant pavidi dum rhinocerota magistri/seque diu magnae colligit ira ferae,/ desperabantur promissi proelia Martis;/sed tandem rediit cognitus ante furor./namque gravem cornu gemino sic extulit ursum,/iactat ut inpositas taurus in astra pilas; 9: praestitit exhibitus tota tibi, Caesar, harena/ quae non promisit proelia rhinoceros./o quam terribilis exarsit pronus in iras!*

quantus erat taurus, cui pila taurus erat!
Cf. *Epigrams* XIV, 52, 53.

15 *CREBM* II, 1930, 411, nos 496–500, pl. 81, nos 16, 17.

16 IX, 21, 2: εἶδον δὲ καὶ ταύρους τούς τε Αἰθιοπικούς, οὓς ἐπὶ τῷ συμβεβηκότι ὀνομάζουσι ῥινόκερως, ὅτ᾽ σφισιν ἐπ᾽ ἀκρᾷ τῇ ῥινὶ ἓν ἑκάστῳ κέρας καὶ ἄλλο ὑπὲρ αὐτὸ οὐ μέγα.

17 SHA, *Antoninus Pius* 10, 9.

18 DCLXXII, 10, 3.

19 DCLXXVII, 6, 2.

20 SHA, *Elagabalus* 28, 3: *habuit ... rhinocerotem et omnia Aegyptia.*

21 SHA, *Gordiani Tres* 33, 1. Since this rhinoceros was shown along with six hippopotamuses it was probably from Egypt.

22 G. V. Gentili, *La villa erculia di Piazza Armerina: i mosaici figurati,* 1959, pl. 27.

CHAPTER IX

1 NH VIII, 39 (95): *in eodem Nilo belua hippopotamus editur;* XXVIII, 31 (121): *est crocodilo cognatio quaedam amnis eiusdem* [*sc.* Nili] *geminique victus cum hippopotamo.*

2 ibid. VIII, 39 (95).

3 I, 35, 8–10.

4 Jennison, 147.

5 J. P. Peters and H. Tiersch, *Painted Tombs in the Necropolis of Marissa,* 1905, pls 12, 13.

6 G. Giulini, *I mosaici di Palestrina,* 1956, pl. 13.

7 Keller I, 158, fig. 57; *RPGR,* 370, no. 1; M. Grant, *Cities of Vesuvius,* 1971, 175 (upper figure); G. E. Rizzo, *La pittura ellenistico-Romana,* 1929, pl. 187b: Pompeii (Casa del Fauno).

8 *RPGR,* 161, no. 5; Alinari, photo 12027, Napoli; A. Maiuri, *La peinture romaine,* 1953, 111; Rizzo,

op. cit., pl. 151a. Cf. S. Aurigemma, *The Baths of Diocletian and the Museo Nazionale Romano,* 1947, pls 10, 11.

9 *RPGR,* 375, no. 2: Herculaneum. Cf. ibid., 377, no. 1; Rizzo, op. cit., pl. 187a: mosaic from the Aventine.

10 S. Aurigemma, *I mosaici di Tripolitania,* 1960, pls 83, 84.

11 NH VIII, 40 (96): *primus eum* [*sc. hippopotamum*] *et quinque crocodiles Romae aedilitatis suae ludis Marcus Scaurus temporario euripo ostendit.*

12 DC LI, 22, 5: ἵππος τε ποτάμιος ἐσφάγη. Dio wrongly states that this was the hippopotamus' first appearance in Rome.

13 Calpurnius Siculus, *Eclogues* VII, 66–8: *spectavi ... et equorum nomine dictum,/sed deforme peius, quod in illo nascitur amne,/qui sata riparum vernantibus irrigat undis.*

14 W. Amelung, *Die Sculpturen des*

vaticanisches Museums I, 1903, 129.
15 J. M. C. Toynbee, *The Hadrianic School*, 1934, 32.
16 ibid., pl. 1, nos 12, 14-18, 20-2.
17 *Gazette Archéologique*, 1880, pl. 25; *RPGR*, 377, no. 1.
18 ibid., 376, no. 1.
19 ibid., 370, no. 2; *PBSR*, 1914, pl. 2, no. 29.
20 ibid., 375, no. 1 (El Alia): ibid., 377, no. 4 and L. Foucher, *Inventaire des mosaiques: Sousse*, 1960, pl. 5 (below).
21 DC LXXII, 10, 3: καὶ πέντε γοῦν ἵππους ποταμίους . . . ταῖς ἑαυτοῦ χερσὶ κατεχρήσατο; 19, 1: ἔσφαξεν ἵππον τε ποτάμιον.
22 SHA, *Elagabalus* 28, 3: *habuit et hippopotamos*.

23 SHA, *Gordiani Tres* 33, 1: *fuerunt sub Gordiano . . . hippopotami sex*.
24 Cf. p. 351, note 84; p. 392, notes 20, 24.
25 SHA, *Firmus* 6, 2: *hippopotamo sedisse*.
26 G. V. Gentili, *La villa erculia di Piazza Armerina: i mosaici figurati*, 1959, pl. 27.
27 *Germania*, 1925, 152-62, fig. 3, nos 1-3; O. Doppelfeld, ed., *Römer am Rhein*, 1967, no. C248, pl. 98. As a symbol of Egypt the hippopotamus features on coins of Juba II of Mauretania: J. Mazard, *Corpus Numorum Numidiae Mauretaniaeque*, 1955, no 347, 348.

CHAPTER X

1 Virgil, *Aeneid* III, 390-3; VIII, 43-5: *litoreis ingens inventa sub ilicibus sus/triginta capitum fetus enixa iacebit/ alba, solo recubans, albi circum ubera nati.*
2 Sala degli Animali: E. Strong, *La scultura romana*, I, 1923, 27, fig. 14; Ny Carlsberg Glyptotek: G. M. A. Richter, *Animals in Greek Sculpture*, 1930, 68 and fig. 119.
3 *CREBM* II, 1930, pl. 6, nos 13, 14 (Vespasian: 3 piglets); pl. 7, no. 3 (Titus: 3 piglets); IV, 1940, pl. 30, no. 10 (Antoninus Pius: 8 piglets); 259 (Antoninus Pius: 11 piglets); pl. 31, no. 6 (Antoninus Pius: 9 piglets); pl. 39, no. 4 (Antoninus Pius: 5 piglets).
4 F. Gnecchi, *I medaglioni romani*, 1912, II, pl. 55, no. 8.
5 ibid., pl. 54, no. 9.
6 *BMQ*, 1928, pl. 52.
7 Virgil, *Aeneid* VIII, 82-5: *candida per silvam cum fetu concolor albo/procubuit viridique in litore conspicitur sus:/ quam pius Aeneas tibi enim, tibi maxima*

Iuno/mactat sacra ferens et cum grege sistit ad aram.
8 *MAAR*, 1955, pl. 10, fig. 21 (Ara Pacis); pl. 15, fig. 28c (Vatican, Belvedere); Gnecchi, op. cit. II, pl. 66, no. 6 (medallion of Marcus Aurelius).
9 Cf. also p. 348, note 12.
10 Petronius, *Satyricon* 40: *secutum est repositorium in quo positus est primae magnitudinis aper, et quidem pilleatus, e cuius dentibus sportellae dependebant duae palmulis textae, alter caryotis, alter thebanis repleta. circa autem minores porcelli ex coptoplacentis facti, quasi uberibus imminerent, scrofam esse positam significabant . . . Carpus . . . ultro latus apri vehementer percussit, ex cuius plaga turdi evolaverunt.*
11 E. A. Sydenham, *Roman Republican Coinage*, 1952, pl. 25, no. 903.
12 *CREBM* I, 1923, pl. 2, no. 14.
13 S. Reinach, *Répertoire de la statuaire grecque et romaine* III, 1904, 219, no. 10; Alinari, photo 19025, Napoli. The marble boar in the

Uffizi, Florence, seated with its hind-legs crumpled up under its hind-quarters, would seem to have been wounded in the chase: Richter, op. cit., 68 and fig. 117.

14 C. Robert, *Die antiken Sarko-phagreliefs* III, 1, 1897; 2, 1904.

15 D. E. Strong, *Roman Imperial Sculpture*, 1961, pl. 81.

16 III, 2: ὁ τῶν συῶν ἐκ τοῦ στόματος ῥέων ἀφρός.

17 LXXI, 36, 2: ὥστε . . . σῦς ἀγρίους ἐν θήρᾳ καταβάλλειν.

18 Gnecchi, op. cit. II, pl. 66, nos 9, 10.

19 R. P. Wright, *Roman Inscriptions of Britain*, I, 1965, no. 1041: Silvano Invicto sacr[um]/Caius Tetius Veturius Micia/nus pr[a]ef[ectus] alae Sebosian/ nae ob aprum eximiae/formae captum quem/multi antecesso/res eius praedari non potuerunt v[oto] s[uscepto] l[ibens] p[osuit].

20 Aldborough: H. Ecroyd Smith, *Reliquiae Isuriacae*, 1852, pl. 25, fig. 16; Colchester (British Museum): *Archaeologia*, 1863, pl. 24, fig. 9; Wattisfield (Ipswich Museum): *JRS*, 1945, pl. 2, fig. 2; Findon (Worthing Museum,: J. M. C. Toynbee, *Art in Britain under the Romans*, 1964, pl. 33b.

21 *Eclogues* VII, 58.

22 *Epigrams* I, 104, 6, 7: et, quantum Calydon tulisse fertur,/ paret purpureis aper capestris.

23 K. Parlasca, *Die römischen Mosai-ken in Deutschland*, 1959, pl. 40, figs 1, 2. Cf. the relief in the Vatican (sala degli Animali) on which a Cupid rides in a light cart drawn by two boars (W. Amelung, *Die Sculpturen des vaticanischen Museums*, plates II, 1908, pl. 38, no. 158).

24 *De Spectaculis* 15, 1, 2: summa tuae, Meleagri, fuit quae gloria famae,/ quantast [how small] Carpophori portio, fusus aper; 12, 1–3: inter Caesareae discrimina saeva Dianae/fixisset gravi-

dam cum levis hasta suem,/exiluit partus miserae de vulnere matris; 14, 1–3: sus fera iam gravior maturi pignore ventris/emisit fetum, vulnere facta parens;/nec iacuit partus, sed matre cadente cucurrit.

25 DC LXXVI, 1: ἐν ταύταις ταῖς θέαις καὶ σύες τοῦ Πλαυτιανοῦ ἑξήκοντα ἄγριοι ἐπάλαισαν ἀλλήλοις ὑπὸ παραγγέλματος.

26 SHA, *Gordiani Tres* 3, 7: apri cen-tum quinquaginta.

27 Claudian, *De Consulatu Stilich-onis* III, 304–6: Germanorumque paludes/eruis et si quis defensus harun-dine Rheni/vastus aper nimio dentes curvaverat aevo.

28 *MAAR*, 1955, pls 8, fig. 17c; 16, fig. 30; 34, fig. 52c; 35, fig. 54a; 36, fig. 55; 37, fig. 56; 38, fig. 57; 40, fig. 59; 41, fig. 61a.

29 E. Strong, op. cit., pl. 31; *MAAR*, 1953, 132, 133.

30 H. B. Walters, *Catalogue of Bronzes, Greek, Roman, and Etruscan, in the British Museum*, 1899, 155, no. 858 with fig.

31 *CREBM* III, 1936, 226, nos 1062–7, pl. 43, nos 10–12; 527, no. 1832A.

32 Cf. note, p. 55.

33 R. Amy, etc., *L'arc d'Orange*, 1962, pls 75, 76, 82a.

34 M. Pobé and J. Roubier, *The Art of Roman Gaul*, 1961, pl. 188: Narbonne Museum.

35 ibid., pl. 193.

36 E.g. G. Macdonald, *The Roman Wall in Scotland*, 1934, pls 66, fig. 1; 67, fig. 2.

37 Keller I, 405, fig. 141.

38 M. Comstock and C. Vermeule, *Greek, Etruscan and Roman Bronzes in the Museum of Fine Arts, Boston*, 1971, no. 92.

39 Alinari, photo 34193, Napoli; J. M. C. Toynbee, *The Art of the Romans*, 1965, pl. 31.

40 *PBSR*, 1948, pl. 10, fig. 28.

41 F. Fremersdorf, *Römisches Bunt-glas in Köln*, 1958, 46, no. 549, pl. 85 (in colour); *Römisches Geformtesglas in Köln*, 1961, 21, no. 549, pl. 7; ed. O. Doppelfeld, *Römer am Rhein*,

1967, no. D, 56, pl. 7 (in colour) opp. p. 192.
42 Fremersdorf, op. cit., 1961, 22, no. 944, pl. 9.
43 ibid., 21, 22, no. 303, pl. 8.

CHAPTER XI

1 *NH* VIII, 26 (67): *camelos inter armenta pascit oriens, quorum duo genera Bactriae et Arabiae differunt, quod illae bina habent tubera in dorso, hae singula et sub pectore alterum cui incumbant . . . omnes autem iumentorum ministeriis dorso funguntur atque etiam equitatus in proeliis.* ('The East produces camels of which there are two breeds, the Bactrian and the Arabian. The former have two humps on their backs, the latter one and also another one below the chest on which they can rest their weight. . . . But all perform the function of beasts of burden by carrying loads on their backs and even of cavalry in battle.')
2 Cicero, *De Natura Deorum* II, 123 : *cameli adiuvantur proceritate collorum.*
3 Lucian, *Prometheus in Verbis* 4: Πτολεμαῖος γοῦν ὁ Λάγου δύο καινὰ ἐς Αἴγυπτον ἄγων, κάμηλόν τε Βακτριανὴν παμμέλαιναν.
4 Athenaeus V, 200F: ἐπῆσαν δὲ καὶ συνωρίδες καμήλων ἕξ, ἐξ ἑκατέρου μέρους τρεῖς.
5 ibid., 201A: κάμηλοι δ'αἱ μὲν ἔφερον λιβανωτοῦ μνᾶς τριακοσίας, σμύρνης τριακοσίας κρόκου καὶ κασίας καὶ κινναμώμου καὶ ἴριδος καὶ τῶν λοιπῶν ἀρωμάτων διακοσίας.
6 W. W. Tarn, *Hellenistic Civilisation*³, 1952, 183.
7 XVII, 1, 45: πρότερον μὲν οὖν ἐνυκτοπόρουν πρὸς τὰ ἄστρα βλέποντες οἱ καμηλέμποροι καὶ καθάπερ οἱ πλέοντες ὥδευον κομίζοντες καὶ ὕδωρ.
8 E. A. Sydenham, *The Roman*

Republican Coinage, 1952, 151, 152, nos 912-14, pl. 25. Another early rendering of a loaded camel in western Roman art is in the monochrome painted landscape frieze in the 'House of Livia' on the Palatine (A. Frova, *L'arte di Roma e del mondo romano*, 1961, 386, fig. 356).
9 J. M. C. Toynbee, *The Hadrianic School*, 1934, pls 2, no. 24; 11, nos 14-18 (the last was struck at Caesarea in Cappadocia).
10 M. Rostovtzeff, *The Social and Economic History of the Roman Empire*, 1926, pls 37, figs 3, 4 (British Museum and Louvre); 38, fig. 1 (Ashmolean Museum, Oxford); 42, figs 1, 2, 5, 6 (from Egypt); *The Social and Economic History of the Hellenistic World*, 1941, I, pl. 56, fig. 1 (Louvre).
11 K. Michalowski, *Palmyra*, 1970, pl. 78.
12 M. Rostovtzeff, *Caravan Cities*, 1932, pl. 22, fig. 1.
13 M. A. R. Colledge, *The Parthians*, 1967, pl. 35; D. Schlumberger, *L'orient hellénisé*, 1970, colour pl. opp. p. 88; Michalowski, op. cit., pl. 74.
14 Rostovtzeff, op. cit., pl. 22, figs 2, 3.
15 *Bulletin of the Cleveland Museum of Art*, 1971, 26, fig. 1; 64, no. 1.
16 E.g. D. E. L. Haynes, *Ancient Tripolitania*, 1947, pl. 26a. For comprehensive surveys of the camel in history and on the monuments of Roman North Africa see *PBSR*, 1954, 126-31, pls 17, 18; *Antiquity*, 1956, 19-21.

17 Livy XXXVII, 40, 12: *cameli quos appellant dromedas. his insidebant Arabes sagittarii.*

18 Plutarch, *Crassus* 25, 1: πολλαὶ κάμηλοι παρεστᾶσι τοξευμάτων πλήρεις, ἀφ'ὧν περιελαύνοντες οἱ πρῶτοι λαμβάνουσι. ('Many camels laden with arrows were at hand, from which [the Parthians] who first encircled [the Romans] took a fresh supply.')

19 Tacitus, *Annals* XV, 12, 2: *magna vis camelorum onusta frumenti.* Cf. Josephus, *Bellum Judaicum* IV, 7, 5 for camels captured by the Roman army from the Jews in A D 68.

20 *Ephemeris Epigraphica* VII, 456–67. For Egyptian documents relating to the requisition of camels for the Roman army in the mid-second and early third centuries see *Latomus*, 1969, 433, 434.

21 C. B. Welles, etc., *The Excavations at Dura-Europos, Final Report V* I, 1959, 28ff.

22 H. P. L'Orange and A. von Gerkan, *Der spätantike Bildschmuck des Konstantinsbogens*, 1939, pls 3a, 6b, 7a.

23 XXX, 15, 16. I have to thank Mr R. E. Walker for calling my attention to this passage.

24 DC LX, 7, 3: ἐν δὲ τῷ ἱπποδρόμῳ κάμηλοί τε ἅπαξ . . . ἠγωνίσαντο.

25 Suetonius, *Nero* 11, 1: *commisitque etiam camelorum quadrigas.*

26 SHA, *Elagabalus* 23, 1: *fertur . . . iunxisse etiam camelos quaternos ad currus.*

27 *MAAR*, 1936, pl. 42, fig. 2; XVII, 1940, pl. 31, fig. 1.

28 G. Caputo and A. Driss, *Tunisia: Ancient Mosaics*, 1962, pl. 9. There are also two camels in the background of the Triumph of Dionysus scene on a sarcophagus in the Museo Capitolino: *PBSR*, 1971, pl. 17a. Cf. p. 44 and p. 351, note 78.

29 F. W. Deichmann, *Repertorium der christlich-antiken Sarkophage* I, 1967, pl. 109, no. 690. Cf. the camels in one of the panels depicting the story of Joseph on the sixth-century ivory throne of Archbishop Maximianus at Ravenna: J. Natanson, *Early Christian Ivories*, 1953, pl. 39; and the kneeling camels in the iconography of St Menas: *PBSR*, 1949, 46 and pl. 8, fig. 1.

30 J. Wilpert, *Die Malereien der Katakomben Roms*, 1903, pl. 229; *RPGR*, 203, no. 8,

31 H. Gerstinger, *Die Wiener Genesis*, 1931, pls 12–14. Cf. pls 19, 20, 22.

32 D. Talbot Rice, etc., *The Great Palace of the Byzantine Emperors, Report 2*, 1958, pl. 45 (below); P. du Bourguet, *Early Christian Painting*, 1965, pl. 150 (in colour).

CHAPTER XII

1 Athenaeus V, 201C: καμηλοπάρδαλις μία.

2 J. P. Peters and H. Thiersch, *Painted Tombs in the Necropolis of Marissa*, 1905, pl. 8.

3 *NH VIII*, 27 (69): *nabun Aethiopes vocant collo similem equo, pedibus et cruribus bovi, camelo capite, albis maculis rutilum colorem distinguentibus, unde appellata camelopardalis, dictatoris*

Caesaris circensibus ludis primum visa Romae. ex eo subinde cernitur aspectu magis quam feritate conspicua, quare etiam ovis ferae nomen invenit.

4 XLIII, 23, 1, 2: τὸ γὰρ ζῷον τοῦτο τὰ μὲν ἄλλα καμήλος ἐστι, πλὴν καθ' ὅσον οὐκ ἐκ τοῦ ἴσου τῶν κώλων ἔχει· τὰ μὲν γὰρ ὀπίσθια αὐτοῦ χθαλαμώτερά ἐστιν. ἀρχόμενον δὲ ἀπὸ τῶν γλουτῶν

ὑψοῦται κατὰ βραχὺ ὥστ᾽ ἀναβαίνοντί ποι ἐοικέναι καὶ μετεωρισθὲν ἐπὶ πλεῖστον. τὸ μὲν ἄλλο σῶμα ἐπὶ τῶν ἐμπροσθίων σκελῶν ἐρείδει, τὸν δὲ αὐχένα ἐς ὕψος αὖ ἴδιον ἀνατείνει. τὴν δὲ δὴ χρόαν κατέστικται ὥσπερ πάρδαλις καὶ διὰ τοῦτο καὶ τὸ ὄνομα ἐπίκοινον ἀμφοτέρων φέρει.

5 *De Lingua Latina* V, 20 (100): *Alexandrea camelopardalis nuper adducta, quod erat figura ut camelus, maculis ut panthera.*

6 *Epistles* II, 1, 195, 196: *diversum confusa genus panthera camelo/sive elephas albus volgi converteret ora.* The white elephant could have been a Siamese beast among those presented to Augustus by the Indian embassy (cf. p. 70).

7 XVI, 4, 16.

8 *Abhandlungen der philosoph.-philologischen Classe der königlich-Bayerischen Akademie der Wissenschaften*, 1858, pl. 1; *RPGR*, 255, no. 6; 355, no. 5; Keller I, 284, fig. 90.

9 IX, 21, 2: καμήλους τε ᾽Ινδικὰς χρῶμα εἰκασμένας παρδάλεσιν.

10 K. Lehmann-Hartleben and E. C. Olsen, *Dionysiac Sarcophagi in Baltimore*, 1942, fig. 7.

11 DC LXXII, 10.3: ἄλλῃ ἡμέρᾳ χωρὶς αὐτὸς ταῖς ἑαυτοῦ χερσὶ κατεχρήσατο . . . καμηλοπάρδαλιν.

12 SHA, *Gordiani Tres* 33, 1: *fuerunt sub Gordiano [tertio] Romae . . . camelopardali decem.*

13 SHA, *Aurelianus* 33, 4: *processerunt . . . camelopardali.*

14 X, 27, 28.

CHAPTER XIII

1 *De Re Rustica* III, 13, 3.

2 E.g. *RPGR*, 28, no. 2; 182, no. 4.

3 E.g. a mosaic pavement found at Leicester: J. M. C. Toynbee, *Art in Roman Britain*, 1963, 197, 198, no. 183, pl. 219.

4 *Aeneid* VII, 483–502.

5 *Epigrams* XIII, 96: *hic erat ille tuo domitus, Cyparisse, capistro/an magis iste tuus, Silvia, cervus erat.*

6 J. M. C. Toynbee, *Roman Medallions*, 1944, pl. 41, no. 2.

7 W. F. Volbach, *Early Christian Art*, 1961, pl. 106.

8 G. V. Gentili, *La villa erculia di Piazza Armerina*, 1959, pl. 20.

9 Contrast the mosaic pavement from Kef, now in the Bardo Museum, Tunis, where hunting dogs are going to be released to dash at the animals, netted stags and ostriches: *Karthago*, 1951/1952, 158–63, figs. 12, 15. Cf. p. 239.

10 *JRS*, 1964, 7–14, pls 2–5 and fig. 1.

11 *De Spectaculis* 30: *concita veloces fugeret cum damma Molossos/et varia lentas necteret arte moras,/Caesaris ante pedes supplex similisque roganti/consitit, et praedam non tetigere canes.* Cf. p. 103. Contrast the famous marble group of hounds slaying a stag from the Casa dei Cervi, Herculaneum: E Kusch, *Herculaneum*, 1960, pl. 48.

12 *Epigrams* IV, 35, 1–5; 74, 1–4.

13 VIII, 17, 4: ἐλάφους δὲ ἐν ᾽Ρώμῃ λευκὰς εἶδόν τε καὶ ἰδὼν θαῦμα ἐποιησάμην, ὁπόθεν δὲ ἢ τῶν ἠπείρων οὖσαι ἢ νησιώτιδες ἐκομίσθησαν, οὐκ ἐπῆλθεν ἐρέσθαι μοι.

14 SHA, *Gordiani Tres* 3, 7.

15 SHA, *Probus* 19, 4.

16 L. Robert, *Les gladiateurs dans l'orient grec*, 1971, 191, no. 1, 191a, C. Possibly the Augustan *denarius* reverse-type of a lion devouring a stag (*CREBM* I, 1923, pl. 2, nos 15, 16) was proximately based on a *venatio* scene.

17 Jennison, 25.

18 *Epigrams* I, 104, 4: *mordent aurea quod lupata cervi.*

19 VII, 18, 12: καὶ ἡ ἱερωμένη παρθένος ὀχεῖται τελευταία τῆς πομπῆς ἐλάφων ὑπὸ τὸ ἅρμα ἐζευγμένων. Cf. the Hadrianic relief from Ephesus, now in Vienna, of Diana driving a chariot drawn by two stags (German Archaeological Institute in Rome: neg. no. 51.197); and Claudian's description of Diana driving a team of stags (*De Consulatu Stilichonis* III, 286: *cervi currum subiere iugales*).

20 K. Parlasca, *Die römischen Mosaiken in Deutschland*, 1959, pls 40, fig. 1; 41, fig. 1.

21 SHA, *Elagabalus* 28, 2: *processit in publicum et quattuor cervis iunctis.*

22 SHA, *Aurelianus* 33, 3: *fuit alius currus quattuor cervis iunctis, . . . quo, ut multi memoriae tradiderunt, Capitolium Aurelianus invectus est.*

23 E. Kusch, op. cit., pls 62, 64: Anderson, photo 25743, Napoli.

24 *Report 1*, 1947, pl. 32.

25 *Illustrated London News*, 14 December 1957, supplement, panel 11.

26 *Eclogues* VII, 59: *hic raram silvis, quibus editur, alcen.*

27 *NH* VIII, 15 (38, 39): *septentrio fert . . . alcen iuvenco similem.*

28 V, 12, 1: τούτοις ἔστιν ἀπιδεῖν μὲν ἐς τὰς ἄλκας τὸ ἐν Κελτικῇ θηρίον . . . ἄλκαι μὲν γὰρ κέρατα ἐπὶ τοῖς ὀφρῦσιν ἔχουσιν οἱ ἄρσενες, τὸ δὲ θῆλου οὐ φύει τὸ παράπαν.

29 SHA, *Gordiani Tres* 3, 7; 31, 1.

30 SHA, *Aurelianus* 33, 4.

31 R. Delbrueck, *Die Consulardiptychen*, 1929, 223–7, no. 58.

32 E.g. Jennison, caption to frontispiece.

33 Athenaeus, V, 200F.

34 VII, 4, 8: ἔστι δὲ τῶν τετραπόδων ὁ καλούμενος κόλος, μεταξὺ ἐλάφου καὶ κριοῦ τὸ

μέγεθος, λευκός, ὀξύτερος τούτων τῷ δρόμῳ.

35 Jennison, 31.

36 *NH* VIII, 79 (214).

37 ibid. X, 94 (201): *orygen perpetuo sitientia Africae generant.*

38 ibid. XI, 45 (124).

39 ibid. XI, 106 (255).

40 *De Re Rustica* IX, 1, 1.

41 *Epigrams* XIII, 95: *matutinarum non ultima praeda ferarum/saevus oryx constat quot mihi morte canum.* ('The savage oryx is not the meanest quarry among the wild beasts of the morning shows: it costs me the death of many dogs.')

42 *Epistolae* IX, 144: *ludos praetorios praeparamus, quorum ornatus peregrina animalia desiderat ut novo cultu Romana splendescat editio. addaces igitur et pygargos studio mihi opto praestari.*

43 E.g. A. Frova, *L'arte di Roma e del mondo romano*, 1961, pl. 5.

44 Gentili, op. cit., pl. 30 and fig. 5.

45 ibid., pl. 32 and fig. 5. Cf. the two *bouboloi* antelopes on the Carthage *venatio* mosaic: *Karthago*, 1952/1953, 129–53, figs 1, 6 (cf. p. 31).

46 Gentili, op. cit., pl. 28 and fig. 5.

47 *DNA* X, 23.

48 ibid. X, 25.

49 ibid. XIV, 14: here Aelian remarks on the animal's speed and the method of capturing it in a net and describes its physical characteristics.

50 ibid. XI, 9.

51 ibid. XVII, 31.

52 *NH* VIII, 79 (214).

53 *Report 1*, 1947, pl. 33.

54 *Epigrams* XIII, 99: *delicium parvo donabis dorcada nato:/iactatis solet hanc mittere turba togis.*

55 Keller I, 287, fig. 91.

56 *Cynegetica* I, 440, 441.

57 *NH* VIII, 79 (214).

58 SHA, *Gordiani Tres* 3, 8.

56 SHA, *Probus* 19, 4.

60 *Report 1*, 1947, pls 28, 38, 53.

61 R. Browning, *Justinian and Theodora*, 1971, pl. on 254.

CHAPTER XIV

1 *De Spectaculis* 23, 3: *illi* [*sc. Carpophoro*] *cessit atrox bubalus* [aurochs here] *atque vison*.

2 *NH* VIII, 15 (38): *Germania insignia tamen boum genera* [*sc. gignit*], *iubatos bisontes*.

3 *Eclogues* VII, 60–3: *vidimus et tauros quibus aut cervice levata/ deformis scapulis torus eminet aut quibus hirtae/iactantur per colla iubae, quibus aspera mento/barba iacet tremulisque rigent palearia saetis*.

4 X, 13, 1, 2.

5 *NH* VIII, 16 (40).

6 *NH* XXVIII, 45 (159): *nec uros aut bisones habuerunt Graeci in experimentis*.

7 *Hippolytus* 64: *villosi terga bisontes*.

8 *Epigrams* I, 104, 8: *turpes esseda quod trahunt visontes*.

9 LXXVI, 1, 5: βίσωντες (βοῶν τι τουτο εἶδος, βαρβαρικὸν τὸ γένος καὶ τὴν ὄψιν).

10 *Bellum Gallicum* VI, 28.

11 *NH* VIII, 15 (38).

12 See note 1, above.

13 See note 6, above.

14 *Georgics* II, 374; III, 532.

15 Athenaeus V, 201C: ὁλόλευκοι βόες Ἰνδικοὶ εἴκοσι ἕξ. There were also 8 Ethiopian oxen, undescribed: βόες Αἰθιοπικοὶ ὀκτώ. The earliest sculptural rendering of a zebu would seem to be that in the lowest register of the Apotheosis of Homer relief in the British Museum, dating from the second century B C: D. Pinkwart, *Das Relief des Archelaos von Priene*, 1965, 43, 44, pl. 1.

16 See note 3, above.

17 *Monuments Piot*, 1934, pl. 9, fig. 1. Cf. the mosaic, also from El-Djem, with sleeping arena-bulls some of which are humped: J. P. V. D. Balsdon, *Life and Leisure in Ancient Rome*, 1969, pl. 15a. A zebu

appears in relief on the fragment of the rim of a marble table-top in Budapest: A. Hekler, *Die Sammlung antiker Skulpturen*, 1929, 147, no. 143 with fig.

18 Pliny, *NH* VIII, 70 (182): *Thessalorum gentis inventum est equo iuxta quadrupedante cornu intorta cervice necare: primus id spectaculum dedit Romae Caesar dictator*.

19 *RPGR*, 297, no. 3. A Roman-age relief from Smyrna, now in the Ashmolean Museum, Oxford, showing several horsemen in pursuit of bulls, indicates the practice of the sport in the eastern provinces: Vigneron, pl. 78b.

20 Claudius: Suetonius, *Claudius* 21, 3: *exhibuit . . . praeterea Thessalos equites, qui feros boves per spatia circi agunt insiliuntque defessos et ad terram cornibus detrahunt*; Nero: DC LXI, 9, 1: ἐν δέ τινι θέᾳ ἄνδρες ταύρους ἀπὸ ἵππων, συμπαραθέοντές σφισι, κατέστρεφον.

21 *ILS* 5053: *in foro tauros, taurocentas*.

22 SHA, *Gallienus* 12, 3–4: *taurum totiens non ferire difficile est*.

23 Pliny, *NH* VIII, 7 (19).

24 *De Spectaculis* 17, 2: *hic* [*sc. elephas*] *modo qui tauro tam metuendus erat*; 19: *qui modo per totam flammis stimulatus harenam/sustulerat raptas taurus in astra pilas,/ occubuit tandem cornuto ardore petitus/dum facilem tolli sic elephanta putat*.

25 *RPGR*, 297, no. 2.

26 *De Ira* III, 43, 2: *videre solemus inter matutina arenae spectacula tauri et ursi pugnam inter se colligatorum*.

27 *RPGR*, 307, no. 2.

28 I, 48, 1; I, 60, 4; I, 104, 20.

29 R. Delbrueck, *Die Consulardiptychen*, 1929, no. 11. For a fight between lions and bulls in open country, see the mosaic from Hadrian's Villa, now in the Vatican: G. E. Rizzo, *La pittura ellenistico romana*, 1929, pl. 184; M. Wheeler, *Roman Art and Architecture*, 1964, pl. 173.

30 *NH* VIII, 70 (182): *vidimus ex imperio dimicantes et ideo demonstratos rotari, cornibus cadentes excipi, iterumque resurgere, modo iacentes ex humo tolli, bigarumque etiam cursu citato, velut aurigas, insistere.*

31 *De Spectaculis* 16: *raptus abit media quod ad aethera taurus arena . . . et nunc Alciden taurus ad astra tulit.*

32 V, 31, 1–4: *aspice quam placidis insultet turba iuvencis/et sua quam facilis pondera taurus amet./cornibus hic pendit summis, vagus ille per armos/ currit et in toto ventilat arma bove.*

33 SHA, *Gordiani Tres* 3, 7: *tauri Cypriaci centum.*

34 G. V. Gentili, *La villa erculia di Piazza Armerina*, 1959, pls 28, 29.

35 *PBSR*, 1948, 36 and pl. 11, fig. 31.

36 E.g. *RPGR*, 184, no. 2; 185, nos 1–4.

37 E.g. the mosaic in the three-apsed reception-room of the Piazza Armerina villa: B. Pace, *I mosaici di Piazza Armerina*, 1955, fig. 11.

38 *RPGR*, 12, no. 4; 14, no. 6.

39 ibid., 183, nos 1–3, 5.

40 *De Spectaculis* 5: *iunctam Pasiphaen Dictaeo credite tauro:/vidimus, accepit fabula prisca fidem./nec se miretur, Caesar, longaeva vetustas:/quidquid fama canit, praestat harena tibi.*

41 E.g. the Parabiago patera in the Soprintenza Office, Milan: W. F. Volbach, *Early Christian Art*, 1961, pl. 107; ivory diptych in the Sens Museum: Delbrueck, op. cit., no. 61.

42 M. J. Vermaseren, *Corpus Inscriptionum et Monumentorum Religionis Mithriacae* I, II, 1956, 1960, *passim*. Cf. the motif of the bull-slaying Victory in Roman public sculpture of the early second cen-

tury: e.g. D. E. Strong, *Roman Imperial Sculpture*, 1961, pl. 67: frieze in Trajan's forum.

43 K. D. White, *Roman Farming*, 1970, 276, 278–80.

44 *Britannia*, 1971, 126, 127, 138–41.

45 *MAAR*, 1955, *passim* and pl. 31, fig. 46 (Ostia mosaic).

46 J. G. Frazer, *The Fasti of Ovid*, 1929, II, 213 (Hercules); II, 197; III, 184, IV, 134 (Juno).

47 Columella, *De Rustica* VI, 24, 4: *quod maxime in operariis vaccis fieri placet.* Cf. ibid. VI, 22, 1, where Columella writes of breaking in barren cows to the plough: *aratro domandae, quoniam laboris et operis non minus quam iuvenci . . . patientes sunt.* Cf. also the relief in the Munich Museum of a peasant driving to market his cow laden with produce: White, op. cit., pl. 73.

48 ibid., 280–2.

49 J. M. C. Toynbee, *Art in Roman Britain*, 1963, 149, no. 54, pl. 60.

50 *MAH*, 1935, 115–25, fig. 1 and pls 1, 2: *La mosaique gréco-romaine*, 1965, fig. 6 after p. 286; P. A. Février, *L'art de l'Algérie antique*, 1971, pl. 83; R. Bianchi Bandinelli, *Roman Art A.D. 200–400*, 1971, pls 234, 236. For ploughing with oxen in the city-founding ritual see, for example, *CREBM* III, 1936, pl. 30, no. 7 (Trajan).

51 Pliny, *NH* XVIII, 48 (172, 173); Palladius VII, 2, 2–4; K. D. White, *Agricultural Implements of the Roman World*, 1967, 157, 158, fig. 119.

52 *De Agricultura* XXII, 3.

53 S. Aurigemma, *I mosaici di Zliten*, 1926, fig. 57.

54 F. W. Deichmann, etc., *Repertorium der christlich-antiken Sarkophage* I, 1967, 3, 4, no. 2, pl. 1: Anderson, photo 24185, Roma.

55 Février, op. cit., pl. 82.

56 Volbach, op. cit., pl. 32: Anderson, photo 83, Roma. F. Gerke, *Der*

Sarkophag des Iunius Bassus, 1936, pl. 32 shows a two-wheeled trolley, loaded with two large baskets of grapes, drawn by two oxen (AD 359).

57 T. L. Shear, 'The Roman Villa', *Corinth*, 1930, pls 3, 4, 5.

58 *CREBM* II, 1930, pls 6, nos 9, 10; 7, no. 1.

59 W. Deonna, *L'art romaine en Suisse*, 1942, pl. 59; V. von Gonzenbach, *Die römischen Mosaiken der Schweiz*, 1961, 175, no. 95, pls 49–51. A third-century sarcophagus relief shows a pair of oxen bringing home a two-wheeled cart loaded with game from the hunting field: Aymard, pl. 7 (above).

60 Gentili, op. cit., fig. 5 and pl. 30.

61 *De Consulatu Stilichonis* III, 238–332.

62 P. du Bourguet, *Early Christian Painting*, 1965, pl. 123.

63 *Bellum Gothicum* I, 26,12.

64 K. Lehmann-Hartleben, *Die Trajanssäule*, 1926, pls 24, 30.

65 C. Caprino, etc., *La Colonna di Marco Aurelio*, 1955, pl. 11, fig. 23.

66 ibid., pl. 17, fig. 35: the vehicle is largely obliterated by a window cut through the frieze.

67 ibid., pl. 56, fig. 111.

68 ibid., pls 67, fig. 133; pl. R (below).

69 ibid., pls 53, fig. 103; 70, fig. 139.

70 F. B. Florescu, *Adamklissi*, 1961, fig. 188.

71 *RPGR*, 114, no. 3.

72 ibid., 106, no. 3.

73 G. Macdonald, *Coin Types*, 1905, fig. 2.

74 *CREBM* I, 1923, pls 10, no. 20; 11, nos 1–6, 14–20; 12, no. 2; 20, no. 22. For bulls as legionary emblems, see S. Weinstock, *Divus Julius*, 1971, 119–21, pls 12; 13, nos 3–6.

75 *CREBM* II, 1930, pls 4, no. 19; 5, nos 5, 6, 7, 10.

76 ibid., pls 3, no. P; 5, nos 11, 12, 17, 18, 19.

77 White, op. cit., pl. 74.

CHAPTER XV

1 Columella, *De Re Rustica* VII, 2, 4–5.

2 Varro, *De Re Rustica* III, 12, 1.

3 SHA, *Gordiani Tres* 3, 7: *oves ferae centum*.

4 SHA, *Probus*, 19, 4: *oves ferae*.

5 Athenaeus V, 201B, C: πρόβατα Αἰθιοπικὰ ἑκατὸν τριάκοντα, Ἀράβια τριακόσια, Εὐβοικὰ εἴκοσι.

6 XVI, 4, 26; XVII, 2, 3.

7 E.g. Horace, *Odes* II, 6, 10–11; Martial, *Epigrams* V, 37, 2; VIII, 28, 1–4 (here the poet enquires of his toga whether it is made of Galaesian wool); XII, 63, 3.

8 E.g. Martial, *Epigrams* XII, 63, 1, 4: *Corduba . . . tinctis gregibus colore vivo*. Cf. VIII, 28, 5–6.

9 *De Re Rustica* VII, 3, 13: *opilio*

villicus teneros . . . agnos, dum adhuc herbae sunt expertes, lanio tradit, quoniam . . . eis submotis fructus lactis ex matribus non minor percipitur.

10 ibid. XII, 13.

11 ibid. VII, 3, 16.

12 *RE*, s.v. 'Schaf', vol. IIA, cols 396–9.

13 E.g. Faunus: Horace, *Odes* I, 4, 11–12; Silvanus: Martial, *Epigrams* X, 92, 6–7.

14 E. Strong, *La scultura romana* I, 1923, 75, fig. 49.

15 F. W. Deichmann, etc., *Repertorium der christlich-antiken Sarkophage* I, 1967, 62, 63, no. 66, pl. 21.

16 *RPGR*, 211, nos 2–6.

17 V, 371, 372.

18 E.g. Virgil, *Georgics* II, 374; *Aeneid* X, 725.

19 *Epigrams* XIII, 98: *pendentem summa capream de rupe videbis:/ caesuram speres, despicit illa canes.*
20 *Georgics* III, 398: *multi etiam excretos perhibent a matribus haedos.*
21 *CREBM* II, 1930, pls 6, no. 17; 7, no. 4.
22 *Archäologischer Anzeiger*, 1940, cols 449, 450, figs 21, 22.
23 F. Gerke, *Die christliche Sarkophage der vorkonstantinischen Zeit*, 1948, pl. 17.
24 *Report 1*, 1947, pl. 28.
25 G. E. Rizzo, *La pittura ellenistico-romano*, 1929, pl. 184; M. Wheeler, *Roman Art and Architecture*, 1964, pl. 174; R. Bianchi Bandinelli, *Roman Art to A.D. 200*, 1970, pl. 307 (detail of a goat in colour).
26 T. L. Shear, 'The Roman Villa', *Corinth*, 1930, pls 3, 6. Cf. the resting goat in an acanthus-scroll on a mosaic from Zliten: S. Aurigemma, *I mosaici di Tripolitania*, 1960, pl. 167.
27 K. D. White, *Roman Farming*, 1970, pl. 71.
28 Gerke, op. cit., pls 18; 24, figs 3, 4.

29 Photo Soprintendenza ai Monumenti di Lazio. A relief from the *Tropaeum Traiani* at Adamklissi shows a lively, if provincial, rendering of two goats reared on their hind-legs for a fight while three rams trot peacefully past them: F. B. Florescu, *Adamklissi*, 1961, fig. 187.
30 Athenaeus V, 200F: συνωρίδες τράγων ἑξήκοντα.
31 *RPGR*, 88, no. 5.
32 Girandon, photo 1440, Louvre. Cf. the goat-carriage carved on a funerary ash-chest at Aquileia: V. S. M. Scrinari, *Sculture romane di Aquileia*, 1972, pl. 317.
33 Keller I, 317, fig. 105.
34 L. Curtius, *Die Wandmalerie Pompejis*, 1929, fig. 213.
35 E.g. Horace, *Odes* I, 4, 12; III, 13, 3; III, 18, 5; Martial, *Epigrams* X, 92, 6–7.
36 *RPGR*, 9, no. 6.
37 ibid., 100, nos 4, 6.
38 F. W. Deichmann, *Frühchristliche Bauten und Mosaiken von Ravenna*, 1958, pl. 174.

CHAPTER XVI

1 DC LXXVI, 14, 3: ἵππους Ἡλίῳ ἱεροὺς τιγροειδεῖς ἐκ τῶν ἐν τῇ Ἐρυθρᾷ θαλάσσῃ νήσων, πέμψας ἑκατοντάρχους, ἐξέκλεψεν.
2 ibid. LXXVII, 6, 2: ἱππότιγριν . . φονευόμενον ἐν τῷ θεάτρῳ.
3 SHA, *Gordiani Tres* 3, 7: *equi feri triginta*; 33, 1.
4 P. A. Février, *L'art de l'Algérie antique*, 1971, pl. 80 (lower register).
5 *De Re Rustica* II, 7, 15: *equi quod alii sunt ad rem militarem idonei, alii ad vecturam, alii ad admissuram, alii ad cursuram.*
6 *Ars Mulomedicina* III, 6, 2: *nam ut viliora ministeria taceamus, equos tribus usibus vel maxime necessarios constat: proeliis circo sellis.*
7 *De Re Rustica* II, 7, 1 and 6.

8 Op. cit. III, 6, 2–4.
9 A. H. M. Jones, *The Later Roman Empire* II, 1964, 706; III, 222, note 44.
10 Vigneron, pl. 8c.
11 *Metamorphoses* XI, 20.
12 *Annals* II, 5, 3: *fessas Gallias ministrandis equis.*
13 K. Lehmann-Hartleben, *Die Trajanssäule*, 1926, pl. 30; J. M. C. Toynbee, *The Hadrianic School*, 1934, pl. 5, nos 10–15.
14 *NH* VIII, 65 (159): *ingenia eorum inenarrabilia. iaculantes obsequia experiuntur difficiles conatus corpore ipso nisuque iuvantium.* ('Their intelligence is quite extraordinary. Mounted javelin-men find them compliant in helping them in difficult attempts with the actual swaying of their bodies.')

15 D. E. Strong, *Roman Imperial Sculpture*, 1961, pl. 123.

16 E.g. *Germania Romana*² III, 1926, pls 6–9; J. M. C. Toynbee, *Art in Roman Britain*, 1963, pls 87, 92; *Art in Britain under the Romans*, 1964, pl. 47a, b.

17 Lehmann-Hartleben, op. cit., pl. 19.

18 Pp. 211–13.

19 *Aeneid* V, 545–603.

20 For a full list of the literary and epigraphical references, see *RE* XIII, cols 2059–67, s.v. 'lusus Troiae'.

21 32–44.

22 J. Keim and H. Klumbach, *Der römische Schatzfund von Straubing*, 1951, pls 1–13 (helmets), 14–18 (greaves and knee-guards). For helmets found in Roman Britain, see J. M. C. Toynbee, *Art in Roman Britain*, 1963, pls 104–10; *Art in Britain under the Romans*, 1964, 290–7, pls 65, 66, 67c, 68.

23 Keim and Klumbach, op. cit., pls 19–35.

24 J. Curle, *A Roman Frontier Post and its People: the Fort at Newstead in the Parish of Melrose*, 1911, pl. 21.

25 *Fasti Archaeologici*, 1958, no. 4636, fig. 93; R. Bianchi Bandinelli, *Roman Art A.D. 200–400*, 1971, pl. 111.

26 ibid., p. 123.

27 ibid., pls 109, 110.

28 Pp. 51–79.

29 Suetonius, *Gaius* 19, 2; *Claudius* 17, 3.

30 X, 18: *spretis . . . equis etiam Thessalicis et aliis iumentis Gallicanis . . . me phaleris aureis et fucatis ephippiis et purpureis tapetis et frenis argenteis et pictilibus balteis et tintinnabulis perargutis exornatum ipse residens . . . affatur.*

31 Caprino, etc., op. cit., pl. E.

32 E.g. Plautus, *Asinaria* 708; Livy II, 6, 8; 20, 2, etc.

33 Vigneron, pls 10b, d; 11–13.

34 Apuleius, *Metamorphoses* VIII, 1; Horace, *Satires* I, 6, 103; II, 8, 72.

35 *De Re Rustica* VI, 30, 1: *nec minus quotidie corpora pecudum quam hominum defricanda sunt ac saepe plus prodest pressa manu subegisse terga.*

36 *De Agricultura* 14, 2; for military stabling see Appendix, Chapter III.

37 *Ars Mulomedicina* I, 56, 3–5; Varro, *De Re Rustica* II, 7. 10.

38 Vigneron, pl. 6a; L. Leschi, *Algérie antique*, 1952, 85.

39 Vigneron, pl. 6b.

40 E.g. ibid., pl. 38b; R. Bianchi Bandinelli, *Roman Art to A.D. 200*, 1970, pls 349, 350. For equestrian figures of emperors in *adventus* scenes on coins and medallions, see e.g. J. M. C. Toynbee, *Roman Medallions*, 1944, pls 17, no. 11; 18, nos 1–9.

41 Vigneron, pl. 36b; J. J. Deiss, *Herculaneum*, 1966, pls on 146, 147.

42 Vigneron, pls 16b, c.

43 *Fasti Archaeologici* IV, 1951, no. 3344, fig. 53; J. M. C. Toynbee, *The Art of the Romans*, 1965, 48; 167, note 17; 248, pl. 30. An imposing life-size bronze statue of a horse, whose reins show that it once had a rider, was found in 1861 at Neuvy-en-Sallias, near Orléans, and is now in the Orléans Museum. Its base is inscribed *Aug[usto] Rudiobo sacrum*, so it was a votive offering to a Celtic god (*Antiquaries Journal*, 1963, 266, 267, pl. 40a).

44 Ammianus Marcellinus XV, 1, 2: *equorum permutatione veloci ut nimietate cogendi quosdam extingueret praecursorius index Mediolanum advenit.*

45 Apuleius, *Metamorphoses* I, 2, 24: *equo . . . admodum fesso . . . desilio, equi sudorem a fronte curiose exfrico, aures remulceo, frenos detraho . . . quod est mihi summe praecipuum, equo . . . faenum atque hordeum acceptis istis nummulis tu, Fotis* [the host's servingmaid], *emito.*

46 G. V. Gentili, *La villa erculia di*

Piazza Armerina, 1959, fig. 5; pl. 30. Cf. Aymard, pl. 27b: mosaic from Lepcis Magna showing a single mounted huntsman with a shield fleeing from a lion and Février, op. cit., pl. 79: mosaic in the Algiers Museum showing a single mounted huntsman with a shield confronting a leopard.

47 Aymard, pl. 19.

48 Arrian, *Cynegetica* 19, 20.

49 *Epigrams* I, 49, 25: *leporemque forti callidum rumpes equo.*

50 ibid. XII, 14: *parcius utaris moneo rapiente veredo,/Prisce, nec in lepores tam violentus eas./. . . quid te frena iuvant temeraria? saepius illis,/Prisce, datum est equitem rumpere quam leporem.*

51 Gentili, op. cit., fig. 4; pls 17, 21.

52 *PBSR*, 1948, pl. 8, fig. 22.

53 ibid., pl. 8, fig. 23.

54 Aymard, pls 20a, 25b, 33b. Cf. also a sarcophagus relief in the Philippeville Museum: Leschi, op. cit., 69.

55 Vigneron, pl. 39a: Leschi, op. cit., p. 149.

56 W. von Massov, *Die Grabmäler von Neumagen*, 1932, pl. 33.

57 F. Chapouthier, *Les Dioscures au service d'une déesse*, 1935.

58 G. I. Kazarov, *Die Denkmäler des thrakischen Rittergottes in Bulgarien*, 1938; D. Krandžalov, 'Les reliefs du cavalier thrace', *Latomus*, 1971, 1057–72, pls 16–39. Cf. also the familiar Gaulish Rider-god mounted on a column.

59 Gentili, op. cit., fig. 12; pls 51, 53.

60 E. Hiller, *Bellerophon: ein griechischer Mythos in der römischen Kunst*, 1970.

61 *Africa Italiana*, 1933, 18, fig. 10; 23, fig. 13.

62 ibid., 19, fig. 11.

63 *Oudheidkundige Mededelingen uit het Rijksmuseum van Oudheiden te Leiden*, 1962, 73; pl. 23, fig. 1.

64 *De Re Rustica* II, 8, 5: *hisce [sc. mulis] binis coniunctis omnia vehicula in viis ducuntur.*

65 Suetonius, *Augustus* 94, 6: *Super laureatum currum bis senis equis candore eximio trahentibus.* For the use of white horses in Roman triumphs, see S. Weinstock, *Divus Julius*, 1971, 68–75.

66 Suetonius, *Nero* 24, 2: *aurigavit . . . Olympiis vero etiam decemiugem.*

67 The renderings in art of mythological *quadrigae* driven by Jupiter and Sol are too familiar to need specifying here.

68 D. E. Strong, *Roman Imperial Sculpture*, 1961, pls 59, 93, 117.

69 E.g. *CREBM* I, 1923, pls 13, nos 3–6; 15, nos 6–8; 24, nos 10, 13; 25, no. 3; J. M. C. Toynbee, *Roman Medallions*, 1944, pls 14, nos 3–7; 42, no. 1; 45, nos 3, 4.

70 Deiss, op. cit., pl. on p. 145; Anderson photos nos 24546, 24549, Venezia.

71 Vigneron, pl. 64.

72 F. S. Maffei, *Museo Veronese*, 1749, pl. 141, no. 6. A small sarcophagus in the cloister of the Museo Nazionale Romano (inv. no. 65199) shows two four-wheeled carriages each containing a family of three and drawn by a pair of spanking horses.

73 XII, 24.

74 *Odes* III, 27, 7; *Epodes* 4, 14.

75 *Amores* II, 16, 49: *rapientibus esseda mannis.*

76 See note 129, below.

77 Cf. *Museum Helveticum*, 1971, 124, 125; cf. also *Journal des Savants*, 1967, 5–42.

78 *Ashmolean Museum: Report of the Visitors*, 1967, pl. 6b.

79 By, for example, Vigneron, op. cit., 190–23, and by H. A. Harris, *Sport in Greece and Rome*, 1972, 201, 202, 210–12.

80 *Halieuticon* 69, 70: *nonne vides*

victor quanto sublimius altum/adtollat caput et vulgi se venditat aurae.

81 IV, 987–9: *quippe videbis equos fortis, cum membra iacebunt/in somnis sudare tamen spirareque semper/et quasi de palma summas contendere vires.*

82 *PBSR*, 1948, 24–37, pls 1–11.

83 E.g. *CIL* VI, 2, 8628, 10047, 10048, 10050, 10052, 10053, 10056, 10069, 10080.

84 A. Audollont, *Defixionum Tabellae*, 1904. Cf. *PBSR*, 1948, pl. 1, fig. 1 (a lead tablet from Beirut).

85 SHA, *Verus* 6, 3, 4.

86 *Epigrams* VII, 7, 10; XII, 36, 12.

87 ibid. XI, 1, 16.

88 *Gaius* 55, 3.

89 DC LXXIV, 4.

90 See note 86, above.

91 DC LXIX, 10, 2; *CIL* XII, no. 1122.

92 Lists of names of racehorses, including names additional to those given in *PBSR*, 1948, 26–33, will be found in *Boletin de la real Academia de la Historia*, 1962, 257–351; J. W. Salomonson, *La mosaique aux chevaux de l'antiquarium de Carthage*, 1965, 81–9.

93 *PBSR*, 1948, 30, 31, pl. 2, fig. 4.

94 ibid., pl. 1, fig. 2.

95 S. Aurigemma, *Le Terme di Diocletiano e il Museo Nazionale Romano* (*Itinerari dei Musei e Monumenti d'Italia*, 78, 1958), 38, no. 82 (124705). The four horse names are 'Italus', 'Euticu[s]', 'Myrsi[s]', 'Anatolichus'.

96 *PBSR*, 1948, pl. 3, fig. 5.

97 Photo Theodor Strübin, Liestal.

98 *Illustrated London News*, 24 December 1955, 1103; O *Arqueólogo Português*, 1962, 335–6, pls 21–6; H.

99 *Epistolae* IV, 58, 60; VII, 48.

100 *Boletin del Seminario de Estudios de Arte y Arqueologia*, 1963, 29–31, pl. between 32 and 33.

101 *PBSR*, 1948, pl. 3, fig. 6.

102 ibid., pl. 5, fig. 10.

103 *Mosaiques de Tunisie*, 1910,

1914, no. 124 with pl.

104 ibid., no. 126, with pl.

105 Vigneron, pl. 9a.

106 Salomonson, op. cit.

107 ibid., 95, fig. 10; 97, 98; pl. 46, fig. 1.

108 ibid., 98, fig. 17; 102; pl. 43, fig. 1.

109 ibid., 55–7, 91.

110 ibid., pl. 64, fig. 5. For the names of racehorses on other mosaics in Africa, Spain and Portugal, Italy and Syria, see ibid., 81, 82, note 1, A–D.

111 ibid., 82, note 2.

112 *Athenischer Mitteilungen*, 1880, pl. 16.

113 *PBSR*, 1948, 30.

114 ibid., pl. 2, fig. 3; Martial, *Epigrams* IV, 67, 5; V, 25, 10; X, 53, 1; X, 74, 5; XI, 1, 16.

115 Salomonson, op. cit., 82, 83, note 3.

116 *PBSR*, 1948, pl. 6, figs 14, 15.

117 ibid., 32, 33, pl. 6, figs 12, 13.

118 ibid., pl. 5, fig. 11.

119 ibid., pl. 7. fig. 20.

120 *Pro Sestio* 59, 126: *non modo gladiatores sed equi ipsi gladiatorum repentinis sibilis extimescebant.*

121 *Gaius* 35, 3; *Claudius* 21, 5.

122 L. Robert, *Les gladiateurs dans l'orient grec*, 1971, 65, 67.

123 C. Daremberg and E. Saglio, *Dictionnaire des antiquités grecques et romaines*, 1877, s.v. *bestiae mansuetae*, 697, fig. 837.

124 LXVI, 25, 2.

125 *Report 1*, 1947, pl. 30; P. du Bourguet, *Early Christian Painting*, 1965, pl. 145.

126 S. Aurigemma, *I mosaici di Zliten*, 1926, fig. 57.

127 Vigneron, pl. 71.

128 *Metamorphoses* IX, 11–13.

129 VIII, 66, 67: *trito ducunt epiraedia collo/segnipedes dignique molam versare nepotes.*

130 *De Re Rustica* VI, 37, 1.

131 *Anthologia Graeca* IX, 19, 20, 21.

132 Ovid, *Metamorphoses* XII, 88–9: *non haec, quam cernis, equinis/fulva iubis cassis*; Vegetius, *De Re Militari* IV, 9: *equorum tamen saetae de caudis ac iubis ad ballistas utiles adseruntur.*

133 E.g. Tacitus, *Histories* IV, 60: *absumptis . . . equis . . . , quae profana foedaque in usum necessitas vertit; Annals* II, 24: *miles . . . fame absumptus nisi quos corpora equorum . . . toleraverant.*

134 *De Rustica* II, 8, 1; 6: *ex equa enim et asino fit mulus: contra ex equo et asina hinnus . . . hinnus . . . est ex equo et asina, minor quam mulus corpore.*

135 Suetonius, *Galba* 4, 2: *cum mula pepererit.*

136 *NH* VIII, 69, 70 (171–4): *ex asino et equa mula gignitur . . . animal viribus in labores eximium . . . equo et asina genitos mares hinnulos antiqui vocabant, contraque mulos, quos asini et equae generarent . . . generantur ex equa et onagris mansuefactis mulae veloces in cursu, duritia eximia pedum, verum strigoso corpore, indomito animo.*

137 Livy V, 25, 9: *honoremque . . . ferunt matronis ut . . . carpentis festo profestoque uterentur.* Cf. XXXIV, 3.

138 Tacitus, *Annals* III, 64.

139 *CREBM* I, 1923, cxxxv, 130, 131, nos 76–8, pl. 23, nos 18, 19.

140 Suetonius, *Gaius* 15, 1: *matri circenses carpentumque quo in pompa traduceretur.*

141 *CREBM* I, 1923, cxlvii, clix, 159, nos 81–7, pl. 30, nos 4–6. Memorial coins featuring a *carpentum* drawn by a pair of mules were also struck for Domitilla, Julia, daughter of Titus, Marciana and Faustina I: ibid. II, 1930, pls 51, nos 8, 9; 80, nos 3, 9; III, 1936, pl. 21, nos 7, 8; IV, 1940, pl. 8, no. 10.

142 Suetonius, *Claudius* 17, 3: *currum eius Messalina uxor carpento secuta est.*

143 Tacitus, *Annals* XII, 42: *carpento Capitolium ingredi.*

144 *CREBM* III, 1936, xlix, 21, 22, nos 119–21, pl. 6, nos 2, 3.

145 M. Rostovtzeff, *The Social and Economic History of the Roman Empire*, 1926, pl. 54, fig. 1.

146 Vigneron, pl. 67a; M. Pobé and J. Roubier, *The Art of Roman Gaul*, 1961, pl. 208.

147 E. Espérandieu, *Receuil général des bas-reliefs, etc. de la Gaule romaine* IV, 1911, 282, no. 3245; Vigneron, pl. 53a. Another side of this block shows two mules walking rightwards and attached to a chain held by a man behind them.

148 Espérandieu, op. cit., 275, 276, no. 3232; Vigneron, pl. 62a.

149 W. von Massow, *Die Grabmäler von Neumagen*, 1932, no. 181, 141, 142, fig. 91, pl. 24.

150 H. Dragendorff and E. Krüger, *Das Grabmal von Igel*, 1924, pl. 12, fig. 1; Vigneron, pl. 54a.

151 Dragendorff and Krüger, op. cit., pl. 12, fig. 2.

152 S. Ferri, *Arte romana sul Danubio*, 1933, 97, fig. 80; Vigneron, pl. 65a.

153 M. E. Mariën, *L'art en Belgique: la sculpture de l'époque romaine*, 1945, pl. 28.

154 ibid., pl. 31.

155 Photo Clément Dessart.

156 *Trierer Zeitschrift*, 1932, pl. 15, fig. 1; H. Schoppa, *Die Kunst der Römerzeit in Gallien, Germanien, und Britannien*, 1957, pl. 60; Vigneron, pl. 55a. (Milestone not shown by Schoppa and Vigneron.)

157 Mariën, op. cit., pl. 30.

158 G. Becatti, *Scavi di Ostia* IV, 1961, pls 107, 108.

159 *Epigrams* V, 22, 7, 8: *vixque datur longas mulorum rumpere mandras/ quaeque trahi multo marmora fune vides.*

160 *Nero* 30, 3: *nunquam minus mille carrucis fecisse iter traditur, soleis mularum argenteis.*

161 *Satires* I, 5, 13: *dum aes exigitur,*

dum mula ligatur, tota abit hora. ('It takes a whole hour to collect the fares and get the mule tied to the boat.')

162 ~XVIII, 27, 5.

163 *Carmina Minora* XVIII (LI).

164 Lehmann-Hartleben, op. cit., pls 22, 24, 30, 31, 50.

165 C. Caprino, etc., *La colonna di Marco Aurelio*, 1955, pls 11, fig. 23 and A; 17, fig. 35; 19, fig. 38; figs 48, 49; 56, fig. 112 and R.

166 Rostovtzeff, op. cit., pl. 54, fig. 3.

167 Cf. Livy VII, 14, 7: *mulis strata detrahi iubet.*

168 Vigneron, pl. 56b; Lehmann-Hartleben, op. cit., pl. 11.

169 *Clitellae dicuntur . . . eae quibus sarcinae conligatae mulis portantur.* Columella states that the male mule is better than the female as a pack-animal (*De Re Rustica* VI, 37, 11: *clitellis aptior mulus*).

170 Vigneron, pl. 56c; Lehmann-Hartleben, op. cit., pl. 64.

171 *Satires* I, 5, 47: *hinc muli Capuae clitellas tempore ponunt.*

172 *Epistles* II, 2, 72: *festinat calidus mulis gerulisque redemptor.*

173 Dragendorff and Krüger, op. cit., pl. 9, fig. 4.

174 E.g. Plautus, *Mostellaria* 780, 781: *nam muliones mulos clitellarios habent.*

175 A. Maiuri, *La peinture romaine*, 1953, colour plate on p. 141.

176 Aymard, pl. 7 (below).

177 ibid., pl. 5 (above); Vigneron, pl. 58b.

178 *Epistles* I, 18, 46: *onerata plagis iumenta*; I, 6, 58–61: *referret/emptum mulus aprum.*

179 *Report* 2, 1958, pls 45 (above) and B.

180 E.g. Livy X, 40, 8 (293 BC); XXV, 36, 7 (212 BC); Caesar, *Bellum Gallicum* VII, 45, 2; *Bellum Civile* I, 81, 7.

181 *Gaius* 43: *ut praetorianae co-*

hortes contra morem iumentis signa imponere . . . cogerentur.

182 Lehmann-Hartleben, op. cit., pls 24, 50; Vigneron, pls 58a, 69a.

183 Photo L. Lefèbvre.

184 Lehmann-Hartleben, op. cit., pl. 8.

185 Suetonius, *Gaius* 39,1.

186 Virgil's location of the wild ass in Italy (*Georgics* III, 409) is, of course, poetic licence.

187 Février, op. cit., pl. 80 (upper register).

188 R. Ghirshman, *Iran: Parthians and Sassanians*, 1962, pl. 62.

189 XXIII, 4, 7: *asini feri cum venatibus agitantur, ita eminus lapides post terga calcitrando emittunt, ut perforent pectora sequentium aut perfractis ossibus capita ipsa displodant.*

190 Arrian, *Cynegetica* 24, 3: τοῖς ὄνοις τοῖς ἀγρίοις . . . βρόχον περιβάλλοντες; Aelian, *DNA* XIV, 10: περιβάλλουσιν αὐτοῖς βρόχον περὶ τὴν δέρην.

191 Varro, *De Re Rustica* II, 6, 3: *in Phrygia et Lycaonia sunt greges multi*; Pliny, *NH* VIII, 69 (174): *sed generator onagro et asina genitus omnes antcellit. onagri in Phrygia et Lycaonia praecipui.*

192 Cf. note 136, above; Varro, loc. cit.: *ad seminationem onagrus idoneus quod et e fero fit mansuetus*; Columella, *De Re Rustica* VI, 37, 3: *mula . . . onagro et equa generatur.*

193 Athenaeus V, 200F: συνωρίδες δ' ὄνων ἀγρίων.

194 Cicero, *Ad Atticum* VI, 1, 25: *nec deerant onagri.*

195 *Epigrams* XIII, 100: *pulcher adest onager.*

196 DC LXXVI, 1,5.

197 SHA, *Gordiani Tres* 3, 7: *onagri triginta*; 33, 1: *onagri viginti.*

198 *NH* VIII, 69 (174): *pullis eorum, ceu praestantibus sapore, Africa gloriatur, quos lalisiones appellet.* Cf. Martial, *Epigrams* XIII, 97.

199 *NH* XVII, 3 (41).

200 *De Re Rustica* III, 17, 6: *ego enim uno servilo, hordeo non multo, aqua domestica meos multinummos alo asinos.*

201 *De Re Rustica* VII, 1.

202 Varro, *De Re Rustica* II, 6, 5, adds Campania as one of the regions in which donkeys plough.

203 *Georgics* I, 273–5: *saepe oleo tardi costas agitator aselli/vilibus aut onerat pomis, lapidumque revertens/ incusum aut atrae massam picis urbe reportat.*

204 *Amores* II, 7, 15, 16: *aspice, ut auritus miserandae sortis asellus/assiduo domitus verbere lentus eat.*

205 *Poenulus* 684; *Pseudolus* 136.

206 *Metamorphoses* VII, 3: *extremae sortis quadripes . . . dolendus atque miserandus.*

207 E.g. ibid. IV, 3–5; VI, 29–31; VII, 17–20.

208 Columella, *De Re Rustica* VII, 1; Varro, *De Re Rustica* II, 1, 14; 6, 1; Pliny, *NH* VIII, 68 (167).

209 Columella, *De Re Rustica* II, 14, 4; X, 81; XI, 3, 12.

210 *NH* VIII, 68 (167).

211 *De Agricultura* 10, 11.

212 *De Re Rustica* II, 6, 5: *greges fiunt fere mercatorum, ut eorum qui e Brundisio aut Apulia asellis dossuariis* [pack-asses] *comportant ad mare oleum aut vinum itemque frumentum aut quid aliut.*

213 *Satires* I, 9, 20, 21: *demitto auriculas ut iniquae mentis asellus,/cum gravius dorso subiit onus.*

214 VII, 17.

215 IX, 32, 33. Trimalchio had on his sideboard the figure of a donkey in Corinthian bronze with two panniers (*bisaccium*), holding black olives on one side, white on the other: Petronius, *Satyricon* 31.

216 X, 1.

217 *Report 1*, pl. 30; du Bourguet, op. cit., pl. 147.

218 *Anthologia Graeca* IX, 301. But on the feast of Vesta (9 June) the mill-donkeys were decked with loaves and garlands and given a week's holiday: Ovid, *Fasti* VI, 311, 347, 348.

219 E. Nash, *A Pictorial Dictionary of Ancient Rome* II, 1962, 330, fig. 1097.

220 G. Calza, *La necropoli del porto di Roma nell'Isola Sacra*, 1940, 255, fig. 154.

221 H. B. Walters, *Catalogue of the Greek and Roman Lamps in the British Museum*, 1914, 105, nos 688, 689, figs 122, 123.

222 *NH* XVIII, 72 (296).

223 *Fasti Archaeologici*, 1960, pl. 31, figs 93, 94; K. D. White, *Agricultural Implements of the Roman World*, 1967, 157, 158, fig. 118, pls 13–16. Rostovtzeff (op. cit., pl. 29, fig. 4) had already suggested that the Arlon fragment might represent a reaping-machine, but thought that the vehicle would have been drawn by a team of oxen.

224 *Metamorphoses* X, 16, 17.

225 ibid. XI, 8.

226 Varro, *De Re Rustica* II, 11, 1.

227 Pliny *NH* XI, 96 (237).

228 Juvenal VI, 468, 469. Cf. Pliny, *NH* XI, 96 (238).

229 Apuleius, *Metamorphoses* VII, 22.

230 G. Caputo and A. Driss, *Tunisia: Ancient Mosaics*, 1962, pl. 13.

231 A. Ferrua, *Le pitture della nuova catacomba di Via Latina*, 1960, pls 26, 104.

232 W. F. Volbach, *Early Christian Art*, 1961, pl. 250 (wrongly captioned as the 'Flight into Egypt').

233 W. Dorigo, *Late Roman Painting* 1971, fig. 211; id., *Kyriakon: Festschrift Johannes Quastin*, 1970, pl. 5.

234 *Antiquité classique*, 1950, 103–12. For Epona as a funerary goddess, see *Ogam*, 1965, 333–6.

235 For an inventory of the Epona monuments, with a bibliography and

many illustrations, see R. Magnen and É. Thevenot, *Épona*, 1953.

236 VIII, 156, 157: *iurat [sc. Lateranus]/solam Eponam et facies olida ad praesepia pictas.*

237 *Metamorphoses* III, 27: *respicio pilae mediae, quae stabuli trabes sustinebat, in ipso fere meditullio Eponae deae simulacrum residens aediculae, quod accurate corollis roseis equidem recentibus fuerat ornatum.*

238 Chapouthier, op. cit., 317, fig. 63; Vigneron, pl. 66e.

239 *Apology* 16, 5: *vos tamen non negabitis et iumenta omnia et totos cantherios cum sua Epona coli a vobis.* Cf. *Ad Nationes* I, 11: *sane vos totos asinos colitis et cum sua Epona.*

240 *Octavius* 28, 7: *vos et totos asinos in stabulis cum vestra vel sua Epona consecratis.*

241 Magnen and Thevenot, op. cit., pl. 17.

242 ibid., pl. 12. The inscription reads: *dea[e] Epon[a]e Satigenus Solemni[s] fil[ius] V[otum Solvit Libens].*

243 ibid., pls 7, 8, 9. For the foal, cf. pls 33–9.

244 ibid., pl. 16.

245 ibid., pls 30, 31.

246 ibid., pl. 47.

247 ibid., pl. 11.

248 ibid., pls 43, 44.

249 ibid., pls 60, 61.

250 ibid., pl. 62.

CHAPTER XVII

1 *De Re Rustica* III, 3, 2.

2 ibid. III, 12, 1–6.

3 *RPGR*, 362, no. 4.

4 Cf. Horace, *Satires* II, 4, 44: *fecunda lepus.*

5 *Eclogues* VII, 58. Cf. Pliny, *NH* VIII, 81 (217) on Alpine hares that are white in winter and turn reddish when the snow melts: *in Alpibus candidi [sc. lepores] qui . . . liquiscente ea [sc. nive] rutilescunt annis omnibus.*

6 Ovid, *Fasti* V, 371, 372.

7 *Georgics* I, 308: *auritosque sequi lepores.*

8 Hinks, 145, 146, no. 57f, fig. 164.

9 R. Bianchi Bandinelli, *Roman Art A.D. 200–400*, 1971, 248, pl. 230. Cf. the group of a huntsman on foot urging on two hounds to seize a hare on the peristyle mosaic of the great palace of the Byzantine emperors at Istanbul: *Report 1*, 1947, pl. 28.

10 Bianchi Bandinelli, op. cit., 245, pl. 227.

11 H. Stern, *Le calendrier de 345*, 1953, pl. 11, fig. 1.

12 F. Gerke, *Der Sarkophag des Iunius Bassus*, 1936, pl. 33.

13 E.g. G. M. A. Hanfmann, *The Season Sarcophagus in Dumbarton Oaks* II, 1951, pls 28, 69, 75, 75a.

14 *RPGR*, 411, no. 9.

15 Martial, *Epigrams* XIII, 92: *inter quadrupides mattea prima lepus.*

16 *RPGR*, 263, no. 7.

17 ibid., 325, nos 6, 7.

18 *Archaeological Journal*, 1946 (1947), 55, pl. 9a; J. M. C. Toynbee, *Art in Britain under the Romans*, 1964, 201, pl. 48b.

19 J. Collingwood Bruce, *Lapidarium Septentrionale*, 1875, 104, no. 196 with fig. The inscription reads: *D[is] M[anibus] Anicio Ingenuo medico ord[inario]/coh[ortis]I Tungr[orum] vix[it] an[nos] XXV.*

20 *Report 1*, 1947, pl. 28.

21 Alinari, photo 6354, Roma.

22 S. Aurigemma, *I mosaici di Tripolitania*, 1960, pl. 64.

23 *RPGR*, 364, no. 11. Cf. a mosaic panel from Zliten in Tripoli-

tania: Aurigemma, op. cit., pl. 128.
24 H. G. Beyen, *Über Stilleben aus Pompeji und Herculaneum*, 1928, pl. 11.
25 F. W, Volbach, *Early Christian Art*, 1961, pls 232-4.
26 *De Re Rustica* III, 12, 6: *tertii generis* [*sc. leporum*] *est quod in Hispania nascitur similis nostro lepori ex quadam parte, sed humile, quem cuniculum appellant.*
27 *Epigrams* XIII, 60: *gaudet in effossis habitare cuniculus antris;/monstravit tacitas hostibus ille vias.*
28 XXXVII, 18.
29 J. M. C. Toynbee, *The Hadrianic School*, 1934, pl. 4, nos 10-23. Cf. the marble group in the British Museum of 'Hispania' reclining and a small boy standing before her and helping her to support on her knee a wicker basket on top of which a rabbit crouches: ibid., pl. 27, fig. 1.
30 III, 2, 6.
31 *NH* VIII, 81 (217, 218).
32 ibid., 43 (104): *Marcus Varro auctor est a cuniculis subfossum in Hispania oppidum.*
33 E. Pfuhl, *Malerei und Zeichnung der Griechen* II, 1923, 862, 863; III, pl. 313, fig. 702a; G. E. Rizzo, *La*

pittura ellenistico-romana, 1929, pl. 153 (above).
34 *Eburacum*, 1962, 100b, pl. 34.
35 E. and J. H. Blanchet, *Catalogue des bronzes antiques de la Bibliothèque Nationale*, 1895, 488, no. 1215 with fig.
36 H. B. Walters, *Catalogue of Bronzes, Greek, Roman, and Etruscan, in the British Museum*, 1899, 254, 255, nos 1858-71. No. 1857 holds a Satyr mask.
37 Aurigemma, op. cit., pl. 165.
38 H. Schoppa, *Die Kunst der Römerzeit in Gallien, Germanien und Britannien*, 1957, pl. 109.
39 Petronius, *Satyricon* 31: *glires melle ac papavere sparsos.*
40 XXVIII, 4, 13: *adpositi . . . glires, quorum magnitudo saepius praedicta.*
41 *Epigrams* III, 58, 36: *somniculosos ille porrigit glires.*
42 ibid. V, 37, 8. Cf. Pliny, *NH* VIII, 82 (224): *nitellis quies est hieme* (i.e. they hibernate).
43 *Epigrams* XIII, 59: *tota mihi dormitur hiems et pinguior illo/tempore sum quo me nil nisi somnus alit.*
44 *De Re Rustica* III, 15.
45 *NH* XVI, 7 (18).
46 See note 21, above.

CHAPTER XVIII

1 *NH* IX, 15 (41): *educat* [*sc. vitulus*] *mammis fetum*; IX, 7 (21): *nutriunt* [*sc. delphini*] *uberibus, sicut balaena*; XI, 95 (235): *balaenae autem vitulique marini mammis nutriunt fetus.*
2 *DNA* V, 4: ἡ φώκαινα ὅμοιον δελφῖνι ζῷόν ἐστι, ἔχει δὲ γάλα καὶ αὐτή. Aelian states that the porpoise frequents the Pontus and seldom strays beyond it.
3 ibid. X, 8.
4 *Halieutica* I, 648, 660-3.
5 ibid., 686-8.

6 *Georgics* IV, 432: *sternunt se somno diversae in litore phocae.*
7 *NH* IX, 6 (19): *vituli marini, quos vocant phocas, spirant ac dormiunt in terra.*
8 ibid., 15 (41): *ipsis* [*sc. vitulis*] *in somno mugitus unde nomen vituli.*
9 III, 238: *eripient somnum . . . vitulisque marinis.*
10 *NH* IX, 15 (41): *accipiunt disciplinam, vocemque pariter ac nutu* [?] *populum salutant, incondito fremitu nomine vocati respondent.*

11 Suetonius, *Augustus* 90.

12 *NH* II, 56 (146).

13 *NH* IX, 7 (23): *rostrum simum, qua de causa nomen Simonis omnes miro modo agnoscunt maluntque ita appellari.*

14 Pliny, *NH* IX, 8 (24): *delphinus non homini tantum amicum animal, verum et musicae arti, mulcetur symphoniae cantu sed praecipue hydrauli sono. hominem non expavescit ut alienum. obviam navigiis venit, alludit exultans, certat etiam et quamvis plena praeterit vela.*

15 ibid., 9, 10 (29–33).

16 *DNA* II, 8.

17 *NH* IX, 8 (25).

18 *NH* IX, 8 (26); Younger Pliny, *Epistolae* IX, 33.

19 E.g. H. Dembeck, *Willingly to School: How Animals are Taught*, 1970, 207, 212–19.

20 G. V. Gentili, *La villa erculia di Piazza Armerina*, 1959, fig. 9; *La villa imperiale di Piazza Armerina*, 1960, 71, fig. 24.

21 *RPGR*, 178, no. 5.

22 ibid., 178, no. 6.

23 ibid., 172, no. 3.

24 S. Aurigemma, *I mosaici di Tripolitania*, 1960, pls 87, 88.

25 B. Cunliffe, *Fishbourne: a Roman Palace and its Garden*, 1971, colour plate I.

26 C. Robert, *Die antike Sarko-*

phagreliefs II, 1890, pl. 1a. For Cupids fishing from dolphin-back, see D. Levi, *Antioch Mosaic Pavements*, 1947, II, pl. 41.

27 *RPGR*, 81, no. 1.

28 ibid., 80, no. 9; 81, nos 4, 6.

29 J. M. C. Toynbee and J. B. Ward-Perkins, *The Shrine of St Peter and the Vatican Excavations*, 1956, pl. 29.

30 E.g. N. Glueck, *Deities and Dolphins*, 1965, pls 1, 11.

31 *NH* IX, 7 (20): *velocissimum omnium animalium, non solum marinorum, est delphinus.*

32 X, 14: *balaena Britannica.*

33 *NH* IX, 2: *plurima autem et maxima animalia in Indico mari, e quibus balaence quaternoum iugerum, pistres ducenorum cubitorum* (the *iuger*= *c.* ⅔ acre, the cubit = 1½ feet!); 3 (8): *maximum animal in Indico mari pistris et balaena est.*

34 ibid.: [*maximum animal*] *in Gallico oceano physeter, ingentis columnae modo se attollens, altiorque navium velis diluviem quandam eructans.*

35 *Mosella* 144: *talis Atlantiaco quondam balaena profundo.*

36 *NH* IX, 5 (12): *balaenae et in nostra maria penetrant.*

37 DC LXXV, 16, 5.

38 Pliny, *NH* IX, 5 (14, 15).

39 *History* VII, 29, 9–16.

CHAPTER XIX

1 *De Re Rustica* III, 5, 12.

2 ibid. III, 17, 2..

3 *NH* IX, 80 (170). *Murena* is sometimes translated, inaccurately, as 'lamprey'.

4 ibid., 79 (168).

5 ibid., 80 (170); Varro, *De Re Rustica* III, 17, 9.

6 *De Re Rustica* III, 16, 1; 17. According to Pliny (*NH* XVIII, 2 (7)

some early imperial *piscinae* were over two *iugera* in extent.

7 *Ad Atticum* I, 19, 6; I, 20, 3.

8 *Epistolae* 90, 7.

9 *Epigrams* X, 30, 16–21.

10 ibid., 22–4.

11 *Ad Atticum* II, 1, 7.

12 *De Re Rustica* III, 17, 5.

13 At the Puteoli market we may visualize wicker baskets piled with

fish, as shown on a mosaic from Zliten in Tripolitania: S. Aurigemma, *I mosaici di Tripolitania*, 1960, pl. 172.

14 *De Re Rustica* III, 17, 3; *NH* IX, 81 (171).

15 *DSA* VIII, 4.

16 *Saturnalia* III, 15, 4.

17 *NH* IX, 81 (172).

18 ibid., 39 (77); Seneca, *De Clementia* I, 18, 2; *De Ira* III, 40, 2; DC LIV, 23, 1.

19 Pliny, *NH* IX, 78 (167).

20 ibid. XXXII, 7 (16).

21 ibid. X, 89 (193).

22 Martial, *Epigrams* IV, 30, 3–7.

23 IV, 39 ff.

24 *Epigrams* XIII, 81: *quamvis lata gerat patella rhombum,/rhombus latior est tamen patella.*

25 ibid., 91: *ad Palatinas acipensem mittite mensas.*

26 ibid., 88: *principium cenae gobius esse solet.*

27 ibid., 84: *hic scarus . . . visceribus bonus est, cetera vile sapit.*

28 Martial, *Epigrams* XIII, 102; Pliny, *NH* XXXI, 43 (94).

29 *Mosella* 75–149.

30 J. M. C. Toynbee, *Death and Burial in the Roman World*, 1971, pl. 65.

31 *Antioch Mosaic Pavements*, 1947, I, 597, 598.

32 G. V. Gentili, *La villa erculia di Piazza Armerina*, 1959, fig. 6, pls 38, 39.

33 G. Becatti, *Scavi di Ostia IV*, 1961, pls 164, 165.

34 G. C. Picard, *L'art romain*, 1962, pl. 30.

36 Levi, op. cit. II, pls 6, 62a.

36 Pernice, pl. 53; G. Gullini, *I mosaici di Palestrina*, 1956, pl. 7, fig. 1; Alinari, photo 12053, Napoli.

37 Keller II, fig. 124; V. Spinazzola, *Le arti decorative in Pompei e nel Museo Nazionale di Napoli*, 1928, pl. 182; Gullini, op. cit., pl. 7, fig. 2; Pernice, pl. 54, fig. 1.

38 Aristotle, *Historia Animalium* VIII, 2, 590B; Pliny, *NH* IX, 88 (185); Aelian, *DNA* I, 32; 'Oppian', *Halieutica* II, 253–320. Cf. *AJA*, 1970, 191, 192.

39 Gullini, op. cit., pls 2, 8–12.

40 Keller II, fig. 147; Victoria and Albert Museum colour postcard.

41 *Africa Italiana*, 1929, 99–101, figs 31, 32; Aurigemma, op. cit., 41, 42, pls 66, 67.

42 F. Staehelin, *Die Schweiz in römischer Zeit*[3], 1948, 402, fig. 89; V. von Gonzenbuch, *Die römischen Mosaiken der Schweiz*, 1961, pl. 17.

43 *Proceedings of the Somersetshire Archaeological and Natural History Society*, 1952, 91–112, pls 7–9.

44 For renderings of the very varied types of sea-fish and other sea-creatures on North African mosaics, see Aurigemma, op. cit., pls 126, 128, 135 (lateral panels of the Zliten Seasons pavement): 136–40 (internal panels of the Zliten gladiators pavement).

45 *NH* IX, 82 (173).

46 *De Re Rustica* III, 14.

47 *Epigrams* IV, 46, 11.

48 Aurigemma, op. cit., pl. 165; *I mosaici di Zliten*, 1926, 211, 219, pl. E and fig. 136.

CHAPTER XX

1 E.g. Ovid, *Metamorphoses* XV, 375; Pliny, *NH* XXXII, 42 (122).

2 *De Divinatione* I, 9, 15.

3 *Satires* I, 5, 14, 15: *ranaeque palustres/avertunt somnos.*

4 E.g. Pliny, *NH* XXVIII, 29 (117); Juvenal III, 44, 45: *ranarum viscera numquam/inspexi.*

5 G. Moretti, *Ara Pacis Augustae*, 1948, pls 11, 13.

6 *NH* XXXVI, 4 (42).

7 British Museum: Keller II, fig. 116; Avenches: F. Staehelin, *Die Sweiz in römischer Zeit³*, 1948, 554, 555, figs 165, 166; Great St Bernard: ibid., 556, fig. 167.

8 ibid., 549, 550, figs 160, 161.

9 Pliny, *NH* XXXVII, 4 (10).

10 *Richborough v*, 1968, 101, nos

183-5, pl. 44; *Verulamium i*, 1972, 122, 123, no. 65, fig. 34.

11 *Bulletin Pro Aventico*, 1967, 93-8, figs 1-7.

12 *Jahrbuch für Antike und Christentum*, 1968/1969, 83-93, pls 11c, 12a, c.

13 *De Re Rustica*, 2, 26.

14 *NH* VIII, 48 (110).

15 ibid. XXXII, 18 (50).

CHAPTER XXI

1 *The Tebtunis Papyri*, 33; A. S. Hunt and C. C. Edgar, *Select Papyri* II, 1934, no. 416.

2 XVII, 1, 38.

3 *DSA* 976B.

4 *DNA* VIII, 4 (ii).

5 XVII, 1, 44.

6 DC LV, 10, 8.

7 SHA, *Antoninus Pius* 10, 9.

8 SHA, *Elagabalus* 28, 3.

9 *Epistolae* IX, 141: *prae ceteris autem, quae Romana spectacula desiderant, crocodillos functio theatralis efflagitat.*

10 ibid. IX, 151: *praetoria donum novum deo iuvante expectat, in qua me crocodillos . . . civibus exhibere. . . .*

11 ibid. VI, 43: *crocodillos theatrali spectaculo publicatos in praesentiam vestram servare temptavimus. sed perseverante inedia, quae illos per dies quinquaginta producta macerabat, secundis ludis congressionum more confecti sunt. duos etiam nunc spirantes in vestrum differimus adventum, licet eos cibi abstinentia longum vivere posse non spondeat.*

12 J. P. Peters and H. Tiersch, *Painted Tombs in the Necropolis of Marissa*, 1905, pl. 12.

13 G. Gullini, *I mosaici di Palestrina*, 1956, pl. 13.

14 E.g. *RPGR*, 161, no. 5; 162, no. 1; 375, nos 1, 2; 377, no. 1; G. E. Rizzo, *La pittura ellenistico–romana*, 1929, pl. 187a; S. Aurigemma, *The*

Baths of Diocletian and the Museo Nazionale Romano, 1947, pls 10, 11; id., *I mosaici di Tripolitania*, 1960, pl. 71; *Scavi di Ostia IV*, 1961, pls 114-18.

15 Unpublished?

16 *CREBM* I, 1923, pls 15, no. 19; 16, nos 1-3 (eastern issues); H. Mattingly, *Roman Coins²*, 1960, pl. 48, no. 3 (Nîmes issues); *Scavi di Ostia IV*, 1961, pl. 122 (Ostia mosaic).

17 *Georgics* IV, 13: *picti squalentia terga lacerti.*

18 34-5: September . . ./captivam filo gaudens religasse lacertam/quae suspensa manu mobile ludit opus ('plays at being actively at work').

19 *NH* XXXIV, 19 (70): *fecit [sc. Praxiteles] et puberem Apollinem subrepenti lacertae comminus sagitta insidiantem quem sauroctonon vocant.*

20 *Epigrams* XIV, 172: *ad te reptanti, puer insidiose, lacertae/parce: cupit digitis illa perire tuis.*

21 W. Amelung, *Die Sculpturen des vaticanischen Museums* I, 3 1903, 495, no. 279.

22 *CIL* VI, 12059.

23 ibid., 24885.

24 ibid., 29417.

25 *NH* XXXII, 14 (32).

26 II, 19, 7: Ἑρμῆς ἐς λύρας ποίησιν χελώνην ἠρκώς.

27 VIII, 30, 6.

28 J. M. C. Toynbee, *Art in Roman Britain*, 1963, pl. 31.

29 ibid., pl. 236.

30 VIII, 54, 7.

31 *Saturae Menippeae*, ed. Riese, 1865, 205, no. iv (3): *in testudineo lecto.*

32 II, 56, 2.

33 II, 737, 738: *pars secreta domus ebore et testudine cultos/tres habuit thalamos.*

34 *Georgics* II, 463: *varios inhiant pulchra testudine postes.*

35 X, 120, 121: *et subfixa manu foribus testudinis Indae/terga sedent crebro maculas disticta zmaragdo.*

36 *De Beneficiis* VII, 9, 2.

37 VI, 80, 81.

38 SHA, *Clodius Albinus* 5, 6, 7.

39 Quintus Curtius Rufus, *Historia Alexandri* IX, 8, 2.

40 Strabo XV, 1, 73.

41 E.g. F. B. Florescu, *Die Trajanssäule*, 1969, pl. 57.

42 *De Divinatione* II, 64, 133.

43 Loc. cit., note 36, above.

44 E. Diehl, *Inscriptiones Latinae Christianae Veteres*, I, 1925, no. 2389a.

45 *Patrologia Latina* XXV, col. 929: *testudo tardigrada et onerata, immo oppressa pondere suo . . . haereticorum gravissima peccata significans.*

46 G. Brusin and P. L. Zovatto, *Monumenti paleocristiani di Aquileia e di Grado*, 1957, 45, fig. 13 (north hall); 75, fig. 31 (south hall).

47 III, 36, 3–7; 37, 1–9.

48 *DNA* XVI, 39.

49 Strabo XV, 1, 73.

50 *Augustus* 43, 4.

51 *Tiberius* 72, 2.

52 *De Ira* II, 31, 6.

53 *Epigrams* VII, 87, 7.

54 *NH* XXIX, 22 (72). Cf. Pausanias II, 28, 1 on the yellowish colour and tameness of the Aesculapian snake.

55 *NH* X, 96 (208).

56 *DNA* XVII, 5.

57 SHA, *Elagabalus* 28, 3.

58 ibid., 23, 2.

59 *Aeneid* VII, 750–5.

60 IX, 619–838.

61 G. M. A. Richter, *Archaic Greek Art*, 1949, fig. 153.

62 *Aeneid*, V, 84–96.

63 III, 457, 458.

64 Alinari, photo 121371, Pompeii; A. Maiuri, *Pompeii*, 1956, 140, fig. 53. For these *lararia* in general, see *MAAR*, 1937.

65 Alinari photo 12190, Napoli; *RPGR*, 102, no. 7. Cf. Persius I, 113: *pinge duos angues.*

66 *MAAR*, 1937, pl. 15.

67 Alinari, photo 9232, Museo Nazionali Napoli; *RPGR*, 117, no. 2.

68 A. Ferrua, *Le pitture della nuova catacomba di Via Latina*, 1960, pl. 102.

69 E.g. J. M. C. Toynbee, *Roman Medallions*, 1944, pl. 26, nos 1, 2; F. Gnecchi, *I medaglioni romani* 1912, II, pl. 69, no. 2.

70 M. Rostovtzeff, *The Social and Economic History of the Roman Empire*, 1926, pl. 12, fig. 1.

71 Toynbee, op. cit., pl. 15, nos 5, 6; Gnecchi, op. cit., pls 57, no. 10; 58, no. 1.

72 F. Cumont, *Les religions orientales dans le paganisme romain*, 1929, pl. 11, fig. 3.

73 M. J. Vermaseren, *Corpus Inscriptionum et Monumentorum Religionis Mithriacae* I, 1956, figs 85, 153, etc.

74 ibid., fig. 190.

75 ibid., figs 102, 106, etc.

76 M. Rostovtzeff, ed., *The Excavations at Dura Europos: Preliminary Report on the Seventh and Eighth Seasons of Work, 1933–35*, 1939, 'The Mithraeum', pls 14, fig. 1; 15.

77 E.g. the relief in the Vatican of an Isiac procession: E. Strong, *La scultura romana* II, 1926, pl. 44; statue from North Africa: Cumont, op. cit., pl. 5, fig. 3.

78 ibid., pl. 6 (central fig.).

79 Keller II, fig. 105.

80 E. A. Sydenham, *The Roman Republican Coinage*, 1952, 193, nos 1197, 1198, pl. 29.

81 Propertius IV, 8, 3-14; Aelian, *DNA* XI, 16.

82 *DNA* XI, 2.

83 Lucian XXXII, *Alexander or the False Prophet*.

84 V. Canarache, *Tezaurul de Sculp-*

turi de la Tomis, 1963, pls 55-7; O. Doppelfeld, ed., *Römer in Rumänien*, 1969, 202, no. F45, pl. 62.

85 F. H. Marshall, *Catalogue of Greek, Etruscan, and Roman Jewellery in the British Museum*, 1911, pls 62, no. 2774; 63, no. 2787; 65, no. 2815; R. A. Higgins, *Greek and Roman Jewellery*, 1961, pls 61 D, E.

CHAPTER XXII

1 *NH* X, 1 (1, 2).

2 Cf. Tenney Frank, *An Economic Survey of Ancient Rome* IV, 1938, 55.

3 *NH* XI, 56 (155).

4 DS II, 50, 3-6; Xenophon, *Anabasis* I, 5, 3.

5 *In Eutropium* II, 310-16.

6 *De Dipsadibus* 2, 6, 7.

7 Athenaeus V, 200F: στρουθῶν συνωρίδες ὀκτώ.

8 *Persa* 198, 199: *vola curriculo* ['run, fly']/*istuc marinus passer per circum solet.*

9 Hinks, 119, 120, no. 45, fig. 137.

10 G. V. Gentili, *La villa erculia di Piazza Armerina*, 1959, fig. 5 and pl. 26. Apropos of one of the reliefs on an ostrich-feather fan from Tutankhamun's tomb, shown in the British Museum in 1972, it is suggested, in the Exhibition Catalogue, no. 23, that the scene showing two men each bearing on his shoulders one of the two birds that the king has shot is unlikely to be realistic, since an Egyptian ostrich is said to weigh about 345 lb. If the birds on the Roman mosaic were of the same breed, that scene, too, would have to be regarded as non-factual.

11 *Epistolae* 133 (*Patrologia Graeca* LXV, LXVI, cols 1521, 1524): στρουθοὺς μεγάλας ἀπὸ τῶν ἐν εἰρήνῃ κυνηγεσίων εἴχομεν. ἀλλ᾽ οὐκ ἦν αὐτὰς στέλλειν ἐπὶ θάλασσαν διὰ τῶν ὅπλων τῶν πολεμίων . . . ἐκπέμψομεν ἂν εἰς ἑτέραν ναῦν . . . τὰς στρουθούς.

12 *Mosaiques d'Algérie*, 1911, 70, no. 298.

13 M. Yacoub, *Musée du Bardo*, 1970, inv. no. 2757, fig. 96; inv. no. 2816.

14 B. Pace, *I mosaici di Piazza Armerina*, 1955, figs 12, 34.

15 *RPGR*, 259, no. 1; 274, no. 7.

16 *Karthago*, 1951/1952, 157-65, figs 12-15.

17 *Illustrated London News*, 29 January 1955, 184, fig. 11.

18 ibid., 185, fig. 21.

19 SHA, *Elagabalus* 22, 1 (10 camels were another prize); 28, 4; 30, 2.

20 SHA, *Firmus* 4, 2.

21 *DNA* XIV, 7.

22 Catullus, 66, 54; Pausanias IX, 31, 1.

23 *Cynegeticus* III, 482-503, especially 490, 491.

24 SHA, *Firmus* 6, 2.

25 *Tusculanae Disputationes* II, 10, 24.

26 *Aeneid* IX, 564.

27 E. Strong, *La scultura romana* I, 1923, 85, fig. 57.

28 G. Lippold, *Die Sculpturen des vaticanischen Museums* III, i, 1936, pl. 40, no. 550.

29 *Archäologischer Anzeiger*, 1938, cols 738, 741, 742, fig. 51.

30 J. M. C. Toynbee, *Art in Roman Britain*, 1963, 150, no. 60, pl. 61.

31 Strong, op. cit. II, 1926, 206, fig. 121.

32 F. Eichler and E. Kris, *Die Kameen im Kunsthistorischen Museum, Wien*, 1927, no. 4, pl. 2.

33 Tacitus, *Annals* II, 17, 2.

34 *Germania Romana*² III, 1926, ʼpl. 5, fig. 3.

35 I. S. Ryberg, *Panel Reliefs of Marcus Aurelius*, 1967, figs 27, 30a (*aquila*); 27, 37a (*signa*).

36 G. C. Picard, *L'art romain*, 1962, pl. 10.

37 Strong, op. cit. I, 1923, 115, fig. 74.

38 ibid. II, 1926, 246, fig. 151. Cf. the two eagles flying heavenward that accompany the *quadriga* which carries up the soul of Julian (?) from the pyre on the British Museum ivory diptych: p. 46 and p. 351, note 89.

39 W. Altmann, *Die römischen Grabaltäre der Kaiserzeit*, 1905, pl. 1. Cf. ibid., figs 40, 62, 64, 74, 75.

40 Strong, op. cit. I, 1923, 130, fig. 83.

41 E.g. J. M. C. Toynbee, *Death and Burial in the Roman World*, 1971, 165 (Igel Monument, near Trier: relief); 173 (Ennii Monument, Celeia: relief); 224 (Hypogeum of the Three Brothers, Palmyra: ceiling painting); 279 (Cologne: limestone group).

42 *Report 2*, 1947, pl. 36; J. M. C. Toynbee, *The Art of the Romans*, 1965, pl. 83.

43 *RPGR*, 362, fig. 4.

44 *DNA* VI, 29.

45 Pliny, *NH* X, 30 (58–60); Plutarch, *DSA* 967C; Aelian, *DNA* III, 13.

46 Cicero, *De Natura Deorum* II, 125; Martial, *Epigrams* XIII, 75; Plutarch, loc. cit.; Aelian, loc. cit.

47 *De Bello Gildonico* I, 475–8.

48 IV, 181, 182.

49 *Epodes* II, 35, 36: *advenam laqueo gruem/ . . . captat.*

50 *NH* XI, 44 (122); X, 69 (135).

51 *NH* X, 30 (60): *mansuefactae lasciviunt, gyrosque quosdam in decoro cursu vel singulae peragunt.*

52 DC LXVI, 25, 1.

53 Horace, *Satires* II, 8, 86, 87; Statius, *Silvae* IV, 6, 9; Aulus Gellius VI, 16, 5: he quotes Marcus Varro as his authority and describes the birds as *Melicae = Medicae*, Median.

54 *NH* X, 30 (60).

55 Varro, *De Re Rustica* III, 2, 14.

56 E.g. mosaic from Zliten: S. Aurigemma, *I mosaici di Tripolitania*, 1960, pl. 134. Cf. Pliny, *NH* X, 30 (58).

57 A. M. Schneider, *The Church of the Multiplication of Loaves and Fishes*, 1937, pl. 15; J. W. Crowfoot, *Early Churches in Palestine*, 1941, pl. 13. Cf. note 83, below.

58 Vize (Archaeological Museum, Istanbul): *Archäologischer Anzeiger*, 1941, cols 165, 166, figs 29, 30; Boscoreale (Louvre): *Monuments Piot*, 1899, pls 11, 12.

59 P. M. Duval, *Les inscriptions antiques de Paris*, 1960, 23, 24, pl. 6A.

60 E. Espérandieu, *Receuil général des bas-reliefs, etc., de la Gaule romaine* VI, 1915, no. 4929 with fig.

61 *DNA* III, 23.

62 Petronius, *Satyricon* 55: *ciconia etiam, grata peregrina hospita/pietaticultrix graciliores crotalistria/avis exul hiemis, titulus tepidi temporis.*

63 E. A. Sydenham, *The Roman Republican Coinage*, 1952, 122, nos 750, 751, pl. 21; 190, nos 1171–4.

64 *CREBM* III, 1936, 473, nos 1531–5; 484, no. 1667; pls 88, no. 10; 90, no. 14; *Jahrbuch für Antike und Christentum* II, 1959, pl. 8, figs c, d.

65 F. van der Meer and C. Mohrmann, *Atlas of the Early Christian World*, 1958, 41, fig. 45.

66 Juvenal XIV, 74, 75; Seneca, *Epistolae* 108, 29.

67 *NH* X, 31 (62).

68 *Satires* II, 2, 49, 50.

69 *NH* X, 79 (164).

70 A. Maiuri, *La peinture romaine*, 1953, colour plate on p. 129; cf. ibid., colour plate on p. 125 for another painted heron at Pompeii (Reg. II, Ins. 6, No. 3).

71 Keller II, 205, fig. 74.

72 Schneider, op. cit., pls A, B, 3, 4, 6, 11, 12; Crowfoot, op. cit., pls 12, 13. Cf. note 83, below. For pairs of herons killing snakes, carved in low relief on the exterior walls of a much restored and worked over marble *aedicula* in the Galleria Lapidaria of the Vatican, see W. Amelung, *Die Sculpturen des vaticanischen Museums* I, 2, 1903, 232–4, pl. 25, nos 91, 91a.

73 *NH* VIII, 41 (97); X, 68 (134). Cf. Strabo XVII, 1, 40.

74 XV, 2, 3: *Aegyptos . . ./pavet saturam serpentibus ibin.*

75 *CREBM* III, 1936, pls 62, nos 15–18; 94, nos 4, 7.

76 Pernice, pl. 68, fig. 2.

77 Op. cit., 61, pl. 10.

78 XI, 139.

79 Pliny, *NH* X, 68 (133); Seneca, *Epistolae* 110, 12; Suetonius, *Vitellius* 13, 2; Martial, *Epigrams* XIII, 71: *dat mihi penna rubens nomen, sed lingua gulosis/nostra sapit* ('I get my name from my red feathers, but it's my tongue that gluttons relish.')

80 *Epigrams* III, 58, 14.

81 Suetonius, *Gaius* 22, 3; 57, 4.

82 M. P. Gauckler, *Catalogue du Musée Alaoui*, Supplément I, 1910, 22, pl. 15, fig. 1.

83 Aurigemma, op. cit., pls 27, 28, 32. For a general view of the whole pavement, see pls 19, 20. Pls 29, 30 show a lively rendering of a crane, pl. 33 shows one of a heron. For another heron on the same mosaic, see *Archaeologia*, 1953, pl. 5b.

84 *NH* X, 63 (129).

85 IX, 388B–D.

86 *DNA* III, 42.

87 *NH* X, 69 (135); 64 (130).

88 *NH* X, 66 (131): *Gallia hos septentrionali proxima oceano mittit.*

89 *Epigrams* XI, 21, 10: *turpe Ravennatis guttur onocrotali.*

90 *Historia Animalium* VIII, 12, 597B: τὸ Ἰνδικὸν ὄρνειον, ἡ ψιττακή, τὸ λεγόμενον ἀνθρωπόγλωττον . . . ἀκολαστότερον δὲ γίνεται, ὅταν πίῃ οἶνον. A second-century B C mosaic pavement from a private house in the Athenian Agora shows, in each of four corners of a square, a pair of parrots perched on the lip of a wine cup: *Hesperia*, 1966, pls 18a, b.

91 *DNA* XVI, 2; 15.

92 ibid. XIII, 18.

93 F. Jacoby, *Fragmenta Historicorum Graecorum* II b, 1929, 709, no. 9.

94 Athenaeus V, 201B: εἶτ᾽ ἐφέροντο ἐν ἀγγείοις ψιττακοί.

95 Pausanias II, 28, 1: παρὰ δὲ Ἰνδῶν μόνων ἄλλα τε κομίζεται καὶ ὄρνιθες οἱ ψιττακοί; Solinus 52, 43–45: *sola India mittit avem psittacum.*

96 *NH* X, 58 (117): *India hanc avem mittit.*

97 *NH* VI, 35 (184): *insulam Gaugadem esse in medio eo tractu . . . inde primum visas aves psittacos.*

98 See note 96, above.

99 See note 95, above.

100 *Florida* 12.

101 *NH* X, 96 (207): *amici . . . turtures et psittaci.*

102 *De Re Rustica* III, 9, 17: *in ornatibus publicis solent poni cum psittacis.*

103 Persius, *Choliambi* 8; *psittaco suum chaere*; *Poetae Latini Minores* LXI (*De Philomela*), 31, 32: *psittacus . . . suo domino chaere sonat vel ave*; Martial, *Epigrams* XIV, 73: *hoc dedici per me dicere 'Caesar have'.*

104 *Amores* II, 6.

105 *tu poteras fragiles pennis habetare smaragdos/tincta gerens rubro punica rostra croco./non fuit in terris vocum*

simulatior ales/reddebas blaeso tam bene
verba sono./ . . . garrulus . . ./plenus
eras minimo: nec prae sermonis amore/in
multos poterant ora vacare cibos.
106 Silvae II, 4.
107 SHA, Elagabalus 20, 6: exhibuit
. . . magides . . . refertas capitibus
psittacorum: 21, 2: psittacis leones
pavit.
108 Altertümer von Pergamon V, 1,
61, pl. 15.
109 JRS, 1949, pls 3, 4.
110 Keller II, fig. 19 (in colour). Cf.
the bright green parrot with red
neck-band and beak on the Justinianic church mosaic at Sabratha:
Aurigemma, op. cit., pl. 25.
111 Hinks, 26, no. 48; 28, fig. 28.
112 F. Wirth, Römische Wandmal-
erei, 1934, pls 24, 34.
113 P. du Bourguet, Early Christian
Painting, 1965, pl. 28.
114 Mosaiques de Tunisie, 1914, pl.
71.
115 ibid., pl. 71d (in colour).
116 E. H. Warmington, Commerce
between the Roman Empire and India,
1928, 143 and pl. opp.
117 E.g. A. de Ridder, Les bronzes
antiques du Louvre I, 1913, nos 995,
996, pl. 60; E. Babelon and J. A.
Blanchet, Catalogue des bronzes antiques de la Bibliothèque Nationale, 1895,
no. 1258 with fig.
118 For a list of examples, see RE
XVIII, 3, 1949, cols 933, 934.
119 D. Levi, Antioch Mosaic Pavements, 1947, II, pls 85c, d; 137d.
120 DNA XVI, 2: γίνονται δὲ
ταῶς ἐν Ἰνδοῖς τῶν πανταχόθεν
μέγιστοι.
121 Athenaeus V, 101B: εἶτ᾽
ἐφέροντο ἐν ἀγγείοις . . . ταοί.
122 Varro, Saturae Menippeae XIII
(18), ed. A. Riese, 1865, 142: ubi
graves pascantur atque alantur pavonum
greges.
123 Varro, De Re Rustica III, 6.
124 De Re Rustica VIII, 11.

125 See note 101, above.
126 SHA, Alexander Severus 41, 7.
127 See note 123, above.
128 Ad Familiares IX, 18, 3 (46 BC).
129 Suetonius, Vitellius 13, 2.
130 I, 143: crudus pavonem in balnea
portas.
131 Epigrams XIII, 70: miraris quo-
tiens gemmantes explicat alas,/et potes
hanc saevo tradere, dure, coco.
132 ibid. XIV, 67: lambere quae
turpes prohibet muscas/alitis eximiae
cauda superba fuit.
133 Suetonius, Gaius 22, 3.
134 Metamorphoses I, 722, 723:
excipit hos [sc. Argus' eyes] volucrisque
suae Saturnia pennis/collocat et gemmis
caudam stellantibus implet; XV, 385:
Iunonis volucrem, quae cauda sidera
portat. Cf. Martial, Epigrams III, 58,
13: gemmei pavones (on Faustinus'
farm at Baiae).
135 See note 123, above.
136 CGCBM: Ionia, 1892, pls 36,
nos 11, 13; 37, no. 5.
137 II, 17, 6: χρυσοῦ δὲ καὶ λίθων
λαμπόντων Ἀδριανὸς βασιλεὺς
ταὼν ἀνέθηκεν.
138 CREBM III, 1936, 438; IV,
1940, pl. 33, no. 9; F. Gnecchi, I
medaglioni romani, 1912, II, pls 42, no.
3; 45, no. 9; III, pls 144, no. 10; 148,
no. 12.
139 CREBM II, 1930, pls 47, no.
11; 61, nos 4, 5. 10; 67, nos 17, 18, 19.
140 Silvae III, 4, 18.
141 CREBM III, 1936, 357.
142 Gnecchi, op. cit. II, pl. 69, no.
10; III, pl. 151, no. 7.
143 ibid. II, pl. 67, no. 7.
144 J. M. C. Toynbee, Roman
Medallions, 1944, pl. 29, no. 8.
145 CREBM IV, 1940, pls 8, no. 7;
10, nos 9–12; 67, no. 20; 68, no. 1;
86, no. 10; p. 653, no. 1570; pl.8 6,
no. 11; V, 1950, pl. 85, no. 5; p.
589; VI, 1962, pl. 37, nos 127, 132,
135.
146 Vatican postcard ser. VI, no. 3.

147 P. Gusman, *L'art décoratif de Rome* I, 1910, pl. 8.

148 Du Bourguet, op. cit., pl. 60.

149 A. Ferrua, *Le pitture della nuova catacomba di Via Latina*, 1960, pl. 101.

150 *Journal of the British Archaeological Association*, 1961, pl. 13, fig. 2.

151 E.g. M. Lawrence, *The Sarcophagi of Ravenna*, 1945, figs 4, 5, 6, 11, 13, 21, 42, 54, 56, 65, 69.

152 G. Brusin and P. L. Zovatto, *Monumenti paleocristiani di Aquileia e di Grado*, 1957, pl. 8. Cf. two roughly contemporary profile peacocks just below the Nilotic scene on the pavement of the north transept of the Tabgha church: Crowfoot, op. cit., pl .12.

153 F. W. Volbach, *Early Christian Art*, 1961, pl. 226.

154 Aurigemma, op. cit., pls 20, 24.

155 ibid., pls 19, 20, 23.

156 *Mosaiques de Tunisie*, 1914, pl. 449.

157 Aquileia Museum, postcard.

158 *Transactions of the Leicestershire Archaeological Society*, 1904-5, 6 with pl. opp.

159 Athenaeus V, 201B: ἐφέροντο ἐν ἀγγείοις . . . μελεαγρίδες.

160 XIV, 655.

161 *De Re Rustica* III, 9, 18. Cf. Petronius, *Satyricon* 93: *Afrae volucres placent palato*.

162 *De Re Rustica* VIII, 2, 2.

163 *NH* X, 38 (74); 67 (132).

164 *Epigrams* III, 58, 15.

165 *Silvae* I, 6, 78 (cf. Horace, *Epodes* 2, 53: *non Afra avis descendat in ventrum meum* ('the guineafowl shan't descend into my stomach'); II, 4, 28.

166 *Gaius* 22, 3.

167 Aurigemma, op. cit., pl. 22.

168 Athenaeus V, 201B: ἐφέροντο ἐν ἀγγείοις . . . φασιανοὶ ὄρνιθες.

169 XIV, 654C.

170 SHA, *Alexander Severus* 41, 7.

171 See note 166, above.

172 *De Re Rustica* VIII, 8, 10: *qui Ponticum Phasim . . . eluant* ('clear of birds').

173 *NH* X, 67 (132).

174 *Silvae* I, 6, 77: pheasants as presents for the people at the Saturnalia.

175 *Epigrams* III, 58, 16: pheasants on Faustinus' Baian farm. Cf. Petronius, *Satyricon* 93: *ales Phasiacis petita Colchis . . . placet palato.*

176 SHA, *Elagabalus* 32, 4: *una die nonnisi de fasianis totum ederet omnesque missus sola fasianorum carne strueret.*

177 ibid., 21, 2: *fasianis leones pavit.*

178 SHA, *Pertinax* 12, 6: *fasianum numquam privato convivio comedit aut alicui misit.*

179 SHA, *Alexander Severus* 37, 6.

180 SHA, *Tacitus* 11, 5: *fasianum avem nisi suo et suorum natali et diebus festissimis non posuit.*

181 Ammianus Marcellinus XVI, 5, 3: *fasianum . . . exigi vetuit et inferri.*

182 M. P. Gauckler, *Catalogue du Musée Alaoui*, supplement I, 1910, 22, no. 268; Keller II, 145, fig. 38.

183 Aurigemma, op. cit., pls 24, 25. Cf. the fine pheasant on one of the vault-mosaics in Santa Costanza in Rome: H. P. L'Orange and P. J. Nordhagen, *Mosaics*, 1966, pl. 43.

184 XV, i, 74: πέρδικά τε μείζω γυπός.

185 Pliny, *NH* XI, 112 (268); XXII, 30 (65); SHA, *Alexander Severus* 41, 5.

186 Statius, *Silvae* II, 4, 20: *quique refert iungens iterata vocabula perdix* ('the partridge which pronounces and joins together the words that it has learnt to repeat').

187 Hinks, 145, 146, no. 57e, fig. 163; Keller II, 157, fig. 45.

188 H. Stern, *Le calendrier de 354*, 1953, pl. 42, fig. 1; *Mosaiques de Tunisie*, 1910, 251-2, no. 752.

189 *NH* X, 68 (133).

190 Horace, *Epodes* 2, 53, 54: *non . . . descendat in ventrum meum attagen*

Ionicus ('the Ionian francolin shan't descend into my stomach'); Martial, *Epigrams* XIII, 61: *inter sapores fertur alitum primus/Ionicarum gustus attagenarum* ('of all the flavours of birds the most tasty is said to be that of the francolin'). The 'painted partridges' (*picta perdix*) that his friend Faustinus kept were doubtless eaten: *Epigrams* III, 58, 15.

191 Keller II, 159, fig. 45b.

192 *NH* X, 29 (56).

193 Suetonius, *Gaius* 22, 3: *hostiae erant . . . tetraones.*

194 *NH* XI, 112 (268): *aliis [sc.* birds] *in pugna vox, ut coturnicibus.*

195 *Wandgemälde der Städte Campaniens*, 1868, 380, no. 1535: Naples Museum.

196 *NH* X, 33 (65, 66).

197 *De Re Rustica* III, 5, 2: *pingues veneunt care ut . . . coturnices* ('fattened birds such as quails fetch high prices').

198 *NH* X, 33 (69): *coturnicibus veneni semen gratissimus cibus, quam ob causam eas damnavere mensae.*

199 *Captivi* 1002, 1003: *pueris . . . coturnices dantur, quicum lusitent*; *Asinaria* 666: *dic mihi igitur tuum . . . coturnicem.*

200 Aurigemma, op. cit., pls 19, 20.

201 ibid., pl. 31 shows two of them.

202 Lucilius, ed. F. Marx, I, 1904, 22, 300, 301: *gallinaceus cum victor se gallus honeste/altius in digitos primoresque erigit ungues.*

203 Columella, *De Re Rustica* VIII, 2, 5: *rixosarum avium lanistae, cuius plerumque totum patrimonium, pignus aleae, victor gallinaceus pyctes abstulit.* Cf. Varro, *De Re Rustica* III, 9, 5 on cocks that were good fighters – *in certamine pugnaces.*

204 Keller, II, 132, fig. 34.

205 P. Ducati, *Pittura etrusca-italo-greca e romana*, 1942, pl. 103.

206 Varro, loc. cit., 2; *gallinae villaticae sunt, quas deinceps rure habent in villis*; Columella, loc. cit., 2 and 4:

cohortalis est avis quae vulgo per omnes fere villas conspicitur . . . villatici generis non spernendus est reditus.

207 Varro, loc. cit., 6 calls them *pulchri et ad proeliandum inter se maxime idonei*; Columella, loc. cit., 4 and 12, who adds Rhodes, says that they possess *procera* [tall] *corpora et animos ad proelia pertinaces* and *corporum speciem* (beauty).

208 Varro, loc. cit., 1; *capiant magnes fructus, ut maxime factitaverunt Deliaci*; Columella, loc. cit., 4: *praecipue celebravere Deliaci.*

209 Varro, *De Re Rustica* III, 9; Columella, *De Re Rustica* VIII, 2–7.

210 *De Agricultura* 89.

211 *NH* X, 74 (147).

212 Loc. cit., 14: *pumiles aves, nisi quem humilitas earum delectat, nec propter fecunditatem nec propter alium reditum nimium probo.*

213 Columella, *De Re Rustica* VIII, 12.

214 Varro, loc. cit., 16.

215 Juvenal 13, 233: *Laribus cristam promittere galli.*

216 E.g. stone reliefs at Cirencester (Corinium) and Gloucester (Glevum): J. M. C. Toynbee, *Art in Britain under the Romans*, 1964, pls 40a, b.

217 Birmingham Museum and Art Gallery, postcard.

218 G. V. Gentili, *La villa erculia di Piazza Armerina*, 1959, pl. 42.

219 Aurigemma, op. cit., pls 19, 34, 29, 30.

220 *NH* X, 52 (104–9).

221 Varro, *De Re Rustica* III, 7, 8; Columella, *De Re Rustica* VIII, 8, 9.

222 *NH* X, 52 (110): *et harum amore insaniunt multi; super tecta exaedificant turres his, nobilitatemque singularum et origines narrant.*

223 Plautus, *Miles Gloriosus* 162; Juvenal 3, 201, 202: *quem tegula sola tuetur/a pluvia, molles ubi reddunt ova columbae* ('from the rain he [the poor man] is protected only by the tiles where the gentle pigeons lay their eggs').

224 *Epigrams* I, 7.

225 Petronius, *Satyricon* 71.

226 E.g. the stele of Maia Severa in the Aquileia Museum: G. Brusin, *Il R. Museo Archeologica di Aquileia*, 1936, fig. 88.

227 G. Kaibel, *Epigrammata Graeca*, 1878, no. 452.

228 Martial, *Epigrams* XIII, 53: *cum pinguis mihi turtur erit, lactuca, valebis.* ('When I get a fat turtle-dove, goodbye, lettuce'.)

229 *Strategems* III, 13, 8.

230 *NH* X, 53 (110).

231 *Epigrams* VIII, 32, 1, 2, 8: *aera per tacitum delapsa sedentis in ipsos/ fluxit Aratullae blanda columba sinus./ ... nuntia venit avis.*

232 J. M. C. Toynbee, *Death and Burial in the Roman World*, 1971, pl. 79.

233 Pliny, *NH* XXXVI, 60 (184).

234 L'Orange and Nordhagen, op. cit., pl. 12a.

235 Aurigemma, op. cit., pl. 166.

236 *NH* X, 32 (63).

237 *Tusculanae Disputationes* I, 30, 73: *cygni, qui non sine causa Apollini dicati sunt, sed quod ab eo divinationem habere videantur, qua providentes quid in morte boni sit, cum cantu et voluptate moriantur.*

238 *RPGR*, 347, no. 8.

239 Strong, op. cit. I, 1923, 43, fig. 23; G. Moretti, *Ara Pacis Augustae*, 1948, pls 1–4, 10–12, 15–18.

240 ibid., pls 17, 23; Strong, op. cit., pl. 6.

241 E. Espérandieu, *Receuil général de bas-reliefs, etc. de la Gaule romaine* I, 1907, no. 140 with fig.; W. Altmann, *Die römische Grabaltäre der Kaiserzeit*, 1905, figs 16, 17; Strong, op. cit., 45, fig. 24; J. Sautel and L. Imbert, *La Provence romaine*, 1929, 64.

242 Altmann, op. cit., fig. 104.

243 Strong, op. cit., pl. 11.

244 E.g. Ovid, *Ars Amatoria* 3, 809, 810; *Metamorphoses* X, 708, 709; Horace, *Odes* III, 28, 14, 15; IV, 1, 9–11.

245 E.g. *RPGR*, 16, nos 7–10; 17, nos 1–8.

246 IX, 393 C: οὐκ ἀπελείποντο δὲ ἡμῶν τοῦ συμποσίου πολάκις οὐδε κύκνοι. ('Even swans were often not lacking at our feasts').

247 Crowfoot, op. cit., pl. 12.

248 Aurigemma, op. cit., pls 29, 31.

249 *Odyssey* XIX, 536, 537.

250 Varro, *De Re Rustica* III, 10; Columella, *De Re Rustica* VIII, 13, 14.

251 Cf. Cato, *De Agricultura* 89: fattening on barley-meal; Pliny, *NH* VIII, 77 (209): fattening on figs and mead; X, 27 (52): stuffing the birds to make the liver grow; Horace, *Satires* II, 8, 88: *pinguibus et ficis pastum iecur anseris albae* ('the white goose's liver is fed on rich figs'). Trimalchio, on the other hand, regarded goose as a very low-class taste: Petronius, *Satyricon* 93: *albus anser ... plebeium sapit.* Cf. note 274, below.

252 H. B. Walters, *Catalogue of the Greek and Etruscan Vases in the British Museum*, 1896, no. F.308; Keller II, 224, fig. 85.

253 *NH* X, 27 (51–4).

254 Cf. note 251, above.

255 ibid., 32 (63).

256 *De Bello Gallico* V, 12, 6: *haec tamen alunt animi voluptatisque causa.*

257 Martial, *Epigrams* III, 58, 12, 13: *vagatur omnis turba sordidae chortis,/ argutus anser.*

258 *Report 1*, 1947, pl. 32.

259 Livy V, 47, 3, 4.

260 J. M. C. Toynbee, *Art in Roman Britain*, 1963, 164, 165, no. 93, pl. 94.

261 *Satyricon* 136, 137.

262 *RPGR*, 160, no. 9.

263 E.g. G. M. A. Hanfmann, *The Season Sarcophagus at Dumbarton Oaks*, 1951, pls 20, 28, 33, 47, 70.

264 H. B. Walters, *Catalogue of the Bronzes, Greek, Roman, and Etruscan, in the British Museum,* 1899, 287, no. 1887; Keller II, 223, fig. 84.

265 *RPGR*, 367, no. 5; Anderson, photo 6389, Roma.

266 Crowfoot, op. cit., pl. 12.

267 Aurigemma, op. cit., pls 26–8, 33.

268 Pliny, *NH* X, 72 (141); Varro, *De Re Rustica* III, 5, 8.

269 ibid., 5, 9–17.

270 ibid. III, 11.

271 *NH* X, 67 (132).

272 *De Re Rustica* VIII, 15.

273 Plautus, *Captivi* 1002, 1003: *pueris . . . anites . . . dantur, quicum lusitent*; *Asinaria* 103: *dic igitur med anaticulum.*

274 Martial, *Epigrams* XIII, 52: *tota quidem ponatur anas, sed pectore tantum/ et cervice sapit: cetera redde coco*; Petronius, *Satyricon* 93: *pictis anas renovata pennis/plebeium sapit* ('the duck which renews its painted feathers is a low-class dish'). Cf. note 251, above.

275 Pliny, *NH* XVIII, 87 (362); Aelian, *DNA* VII, 7.

276 F. W. Volbach, *Early Christian Art,* 1961, pl. 107.

277 Metropolitan Museum of Art, photo.

278 E.g. O. Elia, *Pitture murali e mosaici nel Museo Nazionale di Napoli,* 1932, figs 50, 51.

279 Crowfoot, op. cit., pls 12, 13.

280 *Satires* II, 4, 29, 30.

281 *Domitianus,* 13, 2.

282 *NH* X, 60 (124).

283 *NH* X, 60 (121–3).

284 ibid. X, 60 (124).

285 E.g. Ovid, *Metamorphoses* V, 329: *Delius in corvo est*; II, 545: *Phoebeius ales*; Petronius, *Satyricon* 122: *Delphicus ales*; Statius, *Thebaid* III, 506: *comes obscurus tripodum* ('the dark companion of the tripod'); M. J. Vermaseren, *Corpus Inscriptio-*

num et Monumentorum Religionis Mithriacae I, 1956, figs 47, 49, 102, 106, etc.

286 A. Ross, *Pagan Celtic Britain,* 1967, 249–51.

287 Walters, op. cit., 286, no. 1882.

288 *NH* X, 59 (118).

289 Petronius, *Satyricon* 28: *intrantes salutabat.*

290 *Epigrams* VII, 87, 6; XIV, 76; *pica loquax certa dominum te voce saluto;/si me non videas, esse negabis avem.*

291 *DSA* 19.

292 *Silvae* II, 4, 18, 19: *auditasque memor penitus dimittere voces/sternus.*

293 *NH* X, 59 (120).

294 *NH* X, 43 (81–5).

295 *Epigrams* VII, 87, 8: *luscinio tumulum si Telesilla dedit.*

296 *Satires* II, 3, 245: *luscinias soliti impenso prandere coemptas.*

297 SHA, *Elagabalus* 20, 5: *comedit saepius . . . linguas . . . lusciniarum.*

298 *Life of Apollonius of Tyana* VI, 36: λαλεῖν τε ὅσα ἄνθρωποι καὶ τερετίζειν ὅσα αὐλοί.

299 *Epistolae* IV, 2.

300 Horace, *Ars Poetica* 458, 459; *Satires* II, 8, 91: *vidimus et merulas poni et sine clune palumbas.*

301 Varro, *De Re Rustica* III, 9, 17; cf. p. 248 and note 102, above.

302 *NH* X, 45 (87): *merulae candidae*; Pausanias VIII, 17, 3: κόσσυφοι . . . ὁλόλευκοι.

303 Pliny, *NH* X, 59 (120): *Agrippina Claudii Caesaris turdum habuit, quod numquam ante, imitantem sermones hominum.*

304 *De Re Rustica* III, 2, 15; 4, 2.

305 ibid., 5, 1–6.

306 *NH* X, 30 (60).

307 *Pompey* 2; *Lucullus* 40.

308 Horace, *Epistles* I, 15, 41; *nil melius turdo*; Martial, *Epigrams* XIII, 92: *inter aves turdus . . . mattea prima* ('among birds the thrush is a prime delicacy').

309 Petronius, *Satyricon* 40. Cf. p. 132 and p. 370, note 10.

310 *Epigrams* III, 47, 10: *coronam pinguibus gravem turdis*; XIII, 51: *mihi de turdis facta corona placet* ('I like a wreath made of thrushes').

311 M. P. Gauckler, *Catalogue du Musée Alaoui*, supplément I, 1910, 22, no. 278, pl. 15, fig. 3.

312 Jennison, 117.

313 Catullus 2 and 3.

314 *Asinaria* 666: *dic me igitur tuom passerculum*; *Casina* 138: *meu' pullus passer*.

315 Fronto IV, 6, 2: *quid autem passerculam nostram Gratiam minusculam.*

316 *NH* X, 57 (116).

317 Petronius, *Satyricon* 46.

318 G. E. Rizzo, *La pittura ellenistico-romana*, 1929, colour plate D: Naples Museum. I owe the identification of these birds to the Edward Grey Institute of Ornithology, Oxford. With the smaller bird cf. one with much the same colouring on the Zliten acanthus-scroll mosaic: Aurigemma, op. cit., pl. 162.

319 O. Benndorf and R. Schöne, *Die antiken Bildwerke des lateranischen Museums*, 1867, no. 289; Altmann, op. cit., no. 112, fig. 94. The Lateran collection is now in the Vatican.

320 For other sepulchral relief altars with birds' nests less prominently featured see ibid., nos 41, 43, 46, 53, 60, 75, 203.

321 K. Lehmann-Hartleben and E. C. Olsen, *Dionysiac Sarcophagi in Baltimore*, 1942, fig. 8.

322 Gusman, op. cit. III, 1914, pl. 121; Alinari, photo 6353, Roma.

323 Aurigemma, op. cit., pls 160, 161, 165.

324 I owe this identification to the Edward Grey Institute of Ornith-ology, Oxford. On the early fourth-century mosaic pavement of the 'north hall' of the cathedral at Aquileia there is a partridge's nest on an open flower: G. Brusin and P. L. Zavatto, *Monumenti paleocristiani di Aquileia e di Grado*, 1957, pl. 129, fig. 5.

325 *Monuments Piot*, 1899, 76–9, pls 13, 14; Giraudon, photos 4915, 4916.

326 *RPGR*, 81, no. 3.

327 ibid., 365, no. 8.

328 F. Fremersdorf and others, *Das römische Haus mit den Dionysos-Mosaik vor dem Südportal des Kölner Domes*, 1956; O. Doppelfeld, *The Dionysian Mosaic at Cologne Cathedral*, 1964.

329 Fremersdorf, etc., op. cit., 51, 63, fig. 17 (in colour); Doppelfeld, op. cit., fig. 4; K. Parlasca, *Die römischen Mosaiken in Deutschland*, 1959, pl. 75, fig. 1; *Germania*, 1941, pl. 61. Contrast the Herculaneum parrot, whose toes appear to be correctly rendered: Fremersdorf, op. cit., 63, fig. 20.

330 Fremersdorf, etc., op. cit., 52, fig. 18 (in colour); Parlasca, op. cit., pl. 77, fig. 1; *Germania*, 1941, pl. 62.

331 Gentili, op. cit., pl. 40. A very similar and probably roughly contemporary, but far less well preserved, mosaic from Carthage shows above the *spina* a pair of geese or ducks harnessed to a chariot that is being driven leftwards, below the *spina* a pair of parrots harnessed to a chariot driven towards the right. The birds have no seasonal attributes (*MAH*, 1969, 242–55, fig. 20). Another mutilated mosaic from Volubilis in Morocco presents two chariots drawn by ducks and two by peacocks (ibid., fig. 21).

CHAPTER XXIII

1 A funerary inscription in the Museum Carnuntinum at Bad Deutsch-Altenburg (*c.* 43 km. E. of Vienna) gives circumstantial evidence of belief, or hope, that the next life will be an improvement on this one. The text records a certain Augustania Cassia Marcia, wife of Marcus Antonius Basilides, a member of the secret police attached to the Tenth Legion(*frumentarius Legionis X Geminae*): she died at the age of 34 'having completed the toils of her destiny and hoping for better things' (*dum explesset fati laborem meliora sibi sperans*): A. Schober, *Die römischen Grabsteine von Noricum und Pannonia*, 1923, 47, 48, no. 100, fig. 43.

2 *Bulletino della Commissione Archeologica Comunale di Roma*, 1942, 100, fig. 5.

3 *Archäologischer Anzeiger*, 1940, cols 447–51, figs 21, 22.

4 F. Gerke, *Die christlichen Sarkophage der vorkonstantinischen Zeit*, 1940, pl. 3, fig. 1; Anderson, photo 24185, Roma.

5 E.g. Gerke, op. cit., pls 3, fig. 2; 4, figs 1, 2; 5, figs 1, 2; 17; 18; 19, figs 1–3; 20, fig. 1; 24, figs 1–3.

6 J. Wilpert, *Die Malereien der Katakomben Roms*, 1903, pl. 122; P. du Bourguet, *Early Christian Painting*, 1965, pl. 27.

7 ibid., pl. 59.

8 *AJA*, 1947, pl. 70.

9 *JRS*, 1964, pls 2, 3; 4, figs 1, 2; 5, fig. 3.

10 E.g. J. M. C. Toynbee, *Art in Roman Britain*, 1963, pl. 113; id., *Art in Britain under the Romans*, 1966, pl. 72.

11 4, 22: *nec magnos metuent armenta leones*; 8, 27, 28: *aevoque sequenti/cum canibus timidi venient ad pocula dammae*.

12 16, 33: *credula nec ravos timeant armenta leones*.

13 *Acta Antiqua Academiae Scientiarum Hungaricae*, 1968, 260–2, figs 1, 2.

14 J. W. Crowfoot, *Early Churches in Palestine*, 1941, 142–4, pl. 25. The inscription reads: ΚΑΙ ΛΕΩΝ ΩC ΒΟΥC ΦΑΓ[εται ἄχυρα]. This church has been dated to the seventh century. Cf. the fifth-century mosaic in the church at Korigos (Corycus) in Cilicia with animals and a quotation from Isaiah XI; *Monumenta Asiae Minoris Antiqua* II, 1930, 106, 107, figs 104–7; and the mosaic of *c.* 400 on the podium (altar-emplacement) of the basilica at Mariana in Corsica, with a lion and an ox eating straw from the same manger and a similar quotation in Latin: G. Moracchini-Mazel, *Les monuments paléochrétiens de Corse*, 1967, 22, fig. 23; 24–5, figs 27, 28.

15 D. Levi, *Antioch Mosaic Pavements*, 1947, I, 317–19, fig. 133; II, pls 72, 174a.

16 *Acta Antiqua*, etc. (see note 13, above), 265, fig. 6. Cf. also the sixth-century mosaic in the church of St George at Nebo; S. J. Saller and B. Bagatti, *The Town of Nebo*, 1949, 75, no. 5; 105–6, no. 6; pl. 29, fig. 3.

17 Levi, op. cit. I, 359–63, fig. 149; II, pls 87–9; 135; 136a.

18 *Illustrated London News*, 25 April 1953, 670, 671, figs 3–10; L. Budde, *Antike Mosaiken in Kilikien* I, 1969, figs 186–9; *Anatolian Studies*, 1954, pls 4, fig. 2; 5, fig. 2.

19 *Illustrated London News*, 18 October 1958, 644–6, figs 5–15; Budde, op. cit., figs 182–5; II, 1972, figs 262–71.

20 Crowfoot, op. cit., pl. 20.

21 ibid., 138, pl. 21b. Cf. Budde, op. cit. II, fig. 272.

22 Photo Archives Photographiques, Paris. Cf. the similar mosaic

from Silifke (Seleucia) in Cilicia: Budde, op. cit. II, figs 175–84.

23 Crowfoot, op. cit., 134, pl. 17.

24 *CRAC*, 1970, 64, 66, 67, figs 1, 3, 4.

25 K. Weitzmann, *Ancient Book Illumination*, 1959, 15, 16, pl. 9, fig. 18.

26 Levi, op. cit. II, pl. 137c.

27 D. Mustilli, *Il Museo Mussolini*, 1939, 10, 11, no. 20, pl. 13. A mosaic in the Palazzo dei Conservatori in Rome shows an owl perched on an 'evil. eye' which has been pierced by a spear; other birds and animals are mobbing it: Stuart Jones, ed., *The Sculptures of the Palazzo dei Conservatori*, 1926, pl. 110.

28 Schober, op. cit., 65–7, no. 141, fig. 67: cf. nos 142 (Celeia?), 143 (Petau); A. Conze, *Römische Bildwerke einheimischen Fundorts in Österreich* II, 1875, pl. 5.

29 *Archaeologiai Értesíto*, 1906, 227, fig. 13.

30 *Revue Archéologique*[3], 1895, 77, 78, fig. 1.

31 *De Laudibus Constantini* 14.

32 Wilpert, op. cit., pl. 37.

33 F. W. Deichmann and others, *Repertorium der christlich-antiken Sarkophage* I, 1967, 64, no. 70, pl. 22 (Vatican Museum); 429, 430, no. 1022, pl. 164 (Ostia Museum).

34 G. Pesce, *Sarcofagi romani di Sardegna*, 1957, 102, 103, no. 57, figs 113, 114.

35 Wilpert, op. cit., pl. 229.

36 A. Grabar, *Byzantium*, 1966, pl. 119 (in colour).

37 *Journal of the Warburg and Courtauld Institutes*, 1958, 1–6, pl. 1.

38 *CRAI*, 1970, 68, 69, figs 5, 6.

39 *Epigrams* X, 19, 6–8: *illic Orphea protinus videbis/judi vertice lubricum theatri/mirantesque feras avemque regis.*

40 S. R. Platner and T. Ashby, *A Topographical Dictionary of Ancient Rome*, 1929, 313, 314.

41 *Bulletin du Musée de Beyrouth* 1940, 7–36; pl. 5a (Orpheus); pl. 4 (Hygieia); fig. 14 (*ephebus*); fig. 15 (Naiad); pl. 5b (Achilles and Penthesilea); pl. 6 (male portrait statue); fig. 16 (two heads).

42 III, 49: εἶδες δ'ἂν ἐπὶ μέσων ἀγορῶν κειμέναις κρήναις τὰ τοῦ Καλοῦ Ποιμένος σύμβολα . . . τόν τε Δανιὴλ σὺν αὐτοῖς λέουσιν ἐν χαλκῷ πεπλασμένον χρύσου τε πετάλοις ἐκλάμποντα.

43 G. Mendel, *Musées Imperiaux Ottomans: Catalogue des sculptures grecques, romaines, et byzantines* II, 1914, 412–16, no. 648 with fig.

44 ibid., 420–3, no. 651 with fig. There is also a marble Good Shepherd figure in Alexandria topped by a 'funnel' and with a pedestal similar to that of the Istanbul Good Shepherd: *Jahrbuch für Antike und Christentum* I, 1958, pl. 1d.

45 Sabratha: *Bulletino della Commissione Archeologica Comunale di Roma*, 1941, 61–79 (Museo dell' Impero Romano), figs 1, 2; Athens: ibid., fig. 3.

46 ibid., fig. 4.

47 *Gallia*, 1955, 41–77.

48 *JRS*, 1962, 13–18.

49 *Gallia*, 1971, 138–49, figs 15–34 (Vienne); *BCH*, 1963, 820, fig. 7; 824 (Mytilene); Budde, op. cit. II, 1972, 20–4, text fig. 5, pl. figs 6–18 (Adana); *AJA*, 1972, 197–200, pls 47, 48 (Panik). Sixty-seven Orpheus mosaics are now known, according to *CRAI*, 1970, 70.

50 J. M. C. Toynbee, *Art in Roman Britain*, 1963, pls 221, 222.

51 Horkstow: Hinks, 103–5, figs 112–14; Withington: ibid., 113, 114, figs 125–7; Volubilis: *Gallia*, 1955, 55, fig. 14 (note here the lifelike portrait of an African elephant).

52 E.g. Lepcis Magna: ibid., 60, fig. 17; Palermo: ibid., 51, fig. 10; Ptolemais: *JRS*, 1962, pl. 1 (on this

mosaic Orpheus has a nimbus: cf. pp. 290, 298).

53 E.g. Volubilis: see note 51, above; Tobruk: *JRS*, 1962, 17; Piazza Armerina: G. V. Gentili, *La villa erculia di Piazza Armerina*, 1959, fig. 10.

54 *Gallia*, 1955, 43, fig. 2.

55 See ibid., 54, fig. 12 and note 50, above.

56 Trinquetaille: *Gallia*, 1955, 52, fig. 11; Sant'Anselmo: ibid., 57, fig. 15; Piazza Armerina: see note 53, above.

57 *Gallia*, 1955, 74, fig. 19.

58 See notes 52, 53, above.

59 Gentili, op. cit., pls 44, 45.

60 *MAAR*, 1936, pl. 38, fig. 4. Here there is also a rare (on Orpheus mosaics) rhinoceros.

61 Woodchester: see note 50, above; Ptolemais: *JRS*, 1962, pl. 6, fig. 2. Cf. the similarly engaged bird on the acanthus-scroll mosaic from Zliten: S. Aurigemma, *I mosaici di Tripolitania*, 1960, pl. 164.

62 *RPGR*, 201, no. 7; V. von Gonzenbach, *Die römischen Mosaiken der Schweiz*, 1961, 235, 236, no. 143, pl. 39.

63 P. Gusman, *L'art décoratif de Rome* III, 1914, pl. 121.

64 *Epigrams* V, 37, 13.

65 *NH* VIII, 58 (138); XI, 99 (245).

66 Bobbio: W. F. Volbach, *Early Christian Art*, 1961, pl. 84; Florence: W. F. Volbach, *Elfenbeinearbeiten der Spätantike und des frühen Mittelalters*, 1952, no. 92, pl. 28.

67 J. Natanson, *Early Christian Ivories*, 1953, pl. 3; Volbach, *Elfenbeinarbeiten*, etc., no. 108, pl. 32.

68 ibid., no. 12, pl. 61: Louvre.

69 W. O. Hassall, *The Holkham Bible Picture Book*, 1954, fol. 2 v.

70 See note 52, above.

71 F. Gerke, *Der trierer Agricius Sarkophag*, 1949, pl. 6, fig. 13; F. van der Meer and C. Mohrmann,

Atlas of the Early Christian World, 1958, no. 400 with fig.

72 Imperial-age coins of Apamea in Phrygia show the Ark with Noah and his wife standing outside it, two figures still inside it, and the dove and raven above: B. V. Head, *Historia Numorum*, 1911, 666, 667, fig. 313.

73 Budde, op. cit. I, 1969, 38–57, figs 26–49.

74 C. H. Kraeling, *Gerasa: City of the Decapolis*, 1958, 319–21, pls 63, 64a.

75 H. Gerstinger, *Die Wiener Genesis*, 1931, pl. 4.

76 For detailed descriptions and a catalogue of the sheep-bearing figures of imperial times, on signet-rings, glass vessels, terracotta lamps, in the form of statuettes, and in sarcophagus reliefs, see *Jahrbuch für Antike und Christentum*, 1958, 20–51.

77 ibid., pl. 1e.

78 ibid., pls 1c, f; 2a–f.

79 Byzantine Museum photo.

80 See notes 43, 44 above.

81 *Jahrbuch für Antike und Christentum*, 1960, 125, 126.

82 Hermes/Mercury was friendly to man; but he is *kriophoros* (rambearing) in virtue of his lordship of flocks and herds.

83 Wilpert, op. cit., *passim*.

84 E.g. van der Meer and C. Mohrmann, op. cit., nos 44–6, with figs.

85 San Sebastiano postcard.

86 G. Brusin and P. L. Zovatto, *Monumenti paleocristiani di Aquileia e di Grado*, 1957, 91, fig. 38.

87 *Jahrbuch für Antike und Christentum*, 1962, pls 8–11 and supplementary plate.

88 Van der Meer and Mohrmann, op. cit., no. 78 with fig.

89 ibid., no. 62 with fig.

90 ibid., no. 63 with fig.

91 *Fasti Archaeologici*, 1960, no. 6502, pl. 37, fig. 107.

92 Van der Meer and Mohr-
mann, op. cit., no. 519 with fig.
93 M. Chéhab, Mosaiques de Liban,

1958, 64-6, pls 31-5.
94 ibid., 62, fig. 3.

APPENDIX: CHAPTER I

1 Publius Vegetius Renatus, Diges-
torum Artis Mulomedicinae libri, ed.
E. Lommatzsch, Teubner, 1903.
2 Mulomedicina Chironis, ed. E.
Oder, Teubner, 1901.
3 Apsyrtus, senior army veterinarian to Constantine the Great: E.
Oder, 'Apsyrtus. Lebensbild ˏdes
bedeutendsten altgriecheschen Veter-
inars', Veterinarhistorisches Jahrbuch,
1926, 121-36; G. Bjorck, 'Apsyrtus,
Julius Africanus, et l'hippiatrique
grecque', Universitets Arsskrift (Upp-
sala) IVˏ 1944.
4 Pelagonius, ed. M. Ihm, Teubner,
1892.
5 Columella, De Re Rustica, ed. and
tr. H. B. Ash, 1960.
6 Hippiatrika, ed. E. Oder and C.
Hoppe, in Corpus Hippiatricorum
Graecorum, Teubner, 1924-27, re-
printed 1971. At the command of
Constantine IV (Porphyrogenitus:
AD 911-959) all the surviving
veterinary literature which could be
discovered in the Eastern Empire
was collected together under the
title Hippiatrika. Fragments of books
are thrown together with actual
correspondence between veterinarians, military officers and officials.
Many veterinarians are named, including Apsyrtus, Hierocles, Theomnestus, Pelagonius, Anatolius, Tiberius, Eumelus Archedemus, an Hippo-
crates, Aemilius Hispanus, Africanus,
Didymus, Diophanes, Pamphilus and
Chiron. To many of the names dates
and personal details may be added.
Apsyrtus was born in Prusa in
Bithynia and floruit AD 330-340.
Theomnestus served with Theodoric
the Great AD 454-526 and cam-

paigned from Pannonia into Italy in
AD 488. Hierocles and Bassus appear
to have been both veterinarians and
lawyers. A useful survey of the
Hippiatrika and manuscript locations
is given in Sir Frederick Smith, The
Early History of Veterinary Literature
and its British Development I, 1919.
7 Oder considers that the Mulomedicina is a mixture of several authors
under the name of Claudius Hemerius.
He considers that the original Greek
text may be dated AD 400.
8 Vegetius appears to have grafted
onto Columella's chapters the same
classification of contagious plagues
that he gives for horses. Suspicion is
aroused that by this stage in his
research Vegetius not only felt
obliged to fill an urgent requirement
for knowledge but qualified to invent
some of the necessary expertise!
9 Mago is described by Varro and
Columella as surpassing all others and
the father of husbandry. His twenty-
eight volumes were translated into
Latin by decree of the Senate. Varro
is more detailed, revealing that
Cassius Dionysius of Utica translated
the work of Mago into Greek in
twenty volumes. Diophanes, in
Bithynia, reduced Dionysius to six
volumes and dedicated them to
King Deiotarus. The Greek volumes
of Dionysius in fact only contained
the equivalent of eight of Mago's
books, the remainder being derived
from the other Greek authors in
Varro's bibliography. From this information we may assume Punic influence on Greek theory to have
been much less than on Roman
theory. Mago is quoted some fifteen

times in Columella on a wide variety of subjects.

10 A. Cornelius Celsus, *De Medicina*, ed. and tr. W. G. Spencer, 1960. The author of volumes on agriculture, military arts, rhetoric, philosophy and jurisprudence, he was active early in the first century AD and was a contemporary of Columella. Columella himself was a native of Gades in southern Spain. It is likely that local agricultural practices had been heavily influenced by direct Carthaginian colonization quite apart from any references to Mago.

11 Marcus Terentius Varro (116–27 BC) was an eminent soldier, admiral, public official, scholar and writer. Julius Caesar made him responsible for the future establishment of a great public library of Greek and Latin authors at Rome and Varro thus combined the ability of an antiquarian and scholar with an unrivalled opportunity to study the available literature on any subject. His observations must carry great conviction.

12 *Valerii Maximi dictorum factorumque memorabilium libri novem*, IX, 15, 2: *Herophilus equarius medicus C. Marium septies consulem avum sibi vindicando ita se extulit, ut coloniae veteranorum plures, et municipia splendida, collegiaque fere omnia patronem adoptarent. Quin etiam, cum C. Caesar, Cn. Pompeio adolescente in Hispania oppresso, populum in hortis suis admisisset, proximo intercolumnio paene pari studio frequentiae salutatus est. Quod nisi divinae Caesaris vires huic erubescendae procellae obstitissent, simile vulnus respublica excepisset, atque in Equitio acceperat. Caeterum decreto eius extra Italiam relegatus, postquam ille coelo receptus est, in urbem rediit, et consilium interficiendi senatus capere sustinuit. Quo nomine iussu patrum*

necatus in carcere, seras prompti animi ad omne moliendum scelus poenas pependit. ('Herophilus the horse doctor, claiming that Gaius Marius, holder of seven consulships, was his grandfather, made such a reputation for himself that many veteran colonies and important townships and nearly all the guilds adopted him as their patron. Moreover, when Gaius Caesar, to celebrate his crushing of the young Gnaeus Pompey in Spain, opened his gardens to the populace, a large crowd assembled in the portico next door cheered Herophilus with almost equal enthusiasm. Indeed, had not Caesar's godlike power checked this disgraceful disturbance, the state would have sustained as great a blow as it had suffered in the case of the impostor Equitius. Herophilus was banished from Italy by Caesar's decree. But after Caesar's death and apotheosis he returned to Rome and actually plotted to massacre the Senate. For this he was put to death in prison on the Senate's orders and at long last paid the penalty for his criminal proclivities.')

13 This interesting evidence is discussed by Reinhard Froehner, 'Ueber die tierarztlichen Verrichtungen des Edictum Diocletiani', *Veterinarhistorische Mitteilungen*, 1932, nos 10–11, 83; and by E. Leclainche, *Histoire de la Médicine Vétérinaire*, 1936, 93. VII, 20: *Mulomedico tonsurae et aptaturae pedum in capite uno, den. sex.*; 21: *Depleturae et purgaturae capitis per singula capita, den. biginti.* Translation presents some difficulties, especially in the Greek text which can be shown to be a literal translation made in ignorance of the Latin meaning (see Leclainche). The veterinary sense is, however, quite clear. '20: Clipping [the mane], the preparation [paring] of the feet. Six denarii. 21: Blood-letting and purging the

head. Twenty denarii.' Vegetius I, 56 discusses the importance of correct clipping of the mane and reveals a considerable aesthetic concern. The various procedures related to the feet and the whole question of blood-letting and purging are discussed in the next chapter.

14 *Codex Theodosianus* 8, 5: *De Curso Publico, de angariis et parangariis*, 31: *Iidem* [the emperors Valentinian and Valens] *ad Catafronium Vic. Ital. Nec mulionibus nec carpentariis nec mulomedicis cursui publico deputatis mercedem a quoquam sinceritas tua fuerit* [or *faciet*] *ministrari, cum iuxta publicam dispositionem annonas et vestem, quam hisdem credimus posse sufficere, consequantur. . . . Dat. 18 Kal. Septem. Triviris. Valentiniano et Valente III. A. A. Cons.* ('The same emperors to Cataphronius, Vicar of Italy. "Your sincerity will arrange that no person shall pay any muledriver, wagoner, or veterinarian assigned to the public post, since according to public regulations they obtain subsistence allowances and clothing, which We believe should suffice for them. . . . Given this fifteenth day of August, AD 370."') For a full discussion of the *cursus publicus* see A. H. M. Jones, *The Later Roman Empire* II, 1964, 831.

15 *Digest* 50, 6, 7: In this passage Tarruntenus Paternus, praetorian prefect under Commodus, defines the *immunes*. For a full and authoritative discussion see G. R. Watson, *The Roman Soldier*, 1969, 75 ff.

16 Hygini Gromatici, *Liber de Munitionibus Castrorum, ex recensione*, ed. Gemoll, Teubner, 1879; also von Domazewski, 1887.

17 Inscriptions: Reinhard Froehner, *Kulturgeschichte der Tierheilkunde* I, 1952, has collected together the various Latin and Greek inscriptions

with commentary. *CIL* VI, 9612: . . .]*itius mulom*[*edicus* . . .] *se vibum fecit*; VI, 9611: *Secundinus mulomedicus fecit sibi domum eternam*; VI, 9613: . . . *mulo*[*medicus de*]*positus* . . . *co*[*nsensu senato*[*ris*] [*an*]*nus XLIII*; VI, 9610: *A*]*pollodorus C. Mari C., f Tromentina medicus equarius et venator sibi oll. II*; X, 5919: *L. Vibio L. l. Suro medico veterin. Vettia L. f. uxor dat*; V, 2183: *L. Crassicius Gaiae l. Hermia medicus veterinarius sibi et Abiriae L. l. Maximae uxori vivus fecit et Eugeniae l*; XIII, 7965: *M . . . Ioctavno . . . Medico Peq . . . et Inanna*; X, 6497: *Ap. Quintius Ap. l. Nicephor. medicus iumentarius.*

18 Celsus, *Proemium* 65.

19 The parallel between this description and that of the bull with *nft* in the ancient Egyptian papyrus of Kahun is very striking. The Egyptian treatment of a feverish ox was to bathe it with cold water and rub its body with emollient vegetable extracts (unidentifiable) and to bleed from the head and tail: R. E. Walker, 'The Veterinary Papyrus of Kahun', *The Veterinary Record*, 1964, 198–200.

20 Ammianus Marcellinus XXVIII, 4, 34.

21 Aelian, *DNA* XII, 19, 20. This interesting passage provides an example of the intelligent sophist tampering with a technical text. Democritus is quoted at length in a discussion of the theories offered in ancient times to explain the absence of horns in some breeds of cattle and the interesting phenomenon of horn-shedding among deer. 19: 'Castrated oxen, says Democritus, grow curved, thin and long horns: whereas those of uncastrated oxen are thick at the base, straight, and of shorter length. And he says that these have a much wider forehead than the others, for as there are many veins in that part, the bones are in consequence broader.

And the growth of the horns being thicker makes that part of the animal broader, whereas castrated oxen, in which the circumference at the base of the horns is but small, have a narrower forehead. 20: But hornless bulls, not possessing the "honeycombed" part of the forehead [so Democritus styles it; his meaning would be "porous"] since the entire bone is solid and does not permit the conflux of body juices, are unprotected and destitute of the means of self-defence.' Aelian is presumptuous here, although his intrusion is based on 'atomic' theory. Democritus described the forehead as 'honeycombed' correctly. He had by dissection and observation noticed that the cavities of the frontal sinuses were much larger and more loculated in the ox which bears horns. The frontal sinuses are indeed much smaller in the low-crowned polled ox (hornless). The arrogant sophist is, as it were, caught red-handed! Between the derision of cultivated men such as Ammianus and the meddling of the sophists the pinnacles of technical achievement, modest though they may have been, have been constantly pumiced down, or, where not understandable at all, discarded in pique. The value and interest of Democritus on horns is not that he was right or wrong, but that he was striving to lift human knowledge above the level of naive reasoning. His contemporaries were content to accept that polled oxen had no horns because they originated in cold climates where horns would not grow.

22 Pulpy kidney is the modern popular name for a fatal toxaemia in sheep caused by the toxins of Clostridium perfringens Type D, a bacterium related to the tetanus and gas gangrene family of bacteria. In brief, sheep both adult and infantile on lush pasture or a rich diet of cereals are liable to suffer sudden death from absorption of lethal quantities of toxin produced by the bacterium undergoing a massive increase in numbers in the digestive tract. To the untrained eye the carcase appears healthy. The most common and obvious abnormality is that the kidneys are soft or pulpy (indeed if held under a running water tap the substance of the kidney is washed easily from the hand). The ancient experience of the disease would have been to find sheep suddenly dead. The observation of the condition of the kidneys would arise in the normal course of butchery or kitchen routine. The Greek natural philosophers studied the condition and Aristotle records their opinions. De Partibus Animalium III, 9: 'Now it is an advantage to all animals to have fat kidneys, and often they are completely filled with fat. The sheep is an exception: if this happens to a sheep it dies. But even if the kidneys are as fat as can be there is always some portion which is clear of fat, if not in both kidneys, at any rate in the right one. The reason why this happens solely [or more especially] to sheep is as follows. Some animals have their fat in the form of lard, which is fluid, and thus the wind [pneuma] cannot so easily get shut up within and cause trouble. When this happens, however, it causes rot. Thus, too, in the case of human beings who suffer from their kidneys, although it is an advantage to them to be fat, yet if they become unduly fat pains result which prove fatal. As for the animals whose fat is in the form of suet, none has such dense suet as the sheep has; and, moreover, in the sheep the amount of it is much greater; the fact that they get fat

about the kidneys much more quickly than any other animal shows this. So when the moisture and the wind get shut up within, rot is produced, which rapidly kills the sheep off. The disease makes its way directly to the heart through the aorta and the great blood-vessel, since there are continuous passages leading from these to the kidneys.' *Historia Animalium* III, 7: '. . . sheep die through having their kidneys entirely enveloped in suet. Overfeeding brings on this condition, as

at Leontini in Sicily; that is why they do not turn the sheep out to feed until late in the evening, to reduce the amount they eat.' The predisposing factor has been correctly observed and the precautions would, without doubt, have helped to reduce mortality.

23 The tiny collection of eighteen prescriptions of Gargilius Martialis, *Curae Boum, Ex Corpore Gargili*, is included in the Teubner edition of Vegetius. This is probably an example of an 'empirical' handbook.

CHAPTER II

1 Varro, *De Re Rustica* II, 7; Columella, *De Re Rustica* VI, 27-9; Pliny, *NH* VIII, 66-7; Vegetius, *Mulomedicina* IV, 6, 2 ff. A useful account of horse-breeding is given by K. D. White, *Roman Farming*, 1970, 288-92.

2 I have drawn on H. Isbell, *The Last Poets of Imperial Rome*, 1971.

3 See p. 404, notes 2, 6 and 7.

4 Chiron I; Vegetius I, 21; II, 40.

5 Chiron III, 10-23.

6 Vegetius I, 66.

7 Several examples have been found in Britain. Two farrier's butts (unpublished) are in Dorset County Museum, Dorchester. Another example is illustrated in *Proceedings of the Society of Antiquaries of Scotland*, 1952-53, 29, fig. 6. The example in the Silchester 1900 hoard has a butt with same measure of ornamentation, just recognizable as a griffon's head, on the handle: *Archaeology*, 1911, 248, fig. 6. One of the Dorchester examples has a very slight degree of design work on its handle. On the Continent, in the museums of Bar-le-Duc, Grenoble and Naples are butts lavishly decorated with figures of goddesses and horses on

the shanks and lion or griffon handles of a most elaborate type.

8 R. E. Walker, 'Hipposandals: Some New Evidence for Roman Veterinary Instruments', *Proceedings of the Veterinary History Society*, 1971 (unpublished). The same paper contains 'The *sagitta*: discussion of the bronze *sagitta* in the London Museum with a tentative identification', also '*Ferramenta*: the use and abuse of the boutoir in ancient and modern times'.

9 The *solea* with legs is represented in the Blackburn Mill hoard (B 21), *Proceedings of the Society of Antiquaries of Scotland*, 1952-53, 46, fig. 12. These little legs are not to be interpreted as frost nails.

10 Op. cit.

11 Columella VII, 21, 2.

12 Pliny, *NH* VIII, 70, 177.

13 Columella VI, 24, 4.

14 Columella VI, 26.

15 Op. cit., 207-23.

16 K. D. White, op. cit., refers to Plautus, *Aulularia* II, 85, for a reference to expensive beef, pork and veal in the market; Celsus V, 9 and 13 for veal fat as a medicament; Cicero, *Ad Familiares* IX, 2 for roast veal.

17 A. H. M. Jones, *The Later Roman*

Empire, 1964, describes the sixth-century rations given in *Papyrus Oxyrhyncus*, 2046 as 'gargantuan' but it is possible that consideration should be given to soldiers' servants and women. A similar explanation for the high farm-workers' rations (up to 4 lb. daily) is offered by White, op. cit., 361.

18 Columella I, 6, 4–6; Palladius I, 21; Vitruvius VI, 6, 2.

19 See p. 406, note 19. Also F. L. Griffith, *The Hieratic Papyri of Kahun and Gurob*, 1893, who dates it to about 1900 B C.

20 The word *itn* is unknown but has a speech determinative and must therefore refer to a noise made by the ox. 'Hidden bendings' refers to the contortions of the animal suffering from colic of unknown cause.

21 The context helps us to interpret another unknown word – *kmya*. Possibly it is related to *kmyt* ('gum' or 'resin'): R. O. Faulkner, *Concise Dictionary of Middle Egyptian*, 1962, 279. The context places the word in exact analogy to *uncta*. 'Greased' seems a most reasonable translation.

22 Various types and degrees of virus infection are recognizable in these passages, ranging from the acute form of bovine malignant catarrh to the encephalitic or nervous form of the same disease and typical rinderpest.

23 Vegetius deals with cattle diseases in Book IV. His discussion of plagues is in IV, 1 and 2. the remainder is a copy of Columella VI.

24 Columella VI, 3; Varro II, 2.

25 Varro II, 2, 14.

26 Columella VII, 3, 16.

27 Celsus VII, 29, 5–10.

28 Columella VII, 3, 17.

29 Columella VII, 3, 19.

30 Columella VII, 3, 13.

31 Varro II, 2, 12.

32 Columella VII, 3, 25.

33 A convenient account of the clostridial diseases of sheep is given in D. C. Blood and J. A. Henderson, *Veterinary Medicine*[2], 1963, Chapter 16.

34 Varro II, 2, 19, recommends a stone pavement.

35 Columella VII, 7.

36 The *ceratum* is presumably a composition of wax and other unnamed ingredients, similar to the *cerotum* (= *ceratum*) *album* of Chiron IX, 917 (Teubner numbering), *cerotum album ad omne vulneris et in pessarium* [used in the genital tract].

37 Columella VII, 9, 4.

38 K. D. White, op. cit., 316–21. A. H. M. Jones discusses the 15%–20% rebate in *The Decline of the Ancient World*, 1966, 234, and in *The Later Roman Empire*, 1964, 702, and note 35. The legislation is in *Codex Theodosianus* XIV, 4.10.3.

39 Columella VII, 10, 8.

40 *Bacillus anthracis* causes peracute septicaemia and rapid death in all species. As a spore-forming organism it can lie dormant in soil for several decades and is resistant to procedures such as salting. There can be little doubt that a 'build-up' of contamination would have taken place in the vicinity of farms and tanneries in Roman times and might well have resulted in a serious degree of occurrence in man. Similarly disastrous contamination of fold sites adjacent to homesteads would have occurred in the case of the clostridial diseases. Varro's portable hurdles for fold erection as required in remote areas would have helped considerably in avoiding concentrations of sheep in particular sites (II, 2, 9).

41 H. J. Sevilla, 'L'art vétérinaire antique', *Proceedings of the Third International Congress of the History of Medicine*, 1922; R. Froehner, *Kulturgeschichte der Tierheilkunde* I, 1952; E.

Leclainche, *Histoire de la Médicine Vétérinaire* 1936, 93. Froehner has made the most comprehensive survey of classical literature in recent times.

42 Many of the treatments were without doubt effective. For example those cases of ruminal stasis (oxen whose rumination cycle has ceased with immobility of the stomach wall and no cud production), which were treated with *acetum* (weak wine or vinegar), would have been benefited. The acid reaction of the *acetum* might have countered the alkaline state of the static ruminal contents, thus giving stimulus to resumption of rumination. We may not, however, attribute to the Roman herdsman recognition of the fact that the *acetum* was the active principle of his poly-pharmacy and ruminal stasis was only one of the many forms of indigestion treated in this way. (*Bos si non rumigat*, *Cura Bovum*, Gargilius Martialis, 12; *Cruditas signa* . . . Columella VI, vi.

43 Celsus, *De Medicina, Proemium*. A good account of the medical theories of the Greeks and their impact on Roman life is given in J. Scarborough, *Roman Medicine*, 1969, 15–52. See also E. D. Phillips, *Greek Medicine*, 1973.

CHAPTER III

1 Xenophon, *Hipparchicus*. This treatise covers every aspect of cavalry service and is very insistent on constant training for the horses and men. They are to be able to gallop up and down hills, jump ditches and walls and engage in exercises while on the march.

2 Caesar, *De Bello Civili* I, 41. At first Caesar had only the nine hundred cavalry, drawn from three legions, which he had kept as a bodyguard. These extricated his legionaries from the abortive attack on Ilerda (I, 45). When attacked by Afranius' cavalry the Gauls held their ground and retired in good order (I, 51, 3). The cohort of targeteers was cut off and annihilated (I, 55) in the way recommended by Xenophon (IV, 17). The manoeuvre used is that in which the cavalry divide into two groups. One group attacks and the other holds its ground, remaining uncommitted to the struggle but in a position to prevent the infantry charging and crowding the attacking first group. Xenophon describes this as a vital principle of engaging a superior force. This would appear to have been the manner in which Sulla held the right wing at Cirta and defeated Jugurtha's infantry. Part of Sulla's cavalry charged *turmatim* while the remainder held a line in support and prevented counter-attacks. In effect the cavalry acts in the same way as infantry support. In Caesar's *De Bello Gallico* VIII, 1, cavalry hold their ground in this way by attacking *turmatim*, each *turma* covering its fellows but with the support of light infantry. The cavalry's holding of the countryside is described in I, 69, 3. Four cohorts of targeteers cut off and annihilated after a hard fight by the cavalry: I, 70. Demoralized cavalry of the Pompeians: I, 79.

3 Josephus, *De Bello Judaico* III, 1, 5.

4 Asclepiodotus, *Tactica* I, 3.

5 Tacitus, *Germania* 6.

6 Plíny, *NH* VIII, 65, 159: . . . *iaculantes obsequia experiuntur difficiles conatus corpore ipso nisuque iuvantium*. . . . This would appear to be all that remains of Pliny's manual on the use of the javelin by cavalry, *De Iaculatione Equestri*. We are told that it contained discussion of the appearance of horses (*NH*, VIII, 65, 162) and it may well have been full of remarkable horse lore such as the exploits of chargers who picked up weapons and passed them up to their riders. Xenophon, *On Horsemanship* XII, 13, discusses the throwing of javelins on horseback. He recommends throwing the javelin at the longest range possible so as to give time for the rider to turn his horse and grasp the second javelin. However, he also admits that the javelin is more likely to hit the target if the point is aligned with it at the moment of throwing. Obviously there is an objection to delaying the turn until after throwing the missile, especially when engaging infantry, as the momentum of the horse may carry the rider within the enemy's reach. It would have been better to throw the javelin after turning, when the weight of the rider is pressed down into the saddle and the twisting of the body to the left would increase the grip of the legs. A slight forward throw would also strike the enemy on his right (unshielded) side as the horse galloped across the enemy's front and presented a difficult target for retaliation. Some such manoeuvre must be implied by Pliny.

7 Caesar, *De Bello Gallico* VIII, 1, makes clear that crowding together was a mistake often made in cavalry engagements, which led to inevitable losses in the packed mass. Another example of Caesar's complete understanding of cavalry is his use of the six reserve cohorts to charge the Pompeian cavalry at Pharsalus (*De Bello Civili* III, 93): caught without room to deploy, the horsemen were overthrown.

8 Josephus, *De Bello Iudaico* III, 7,

24: πάντοθεν πεφραγμένους τοῖς ὅπλοις καὶ τοὺς κοντοὺς προίσχοντας.

9 The whole question of artillery is amply discussed by E. W. Marsden, *Greek and Roman Artillery, A Historical Development*, 1969, 174-98. Whether the *ballistarii* of the late Empire were field artillery-men or the forerunners of the medieval crossbowmen, they must have presented an appalling problem for the cavalry. Evidence for the existence of the crossbow in Roman times is given by two reliefs in the Musée Crozatier, Le Puy, which depict the weapon being used by a huntsman: P.-L. Duchartre, *Histoire des armes de de chasse et de leurs emplois*, 1955, figs 85-6. I am grateful to Mr Vesey Norman for this reference.

10 J. W. Eadie, 'The Development of Roman Mailed Cavalry', *JRS*, 1967, 161-73, surveys evidence for *cataphractarii* and *clibanarii*. A very detailed discussion of cavalry tactics in classical times is given by P. Vigneron, *Le cheval dans l'antiquité greco-romaine* I, 1968, 235-314.

11 The *basilica equestris exercitatatoria*. An inscription in Carlisle Museum originally erected at Netherby (Castra Exploratorum) by the *Cohors I Aelia Hispanorum milliaria*, names this building: Colingwood and Wright, *RIB*, n. 978. Further evidence for such buildings and for the training areas outside every fort is reviewed by R. W. Davies, 'Training Grounds of the Roman Cavalry', *Archaeological Journal*, 1969, 73ff. A unique example of a *gyrus* has been discovered in England: 'Excavations at "The Lunt", Bagington, Warwickshire, 1968-71, Second Interim Report', *Transactions of the Birmingham Archaeological Society*, 1970-71, 7-92. This *gyrus* was large enough to accommodate a number of *equites* and had a high barrier for javelin practice around its circumference. I am grateful to Mr Brian Hobley, Keeper of Field Archaeology, Coventry Museum, for this reference.

12 *ILS*, 2487 (= *CIL* VIII, 18092); E. M. Smallwood, *Documents illustrating the Principates of Nerva, Trajan and Hadrian*, 1966, 328.

13 A good account of the Dacian Wars is given in L. Rossi, *Trajan's Column and the Dacian Wars*, 1971.

14 Vigneron, op. cit. II.

15 Polybius VI, 39, 3.

16 Xenophon, *On Horsemanship* X, 6.

17 Xenophon, *Hipparchicus* I, 3.

18 *The Excavations at Dura-Europos, Final Report V*, I, *The Parchments and Papyri*, ed. C. G. Welles, R. O. Fink and J. F. Gilliam, 1959, 97, 296. A Latin list of men and mounts in A D 251: *Yale Classical Studies*, 1950, 189–209; *CIL* 325. R. W. Davies, *Latomus*, 1969, discusses the list and the difficulties that might be posed by mares. Allowing that the reading *equum* might designate neutered males (although the accusative case is used for the mares), the difficulties are exaggerated. Varro II, 7, 15, is quite clear that spirited horses are required by the army and that docile horses are required for road service: *Propter quod discrimen maxime institutum ut castrentur equi*. In the veterinary literature the castration of horses is given very little attention in comparison with the castration of oxen and pigs. It seems to have been performed seldom and solely for the provision of docile hacks for travelling.

19 Eadie, op. cit., 170, discusses the horse-armour (iron plates stitched to cloth) discovered at Dura-Europos in 1932 and compares it with the descriptions of Heliodorus, *Aethiopica* 9, 15. This armour is illustrated in G.

Webster, *The Roman Imperial Army*, 1969, pl. XX, 192.

20 Arrian, *Tactica* 4.

21 The tomb of Payava (British Museum 956) has some interesting but inconclusive features. On the east side a horseman gallops from left to right with his right thigh protected. It may be that the protection is no more than a shield carried attached to the saddle in a rather unusual fashion. On the west side of the roof of the tomb a small frieze of horsemen galloping from right to left appear to be led by a man whose left leg is covered by a rectangular object unlike a shield. This may represent some protection of the type mentioned by Xenophon.

22 The first known use of *clibanarii* is by Maxentius against Constantine near Turin in 312. The subsequent battle of the Milvian Bridge is depicted on the Arch of Constantine. Here the horses are hidden in the river amid the chaotic mass of bodies as a bridge of boats collapses, and the heads of two horses which are discernible bear no evidence of armour.

23 Sir Ian Richmond, *Hod Hill* II, 1968, 82–4.

24 *Hod Hill*, pl. 30b shows the stable floor.

25 Columella *De Re Rustica* VI, 19, describes the *machina* for restraining animals for treatment and gives the measurements of this indispensable piece of equipment.

26 Polybius VI, 39, 12–14.

27 Pliny, *NH* XVIII, 11, 62, gives an average weight of 15 *librae* for a modius of *barley*. A *libra* = $\frac{3}{4}$ lb.

28 *Papyrus Oxyrhyncus*, 2046. A full discussion of late evidence of this type is given by A. H. M. Jones, *The Later Roman Empire*, 1964, 629 ff.

29 *Papryus Amherst* II, 107: receipt for barley issued to the *duplicarius*

Justinus on behalf of Valerius Frontinus, prefect of the *ala Heracliana*.
30 *De Munitionibus Castrorum* 16.
The importance of calculating the
officers' remounts is obvious. The *ala
quingenaria* must accommodate and
feed 64 extra horses. The *ala milliaria*,
having 24 *turmae*, has 96 extra horses
which is equivalent to three extra
turmae. In order to calculate ration
strengths some scale of definite paper
establishments must have existed. The
only possible system would have
been to provide rations in advance on
the basis of a full establishment.
Additional requisitions in the event of
miscalculation would have been
extremely unpopular. Pack-animals
would have been fed ordinary fodder
which was collected by the unit from
the surrounding countryside, and
private ownership of extra mounts
would have been the responsibility of
the personnel concerned. No doubt
purchase of extra fodder from local
farmers would have presented no
problems. Similarly the equestrian
prefect's chargers would have been
his own property and the scale of his
household would have depended on
his purse and the degree to which his
salary would cover his needs.
31 Further information on remounts is given by R. W. Davies,
'The Supply of Animals to the
Roman Army and the Remount
System', *Latomus*, 1969, 429 ff. Davies
suggests that Roman cavalry horses
were castrated, which is not acceptable. Richmond, op. cit., 83, note 3,
refers to Trajan's Column, on which
an unmistakable stallion is depicted;
Traianssäule, Taf. 29, or F. Fremersdorf, *Denkmaler des römischen Koln²*,
*Urkunden zur Kolner Stadtgeschichte
aus römischer Zeit*, 1963, Taf. 25, pl.
46a. On the subject of the strength
of the *turma*, Polybius gives a figure
of 30 including officers. Varro, *De*

Lingua Latina V, 91, gives an incor-
rect etymology for *turma* which is,
however, based on the tacit acceptance of 30 as the strength. It is clear
from this passage that each decurion
led a file with the aid of an *optio*.
The division of the *turma* into 3 files
and the traditional allotment of 3
remounts may explain the arrangement of horses in groups of 3 in the
stables. Evidence, often claimed, for
32 as the *turma* strength is a remark by
Arrian, *Tactica* 18, in which he points
out that the Macedonian *hipparchia*
was what the Romans called an *ala*.
The fact that the Macedonian cavalry
was based on a troop or *ila* of 64
gave by progression a strength of
512 for the *hipparchia*. Arrian does
not say that the *ala* was 512 strong.
The only direct evidence for 32 is
Vegetius, *Militaria*, in which he
says that he would attach 32 troopers
to each of his cohorts (five centuries
strong) in a legion whose organization appears to be the conception of
the author rather than an actual
military institution.
32 *Papyrus Oxyrhyncus*, 2046.
33 H. C. B. Rogers, *The Mounted
Troops of the British Army 1066–1945*
(The Imperial Services Library, vol.
III), 1959. This work provides a most
convenient introduction to the history of cavalry.
34 J. Curle, *A Roman Frontier Post
and Its People: The Fort of Newstead in
the Parish of Melrose*, 1911, 362.
35 Fattening ration: *Mulomedicina*
I, 56, 23; on the subject of size and
breeding Vegetius' complaints in
the preface to his second Book are
interesting. It is clear that Roman
horses were not as hardy as those
of the Huns and other barbarous
nations. Vegetius attributes this to the
fact that the barbarians did not house
their horses and pamper them; but it
is more likely that the difference was

simply that the Romans had 'improved' their horses whereas the barbarians were still employing small, hardy ponies. In this connection the remarks of W. Youatt, *The Horse*, 1848, 93, are of interest; 'Our cavalry horses were formerly large and heavy. . . . A considerable change has taken place in the character of our troop horses . . . lightness and activity will succeed to bulk and strength, and for skirmishing and sudden attack the change will be an improvement. It is particularly found to be so in long and rapid marches, which the lighter troops scarcely regard, while the heavier horses with their more than comparative additional weight to carry are knocked up.'

36 Rogers, op. cit., 210, cites Sir Walter Gilbey, *Small Horses in Warfare*, 1900.

37 op. cit., 217.

38 Pliny, *NH* VIII, 65, 162.

39 Rogers, op. cit., 197.

40 A fourth-century attempt to economize on fodder is represented in the *Codex Theodosianus* VIII, 4, 8, which directs that no fodder is to be issued to cavalry before 1 August. This type of practice was common in Britain in the eighteenth century and was known as 'marching to grass' since the horses were turned out to pasture. Rogers, 132, cites the order book of the 10th Light Dragoons for 1784–88. He points out that a grass-fed horse was able to patrol and undergo slow troop training without detriment. Presumably sustained hard training or active service must have been considered to be unlikely in the Eastern Empire at the time of the directive. It should be noted, however, that the Boer horsemen rode small horses, rarely over $14\frac{1}{2}$ hands and capable of marching forty miles a day without losing condition. The horses were fed as far as possible by grazing and this diet was supplemented by oat straw. Oats were cut just before ripening and tied into 6 lb bundles. One such bundle was one day's ration for a horse (Rogers, op. cit., 227).

Additional Note to p. 49

With the loaded elephant on the Baltimore sarcophagus there may be compared a relief, formerly in the Lateran, of a reticulated Indian elephant marching leftwards with seven tusks in a box strapped on its back: Alinari, photo 47194, Roma.

SOURCES OF ILLUSTRATIONS

INDICES

I PLACES AND ANCIENT PERSONS

(Note: authors and places constantly referred to are not included. The notes are indexed only for material not cited in the text. The Appendix is separately indexed)

II ANIMALS AND GREEK AND LATIN TERMS

(The names of individual animals are not included)

III THE APPENDIX